A LIBRARY

OF

AMERICAN LITERATURE

Vol. II.

Eng^d by H.B.Hall's Sons. New York.

Cotton Mather.

A LIBRARY OF

36

AMERICAN LITERATURE

FROM THE EARLIEST SETTLEMENT
TO THE PRESENT TIME

COMPILED AND EDITED BY

EDMUND CLARENCE STEDMAN AND
ELLEN MACKAY HUTCHINSON

IN ELEVEN VOLUMES

VOL. II

NEW-YORK

CHARLES L. WEBSTER & COMPANY

1891

r 810.8

S918

V.2

r
PS504
S7
1894

vol 2

PRINTED BY
D. G. F. CLASS.
NEW YORK.

CONTENTS OF VOLUME II.

Later Colonial Literature.

CONTENTS OF VOLUME II.

Portraits in this Volume.

ON STEEL.

MISCELLANEOUS.

LATER

COLONIAL LITERATURE

1676—1764

ON THE PROSPECT OF PLANTING ARTS AND LEARNING IN AMERICA.

THE Muse, disgusted at an age and clime
  Barren of every glorious theme,
    In distant lands now waits a better time,
    Producing subjects worthy fame :

In happy climes, where from the genial sun
  And virgin earth such scenes ensue,
The force of art by nature seems outdone,
  And fancied beauties by the true :

In happy climes, the seat of innocence,
  Where nature guides and virtue rules,
Where men shall not impose for truth and sense
  The pedantry of courts and schools :

There shall be sung another golden age,
  The rise of empire and of arts,
The good and great inspiring epic rage,
  The wisest heads and noblest hearts.

Not such as Europe breeds in her decay ;
  Such as she bred when fresh and young,
When heavenly flame did animate her clay,
  By future poets shall be sung.

Westward the course of empire takes its way ;
  The four first Acts already past,
A fifth shall close the Drama with the day ;
  Time's noblest offspring is the last.

GEORGE BERKELEY. A D. 17—

From the Oxford Text.

LATER

COLONIAL LITERATURE.

Michael Wigglesworth.

BORN in England, 1631. DIED at Malden, Mass., 1705.

THE DAY OF DOOM.

[The Day of Doom ; or, a Poetical Description of the Great and Last Judgment. 1662.]

SOUNDING OF THE LAST TRUMP.

STILL was the night, Serene & Bright,
  when all Men sleeping lay ;
Calm was the season, & carnal reason
  thought so 'twould last for ay.
Soul, take thine ease, let sorrow cease,
  much good thou hast in store :
This was their Song, their Cups among,
  the Evening before.

The Security of the World before Christ's coming to Judgment. Luke 12. 19.

Wallowing in all kind of sin,
  vile wretches lay secure :
The best of men had scarcely then
  their Lamps kept in good ure.
Virgins unwise, who through disguise
  amongst the best were number'd
Had clos'd their eyes ; yea, and the wise
  through sloth and frailty slumber'd.

Mat. 25. 5.

Like as of old, when Men grow bold
  God's threatenings to contemn,
Who stop their Ear, and would not hear,
  when Mercy warned them :

Mat. 24. 37, 38.

But took their course without remorse,
    till God began to powre
Destruction the World upon
    in a tempestuous showre.

1. Thes. 5. 8.

They put away the evil day,
    and drown'd their care and fears,
Till drown'd were they, and swept away
    by vengeance unawares:
So at the last, whilst Men sleep fast
    in their security,
Surpriz'd they are in such a snare
    as cometh suddenly.

The Suddenness, Majesty, & Terror of Christ's appearing. Mat. 25. 6. 2 Pet. 3. 10.

For at midnight brake forth a Light,
    which turn'd the night to day,
And speedily an hideous cry
    did all the world dismay.
Sinners awake, their hearts do ake,
    trembling their loynes surprizeth;
Amaz'd with fear, by what they hear,
    each one of them ariseth.

They rush from Beds with giddy heads,
    and to their windows run,
Viewing this light, which shines more bright
    then doth the Noon-day Sun.
Straightway appears (they see't with tears)
Mat. 24. 29, 30.   the Son of God most dread;
Who with his Train comes on amain
    to Judge both Quick and Dead.

Before his face the Heav'ns gave place,
    and Skies are rent asunder,
With mighty voice, and hideous noise,
    more terrible than Thunder.
2 Pet. 3. 10.   His brightness damps heav'ns glorious lamps
    and makes them hide their heads,
As if afraid and quite dismay'd,
    they quit their wonted steads.

Ye sons of men that durst contemn
    the Threatnings of Gods Word.
How chear you now ? your hearts, I trow,
    are thrill'd as with a sword,
Now Athist blind, whose brutish mind
    a God could never see,
Dost thou perceive, dost now believe
    that Christ thy judge shall be ?

Stout Courages, (whose hardiness
   could Death and Hell out-face)
Are you as bold now you behold
   your Judge draw near apace ?
They cry, no, no: Alas! and wo!
   our courage all is gone :
Our hardiness (fool hardiness)
   hath us undone, undone.

No heart so bold, but now grows cold   Rev. 6. 15.
   and almost dead with fear :
No eye so dry, but now can cry,
   and pour out many a tear.
Earth's Potentates and pow'rful States,
   Captains and Men of Might
Are quite abasht, their courage dasht
   at this most dreadful sight.

Mean men lament, great men do rent   Mat. 24. 30.
   their Robes, and tear their hair :
They do not spare their flesh to tear
   through horrible despair.
All Kindreds wail : all hearts do fail :
   horror the world doth fill
With weeping eyes, and loud out-cries,
   yet knows not how to kill.

Some hide themselves in Caves and Delves,   Rev. 6. 15. 16.
   in places under ground :
Some rashly leap into the Deep,
   to scape by being drown'd :
Some to the Rocks (O senseless blocks !)
   and woody Mountains run,
That there they might this fearful sight,
   and dreaded Presence shun.

In vain do they to Mountains say,
   fall on us and us hide
From Judges ire, more hot than fire,
   for who may it abide ?
No hiding place can from his Face
   sinners at all conceal,
Whose flaming Eye hid things doth 'spy
   and darkest things reveal.

The Judge draws nigh, exalted high,   Mat. 25. 21.
   upon a lofty Throne,
Amidst the throng of Angels strong,
   lo, Israel's Holy One !

The excellence of whose presence
   and awful Majesty,
Amazeth Nature, and every Creature,
   doth more than terrify.

Rev. 6. 14.

The Mountains smoak, the Hills are shook,
   the Earth is rent and torn,
As if she should be clear dissolv'd,
   or from the Center born.
The Sea doth roar, forsakes the shore,
   and shrinks away for fear ;
The wild beasts flee into the Sea,
   so soon as he draws near.

Whose Glory bright, whose wondrous might,
   whose power Imperial,
So far surpass whatever was
   in Realms Terrestrial ;
That tongues of men (nor angels pen)
   cannot the same express,
And therefore I must pass it by,
   lest speaking should transgress.

1 Thes. 4. 16.
Resurrection
of the dead.
John 5. 28, 29.

Before his Throne a Trump is blown,
   Proclaiming the day of Doom :
Forthwith he cries, Ye dead arise,
   and unto Judgment come.
No sooner said, but 'tis obey'd ;
   Sepulchres opened are :
Dead bodies all rise at his call,
   and's mighty power declare.

Both Sea and Land, at his Command,
   their Dead at once surrender :
The Fire and Air constrained are
   also their dead to tender.
The mighty word of this great Lord
   links Body and Soul together
Both of the Just, and the unjust,
   to part no more for ever.

The living
Changed.
Luke 20. 36.
1 Cor. 15. 52.

The same translates, from Mortal states
   to Immortality,
All that survive, and be alive,
   i' th' twinkling of an eye :
That so they may abide for ay
   to endless weal or woe ;
Both the Renate and Reprobate
   are made to dy no more.

His winged Hosts flie through all Coasts,
   together gethering
Both good and bad, both quick and dead,
   and all to Judgment bring.
Out of their holes those creeping Moles,
   that hid themselves for fear,
By force they take, and quickly make
   before the Judge appear.

all brought to
Judgment.
Mat. 24. 31.

Thus every one before the Throne
   of Christ the Judge is brought,
Both righteous and impious
   that good or ill hath wrought.
A separation, and diff'ring station
   by Christ appointed is
(To sinners sad) 'twixt good and bad,
   'twixt Heirs of woe and bliss.

2 Cor. 5. 10.
The sheep
separated
from the
Goats. Mat.
25. 32.

•   •   •   •   •   •   •

THE HEATHEN'S VAIN DEFENCE.

These words appall and daunt them all ;
   dismai'd, and all amort,
Like stocks that stand at Christ's left hand
   and dare no more retort.
Then were brought near with trembling fear
   a number numberless
Of blind Heathen, and bruitish men,
   that did God's Laws transgress.

Whose wicked ways Christ open layes,
   and makes their sins appear,
They making pleas their case to ease,
   if not themselves to clear.
Thy written Word (say they) good Lord,
   we never did enjoy :
We nor refus'd nor it abus'd
   Oh, do not us destroy.

Heathen men
plead want of
the written
Word.

You ne'r abus'd nor yet refus'd
   my written Word, you plead,
That's true (quoth he) therefore shall ye
   the less be punished.
You shall not smart for any part
   of other mens offence,
But for your own transgression
   receive due recompence.

Mat. 11. 22.
Luke 12. 48.

But we were blind, say they, in mind,
  too dim was Natures Light,
Our only guide, as hath been try'd
  to bring us to the sight

1 Cor. 1. 21.
And insuffici-
ency of the
Light of Na-
ture.

Of our estate degenerate,
  and curst by Adam's fall ;
How we were born and lay forlorn
  in bondage and in thrall.

We did not know a Christ till now,
  nor how faln men be saved,
Else would we not, right well we wot,
  have so our selves behaved.

Mat. 11. 22.

We should have mourn'd, we should have turn'd
  from sin at thy Reproof,
And been more wise through thy advice,
  for our own Souls behoof.

But Natures Light shin'd not so bright
  to teach us the right way :
We might have lov'd it, and well improv'd it,
  and yet have gone astray.

They are an-
swered.

The Judge most High makes this Reply,
  you ignorance pretend,
Dimness of sight, and want of light
  your course Heav'nward to bend.

How came your mind to be so blind ?
  I once you knowledge gave,

Gen. 1. 27.
Eccl. 7. 29.
Hos. 13. 9.

Clearness of sight, and judgment right ;
  who did the same deprave ?
If to your cost you have it lost,
  and quite defac'd the same ;
Your own desert hath caus'd the smart,
  you ought not me to blame.

Your selves into a pit of woe,
  your own transgression led :
If I to none my Grace had shown,
  who had been injured ?

Mat. 1. 25 com-
pared with 20,
& 15.

If to a few, and not to you,
  I shew'd a way of life,
My Grace so free, you clearly see,
  gives you no ground of strife.

'Tis vain to tell, you wot full well,
  if you in time had known,
Your Misery and Remedy,
  your actions had it shown.

You, sinful Crew, have not been true,
　　unto the Light of Nature,
Nor done the good you understood,
　　nor owned your Creator.

Rom. 1. 20, 21,
22.

He that the Light, because 'tis Light,
　　hath used to despize,
Would not the Light shining more bright,
　　be likely for to prize.
If you had lov'd, and well improv'd
　　your knowledge and dim sight,
Herein your pain had not been vain,
　　your plagues had been more light.

Rom. 2. 12, 15,
& 1. 32.
Mat. 12. 41.

PLEA OF THE INFANTS.

Then to the Bar, all they drew near
　　Who dy'd in infancy,
And never had or good or bad
　　effected pers'nally.
But from the womb unto the tomb
　　were straightway carried,
(Or at the least e'er they transgrest)
　　who thus began to plead :

Reprobate In-
fants plead
for them-
selves.
Rev. 20. 12, 15.
compared
with Rom. 5.
12, 14, & 9. 11,
13.
Ezek. 18. 2.

If for our own transgression,
　　or disobedience,
We here did stand at thy left hand
　　just were the Recompence :
But Adam's guilt our souls hath spilt,
　　his fault is charg'd on us :
And that alone hath overthrown,
　　and utterly undone us.

Not we, but he ate of the Tree,
　　whose fruit was interdicted :
Yet on us all of his sad Fall,
　　the punishment's inflicted.
How could we sin that had not been
　　or how is his sin our
Without consent, which to prevent,
　　we never had a pow'r ?

O great Creator, why was our Nature
　　depraved and forlorn ?
Why so defil'd, and made so vil'd
　　whilst we were yet unborn ?

If it be just, and needs we must
   transgressors reck'ned be,

Psal. 51. 5.

Thy Mercy Lord, to us afford,
   which sinners hath set free.

Behold we see Adam set free,
   and sav'd from his trespass,
Whose sinful Fall hath spilt us all,
   and brought us to this pass.
Canst thou deny us once to try,
   or Grace to us to tender,
When he finds grace before thy face,
   that was the chief offender ?

Then answered the Judge most dread,
   God doth such doom forbid,

Their Argu-
ments taken
off.
Ezek. 18. 20.
Rom. 5. 12, 19.

That men should dye eternally
   for what they never did.
But what you call old Adam's Fall,
   and only his Trespass,
You call amiss to call it his,
   both his and yours it was.

He was design'd of all Mankind
   to be a publick Head,

1 Cor. 15. 48,
49.

A common Root, whence all should shoot,
   and stood in all their stead.
He stood and fell, did ill or well,
   Not for himself alone,
But for you all, who now his Fall,
   and trespass would disown.

If he had stood, then all his brood
   had been established
In Gods true love never to move,
   nor once awry to tread :
Then all his Race, my Fathers Grace,
   should have enjoy'd for ever,
And wicked Sprights by subtile sleights
   could them have harmed never.

Would you have griev'd to have receiv'd
   through Adam so much good,
As had been your for evermore,
   if he at first had stood ?
Would you have said, we ne'er obey'd,
   nor did thy Laws regard ;
It ill befits with benefits,
   us, Lord, so to reward.

Since then to share in his welfare,
 you could have been content,
You may with reason share in his treason,
 and in the punishment.   Rom. 5. 12.
             Psal. 51. 5.
Hence you were born in state forlorn, Gen. 5. 3.
 with Natures so depraved :
Death was your due, because that you
 had thus your selves behaved.

You think if we had been as he,
 whom God did so betrust,
We to our cost would ne'er have lost
 all for a paltry Lust.
Had you been made in Adam's stead, Mat. 23. 30, 31.
 you would like things have wrought,
And so into the self same wo,
 your selves and yours have brought.

I may deny you once to try,
 or Grace to you to tender,
Though he finds Grace before my face, Rom. 9. 15, 18.
             The free gift.
 who was the chief offender :   Rom. 5. 15.
Else should my Grace cease to be Grace ;
 for it should not be free,
If to release whom I should please,
 I have no libertie.

If upon one what's due to none
 I frankly shall bestow,
And on the rest shall not think best,
 compassions skirts to throw,
Whom injure I ? will you envy,
 and grudge at others weal ?
Or me accuse, who do refuse
 your selves to help and heal.

Am I alone of what's my own,
 no Master or no Lord ?   Mat. 20. 15.
O if I am, how can you claim
 what I to some afford ?
Will you demand Grace at my hand,
 and challenge what is mine ?
Will you teach me whom to set free,
 and thus my grace confine ?

You sinners are, and such a share   Psl. 58. 3.
 as sinners may expect,   Rom. 6. 23.
             Gal. 3. 10.
Such you shall have ; for I do save Rom. 8. 29, 30,
             & 11. 7.
 none but my own Elect.   Rev. 21. 27.

Yet to compare your sin with their
   who liv'd a longer time,
I do confess yours is much less,
   though every sin's a crime.

A Crime it is, therefore in bliss
   you may not hope to dwell ;
But unto you I shall allow
   the easiest room in Hell.
The glorious King thus answering,
   they cease and plead no longer :
Their Consciences must needs confess
   his Reasons are the stronger.

Thus all mens Pleas the Judge with ease
   doth answer and confute,
Until that all, both great and small,
   are silenced and mute.
Vain hopes are cropt, all mouths are stopt,
   sinners have nought to say,
But that 'tis just, and equal most
   they should be damn'd for ay.

SENTENCE AND TORMENT OF THE CONDEMNED.

Where tender love mens hearts did move
   unto a sympathy,
And bearing part of others smart
   in their anxiety ;

Now such compassion is out of fashion,
   and wholly laid aside :
No Friends so near, but Saints to hear
   their Sentence can abide.

One natural Brother beholds another
   in his astonied fit,

Yet sorrows not thereat a jot,
   nor pities him a whit.
The godly wife conceives no grief,
   nor can she shed a tear
For the sad state of her dear Mate,
   when she his doom doth hear.

He that was erst a Husband pierc't
   with sense of Wives distress,
Whose tender heart did bear a part
   of all her grievances,

Shall mourn no more as heretofore
   because of her ill plight ;
Although he see her now to be
   a damn'd forsaken wight.

The tender Mother will own no other
   of all her numerous brood,
But such as stand at Christ's right hand
   acquitted through his Blood.   Luk. 16. 25.
The pious father had now much rather
   his graceless son should ly
In Hell with Devils, for all his evils,
   burning eternally.

Then God most high should injury,
   by sparing him sustain ;
And doth rejoice to hear Christ's voice   Psal. 58. 10.
   adjudging him to pain.
Who having all both great and small,
   convinc'd and silenced,
Did then proceed their Doom to read,
   and thus it uttered.

Ye sinful wights, and cursed sprights,   The Judge
   that work iniquity,   pronounceth
                               the Sentence
Depart together from me for ever   of condemna-
   to endless Misery ;   tion.
Your portion take in yonder Lake,   Mat. 25. 41.
   where Fire and Brimstone flameth :
Suffer the smart, which your desert
   as it's due wages claimeth.

Oh piercing words more sharp than swords !   The terrour of
   what, to depart from thee,   it.
Whose face before for evermore
   the best of Pleasures be !
What ? to depart (unto our smart)
   from thee Eternally :
To be for aye banish'd away,
   with Devils company !

What ? to be sent to Punishment,
   and flames of Burning Fire,
To be surrounded, and eke confounded
   with Gods Revengeful ire !
What ? to abide, not for a tide
   these Torments, but for Ever :
To be released, or to be eased,
   not after years, but Never.

Oh fearful Doom ! now there's no room
   for hope or help at all :
Sentence is past which aye shall last,
   Christ will not it recall.
There might you hear them rent and tear
   the Air with their out-cries :
The hideous noise of their sad voice
   ascendeth to the Skies.

Luke 13. 28.
Prov. 1. 26.

They wring their hands, their caitiff-hands,
   and gnash their teeth for terrour ;
They cry, they roar for anguish sore,
   and gnaw their tongues for horrour.
But get away without delay,
   Christ pities not your cry :
Depart to Hell, there may you yell,
   and roar Eternally.

It is put in
Execution.
Mat. 25. 46.

That word, Depart, maugre their heart,
   drives every wicked one,
With mighty pow'r, the self-same hour,
   far from the Judge's Throne.
Away they're chast'd by the strong blast
   of his Death-threatning mouth :
They flee full fast, as if in haste,
   although they be full loath.

Mat. 13. 41, 42.

As chaff that's dry, and dust doth fly
   before the Northern wind :
Right so are they chased away,
   and can no Refuge find.
They hasten to the Pit of Woe,
   guarded by Angels stout ;
Who to fulfil Christ's holy will,
   attend this wicked Rout.

HELL.
Mat. 25. 30.
Mark 9. 42.
Isa. 30. 33.
Rev. 21. 8.

Whom having brought as they are taught,
   unto the brink of Hell,
(That dismal place far from Christ's face,
   where Death and Darkness dwell :
Where God's fierce Ire kindleth the fire,
   and vengeance feeds the flame
With piles of Wood and Brimstone Flood.
   that none can quench the same,)

Wicked Men
and Devils
cast into it for
ever.
Mat. 22. 13. &
25. 46.

With Iron bands they bind their hands,
   and cursed feet together,
And cast them all both great and small,
   into that Lake for ever,

Where day and night, without respite,
　　they wail, and cry, and howl
For tort'ring pain which they sustain
　　in body and in Soul.

For day and night, in their despight,
　　their torments smoak ascendeth.
Their pain and grief have no relief,　　　Rev. 14. 10, 11.
　　their anguish never endeth.
There must they ly, and never dy,
　　though dying every day :
There must they dying ever ly,
　　and not consume away.

Dy fain they would, if dy they could,
　　but death will not be had.
God's direful wrath their bodies hath
　　for ev'r Immortal made.
They live to ly in misery,
　　and bear eternal wo ;
And live they must whilst God is just,
　　that he may plague them so.

But who can tell the plagues of Hell,　　The insuffer-
　　and torments exquisite ?　　　　　　able torments
Who can relate their dismal state,　　　of the damn-
　　and terrours infinite ?　　　　　　　ed.
Who fare the best, and feel the least,　Luk. 16. 24.
　　yet feel that punishment　　　　　　Jude 7.
Whereby to nought they should be brought,
　　if God did not prevent.

The least degree of misery
　　there felt's incomparable,
The lightest pain they there sustain　　Isa. 33. 14.
　　more than intolerable.　　　　　　　Mark 9. 43, 44.
But God's great pow'r from hour to hour
　　upholds them in the fire,
That they shall not consume a jot,
　　nor by it's force expire.

．　．　．　．　．　．　．　．

THE SAINTS ASCEND TO HEAVEN.

The Saints behold with courage bold,　　The Saints re-
　　and thankful wonderment,　　　　　joyce to see
To see all those that were their foes　Judgment
　　thus sent to punishment ;　　　　　executed
　　　　　　　　　　　　　　　　　　　　upon the
　　　　　　　　　　　　　　　　　　　　wicked
　　　　　　　　　　　　　　　　　　　　World.

Psal. 58. 10.
Rev. 10. 1, 2, 3.

Then do they sing unto their King
    a Song of endless Praise :
They praise his Name, and do proclaim
    that just are all his ways.

They ascend
with Christ
into Heaven
triumphing.
Mat. 25. 46.

Thus with great joy and melody
    to Heav'n they all ascend,
Him there to praise with sweetest layes,
    and Hymns that never end.
Where with long rest they shall be blest.
    and nought shall them annoy :
Where they shall see as seen they be,
    and whom they love enjoy.

1 Joh. 3. 2.
1 Cor. 13. 12.
Their Eternal
happiness and
incomparable
Glory there.

O glorious Place ! where face to face
    Jehovah may be seen,
By such as were sinners while here
    and no dark veil between.
Where the Sun shine and light Divine,
    of Gods bright countenance,
Doth rest upon them every one,
    with sweetest influence.

O blessed state of the Renate !
    O wond'rous Happiness,
To which they're brought beyond what **thought**
    can reach, or words express !

Rev. 21. 4.

Griefs water-course, and sorrows source,
    are turn'd to joyful streams.
Their old distress and heaviness
    are vanished like dreams.

For God above in arms of love
    doth dearly them embrace,

Psal. 16. 11.

And fills their sprights with such **delights,**
    and pleasures in his grace ;
As shall not fail, nor yet grow stale
    through frequency of use :
Nor do they fear Gods favour there,
    to forfeit by abuse.

For there the Saints are perfect Saints,
    and holy ones indeed,

Heb. 12. 23.

From all the sin that dwelt within
    their mortal bodies freed :

Rev. 1. 6, &
22. 5.

Made Kings and Priests to God through **Christs**
    dear loves transcendency,
There to remain and there to reign
    with him Eternally.

VANITY OF VANITIES.

[Appended to " The Day of Doom," Sixth Edition, 1715.]

VAIN, frail, short-liv'd, and miserable Man,
    Learn what thou art when thy estate is best :
A restless Wave o' th' troubled Ocean,
A Dream, a lifeless Picture finely drest.

A Wind, a Flower, a Vapour and a Bubble,
A Wheel that stands not still, a trembling Reed,
A trolling Stone, dry Dust, light Chaff and Stuff,
A shadow of something but truly nought indeed.

Learn what deceitful Toyes, and empty things,
This World, and all its best Enjoyments be :
Out of the Earth no true Contentment springs,
But all things here are vexing Vanitie.

For what is Beauty, but a fading Flower ?
Or what is Pleasure, but the Devils bait,
Whereby he catcheth whom he would devour,
And multitudes of Souls doth ruinate ?

And what are Friends, but mortal men, as we,
Whom Death from us may quickly separate ;
Or else their hearts may quite estranged be,
And all their love be turned into hate.

And what are Riches to be doted on ?
Uncertain, fickle, and ensnaring things ;
They draw Mens Souls into Perdition,
And when most needed, take them to their wings.

Ah foolish man ! that sets his heart upon
Such empty shadows, such wild Fowl as these,
That being gotten will be quickly gone,
And whilst they stay increase but his disease.

As in a Dropsie, drinking draughts begets,
The more he drinks, the more he still requires ;
So on this World whoso affection sets,
His Wealths encrease, encreaseth his desires.

O happy Man, whose portion is above,
Where Floods, where Flames, where Foes cannot bereave him :
Most wretched Man that fixed hath his love
Upon this World, that surely will deceive him.

For what is Honour? what is Sov'raignty,
Whereto mens hearts so restlessly aspire?
Whom have they Crowned with Felicity?
When did they ever satisfie desire?

The Ear of Man with hearing is not fill'd;
To see new Lights still coveteth the Eye:
The craving Stomach though it may be still'd,
Yet craves again without a new supply.

All Earthly Things man's cravings answer not,
Whose little heart would all the World contain,
(If all the World should fall to one Man's Lott)
And notwithstanding empty still remain.

The Eastern Conquerour was said to weep,
When he the Indian Ocean did view,
To see his Conquest bounded by the Deep,
And no more Worlds remaining to subdue.

Who would that man in his Enjoyment bless,
Or envy him, or covet his estate,
Whose gettings do augment his greediness,
And make his wishes more intemperate.

Such is the wonted and the common guise
Of those on Earth that bear the greatest sway;
If with a few the case be otherwise,
They seek a Kingdom that abides for ay.

Moreover they, of all the Sons of Men,
That Rule, and are in Highest Places set,
Are most enclin'd to scorn their Bretheren;
And God himself (without great Grace) forget.

For as the Sun doth blind the gazers eyes,
That for a time they nought discern aright;
So Honour doth befool and blind the Wise,
And their own lustre 'reaves them of their sight.

Great are their Dangers, manifold their Cares,
Thro' which, whilst others sleep, they scarcely Nap,
And yet are oft surprized unawares,
And fall unwilling into Envies Trap.

The mean Mechanick finds his kindly rest,
All void of fear sleepeth the Country Clown,
When greatest Princes often are distrest,
And cannot sleep upon their Beds of Down.

Could Strength or Valour men Immortalize,
Could Wealth or Honour keep them from decay,
There were some cause the same to Idolize,
And give the lie to that which I do say.

But neither can such things themselves endure,
Without the hazard of a Change one hour,
Nor such as trust in them can they secure
From dismal days, or Death's prevailing pow'r.

If Beauty could the Beautiful defend
From Death's dominion, then fair Absalom
Had not been brought to such a shameful end :
But fair and foul unto the Grave must come.

If Wealth or Scepters could Immortal make,
Then wealthy Crœsus, wherefore art thou dead ?
If Warlike-force which makes the World to quake,
Then why is Julius Cæsar perished ?

Where are the Scipio's Thunder-bolts of War ?
Renowned Pompey, Cæsars Enemy ?
Stout Hannibal, Rome's Terror known so far ?
Great Alexander, what's become of thee ?

If Gifts and Bribes Death's favour might but win,
If Pow'r, if Force, or Threatnings might it fray,
All these, and more had still surviving been :
But all are gone, for Death will have no Nay.

Such is this World with all her Pomp & Glory ;
Such are the men whom worldly eyes admire,
Cut down by time, and now become a story,
That we might after better things aspire.

Go boast thy self of what thy heart enjoys,
Vain Man ! triumph in all thy Worldly Bliss :
Thy best Enjoyments are but Trash and Toys,
Delight thyself in that which worthless is.

  Omnia prætereunt præter amare Deum.

Jonathan Mitchell.

BORN in Yorkshire, England, about 1625. DIED at Cambridge, Mass., 1668.

ON LOOKING UP STEADFASTLY INTO HEAVEN.

[A Discourse of the Glory to which God hath called Believers by Jesus Christ. 1677.]

THERE is no certainty of any thing in this world. Riches have wings, the top of honor is a slippery place, life itself is but a vapor. All things here lie within the reach of many devourers and destroyers, moth and rust, and thieves, pirates at sea, and other sons of violence at land. And what is saved from other destroyers is but reserved for the fire, that must be the end of all the possessions upon earth. All earthly possessions must turn into a blaze and end in smoke. At the great day of judgment there shall be an universal burning (all the earth on a light fire) in particular, previous days of judgment here (which are tastes and hansells of that) the Lord often contends by fire. Why, if men will not see by the light of the word, one would think they should see by the flames of devouring fire (though indeed seldom do men see by the latter, or by any destroying judgments, that have obstinately refused the light and voice of the former. But in itself it is a wonderful help to see, and it will be so to them that regard the word) the vanity, uncertainty and perishing nature of all things here. But to be sure our enjoyment of all things in this world (at best) hangs but upon the twine-thread of our life, which there are so many sharp edged tools (sicknesses, diseases, sad accidents) continually ready to cut asunder, we are not sure to have it continued one hour longer. Had we not need be sure of something when all these things shall fail, as Luke xvi. 9? Paul knows what he hath to trust to when this world turns him out of doors (he hath then an house to hide his head in), II. Cor. v. 1. Oh, it is a comfortable thing, when temporal habitations fail, to be sure of eternal ones! Imagine you were now to die, this moment leaving the world, how glad would you be to be sure of Heaven and of a better life! Why, that must be ere long, and you cannot think to be sure of it then, in a dying hour, if you do not labor to make it sure now in a time of health and peace. When David looks over the world and sees the vanity fading uncertainty of all portions (of riches, glory, honor, fair dwellings, etc.) here, what a thing is it to him to be sure of a God to receive him into arms of love and mercy when he dies, and of an happy waking in the morning of the Resurrection to eternal glory.

When you see men stand in slippery places, and one tumbling down after another (the rich tumbling into poverty, the great into contempt), then look to your feet and to your standing; what foothold have you, what sure bottom and foundation have you to stand steady upon, as Psal. xxvi. 12? The wicked stand in slippery places, but the godly that walk with God in integrity, stand in an even place. The covenant is sure, the state of grace is a sure standing. Indeed in regard of themselves they would fall as soon as any, but they have a sure hand to hold them.

Should not we make this use of the times we live in, to quicken us to make sure of Heaven? May we not get this meat out of the eater, this good out of all the evils and troubles that are in the world? Is it now a time to walk at peradventures with God, to live at uncertainties, to hang between Heaven and earth, to be to seek of a resting place when trouble fills the whole earth? When the Lord's anger is burning up and down the world, and his fury poured out like fire everywhere, and the rocks thrown down by him. Had we not need make sure of his love, and be able to say, the Lord is good and my stronghold, etc.? When hypocrites cannot stand (as they cannot before God appearing in his dreadful and devouring wrath) had we need not make sure of sincerity of grace? You may bear up your head for a time, and go up and down carelessly, but sooner or later, one way or other, there will come such a devouring fire, such an appearance of wrath, such dreadful judgments as no false heart, no slight chaffy professor shall be able to stand before. He had need have gold tried in the fire, grace that is of golden solidity and purity. Dross and chaff will not bide the fire that is kindled in the day of God's judgments; when He takes his fan into his hand to sever, purge out and burn up the chaff (the hypocrites and sinners in Sion) that is mixed with the wheat, and found on the floor of the visible church. When Jerusalem's sins are ripe for judgment and God hath waited his time upon obstinate sinners and despisers of the Gospel (as He did on the Jews in and after Christ's time), then a threshing and winnowing, fanning, and to the chaff a burning time comes. Then indeed the Lord will lose never a grain of sound wheat (it had need be sound and solid wheat that can bear the tossings of the fan and the blasts of the wind, and not be heaved and driven quite away). But chaffy hypocrites and sinners will not be able to stand or abide such a time, Amos. ix. 9, ("for I will fan the house of Israel as corn is fanned, tossed in a fan") 10. Oh, we had need be sure to be good and sound wheat at such a time, be settled, strengthened, stablished in grace, well built and founded; as Peter prays for them here in text, to a time of great afflictions, sufferings, and troubles, I. Pet. v. 9, 10, in a time when judgment was begun at the house of God, I. Pet. iv. 17, and of fiery trials, v. 12. Oh, at such a time it is a suitable and a precious thing to have a lively inheritance, as he begins the Epistle, I. Pet. i. 1–6. When the earth looks uncomfortably, when the face of things in this lower world hath terror, trouble, and blackness in it (and was it ever blacker than at this day?), it is then seasonable to be looking up steadfastly into Heaven, and to get a clear sight of the glory there and of our interest in it. Oh, we might make a gain of all the troubles of the times, did we turn them this way, to lift up our eyes to Heaven, and to awaken our souls to make sure of a portion there!

Joshua Scottow.

BORN in England about 1615. DIED in Boston, Mass., 1698.

THE NURSING FATHERS OF THE NEW WORLD.

[*A Narrative of the Planting of the Massachusetts Colony.* 1694.]

MEN of narrow spirits, of mean capacities and fortunes, had not been capable to officiate in so great a work, that such and so many gentlemen of ancient and worshipful families, of name and number, of character and quality, should combine and unite in so desperate and dangerous a design, attended with such insuperable difficulties and hazards in the plucking up of their stakes, leaving so pleasant and profitable a place as their native soil, parting with their patrimonies, inheritances, plentiful estates, and settlement of houses well furnished, of land well stocked, and with comfortable ways of subsistence, which the first planters deserted; and not a few did leave all their worldly hopes to come into this desert and unknown land, and smoky cottages, to the society of cursed cannibals (as they have proved to be), and at best wild Indians. What less than a Divine Ardor could inflame a people thus circumstanced to a work so contrary to flesh and blood?

Infinite wisdom and prudence contrived and directed this mysterious work of Providence; divine courage and resolution managed it; superhuman sedulity and diligence attended it, and angelical swiftness and dispatch finished it. Its wheels stirred not, but according to the Holy Spirit's motion in them; yea, there was the involution of a wheel within a wheel. God's ways were a great depth, and high above the eagle or vulturous eye; and such its immensity as man's cockle-shell is infinitely unable to empty this ocean.   .   .   .   .

The leaders of this people, upon serious debate, drew up a determination to settle the corporation and government upon the place; and accordingly made choice of a governor and deputy to abide there, which being effected, and divinely directed in such a choice of the governor, the famous pattern of wisdom, justice, and liberality, and of a deputy governor who, by his experience at home and travels abroad, with his natural and acquired abilities, was a gentleman qualified above others for the chief rule and government, wherein, according to his just deserts, he shared more than others,—the fame whereof being come abroad in the nation to such whose hearts God had touched,—this being upon the wing, there wanted not number of persons of all occupations, skilled in all faculties needful for the planting of a colony, who filled up a fleet of eleven ships, of considerable burthen, besides their attenders ; some of them about four hundred tons, the rest not much inferior ; some carrying near two hundred passengers, the rest proportionably. The wheels of Providence were lifted up very high, and also were radiantly magnificent.

These tarting travellers' removal, carrying so great a resemblance of departure into another world, they were not stupid Stoics, but abounded with that which grace doth not destroy, but direct. What showers of melting tears dropped into the bosoms of each other, whose souls as Jonathan and David clave one to another, yet alleviated with consideration ; though they were "absent in body, yet present in spirit," and of their mutual access to the Throne of Grace, and of "meeting at the assembly of the first-born and spirits of just men made perfect." Some of their choice friends, as the Reverend Mr. Cotton, and others, went along with them from Boston in Lincolnshire to Southampton, where they parted, and he preached his farewell sermon.

That so many eminent persons, some of noble extract, should upon sea-bridges pass over the largest ocean in the Universe, by the good hand of their God upon them, having sought of him a right way for themselves, little ones, and substance ; yea, above three thousand in one year, and that above three hundred ships since that time, all laden with jewels of invaluable value, far above the gold of Ophir—that each individual one should have a Celestial Convoy, under the flaming swords of flying Cherubims, turning every way, to keep them in their way, so as they all at their port safely arrived. Not one foundered in the sea, split upon rocks, were sucked in by sands, overset by sudden gusts, nor taken and plundered by pirates or robbers, except one called the "Angel Gabriel," whose tutelar guardianship failed (if any aboard put trust therein). She was laden with passengers for Boston, but put in at Pemiquid, where the ship and whole cargo perished, but not one soul of seamen or passengers miscarried. They met with an hurricane, before or since not known in this country, raised by the power of him who holds the wind in his hand and commissioneth the Prince of the Air, by raising "stormy winds to fulfil his Word." It's said the tide rose twenty foot perpendicular above its ordinary height. The same time another great

ship laden with passengers was wonderfully preserved, when as ready
to be split in pieces upon rocks at the "Isle of Shoals;" at the prayer
of the distressed Saints aboard God caused the winds to veer a point
or two about the compass, so as she cleared them, and they were
saved.   .   .   .   .

Our ancestors were men of God, made partakers of the divine nature;
Christ was formed and visibly legible in them; they served God in
houses of the first edition, without large chambers, or windows, ceiled
with cedar, or painted with vermilion; a company of plain, pious, humble and open-hearted Christians, called Puritans. When news was
brought hither, that the church at Bermudas was banished thence into
a desert island, and full of straits, forthwith they sent a vessel of good
burthen to them, fully laden with provisions of all sorts, each striving
who should be forwardest in so good a work; which supply came unto
them, when as all the meal in their barrels and oil in their cruise was
spent; and it was brought to them upon a Lord's-day, when as their
faithful pastor had finished his exhortation from Psalm xxiii.: "To trust
upon Jehovah their Shepherd, who would not trust his flock to want;"
thus the Lord set his seal to their faith and progress.

The gravity of their habit and calendar reformation, by Satan's policy,
hath since been imitated by the Quakers, that our Fathers might be listed
among those fanatics and enthusiasts; but they owned no Spirit within
them, but to be tried by the Word without them, and no Word without
them, but accorded with the Spirit within them; no word of promise to
them without a work of grace upon them, neither without the Holy
Spirit's dwelling in them and testifying to them. They minded the ornament of the meek and quiet Spirit; they were not acquainted with the
toys and fancies of this age; they were glorious within; their clothing
was of wrought gold; they were brought in unto the King in raiment of
needle-work, wrought with tender pricks of conscience; the least vain
fashion, wanton, or wicked thought touched them to the quick.   .   .

It's historied of our Pagan progenitors, that Gregory the Great, the last
of the good, and first of bad Popes, seeing strange lads of a comely countenance produced publicly to be sold, he inquired of what nation they
were of. Being told they were *Angli*, "English," looking upon their fair
faces, he said they were *Angeli*, Angels, and pitying them that they were
vassals of Satan, he took order for the conversion of our nation to the
Christian faith; but as for us *Nov Angli*, "New English," by our smutty
deformity and Hell's blackness, we have rendered ourselves *Diaboli Vet-
erani*, Old Devils. New England will be called new Witch-land, Em-
manuel's Land will be titled the Land of *Abaddon;* Salem Village and
Andover will be called the Swedish *Mohra* and *Bokul;* the country whose
native and natural smell was as of a field which the Lord hath blessed;

a promenado abroad, after rain, would have revived a man's spirits, as some have experienced it; yea, the whole Continent which, long after our first coming hither, was so full, not only of internal, but of external flavor and sweet odor; so as when ships were divers leagues distant and had not made land, so fragrant and odoriferous was the land to the mariners, that they knew they were not far from the shore; such was the plenty of sweet fern, laurel, and other fragrant simples this land then abounded with, especially near the sea-side; such was the scent of our aromatic and balsam-bearing pines, spruces, and larch trees, with our tall cedars, exceeding all in Europe. But our sweet scent is gone, we smell rank of hellebore, henbane, and poisonful hemlock, as if we were laid out to be the American *Anticyra.*

William Hubbard.

BORN in Essex, England, 1621. DIED at Ipswich, Mass., 1704.

CAPTAIN MILES STANDISH HIS TEMPER.

[*History of New England. Completed* 1680.]

DURING this whole lustre of years, from 1625, there was little matter of moment acted in the Massachusetts, till the year 1629, after the obtaining the patent; the former years being spent in fishing and trading by the agents of the Dorchester merchants and some others of the west country.

In one of the fishing voyages about the year 1625, under the charge and command of one Mr. Hewes, employed by some of the west country merchants, there arose a sharp contest between the said Hewes and the people of New Plymouth, about a fishing-stage, built the year before about Cape Anne by Plymouth men, but was now, in the absence of the builders made use of by Mr. Hewes his company; which the other, under the conduct of Capt. Standish, very eagerly and peremptorily demanded. For the Company of New Plymouth, having themselves obtained a useless patent for Cape Anne about the year 1623, sent some of the ships, which their Adventurers employed to transport passengers over to them, to make fish there; for which end they built a stage there in the year 1624. The dispute grew to be very hot, and high words passed between them; which might have ended in blows, if not in blood and slaughter, had not the prudence and moderation of Mr. Roger Conant, at that time there present, and Mr. Peirce's interposition, that lay just by with his ship, timely prevented. For Mr. Hewes had barricadoed his company with hogsheads on the stage-head, while the demandants stood upon the land, and might easily have been cut off. But the ship's crew, by advice, promising to help them build another, the difference was thereby ended. Capt. Standish had been bred a soldier in the Low Countries, and never entered the school of our Saviour Christ, or of John Baptist, his harbinger; or, if he was ever there, had forgot his first lessons, to offer violence to no man, and to part with the cloak rather than needlessly contend for the coat, though taken away without order. A little chimney is soon fired; so was the Plymouth captain, a man of very little stature, yet of a very hot and angry temper. The fire of his passion soon kindled, and blown up into a flame by hot words, might easily have consumed all, had it not been seasonably quenched.

TAKING OF THE NARRAGANSET FORT.

[A Narrative of the Troubles with the Indians in New-England. 1677.]

THE whole number of all our forces being now come, the want of provision with the sharpness of the cold minded them of expedition; wherefore the very next day, the whole body of the Massachusets and Plimouth Forces marched away to Pettiquamscot, intending to engage the enemy upon the first opportunity that next offered itself: To the which resolution those of Connecticut presently consented, as soon as they met together, which was about five o'clock in the afternoon. Bulls House, intended for their general rendezvouz, being unhappily burnt down two or three days before, there was no shelter left either for officer or private soldier, so as they were necessitated to march on towards the enemy through the snow in a cold stormy evening, finding no other defence all that night, save the open air, nor other covering than a cold and moist fleece of snow. Through all these difficulties they marched from the break of the next day, December 19th, till one of the clock in the afternoon, without either fire to warm them, or respite to take any food save what they could chew in their march. Thus having waded fourteen or fifteen mile through the country of the old Queen, or Sunke Squaw of Narhaganset, they came at one o'clock upon the edge of the swamp, where their guide assured them they should find Indians enough before night.

Our forces chopping thus upon the seat of the enemy, upon the sudden, they had no time either to draw up in any order or form of battle, nor yet opportunity to consult where or how to assault. As they

marched, Capt. Mosley and Capt. Davenport led the van; Major Appleton and Capt. Oliver brought up the rear of the Massachuset forces;
General Winslow with the Plimouth forces marched in the centre; those
of Connecticut came up in the rear of the whole body.   But the frontiers discerning Indians in the edge of the swamp fired immediately
upon them, who answering our men in the same language retired presently into the swamp; our men followed them in amain without staying
for the word of command, as if every one were ambitious who should
go first, never making any stand till they came to the sides of the
fort, into which the Indians that first fired upon them betook themselves.

It seems that there was but one entrance into the Fort, though the
enemy found many ways to come out; but neither the English nor their
guide well knew on which side the entrance lay, nor was it easy to have
made another; wherefore the good providence of Almighty God is the
more to be acknowledged, who, as he led Israel sometime by the Pillar
of Fire and the Cloud of his Preference a right way through the wilderness, so did he now direct our forces upon that side of the Fort,
where they might only enter, though not without utmost danger and
hazard.   The Fort was raised upon a kind of island of five or six acres
of rising land in the midst of a swamp; the sides of it were made of
palisades set upright, the which was compassed about with an hedge of
almost a rod thickness, through which there was no passing, unless they
could have fired away through, which then they had no time to do.   The
place where the Indians used ordinarily to enter themselves was over a
long tree upon a place of water, where but one man could enter at a
time, and which was so way-laid that they would have been cut off that
had ventured there.   But at one corner there was a gap made up only
with a long tree, about four or five foot from the ground, over which
men might easily pass.   But they had placed a kind of block-house
right over against the said tree, from whence they sorely galled our men
that first entered; some being shot dead upon the tree, as Capt. Johnson,
and some as soon as they entered, as was Capt. Davenport, so as they
that first entered were forced presently to retire and fall upon their bellies
till the fury of the enemies' shot was pretty well spent, which some companies that did not discern the danger, not observing, lost sundry of
their men; but at the last, two companies being brought up besides the
four that first marched up, they animated one another to make another assault, one of the commanders crying out, *They run, they
run;* which did so encourage the Soldiers that they presently entered amain.   After a considerable number were well entered, they
presently beat the enemy out of a flanker on the left hand, which did a
little shelter our men from the enemies' shot till more company came up,

and so by degrees made up higher, first into the middle, and then into
the upper end of the Fort, till at last they made the enemy all retire
from their sconces and fortified places, leaving multitudes of their dead
bodies upon the place.   Connecticut soldiers marching up in the rear,
being not aware of the dangerous passage over the tree in command of
the block-house, were at their first entrance many of them shot down,
although they came on with as gallant resolution as any of the rest, under the conduct of their wise and valiant leader, Major Treat.

The brunt of the battle or danger that day lay most upon the commanders, whose part it was to lead on their several companies in the very
face of death, or else all had been lost; so as all of them with great valor
and resolution of mind, as not at all afraid to die in so good a cause,
bravely led on their men in that desperate assault, leaving their lives in
the place as the best testimony of their valor, and of love to the cause
of God and their Country.   No less than six brave captains fell that day
in the assault, viz.: Capt. Davenport, Capt. Gardner, Capt. Johnson of
the Massachusets, besides Lieutenant Upham, who died some months
after of his wounds received at that time.   Capt. Gallop also, and Capt.
Siely, and Capt. Marshal were slain of those that belonged to Connecticut
Colony.   It is usually seen that the valor of the soldiers is much
wrapped up in the lives of their commanders ; yet it was found here
that the soldiers were rather enraged than discouraged by the loss of
their commanders, which made them redouble their courage, and not give
back after they were entered the second time, till they had driven out
their enemies.   So as after much blood and many wounds dealt on both
sides, the English, feeling their advantage, began to fire the wigwams,
where was supposed to be many of the enemies' women and children
destroyed, by the firing of at least five or six hundred of those smoky
cells.

It is reported by them that first entered the Indians' Fort, that our
soldiers came upon them when they were ready to dress their dinner;
but one sudden and unexpected assault put them besides that work,
making their cook-rooms too hot for them at that time, when they and
their mitchin fried together ; and probably some of them eat their suppers in a colder place that night, most of their provisions as well as their
huts being then consumed with fire ; and those that were left alive
forced to hide themselves in a cedar swamp, not far off, where they had
nothing to defend them from the cold but boughs of spruce and pine
trees.   For after two or three hours' fight the English became masters of
the place ; but not judging it tenable, after they had burned all they
could set fire upon, they were forced to retreat, after the day-light was
almost quite spent, and were necessitated to retire to their quarters, full
fifteen or sixteen miles off, some say more, whither with their dead and

wounded men they were to march, a difficulty scarce to be believed, as not to be paralleled almost in any former age.

It is hard to say who acquitted themselves best in that day's service, either the soldiers for their manlike valor in fighting, or the commanders for their wisdom and courage; leading on in the very face of death. There might one have seen the whole body of that little regimental army, as busy as bees in a hive, some bravely fighting with the enemy, others hauling off and carrying away the dead and wounded men; which I rather note, that none may want the due testimony of their valor and faithfulness, though all ought to say, "Not unto us, but unto thy Name, O Lord," etc.

For though there might not be above three or four hundred at any time within the Fort at once, yet the rest in their turns came up to do what the exigency of the service required in bringing off the dead and wounded men. The Major of the Massachusets regiment, together with Capt. Mosely, was very serviceable; for by that means the Fort being clear of the dead bodies, it struck a greater terror into the enemy to see but eight or ten dead bodies of the English left, than to meet with so many hundreds of their own slain and wounded carcasses. The number of the slain was not then known on the enemies side, because our men were forced to leave them on the ground; but our victory was found afterwards to be much more considerable than at the first was apprehended; for although our loss was very great, not only because of the desperateness of the attempt itself (in such a season of the year, and at such a distance from our quarters, whereby many of our wounded men perished, which might otherwise have been preserved, if they had not been forced to march so many miles in a cold and snowy night, before they could be dressed) yet the enemy lost so many of their principal fighting men,—their provision also was, by the burning of their wigwams, so much of it spoiled at the taking of their Fort, and by surprising so much of their corn about that time also,—that it was the occasion of their total ruin afterwards; they being at that time driven away from their habitations and put by from planting for that next year, as well as deprived of what they had in store for the present winter. What numbers of the enemy were slain is uncertain; it was confessed by one Potock a great councillor among them, afterwards taken at Road Island and put to death at Boston, that the Indians lost seven hundred fighting men that day, besides three hundred that died of their wounds the most of them; the number of men, women and children, that perished either by fire, or that were starved with hunger and cold, none of them could tell. There were above eighty of the English slain, and a hundred and fifty wounded that recovered afterwards.

SUBTLETY AND COURAGE OF THE FRIENDLY INDIANS.

[From the Same.]

IT is worth noting, what faithfulness and courage some of the Christian Indians with the said Capt. Peirce showed in the fight [at Abbot's Run]. One of them, Amos by name, after the Captain was shot in his leg or thigh, so he was not able to stand any longer, would not leave him, but charging his gun several times, fired stoutly upon the enemy, till he saw that there was no possibility for him to do any further good to Capt. Peirce, nor yet to save himself, if he stayed any longer; therefore he used this policy, perceiving the enemy had all blacked their faces, he also stooping down, pulled out some blacking out of a pouch he carried with him, discolored his face therewith, and, so making himself as like *Hobamacko* as any of his enemies, he ran among them a little while, and was taken for one of themselves, as if he had been searching for the English, until he had an opportunity to escape away among the bushes; therein imitating the cuttle-fish, which when it is pursued, or in danger, casteth out of its body a thick humor as black as ink, through which it passes away unseen by the pursuer.

It is reported of another of these Cape Indians (friends to the English of Plimouth) that being pursued by one of the enemies, he betook himself to a great rock, where he sheltered himself for a while; at last perceiving that his enemy lay ready with his gun on the other side, to discharge upon him, as soon as he stirred never so little away from the place where he stood; in the issue he thought of this politic stratagem to save himself and destroy his enemy (for as Solomon said of old, "Wisdom is better than Weapons of War"), he took a stick, and hung his hat upon it, and then by degrees gently lifted it up, till he thought it would be seen and so become a fit mark for the other that watched to take aim at him. The other taking it to be his head fired a gun, and shot through the hat; which our Christian Indian perceiving, boldly held up his head and discharged his own gun upon the real head, not the hat of his adversary, whereby he shot him dead upon the place, and so had liberty to march away with the spoils of his enemy.

The like subtle device was used by another of the Cape Indians at the same time, being one of them that went out with Capt. Peirce; for being in like manner pursued by one of Philip's Indians, as the former was, he nimbly got behind the but-end of a tree newly turned up by the roots, which carried a considerable breadth of the surface of the earth along with it (as is very useful in these parts, where the roots of the trees lie very fleet in the ground) which stood up above the Indian's height in form of a large shield, only it was somewhat too heavy to be easily wielded or removed; the enemy-Indian lay with his gun ready to shoot him down upon his first deserting his station; but a subtle wit taught our Christian *Netop* a better device; for, boring a little hole through this his broad shield, he discerned his enemy, who could not so easily discern him; a good musketeer need never desire a fairer mark to shoot at; whereupon discharging his gun, he shot him down: what can be more just than that he should himself be killed, who lay in wait to kill another man?

> —— *Neque enim Lex justior ulla est,*
> *Quam necis Artifices arte perire sua.*

Instances of this nature show the subtility and dexterousness of these natives, if they were improved in feats of arms: and possibly if some of the English had not been too shy in making use of such of them as were well affected to their own interest, they need never have suffered so much from their enemies: it having been found upon late experience that many of them have proved not only faithful, but very serviceable and helpful to the English; they usually proving good seconds, though they have not ordinarily confidence enough to make the first onset.

HOW AN INDIAN BORE HIMSELF UNDER TORTURE.

[From the Same.]

AMONGST the rest of the prisoners then taken was a young sprightly fellow, seized by the Mohegans; who desired of the English commanders that he might be delivered into their hands, that they might put him to death, *more majorum;* sacrifice him to their cruel Genius of Revenge, in which brutish and devilish passion they are most of all delighted. The English, though not delighted in blood, yet at this time were not unwilling to gratify their humor, lest by a denial they might disoblige their Indian friends, of whom they lately made so much use; partly also that they might have an ocular demonstration of the savage, barbarous cruelty of these Heathen. And indeed, of all the enemies that have been the subjects of the precedent discourse, this villain did most deserve to become an object of justice and severity; for he boldly told them that he had with his gun dispatched nineteen English, and that he had charged it for the twentieth; but not meeting with any of ours, and unwilling to lose a fair shot, he had let fly at a Mohegan and killed him, with which, having made up his number, he told them he was fully satisfied. But, as is usually said, justice vindictive hath iron hands, though leaden feet; this cruel monster is fallen into their power, that will repay him seven-fold. In the first place, therefore, making a great circle, they placed him in the middle, that all their eyes might at the same time be pleased with the utmost revenge upon him. They first cut one of his fingers round in the joint, at the trunk of his hand, with a sharp knife, and then broke it off, as men used to do with a slaughtered beast before they uncase him; then they cut off another and another, till they had dismembered one hand of all its digits, the blood sometimes spurting out in streams a yard from his hand, which barbarous and unheard of cruelty the English were not able to bear, it forcing tears from their eyes. Yet did not the sufferer ever relent, or show any sign of anguish; for being asked by some of his tormentors, how he liked the war? he might have replied, as the Scotch gentleman did after the loss of a battle, that being asked how he liked the match, *sc.* with our Prince of Wales (which then was the occasion of the quarrel), made answer, he liked the match well enough, but no whit liked the manner of the wooing written by such lines of blood. But this unsensible and hard-hearted monster answered, He liked it very well, and found it as sweet as Englishmen did their sugar. In this frame he continued, till his executioners had dealt with the toes of his feet as they had done with the fingers of his hands; all the while making him dance round the circle and sing, till he had wearied both himself and them. At last they broke the bones of his legs, after which he was forced to sit down, which 'tis said he silently did till they had knocked out his brains. Instances of this nature should be incentive unto us to bless the Father of Lights, who hath called us out of the dark places of the earth, full of the habitations of cruelty. When the Day-spring from on high shall visit those that sit in this region of darkness, another Spirit will be poured upon them, and then the feet of them that bring the glad tidings of gospel-salvation will appear more beautiful to them than at present they seem to do. And when these mountains of prey shall become the holy mountain of the Lord, they shall neither hurt, nor destroy, nor exercise cruelty therein.

———

Benjamin Tompson.

BORN in Braintree, Mass., 1642. Our first native Poet. DIED at Roxbury, Mass., 1714.

ON THE WOMEN FORTIFYING BOSTON NECK.

[New England's Crisis. About 1675.]

A GRAND attempt some Amazonian Dames
   Contrive whereby to glorify their names,
A ruff for Boston Neck of mud and turfe,
Reaching from side to side, from surf to surf,
Their nimble hands spin up like Christmas pyes,
Their pastry by degrees on high doth rise.
The wheel at home counts in an holiday,
Since while the mistress worketh it may play.
A tribe of female hands, but manly hearts,
Forsake at home their pastry crust and tarts,
To kneed the dirt, the samplers down they hurl,
Their undulating silks they closely furl.
The pick-axe one as a commandress holds,
While t'other at her awk'ness gently scolds.
One puffs and sweats, the other mutters why
Cant you promove your work so fast as I ?
Some dig, some delve, and others' hands do feel
The little wagon's weight with single wheel.
And least some fainting-fits the weak surprize,
They want no sack nor cakes, they are more wise.
These brave essays draw forth male, stronger hands,
More like to dawbers than to marshal bands ;
These do the work, and sturdy bulwarks raise,
But the beginners well deserve the praise.

THE ALARMING PROGRESS OF LUXURY IN NEW ENGLAND.

[From the Same.]

THE times wherin old Pompion was a saint,
   When men fared hardly yet without complaint,
On vilest cates ; the dainty Indian maize
Was eat with clamp-shells out of wooden trays,
Under thatch'd hutts without the cry of rent,
And the best sawce to every dish, content.
When flesh was food and hairy skins made coats,
And men as well as birds had chirping notes.

When Cimnels were accounted noble bloud ;
Among the tribes of common herbage food.
Of Ceres' bounty form'd was many a knack.
Enough to fill poor Robin's Almanack.
These golden times (too fortunate to hold)
Were quickly sin'd away for love of gold.
'Twas then among the bushes, not the street,
If one in place did an inferior meet,
" Good morrow, brother, is there aught you want ?
" Take freely of me, what I have you ha'nt."
Plain Tom and Dick would pass as current now,
As ever since " Your Servant, Sir," and bow.
Deep-skirted doublets, puritanic capes,
Which now would render men like upright apes,
Was comlier wear, our wiser fathers thought,
Than the cast fashions from all Europe brought.
'Twas in those days an honest grace would hold
Till an hot pudding grew at heart a cold.
And men had better stomachs at religion,
Than I to capon, turkey-cock, or pigeon ;
When honest sisters met to pray, not prate,
About their own and not their neighbour's state.
During Plain Dealing's reign, that worthy stud
Of the ancient planter's race before the flood,
Then times were good, merchants car'd not a rush
For other fare than Jonakin and Mush.
Although men far'd and lodged very hard,
Yet innocence was better than a guard.
'Twas long before spiders and worms had drawn
Their dungy webs, or hid with cheating lawne
New England's beautyes, which still seem'd to me
Illustrious in their own simplicity.
'Twas ere the neigbouring Virgin-Land had broke
The hogsheads of her worse than hellish smoak.
'Twas ere the Islands sent their presents in,
Which but to use was counted next to sin.
'Twas ere a barge had made so rich a freight
As chocolate, dust-gold and bitts of eight.
Ere wines from France and Muscovadoe to,
Without the which the drink will scarsly doe.
From western isles ere fruits and delicacies
Did rot maids' teeth and spoil their handsome faces.
Or ere these times did chance, the noise of war
Was from our towns and hearts removed far.
No bugbear comets in the chrystal air
Did drive our christian planters to despair.
No sooner pagan malice peeped forth
But valour snib'd it. Then were men of worth
Who by their prayers slew thousands angel-like ;
Their weapons are unseen with which they strike.

Then had the churches rest ; as yet the coales
Were covered up in most contentious souls :
Freeness in judgment, union in affection,
Dear love, sound truth, they were our grand protection
Then were the times in which our councells sate,
These gave prognosticks of our future fate.
If these be longer liv'd our hopes increase,
These warrs will usher in a longer peace.
But if New England's love die in its youth,
The grave will open next for blessed truth.
This theame is out of date, the peacefull hours
When castles needed not, but pleasant bowers.
Not ink, but bloud and tears now serve the turn
To draw the figure of New England's urne.
New England's hour of passion is at hand ;
No power except divine can it withstand.
Scarce hath her glass of fifty years run out,
But her old prosperous steeds turn heads about,
Tracking themselves back to their poor beginnings,
To fear and fare upon their fruits of sinnings.
So that the mirror of the christian world
Lyes burnt to heaps in part, her streamers furl'd.
Grief sighs, joyes flee, and dismal fears surprize
Not dastard spirits only, but the wise.
Thus have the fairest hopes deceiv'd the eye
Of the big-swoln expectant standing by :
Thus the proud ship after a little turn,
Sinks into Neptune's arms to find its urne :
Thus hath the heir to many thousands born
Been in an instant from the mother torn :
Even thus thine infant cheeks began to pale,
And thy supporters through great losses fail.
This is the *Prologue* to thy future woe,
The *Epilogue* no mortal yet can know.

IN PRAISE OF THE RENOWNED COTTON MATHER.

[*Prefixed to the " Magnalia Christi Americana." 1702.*]

IS the bless'd MATHER necromancer turn'd,
 To raise his country's fathers' ashes urn'd ?
Elisha's dust, life to the dead imparts ;
This prophet, by his more familiar arts,
Unseals our heroes' tombs, and gives them air ;
They rise, they walk, they talk, look wondrous fair ;
Each of them in an orb of light doth shine,
In liveries of glory most divine.

When ancient names I in thy pages met,
Like gems on Aaron's costly breastplate set,
Methinks heaven's open, while great saints descend,
To wreathe the brows by which their acts were penn'd.

Urian Oakes.

BORN in England, 1631–2.   DIED at Cambridge, Mass., 1681.

ELEGY ON THE DEATH OF THOMAS SHEPARD.

[An Elegie upon The Death of the Reverend Mr. Thomas Shepard. 1677.]

OH ! that I were a poet now in grain !
   How would I invocate the Muses all
To deign their presence, lend their flowing vein ;
And help to grace dear Shepard's funeral !
      How would I paint our griefs, and succours borrow
      From art and fancy, to limn out our sorrow !

Now could I wish (if wishing would obtain)
The sprightliest efforts of poetick rage,
To vent my griefs, make others feel my pain,
For this loss of the glory of our age.
      Here is a subject for the loftiest verse
      That ever waited on the bravest hearse.

And could my pen ingeniously distill
The purest spirits of a sparkling wit
In rare conceits, the quintessence of skill
In elegiack strains ; none like to it :
      I should think all too little to condole
      The fatal loss (to us) of such a soul.

Could I take highest flights of fancy, soar
Aloft ; if wit's monopoly were mine ;
All would be much too low, too light, too poor,
To pay due tribute to this great divine.
      Ah ! wit avails not, when th' heart's like to break,
      Great griefs are tongue-tied, when the lesser speak.

      .   .   .   .

Here need no spices, odours, curious arts,
No skill of Egypt, to embalm the name
Of such a worthy : let men speak their hearts,
They'l say, he merits an immortal fame.
      When Shepard is forgot, all must conclude,
      This is prodigious ingratitude.

But live he shall in many a grateful breast
Where he hath rear'd himself a monument,
A monument more stately than the best
On which immensest treasures have been spent.
    Could you but into th' hearts of thousands peep,
    There would you read his name engraven deep.

Oh ! that my head were waters, and mine eyes
A flowing spring of tears, still issuing forth
In streams of bitterness, to solemnize
The obits of this man of matchless worth !
    Next to the tears our sins do need and crave,
    I would bestow my tears on Shepard's grave.

Not that he needs our tears : for he hath dropt
His measure full ; not one tear more shall fall
Into God's bottle from his eyes ; Death stopt
That water-course, his sorrows ending all.
    He fears, he cares, he sighs, he weeps no more :
    Hee's past all storms, arriv'd at th' wished shoar.

Dear Shepard ! could we reach so high a strain
Of pure seraphick love, as to divest
Ourselves, and love, of self respects, thy gain
Would joy us, though it cross our interest.
    Then would we silence all complaints with this,
    Our dearest friend is doubtless gone to bliss.

Ah ! but the lesson's hard, thus to deny
Our own dear selves, to part with such a loan
Of Heaven (in time of such necessity)
And love thy comforts better than our own.
    Then let us moan our loss, adjourn our glee,
    Till we come thither to rejoice with thee.

As when some formidable comet's blaze,
As when portentous prodigies appear,
Poor mortals with amazement stand and gaze,
With hearts affrighted, and with trembling fear :
    So are we all amazed at this blow,
    Sadly portending some approaching woe.

We shall not summon bold astrologers
To tell us what the stars say in the case,
(Those cousen-germans to black conjurers).
We have a sacred Oracle that sayes,
    When th' righteous perish, men of mercy go,
    It is a sure presage of coming wo.

He was (ah, woful word ! to say he was)
Our wrestling Israel, second unto none,

The man that stood i' th' gap, to keep the pass,
To stop the troops of judgments rushing on.
 This man the honour had to hold the hand
 Of an incensed God against our Land.

When such a pillar's faln (oh such an one !)
When such a glorious, shining light's put out,
When chariot and horsemen thus are gone,
Well may we fear some downfal, darkness, rout.
 When such a bank's broke down, there's sad occasion
 To wail, and dread some grievous inundation.

What ! must we with our God, and glory part ?
Lord ! is thy treaty with New-England come
Thus to an end ? And is war in thy heart
That this embassadour is called home ?
 So earthly Gods (Kings), when they war intend,
 Call home their ministers, and treaties end.

Oh for the raptures, transports, inspirations
Of Israel's Singer, when his Jonathan's fall
So tun'd his mourning harp ! what Lamentations
Then would I make for Shepard's funeral !
 How truly can I say, as well as he,
 " My dearest brother, I am distress'd for thee."

How lovely, worthy, peerless, in my view !
How precious, pleasant hast thou been to me !
How learned, prudent, pious, grave, and true !
And what a faithful friend ! who like to thee !
 Mine eye's desire is vanish'd : who can tell
 Where lives my dearest Shepard's parallel ?

'Tis strange to think : but we may well believe,
That not a few, of different perswasions
From this great worthy, do now truely grieve
I' th' mourning crowd, and joyn their lamentations.
 Such powers magnetick had he to draw to him
 The very hearts, and souls, of all that knew him !

Art, nature, grace, in him were all combin'd
To shew the world a matchless paragon :
In whom of radiant virtues no less shin'd
Than a whole constellation: but hee's gone !
 Hee's gone alas ! Down in the dust must ly
 As much of this rare person as could dy.

If to have solid judgment, pregnant parts,
A piercing wit, and comprehensive brain ;
If to have gone the round of all the arts,
Immunity from Death's arrest would gain,

Shepard would have been death-proof, and secure
From that all-conquering hand, I'm very sure.

If holy life, and deeds of charity,
If grace illustrious, and virtue tried,
If modest carriage, rare humility,
Could have brib'd Death, good Shepard had not died.
  Oh! but inexorable Death attacks
  The best men, and promiscuous havock makes.

Come tell me, Criticks, have you ever known
Such zeal, so temper'd well with moderation?
Such prudence, and such innocence met in one?
Such parts, so little pride and ostentation?
  Let Momus carp, and Envy do her worst,
  And swell with spleen and rancour till she burst.

To be descended well, doth *that* commend?
Can sons their fathers' glory call their own?
Our Shepard justly might to this pretend,
(His blessed father was of high renown,
  Both Englands speak him great, admire his name),
  But his own personal worth's a better claim.

Great was the father, once a glorious light
Among us, famous to an high degree:
Great was this son: indeed (to do him right)
As great and good (to say no more) as he.
  A double portion of his father's spirit
  Did this (his eldest) son, through grace, inherit.

His look commanded reverence and awe,
Though mild and amiable, not austere:
Well-humour'd was he as I ever saw
And rul'd by love and wisdome, more than fear,
  The Muses, and the Graces too, conspir'd
  To set forth this rare piece, to be admir'd,

He govern'd well the tongue (that busie thing,
Unruly, lawless and pragmatical),
Gravely reserv'd, in speech not lavishing,
Neither too sparing, nor too liberal.
  His words were few, well season'd, wisely weigh'd,
  And in his tongue the law of kindness sway'd.

Learned he was beyond the common size,
Befriended much by nature in his wit,
And temper (sweet, sedate, ingenious, wise),
And (which crown'd all) he was Heavens favourite;
  On whom the God of all Grace did command,
  And show'r down blessings with a liberal hand.

Wise he, not wily, was; grave, not morose ;
Not stiffe, but steady ; serious, but not sowre ;
Concern'd for all, as if he had no Foes ;
(Strange if he had!) and would not wast an hour.
     Thoughtful and active for the common good:
     And yet his own place wisely understood.

Nothing could make him stray from duty; Death
Was not so frightful to him, as omission
Of ministerial work ; he fear'd no breath,
Infectious, i' th' discharge of his commission.
     Rather than run from's work, he chose to dy,
     Boldly to run on death, than duty fly.

(Cruel Disease! that didst (like high-way-men)
Assault the honest traveller in his way,
And rob dear Shepard of his life (ah !) then,
When he was on the road where duty lay.
     Forbear, bold pen ! 'twas God that took him thus,
     To give him great reward, and punish us.)

Zealous in God's cause, but meek in his own ;
Modest of nature, bold as any lion
Where conscience was concern'd: and there were none
More constant mourners for afflicted Sion:
     So general was his care for th' Churches all,
     His spirit seemed apostolical.

Large was his heart, to spend without regret,
Rejoycing to do good: not like those moles
That root i' th' earth, or roam abroad, to get
All for themselves (those sorry, narrow souls!)
     But he, like th' sun (i' th' center, as some say)
     Diffus'd his rayes of goodness every way.

He breath'd love, and pursu'd peace in his day,
As if his soul were made of harmony:
Scarce ever more of goodness crouded lay
In such a piece of frail mortality.
     Sure Father Wilson's genuine son was he,
     New-England's Paul had such a Timothy.

No slave to th' world's grand idols ; but he flew
At fairer quarries, without stooping down
To sublunary prey: his great soul knew
Ambition none, but of the heavenly crown:
     Now he hath won it, and shall wear 't with honour
     Adoring grace, and God in Christ, the donour.

A friend to truth, a constant foe to errour,
Powerful i' th' pulpit, and sweet in converse,

To weak ones gentle, to th' profane a terrour,—
Who can his vertues and good works rehearse?
    The Scripture—Bishop's character read o're,
    Say this was Shepard's : what need I say more?

I say no more; let them that can declare
His rich and rare endowments, paint this sun
With all its dazzling rayes: but I despair,
Hopeless by any hand to see it done.
    They that can Shepard's goodness well display
    Must be as good as he ; but who are they?

See where our Sister Charlstown sits and moans !
Poor widow'd Charlstown! all in dust, in tears !
Mark how she wrings her hands! hear how she groans !
See how she weeps ! what sorrow like to hers !
    Charlstown, that might for joy compare of late
    With all about her, now looks desolate.

As you have seen some pale, wan, ghastly look,
When grisly death, that will not be said nay,
Hath seiz'd all for itself, possession took,
And turn'd the soul out of its house of clay:
    So visag'd is poor Charlstown at this day;
    Shepard, her very soul, is torn away.

Cambridge groans under this so heavy cross,
And sympathizes with her Sister dear ;
Renews her griefs afresh for her old loss
Of her own Shepard, and drops many a tear.
    Cambridge and Charlstown now joint mourners are,
    And this tremendous loss between them share.

Must Learnings friend (ah! worth us all) go thus?
That great support to Harvard's nursery!
Our Fellow (that no fellow had with us)
Is gone to Heaven's great University.
    Ours now indeed's a lifeless Corporation,
    The soul is fled, that gave it animation!

Poor Harvard's sons are in their mourning dress:
Their sure friend's gone! their hearts have put on mourning;
Within their walls are sighs, tears, pensiveness;
Their new foundations dread an overturning.
    Harvard! where's such a fast friend left to thee?
    Unless thy great friend LEVERET, it be.

We must not with our greatest Soveraign strive,
Who dare find fault with him that is most high?
That hath an absolute prerogative,
And doth his pleasure : none may ask him, why?

We're clay-lumps, dust-heaps, nothings in his sight:
The Judge of all the earth doth always right.

.Ah! could not prayers and tears prevail with God!
Was there no warding off that dreadful blow!
And was there no averting of that rod!
Must Shepard dy! and that good angel go!
  Alas! Our heinous sins (more than our hairs)
  It seems, were louder, and out-cried our prayers.

See what our sins have done! what ruines wrought
And how they have pluck'd out our very eyes!
Our sins have slain our Shepard! we have bought,
And dearly paid for, our enormities.
  Ah, cursed sins! that strike at God and kill
  His servants, and the blood of prophets spill.

As you would loath the sword that's warm and red,
As you would hate the hands that are embrued
I' th' heart's-blood of your dearest friends: so dread,
And hate your sins; Oh! let them be pursued:
  Revenges take on bloody sins: for there's
  No refuge-city for these murtherers.

In vain we build the prophets' sepulchers,
In vain bedew their tombs with tears, when dead;
In vain bewail the deaths of ministers,
Whilest prophet-killing sins are harboured.
  Those that these murtherous traitors favour, hide;
  Are with the blood of Prophets deeply dy'd.

New-England! know thy heart-plague: feel this blow;
A blow that sorely wounds both head and heart,
A blow that reaches all, both high and low,
A blow that may be felt in every part.
  Mourn that this great man's faln in Israel:
  Let it be said, "with him New-England fell!"

Farewell, dear Shepard! Thou art gone before,
Made free of Heaven, where thou shalt sing loud hymns
Of high triumphant praises ever more,
In the sweet quire of saints and seraphims.
  Lord! look on us here, clogg'd with sin and clay,
  And we, through grace, shall be as happy as they.

My dearest, inmost, bosome-friend is gone!
Gone is my sweet companion, soul's delight!
Now in an hud'ling croud I'm all alone,
And almost could bid all the world "Goodnight."
  Blest be my Rock! God lives: O let him be,
  As He is All, so All in All to me!

A CONTRITE SPIRIT BETTER THAN OUTWARD SEEMING.

[*Sincerity and Delight in the Service of God.* 1682.]

MEN may do many duties and yet do none of them well, and consequently do none at all in God's estimation. Men may go the round of duty and plod on in a course of religious performances, and yet do nothing the while to any purpose. In all the duties of worship, it is not the bare outward action, but the manner of performance that gives the denomination and is regarded especially of the Lord. Hence Luther's saying, that adverbs are of more account with God than verbs, meaning that the manner of our performances (which is commonly denoted by this or that adverb) is more available with God than the bare performance of duty, which is usually expressed by some verb or other. There are many necessary requisites to, and essential ingredients in the true worship of God, which, if they be wanting, the external performance of it is as a thing of naught in God's valuation. Though the worship be materially good, not idolatrous, superstitious, uncommanded, or unlawful in itself, but such as God hath instituted and enjoined ; yet it may be formally evil and want such conditions and qualifications as would render it acceptable to God. Men may pray, hear, receive sacraments, be much in duties of worship, and yet do nothing from a principle of grace, in obedience to God, with a due respect to his glory. And is not all this (think you) as good as nothing in point of acceptation with the Lord ?

A man may be doing every day, and yet do nothing in religion. All his prayers may be nothing else but the lazy wishings and wouldings of sinful sloth, the babblings of formality, the cravings, inordinate, selfish, greedy cravings of his lusts, the discontented murmurings and grumblings of the flesh, or howlings in a time of affliction. Yea, as the plowing of the wicked is sin, so is his praying also. "The sacrifice of the wicked is an abomination to the Lord," Prov. xv., 8. God looks with a gracious aspect on him that is poor and of a contrite spirit, and trembles at his word : but he that, without these inward, holy dispositions of spirit, slayeth an ox, is as if he slew a man, etc. Of so little account with God is external worship without the internal, as He will hardly allow it the name of invocation and worship, but gives it very hard names, importing that such invocation is indeed a great provocation of God. All the use that I would make of it is in these words :

This may serve to check the pride and petulancy, to beat down the confidence and conceit of hypocrites, that glory in their performances and reckon God indebted to them for their services, that think they have done some great matter when they have prayed, fasted, heard God s

word, done these or those duties, and bear themselves high upon the
frequency of their external devotion, and think God doth them great
wrong, if He doth not consider and reward their diligence and dutifulness.
No hypocrite acts beyond the sphere of the covenant of works, but
thinks to win it and wear it, and is (whatever he professeth) of a mer-
cenary spirit, and quarrels with God, if He do not hear his prayers and
reward his services.   So those supercilious, proud hypocrites: "Wherefore have we fasted" (saith they) "and thou seest not? Wherefore have
we afflicted our soul, and thou takest no knowledge?"   Thus they fly
out and expostulate with God, because their external humiliations and
hypocritical performances were not regarded and rewarded according to
their mind.   There is this saucy spirit in all hypocrites.   Ah! poor
proud man, thou mayest boast of thy prayers and duties, and quarrel
with God that He doth not hear and reward, but thou hast no reason;
for take this home with thee: thou hast never prayed in thy life, never
called upon God to this day, thou has done much in a way of duty, in thy
kind and fond opinion of thyself, but as good as nothing in God's account.   Thou hast more reason to admire the patience and mercy of God,
for not punishing thee for such simple, as well as insignificant performances, than expostulate with him and question his justice and faithful·
ness, because He hath not rewarded them.

John Rogers.

BORN in Essex, England, about 1630. DIED at Cambridge, Mass., 1684.

UPON MRS. ANNE BRADSTREET HER POEMS.

[Prefixed to the Posthumous Edition of Anne Bradstreet's Poems. 1678.]

MADAM, twice through the Muses' grove I walked ;
    Under your blissful bowers, I shrouding there,
It seemed with nymphs of Helicon I talked :
    For there those sweet-lipped Sisters sporting were ;
Apollo with his sacred lute sate by ;
On high they made their heavenly sonnets fly ;
Posies around they strewed, of sweetest poesy.

Twice have I drunk the nectar of your lines,
    Which high sublimed my mean-born fantasy.
Flushed with the streams of your Maronean wines,
    Above myself rapt to an ecstasy,
Methought I was upon Mount Hybla's top,
There where I might those fragrant flowers lop,
Whence did sweet odors flow, and honey spangles drop.

To Venus' shrine no altars raised are,
    Nor venomed shafts from painted quiver fly,
Nor wanton doves of Aphrodite's car
    Are fluttering there, nor here forlornly lie
Lorn paramours, nor chatting birds tell news
How sage Apollo Daphne hot pursues,
Or stately Jove himself is wont to haunt the stews.

Nor barking Satyr's breath, nor dreary clouds
    Exhaled from Styx, their dismal drops distil
Within these fairy, flowery fields, nor shrouds
    The screeching night raven, with his shady quill :
But lyric strings here Orpheus nimbly hits,
Orion on his saddled Dolphin sits,
Chanting as every humor, age, and season fits.

Here silver swans with nightingales set spells,
    Which sweetly charm the traveller, and raise
Earth's earthed monarchs from their hidden cells,
    And to appearance summon lapsed days ;
There heavenly air becalms the swelling frays,
And fury fell of elements allays
By paying every one due tribute of his praise.

This seemed the site of all those verdant vales
    And purled springs, whereat the Nymphs do play,
With lofty hills, where Poets read their tales
    To heavenly vaults, which heavenly sounds repay
By echo's sweet rebound ; here Ladies kiss,
Circling, nor songs nor dance's circle miss ;
But whilst those Siren's sung, I sunk in sea of bliss.

   .   .   .   .

Your only hand those poesies did compose,
    Your head the source whence all those springs did flow ;
Your voice, whence change's sweetest notes arose ;
    Your feet, that kept the dance alone, I trow :
Then vail your bonnets, Poetasters all ;
Strike, lower amain, and at these humbly fall,
And deem yourselves advanced to be her pedestal.

Should all with lowly congies laurels bring,
    Waste Flora's magazine to find a wreath,
Or Pineus' banks, 'twere too mean offering ;
    Your Muse a fairer garland doth bequeath
To guard your fairer front ; here 'tis your name
Shall stand immarbled ; this your little frame
Shall great Colossus be, to your eternal fame.

I'll please myself, though I myself disgrace,
What errors here be found, are in *Errata's* place.

John Norton.

BORN 1651.   Minister at Hingham, Mass.   DIED there, 1716.

DIRGE FOR THE TENTH MUSE.

Anne Bradstreet

[Appended to the Posthumous Edition of Anne Bradstreet's Poems. 1678.]

ASK not why hearts turn magazines of passions,
    And why that grief is clad in several fashions ;
Why she on progress goes, and doth not borrow
The smallest respite from th' extremes of sorrow.
Here misery is got to such an height
As makes the earth groan to support its weight ;
Such storms of woe so strongly have beset her,
She hath no place for worse, nor hope for better ;
Her comfort is, if any for her be,
That none can show more cause of grief than she.
Ask not why some in mournful black are clad ;
The sun is set, there needs must be a shade.
Ask not why every face a sadness shrouds ;
The setting sun o'er-cast us hath with clouds.
Ask not why the great glory of the sky,
That gilds the stars with heavenly alchemy,
Which all the world doth lighten with his rays,
The Persian God, the Monarch of the days, —
Ask not the reason of his ecstasy,
Paleness of late, in midnoon majesty,
While that the pale-faced Empress of the night
Disrobed her brother of his glorious light.
Did not the language of the stars foretell
A mournful scene, when they with tears did swell ?
Did not the glorious people of the sky
Seem sensible of future misery ?
Did not the lowering heavens seem to express
The world's great loss, and their unhappiness ?
Behold how tears flow from the learned hill,
How the bereaved Nine do daily fill
The bosom of the fleeting air with groans
And woful accents, which witness their moans.
How do the Goddesses of verse, the learned choir
Lament their rival quill, which all admire !
Could Maro's Muse but hear her lively strain,
He would condemn his works to fire again.
Methinks I hear the Patron of the Spring,
The unshorn Deity, abruptly sing.
Some do for anguish weep, for anger I
That Ignorance should live, and Art should die.

Black, fatal, dismal, inauspicious day,
Unblest forever by Sol's precious ray,
Be it the first of miseries to all,
Or last of life, defamed for funeral.
When this day yearly comes, let every one
Cast in their urn the black and dismal stone,—
Succeeding years, as they their circuit go,
Leap o'er this day, as a sad time of woe.
Farewell, my Muse, since thou hast left thy shrine,
I am unblest in one, but blest in nine.
Fair Thespian Ladies, light your torches all,
Attend your glory to its funeral,
To court her ashes with a learned tear,
A briny sacrifice,—let not a smile appear.
Grave Matron, whoso seeks to blazon thee,
Needs not make use of wit's false heraldry ;
Whoso should give thee all thy worth would swell
So high, as 'twould turn the world infidel.
Had he great Maro's Muse, or Tully's tongue,
Or raping numbers like the Thracian song,
In crowning of her merits he would be
Sumptuously poor, low in hyperbole.
To write is easy ; but to write on thee,
Truth would be thought to forfeit modesty.
He'll seem a Poet that shall speak but true ;
Hyperboles in others, are thy due.
Like a most servile flatterer he will show,
Though he write truth, and make the subject, **You.**
Virtue ne'er dies, time will a Poet raise,
Born under better stars, shall sing thy praise.
Praise her who list, yet he shall be a debtor,
For Art ne'er feigned, nor Nature framed, a better.
Her virtues were so great, that they do raise
A work to trouble fame, astonish praise,
When as her name doth but salute the ear,—
Men think that they perfection's abstract hear.
Her breast was a brave palace, a Broad-street,
Where all heroic ample thoughts did meet,
Where nature such a tenement had ta'en,
That other's souls, to hers, dwelt in a lane.
Beneath her feet pale envy bites her chain,
And poison malice whets her sting in vain.
Let every laurel, every myrtle bough
Be stripped for leaves to adorn and load her brow,
Victorious wreaths, which, 'cause they never fade,
Wise elder times for Kings and Poets made.
Let not her happy memory e'er lack
Its worth in Fame's eternal almanac,
Which none shall read, but straight their loss deplore,
And blame their fates they were not born before.

Do not old men rejoice their fates did last,
And infants too, that theirs did make such haste,
In such a welcome time to bring them forth,
That they might be a witness to her worth?
Who undertakes this subject to commend
Shall nothing find so hard as how to end.

Charles Wolley.

BORN in Lincolnshire, England. Chaplain of Fort James, New York, 1678–80.

FELLOW-PASSENGERS TO ENGLAND.

[A Two Years Journal in New-York. 1701.]

OLD CLAUS, the Indian, made me the owner of a couple of well-grown bear's cubs, two or three days before I took shipping for England, he thinking I would have brought them along with me; which present I accepted with a great deal of ceremony (as we must everything from their hands) and ordered my negro boy about twelve years old to tie them under the crib by my horse, and so left them to any one's acceptance upon my going aboard. I brought over with me a gray squirrel, a parrot and a rackoon. The first the Lady Sherard had some years at Sapleford, the second, I left at London; the last I brought along with me to Alford, where one Sunday in prayer time, some boys giving it nuts, it was choked with a shell. It was by nature a very curious cleanly creature, never eating anything but first washed it with its forefeet very carefully. The Parrot was a prattling familiar bird, and diverting company in my solitary intervals upon our voyage home. As I was talking with it upon the quarter deck, by a sudden rolling of the ship, down drops Poll overboard into the sea and cried out amain, "poor Poll." The ship being almost becalmed, a kind seaman threw out a rope, and Poll seized it with his beak and came safe aboard again; this for my own diversion.

KNICKERBOCKER CUSTOMS IN THE PLEASANT OLDEN TIME.

[From the Same.]

TO return from the wilderness into New York, a place of as sweet and agreeable air as ever I breathed in, and the inhabitants, both English and Dutch, very civil and courteous, as I may speak by experience, amongst whom I have often wished myself and family, to whose tables I was frequently invited, and always concluded with a generous bottle of Madeira. I cannot say I observed any swearing or quarrelling, but what was easily reconciled and recanted by a mild rebuke, except once betwixt two Dutch Boors (whose usual oath is "Sacrament") which, abating the abusive language, was no unpleasant scene. As soon as they met (which was after they had alarmed the neighborhood) they seized each other's hair with their forefeet, and down they went to the sod, their vrows and families crying out because they could not part them; which fray happening against my chamber window, I called up one of my acquaintance, and ordered him to fetch a kit full of water and discharge it at them, which immediately cooled their courage and loosed their grapples; so we used to part our mastiffs in England. In the same City of New York where I was minister to the English, there were two other ministers, or dominies as they were called there, the one a Lutheran, a German, or High-Dutch, the other a Calvinist, an Hollander, or Low-Dutchman; who behaved themselves one towards another so shyly and uncharitably as if Luther and Calvin had bequeathed and entailed their virulent and bigoted spirits upon them and their heirs forever. They had not visited or spoken to each other with any respect for six years together before my being there; with whom I being much acquainted, I invited them both with their vrows to a supper one night unknown to each other, with an obligation, that they should not speak one word in Dutch, under the penalty of a bottle of Madeira, alleging I was so imperfect in that language that we could not manage a sociable discourse; so accordingly they came, and at the first interview they stood so appalled as if the ghosts of Luther and Calvin had suffered a transmigration, but the amaze soon went off with a *salve tu quoque* and a bottle of wine, of which the Calvinist dominie was a true Carouzer, and so we continued our *Mensalia* the whole meeting in Latine, which they both spoke so fluently and promptly that I blushed at myself with a passionate regret, that I could not keep pace with them; and at the same time could not forbear reflecting upon our English schools and universities, who indeed write Latine elegantly, but speak it as if they were confined to mood and figure, forms and phrases, whereas it should be their common talk in their seats and halls, as well as in their school disputations and themes. This with all deference to these repositories of learning. As to the Dutch language, in which I was but a smatterer, I think it lofty, majestic and emphatical, especially the German or High-Dutch, which as far as I understand it is very expressive in the Scripture, and so underived that it may take place next the Oriental languages and the Septuagint. The name of the Calvinist was Newenhouse, of the Lutheran, Bernhardus Frazius, who was of a genteel personage, and a very agreeable behaviour in conversation. I seldom knew of any lawsuits, for indeed attorneys were denied the liberty of pleading. The English observed one anniversary custom, and that without superstition, I mean the *strenarum commercium,* as Suetonius calls them, a neighbourly commerce of presents every New-Years day:

Totus ab auspicio, ne foret annus iners.—Ovid, Fastor.

Some would send me a sugar-loaf, some a pair of gloves, some a bottle or two of wine. In a word, the English merchants and factors (whose names are at the beginning) were very unanimous and obliging. There was one person of quality, by name, Mr. Russell, younger brother to the late Lord Russell, a gentleman of a comely personage, and very obliging, to whose lodgings I was often welcome. But I suppose his fortune was that of a younger brother, according to Henry the VIII's constitution, who abolished and repealed the Gavelkind custom, whereby the lands of the father were equally divided among all his sons, so that ever since the Cadets or younger sons of the English nobility and gentry, have only that of the poet to bear up their spirits.

> *Sum pauper, non culpa mea est, sed culpa parentum*
> *Qui me fratre meo non genuere prius.*

In my rude English rhyming thus:

> I'm poor (my dad) but that's no fault of mine,
> If any fault there be, the fault is thine,
> Because thou didst not give us Gavelkine.

The Dutch in New York observe this custom, an instance of which I remember in one Frederick Philips, the richest Myn Heer in that place, who was said to have whole hogsheads of Indian money or Wampam, who having one son and daughter, I was admiring what a heap of wealth the son would enjoy, to which a Dutchman replied, that the daughter must go halves, for so was the manner amongst them, they standing more upon nature than names; that as the root communicates itself to all its branches, so should the parent to all his offspring, which are the olive branches round about his table, and if the case be so, the minors and infantry of the best families might wish they had been born in Kent, rather than in such a Christendom as entails upon them their elder brother's old clothes, or some superannuated incumbent reversion; but to invite both elder and younger brothers to this sweet climate of New York, when they arrive there, if they are induced to settle a plantation, they may purchase a tract of ground at a very small rate, in my time at two-pence or three-pence the acre, for which they have a good patent or deed from the governor.

NEW YORK AND THE PRODIGIOUS VOYAGE THITHER.

[From the Same.]

THE City of New York in my time was as large as some market towns with us, all built the London way; the garrison side of a high situation and a pleasant prospect, the island it stands on all a level and champaign. The diversion especially in the winter season used by the Dutch is aurigation, i. e. riding about in wagons, which is allowed by physicians to be a very healthful exercise by land. And upon the ice it's admirable to see men and women as it were flying upon their skates from place to place, with markets upon their heads and backs. In a word, it's a place so every way inviting that our English gentry, merchants and clergy (especially such as have the natural stamina of a consumptive propagation in them; or an hypochondriacal consumption) would flock thither for self-preservation. This I have all the reason to affirm and believe from the benign effectual influence it had upon my own constitution; but O the passage, the passage thither, *hic labor, hoc opus est:* there is the timorous objection. The ship may founder by springing a leak, be wrecked by a storm or taken by a pickeroon; which are plausible pleas to flesh and blood, but if we would examine the bills of mortality and compare the several accidents and diseases by the land, we should find them almost a hundred for one to what happens by sea, which deserves a particular essay, and, if we will believe the ingenious Dr. Carr in his *Epistolæ Medicinales*, there is an "Emetic Vomitory" virtue in the sea-water itself, which by the motion of the ship operates upon the stomach and ejects whatever is offensive, and so extimulates and provokes or recovers the appetite, which is the chiefest defect in such constitutions: and besides, there is a daily curiosity in contemplating the wonders of the deep, as to see a whale wallowing and spouting cataracts of water, to see the dolphin, that hieroglyphick of celerity, leaping above water in chase of the flying-fish, which I have sometimes tasted of as they flew aboard, where they immediately expire out of their element; and now and then to hale up that Cannibal of the sea, I mean the shark, by the bait of a large gobbet of beef or pork; who makes the deck shake again by his flapping violence, and opens his devouring mouth with double rows of teeth, in shape like a skate or flare as we call them in Cambridge; of which dreadful fish I have often made a meal at sea, but indeed it was for want of other provisions.

Mary Rowlandson.

BORN in Mass., about 1636. Wife of the Rev. Joseph Rowlandson. Made captive by the Indians at the Destruction of Lancaster, Mass., Feb. 21, 1676.

STORY OF HER CAPTIVITY, SUFFERINGS, AND RESTORATION.

[*Narrative of the Captivity and Restouration of Mrs. Mary Roulandson*. 1682.]

THE DOLEFUL ONSLAUGHT OF THE INDIANS.

ON the 10th of February, 1675 [o. s.], came the Indians with great numbers upon Lancaster: their first coming was about sun-rising; hearing the noise of some guns we looked out; several houses were burning, and the smoke ascending to heaven. There were five persons taken in one house, the father and mother and a suckling child they knocked on the head, the other two they took and carried away alive. There were two others, who, being out of their garrison upon occasion, were set upon, one was knocked on the head, the other escaped. Another there was who, running along, was shot and wounded, and fell down; he begged of them his life, promising them money (as they told me), but they would not hearken to him, but knocked him on the head, stripped him naked, and split open his bowels. Another seeing many of the Indians about his barn ventured and went out, but was quickly shot down. There were three others belonging to the same garrison who were killed; the Indians, getting up upon the roof of the barn, had advantage to shoot down upon them over their fortification. Thus these murtherous wretches went on burning and destroying all before them.

At length they came and beset our house, and quickly it was the dolefulest day that ever mine eyes saw. The house stood upon the edge of a hill; some of the Indians got behind the hill, others into the barn, and others behind anything that would shelter them; from all which places they shot against the house, so that the bullets seemed to fly like hail, and quickly they wounded one man among us, then another, then a third. About two hours (according to my observation in that amazing time) they had been about the house before they prevailed to fire it, (which they did with flax and hemp which they brought out of the barn, and there being no defence about the house, only two flankers at two opposite corners, and one of them not finished) they fired it once, and one ventured out and quenched it, but they quickly fired it again, and that took. Now is the dreadful hour come that I have often heard of (in time of the war, as it was the case of others) but now mine eyes see it. Some in our house were fighting for their lives, others wallowing in blood, the house on fire over our heads, and the bloody heathen ready to knock us on the head if we stirred out. Now might we hear mothers and children crying out for themselves and one another, Lord, what shall we do! Then I took my children (and one of my sisters hers) to go forth and leave the house: but, as soon as we came to the door and appeared, the Indians shot so thick that the bullets rattled against the house as if one had taken a handful of stones and threw them, so that we were forced to give back. We had six stout dogs belonging to our garrison, but none of them would stir, though at another time if an Indian had come to the door, they were ready to fly upon him and tear him down. The Lord hereby would make us the more to acknowledge his hand, and to see that our help is always in him. But out we must go, the fire increasing, and coming along behind us roaring, and the Indians gaping before us with their guns, spears, and hatchets to devour us. No sooner were we out of the house, but my brother-in-law (being before wounded in defending the house, in or near the throat) fell down dead, whereat the Indians scornfully shouted and hallowed, and were presently upon him, stripping off his clothes. The bullets flying thick, one went through my side, and the same (as would seem) through the bowels and hand of my poor child in my arms. One of my elder sister's children (named William) had then his leg broke, which the Indians perceiving they knocked him on the head. Thus were we butchered by those merciless heathens, standing amazed, with the blood running down to our heels. My eldest sister being yet in the house, and seeing those woful sights, the infidels hauling mothers one way and children another, and some wallowing in their blood; and her eldest son telling her that her son William was dead, and myself was wounded, she said, "and Lord, let me die with them;" which was no sooner said, but she was struck with a bullet, and fell down dead over the threshold. I hope she is reaping the fruit of her good labors, being faithful to the service of God in her place.   .   .   .   .

Oh! the doleful sight that now was to behold at this house! Come, behold the works of the Lord, what desolations he has made in the earth. Of thirty-seven persons who were in this one house, none escaped either present death, or a bitter captivity, save only one, who might say as in Job i. 15: "And I only am escaped alone to tell the news." There were twelve killed, some shot, some stabbed with their spears, some knocked down with their hatchets. When we are in prosperity, Oh the little that we think of such dreadful sights, to see our dear friends and relations lie bleeding out their heart's-blood upon the ground. There was one who was chopped in the head with a hatchet, and stripped naked, and yet was crawling up and down. It was a solemn sight to see so many Christians lying in their blood, some here and some there, like a company of sheep torn by wolves. All of them stripped naked by a company of hell-hounds, roaring, singing, ranting, and insulting, as if they would have torn our very hearts out; yet the Lord, by his almighty power, preserved a number of us from death, for there were twenty-four of us taken alive and carried captive.

I had often before this said, that if the Indians should come, I should choose rather to be killed by them than taken alive, but when it came to the trial, my mind changed; their glittering weapons so daunted my spirit, that I chose rather to go along with those (as I may say) ravenous bears, than that moment to end my days. And that I may the better declare what happened to me during that grievous captivity, I shall particularly speak of the several Removes we had up and down the wilderness.

THE FIRST REMOVE.

Now away we must go with those barbarous creatures, with our bodies wounded and bleeding, and our hearts no less than our bodies. About a mile we went that night, up upon a hill, within sight of the town, where we intended to lodge. There was hard by a vacant house (deserted by the English before, for fear of the Indians); I asked them whether I might not lodge in the house that night? to which they answered, "What, will you love Englishmen still?" This was the dolefulest night that ever my eyes saw. Oh, the roaring and singing, and dancing, and yelling of those black creatures in the night, which made the place a lively resemblance of hell. And miserable was the waste that was there made, of horses, cattle, sheep, swine, calves, lambs, roasting pigs, and fowls (which they had plundered in the town), some roasting, some lying and burning, and some boiling, to feed our merciless enemies; who were joyful enough, though we were disconsolate. To add to the dolefulness of the former day, and the dismalness of the present night, my thoughts ran upon my losses and sad, bereaved condition. All was gone, my husband gone (at least separated from me, he being in the Bay; and to add to my grief, the Indians told me they would kill him as he came homeward), my children gone, my relations and friends gone, our house and home, and all our comforts within door and without, all was gone (except my life), and I knew not but the next moment that might go too.

There remained nothing to me but one poor, wounded babe, and it seemed at present worse than death, that it was in such a pitiful condition, bespeaking compassion, and I had no refreshing for it, nor suitable things to revive it. Little do many think, what is the savageness and brutishness of this barbarous enemy, those even that seem to profess more than others among them, when the English have fallen into their hands. . . . .

THE SECOND REMOVE.

But now (the next morning) I must turn my back upon the town, and travel with them into the vast and desolate wilderness, I know not whither. It is not my tongue or pen can express the sorrows of my heart, and bitterness of my spirit, that I had at this departure; but God was with me in a wonderful manner, carrying me along and bearing up my spirit, that it did not quite fail. One of the Indians carried my poor wounded babe upon a horse; it went moaning all along: "I shall die, I shall die." I went on foot after it, with sorrow that cannot be expressed. At length I took it off the horse, and carried it in my arms, till my strength failed and I fell down with it. Then they set me upon a horse with my wounded child in my lap, and there being no furniture on the horse's back, as we were going down a steep hill, we both fell over the horse's head, at which they, like inhuman creatures, laughed, and rejoiced to see it, though I thought we should there have ended our days, overcome with so many difficulties. But the Lord renewed my strength still, and carried me along, that I might see more of his power, yea so much that I could never have thought of, had I not experienced it.

After this it quickly began to snow, and when night came on they stopped: and now down I must sit in the snow by a little fire, and a few boughs behind me, with my sick child in my lap and calling much for water, being now (through the wound) fallen into a violent fever. My own wound also growing so stiff that I could scarce sit down or rise up, yet so it must be, that I must sit all this cold winter night, upon the cold snowy ground, with my sick child in my arms, looking that every hour would be the last of its life; and having no Christian friend near me, either to comfort or help me. Oh, I may see the wonderful power of God, that my spirit did not utterly sink under my affliction; still the Lord upheld me with his gracious and merciful spirit, and we were both alive to see the light of the next morning. ·　·　·　·

THE EIGHTH REMOVE.—A VISIT TO KING PHILIP.

On the morrow morning we must go over Connecticut river to meet with King Philip; two canoes full they had carried over, the next turn myself was to go; but as my foot was upon the canoe to step in, there was a sudden out-cry among them, and I must step back; and instead of going over the river, I must go four or five miles up the river farther northward. Some of the Indians ran one way, and some another. The cause of this rout was, as I thought, their espying some English scouts who were thereabouts. In this travel up the river, about noon the com-

pany made a stop and sat down, some to eat and others to rest them.
As I sat amongst them, musing on things past, my son Joseph unexpectedly came to me. We asked of each other's welfare, bemoaning our
doleful condition and the change that had come upon us. We had
husband and father, and children and sisters, and friends and relations,
and house and home, and many comforts of this life; but now we might
say as Job, " Naked came I out of my mother's womb, and naked shall
I return: The Lord gave, and the Lord hath taken away, blessed be the
name of the Lord." I asked him whether he would read? he told me
he earnestly desired it. I gave him my Bible, and he lighted upon that
comfortable scripture, Psalm cxviii. 17, 18: "I shall not die, but live,
and declare the works of the Lord: The Lord hath chastened me sore,
yet he hath not given me over unto death." Look here, mother (says he),
did you read this? And here I may take occasion to mention one principal ground of my setting forth these lines, even as the Psalmist says,
to declare the works of the Lord, and his wonderful power in carying us
along, preserving us in the wilderness while under the enemy's hand, and
returning of us in safety again; and his goodness in bringing to my hand
so many comfortable and suitable scriptures in my distress.

But to return: We traveled on till night, and in the morning we
must go over the river to Philip's crew. When I was in the canoe, I
could not but be amazed at the numerous crew of Pagans that were on
the bank on the other side. When I came ashore, they gathered all
about me, I sitting alone in the midst: I observed they asked one another questions, and laughed, and rejoiced over their gains and victories.
Then my heart began to fail, and I fell a weeping; which was the first
time, to my remembrance, that I wept before them; although I had met
with so much affliction, and my heart was many times ready to break,
yet could I not shed one tear in their sight, but rather had been all this
while in a maze, and like one astonished; but now I may say as Psal.
cxxxvii. 1: "By the river of Babylon, there we sat down, yea, we wept,
when we remembered Zion." There one of them asked me why I wept?
I could hardly tell what to say; yet I answered, they would kill me:
No, said he, none will hurt you. Then came one of them, and gave me
two spoonfuls of meal (to comfort me) and another gave me half a pint
of peas, which was worth more than many bushels at another time.
Then I went to see King Philip; he bade me come in and sit down,
and asked me whether I would smoke it? (a usual compliment now a
days, among the saints and sinners), but this no way suited me. For
though I had formerly used tobacco, yet I had left it ever since I was
first taken. It seems to be a bait the devil lays to make men lose their
precious time. I remember with shame how formerly, when I had
taken two or three pipes, I was presently ready for another; such a be-

witching thing it is : but I thank God, He has now given me power over it ; surely there are many who may be better employed than to sit suck-ing a stinking tobacco-pipe.

Now the Indians gathered their forces to go against Northampton. Over night one went about yelling and hooting to give notice of the de-sign. Whereupon they went to boiling of ground-nuts, and parching corn (as many as had it) for their provision: and in the morning away they went. During my abode in this place, Philip spake to me to make a shirt for his boy, which I did; for which he gave me a shilling. I offered the money to my mistress, but she bid me keep it, and with it I bought a piece of horse-flesh. Afterward he asked me to make a cap for his boy, for which he invited me to dinner; I went, and he gave me a pancake, about as big as two fingers; it was made of parched wheat, beaten and fried in bear's grease, but I thought I never tasted pleasanter meat in my life. There was a squaw who spake to me to make a shirt for her sannup; for which she gave me a piece of beef. Another asked me to knit a pair of stockings, for which she gave me a quart of peas. I boiled my peas and beef together, and invited my master and mistress to dinner; but the proud gossip, because I served them both in one dish, would eat nothing, except one bit that he gave her upon the point of his knife. Hearing that my son was come to this place, I went to see him, and found him lying flat on the ground; I asked him how he could sleep so? he answered me, that he was not asleep, but at prayer; and that he lay so, that they might not observe what he was doing. I pray God he may remember these things now he is returned in safety. At this place (the sun now getting higher) what with the beams and heat of the sun, and smoke of the wigwams, I thought I should have been blinded. I could scarce discern one wigwam from another. There was one Mary Thurston, of Medfield, who, seeing how it was with me, lent me a hat to wear ; but as soon as I was gone, the squaw that owned that Mary Thurston came running after me, and got it away again. Here was a squaw who gave me a spoonful of meal; I put it in my pocket to keep it safe, yet notwithstanding somebody stole it, but put five in-dian corns in the room of it ; which corns were the greatest provision I had in my travel for one day.

The Indians returning from Northampton brought with them some horses, and sheep, and other things which they had taken; I desired them that they would carry me to Albany upon one of those horses, and sell me for powder; for so they had sometimes discoursed. I was utterly helpless of getting home on foot, the way that I came. I could hardly bear to think of the many weary steps I had taken to this place. .   .   .   .

THE NINETEENTH REMOVE.—A ROYAL PROMISE.

They said, when we went out, that we must travel to Wachuset this day. But a bitter weary day I had of it, traveling now three days together, without resting any day between. At last, after many weary steps, I saw Wachuset hills, but many miles off. Then we came to a great swamp, through which we traveled up to our knees in mud and water, which was heavy going to one tired before. Being almost spent, I thought I should have sunk down at last, and never got out; but I may say as in Psalm xciv. 18. "When my foot slipped, thy mercy, O Lord, held me up." Going along, having indeed my life, but little spirit, Philip (who was in the company) came up, and took me by the hand, and said "two weeks more and you shall be mistress again." I asked him if he spoke true? he said yes, and quickly you shall come to your master again, who had been gone from us three weeks. After many weary steps we came to Wachuset, where he was, and glad was I to see him. He asked me when I washed me? I told him not this month; then he fetched me some water himself, and bid me wash, and gave me a glass to see how I looked, and bid his squaw to give me something to eat. So she gave me a mess of beans and meat, and a little ground-nut cake. I was wonderfully revived with this favor showed me. Psalm cvi. 46: "He made them also to be pitied of all those that carried them away captive."

My master had three squaws, living sometimes with one and sometimes with another. Onux, this old squaw at whose wigwam I was, and with whom my master had been these three weeks: Another was Wettimore, with whom I had lived and served all this while. A severe and proud dame she was; bestowing every day in dressing herself near as much time as any of the gentry of the land: powdering her hair and painting her face, going with her necklaces, with jewels in her ears, and bracelets upon her hands. When she had dressed herself, her work was to make girdles of wampum and beads. The third squaw was a younger one, by whom he had two papooses. By that time I was refreshed by the old squaw, Wettimore's maid came to call me home, at which I fell a weeping. Then the old squaw told me to encourage me, that when I wanted victuals, I should come to her, and that I should lie in her wigwam. Then I went with the maid, and quickly I came back and lodged there. The squaw laid a mat under me, and a good rug over me; the first time that I had any such kindness showed me. I understood that Wettimore thought that, if she should let me go and serve with the old squaw, she should be in danger to lose (not only my service) but the redemption pay also. And I was not a little glad to hear this; being by it raised in my hopes that, in God's due time, there would be an end of this sorrowful hour. Then came an Indian and asked me to knit him three pair of stockings, for which I had a hat and a silk handkerchief. Then another asked me to make her a shift, for which she gave me an apron.

Then came Tom and Peter with the second letter from the council, about the captives. Though they were Indians, I got them by the hand, and burst out into tears; my heart was so full that I could not speak to them; but recovering myself I asked them how my husband did? and all my friends and acquaintances? They said they were well, but very melancholy. They brought me two biscuits and a pound of tobacco; the tobacco I soon gave away. When it was all gone one asked me to give him a pipe of tobacco, I told him it was all gone; then he began to rant and threaten; I told him when my husband came I would give him some. Hang him, rogue, says he, I will knock out his brains, if he comes here. And then again at the same breath they would say that if there should come an hundred without guns they would do them no hurt. So unstable and like madmen they were. So that fearing the worst, I durst not send to my husband, though there were some thoughts of his coming to redeem and fetch me, not knowing what might follow; for there was little more trust to them than to the master they served. When the letter was come, the Saggamores met to consult about the captives, and called me to them, to enquire how much my husband would give to redeem me. When I came I sat down among them, as I was wont to do, as their manner is. Then they bid me stand up, and said they were the general court. They bid me speak what I thought he would give. Now knowing that all we had was destroyed by the Indians, I was in a great strait. I thought if I should speak of but a little, it would be slighted and hinder the matter; if of a great sum, I knew not where it would be procured; yet at a venture I said twenty pounds, yet desired them to take less; but they would not hear of that, but sent the message to Boston that for twenty pounds I should be redeemed. It was a praying Indian that wrote their letters for them. There was another praying Indian, who told me that he had a brother, that would not eat horse, his conscience was so tender and scrupulous, though as large as hell for the destruction of poor Christians, then, he said, he read that scripture to him, II. Kings vi. 25: "There was a famine in Samaria, and behold they besieged it, until an ass's head was sold for fourscore pieces of silver, and the fourth part of a cab of dove's dung for five pieces of silver." He expounded this place to his brother, and shewed him that it was lawful to eat that in a famine, which it is not at another time. And now, says he, he will eat horse with any Indian of them all. There was another praying Indian who, when he had done all the mischief that he could, betrayed his own father into the English's hands, thereby to purchase his own life. Another praying Indian was at Sudbury fight, though, as he deserved, he was afterwards hanged for it. There was another praying Indian, so wicked and cruel as to wear a string about his neck, strung with Christian fingers. Another praying Indian, when they went to Sudbury fight, went with them, and his squaw also with him, with her papoose at her back.   .   .   .   .

RETURN TO HOME AND FRIENDS.

But to return again to my going home; where we may see a remarkable change of providence: At first they were all against it, except my husband would come for me; but afterward they assented to it, and seemed to rejoice in it. Some asking me to send them some bread, others some tobacco, others shaking me by the hand, offering me a hood and scarf to ride in; not one moving hand or tongue against it. Thus hath the Lord answered my poor desires, and the many earnest requests of others put up unto God for me. In my travels an Indian came to me and told me, if I were willing, he and his squaw would run away, and go home along with me. I told them no, I was not willing to run away, but desired to wait God's time that I might go home quietly, and without fear. And now God hath granted me my desire. Oh, the wonderful power of God that I have seen, and the experiences that I have had! I have been in the midst of those roaring lions and savage bears, that feared neither God, nor man, nor the devil, by night and day, alone and in company; sleeping all sorts together, and yet not one of them ever offered the least abuse of unchastity to me in word or action. Though some are ready to say I speak it for my own credit; but I speak it in the presence of God, and to his glory. God's power is as great now as it was to save Daniel in the lion's den, or the three children in the fiery furnace. Especially that I should come away in the midst of so many hundreds of enemies, and not a dog move his tongue. So I took my leave of them, and in coming along my heart melted into tears, more than all the while I was with them, and I was almost swallowed up with the thoughts that ever I should go home again. About the sun's going down, Mr. Hoar, myself, and the two Indians, came to Lancaster, and a solemn sight it was to me. There had I lived many comfortable years among my relations and neighbors; and now not one Christian to be seen, or one house left standing. We went on to a farm house that was yet standing, where we lay all night; and a comfortable lodging we had, though nothing but straw to lie on. The Lord preserved us in safety that night, raised us up again in the morning, and carried us along, that before noon we came to Concord. Now was I full of joy and yet not without sorrow: joy, to see such a lovely sight, so many Christians together, and some of them my neighbors. There I met with my brother, and brother-in-law, who asked me if I knew where his wife was. Poor heart! he had helped to bury her and knew it not; she, being shot down by the house, was partly burned, so that those who were at Boston at the desolation of the town, came back afterward and buried the dead, did not know her. Yet I was not without sorrow, to think how many were looking and longing, and my own children among the rest, to enjoy that deliverance that I had now received; and I did not know whether ever I should see them again. Being recruited with food and raiment, we went to Boston that day, where I met with my dear husband; but the thoughts of our dear children, one being dead, and the other we could not tell where, abated our comfort in each other. I was not before so much hemmed in by the merciless and cruel heathen, but now as much with pitiful, tender-hearted, and compassionate Christians. In that poor and beggarly condition, I was received in, I was kindly entertained in several houses. So much love I received from several (many of whom I knew not) that I am not capable to declare it. But the Lord knows them all by name; the Lord reward them seven-fold into their bosoms of his spirituals, for their temporals. The twenty pounds, the price of my redemption, was raised by some Boston gentlewomen, and Mr. Usher, whose bounty and charity I would not forget to make mention of. . . . We were now in the midst of love, yet not without much and frequent heaviness of heart for our poor children and other relations, who were still in affliction. The week following, after my coming in, the governor and council sent to the Indians again, and that not without success; for they brought in my sister and good wife Kettle. Their not knowing where our children were, was a sore trial to us still; and yet we were not without secret hopes of seeing them again. That which was dead lay heavier upon my spirits, than those which were alive among the heathen; thinking how it suffered with its wounds, and I was not able to relieve it, and how it was buried by the heathen in the wilderness from among all Christians. We were hurried up and down in our thoughts, sometimes we should hear a report that they were gone this way and sometimes that; and that they were come in this place or that; we kept inquiring and listening to hear concerning them, but no certain news as yet. About this time the council had ordered a day of public thanksgiving, though I had still cause of mourning; and being unsettled in our minds we thought we would ride eastward to see if we could hear anything concerning our children. As we were riding along between Ipswich and Rowley, we met with William Hubbard, who told us our son Joseph and my sister's son were come into Major Waldren's; I asked him how he knew it? He said the Major himself told him so. So along we went till we came to Newbury; and, their minister being absent, they desired my husband to preach the thanksgiving for them; but he was not willing to stay there that night, but he would go over to Salisbury to hear father, and come again in the morning, which he did, and preached there that day. At night when he had done one came and told him that his daughter was come into Providence. Here was mercy on both hands. Now we were between them, the one on the east, and the other on the west; our son being nearest, we went to him first, to Portsmouth, where we met with him and with the major also, who told us he had done what he could, but could not redeem him under seven pounds, which the good people thereabouts were pleased to pay. The Lord reward the major, and all the rest, though unknown to me, for their labor of love. My sister's son was redeemed for four pounds, which the council gave order for the payment of. Having now received one of our children, we hastened toward the other. Going back through Newbury, my husband preached there on the Sabbath Day, for which they rewarded him manifold.

On Monday we came to Charlestown, where we heard that the governor of Rhode Island had sent over for our daughter, to take care of her, being now within his jurisdiction; which should not pass without our acknowledgments. But she being nearer Rehoboth than Rhode Island, Mr. Newman went over and took care of her, and brought her to his own house. And the goodness of God was admirable to us in our low estate, in that He raised up compassionate friends on every side, when we had nothing to recompense any for their love. The Indians were now gone that way, that it was apprehended dangerous to go to her; but the carts which carried provision to the English army, being guarded, brought her with them to Dorchester, where we received her safe; blessed be the Lord for it. Her coming in was after this manner: She was traveling one day with the Indians, with her basket on her back; the company of Indians were got before her and gone out of sight, all except one squaw. She followed the squaw till night, and then both of them lay down, having nothing over them but the heavens, nor under them but the earth. Thus she traveled three days together, having nothing to eat or drink but water and green whortleberries. At last they came into Providence, where she was kindly entertained by several of that town. The Indians often said that I should never have her under twenty pounds, but now the Lord hath brought her in upon free cost, and given her to me the second time. The Lord make us a blessing indeed to each other. Thus hath the Lord brought me and mine out of the horrible pit, and hath set us in the midst of tender-hearted and compassionate Christians. 'Tis the desire of my soul that we may walk worthy of the mercies received, and which we are receiving.

Benjamin Church.

BORN in Plymouth, Mass., 1639. DIED at Little Compton, R. I., 1718.

A DEATH-GRAPPLE.

[Entertaining Passages Relating to Philip's War. 1716.]

IN this march, the first thing remarkable was, they came to an Indian town, where there were many wigwams in sight, but an icy swamp, lying between them and the wigwams, prevented their running at once upon it as they intended. There was much firing upon each side before they passed the swamp. But at length the enemy all fled and a certain Mohegan, that was a friend Indian, pursued and seized one of the enemy that had a small wound in his leg, and brought him before the General, where he was examined. Some were for torturing of him to bring him to a more ample confession of what he knew concerning his countrymen. Mr. Church, verily believing he had been ingenuous in his confession, interceded and prevailed for his escaping torture. But the army being bound forward in their march, and the Indian's wound somewhat disenabling him for travelling, it was concluded he should be knocked on the head. Accordingly he was brought before a great fire, and the Mohegan that took him was allowed, as he desired to be, the executioner. Mr. Church, taking no delight in the sport, framed an errand at some distance among the baggage horses, and when he had got some ten rods, or thereabouts, from the fire, the executioner fetching a blow with his hatchet at the head of the prisoner, he, being aware of the blow, dodged his head aside, and the executioner missing his stroke, the hatchet flew out of his hand, and had like to have done execution where it was not designed. The prisoner upon his narrow escape broke from them that held him, and, notwithstanding his wound, made use of his legs, and happened to run right upon Mr. Church, who laid hold on him, and a close scuffle they had; but the Indian having no clothes on slipped from him and ran again, and Mr. Church pursued [him], although being lame there was no great odds in the race, until the Indian stumbled and fell, and they closed again—scuffled and fought pretty smartly, until the Indian, by the advantage of his nakedness, slipped from his hold again, and set out on his third race, with Mr. Church close at his heels, endeavoring to lay hold on the hair of his head, which was all the hold could be taken of him. And running through a swamp that was covered with hollow ice, it made so loud a noise that Mr. Church expected (but in vain) that some of his English friends would follow the noise and come to his assistance But the Indian happened to run athwart a mighty tree that lay fallen near breast high, where he stopped and cried out aloud for help. But Mr. Church being soon upon him again, the Indian seized him fast by the hair of his head, and endeavored by twisting to break his neck. But though Mr. Church's wounds had somewhat weakened him, and the Indian a stout fellow, yet he held him well in play and twisted the Indian's neck as well, and took the advantage of many opportunities, while they hung by each other's hair, to give him notorious bunts in the face with his head. But in the heat of this scuffle they heard the ice break, with somebody's coming apace to them, which when they heard, Church concluded there was help for one or other of them, but was doubtful which of them must now receive the fatal stroke —anon somebody comes up to them, who proved to be the Indian that had first taken the prisoner; without speaking a word, he felt them out (for it was so dark he could not distinguish them by sight, the one being clothed and the other naked), he felt where Mr. Church's hands were fastened in the Netop's hair and with one blow settled his hatchet in between them, and ended the strife. He then spoke to Mr. Church and hugged him in his arms, and thanked him abundantly for catching his prisoner, and cut off the head of his victim and carried it to the camp, and, giving an account to the rest of the friend Indians in the camp how Mr. Church had seized his prisoner, etc., they all joined in a mighty shout.

THE DEATH OF KING PHILIP.

[*From the Same.*]

CAPTAIN CHURCH being now at Plymouth again, weary and worn, would have gone home to his wife and family; but the government being solicitous to engage him in the service until Philip was slain, and promising him satisfaction and redress for some mistreatment that he had met with, he fixes for another expedition.

He had soon volunteers enough to make up the company he desired, and marched through the woods, until he came to Pocasset. And not seeing or hearing of any of the enemy, they went over the ferry to Rhode Island, to refresh themselves. The Captain, with about half a dozen in his company, took horses and rid about eight miles down the island to Mr. Sanford's, where he had left his wife. Who no sooner saw him, but fainted with surprise; and by that time she was a little revived, they spied two horsemen coming a great pace. Captain Church told his company, that "Those men (by their riding) come with tidings." When they came up, they proved to be Major Sanford and Captain Golding.

Who immediately asked Captain Church, what he would give to hear some news of Philip? He replied that was what he wanted. They told him, they had rid hard with some hopes of overtaking him, and were now come on purpose to inform him, that there were just now tidings from Mount-hope. An Indian came down from thence (where Philip's camp now was) on to Sandy point, over against Trip's, and hallooed, and made signs to be fetched over. And being fetched over, he reported, that he was fled from Philip, "who (said he) has killed my brother just before I came away, for giving some advice that displeased him." And said, he was fled for fear of meeting with the same his brother had met with. Told them also, that Philip was now in Mount-hope Neck. Captain Church thanked them for their good news, and said he hoped by to-morrow morning to have the rogue's head. The horses that he and his company came on, standing at the door (for they had not been unsaddled), his wife must content herself with a short visit, when such game was ahead. They immediately mounted, set spurs to their horses, and away.

The two gentlemen that brought him the tidings told him, they would gladly wait upon him to see the event of this expedition. He thanked them, and told them he should be as fond of their company as any men's; and (in short) they went with him. And they were soon at Trip's ferry, (with Captain Church's company) where the deserter was. Who was a fellow of good sense, and told his story handsomely. He offered Captain Church, to pilot him to Philip, and to help to kill him, that he might revenge his brother's death. Told him, that Philip was now upon a little spot of upland, that was in the south end of the miry swamp, just at the foot of the mount, which was a spot of ground that Captain Church was well acquainted with.

By that time they were got over the ferry, and came near the ground, half the night was spent. The Captain commands a halt, and bringing the company together, he asked Major Sanford's and Captain Golding's advice, what method was best to take in making the onset; but they declined giving any advice; telling him, that his great experience and success forbid their taking upon them to give advice. Then Captain Church offered Captain Golding that he should have the honor (if he would please accept of it) to beat up Philip's headquarters. He accepted the offer and had his allotted number drawn out to him, and the pilot. Captain Church's instructions to him were, to be very careful in his approach to the enemy, and be sure not to show himself, until by daylight they might see and discern their own men from the enemy; told him also, that his custom in the like cases was, to creep with his company, on their bellies, until they came as near as they could; and that as soon as the enemy discovered them, they would cry out, and that was the

word for his men to fire and fall on. He directed him, that when the
enemy should start and take into the swamp, they should pursue with
speed; every man shouting and making what noise he could; for he
would give orders to his ambuscade to fire on any that should come
silently.

Captain Church, knowing that it was Philip's custom to be foremost
in the flight, went down to the swamp, and gave Captain Williams of
Scituate the command of the right wing of the ambush, and placed an
Englishman and an Indian together behind such shelters of trees, etc., as
he could find, and took care to place them at such distance that none
might pass undiscovered between them; charged them to be careful of
themselves, and of hurting their friends, and to fire at any that should
come silently through the swamp. But it being somewhat farther
through the swamp than he was aware of, he wanted men to make up
his ambuscade.

Having placed what men he had, he took Major Sanford by the hand,
and said, "Sir, I have so placed them that it is scarce possible Philip
should escape them." The same moment a shot whistled over their
heads, and then the noise of a gun towards Philip's camp. Captain
Church, at first, thought it might be some gun fired by accident; but,
before he could speak, a whole volley followed, which was earlier than
he expected. One of Philip's gang going forth to ease himself, when he
had done, looked round him, and Captain Golding thought that the Indian
looked right at him, (though probably it was but his conceit); so fired at
him; and upon his firing, the whole company that were with him fired upon
the enemy's shelter, before the Indians had time to rise from their sleep,
and so over-shot them. But their shelter was open on that side next the
swamp, built so on purpose for the convenience of flight on occasion.
They were soon in the swamp, and Philip the foremost, who, starting at
the first gun, threw his *petunk* and powderhorn over his head, catched
up his gun, and ran as fast as he could scamper, without any more
clothes than his small breeches and stockings; and ran directly upon
two of Captain Church's ambush. They let him come fair within shot,
and the Englishman's gun missing fire, he bid the Indian fire away, and
he did so to the purpose; sent one musket bullet through his heart, and
another not above two inches from it. He fell upon his face in the mud
and water, with his gun under him.

By this time the enemy perceived they were waylaid on the east side
of the swamp, and tacked short about. One of the enemy, who seemed
to be a great, surly old fellow, hallooed with a loud voice, and often
called out, "*Iootash, Iootash.*" Captain Church called to his Indian,
Peter, and asked him, who that was that called so? He answered, it
was old Annawon, Philip's great Captain; calling on his soldiers to

stand to it, and fight stoutly. Now the enemy finding that place of the swamp which was not ambushed, many of them made their escape in the English tracks.

The man that had shot down Philip ran with all speed to Captain Church, and informed him of his exploit, who commanded him to be silent about it and let no man more know it, until they had driven the swamp clean. But when they had driven the swamp through, and found the enemy had escaped, or, at least, the most of them, and the sun now up, and so the dew gone, that they could not easily track them, the whole company met together at the place where the enemy's night shelter was, and then Captain Church gave them the news of Philip's death. Upon which the whole army gave three loud huzzas.

Captain Church ordered his body to be pulled out of the mire on to the upland. So some of Captain Church's Indians took hold of him by his stockings, and some by his small breeches (being otherwise naked) and drew him through the mud to the upland; and a doleful, great, naked, dirty beast he looked like. Captain Church then said that, forasmuch as he had caused many an Englishman's body to lie unburied, and rot above ground, not one of his bones should be buried. And, calling his old Indian executioner, bid him behead and quarter him. Accordingly he came with his hatchet and stood over him, but before he struck he made a small speech directing it to Philip, and said, "he had been a very great man, and had made many a man afraid of him, but so big as he was, he would now chop him to pieces." And so went to work and did as he was ordered.

Philip, having one very remarkable hand, being much scarred, occasioned by the splitting of a pistol in it formerly, Captain Church gave the head and that hand to Alderman, the Indian who shot him, to show to such gentlemen as would bestow gratuities upon him; and accordingly he got many a penny by it.

This being on the last day of the week, the Captain with his company, returned to the island, tarried there until Tuesday; and then went off and ranged through all the woods to Plymouth, and received their premium, which was thirty shillings per head, for the enemies which they had killed or taken, instead of all wages; and Philip's head went at the same price. Methinks it is scanty reward, and poor encouragement; though it was better than what had been some time before. For this march they received four shillings and sixpence a man, which was all the reward they had, except the honor of killing Philip. This was in the latter end of August, 1676.

CAPTURE AND FATE OF THE GREAT ANNAWON.

[From the Same.]

THE Captain was now in great strait of mind what to do next; he had a mind to give Annawon a visit, now he knew where to find him. But his company was very small, but half a dozen men beside himself, and was under a necessity to send some body back to acquaint his Lieutenant and company with his proceedings. However, he asked his small company that were with him, whether they would willingly go with him and give Annawon a visit? They told him they were always ready to obey his commands, etc.; but withal told him, that they knew this Captain Annawon was a great soldier; that he had been a valiant Captain under Asuhmequin, Philip's father; and that he had been Philip's chieftain all this war. A very subtle man, and of great resolution, and had often said, that he would never be taken alive by the English. And moreover they knew that the men that were with him were resolute fellows, some of Philip's chief soldiers; and therefore feared whether it was practicable to make an attempt upon him with so small a handful of assistants as now were with him. Told him further, that it would be a pity, after all the great things he had done, he should throw away his life at last. Upon which he replied, that he doubted not Annawon was a subtle and valiant man; that he had a long time, but in vain, sought for him, and never till now could find his quarters, and he was very loath to miss of the opportunity; and doubted not that, if they would cheerfully go with him, the same Almighty Providence that had hitherto protected and befriended them, would do so still, etc.

Upon this with one consent they said they would go. Captain Church then turned to one Cook of Plymouth, (the only Englishman then with him) and asked him, what he thought of it? Who replied, "Sir, I am never afraid of going any where when you are with me." Then Captain Church asked the old Indian, if he could carry his horse with him? (For he conveyed a horse thus far with him.) He replied that it was impossible for one horse to pass the swamps. Therefore, he sent away his new Indian soldier with his father, and the Captain's horse, to his Lieutenant, and orders for him to move to Taunton with the prisoners, to secure them there, and to come out in the morning in the Rehoboth Road, in which he might expect to meet him, if he were alive and had success. The Captain then asked the old fellow if he would pilot him unto Annawon? He answered, that he having given him his life, he was obliged to serve him. He bid him move on then, and they followed. The old man would out-travel them so far sometimes that they were almost out of sight; looking over his shoulder, and seeing them behind, he would halt.

Just as the sun was setting, the old man made a full stop and sat down; the company coming up, also sat down, being all weary. Captain Church asked, "What news?" He answered, that about that time in the evening, Captain Annawon sent out his scouts to see if the coast were clear, and as soon as it began to grow dark, the scouts returned; "and then" (said he) "we may move again securely." When it began to grow dark, the old man stood up again, and Captain Church asked him if he would take a gun and fight for him? He bowed very low, and prayed him not to impose such a thing upon him, as to fight against Captain Annawon his old friend. "But," says he, "I will go along with you, and be helpful to you, and will lay hands on any man that shall offer to hurt you."

It being now pretty dark, they moved close together;—anon they heard a noise. The Captain stayed the old man with his hand, and asked his own men what noise they thought it might be? They concluded it to be the pounding of a mortar. The old man had given Captain Church a description of the place where Annawon now lay, and of the difficulty of getting at him. Being sensible that they were pretty near them, with two of his Indians he creeps to the edge of the rocks, from whence he could see their camps. He saw three companies of Indians at a little distance from each other; being easy to be discovered by the light of their fires. He saw also the great ANNAWON and his company, who had formed his camp or kenneling place by falling a tree under the side of the great cliffs of rocks, and setting a row of birch bushes up against it; where he himself, his son, and some of his chiefs had taken up their lodgings, and made great fires without them, and had their pots and kettles boiling, and spits roasting. Their arms also he discovered, all set together, in a place fitted for the purpose, standing up an end against a stick lodged in two crotches, and a mat placed over them, to keep them from the wet or dew. The old Annawon's feet and his son's head were so near the arms, as almost to touch them. But the rocks were so steep that it was impossible to get down, only as they lowered themselves by the boughs, and the bushes that grew in the cracks of the rocks. Captain Church, creeping back again to the old man, asked him, if there was no possibility of getting at them some other way? He answered, "No." That he, and all that belonged to Annawon, were ordered to come that way, and none could come any other way without difficulty, or danger of being shot.

Captain Church then ordered the old man and his daughter to go down foremost with their baskets at their backs, that when Annawon saw them with their baskets he should not mistrust the intrigue. Captain Church and his handful of soldiers crept down also, under the shadow of those two and their baskets. The Captain himself crept close behind the old man, with his hatchet in his hand, and stepped over the young man's head to the arms. The young Annawon, discovering of him, whipped his blanket over his head and shrunk up in a heap. The old Captain Annawon started up on his breech, and cried out, "Howoh," and, despairing of escape, threw himself back again, and lay silent until Captain Church had secured all the arms, etc. And having secured that company, he sent his Indian soldiers to the other fires and companies, giving them instructions what to do and say. Accordingly they went into the midst of them. When they discovered themselves to the enemy, they told them that their Captain Annawon was taken, and it would be best for them quietly and peaceably to surrender themselves, which would procure good quarter for them; otherwise, if they should pretend to resist or make their escape, it would be in vain, and they could expect no other but that Captain Church, with his great army, who had now entrapped them, would cut them to pieces. Told them also, if they would submit themselves, and deliver up all their arms unto them, and keep every man in his place until it was day, they would assure them that their Captain Church, who had been so kind to themselves when they surrendered to him, should be as kind unto them. Now they being old acquaintance, and many of them relations, did much the readier give heed to what they said; and complied, and surrendered up their arms unto them, both their guns and hatchets, etc., and were forthwith carried to Captain Church. . . . .

Supper being over, Captain Church sent two of his men to inform the other companies that he had killed Philip, and had taken their friends in Mount-hope Neck, but had spared their lives, and that he had subdued now all the enemy (he supposed), except this company of Annawon's; and now if they would be orderly and keep their places until morning, they should have good quarter, and that he would carry them to Taunton, where they might see their friends again, etc. The messengers returned, that the Indians yielded to his proposals.

Captain Church thought it was now time for him to take a nap, having had no sleep in two days and one night before. Told his men, that if they would let him sleep two hours, they should sleep all the rest of the night. He laid himself down and endeavoured to sleep, but all disposition to sleep departed from him. After he had lain a little while, he looked up to see how his watch managed, but found them all fast asleep. Now Captain Church had told Captain Annawon's company, as he had ordered his Indians to tell the others, that their lives should all be spared, excepting Captain Annawon's, and it was not in his power to promise him his life, but he must carry him to his masters at Plymouth, and he would entreat them for his life.

Now, when Captain Church found not only his own men, but all the

Indians, fast asleep, Annawon only excepted, who, he perceived, was as broad awake as himself; and so they lay looking one upon the other, perhaps an hour. Captain Church said nothing to him, for he could not speak Indian, and thought Annawon could not speak English.

At length Annawon raised himself up, cast off his blanket, and with no more clothes than his small breeches, walked a little way back from the company. . . . But by and by he was gone out of sight and hearing, and then Captain Church began to suspect some ill design in him; and got all the guns close to him, and crowded himself close under young Annawon; that if he should anywhere get a gun, he should not make a shot at him, without endangering his son. Lying very still awhile, waiting for the event, at length he heard somebody coming the same way that Annawon went. The moon now shining bright, he saw him at a distance coming with something in his hands, and coming up to Captain Church, he fell upon his knees before him, and offered him what he had brought, and speaking in plain English, said, "Great Captain, you have killed Philip, and conquered his country; for I believe that I and my company are the last that war against the English, so suppose the war is ended by your means; and therefore these things belong unto you." Then opening his pack, he pulled out Philip's belt, curiously wrought with wompom, being nine inches broad, wrought with black and white wompom, in various figures, and flowers and pictures of many birds and beasts. This, when hung upon Captain Church's shoulders, it reached his ankles; and another belt of wompom he presented him with, wrought after the former manner, which Philip was wont to put upon his head. It had two flags on the back part, which hung down on his back, and another small belt with a star upon the end of it, which he used to hang on his breast, and they were all edged with red hair, which Annawon said they got in the Mohawk's country. Then he pulled out two horns of glazed powder, and a red cloth blanket. He told Captain Church these were Philip's royalties, with which he was wont to adorn himself with, when he sat in state; that he thought himself happy that he had an opportunity to present them to Captain Church, who had won them, etc. They spent the remainder of the night in discourse. And Captain Annawon gave an account of what mighty success he had formerly in wars against many nations of Indians, when he served Asuhmequin, Philip's father, etc.   .   .   .   .   .

But when Captain Church returned from Boston, he found, to his grief, the heads of Annawon, Tispaquin, etc., cut off, which were the last of Philip's friends.

Nathaniel Byfield.

BORN in Long Ditten, Surrey, England, 1653.   DIED in Boston, Mass., 1733.

THE REVOLT AGAINST SIR EDMUND ANDROS.

[*An Account of the Late Revolution in New-England.   Written, from Bristol, R. I.,
to friends in London.   1689.*]

GENTLEMEN:—Here being an opportunity of sending for London,
by a vessel that loaded at Long Island and for want of a wind put
in here; and not knowing that there will be the like from this country
suddenly, I am willing to give you some brief account of the most remarkable things that have happened here within this fortnight last past;
concluding that, till about that time, you will have received, per Carter, a
full account of the management of affairs here.   Upon the 18th instant,
about eight of the clock in the morning, in Boston, it was reported at the
south end of the town, that at the north end they were all in arms; and
the like report was at the north end, respecting the south end.   Whereupon
Captain John George was immediately seized, and about nine of the clock
the drums beat through the town; and an ensign was set up upon the
beacon.   Then Mr. Bradstreet, Mr. Danforth, Major Richards, Dr. Cooke,
and Mr. Addington, etc., were brought to the council-house by a company
of soldiers under the command of Captain Hill.   The meanwhile the
people in arms did take up and put into jail Justice Bullivant, Justice
Foxcroft, Mr. Randolf, Sheriff Sherlock, Captain Ravenscroft, Captain
White, Farewel, Broadbent, Crafford, Larkin, Smith, and many more, as
also Mercey the then jail-keeper, and put Scates the bricklayer in his
place.   About noon, in the gallery at the council-house, was read the
declaration here inclosed.   Then a message was sent to the fort to Sir
Edmund Andros, by Mr. Oliver and Mr. Eyres, signed by the Gentlemen then in the council-chamber, . . . to inform him how un-
safe he was like to be if he did not deliver up himself, and fort and
government forthwith, which he was loath to do.   By this time, being
about two of the clock (the lecture being put by) the town was generally
in arms, and so many of the country came in that there was twenty companies in Boston, besides a great many that appeared at Charlestown
that could not get over (some say fifteen hundred).   There then came
information to the soldiers, that a boat was come from the frigate that
made towards the fort, which made them haste thither, and come to the
sconce soon after the boat got thither; and 'tis said that Governor Andros and about half a score gentlemen were coming down out of the
fort; but the boat being seized, wherein were small arms, hand-grenades,

and a quantity of match, the Governor and the rest went in again; whereupon Mr. John Nelson, who was at the head of the soldiers, did demand the fort and the Governor, who was loath to submit to them; but at length did come down, and was with the gentlemen that were with him conveyed to the council-house, where Mr. Bradstreet and the rest of the gentlemen waited to receive him; to whom Mr. Stoughton first spake, telling him, he might thank himself for the present disaster that had befallen him, etc. He was then confined for that night to Mr. John Usher's house under strong guards, and the next day conveyed to the fort (where he yet remains, and with him Lieutenant-Colonel Ledget), which is under the command of Mr. John Nelson; and at the castle, which is under the command of Mr. John Fairweather, is Mr. West, Mr. Graham, Mr. Palmer, and Captain Tryfroye. At that time Mr. Dudley was out upon the circuit, and was holding a court at Southold on Long Island. And on the 21st instant he arrived at Newport, where he heard the news. The next day letters came to him, advising him not to come home; he thereupon went over privately to Major Smith's at Naraganzett, and advice is this day come hither, that yesterday about a dozen young men, most of their own heads, went thither to demand him; and are gone with him down to Boston. We have also advice, that on Friday last towards evening Sir Edmund Andros did attempt to make an escape in woman's apparel, and passed two guards, and was stopped at the third, being discovered by his shoes, not having changed them. We are here ready to blame you sometimes, that we have not to this day received advice concerning the great changes in England, and in particular how it is like to fare with us here; who do hope and believe that all these things will work for our good; and that you will not be wanting to promote the good of a country that stands in such need as New England does at this day. The first day of May, according to former usage, is the election-day at Road Island; and many do say they intend their choice there then. I have not farther to trouble you with at present, but recommending you, and all our affairs with you, to the direction and blessing of our most gracious God, I remain

Gentlemen,

Your most humble servant at command,
NATHANIEL BYFIELD.

BRISTOL, *April* 29, 1689.

Through the goodness of God, there has been no blood shed. Nath. Clark is in Plymouth jail, and John Smith in jail here, all waiting for news from England.

Samuel Willard.

BORN in Concord, Mass., 1640. DIED in Boston, Mass., 1707.

AUTHORITY MUST TAKE PATTERN FROM ON HIGH.

[*The Character of a Good Ruler.* 1694.]

NOW that all these may be just, it is firstly required that they have a principle of moral honesty in them and swaying of them; that they "love righteousness and hate iniquity"; that they be "men of truth," Exod. xviii., 21, for every man will act in his relation, according to the principle that rules in him: so that an unrighteous man will be an unrighteous ruler, so far as he hath an opportunity.

They must also be acquainted with the rules of righteousness; they must know what is just and what is unjust, be "able men," Exod. xviii., 21. For, though men may know and not do, yet "without knowledge the mind cannot be good." Ignorance is a foundation for error, and will likely produce it, when the man applies himself to act; and if he do right at any time it is but by guess, which is a very poor commendation.

Again, he must be one that respects the cause, and not the persons, in all his administrations, Deut. i., 17: "Ye shall not respect persons in judgment," etc. If his affections oversway his judgment at any time, they will be a crooked bias, that will turn him out of the way, and that shall be justice in one man's case, which will not be so in another.

Farthermore, he must be one whom neither flattery nor bribery may be able to remove out of his way, Deut. xvi., 19: "Thou shalt not wrest judgment, thou shalt not respect persons, neither take a gift;" and hence he must be one who hates both ambition and covetousness; Exod. xviii. 21, "Hating covetousness," which word signifies, a greedy desire, and is applicable to both the fore-cited vices; for if these rule him, he will never be a just ruler.

Finally, he must be one who prefers the public benefit above all private and separate interests whatsoever. Every man in his place owes himself to the good of the whole, and if he doth not so devote himself, he is unjust; and he who either to advance himself, or to be revenged on another, will push on injurious laws, or pervert the true intention of such as are in force, is an unjust man; and he who is under the influence of a narrow spirit, will be ready to do so, as occasion offers.

Nor is this justice to be looked upon as separate from the fear of God, but as influenced and maintained by it. He therefore that "ruleth in the fear of God," is one who acknowledgeth God to be his sovereign, and carries in his heart an awful fear of him; who owns his commission to be from him, and expects ere long to be called to give in an account of his managing of it; which maketh him to study in all things to please him, and to be afraid of doing any thing that will provoke him.

And accordingly he is a student in the Law of God, and "meditates in it day and night;" making it the rule into which he ultimately resolves all that he doth in his place. We find that in the old law, the king was to *write* a copy of it with his own hand, and to make use of it at all times; Deut. xvii., 18, 19.

If he hath any thing to do in the making of laws, he will consult a good conscience, and what may be pleasing to God, and will be far from "framing mischief by a law." And if he be to execute any laws of men, he will not dare to give a judgment for such an one as directly crosseth the command of God, but counts it *ipso facto* void, and his conscience acquitted of his oath.

Yea, the fear of God will make him not to think himself lawless; nor dare to bear witness, by laws and penalties, against sins in others, which he countenanceth and encourageth by living in the practice of himself. But to use utmost endeavors that his own life may be an exemplification of obedience, and others may learn by him what a veneration he hath for the laws that are enacted for the good of mankind.

In a word, he is one that will take care to promote piety, as well as honesty, among men; and do his utmost that the true religion may be countenanced and established and that all ungodliness, as well as unrighteousness, may have a due testimony borne against it at all times. So he resolves, Psal. lxxv., 10: "All the horns of the wicked also will I cut off; but the horns of the righteous shall be exalted."

Increase Mather.

BORN in Dorchester, Mass., 1639.   DIED in Boston, Mass., 1723.

THE SIGN OF THE BLAZING STAR.

[*Heavens Alarm to the World.* 1681.]

SOMETIMES such signs in heaven are presages of miserable dearths and scarcity. That blazing star impending over Jerusalem which the text hath reference unto was attended with a terrible famine, whereby multitudes perished. And therefore such signs are frequently portentous of those judgments which cause want and scarcity: *e. gr.* of sore droughts and blastings and the multiplication of noxious creatures that destroy the fruits of the earth. All which particulars I could confirm unto you by approved history which declareth how they have all been presaged by "blazing stars" in heaven.

Lamentable deaths and destructions amongst men have been oftentimes presaged by such sights in heaven. Sudden and amazing ruins by earth-quakes, by inundations, by fire and the like awful visitations have been thereby portended. Especially destructions by mortal and contagious diseases. That strange disease known by the name of *Sudor Anglicanus*, which in a peculiar manner pursued those of the English nation, even when in strange lands (whence they were dreaded in all places where they came), there was a "blazing star" that did precede it. Especially that which is of all diseases miserable mortals are subject unto the most ter-rible (I mean the plague of pestilence), it is frequently thus presaged. Such sights are "Heaven's Alarm" to a sinful world, to give notice that God hath bent his bow and made his arrows ready and that if sinners turn not the arrows of pestilence and death shall fall down upon them speedily. This might be confirmed by a multitude of instances but it needs not. Our own experience is enough. We cannot but remember the "blazing star" that was seen but sixteen years ago, and a terrible plague followed; so that in our own nation near upon an hundred thou-sand were swept away in one city and in one year. And it is reported that immediately after that great blazing star which appeared above threescore years ago God sent the plague amongst the natives in this land, which swept them away in such multitudes, as that the living were not enough to bury the dead. So did the Lord cast out the heathen before this his people, that the way might thereby be prepared unto our more peaceable settlement here.

***

CONCERNING REMARKABLE JUDGMENTS.

[An Essay for the Recording of Illustrious Providences. 1684.]

THOSE memorable judgments which the hand of Heaven has exe-cuted upon notorious sinners are to be reckoned amongst Remark-able Providences. *Lubricus hic locus et difficilis.* He undertakes a diffi-cult province that shall relate all that might be spoken on such a subject, both in that it cannot but be gravaminous to surviving relations when such things are published, also in that men are apt to misapply the unsearchable judgments of God, which are a great deep, as Job's friends did; and wicked Papists have done the like with respect to the

Increase Mather

Tuis ad aras
Crescentius Matherus

untimely death of famous Zuinglius. We may not judge of men merely by outward accidents which befal them in this world, since all things happen alike unto all, and no man knoweth either love or hatred by all that is before them. We have seen amongst ourselves that the Lord's faithful servants have sometimes been the subjects of very dismal dispensations. There happened a most awful providence at Farmington in Connecticut colony, Dec. 14, 1666, when the house of Serjeant John Hart taking fire in the night, no man knows how (only it is conjectured that it might be occasioned by an oven), he and his wife and six children were all burned to death before the neighbours knew anything of it, so that his whole family had been extinguished by the fatal flames of that unhappy night had not one of his children been providentially from home at that time. This Hart was esteemed a choice Christian, and his wife also a good woman. Such things sometimes fall upon those that are dear unto God, to intimate, "If this be done to the green tree, what shall be done to the dry? that is, fit for nothing but the fire." Nevertheless, a judgment may be so circumstanced as that the displeasure of Heaven is plainly written upon it in legible characters; on which account it is said, "That the wrath of God is revealed from heaven against all ungodliness and unrighteousness of men." .   .   .   .

It hath been by many observed, that men addicted to horrid cursings and execrations have pulled down the imprecated vengeance of Heaven upon themselves. Sundry very awful examples of this kind have lately happened : I shall here mention one or two.

The hand of God was very remarkable in that which came to pass in the Narraganset country in New England, not many weeks since; for I have good information, that on August 28, 1683, a man there (viz. Samuel Wilson) having caused his dog to mischief his neighbour's cattle was blamed for his so doing. He denied the fact with imprecations, wishing that he might never stir from that place if he had so done. His neighbour being troubled at his denying the truth, reproved him, and told him he did very ill to deny what his conscience knew to be truth. The atheist thereupon used the name of God in his imprecations, saying, "He wished to God he might never stir out of that place, if he had done that which he was charged with." The words were scarce out of his mouth before he sunk down dead, and never stirred more; a son-in-law of his standing by and catching him as he fell to the ground.

A thing not unlike this hapned (though not in New England yet) in America, about a year ago; for in September, 1682, a man at the Isle of Providence, belonging to a vessel, whereof one Wollery was master, being charged with some deceit in a matter that had been committed to him, in order to his own vindication, horridly wished "that the devil might put out his eyes if he had done as was suspected concerning him." That very night a rhume fell into his eyes, so that within a few days he became stark blind. His company being astonished at the Divine hand which thus conspiciously and signally appeared, put him ashore at Providence, and left him there. A physitian being desired to undertake his cure, hearing how he came to lose his sight, refused to meddle with him. This account I lately received from credible persons, who knew and have often seen the man whom the devil (according to his own wicked wish) made blind, through the dreadful and righteous judgment of God.

Moreover, that worse than brutish sin of drunkenness hath been witnessed against from heaven by severe and signal judgments. It was a sign of the fearful wrath of God upon that notorious drunkard at a place called Seatucket in Long Island; who, as he was in drink, fell into the fire (the people in the house then being in bed and asleep), and so continued for some considerable time, until he received his death's wound. At his first awakening he roared out, "Fire! Fire!" as if it had been one in hell, to the great astonishment of all that heard him. One in the house flung a pail of water on him to quench his clothes, but that added to his torment; so he continued yelling after an hideous manner, "Fire! Fire!" and within a day or two died in great misery. And though this drunkard died by fire, it is remarkable that many of those who have loved drink have died by water, and that at the very time when their understandings have been drowned with drink. It is an awful consideration that there have been at several times above forty persons in this land whom death hath found in that woful plight, so that their immortal souls have gone out of drunken bodies to appear before God, the judge of all.

That remarkable judgment hath first or last fallen upon those who have sought the hurt of the people of God in New England, is so notorious as that it is become the observation of every man. This Israel in the wilderness hath eat up the nations his enemies; he hath broke their bones, and pierced them through with his arrows. Some adversaries have escaped longer unpunished than others; but then their ends have been of all the most woful and tragical at last. I shall instance only in what hath lately come to pass with respect unto the heathen who rose up against us, thinking to swallow us up quick when their wrath was kindled against us. Blessed be the Lord, who hath not given us a prey to their teeth! The chieftains amongst them were all cut off, either by sword or sickness, in the war time, excepting those in the eastern parts, whose ringleaders outlived their fellows; but now God hath met with them. There were in special two of those Indians who shed much innocent blood, viz. Simon and Squando. As for bloody

Simon, who was wont to boast of the mischiefs he had done, and how he had treacherously shot and killed such and such Englishmen, he died miserably the last winter. Another Indian discharging a gun, hapned to shoot Simon, so as to break his arm. After which he lived two years, but in extremity of pain, so as that the Indians when enquired of how Simon did, their usual answer was, "Worse than dead." He used all means that earth and hell (for he betook himself to *powaws*) could afford him for his recovery, but in vain. Thus was the wickedness of that murtherer at last returned upon his own head.

Concerning Squando, the Sachem of the Indians at Saco, the story of him is upon sundry accounts remarkable. Many years ago, he was sick and near unto death, after which he said, that one pretending to be the Englishman's God appeared to him in the form of an English minister, and discoursed with him, requiring him to leave off his drinking of rum, and religiously to observe the Sabbath-day, and to deal justly amongst men, withal promising him that if he did so, then at death his soul should go upwards to an happy place; but if he did not obey these commandments, at death his soul should go downwards, and be for ever miserable. But this pretended God said nothing to him about Jesus Christ. However, this apparition so wrought upon Squando, as that he left his drunkenness, and became a strict observer of the Sabbath-day; yea, so as that he always kept it as a day of fast, and would hear the English ministers preach, and was very just in his dealing. But in the time of the late Indian war, he was a principal actor in the bloody tragedies in that part of the country. The last year the pretended Englishman's God appeared to him again, as afore, in the form of a minister, requiring him to kill himself, and promising him that if he did obey, he should live again the next day, and never die more. Squando acquainted his wife and some other Indians with this new apparition; they most earnestly advised him not to follow the murderous counsel which the spectre had given. Nevertheless, he since hath hanged himself, and so is gone to his own place. This was the end of the man that disturbed the peace of New England.

THE DÆMON AT WILLIAM MORSE HIS HOUSE.

[From the Same.]

AS there have been several persons vexed with evil spirits, so divers houses have been wofully haunted by them. In the year 1679, the house of William Morse, in Newberry in New England, was strangely disquieted by a dæmon. After those troubles began, he did, by the advice of friends, write down the particulars of those unusual accidents. And the account which he giveth thereof, is as followeth :—

On December 3, in the night time, he and his wife heard a noise upon the roof of their house, as if sticks and stones had been thrown against it with great violence; whereupon he rose out of his bed, but could see nothing. Locking the doors fast, he returned to bed again. About midnight they heard an hog, making a great noise in the house, so that the man rose again, and found a great hog in the house; the door being shut, but upon the opening of the door it ran out.

On December 8, in the morning, there were five great stones and bricks by an invisible hand thrown in at the west end of the house while the man's wife was making the bed; the bedstead was lifted up from the floor, and the bedstaff flung out of the window, and a cat was hurled at her; a long staff danced up and down in the chimney; a burnt brick, and a piece of weather-board, were thrown in at the window. The man, at his going to bed, put out his lamp, but in the morning found that the saveall of it was taken away, and yet it was unaccountably brought into its former place. On the same day the long staff, but now spoken of, was hang'd up by a line, and swung to and fro; the man's wife laid it in the fire, but she could not hold it there, inasmuch as it would forcibly fly out; yet after much ado, with joynt strength they made it to burn. A shingle flew from the window, though no body near it; many sticks came in at the same place, only one of these was so scragged that it could enter the hole but a little way, whereupon the man pusht it out; a great rail likewise was thrust in at the window, so as to break the glass.

At another time an iron crook that was hanged on a nail violently flew up and down; also a chair flew about, and at last lighted on the table where victuals stood ready for them to eat, and was likely to spoil all, only by a nimble catching they saved some of their meal with the loss of the rest and the overturning of their table.

People were sometimes barricado'd out of doors, when as yet there was nobody to do it; and a chest was removed from place to place, no hand touching it. Their keys being tied together, one was taken from the rest, and the remaining two would fly about making a loud noise by knocking against each other. But the greatest part of this devil's feats were his mischievous ones, wherein indeed he was sometimes antick enough too, and therein the chief sufferers were the man and his wife, and his grand-son. The man especially had his share in these diabolical molestations. For one while they could not eat their suppers quietly, but had the ashes on the hearth before their eyes thrown into their victuals, yea, and upon their heads and clothes, insomuch that they were forced up into their chamber, and yet they had no rest there; for one of the man's shoes being left below, it was filled with ashes and coals, and thrown up after them. Their light was beaten out, and, they being laid in their bed with their little boy between them, a great stone (from the floor of the loft) weighing above three pounds was thrown upon the man's stomach, and he turning it down upon the floor, it was once more thrown upon him. A box and a board were likewise thrown upon them all; and a bag of hops was taken out of their chest, therewith they were beaten, till some of the hops were scattered on the floor, where the bag was then laid and left.

In another evening, when they sat by the fire, the ashes were so whirled at them, that they could neither eat their meat nor endure the house. A peel struck the man in the face. An apron hanging by the fire was flung upon it, and singed before they could snatch it off. The man being at prayer with his family, a beesom gave him a blow on his head behind, and fell down before his face.

On another day, when they were winnowing of barley, some hard dirt was thrown in, hitting the man on the head, and both the man and his wife on the back; and when they had made themselves clean, they essayed to fill their half-bushel; but the foul corn was in spite of them often cast in amongst the clean, and the man, being divers times thus abused, was forced to give over what he was about.

On January 23 (in particular), the man had an iron pin twice thrown at him, and his inkhorn was taken away from him while he was writing; and when by all his seeking it he could not find it, at last he saw it drop out of the air down by the fire. A piece of leather was twice thrown at him; and a shoe was laid upon his shoulder, which he catching at, was suddenly rapt from him. An handful of ashes was thrown at his face, and upon his clothes; and the shoe was then clapt upon his head, and upon it he clapt his hand, holding it so fast, that somewhat unseen pulled him with it backward on the floor.

On the next day at night, as they were going to bed, a lost ladder was thrown against the door, and their light put out; and when the man was a bed, he was beaten with an heavy pair of leather breeches, and pull'd by the hair of his head and beard, pinched and scratched, and his bed-board was taken away from him. Yet more: in the next night, when the man was likewise a bed, his bed-board did rise out of its place, notwithstanding his putting forth all his strength to keep it in; one of his awls was brought out of the next room into his bed, and did prick him; the clothes wherewith he hoped to save his head from blows, were violently pluckt from thence. Within a night or two after, the man and his wife received both of them a blow upon their heads, but it was so dark that they could not see the stone which gave it. The man had his cap pulled off from his head while he sat by the fire.

The night following, they went to bed undressed, because of their late disturbances, and the man, wife, boy, presently felt themselves pricked, and upon search, found in the bed a bodkin, a knitting needle, and two sticks picked at both ends; he received also a great blow, as on his thigh, so on his face, which fetched blood; and while he was writing, a candlestick was twice thrown at him; and a great piece of bark fiercely smote him; and a pail of water turned up without hands.   .   .   .

February 2.   While he and his boy were eating of cheese, the pieces which he cut were wrested from them, but they were afterwards found upon the table, under an apron and a pair of breeches; and also from the fire arose little sticks and ashes, which flying upon the man and his boy, brought them into an uncomfortable pickle.   But as for the boy, which the last passage spoke of, there remains much to be said concerning him and a principal sufferer in these afflictions; for on the 18th of December, he, sitting by his grandfather, was hurried into great motions, and the man thereupon took him, and made him stand between his legs; but the chair danced up and down, and had like to have cast both man and boy into the fire; and the child was afterwards flung about in such a manner, as that they feared that his brains would have been beaten out; and in the evening he was tossed as afore, and the man tried the project of holding him, but ineffectually.   The lad was soon put to bed, and they presently heard an huge noise, and demanded what was the matter? and he answered, that his bedstead leaped up and down; and they (i. e., the man and his wife) went up, and at first found all quiet, but before they had been there long, they saw the board by his bed trembling by him, and the bed-clothes flying off him; the latter they laid on immediately, but they were no sooner on than off; so they took him out of his bed for quietness.

December 29.   The boy was violently thrown to and fro, only they carried him to the house of a doctor in the town, and there he was free from disturbances; but returning home at night, his former trouble began, and the man taking him by the hand, they were both of them almost tript into the fire.   They put him to bed, and he was attended with the same iterated loss of his clothes, shaking off his bed-board, and noises that he had in his last conflict; they took him up, designing to sit by the fire, but the doors clattered, and the chair was thrown at him; wherefore they carried him to the doctor's house, and so for that night all was well.   The next morning he came home quiet; but as they were doing somewhat, he cried out that he was prickt on the back; they looked, and found a three-tin'd fork sticking strangely there; which being carried to the doctor's house, not only the doctor himself said that it was his, but also the doctor's servant affirmed it was seen at home after the boy was gone.   The boy's vexations continuing, they left him at the doctor's, where he remained well till awhile after, and then he complained he was pricked; they looked and found an iron spindle sticking below his back: he complained he was pricked still; they looked, and found there a long iron, a bowl of a spoon, and a piece of a pansheard. They lay down by him on the bed, with the light burning, but he was twice thrown from them, and the second time thrown quite under the bed. In the morning the bed was tossed about, with such a creaking noise as was heard to the neighbour's. In the afternoon their knives were, one after another, brought, and put into his back, but pulled out by the spectators; only one knife, which was missing, seemed to the standers by to come out of his mouth. He was bidden to read; his book was taken and thrown about several times, at last hitting the boy's grandmother on the head. Another time he was thrust out of his chair, and rolled up and down, with outcries, that all things were on fire; yea, he was three times very dangerously thrown into the fire, and preserved by his friends with much ado. The boy also made, for a long time together, a noise like a dog, and like an hen with her chickens, and could not speak rationally.

Particularly, on December 26, he barked like a dog, and clock't like an hen; and after long distraining to speak, said: " There's Powel, I am pinched." His tongue likewise hung out of his mouth, so as that it could by no means be forced in till his fit was over, and then he said 'twas forced out by Powel. He and the house also after this had rest till the 9th of January; at which time the child, because of his intolerable ravings, lying between the man and his wife, was pulled out of bed, and knockt vehemently against the bedstead boards, in a manner very perillous and amazing. In the day-time he was carried away beyond all possibility of their finding him. His grandmother at last saw him creeping on one side, and drag'd him in, where he lay miserable lame; but recovering his speech, he said, that he was carried above the doctor's house, and that Powel carried him; and that the said Powel had him into the barn, throwing him against the cart-wheel there, and then thrusting him out at an hole; and accordingly they found some of the remainders of the threshed barley, which was on the barn-floor, hanging to his clothes.

At another time he fell into a swoon; they forced somewhat refreshing into his mouth, and it was turned out as fast as they put it in; e're long he came to himself, and expressed some willingness to eat, but the meat would forcibly fly out of his mouth; and when he was able to speak, he said Powel would not let him eat. Having found the boy to be best at a neighbour's house, the man carried him to his daughter's, three miles from his own. The boy was growing antick as he was on the journey, but before the end of it he made a grievous hollowing ; and when he lighted, he threw a great stone at a maid in the house, and fell on eating of ashes.　Being at home afterwards, they had rest awhile ; but on the 19th of January, in the morning, he swooned, and coming to himself, he roared terribly, and did eat ashes, sticks, rug-yarn.　．　．

All this while the devil did not use to appear in any visible shape, only they would think they had hold of the hand that sometimes scratched them ; but it would give them the slip.　And once the man was discernably beaten by a fist, and an hand got hold of his wrist, which he saw but could not catch ; and the likeness of a blackmore child did appear from under the rug and blanket, where the man lay, and it would rise up, fall down, nod, and slip under the clothes, when they endeavoured to clasp it, never speaking anything.

Neither were there many words spoken by Satan all this time ; only once, having put out their light, they heard a scraping on the boards, and then a piping and drumming on them, which was followed with a voice, singing, "Revenge !　Revenge !　Sweet is revenge !"　And they being well terrified with it, called upon God : the issue of which was, that suddenly, with a mournful note, there were six times over uttered such expressions as, " Alas !　me knock no more !　me knock no more !" and now all ceased.

The man does, moreover, affirm that a seaman (being a mate of a ship) coming often to visit him told him, that they wronged his wife who suspected her to be guilty of witchcraft ; and that the boy (his grandchild) was the cause of this trouble ; and that if he would let him have the boy one day, he would warrant him his house should be no more troubled as it had been.　To which motion he consented. The mate came the next day betimes, and the boy was with him until night ; since which time his house, he saith, has not been molested with evil spirits.

Thus far is the relation concerning the dæmon at William Morse his house in Newberry.　The true reason of these strange disturbances is as yet not certainly known : some (as has been hinted) did suspect Morse's wife to be guilty of witchcraft.

One of the neighbours took apples, which were brought out of that house, and put them into the fire ; upon which, they say, their houses were much disturbed.　Another of the neighbours caused an horse-shoe to be nailed before the doors ; and as long as it remained so, they could not perswade the suspected person to go into the house ; but when the horse-shoe was gone, she presently visited them.　I shall not here inlarge upon the vanity and superstition of those experiments, reserving that for another place ; all that I shall say at present is, that the dæmons, whom the blind Gentiles of old worshipped, told their servants, that such things as these would very much affect them; yea, and that certain characters, signs, and charms, would render their power ineffectual; and, accordingly, they would become subject, when their own directions were obeyed. It is sport to the devils when they see silly men thus deluded and made fools of by them. Others were apt to think that a seaman, by some suspected to be a conjurer, set the devil on work thus to disquiet Morse's family; or, it may be, some other thing, as yet kept hid in the secrets of Providence, might be the true original of all this trouble.

THAT THERE BE DÆMONS AND POSSESSED PERSONS.

[*From the Same.*]

THE Sadduces of these days being like unto Avicenna, and Averroes, and other atheistical philosophers in former times, say that there are no spirits, and that all stories concerning them are either fabulous or to be ascribed unto natural causes. Amongst many others, the learned Voetius (*in Disp. de operationibus Dæmonum*) has sufficiently refuted them. And as the experience of other ages and places of the world, so the things which Divine Providence hath permitted and ordered to come to pass amongst ourselves, if the Scriptures were silent, make it manifest beyond all contradiction, that there are devils infesting this lower world. Most true it is, that Satan and all his wicked angels are limited by the providence of God, so as that they cannot hurt any man or creature, much less any servant of his, without a commission from him, whose kingdom is over all. It is a memorable passage, which Chytræus relateth concerning Luther, that when he was sought after by his popish and implacable enemies (being then hid by the Duke of Saxony), they consulted with magicians that so they might find where Luther absconded, but the wizards confessed they could not discover him. Undoubtedly the devils knew where Luther hid himself; only God would not suffer them to reveal it. Nevertheless the Lord doth, for wise and holy ends, sometimes lengthen the chain which the infernal lions are bound fast in. And as there are many tremendous instances confirming the truth hereof, so that of Satan's taking bodily possession of men is none of the least. Sometimes indeed it is very hard to discern between natural diseases and satanical possessions; so as that persons really possessed have been thought to be only molested with some natural disease, without any special finger of the evil spirit therein. Fernelius (*de Abditis Rerum Causis*, lib. 2, cap. 16) speaketh of a certain young gentleman that was taken with strange convulsions, which did surprise him at least ten times in a day.　In his fits he had the use of his speech and reason free; otherwise his disease would have been judged no other than an ordinary epilepsy.　Much means was used by skilful physitians for his relief, but without success for three months together; when all on a sudden, a dæmon began to speak out of the miserable patient; and that with not only Latin but Greek sentences, which the afflicted party himself had no knowledge of; and the dæmon discovered many secrets both of the physitians and of other persons that attended, deriding them for their vain attempts to cure a man whom he had the possession of.　There are sundry authors (in special Balduinus in his cases of conscience, and Darrel in his history of the "Seven Possessed Persons in Lancashire") who have endeavoured to describe and characterise possessed persons.　And such particulars as these following are by them mentioned as signs of possession :

1.　If the party concerned shall reveal secret things, either past or future, which without supernatural assistance could not be known, it argueth possession.

2.　If he does speak with strange languages, or discover skill in arts and sciences never learned by him.

3.　If he can bear burthens, and do things which are beyond human strength.

4.　Uttering words without making use of the organs of speech, when persons shall be heard speaking, and yet neither their lips nor tongues have any motion, 'tis a sign that an evil spirit speaketh in them.

5.　When the body is become inflexible.

6.　When the belly is on a sudden puft up, and instantly flat again.

These are thought to be certain arguments of an energumenical person.　Some other signs are mentioned by Thyræus (*De Obsessis*, part 2, cap. 25, 26).

There are who conceive (and that as they suppose upon scripture grounds) that men may possibly be dæmoniacal, when none of those mentioned particulars can be affirmed of them.　The excellently learned and judicious Mr. Mede is of opinion, that the dæmoniacks whom we read so frequently of in the New Testament, were the same with epilepticks, lunaticks, and mad men.　　.　　　.　　　.　　　.

There are that acknowledge the existence of spirits, and that the bodies of men are sometimes really possessed thereby, who, nevertheless, will not believe there are any such woful creatures *in rerum naturâ* as witches, or persons confederate with the devil.　I have read of a famous wizard, whose name was William de Lure, that after he had laboured much in opposing their opinion, who think that there are men on earth joyned in an explicit confederacy with the fiends of hell, was himself convicted and condemned for that crime which he designed to make the world believe that no man was or could be guilty of. I shall not suspect all those as guilty of witchcraft, nor yet of heresie, who call the received opinion about witches into question. There are four or five English writers, viz. Mr. Scot, Ady, and of late, Wagstaff and Webster, and another anonymous author, who do, with great vehemence, affirm, that never any did maintain that familiarity with the evil spirits which is commonly believed. Wierus (otherwise a judicious author) conceiveth that all those things supposed to be done by witches are done by the evil spirits themselves, without any confederates. But he is sufficiently refuted by Binsfieldius, Bodinus, Sennertus, and others.   .   .   .

Experience has too often made it manifest that there are such in the world as hold a correspondence with hell. There have bin known wizards; yea, such as have taught others what ceremonies they are to use in maintaining communion with devils. Trithemius his book *de Septem Intelligentiis*, and Cornelius Agrippa's books of occult philosophy, wherein too much of these nefandous abominations is described, are frequently in the hands of men. Several other books there are extant which do professedly teach the way of familiarity with dæmons; the titles whereof, as also the names of the authors that have published them, I designedly forbear to mention, lest haply any one into whose hands this discourse may come, should out of wicked curiosity seek after them to the ruine of his soul. There are famous histories of several who had their *paredri* or familiar spirits, some in one likeness, some in another, constantly attending them: thus had Apollonius, Thyanæus of old; and of later times, Mich. Scot and Josephus Niger. Likewise Cardanus (*de Subtilitate*, lib. xix, p. 963) writeth, that his own father had such a familiar for thirty years together. So had Christopher Waganeer a familiar in the form of an ape for seven years attending him; so had Tolpardus, which two were at last carried away body and soul by the devil, unto whose service they had devoted their lives. There is also a true (as well as a romantick) story of Faustus. The excellent Camerarius, in his *Horæ Subsecivæ*, cent. i, cap. 70, relateth strange things of him, which he received from those who knew Faustus, and were eye-witnesses of his magical and diabolical impostures. He also had a familiar devil, in form of a monk, accompanying of him for the space of twenty-four years. Hausdorfius and Lonicer *ad* 2 *præc.* p. 167, speak of Faustus. Melancthon declares that he knew the man; so that Naudeus is to be convinced of vanity, in denying that ever there was such a person in the world. In a word, it is a thing known, that there have been men who would discourse in languages and reason notably about sciences which they never learned; who have revealed secrets, discovered hidden treasures, told whither stolen goods have been conveyed, and by whom; and that have caused bruit creatures, nay statues or images, to speak and give rational answers. The Jews' *teraphims* oftentimes did so.   .   .   .   .

There have been many in the world who have, upon conviction, confessed themselves guilty of familiarity with the devil. A multitude of instances this way are mentioned by Bodinus, Codronchus, Delrio, Jacquerius, Remigius, and others. Some in this country have affirmed that they knew a man in another part of the world, above fifty years ago, who having an ambitious desire to be thought a wise man, whilest he was tormented with the itch of his wicked ambition, the devil came to him with promises that he should quickly be in great reputation for his wisdom, in case he would make a covenant with him; the conditions whereof were, that when men came to him for his counsel, he should labour to perswade them that there is no God, nor devil, nor heaven, nor hell; and that, such a term of years being expired, the devil should have his soul. The articles were consented to: the man continuing after this to be of a very civil conversation, doing hurt to none, but good to many; and by degrees began to have a name to be a person of extraordinary sagacity, and was sought unto far and near for counsel, his words being esteemed oracles by the vulgar. And he did according to his covenant upon all occasions secretly disseminate principles of atheism, not being suspected for a wizard. But a few weeks before the time indented with the devil was fulfilled, inexpressible horror of conscience surprized him, so that he revealed the secret transactions which had passed betwixt himself and the devil. He would sometimes, with hideous roarings, tell those that came to visit him, that now he knew there was a God, and a devil, and an heaven, and an hell. So did he die a miserable spectacle of the righteous and fearful judgment of God. And every age does produce new examples of those that have by their own confession made the like cursed covenants with the prince of darkness.

In the year 1664, several who were indicted at the assizes, held at Taunton in Somersetshire, confessed that they had made an explicit league with the devil; and that he did baptise pictures of wax with oyl, giving them the names of those persons they did intend mischief unto.

Anno 1678 one John Stuart, and his sister, Annibal Stuart, at the assizes held at Paysley in Scotland, confessed that they had been in confederacy with the devil; and that they had made an image of wax, calling it by the name of Sir George Maxwel, sticking pins in the sides and on the breast of it. Such an image, with pins in it, was really found in the witches' houses; and upon the removal of it, the pins being taken out, Sir George had immediate ease, and recovered his health.

There is lately published (by Dr. Horneck) the "History of the

Witches in Sweden;" by whose means that kingdom was fearfully plagued. Upon examination, they confessed their crime, and were executed in the year 1670.

And no longer since than the last year, viz. on Aug. 25, 1682, three women, who were executed at Exon in Devonshire, all of them confessed that they had had converses and familiarities with the devil.

But the instance of the witch executed in Hartford, here in New England (of which the preceding chapter giveth an account), considering the circumstances of that confession, is as convictive a proof as most single examples that I have met with. It is a vain thing for the patrons of witches to think that they can sham off this argument, by suggesting that these confessions did proceed from the deluded imaginations of mad and melancholly persons. Some of them were as free from distemperature in their brains as their neighbours. That divers executed for witches have acknowledged things against themselves which were never so, I neither doubt or deny; and that a deluded phansie may cause persons verily to think they have seen and done these things which never had any existence except in their own imaginations, is indisputable. I fully concur with a passage which I find in worthy Dr. Owen's late excellent discourse about the work of the Spirit in prayer (p. 202), where he has these words:—"We find by experience that some have had their imaginations so fixed on things evil and noxious by satanical delusions, that they have confessed against themselves things and crimes that have rendered them obnoxious to capital punishment, whereof they were never really and actually guilty." This, notwithstanding that persons, whose judgment and reason have been free from disturbance by any disease, should not only voluntarily acknowledge their being in cursed familiarities with Satan, but mention the particular circumstances of those transactions, and give ocular demonstration of the truth of what they say, by discovering the *stigmata* made upon their bodies by the devil's hand; and that, when more than one or two have been examined apart, they should agree in the circumstances of their relations; and yet that all this should be the mere effect of melancholly or phrensie, cannot, without offering violence to reason and common sense, be imagined. And as there are witches, so, many times, they are the causes of those strange disturbances which are in houses haunted by evil spirits, such as those mentioned in the former chapter. Instances concerning this may be seen in Mr. Glanvil's "Collections," together with the continuation thereof, published the last year by the learned Dr. Henry More. Sometimes Providence permits the devil himself (without the use of instruments) to molest the houses of some, as a punishment for sin committed, most commonly either for the sin of murder: Plutarch writes, that the house of Pausanias was haunted by an evil spirit after he had murdered his wife; many like instances have been reported and recorded by credible authors; or else for the sin of theft. As for Walton, the Quaker of Portsmouth, whose house has been so strangely troubled, he suspects that one of his neighbours has caused it by witchcraft; she (being a widow-woman) chargeth him with injustice in detaining some land from her. It is none of my work to reflect upon the man, nor will I do it; only, if there be any late or old guilt upon his conscience, it concerns him by confession and repentance to give glory to that God who is able in strange ways to discover the sins of men.

OF THE WORKINGS OF SATAN.

[Cases of Conscience concerning Evil Spirits. 1693.]

THAT evil angels have sometimes appeared in the likeness of living absent persons, is a thing abundantly confirmed by history.

Austin tells us of one that went for resolution in some intricate questions to a philosopher, of whom he could get no answer; but in the night the philosopher comes to him, and resolves all his doubts. Not long after, he demanded the reason why he could not answer him in the day as well as in the night; the philosopher professed he was not with him in the night, only acknowledged that he dreamed of his having such conversation of his friend, but he was all the time at home and asleep. Paulus and Palladius did both of them profess to Austin, that one in his shape had divers times and in divers places appeared to them. Thyreus mentions several apparitions of absent living persons, which happened in his time, and which he had the certain knowledge of. A man that is in one place cannot (*Autoprosopos*) at the same time be in another. It remains then that such spectres are prodigious and supernatural, and not without diabolical operation. It has been controverted among learned men, whether innocent persons may not by the malice and deluding power of the devil be represented as present amongst witches at their dark assemblies. The mentioned Thyreus says, that the devil may and often does represent the forms of innocent persons out of those conventions, and that there is no question to be made of it, but as to his natural power and art he is able to make their shapes appear amongst his own servants, but he supposeth the providence of God will not suffer such an injury to be done to an innocent person. With him Delrio, and Spineus concur. But Cumanus in his *Lucerna Inquisitorum* (a book which I have not yet seen) defends the affirmative in this question. Bins Fieldius in his

Treatise, concerning the Confession of Witches, inclines to the negative, only he acknowledges *Dei extraordinaria permissione posse innocentes sic representari*. And he that shall assert, that Great and Holy God never did nor ever will permit the devil thus far to abuse an innocent person, affirms more than he is able to prove. The story of Germanus his discovering a diabolical illusion of this nature, concerning a great number of persons that seemed to be at a feast when they were really at home and asleep, is mentioned by many authors. But the particulars insisted on do sufficiently evince the truth of what we assert, viz. : That the devil may by divine permission appear in the shape of innocent and pious persons. Nevertheless, it is evident from another Scripture, viz., that in II. Cor. xi. 14, "For Satan himself is transformed into an angel of light." He seems to be what he is not, and makes others seem to be what they are not. He represents evil men as good, and good men as evil. The angels of heaven (who are the angels of light) love truth and righteousness, the devil will seem to do so too ; and does therefore sometimes lay before men excellent good principles and exhort them (as he did Theodore Maillit) to practise many things, which by the law of righteousness they are obliged unto, and hereby he does more effectually deceive. Is it not strange, that he has sometimes intimated to his most devoted servants, that if they would have familiar conversation with him, they must be careful to keep themselves from enormous sins, and pray constantly for divine protection? But so has he transformed himself into an angel of light, as Boissardus sheweth. He has frequently appeared to men pretending to be a good angel, so to Anatolius of old ; and the late instances of Dr. Dee and Kellet are famously known. How many deluded enthusiasts both in former and latter times have been imposed on by Satan's appearing visibly to them, pretending to be a good angel. And moreover, he may be said to transform himself into an angel of light, because of his appearing in the form of holy men, who are the children of light, yea in the shape and habit of eminent ministers of God. So did he appear to Mr. Earl of Colchester in the likeness of Mr. Liddal an holy man of God, and to the Turkish Chaous baptized at London, Anno 1658, pretending to be Mr. Dury, an excellent minister of Christ. And how often has he pretended to be the Apostle Paul or Peter or some other celebrated saint? Ecclesiastical histories abound with instances of this nature. Yea, sometimes he has transfigured himself into the form of Christ. It is reported that he appeared to St. Martin gloriously arrayed, as if he had been Christ. So likewise to Secundellus, and to another saint, who suspecting it was Satan transforming himself into an angel of light had this expression, "If I may see Christ in heaven it is enough, I desire not to see him in this world"; whereupon the spectre vanished. It has been related of Luther, that after he had been fasting and pray-

ing in his study, the devil come pretending to be Christ, but Luther saying, "Away thou confounded devil, I acknowledge no Christ but what
is in my Bible," nothing more was seen. Thus then the devil is able (by
divine permission) to change himself into what form or figure he pleaseth.

Omnia transformat sese in miracula rerum.

A third Scripture to our purpose is that in Rev. xii. 10, where the devil
is called the Accuser of the Brethren. Such is the malice and impudence of the devil, as that he does accuse good men, and that before God,
and that not only of such faults as they really are guilty of (he accused
Joshua with his filthy garments, when through his indulgence some of
his family had transgressed by unlawful marriages), but also with such
crimes as they are altogether free from. He represented the Primitive
Christians as the vilest of men, and as if at their meetings they did commit the most nefandous villanies that ever were known; and that not
only innocent, but eminently pious persons should through the malice of
the devil be accused with the crime of witchcraft, is no new thing. Such
an affliction did the Lord see meet to exercise the great Athanasius with,
only the divine providence did wonderfully vindicate him from that as
well as from some other foul aspersions. The Waldenses (although the
Scriptures called them saints, Rev. xiii. 7), have been traduced by Satan
and by the world as horrible witches; so have others in other places,
only because they have done extraordinary things by their prayers. It
is by many authors related that a city in France was molested with a
diabolical spectre, which the people were wont to call Hugon; near that
place a number of Protestants were wont to meet to serve God, whence
the professors of the true reformed religion were nic-named Hugonots
by the Papists, who designed to render them before the world, as the
servants and worshippers of that dæmon, that went under the name of
Hugon. And how often have I read in books written by Jesuits, that
Luther was a wizard, and that he did himself confess that he had familiarity with Satan! Most impudent untruths! nor are these things to be
wondered at, since the Holy Son of God himself was reputed a magician,
and one that had familiarity with the greatest of devils. The blasphem-
ing Pharisees said, "He casts out the devils through the prince of devils,"
Matth. ix. 34. There is, then, not the best saint on earth (man or woman)
that can assure themselves that the devil shall not cast such an imputation upon them. "It is enough for the disciple that he be as his master,
and the servant as his Lord: If they have called the master of the house
Beelzebub, how much more them of his household," Matth. x. 25. It is
not for men to determine how far the Holy God may permit the wicked
one to proceed in his accusations. The sacred story of Job giveth us to
understand that the Lord, whose ways are past finding out, does for wise

and holy ends suffer Satan by immediate operation (and consequently by witchcraft) greatly to afflict innocent persons, as in their bodies and estates, so in their reputations.   I shall mention but one Scripture more to confirm the truth in hand.   It is that in Eccles. ix. 2, 3, where it is said, "All things come alike to all: there is one event to the righteous and to the wicked: as is the good, so is the sinner: this is an evil amongst all things under the sun, that there is one event happeneth to all." And in Eccles. vii. 15, 'tis said, "There is a just man that perisheth in his righteousness."

From hence we infer that there is no outward affliction whatsoever but may befall a good man; now to be represented by Satan as a tormentor of bewitched or possessed persons, is a sore affliction to a good man.   To be tormented by Satan is a sore affliction, yet nothing but what befell Job, and a daughter of Abraham, whom we read of in the gospel.   To be represented by Satan as tormenting others is an affliction like the former; the Lord may bring such extraordinary temptations on his own children, to afflict and humble them, for some sin they have been guilty of before him.   A most wicked person in St. Ives got a knife, and went with it to a minister's house, designing to stab him, but was disappointed; afterwards conscience being awakened, the devil appears to this person in the shape of that minister, with a knife in his hand exhorting to self-murder.   Was not here a punishment suitable to the sin which that person had been guilty of?   Perhaps some of those whom Satan has represented as committing witchcrafts, have been tampering with some foolish and wicked sorceries, though not to that degree which is criminal and capital by the laws both of God and men; for this Satan may be permitted so to scourge them; or, it may be, they have misrepresented and abused others, for which cause the Holy God may justly give Satan leave falsely to represent them.

Have we not known some that have bitterly censured all that have been complained of by bewitched persons, saying it was impossible they should not be guilty; soon upon which themselves or some near relations of theirs have been to the lasting infamy of their families accused after the same manner, and personated by the devil!   Such tremendous rebukes on a few should make all men to be careful how they joyn with Satan in condemning the innocent.   .   .   .   .

If Satan may not represent one that is not a covenant servant of his, as afflicting those that are bewitched or possessed, then it is either because he wants will or power to do this, or because God will never permit him thus to do.   No man but a Sadduce doubts of the ill will of devils; nothing is more pleasing to the malice of those wicked spirits than to see innocency wronged.   And the power of the enemy is such, as that having once obtained a divine concession to use his art, he can do this and much more than this amounts unto. We know by Scripture-revelation, that the sorcerers of Egypt caused many untrue and delusive representations before Pharaoh and his servants. And we read of the working of Satan in all power and signs, and lying wonders. His heart is beyond what the wisest of men may pretend unto. He has perfect skill in opticks, and can therefore cause that to be visible to one, which is not so to another, and things also to appear far otherwise than they are. He has likewise the art of limning in the perfection of it, and knows what may be done by colors. It is an odd passage which I find in the *Acta Eruditorum*, printed by Lipsick, that about thirty-two years ago an indigent merchant in France was instructed by a dæmon that with water of borax he might color taffities, so as to cause them to glister and look very gay. He searcheth into the nature, causes, and reasons of things, whereby he is able to produce wonderful effects. So that if he does not form the shape of an innocent person as afflicting others, it is not from want of either will or power. They that affirm that God never did, nor ever will permit him thus to do, allege that it is inconsistent with the righteousness and providence of God, in governing human affairs thus to suffer men to be imposed on. It must be acknowledged that the divine providence has taken care that the greatest part of mankind shall not be left to unavoidable deception, so as to be always abused by the mischievous agents of hell, in the objects of plain sence. But yet it is not for sinful and silly mortals to prescribe rules to the Most High in his government of the world, or to direct him how far he may permit Satan to use his power. I am apt to think that there are some amongst us, who if they had lived in Job's days, and seen the devil tormenting of him, and heard him complaining of being scared with dreams, and terrified with night-visions, they would have joined with his uncharitable friends in censuring him as a most guilty person. But we should consider, that the most high God doth sometimes deal with men in a way of absolute sovereignty, performing the thing which is appointed for them, and many such things are with him. If he does destroy the perfect with the wicked, and laugh at the tryal of the innocent (Job ix. 22, 23). Who shall enter into his councils! who has given him a charge over the earth! or who has disposed the whole world! Men are not able to give an account of his ordinary works, much less of his secret counsels and the dark dispensations of his providence. They do but darken counsel by words without knowledge when they undertake it. If we are not able to see how this or that can stand with the righteousness of him that governs the world, shall we say that the Almighty will pervert judgment? or that he that governs the earth hateth right? Shall we condemn him that is most just? But whereas 'tis objected, where is Providence? And how shall men live on the earth, if the devil may be permitted to use

such power? I demand, where was Providence, when Satan had power
to cause sons of Belial to lye and swear away the life of innocent Naboth,
laying such crimes to his charge as he was never guilty of? And what
an hour of darkness was it? How far was the power of hell permitted
to prevail, when Christ the Son of God was accused, condemned, and
hanged for a crime that he never was guilty of? That was the strangest
providence that has happened since the world began, and yet in the issue
the most glorious. We must therefore distinguish between what does
ordinarily come to pass by the providence of God, and things which are
extraordinary. It is not an usual thing for a Naboth to have his life
taken from him by false accusations, or for an Athanasius or a Susanna
to be charged, and perhaps brought before courts of judicature for crimes
of which they were altogether innocent.

But if we therefore conclude, that such a thing as this can never
happen in the world, we shall offend against the generation of the just.
It is not ordinary for devils to be permitted to reveal the secret sins of
men; yet this has been done more than once or twice. Nor is it ordinary
for dæmons to steal money out of men's pockets, and purses, or wine and
cyder out of their cellars. Yet some such instances have there been
amongst ourselves. It is not usual for Providence to permit the devil
to come from hell and to throw fire on the tops of houses, and to cause a
whole town to be burnt to ashes thereby; there would (it must be confessed) be no living in the world, if evil angels should be permitted to do
thus when they had a mind to it; nevertheless, authors worthy of credit
tell us that this has sometimes happened. Both Erasmus and Cardanus
write that the town of Schiltach in Germany was in the month of April,
1533, set on fire by a devil, and burnt to the ground in an hour's space.
'Tis also reported by Sigibert, Aventinus and others, that some cottages
and barns in a town called Bingus were fired by a wicked genius; that
spiteful dæmon said it was for the impieties of such a man whom he
named, that he was sent to molest them. The poor man to satisfie his
neighbours, who were ready to stone him, carried an hot iron in his hand,
but receiving no hurt thereby, he was judged to be innocent. It is not
ordinary for a devil, upon the dying curse of a servant, to have a commission from heaven to tear and torment a bloody cruel master; yet such
a thing may possibly come to pass. There is a fearful story to this purpose, in the account of the Bucuneers of America, wherein my author
relates that a servant, who was spirited or kidnapt (as they call it) into
America, falling into the hands of a tyrannical master, he ran away from
him, but being taken and brought back, the hard-hearted tyrant lashed
him on his naked back until his body ran in an entire stream of blood;
to make the torment of this miserable creature intolerable, he anointed
his wounds with juice of lemon mingled with salt and pepper, being

ground small together, with which torture the miserable wretch gave up the ghost, with these dying words, "I beseech the Almighty God, Creator of heaven and earth, that he permit a wicked spirit to make thee feel as many torments before thy death, as thou hast caused me to feel before mine." Scarce four days were past after this horrible fact, when the Almighty Judge gave permission to the father of wickedness to possess the body of that cruel master, and to make him lacerate his own flesh until he died, belike surrendering his ghost into the hands of the infernal spirit, who had tormented his body. But of this tragical story enough.

To proceed, It is not usual for persons after their death to appear unto the living. But it does not therefore follow, that the great God will not suffer this to be. For both in former and latter ages examples thereof have not been wanting. No longer since than the last winter, there was much discourse in London concerning a gentlewoman, unto whom her dead son (and another whom she knew not) had appeared. Being then in London, I was willing to satisfie myself, by enquiring into the truth of what was reported; and on Febr. 23, 1691, my brother (who is now a pastor to a congregation in that city) and I discoursed the gentlewoman spoken of; she told us, that a son of hers, who had been a very civil young man, but more airy in his temper than was pleasing to his serious mother, being dead, she was much concerned in her thoughts about his condition in the other world; but a fortnight after his death he appeared to her, saying, "Mother, you are solicitous about my spiritual welfare; trouble yourself no more, for I am happy," and so vanished; should there be a continual intercourse between the visible and invisible world, it would breed confusion. But from thence to infer, that the great Ruler of the Universe will never permit anything of this nature to be, is an inconsequent conclusion. It is not usual for devils to be permitted to come and violently carry away persons through the air, several miles from their habitations; nevertheless, this was done in Sweedland about twenty years ago, by means of a cursed knot of witches there. And a learned physician now living giveth an account of several children, who by diabolical frauds were stolen from their parents, and others left in their room. And of two, that in the night-time a line was by invisible hands put about their necks, with which they had been strangled, but that some near them happily prevented it.

Let me further add here: It has very seldom been known, that Satan has personated innocent men doing an ill thing, but Providence has found out some way for their vindication; either they have been able to prove that they were in another place when that fact was done, or the like. So that perhaps there never was an instance of any innocent person condemned in any court of judicature on earth, only through Satan's deluding and imposing on the imaginations of men, when, nevertheless, the witnesses, juries, and judges, were all to be excused from blame.

It is certain both from Scripture and history, that magicians by their inchantments and hellish conjurations may cause a false representation of persons and things. An inchanted eye shall see such things as others cannot discern; it is a thing too well known to be denied, that some by rubbing their eyes with a bewitched water have immediately thereupon seen that which others could not discern; and there are persons in the world, who have a strange spectral sight. Mr. Glanvil speaks of a Dutchman that could see ghosts which others could perceive nothing of. There are in Spain a sort of men whom they call Zahurs, these can see into the bowels of the earth; they are able to discover minerals and hidden treasures; nevertheless, they have their extraordinary sight only on Tuesdays and Fridays, and not on the other days of the week. Delrio saith, that when he was at Madrid, Anno Dom. 1575, he saw some of these strange sighted creatures. Mr. George Sinclare, in his book entituled, "Satans Invisible World discovered," has these words, "I am undoubtedly informed, that men and women in the High-lands can discern fatality approaching others, by seeing them in the waters or with winding sheets about them. And that others can lecture in a sheep's shoulder-bone a death within the parish seven or eight days before it come. It is not improbable but that such preternatural knowledge comes first by a compact with the devil, and is derived downward by succession to their posterity. Many such I suppose are innocent, and have this sight against their will and inclination." Thus Mr. Sinclare. I concur with his supposal, that such knowledge is originally from Satan, and perhaps the effect of some old inchantment. There are some at this day in the world, that if they come into a house where one of the family will die within a fortnight, the smell of a dead corpse offends them to such a degree, as that they cannot stay in that house. It is reported that near unto the Abby of Maurice in Burgundy there is a fishpond in which are fishes put according to the number of the monks of that place; if any one of them happened to be sick, there is a fish seen to float and swim above water half dead, and if the monk shall die, the fish a few days before dieth. In some parts in Wales death-lights or corpse candles (as they call them) are seen in the night time going from the house where some body will shortly die, and passing in to the church-yard. Of this, my honoured and never to be forgotten friend, Mr. Richard Baxter, has given an account in his book about witchcrafts lately published: what to make of such things, except they be the effect of some old inchantment, I know not; nor what natural reason to assign for that which I find amongst the Observations of the Imperial Academy for the year 1687, viz. that in an orchard where are choice Damascen plumbs, the master of the family being sick of a quartan ague, whilst he continued very ill, four of his plumb-trees instead of Damascens brought forth a vile sort of yellow plumbs: but recovering health, the next year the tree did (as formerly) bear Damascens again; but when after that he fell into a fatal dropsie, on those trees were seen not Damascens, but another sort of fruit. The same author gives instances of which he had the certain knowledge, concerning apple-trees and pear-trees, that the fruit of them would on a sudden wither as if they had been baked in an oven, when the owners of them were mortally sick. It is no less strange that in the illustrious Electoral House of Brandenburg before the death of some one of the family feminine spectres appeared. And often in the houses of great men, voices and visions from the invisible world have been the harbingers of death. When any heir in the worshipful family of the Breertons in Cheshire is near his death, there are seen in a pool adjoyning, bodies of trees swimming for certain days together, on which learned Cambden has this note, "These and such like things are done either by the holy tutelar angels of men, or else by the devils, who by God's permission mightily show their power in this inferiour world." As for Mr. Sinclare's notion that some persons may have a second sight (as 'tis termed), and yet be themselves innocent, I am satisfied that he judgeth right; for this is common amongst the Laplanders, who are horribly addicted to magical incantations. They bequeath their dæmons to their children as a legacy, by whom they are often assisted (like bewitched persons as they are) to see and do things beyond the power of nature. An historian who deserves credit relates, that a certain Laplander gave him a true and particular account of what had happened to him in his journey to Lapland; and further complained to him with tears, that things at great distance were represented to him, and how much he desired to be delivered from that diabolical sight, but could not; this doubtless was caused by some inchantment. But to proceed to what I intend; the eyes of persons, by reason of inchanting charms, may not only see what others do not, but be under such power of fascination, as that things which are not shall appear to them as real. The apostle speaks of bewitched eyes, Gal. iii. 1, and we know from Scripture, that the imaginations of men have by inchantments been imposed upon; and histories abound with very strange instances of this nature. The old witch Circe by an inchanted cup caused Ulysses his companions to imagine themselves to be turned into swine; and how many witches have been themselves so bewitched by the devil, as really to believe that they were transformed into wolves, or dogs, or cats. It is reported of Simon Magus, that by his sorceries he would so impose on the imaginations of people, as that they thought he had really changed himself into another sort of creature. Opollonius of Tyana could outdo Simon with his magick. The great Bohemian conjurer Zyto by his inchantments caused certain persons whom he had a mind to try his art upon, to imagine that their hands were turned into the feet of an ox, or into the hoofs of a horse, so that they could not reach to the dishes before them to take any thing thence; he sold wisps of straw to a butcher who bought them for swine; that many such prestigious pranks were played by the unhappy Faustus, is attested by Camerarius, Wyerus, Voetius, Lavater, and Lonicer.

There is newly published a book (mentioned in the *Acta Eruditorum*) wherein the author (Wiechard Valvassor) relates, that a Venetian Jew instructed him (only he would not attend his instructions) how to make a magical glass which should represent any person or thing according as he should desire. If a magician by an inchanted glass can do this, he may as well by the help of a dæmon cause false idæas of persons and things to be impressed on the imaginations of bewitched persons; the blood and spirits of a man, that is bitten with a mad-dog, are so envenomed, as that strange impressions are thereby made on his imagination. Let him be brought into a room where there is a looking-glass, and he will (if put upon it) not only say but swear that he sees a dog, though in truth there is no dog it may be within 20 miles of him; and is it not then possible for the dogs of hell to poyson the imaginations of miserable creatures, so as that they shall believe and swear that such persons hurt them as never did so?

OF THE DISCOVERY OF WITCHES.

[From the Same.]

IF the things which nave been mentioned are not infallible proofs of guilt in the accused party, it is then queried, Whether there are any discoveries of this crime, which jurors and judges may with a safe conscience proceed upon to the conviction and condemnation of the persons under suspicion?

Let me here premise two things,

1. The evidence in this crime ought to be as clear as in any other crimes of a capital nature. The Word of God does nowhere intimate, that a less clear evidence, or that fewer or other witnesses may be taken as sufficient to convict a man of sorcery, which would not be enough to convict him were he charged with another evil worthy of death; if we may not take the oath of a distracted person, or of a possessed person in a case of murder, theft, felony of any sort, then neither may we do it in the case of witchcraft.

2. Let me premise this also, that there have been ways of trying witches long used in many nations, especially in the dark times of Paganism and Popery, which the righteous God never approved of. But which (as judicious Mr. Perkins expresseth it in plain English) were invented by the devil, that so innocent persons might be condemned, and some notorious witches escape. Yea, many superstitious and magical experiments have been used to try witches by. Of this sort is that of scratching the witch, . . . yea, and that way of discovering witches by tying their hands and feet, and casting them on the water, to try whether they will sink or swim. I did publickly bear my testimony against this superstition in a book printed at Boston eight years past.

I hear that of late some in a neighbour colony have been playing with this diabolical invention. It is to be lamented that, in such a land of uprightness as New-England once was, a practice which Protestant writers generally condemn as sinful, and which the more sober and learned men amongst Papists themselves have not only judged unlawful, but (to express it in their own terms) to be no less than a mortal sin, should ever be heard of. Were it not that the coming of Christ to judge the earth draweth near, I should think that such practices are an unhappy omen that the devil and Pagans will get these dark territories into their possession again. But that I may not be thought to have no reason for my calling the impleaded experiment into question, I have these things further to allege against it.

1. It has been rejected long agone by Christian nations as a thing superstitious and diabolical. In Italy and Spain it is wholly disused; and in the Low-Countries, and in France, where the judges are men of learning. In some parts of Germany old paganism customs are observed more than in other countries, nevertheless all the academies throughout Germany have disapproved of this way of purgation.

2. The devil is in it, all superstition is from him; and when secret things or latent crimes are discovered by superstitious practices, some compact and communion with the devil is the cause of it, as Austin has truly intimated; and so it is here; for if a witch cannot be drowned, this must proceed either from some natural cause, which it doth not, for it is against nature for human bodies, when hands and feet are tied, not to sink under the water. Besides, they that plead for this superstition say that if witches happen to be condemned for some other crime and not for witchcraft, they will not swim like a cork above water, which cause sheweth that the cause of this natation is not physical. And if not, then either it must proceed from a divine miracle to save a witch from drowning; or lastly, it must be a diabolical wonder. This superstitious experiment is commonly known by the name of "The Vulgar Probation," because it was never appointed by any lawful authority, but from the

suggestion of the devil taken up by the rude rabble. And some learned men are of opinion, that the first explorator (being a white witch) did explicitly covenant with the devil, that he should discover latent crimes in this way. And that it is by virtue of that first contract that the devil goeth to work to keep his servants from sinking, when this ceremony of his ordaining is used. Moreover, we know that *Diabolus est Dei simia*, the devil seeks to imitate divine miracles. We read in ecclesiastical story that some of the martyrs, when they were by persecutors ordered to be drowned, prov'd to be immersible. This miracle would the devil imitate in causing witches, who are his martyrs, not to sink when they are cast into the waters.

3. This way of purgation is of the same nature with the old ordeals of the Pagans. If men were accused with any crime, to clear their innocency, they were to take an hot iron into their hands, or to suffer scalding water to be poured down their throats, and if they received no hurt thereby they were acquitted. This was the devil's invention, and many times (as the devil would have it) they that submitted to these tryals suffered no inconvenience. Nevertheless, it is astonishing to think what innocent blood has been shed in the world by means of this satanical device. Witches have often (as Sprenger observes) desired that they might stand or fall by this tryal by hot iron, and sometimes come off well. Indeed, this ordeal was used in other cases, and not in cases of witchcraft only. And so was "The Vulgar Probation" by casting into the water practiced upon persons accused with other crimes as well as that of witchcraft. How it came to be restrained to that of witchcraft I cannot tell; it is as supernatural for a body whose hands and feet are tied to swim above the water, as it is for their hands not to feel a red hot iron. If the one of these ordeals is lawful to be used, then so is the other too. But as for the fiery ordeal it is rejected and exploded out of the world; for the same reason then the tryal by water should be so.

4. It is a tempting of God when men put the innocency of their fellow-creatures upon such tryals; to desire the Almighty to shew a miracle to clear the innocent or to convict the guilty, is a most presumptuous tempting of him. Was it not a miracle when Peter was kept from sinking under the water by the omnipotency of Christ? As for Satan, we know that his ambition is to make his servants believe that his power is equal to God's, and that therefore he can preserve whom he pleaseth. I have read of certain magicians, who were seen walking on the water. If then guilty persons shall float on the waters, either it is the devil that causes them to do so (as no doubt it is), and what have men to do to set the devil on work; or else it is a divine miracle, like that of Peter's not sinking, or that of the iron that swam at the word of Elisha. And shall men try whether God will work a miracle to make a discovery? If a crime

cannot be found out but by miracle, it is not for any judge on earth to usurp that judgment which is reserved for the divine throne.

5. This pretended gift of immersibility attending witches is a most fallible deceitful thing; for many a witch has sunk under the water. Godelmannus giveth an account of six notorious and clearly convicted witches, that when they were brought to their vulgar probation, sunk down under the water like other persons; Althusius affirms the like concerning others; in the Bohemian history it is related that Uratslaus, the King of Bohemia, extirpated witches out of his kingdom, some of which he delivered to the ax, others of them to the fire, and others of them he caused to be drowned. If witches are immersible, how came they to die by drowning in Bohemia? Besides, it has sometimes been known that persons who have floated on the water when the hangman has made the experiment on them, have sunk down like a stone, when others have made the tryal.

6. The reasons commonly alleged for this superstition are of no moment. It is said they hate the water; whereas they have many times desired that they might be cast on the water in order to their purgation. It is alleged, that water is used in baptism, therefore witches swim. A weak phansie; all the water in the world is not consecrated water. Cannot witches eat bread or drink wine, notwithstanding those elements are made use of in the Blessed Sacrament? But (say some) the devils by sucking of them make them so light that the water bears them; whereas some witches are twice as heavy as many an innocent person. Well, but then they are possessed with the devil. Suppose so; is the devil afraid if they should sink, that he should be drowned with them? But why then were the Gadaren's hogs drowned when the devil was in them?

These things being premised, I answer the question affirmatively: There are proofs for the conviction of witches which jurors may with a safe conscience proceed upon, so as to bring them in guilty. The Scripture which saith, "Thou shalt not suffer a witch to live," clearly implies, that some in the world may be known and proved to be witches. For until they be so, they may and must be suffered to live. Moreover we find in Scripture, that some have been convicted and executed for witches. "For Saul cut off those that had familiar spirits, and the wizards out of the land," I. Sam. xxviii. 9. . . . .

But then the enquiry is, What is sufficient proof?

This case has been with great judgment answered by several divines of our own, particularly by Mr. Perkins and Mr. Bernard; also Mr. John Gaul, a worthy minister at Staughton, in the county of Huntington, has published a very judicious discourse, called, "Select Cases of Conscience touching Witches and Witchcrafts," Printed at London A.D. 1646, wherein he does with great prudence and evidence of Scripture light handle this and other cases.   Such jurors as can obtain those books, I would advise them to read, and seriously as in the fear of God to consider them, and so far as they keep to the law and to the testimony, and speak according to that word, receive the light which is in them.   But the books being now rare to be had, let me express my concurrence with them in these two particulars.

1. That a free and voluntary confession of the crime made by the person suspected and accused after examination, is a sufficient ground of conviction.

Indeed, if persons are distracted, or under the power of phrenetick melancholy, that alters the case; but the jurors that examine them, and their neighbours that know them, may easily determine that case; or if confession be extorted, the evidence is not so clear and convictive; but if any persons out of remorse of conscience, or from a touch of God in their spirits, confess and shew their deeds, as the converted magicians in Ephesus did, nothing can be more clear. Suppose a man to be suspected for murder, or for committing a rape, or the like nefandous wickedness, if he does freely confess the accusation, that's ground enough to condemn him.   The Scripture approveth of judging the wicked servant out of his own mouth.   It is by some objected, that persons in discontent may falsely accuse themselves.   I say, if they do so, and it cannot be proved that they are false accusers of themselves, they ought to die for their wickedness, and their blood will be upon their own heads; the jury, the judges, and the land is clear.   I have read a very sad and amazing, and yet a true story to this purpose.

There was in the year 1649, in a town called Lauder in Scotland, a certain woman accused and imprisoned on suspicion of witchcraft, when others in the same prison with her were convicted, and their execution ordered to be on the Monday following, she desired to speak with a minister, to whom she declared freely that she was guilty of witchcraft, acknowledging also many other crimes committed by her, desiring that she might die with the rest.   She said particularly that she had covenanted with the devil, and was become his servant about twenty years before, and that he kissed her and gave her a name, but that since he had never owned her.   Several ministers who were jealous that she accused herself untruly, charged it on her conscience, telling her that they doubted she was under a temptation of the devil to destroy her own body and soul, and adjuring her in the name of God to declare the truth. Notwithstanding all this, she stifly adhered to what she had said, and was on Monday morning condemned, and ordered to be executed that day. When she came to the place of execution, she was silent until the prayers were ended, then going to the stake where she was to be burnt, she thus expressed herself: "All you that see me this day ! Know ye that

I am to die as a witch, by my own confession! and I free all men, especially the ministers and magistrates, from the guilt of my blood, I take it wholly on myself, and as I must make answer to the God of heaven, I declare I am as free from witchcraft as any child, but being accused by a malicious woman, and imprisoned under the name of a witch, my husband and friends disowned me, and seeing no hope of ever being in credit again, through the temptation of the devil, I made that confession to destroy my own life, being weary of it, and choosing rather to die than to live." This her lamentable speech did astonish all the spectators, few of whom could restrain from tears. The truth of this relation (saith my author) is certainly attested by a worthy divine now living, who was an eye and an ear-witness of the whole matter; but thus did that miserable creature suffer death, and this was a just execution. When the Amalekite confessed that he killed Saul, whom he had no legal authority to meddle with, although 'tis probable that he belyed himself, David gave order for his execution, and said to him, "Thy blood be upon thy head, for thy mouth hath testified against thee." But as for the testimony of confessing witches against others, the case is not so clear as against themselves, they are not such credible witnesses, as in a case of life and death is to be desired. It is beyond dispute, that the devil makes his witches to dream strange things of themselves and others which are not so. There was (as authors beyond exception relate) in appearance a sumptuous feast prepared, the wine and meat set forth in vessels of gold; a certain person whom an amorous young man had fallen in love with, was represented and supposed to be really there; but Apollonius Tyanæus discovered the witchery of the business, and in an instant all vanished, and nothing but dirty coals were to be seen.　　.　　.　　.　　.

What credit can be given to those that say they can turn men into horses? If so, they can as well turn horses into men; but all the witches on earth in conjunction with all the devils in hell, can never make or unmake a rational soul, and then they cannot transform a brute into a man, nor a man into a brute; so that this transmutation is fantastical. The devil may and often does impose on the imagination of his witches and vassals, that they believe themselves to be converted into beasts, and reverted into men again; as Nebuchadnezzar whilst under the power of a dæmon really imagined himself to be an ox, and would lye out of doors and eat grass. The devil has inflicted on many a man the disease called lycanthropia, from whence they have made lamentable complaints of their being wolves. In a word, there is no more reality in what many witches confess of strange things seen or done by them, whilst Satan had them in his full power, than there is in Lucian's ridiculous fable of his being bewitched into an asse, and what strange feats he then played; so that what such persons relate concerning persons and things at witch-meetings, ought not to be received with too much credulity.

I could mention dismal instances of innocent blood which has been shed by means of the lies of some confessing witches; there is a very sad story mentioned in the preface to the relation of the witchcrafts in Sweedland, how that in the year 1676, at Stockholm, a young woman accused her own mother (who had indeed been a very bad woman, but not guilty of witchcraft), and swore that she had carried her to the nocturnal meetings of witches, upon which the mother was burnt to death. Soon after the daughter came crying and howling before the judges in open court, declaring, that to be revenged on her mother for an offence received, she had falsely accused her with a crime which she was not guilty of; for which she also was justly executed. A most wicked man in France freely confessed himself to be a magician, and accused many others, whose lives were thereupon taken from them; and a whole province had like to have been ruined thereby, but the impostor was discovered. The confessing pretended wizard was burnt at Paris in the year 1668. I shall only take notice further of an awful example mentioned by A. B. Spotswood in his History of Scotland, p. 449. His words are these: "This summer (viz. Anno 1597), there was a great business for the tryal of witches, amongst others, one Margaret Atkin being apprehended on suspicion, and threatened with torture, did confess herself guilty; being examined touching her associates in that trade, she named a few, and perceiving her delations find credit, made offer to detect all of that sort, and to purge the country of them; so she might have her life granted. For the reason of her knowledge, she said, ·That they had a secret mark all of that sort in their eyes, whereby she could surely tell, how soon she looked upon any, whether they were witches or not'; and in this she was so readily believed, that for the space of 3 or 4 months she was carried from town to town to make discoveries in that kind; many were brought in question by her delations, especially at Glasgow, where divers innocent women, through the credulity of the minister Mr. John Cowper, were condemned and put to death; in the end she was found to be a mere deceiver, and sent back to Fife, where she was first apprehended. At her tryal she affirmed all to be false that she had confessed of herself or others, and persisted in this to her death, which made many fore-think their too great forwardness that way, and moved the king to recall his commission given out against such persons, discharging all proceedings against them, except in case of a voluntary confession, till a solid order should be taken by the estates touching the form that should be kept in their tryal." Thus that famous historian.

2. If two credible persons shall affirm upon oath that they have seen

the party accused speaking such words, or doing things which none but such as have familiarity with the devil ever did or can do, that's a sufficient ground for conviction.

Some are ready to say, that wizards are not so unwise as to do such things in the sight or hearing of others, but it is certain that they have very often been known to do so. How often have they been seen by others using inchantments? Conjuring to raise storms? And have been heard calling upon their familiar spirits? And have been known to use spells and charms? And to shew in a glass or in a shew-stone persons absent? And to reveal secrets which could not be discovered but by the devil? And have not men been seen to do things which are above human strength, that no man living could do without diabolical assistances? Claudia was seen by witnesses enough to draw a ship which no human strength could move. Tuccia a vestal virgin was seen to carry water in a sieve. The devil never assists men to do supernatural things undesired. When therefore such like things shall be testified against the accused party, not by spectres which are devils in the shape of persons either living or dead, but by real men or women who may be credited, it is proof enough that such an one has that conversation and correspondence with the devil, as that he or she, whoever they be, ought to be exterminated from amongst men. This notwithstanding I will add: It were better that ten suspected witches should escape, than that one innocent person should be condemned.

Deodat Lawson.

Minister at Salem Village (now Danvers), Mass., 1683, and at Scituate, Mass., 1686-98.

WITCHCRAFT IN SALEM.

[Appendix to " Christ's Fidelity the only Shield against Satan's Malignity." 1704.]

IT pleased God in the year of our Lord 1692 to visit the people at a place called Salem Village in New-England with a very sore and grievous affliction, in which they had reason to believe that the sovereign and holy God was pleased to permit Satan and his instruments to affright and afflict those poor mortals in such an astonishing and unusual manner.

Now, I having for some time before attended the work of the ministry in that village, the report of those great afflictions came quickly to my notice; and the more readily because the first person afflicted was in the minister's family, who succeeded me after I was removed from them.   In pity, therefore, to my Christian friends and former acquaintance there, I was much concerned about them, frequently consulted with them, and fervently (by Divine assistance) prayed for them; but especially my concern was augmented when it was reported at an examination of a person suspected for witchcraft that my wife and daughter, who died three years before, were sent out of the world under the malicious operations of the infernal powers, as is more fully represented in the following remarks.   I did then desire and was also desired by some concerned in the court, to be there present that I might hear what was alleged in that respect; observing, therefore, when I was amongst them that the case of the afflicted was very amazing and deplorable, and the charges brought against the accused such as were ground of suspicions yet very intricate and difficult to draw up right conclusions about them.   .   .   .   .

One or two of the first that were afflicted complaining of unusual illness, their relations used physic for their cure, but it was altogether in vain.

They were oftentimes very stupid in their fits and could neither hear nor understand in the apprehension of the standers by, so that when prayer hath been made with some of them in such a manner as might be audible in a great congregation, yet when their fit was off they declared they did not hear so much as one word thereof.

It was several times observed that when they were discoursed with about God or Christ or the things of Salvation they were presently afflicted at a dreadful rate, and hence were oftentimes outrageous if they were permitted to be in the congregation in the time of the public worship.   .   .   .   .

They affirmed that they saw the ghosts of several departed persons, who, at their appearing, did instigate them to discover such as (they said) were instruments to hasten their deaths; threatening sorely to afflict them if they did not make it known to the magistrates.   They did affirm at the examination and again at the trial of an accused person that they saw the ghosts of his two wives (to whom he had carried very ill in their lives as was proved by several testimonies) and also that they saw the ghosts of my wife and daughter (who died above three years before) and they did affirm that when the very ghosts looked on the prisoner at the bar they looked red, as if the blood would fly out of their faces with indignation at him.   The manner of it was thus : Several afflicted being before the prisoner at the bar, on a sudden they fixed all their eyes together on a certain place of the floor before the prisoner, neither moving their eyes nor bodies for some few minutes nor answering to any question which was asked them.   So soon as that trance was over, some being removed out of sight and hearing, they were all one after another asked what they saw and they did all agree that they saw those ghosts above mentioned. I was present and heard and saw the whole of what passed upon that account during the trial of that person who was accused to be the instrument of Satan's malice therein.

In this (worse than Gallick) persecution by the Dragoons of Hell, the persons afflicted were harassed at such a dreadful rate to write their names in a devil-book presented by a spectre unto them; and one in my hearing said: "I will not, I will not write; it is none of God's Book, it is none of God's Book; it is the devil's book for aught I know." And when they steadfastly refused to sign they were told if they would but touch or take hold of the book it should do. And lastly, the diabolical propositions were so low and easy that if they would but let their clothes or any thing about them touch the book, they should be at ease from their torments, it being their consent that is aimed at by the devil in those representations and operations.

One who had been long afflicted at a stupendious rate by two or three spectres, when they were (to speak after the manner of men) "tired out" with tormenting of her, to force or fright her to sign a covenant with the prince of darkness, they said to her as in a diabolical and accursed passion: "Go your ways and the devil go with you, for we will be no more pestered and plagued about you." And ever after that she was well and no more afflicted that ever I heard of.

Sundry pins have been taken out of the wrists and arms of the afflicted and one in time of examination of a suspected person had a pin run through both her upper and her lower lip when she was called to speak; yet no apparent festering followed thereupon after it was taken out.

Some of the afflicted, as they were striving in their fits in open court, have (by invisible means) had their wrists bound fast together with a real cord, so as it could hardly be taken off without cutting. Some afflicted have been found with their arms tied and hanged upon an hook, from whence others have been forced to take them down that they might not expire in that posture.

Some afflicted have been drawn under tables and beds by undiscerned force, so as they could hardly be pulled out. And one was drawn half way over the side of a well and was with much difficulty recovered back again.

When they were most grievously afflicted, if they were brought to the accused and the suspected person's hand but laid upon them they were immediately relieved out of their tortures; but if the accused did but look on them they were instantly struck down again. Wherefore they use to cover the face of the accused while they laid their hands on the afflicted and then it obtained the desired issue. For it hath been experienced (both in examinations and trials) that so soon as the afflicted came in sight of the accused they were immediately cast into their fits. Yea, though the accused were among the crowd of people, unknown to the sufferers, yet on the first view were they struck down; which was observed in a child of four or five years of age, when it was apprehended that so many as she would look upon, either directly or by turning her head, were immediately struck into their fits.

An iron spindle of a woolen wheel, being taken very strangely out of an house at Salem Village, was used by a spectre as an instrument of torture to a sufferer, not being discernable to the standers by until it was by the said sufferer snatched out of the spectre's hand and then it did immediately appear to the persons present to be really the same iron spindle.

Sometimes in their fits they have had their tongues drawn out of their mouths to a fearful length, their heads turned very much over their shoulders, and while they have been so strained in their fits, and had their arms and legs, etc., wrested as if they were quite dislocated, the blood hath gushed plentifully out of their mouths for a considerable time together; which some, that they might be satisfied that it was real blood, took upon their finger and rubbed on their other hand. I saw several together thus violently strained and bleeding in their fits, to my very great astonishment that my fellow mortals should be so grievously distressed by the invisible powers of darkness. For certainly all considerate persons who beheld these things must needs be convinced that their motions in their fits were preternatural and involuntary, both as to the manner which was so strange, as a well person could not (at least without great pain) screw their bodies into; and as to the violence also they were preternatural motions, being much beyond the ordinary force of the same persons when they were in their right minds. So that being such grievous sufferers, it would seem very hard and unjust to censure them of consenting to or holding any voluntary converse or familiarity with the devil.

Their eyes were for the most part fast closed in their trance fits, and when they were asked a question they could give no answer. And I do verily believe they did not hear at that time, yet did they discourse with the spectres as with real persons; asserting things and receiving answers affirmative or negative, as the matter was. For instance, one in my hearing thus argued with and railed at a spectre: " Goodn—— be gone! Be gone! Be gone! Are you not ashamed, a woman of your profession, to afflict a poor creature so? What hurt did I ever do you in my life? You have but two years to live and then the devil will torment your soul for this. Your name is blotted out of God's Book and it shall never be put into God's Book again. Be gone! For shame! Are you not afraid of what is coming upon you? I know, I know what will make you afraid—the wrath of an angry God! I am sure that will make you afraid. Be gone! Do not torment me; I know what you would have," (we judged she meant her soul), "but it is out of your reach, it is clothed with the white robes of Christ's righteousness." This sufferer I was well acquainted with and knew her to be a very sober and pious woman, so far as I could judge; and it appears that she had not in that fit voluntary converse with the devil. For then she might have been helped to a better guess about that woman above said, as to her living but two years, for she lived not many months after that time.   .   .   .   .

Some of them were asked how it came to pass that they were not affrighted when they saw the Black-man. They said they were at first but not so much afterwards.

Some of them affirmed they saw the Black-man sit on the gallows and that he whispered in the ears of some of the condemned persons when they were just ready to be turned off—even while they were making their last speech.   .   .   .   .

Some of them have sundry times seen a White-man appearing amongst the spectres, and as soon as he appeared, the Black-Witches vanished; they said this White-man had often foretold them what respite they should have from their fits; as sometimes a day or two or more, which fell out accordingly. One of the afflicted said she saw him in her fit and was with him in a glorious place which had no candle or sun, yet was full of light and brightness, where there was a multitude in "white glittering robes," and they sang the song in Rev. v. 9, Psal. cx. Psal. cxlix. She was loth to leave that place and said: "How long shall I stay here, let me be along with you?" She was grieved she could stay no longer in that place and company.

A young woman that was afflicted at a fearful rate had a spectre appear to her with a white sheet wrapped about it, not visible to the standers by, until this sufferer (violently striving in her fit) snatched at, took hold, and tore off a corner of that sheet. Her father being by her endeavored to lay hold upon it with her that she might retain what she had gotten; but at the passing away of the spectre he had such a violent twitch of his hand as if it would have been torn off. Immediately thereupon appeared in the sufferer's hand the corner of a sheet, a real cloth, visible to the spectators, which (as it is said) remains still to be seen.   .   .   .   .

A woman being brought upon public examination desired to go to prayer. The magistrates told her they came not there to hear her pray but to examine her in what was alleged against her, relating to suspicions of witchcraft.

It was observed both in times of examination and trial that the accused seemed little affected with what the sufferers underwent or what was charged against them, as being the instruments of Satan therein. So that the spectators were grieved at their unconcernedness. . . . .

They were accused by the sufferers to keep days of hellish fasts and thanksgivings and upon one of their fast-days they told a sufferer she must not eat, it was fast-day. She said she would; they told her they would choke her then; which when she did eat was endeavored.

They were also accused to hold and administer diabolical sacraments, viz., a mock-baptism and a devil-supper at which cursed imitations of the sacred institutions of our blessed Lord they used forms of words to be trembled at, in the very rehearsing. . . . At their cursed supper they were said to have red bread and red drink, and when they pressed an afflicted person to eat and drink thereof, she turned away her head and spit at it, and said : "I will not eat, I will not drink. It is blood. That is not the Bread of Life, that is not the Water of Life, and I will have none of yours." Thus horribly doth Satan endeavor to have his kingdom and administrations to resemble those of our Lord Jesus Christ. . . . .

Several of the accused would neither in time of examination nor trial confess any thing of what was laid to their charge. Some would not admit of any minister to pray with them, others refused to pray for themselves. It was said by some of the confessing-witches that such as have received the Devil-Sacrament can never confess. Only one woman condemned, after the death warrant was signed, freely confessed, which occasioned her reprieval for some time; and it was observable this woman had one lock of hair of a very great length, viz., four foot and seven inches long, by measure. This lock was of a different color from all the rest (which was short and gray). It grew on the hinder part of her head and was matted together like an elf-lock. The court ordered it to be cut off, to which she was very unwilling and said she was told if it were cut off she should die or be sick ; yet the court ordered it so to be.

A person who had been frequently transported to and fro by the devils for the space of near two years was struck dumb for about nine months of that time; yet he after that had his speech restored to him and did depose upon oath that in the time while he was dumb he was many times bodily transported to places where the witches were gathered together, and that he there saw feasting and dancing and, being struck on the back or shoulder, was thereby made fast to the place and could only see and hear at a distance. He did take his oath that he did with his bodily eyes see some of the accused at those witch-meetings several times. I was present in court when he gave his testimony. He also proved by sundry persons that at those times of transport he was bodily absent from his abode and could nowhere be found, but being met with by some on the road at a distance from his home, was suddenly conveyed away from them.　　.　　　.　　　.　　　.

Whilst a godly man was at prayer with a woman afflicted, the daughter of that woman (being a sufferer in the like kind) affirmed that she saw two of the persons accused at prayer to the devil.

It was proved by substantial evidences against one person accused that he had such an unusual strength (though a very little man) that he could hold out a gun with one hand behind the lock, which was near seven foot in the barrel, being as much as a lusty man could command with both hands after the usual manner of shooting. It was also proved that he lifted barrels of meat and barrels of molasses out of a canoe alone; and that putting his fingers into a barrel of molasses, full within a finger's length according to custom, he carried it several paces. And that he put his finger into the muzzle of a gun which was more than five foot in the barrel and lifted up the butt end thereof, lock, stock and all, without any visible help to raise it. It was also testified that being abroad with his wife and his wife's brother, he occasionally stayed behind letting his wife and her brother walk forward; but suddenly coming up with them, he was angry with his wife for what discourse had passed betwixt her and her brother. They wondering how he should know it, he said: "I know your thoughts," at which expression they, being amazed, asked him how he could do that he said: "My God whom I serve makes known your thoughts to me."

I was present when these things were testified against him and observed that he could not make any plea for himself in these things, that had any weight. He had the liberty of challenging his jurors before empanelling according to the statute in that case, and used his liberty in challenging many; yet the jury that were sworn brought him in guilty.　　.　　　.　　　.　　　.

It pleased God for the clearer discovery of those mysteries of the kingdom of darkness so to dispose that several persons, men, women and children, did confess their hellish deeds as followeth.

They confessed against themselves that they were witches; told how long they had been so, and how it came about that the devil appeared to them, viz., sometimes upon discontent at their mean condition in the world; sometimes about fine clothes; sometimes for the gratifying other carnal and sensual lusts. Satan then, upon his appearing to them, made them fair though false promises that if they would yield to him and sign his book, their desires should be answered to the uttermost, whereupon they signed it; and thus the accursed confederacy was confirmed betwixt them and the prince of darkness.

Some did affirm that there were some hundreds of the society of witches, considerable companies of whom were affirmed to muster in arms by beat of drum. In time of examinations and trials they declared that such a man was wont to call them together from all quarters to witch-meetings with the sound of a diabolical trumpet.

Being brought to see the prisoners at the bar, upon their trials they did affirm in open court (I was then present) that they had oftentimes seen them at witch-meetings, where was feasting, dancing and jollity, as also at devil sacraments ; and particularly that they saw such a man —— amongst the rest of the cursed crew, and affirmed that he did administer the sacrament of Satan to them, encouraging them to go on in their way and they should certainly prevail. They said also that such a woman —— was a deacon and served in distributing the diabolical element. They affirmed that there were great numbers of the witches.

They affirmed that many of those wretched souls had been baptized at Newbury Falls and at several other rivers and ponds ; and as to the manner of administration, the great officer of hell took them up by the body and, putting their heads into the water, said over them : " Thou art mine and I have full power over thee ; " and thereupon they engaged and covenanted to renounce God, Christ, their sacred baptism and the whole way of Gospel Salvation, and to use their utmost endeavors to oppose the kingdom of Christ, and to set up and advance the kingdom of Satan.

Some after they confessed were very penitent, and did wring their hands and manifest a distressing sense of what they had done, and were by the mercies of God recovered out of those snares of the kingdom of darkness.

Several have confessed against their own mothers, that they were instruments to bring them into the devil's covenant to the undoing of them body and soul. And some girls of eight or nine years of age did declare that after they were so betrayed by their mothers to the power of Satan they saw the devil go in their own shapes to afflict others. . . . .

Some of them confessed that they did afflict the sufferers according to the time and manner they were accused thereof, and being asked what they did to afflict them some said that they pricked pins into puppets made with rags, wax and other materials. One that confessed after the signing the death warrant, said she used to afflict them by clutching and pinching her hands together, and wishing in what part and after what manner she would have them afflicted, and it was done.

They confessed the design was laid by this witchcraft to root out the interest of Christ in New England and that they began at the village, in order to settling the kingdom of darkness and the powers thereof, de-

claring that such a man —— was to be head conjurer, and for his activity
in that affair was to be crowned King of Hell, and that such a woman
—— was to be Queen of Hell.

Thus I have given my reader a brief and true account of those fearful and amazing operations and intrigues of the Prince of Darkness; and
I must call them so, for let some persons be as incredulous as they please
about the powerful and malicious influence of evil angels upon the minds
and bodies of mankind, sure I am, none that observed those things above
mentioned could refer them to any other head than the sovereign permission of the Holy God and the malicious operations of His and our
implacable Enemy.

Cotton Mather.

BORN in Boston, Mass., 1663.   DIED there, 1728.

OF BEELZEBUB AND HIS PLOT.

[*The Wonders of the Invisible World.* 1693.]

THE New-Englanders are a people of God settled in those, which were
once the devil's territories; and it may easily be supposed that the
devil was exceedingly disturbed when he perceived such a people here
accomplishing the promise of old made unto our blessed Jesus, that he
should have the utmost parts of the earth for his possession.   There was
not a greater uproar among the Ephesians, when the gospel was first
brought among them, than there was among the powers of the air (after
whom those Ephesians walked) when first the silver trumpets of the
gospel here made the joyful sound.   The devil thus irritated, immediately try'd all sorts of methods to overturn this poor plantation; and
so much of the church, as was fled into this wilderness, immediately
found the serpent cast out of his mouth a flood for the carrying of it
away.   I believe, that never were more satanical devices used for the
unsetling of any people under the sun, than what have been employ'd
for the extirpation of the vine which God has here planted, casting out
the heathen, and preparing a room for it, and causing it to take deep
root and fill the land, so that it sent its boughs unto the Atlantic sea
eastward, and its branches unto the Connecticut river westward, and the
hills were covered with the shadow thereof.   But all those attempts of
hell have hitherto been abortive, many an Ebenezer has been erected
unto the praise of God, by his poor people here; and, having obtained

help from God, we continue to this day. Wherefore the devil is now
making one attempt more upon us; an attempt more difficult, more surprizing, more snarl'd with unintelligible circumstances than any that we
have hitherto encountered; an attempt so critical, that if we get well
through, we shall soon enjoy halcyon days with all the vultures of hell
trodden under our feet. He has wanted his incarnate legions to perse-
cute us as the people of God have in the other hemisphere been persecuted. He has therefore drawn forth his more spiritual ones to make an
attacque upon us.

We have been advised by some credible Christians yet alive, that a
malefactor, accused of witchcraft as well as murder, and executed in this
place more than forty years ago, did then give notice of an horrible plot
against the country by witchcraft, and a foundation of witchcraft then
laid, which if it were not seasonably discovered would probably blow
up and pull down all the churches in the country. And we have now
with horror seen the discovery of such a witchcraft! An army of devils
is horribly broke in upon the place which is the centre, and, after a sort,
the first-born of our English settlements; and the houses of the good
people there are fill'd with the doleful shrieks of their children and servants, tormented by invisible hands, with tortures altogether preternatural. After the mischiefs there endeavoured, and since in part conquered,
the terrible plague, of evil angels, hath made its progress into some other
places, where other persons have been in like manner diabolically handled.
These our poor afflicted neighbours, quickly after they become infected
and infested with these dæmons, arrive to a capacity of discerning those
which they conceive the shapes of their troublers; and notwithstanding
the great and just suspicion, that the dæmons might impose the shapes
of innocent persons in their spectral exhibitions upon the sufferers (which
may perhaps prove no small part of the witch-plot in the issue), yet many
of the persons thus represented being examined, several of them have
been convicted of a very damnable witchcraft. Yea, more than one
twenty have confessed that they have signed unto a book which the
devil show'd them, and engaged in his hellish design of bewitching and
ruining our land. We know not, at least I know not, how far the delusions of Satan may be interwoven into some circumstances of the confessions; but one would think all the rules of understanding human affairs
are at an end, if after so many most voluntary harmonious confessions,
made by intelligent persons of all ages, in sundry towns, at several times,
we must not believe the main strokes wherein those confessions all agree;
especially when we have a thousand preternatural things every day
before our eyes, wherein the confessors do acknowledge their concernment, and give demonstration of their being so concerned. If the devils
now can strike the minds of men with any poisons of so fine a composi-

tion and operation, that scores of innocent people shall unite in confessions of a crime which we see actually committed, it is a thing prodigious, beyond the wonders of the former ages, and it threatens no less than a sort of dissolution upon the world. Now, by these confessions 'tis agreed that the devil has made a dreadful knot of witches in the country, and by the help of witches has dreadfully increased that knot; that these witches have driven a trade of commissioning their confederate spirits, to do all sorts of mischiefs to the neighbours, whereupon there have ensued such mischievous consequences upon the bodies and estates of the neighbourhood, as could not otherwise be accounted for. Yea, that at prodigious witch-meetings, the wretches have proceeded so far as to concert and consult the methods of rooting out the Christian religion from this country, and setting up instead of it, perhaps a more gross diabolesm than ever the world saw before. And yet it will be a thing little short of miracle, if in so spread a business as this, the devil should not get in some of his juggles to confound the discovery of all the rest. .   .   .   .

I have now published a most awful and solemn warning for ourselves at this day; which has four propositions comprehended in it.

Proposition I. That there is a devil, is a thing doubted by none but such as are under the influences of the devil. For any to deny the being of a devil must be from an ignorance or profaneness, worse than diabolical. A devil. What is that? We have a definition of the monster, in Eph. vi. 12. A spiritual wickedness, that is, a wicked spirit. A devil is a fallen angel, an angel fallen from the fear and love of God, and from all celestial glories; but fallen to all manner of wretchedness and cursedness. He was once in that order of heavenly creatures which God in the beginning made ministering spirits, for his own peculiar service and honour, in the management of the universe; but we may now write that epitaph upon him, "How art thou fallen from heaven! thou hast said in thine heart, I will exalt my throne above the stars of God; but thou art brought down to hell!" A devil is a spiritual and rational substance, by his apostacy from God inclined unto all that is vicious, and for that apostacy confined unto the atmosphere of this earth, in chains unto darkness, unto the judgment of the great day. This is a devil; and the experience of mankind, as well as the testimony of Scripture, does abundantly prove the existence of such a devil.

About this devil, there are many things whereof we may reasonably and profitably be inquisitive; such things, I mean, as are in our Bibles reveal'd unto us; according to which if we do not speak, on so dark a subject, but according to our own uncertain and perhaps humoursome conjectures, there is no light in us. I will carry you with me but unto one paragraph of the Bible, to be informed of three things relating to the devil; 'tis the story of the Gadaren Energumen, in the fifth chapter of Mark.

First, then, 'tis to be granted; the devils are so many, that some thousands can sometimes at once apply themselves to vex one child of man. It is said, in Mark v. 15, he that was possessed with the devil had the legion. Dreadful to be spoken! A legion consisted of twelve thousand five hundred people; and we see that in one man or two, so many devils can be spared for a garrison. As the prophet cryed out, "Multitudes, multitudes, in the Valley of Decision!" So I say, there are multitudes, multitudes, in the valley of destruction, where the devils are! When we speak of the devil, 'tis a name of multitude; it means not one individual devil, so potent and scient, as perhaps a Manichee would imagine; but it means a kind which a multitude belongs unto. Alas, the devils they swarm about us, like the frogs of Egypt, in the most retired of our chambers. Are we at our boards? There will be devils to tempt us unto sensuality. Are we in our beds? There will be devils to tempt us unto carnality. Are we in our shops? There will be devils to tempt us unto dishonesty. Yea, though we get into the church of God, there will be devils to haunt us in the very temple itself, and there tempt us to manifold misbehaviours. I am verily perswaded that there are very few human affairs whereinto some devils are not insinuated. There is not so much as a journey intended, but Satan will have an hand in hindering or furthering of it.

Secondly, 'Tis to be supposed, that there is a sort of arbitrary, even military government, among the devils. This is intimated, when in Mar. v. 9, the unclean spirit said, "My name is Legion." They are such a discipline as legions use to be. Hence we read about the prince of the power of the air. Our air has a power? or an army of devils in the high places of it; and these devils have a prince over them, who is king over the children of pride. 'Tis probable that the devil, who was the ringleader of that mutinous and rebellious crew which first shook off the authority of God, is now the general of those hellish armies; our Lord that conquered him has told us the name of him; 'tis Belzebub; 'tis he that is the devil and the rest are his angels, or his souldiers. Think on vast regiments of cruel and bloody French dragoons, with an intendant over them, overrunning a pillaged neighborhood, and you will think a little what the constitution among the devils is.

Thirdly, 'tis to be supposed that some devils are more peculiarly commission'd, and perhaps qualify'd, for some countries, while others are for others. This is intimated when in Mar. v. 10 the devils besought our Lord much, that he would not send them away out of the country. Why was that? But in all probability, because these devils were more able to do the works of the devil, in such a country, than in another.

It is not likely that every devil does know every language; or that every
devil can do every mischief. 'Tis possible that the experience, or, if I
may call it so, the education of all devils is not alike, and that there may
be some difference in their abilities. If one might make an inference
from what the devils do, to what they are, one cannot forbear dreaming
that there are degrees of devils. Who can allow that such trifling
dæmons, as that of Mascon, or those that once infested our Newberry,
are of so much grandeur, as those dæmons, whose games are mighty
kingdoms? Yea, 'tis certain, that all devils do not make a like figure in
the invisible world. Nor does it look agreeably that the dæmons, which
were the familiars of such a man as the old Apollonius, differ not from
those baser goblins that choose to nest in the filthy and loathsome rags of
a beastly sorceress. Accordingly, why may not some devils be more
accomplished for what is to be done in such and such places, when
others must be detach'd for other territories? Each devil, as he sees his
advantage, cries out, "Let me be in this country, rather than another."
But enough, if not too much, of these things.   .   .   .   .

Indeed, as the devil does begrutch us all manner of good, so he does
annoy us with all manner of woe, as often as he finds himself capable of
doing it. But shall we mention some of the special woes with which the
devil does usually infest the world! Briefly then: plagues are some of
those woes with which the devil troubles us. It is said of the Israelites,
in I. Cor. x. 10, "They were destroyed of the destroyer." That is, they
had the plague among them. 'Tis the destroyer, or the devil, that scat-
ters plagues about the world. Pestilential and contagious diseases, 'tis
the devil who does oftentimes invade us with them. 'Tis no uneasy
thing for the devil to impregnate the air about us with such malignant
salts, as meeting with the salt of our microcosm shall immediately cast
us into that fermentation and putrefaction, which will utterly dissolve all
the vital tyes within us; ev'n as an aqua-fortis, made with a conjunction
of nitre and vitriol, corrodes what it seizes upon. And when the devil
has raised those arsenical fumes, which become venomous quivers full of
terrible arrows, how easily can he shoot the deleterious miasms into those
juices or bowels of men's bodies, which will soon enflame them with a
mortal fire! Hence come such plagues as that beesom of destruction,
which within our memory swept away such a throng of people from one
English city in one visitation. And hence those infectious fevers, which
are but so many disguised plagues among us, causing epidemical desolations. Again, wars are also some of those woes, with which the devil
causes our trouble. It is said in Rev. xii. 17, "The dragon was wrath,
and he went to make war"; and there is in truth scarce any war, but
what is of the dragon's kindling. The devil is that Vulcan, out of whose
forge comes the instruments of our wars, and it is he that finds us em-

ployments for those instruments We read concerning dæmoniacks, or people in whom the devil was, that they would cut and wound themselves; and so, when the devil is in men, he puts 'em upon dealing in that barbarous fashion with one another. Wars do often furnish him with some thousands of souls in one morning from one acre of ground; and for the sake of such Thyestæan banquets, he will push us upon as many wars as he can.

Once more, why may not storms be reckoned among those woes, with which the devil does disturb us? It is not improbable that natural storms on the world are often of the devils raising. We are told in Job i. 11, 12, 19, that the devil made a storm, which hurricano'd the house of Job upon the heads of them that were feasting in it. Paracelsus could have have informed the devil, if he had not been informed, as be sure he was before, that if much aluminious matter, with salt petre not throughly prepared, be mixed, they will send up a cloud of smoke, which will come down in rain. But undoubtedly the devil understands as well the way to make a tempest as to turn the winds at the solicitation of a Laplander; whence perhaps it is, that thunders are observed oftner to break upon churches than upon any other buildings; and besides many a man, yea, many a ship, yea, many a town has miscarried, when the devil has been permitted from above to make an horrible tempest. However, that the devil has raised many metaphorical storms upon the church, is a thing than which there is nothing more notorious. It was said unto believers in Rev. ii. 10, " The devil shall cast some of you into prison." The devil was he that at first set Cain upon Abel to butcher him, as the apostle seems to suggest, for his faith in God, as a rewarder. And in how many persecutions, as well as heresies, has the devil been ever since engaging all the children of Cain! That serpent the devil has acted his cursed seed in unwearied endeavours to have them, of whom the world is not worthy, treated as those who are not worthy to live in the world. By the impulse of the devil 'tis that first the old heathens, and then the mad Arians were pricking briars to the true servants of God; and that the Papists that came after them have out done them all for slaughters upon those that have been accounted as the sheep for the slaughterers. The late French persecution is perhaps the horriblest that ever was in the world. And as the devil of Mascon seems before to have meant it in his out-cries upon the miseries preparing for the poor Hugonots! Thus it has been all acted by a singular fury of the old dragon inspiring of his emissaries.

THE TRIAL OF GEORGE BURROUGHS.

[From the Same.]

GLAD should I have been if I had never known the name of this man; or never had this occasion to mention so much as the first letters of his name. But the government requiring some account of his trial to be inserted in this book, it becomes me with all obedience to submit unto the order.

This G. B. was indicted for witch-craft, and in the prosecution of the charge against him he was accused by five or six of the bewitched, as the author of their miseries; he was accused by eight of the confessing witches, as being an head actor at some of their hellish randezvouzes, and one who had the promise of being a king in Satan's kingdom, now going to be erected. He was accused by nine persons for extraordinary lifting, and such feats of strength as could not be done without a diabolical assistance. And for other such things he was accused, until about thirty testimonies were brought in against him; nor were these judg'd the half of what might have been considered for his conviction. However they were enough to fix the character of a witch upon him according to the rules of reasoning, by the judicious Gaule, in that case directed.

The Court being sensible that the testimonies of the parties bewitched use to have a room among the suspicions or presumptions brought in against one indicted for witch-craft, there were now heard the testimonies of several persons, who were most notoriously bewitched, and every day tortured by invisible hands, and these now all charged the spectres of G. B. to have a share in their torments. At the examination of this G. B. the bewitched people were grievously harassed with preternatural mischiefs, which could not possibly be dissembled; and they still ascribed it unto the endeavours of G. B. to kill them. And now upon the tryal one of the bewitched persons testified that in her agonies, a little black hair'd man came to her, saying his name was B. and bidding her set her hand to a book which he shewed unto her; and bragging that he was a conjurer above the ordinary rank of witches; that he often persecuted her with the offer of that book, saying, "She should be well, and need fear nobody, if she would but sign it." But he inflicted cruel pains and hurts upon her because of her denying so to do. The testimonies of the other sufferers concurred with these; and it was remarkable that, whereas biting was one of the ways which the witches used for the vexing of the sufferers, when they cry'd out of G. B. biting them, the print of the teeth would be seen on the flesh of the complainers, and just such a set of teeth as G. B.'s would then appear upon them, which could be distinguished from those of some other men's. Others of them testified that in their torments G. B. tempted them to go unto a sacrament, unto which they perceived him with a sound of trumpet summoning of other witches, who quickly after the sound would come from all quarters unto the rendezvous. One of them falling into a kind of trance affirmed that G. B. had carried her away into a very high mountain, where he shewed her mighty and glorious kingdoms, and said, "He would give them all to her, if she would write in his book"; but she told him, "They were none of his to give"; and refused the motions; enduring of much misery for that refusal.

It cost the Court a wonderful deal of trouble, to hear the testimonies of the sufferers; for when they were going to give in their depositions, they would for a long time be taken with fits that made them uncapable of saying any thing. The chief judge asked the prisoner, who he thought hindered these witnesses from giving their testimonies? And he answered, "He supposed it was the devil." That honourable person replied, "How comes the devil then to be so loath to have any testimony borne against you?" Which cast him into very great confusion.

It has been a frequent thing for the bewitched people to be entertained with apparitions of ghosts of murdered people, at the same time that the spectres of the witches trouble them. These ghosts do always affright the beholders more than all the other spectral representations; and when they exhibit themselves, they cry out of being murthered by the witchcrafts or other violences of the persons who are then in spectre present. It is further considered that once or twice these apparitions have been seen by others, at the very same time they have shewn themselves to be bewitched; and seldom have there been these apparitions, but when something unusual or suspected have attended the death of the party thus appearing. Some that have been accused by these apparitions accosting of the bewitched people, who had never heard a word of any such persons ever being in the world, have upon a fair examination freely and fully confessed the murthers of those very persons, although these also did not know how the apparitions had complained of them. Accordingly several of the bewitched had given in their testimony, that they had been troubled with the apparitions of two women, who said that they were G. B.'s two wives, and that he had been the death of them; and that the magistrates must be told of it, before whom if B. upon his tryal denied it, they did not know but that they should appear again in Court. Now, G. B. had been infamous for the barbarous usage of his two late wives, all the country over. Moreover, it was testified, the spectre of G. B. threatning of the sufferers told them he had killed (besides others) Mrs. Lawson and her daughter Ann. And it was noted, that these were the vertuous wife and daughter of one at whom this G. B. might have a prejudice for his being serviceable at Salem Village, from whence himself had in ill terms removed some years before; and that when they dy'd, which was long since, there were some odd circumstances about them, which made some of the attendents there suspect something of witch-craft, though none imagined from what quarter it should come.

Well, G. B. being now upon his tryal, one of the bewitched persons was cast into horror at the ghost of B.'s two deceased wives then appearing before him, and crying for vengeance against him. Hereupon several of the bewitched persons were succesively called in, who all, not knowing what the former had seen and said, concurred in their horror of the apparition, which they affirmed that he had before him. But he, though much appalled, utterly deny'd that he discern'd any thing of it; nor was it any part of his conviction.

Judicious writers have assigned it a great place in the conviction of witches, when persons are impeached by other notorious witches to be as ill as themselves; especially, if the persons have been much noted for neglecting the worship of God. Now, as there might have been testimonies enough of G. B.'s antipathy to prayer, and the other ordinances of God, though by his profession singularly obliged thereunto; so there now came in against the prisoner the testimonies of several persons, who confessed their own having been horrible witches, and ever since their confessions had been themselves terribly tortured by the devils and other witches, even like the other sufferers; and therein undergone the pains of many deaths for their confessions.

These now testified that G. B. had been at witch-meetings with them, and that he was the person who had seduc'd and compell'd them into the snares of witchcraft; that he promised them fine cloaths for doing it; that he brought poppets to them, and thorns to stick into those poppets, for the afflicting of other people; and that he exhorted them with the rest of the crew to bewitch all Salem Village, but be sure to do it gradually, if they would prevail in what they did.

When the Lancashire witches were condemn'd, I don't remember that there was any considerable further evidence than that of the bewitched, and than that of some that confessed. We see so much already against G. B. But this being indeed not enough, there were other things to render what had been already produced credible.

A famous divine recites this among the convictions of a witch: "The testimony of the party bewitched, whether pining or dying; together with the joint oaths of sufficient persons that have seen certain prodigious pranks or feats wrought by the party accused." Now, God had been pleased so to leave this G. B. that he had ensnared himself by several instances, which he had formerly given of a preternatural strength, and which were now produced against him. He was a very puny man, yet he had often done things beyond the strength of a giant. A gun of about seven foot barrel, and so heavy that strong men could not steadily nold it out with both hands; there were several testimonies, given in by persons of credit and honor, that he made nothing of taking up such a gun behind the lock with but one hand, and holding it out like a pistol at arms-end. G. B. in his vindication was so foolish as to say, "That an Indian was there, and held it out at the same time." Whereas none of the spectators ever saw any such Indian; but they supposed, the "Black Man" (as the witches call the devil; and they generally say he resembles an Indian) might give him that assistance. There was evidence likewise brought in, that he made nothing of taking up whole barrels fill'd with molasses or cider in very disadvantageous postures and carrying of them through the difficultest places out of a canoe to the shore.

Yea, there were two testimonies, that G. B. with only putting the fore-finger of his right hand into the muzzle of an heavy gun, a fowling-piece of about six or seven foot barrel, did lift up the gun, and hold it out at arms-end; a gun which the deponents thought strong men could not with both hands lift up and hold out at the butt-end, as is usual. Indeed, one of these witnesses was over-perswaded by some persons to be out of the way upon G. B.'s tryal; but he came afterwards with sorrow for his withdraw, and gave in his testimony. Nor were either of these witnesses made use of as evidences in the trial.

There came in several testimonies relating to the domestick affairs of G. B. which had a very hard aspect upon him; and not only prov'd him a very ill man; but also confirmed the belief of the character which had been already fastened on him.

'Twas testified that, keeping his two successive wives in a strange kind of slavery, he would when he came home from abroad pretend to tell the talk which any had with them; that he has brought them to the point of death, by his harsh dealings with his wives, and then made the people about him to promise that in case death should happen, they would say nothing of it; that he used all means to make his wives write, sign, seal, and swear a covenant never to reveal any of his secrets; that his wives had privately complained unto the neighbours about frightful appari-tions of evil spirits with which their house was sometimes infested; and that many such things have been whispered among the neighbourhood. There were also some other testimonies relating to the death of people whereby the consciences of an impartial jury were convinced that G. B. had bewitched the persons mentioned in the complaints. But I am forced to omit several passages, in this, as well as in all the succeeding tryals, because the scribes who took notice of them have not supplied me.

One Mr. Ruck, brother-in-law to this G. B., testified that G. B. and himself, and his sister, who was G. B.'s wife, going out for two or three

miles to gather straw-berries, Ruck with his sister, the wife of G. B., rode
home very softly, with G. B. on foot in their company, G. B. stept aside
a little into the bushes; whereupon they halted and halloo'd for him.
He not answering, they went away homewards with a quickened pace,
without expectation of seeing him in a considerable while; and yet when
they were got near home, to their astonishment, they found him on foot
with them, having a basket of straw-berries. G. B. immediately then fell
to chiding his wife, on the account of what she had been speaking to her
brother, of him, on the road. Which when they wondered at, he said,
"He knew their thoughts." Ruck being startled at that, made some
reply, intimating that the devil himself did not know so far; but G. B.
answered, "My God makes known your thoughts unto me." The prisoner now at the bar had nothing to answer, unto what was thus witnessed against him, that was worth considering. Only he said, "Ruck,
and his wife left a man with him, when they left him." Which Ruck
now affirm'd to be false; and when the Court asked G. B. "What the
man's name was?" his countenance was much altered; nor could he say,
who 'twas. But the Court began to think that he then step'd aside only
that, by the assistance of the black man, he might put on his invisibility,
and in that fascinating mist gratifie his own jealous humour to hear
what they said of him. Which trick of rendering themselves invisible,
our witches do in their confessions pretend, that they sometimes are
masters of; and it is the more credible, because there is demonstration
that they often render many other things utterly invisible.

Faltering, faulty, unconstant, and contrary answers upon judicial and
deliberate examination, are counted some unlucky symptoms of guilt, in
all crimes, especially in witchcrafts. Now there never was a prisoner
more eminent for them than G. B. both at his examination and on his
trial. His tergiversations, contradictions, and falsehoods were very sensible. He had little to say, but that he had heard some things that he
could not prove, reflecting upon the reputation of some of the witnesses.

Only he gave in a paper to the jury; wherein, although he had many
times before granted, not only that there are witches, but also that the
present sufferings of the country are the effects of horrible witchcrafts,
yet he now goes to evince it, "That there neither are, nor ever were
witches, that having made a compact with the devil can send a devil to
torment other people at a distance." This paper was transcribed out of
Ady; which the Court presently knew, as soon as they heard it. But
he said, he had taken none of it out of any book; for which his evasion
afterwards was, that a gentleman gave him the discourse in a manuscript,
from whence he transcribed it.

The jury brought him in guilty. But when he came to die, he utterly
deni'd the fact whereof he had been thus convicted.

HOW MARTHA CARRIER WAS TRIED.

[*From the Same.*]

MARTHA CARRIER was indicted for the bewitching certain persons, according to the form usual in such cases pleading not guilty to her indictment; there were first brought in a considerable number of the bewitched persons; who not only made the Court sensible of an horrid witchcraft committed upon them, but also deposed that it was Martha Carrier or her shape that grievously tormented them by biting, pricking, pinching and choaking of them. It was further deposed that while this Carrier was on her examination before the magistrates, the poor people were so tortured that every one expected their death upon the very spot, but that upon the binding of Carrier they were eased. Moreover the look of Carrier then laid the afflicted people for dead; and her touch, if her eye at the same time were off them, raised them again. Which things were also now seen upon her tryal. And it was testified, that upon the mention of some having their necks twisted almost round by the shape of this Carrier, she replyed, "It's no matter though their necks had been twisted quite off."

Before the trial of this prisoner several of her own children had frankly and fully confessed, not only that they were witches themselves, but that this their mother had made them so. This confession they made with great shews of repentance, and with much demonstration of truth. They related place, time, occasion; they gave an account of journeys, meetings and mischiefs by them performed, and were very credible in what they said. Nevertheless, this evidence was not produced against the prisoner at the bar, inasmuch as there was other evidence enough to proceed upon.

Benjamin Abbot gave his testimony that last March was a twelvemonth this Carrier was very angry with him upon laying out some land, near her husband's. Her expressions in this anger were, "That she would stick as close to Abbot as the bark stuck to the tree; and that he should repent of it afore seven years came to an end, so as Doctor Prescot should never cure him." These words were heard by others besides Abbot himself; who also heard her say, "She would hold his nose as close to the grindstone as ever it was held since his name was Abbot." Presently after this he was taken with a swelling in his foot, and then with a pain in his side, and exceedingly tormented. It bred into a sore, which was lanced by Doctor Prescot, and several gallons of corruption ran out of it. For six weeks it continued very bad, and then another sore bred in the groin, which was also lanced by Doctor Prescot. Another sore then bred in his groin, which was likewise cut, and put him to very great misery. He was brought unto death's door, and so remained until Carrier was taken and carried away by the constable, from which very day he began to mend and so grew better every day, and is well ever since.

Sarah Abbot also, his wife, testified that her husband was not only all this while afflicted in his body, but also that strange extraordinary and unaccountable calamities befell his cattle; their death being such as they could guess at no natural reason for.

Allin Toothaker testify'd that Richard, the son of Martha Carrier, having some difference with him, pull'd him down by the hair of the head. When he rose again he was going to strike at Richard Carrier; but fell down flat on his back to the ground and had not power to stir hand or foot, until he told Carrier he yielded; and then he saw the shape of Martha Carrier go off his breast.

This Toothaker had received a wound in the wars; and he now testify'd that Martha Carrier told him he should never be cured. Just afore the apprehending of Carrier, he could thrust a knitting needle into his wound, four inches deep; but presently after her being seized, he was thoroughly healed.

He further testify'd, that when Carrier and he sometimes were at variance, she would clap her hands at him, and say, "He should get nothing by it." Whereupon he several times lost his cattle by strange deaths, whereof no natural causes should be given.

John Rogger also testifyed that upon the threatning words of this malicious Carrier, his cattle would be strangely bewitched; as was more particularly then described.

Samuel Preston testify'd that about two years ago, having some difference with Martha Carrier, he lost a cow in a strange preternatural unusual manner; and about a month after this the said Carrier, having again some difference with him, she told him, "He had lately lost a cow and it should not be long before he lost another"; which accordingly came to pass; for he had a thriving and well-kept cow, which without any known cause quickly fell down and dy'd.

Phebe Chandler testify'd that about a fortnight before the apprehension of Martha Carrier, on a Lord's-day, while the psalm was singing in the church, this Carrier then took her by the shoulder and shaking her asked her where she lived. She made her no answer, although as Carrier, who lived next door to her father's house, could not in reason but know who she was. Quickly after this, as she was at several times crossing the fields, she heard a voice, that she took to be Martha Carrier's, and it seem'd as if it was over her head. The voice told her she should within two or three days be poisoned. Accordingly, within such a little time, one half of her right hand became greatly swollen, and very painful; as also part of her face; whereof she can give no account how it came. It continued very bad for some dayes; and several times since she has had a great pain in her breast; and been so seized on her legs that she has hardly been able to go. She added that lately, going well to the house of God, Richard, the son of Martha Carrier, look't very earnestly upon her, and immediately her hand, which had formerly been poisoned, as is abovesaid, began to pain her greatly, and she had a strange burning at her stomach; but was then struck deaf so that she could not hear any of the prayer, or singing, till the two or three last words of the psalm.

One Foster, who confessed her own share in the witchcraft for which the prisoner stood indicted, affirm'd that she had seen the prisoner at some of their witch-meetings, and that it was this Carrier, who perswaded her to be a witch. She confess'd, that the devil carry'd them on a pole to a witch-meeting; but the pole broke, and she hanging about Carrier's neck, they both fell down, and she then received an hurt by the fall whereof she was not at this very time recovered.

One Lacy, who likewise confessed her share in this witchcraft, now testify'd that she and the prisoner were once bodily present at a witch-meeting in Salem Village; and that she knew the prisoner to be a witch, and to have been at a diabolical sacrament, and that the prisoner was the undoing of her and her children, by enticing them into the snare of the devil.

Another Lacy, who also confessed her share in this witchcraft, now testify'd that the prisoner was at the witch-meeting, in Salem Village, where they had bread and wine administered unto them.

In the time of this prisoner's tryal, one Susanna Sheldon in open Court had her hands unaccountably ty'd together with a wheel-band, so fast that without cutting it could not be loosed. It was done by a spectre; and the sufferer affirm'd it was the prisoner's.

Memorandum. This rampant hag, Martha Carrier, was the person, of whom the confessions of the witches, and of her own children among the rest, agreed, that the devil had promised her she should be Queen of Hell.

THE INVISIBILIZING OF WITCHES.

[From the Same.]

IN all the witchcraft which now grievously vexes us, I know not whether anything be more unaccountable than the trick which the witches have to render themselves, and their tools invisible. Witchcraft seems to be the skill of applying the plastic spirit of the world unto some unlawful purposes by means of a confederacy with evil spirits. Yet one would wonder how the evil spirits themselves can do some things; especially at invisibilizing of the grossest bodies. I can tell the name of an ancient author who pretends to show the way how a man may come to walk about invisible, and I can tell the name of another ancient author who pretends to explode that way. But I will not speak too plainly lest I should unawares poison some of my readers, as the pious Hemingius did one of his pupils, when he only by way of diversion recited a spell which, they had said, would cure agues. This much I will say: The notion of procuring invisibility, by any natural expedient yet known, is, I believe, a mere Plinyism; how far it may be obtained by a magical sacrament is best known to the dangerous knaves that have try'd it. But our witches do seem to have got the knack; and this is one of the things that make me think witchcraft will not be fully understood, until the day when there shall not be one witch in the world.

There are certain people very dogmatical about these matters; but I'll give them only these three bones to pick.

First, one of our bewitched people was cruelly assaulted by a spectre that, she said, ran at her with a spindle; though no body else in the room could see either the spectre or the spindle. At last, in her miseries giving a snatch at the spectre, she pull'd the spindle away, and it was no sooner got into her hand but the other people then present beheld that it was indeed a real, proper, iron spindle, belonging they knew to whom; which when they lock'd up very safe, it was nevertheless by demons unaccountably stole away, to do further mischief.

Secondly, another of our bewitched people was haunted with a most abusive spectre, which came to her, she said, with a sheet about her. After she had undergone a deal of teaze from the annoyance of the spectre, she gave a violent snatch at the sheet that was upon it; wherefrom she tore a corner, which in her hand immediately became visible to a roomful of spectators; a palpable corner of a sheet. Her father, who was now holding her, catch'd that he might keep what his daughter had so strangely seized, but the unseen spectre had like to have pull'd his hand off by endeavouring to wrest it from him; however he still held it, and I suppose has it still to show; it being but a few hours ago, namely about the beginning of this October, that this accident happened in the family of one Pitman, at Manchester.

Thirdly, a young man, delaying to procure testimonials for his parents, who, being under confinement on suspicion of witchcraft, required him to do that service for them, was quickly pursued with odd inconveniences. But once above the rest, an officer going to put his brand on the horns of some cows belonging to these people, which though he had seiz'd for some of their debts, yet he was willing to leave in their possession, for the subsistance of the poor family; this young man help'd in holding the cows to be thus branded. The three first cows he held well enough; but when the hot brand was clap'd upon the fourth he winc'd and shrunk at such a rate as that he could hold the cow no longer. Being afterwards examined about it, he confessed, that at that very instant when the brand entered the cow's horn, exactly the like burning brand was clap'd upon his own thigh; where he has expos'd the lasting marks of it, unto such as asked to see them.

Unriddle these things,—*Et eris mihi magnus Apollo.*

THE STORY OF MARGARET RULE.

[From the Text given in Calef's " More Wonders of the Invisible World." 1700.]

THERE was one in the north part of Boston seized by the evil angels many months after the general storm of the late enchantments was over, and when the country had long lain pretty quiet, both as to molestations and accusations from the invisible world: her name was Margaret Rule, a young woman: she was born of sober and honest parents, yet living; but what her own character was before her visitation I can speak with the less confidence of exactness, because I observe that wherever the devils have been let loose, to worry any poor creature amongst us, a great part of the neighbourhood presently set themselves to inquire, and relate all the little vanities of their childhood, with such unequal exaggerations, as to make them appear greater sinners than any whom the pilot of hell has not yet preyed upon. But it is affirmed, that, for about half a year before her visitation, she was observably improved in the hopeful symptoms of a new creature; she was become furiously concerned for the everlasting salvation of her soul, and careful to avoid the snares of evil company.   .   .   .   .

'Twas upon the Lord's day, the 10th of September, in the year 1693, that Margaret Rule, after some hours of previous disturbance in the public assembly, fell into odd fits, which caused her friends to carry her home, where her fits in a few hours grew into a figure that satisfied the spectators of their being preternatural. Some of the neighbours were forward enough to suspect the rise of this mischief in an house hard by, where lived a miserable woman, who had been formerly imprisoned, on the suspicion of witchcraft, and who had frequently cured very painful hurts, by muttering over them certain charms, which I shall not endanger the poisoning of my reader by repeating. This woman had, the evening before Margaret fell into her calamities, very bitterly treated her, and threatened her; but the hazard of hurting a poor woman, that might be innocent, notwithstanding surmises that might have been more strongly grounded than those, caused the pious people in the vicinity to try, rather, whether incessant supplication to God alone might not procure a quicker and safer ease to the afflicted, than hasty prosecution of any supposed criminal; and accordingly that unexceptionable course was all that was ever followed; yea, which I looked on as a token for good, the afflicted family was as averse, as any of us all, to entertain thoughts of any other course.

The young woman was assaulted by eight cruel spectres, whereof she imagined that she knew three or four; but the rest came still with their faces covered, so that she could never have a distinguishing view of the countenance of those whom she thought she knew; she was very careful of my reiterated charges, to forbear blazing the names, lest any good person should come to suffer any blast of reputation, through the cunning malice of the great accuser; nevertheless, having since privately named them to myself, I will venture to say this of them, that they are a sort of wretches, who for these many years have gone under as violent presumptions of witchcraft, as perhaps any creatures yet living upon earth; although I am far from thinking that the visions of this young woman were evidence enough to prove them so. These cursed spectres now brought unto her a book about a cubit long—a book red and thick, but not very broad; and they demanded of her, that she would set her hand to that book, or touch it at least with her hand, as a sign of her becoming a servant of the devil. Upon her peremptory refusal to do what they asked, they did not after renew the proffers of the book unto her, but instead thereof they fell to tormenting of her in a manner too hellish to be sufficiently described—in those torments confining her to her bed for just six weeks together.

Sometimes, but not always, together with the spectres, there looked in upon the young woman (according to her account) a short and a black man, whom they called their master—a wight, exactly of the same dimensions and complexion and voice, with the devil that has exhibited himself unto other infested people, not only in other parts of this country, but also in other countries, even of the European world, as the relation of the enchantments there informs us. They all professed themselves vassals of this devil, and in obedience unto him they addressed themselves unto various ways of torturing her. Accordingly she was cruelly pinched with invisible hands, very often in a day, and the black and blue marks of the pinches became immediately visible unto the standers-by. Besides this, when her attendants had left her without so much as one pin about her, that so they might prevent some feared inconveniences, yet she would ever now and then be miserably hurt with pins, which were found stuck into her neck, back and arms; however, the wounds made by the pins would in a few minutes ordinarily be cured; she would also be strangely distorted in her joints, and thrown into such exorbitant convulsions as were astonishing unto the spectators in general. They that could behold the doleful condition of the poor family without sensible compassions, might have entrails indeed; but I am sure they could have no true bowels in them.

It were a most unchristian and uncivil, yea, a most unreasonable thing, to imagine, that the fits of the young woman were but mere impostures; and I believe scarce any but people of a particular dirtiness will harbour such an uncharitable censure. However, because I know not how far the devil may drive the imagination of poor creatures, when he has possession of them, that at another time, when they are themselves, would scorn to dissemble any thing, I shall now confine my narrative unto passages wherein there could be no room left for any dissimulation. Of these, the first that I'll mention shall be this: From the time that Margaret Rule first found herself to be formally besieged by the spectres, until the ninth day following, namely, from the 10th of September to the 18th, she kept an entire fast, and yet she was unto all appearance as fresh, as lively, as hearty, at the nine days' end, as before they began; in all this time, though she had a very eager hunger upon her stomach, yet, if any refreshment were brought unto her, her teeth would be set, and she would be thrown into many miseries; indeed once or twice or so in all this time, her tormentors permitted her to swallow a mouthful of somewhat that might increase her miseries, whereof a spoonful of rum was the most considerable; but otherwise, as I said, her fast unto the ninth day was very extreme and rigid: however, afterwards there scarce passed a day wherein she had not liberty to take something or other for her sustentation. And I must add this, further, that this business of her fast was carried so, that it was impossible to be dissembled without a combination of multitudes of people, unacquainted with one another, to support the juggle; but he that can imagine such a thing of a neighbourhood, so filled with virtuous people, is a base man— I cannot call him any other.

But if the sufferings of this young woman were not imposture, yet might they not be pure distemper? I will not here inquire of our Sadducees, what sort of a distemper 'tis shall stick the body full of pins without any hand that could be seen to stick them; or whether all the pin-makers in the world would be willing to be evaporated into certain ill habits of body, producing a distemper; but of the distemper my reader shall be judge, when I have told him something further of those unusual sufferings. I do believe that the evil angels do often

take advantage, from natural distempers in the children of men, to
annoy them with such further mischiefs, as we call preternatural.
The malignant vapours and humours of our diseased bodies may be
used by devils, thereinto insinuating as engines of the execution of
their malice upon those bodies ; and perhaps, for this reason, one sex
may suffer more troubles of some kinds from the invisible world than
the other ; as well as for that reason, for which the old serpent made,
where he did, his first address.   But I pray, what will you say to
this ?   Margaret Rule would sometimes have her jaws forcibly pulled
open, whereupon something invisible would be poured down her
throat ; we all saw her swallow, and yet we saw her try all she could,
by spitting, coughing and shrieking, that she might not swallow ; but
one time the standers-by plainly saw something of that odd liquor
itself on the outside of her neck : she cried out of it, as of scalding
brimstone poured into her, and the whole house would immediately
scent so hot of brimstone that we were scarce able to endure it—
whereof there are scores of witnesses ; but the young woman herself
would be so monstrously inflamed, that it would have broke a heart
of stone to have seen her agonies.   This was a thing that several
times happened ; and several times, when her mouth was thus pulled
open, the standers-by clapping their hands close thereupon, the distresses that otherwise followed would be diverted.   Moreover there
was a whitish powder, to us invisible, sometimes cast upon the eyes
of this young woman, whereby her eyes would be extremely incom-
moded ; but one time some of this powder was fallen actually visible
upon her cheek, from whence the people in the room wiped it with
their handkerchiefs ; and sometimes the young woman would also be
so bitterly scorched with the unseen sulphur thrown upon her, that
very sensible blisters would be raised upon her skin, whereto her
friends found it necessary to apply the oils proper for common burn-
ings ; but the most of these hurts would be cured in two or three
days at farthest.   I think I may without vanity pretend to have read
not a few of the best systems of physick that have been yet seen in
these American regions, but I must confess that I have never yet
learned the name of the natural distemper whereto these odd symptoms do belong : however, I might suggest perhaps many a natural
medicine which would be of singular use against many of them.

But there fell out some other matters far beyond the reach of natural
distemper.   This Margaret Rule once in the middle of the night lamented
sadly that the spectres threatened the drowning of a young man in the
neighbourhood, whom she named unto the company : well, it was afterwards found that at that very time this young man, having been pressed
on board a man of war, then in the harbour, was out of some dissatis-

faction attempting to swim ashore, and he had been drowned in the attempt, if a boat had not seasonably taken him up; it was by computation a minute or two after the young woman's discourse of the drowning, that the young man took the water. At another time she told us, that the spectres bragged and laughed in her hearing about an exploit they had lately done, by stealing from a gentleman his will soon after he had written it; and within a few hours after she had spoken this, there came to me a gentleman with a private complaint, that having written his will, it was unaccountably gone out of the way; how, or where, he could not imagine; and besides all this, there were wonderful noises every now and then made about the room, which our people could ascribe to no other authors but the spectres; yea, the watchers affirm, that they heard those fiends clapping their hands together with an audibleness wherein they could not be imposed upon; and once her tormentors pulled her up to the ceiling of the chamber, and held her there, before a very numerous company of spectators, who found it as much as they could all do to pull her down again. There was also another very surprising circumstance about her, agreeable to what we have not only read in several histories concerning the imps that have been employed in witchcraft, but also known in some of our own afflicted; we once thought we perceived something stir upon her pillow at a little distance from her; whereupon one present laying his hand there, he to his horror apprehended that he felt, though none could see it, a living creature not altogether unlike a rat, which nimbly escaped from him; and there were divers other persons who were thrown into a great consternation by feeling, as they judged, at other times, the same invisible animal.   .   .   .   .

Not only in the Swedish, but also in the Salem witchcraft, the enchanted people have talked much of a white spirit, from whence they received marvellous assistances in their miseries. What lately befell Mercy Short, from the communications of such a spirit, hath been the just wonder of us all; but by such a spirit was Margaret Rule now also visited. She says that she could never see his face; but that she had a frequent view of his bright, shining and glorious garments; he stood by her bedside continually heartening and comforting of her, and counselling her to maintain her faith and hope in God, and never comply with the temptations of her adversaries. She says he told her that God had permitted her afflictions to befall her for the everlasting and unspeakable good of her own soul, and for the good of many others, and for his own immortal glory; and that she should therefore be of good cheer, and be assured of a speedy deliverance; and the wonderful resolution of mind wherewith she encountered her afflictions was but agreeable to such expectations. Moreover, a minister having one day with some importunity prayed for the deliverance of this young woman, and pleaded that as she belonged to his flock and charge, he had so far a right unto her as that he was to do the part of a minister of our Lord for the bringing of her home unto God, only now the devil hindered him in doing that which he had a right thus to do; and whereas he had a better title unto her to bring her home to God, than the devil could have unto her to carry her away from the Lord, he therefore humbly applied himself unto God, who alone could right this matter, with a suit that she might be rescued out of Satan's hands. Immediately upon this, though she heard nothing of this transaction, she began to call that minister her father and that was the name whereby she every day before all sorts of people distinguished him. The occasion of it she says was this: the white spirit presently upon this transaction did after this manner speak to her: "Margaret, you now are to take notice that (such a man) is your father; God has given you to him; do you from this time look upon him as your father, obey him, regard him, as your father; follow his counsels, and you shall do well." And though there was one passage more, which I do as little know what to make of as any of the rest, I am now going to relate it: more than three times have I seen it fulfilled in the deliverance of enchanted and possessed persons, whom the providence of God has cast into my way, that their deliverance could not be obtained before the third fast kept for them, and the third day still obtained the deliverance; although I have thought of beseeching of the Lord thrice, when buffetted by Satan: yet I must earnestly entreat all my readers to beware of any superstitious conceits upon the number *three:* if our God will hear us upon once praying and fasting before him, 'tis well; and if he will not vouchsafe his mercy upon our thrice doing so, yet we must not be so discouraged as to throw by our devotion; but if the sovereign grace of our God will in any particular instances count our patience enough tried when we have solemnly waited upon him for any determinate number of times, who shall say to him, What doest thou? And if there shall be any number of instances wherein this grace of our God has exactly holden the same course, it may have a room in our humble observations, I hope, without any superstition. I say, then, that after Margaret Rule had been more than five weeks in her miseries, this white spirit said unto her, "Well, this day such a man (whom he named) has kept a third day for your deliverance; now be of good cheer, you shall speedily be delivered." I inquired whether what had been said of that man were true, and I gained exact and certain information that it was precisely so; but I doubt lest in relating this passage that I have used more openness than a friend should be treated with, and for that cause I have concealed several of the most memorable things that have occurred, not only in this but in some former histories, although indeed I am not so well satisfied about the true nature of this white spirit, as to count that I can do a friend much honour by reporting what notice this white spirit may have thus taken of him.

On the last day of the week her tormentors (as she thought and said) approaching towards her, would be forced still to recoil and retire as unaccountably unable to meddle with her; and they would retire to the fire side with their poppets; but going to stick pins into those poppets, they could not (according to their visions) make the pins to enter. She insulted over them with a very proper derision, daring them now to do their worst, while she had the satisfaction to see their black master strike them and kick them, like an overseer of so many negroes, to make them do their work, and renew the marks of his vengeance on them when they failed of doing it. At last, being as it were tired with their ineffectual attempts to mortify her, they furiously said, "Well, you shan't be the last." And after a pause they added, "Go, and the devil go with you, we can do no more;" whereupon they flew out of the room, and she, returning perfectly to herself, most affectionately gave thanks to God for her deliverance. Her tormentors left her extreme weak and faint, and overwhelmed with vapours, which would not only cause her sometimes to swoon away, but also now and then for a little while discompose the reasonableness of her thoughts. Nevertheless, her former troubles returned not; but we are now waiting to see the good effects of those troubles upon the souls of all concerned. And now I suppose that some of our learned witlings of the coffee-house, for fear lest these proofs of an invisible world should spoil some of their sport, will endeavour to turn them all into sport; for which buffoonery their only pretence will be, "They can't understand how such things as these could be done;" whereas indeed he that is but philosopher enough to have read but one little treatise, published in the year 1656, by no other man than the chirurgeon of an army, or but one chapter of Helmont, which I will not quote at this time too particularly, may give a far more intelligible account of these appearances than most of these blades can give why and how their tobacco makes them spit, or which way the flame of their candle becomes illuminating. As for that cavil, "The world would be undone if the devils could have such power as they seem to have in several of our stories," it may be answered, that as to many things, the lying devils have only known them to be done, and then pretended unto the doing of those things; but the true and best answer is, that by these things we only see what the devils could have powers to do, if the great God should give them those powers; whereas now our histories afford a glorious evidence for the being of a God. The world would indeed be undone, and horribly undone, if these devils, who now and then get liberty to play some very mischievous pranks, were not under a daily restraint of some Almighty Superior from doing more of such mischiefs. Wherefore, instead of all apish shouts and jeers at histories which have such undoubted confirmation, as that no man that has breeding enough to regard the common laws of human society, will offer to doubt of them, it becomes us rather to adore the goodness of God, who does not permit such things every day to befall us all, as he sometimes did permit to befall some few of our miserable neighbours.

And what, after all my unwearied cares and pains to rescue the miserable from the lions and bears of hell, which had seized them, and after all my studies to disappoint the devils in their designs to confound my neighbourhood, must I be driven to the necessity of an apology? Truly the hard representations wherewith some ill men have reviled my conduct, and the countenance which other men have given to these representations, oblige me to give mankind some account of my behaviour. No Christian can (I say none but evil workers can) criminate my visiting such of my poor flock as have at any time fallen under the terrible and sensible molestations of evil angels: let their afflictions have been what they will, I could not have answered it unto my glorious Lord, if I had withheld my just counsels and comforts from them; and if I have also with some exactness observed the methods of the invisible world, when they have thus become observable, I have been but a servant of mankind in doing so; yea, no less a person than the venerable Baxter has more than once or twice in the most publick manner invited mankind to thank me for that service. I have not been insensible of a greater danger attending me in this fulfilment of my ministry, than if I had been to take ten thousand steps over a rocky mountain filled with rattlesnakes; but I have considered, he that is wise will observe things; and the surprising explication and confirmation of the biggest part of the Bible, which I have seen given in these things, has abundantly paid me for observing them. Now, in my visiting of the miserable, I was always of this opinion, that we were ignorant of what powers the devils might have to do their mischiefs in the shapes of some that had never been explicitly engaged in diabolical confederacies, and that therefore, though many witchcrafts had been fairly detected on inquiries provoked and begun by spectral exhibitions, yet we could not easily be too jealous of the snares laid for us in the devices of Satan. The world knows how many pages I have composed and published, and particular gentlemen in the government know how many letters I have written, to prevent the excessive credit of spectral accusations; wherefore I have still charged the afflicted that they should cry out of nobody for afflicting of them; but that, if this might be any advantage, they might privately tell their minds to some one person of discretion enough to make no ill use of their communications; accordingly there has been this effect of it, that the name of no one good person in the world ever came under any blemish by means of any afflicted person that fell under my particular cognizance; yea, no one man, woman or child ever came into any trouble for the sake of any that were afflicted, after I had once begun to look after them. How often have I had this thrown into my dish, that many years ago I had an opportunity to have brought forth such people as have in the late storm of witchcraft been complained of, but that I smothered all; and after that storm was raised at Salem, I did myself offer to provide meat, drink and lodging for no less than six of the afflicted, that so an experiment might be made, whether prayer with fasting, upon the removal of the distressed, might not put a period to the trouble then rising, without giving the civil authority the trouble of prosecuting those things which nothing but a conscientious regard unto the cries of miserable families could have overcome the reluctancies of the honourable judges to meddle with. In short, I do humbly but freely affirm it, there is not that man living in this world who has been more desirous than the poor man I to shelter my neighbours from the inconveniencies of spectral outcries; yea, I am very jealous I have done so much that way, as to sin in what I have done; such have been the cowardice and fearfulness whereunto my regard unto the dissatisfactions of other people has precipitated me. I know a man in the world, who has thought he has been able to convict some such witches as ought to die; but his respect unto the publick peace has caused him rather to try whether he could not renew them by repentance; and as I have been studious to defeat the devils of their expectations to set people together by the ears, thus, I have also checked and quelled those forbidden curiosities which would have given the devil an invitation to have tarried amongst us, when I have seen wonderful snares laid for curious people, by the secret and future things discovered from the mouths of damsels possest with a spirit of divination. Indeed I can recollect but one thing wherein there could be given so much as a shadow of reason for exceptions, and that is, my allowing of so many to come and see those that were afflicted. Now for that I have this to say, that I have almost a thousand times entreated the friends of the miserable, that they would not permit the intrusion of any company, but such as by prayers or other ways might be helpful to them; nevertheless I have not absolutely forbid all company from coming to your haunted chambers; partly because the calamities of the families was such as required the assistance of many friends; partly because I have been willing that there should be disinterested witnesses of all sorts, to confute the calumnies of such as would say all was but imposture; and partly because I saw God had sanctified the spectacle of the miseries on the afflicted unto the souls of many that were spectators; and it is a very glorious thing that I have now to mention: The devils have with most horrendous operations broke in upon our neighbourhood, and God has at such a rate overruled all the fury and malice of those devils, that all the afflicted have not only been delivered, but I hope also sav-

ingly brought home unto God, and the reputation of no one good person
in the world has been damaged; but instead thereof the souls of many,
especially of the rising generation, have been thereby awakened unto
some acquaintance with religion; our young people, who belonged unto
the praying meetings, of both sexes, a part would ordinarily spend whole
nights by whole weeks together in prayers and psalms upon these occasions, in which devotions the devils could get nothing, but, like fools, a
scourge for their own backs; and some scores of other young people,
who were strangers to real piety, were now struck with the lively demonstrations of hell evidently set forth before their eyes, when they saw persons cruelly frighted, wounded and starved by devils, and scalded with
burning brimstone; and yet so preserved in this tortured state, as that,
at the end of one month's wretchedness, they were as able still to undergo another; so that of these also it might now be said, "Behold they
pray." In the whole—the devil got just nothing—but God got praises,
Christ got subjects, the Holy Spirit got temples, the church got addition,
and the souls of men got everlasting benefits. I am not so vain as to say
that any wisdom or virtue of mine did contribute unto this good order
of things; but I am so just as to say, I did not hinder this good. When
therefore there have been those that picked up little incoherent scraps
and bits of my discourses in this fruitful discharge of my ministry, and
so travestied them in their abusive pamphlets as to persuade the town that
I was their common enemy in those very points, wherein, if in any one
thing whatsoever, I have sensibly approved myself as true a servant unto
them as possibly I could, though my life and soul had been at stake for it
—yea to do like Satan himself, by sly, base, unpretending insinuations,
as if I wore not the modesty and gravity which became a minister of the
gospel—I could not but think myself unkindly dealt withal, and the neg-
lects of others to do me justice in this affair has caused me to conclude
this narrative with complaints in another hearing of such monstrous injuries.

A CITY HELPED OF THE LORD.

[*Magnalia Christi Americana.* 1702.]

LET us thankfully, and agreeably, and particularly acknowledge what
help we have received from the God of heaven, in the years that
have rolled over us. While the blessed Apostle Paul was, as it should
seem, yet short of being threescore years old, how affectionately did he
set up an Ebenezer, with an acknowledgment in Acts xxvi. 22: "Having
obtained help of God, I continue to this day!" Our town is now three-

score and eight years old; and certainly 'tis time for us, with all possible affection, to set up our Ebenezer, saying, "Having obtained help from God, the town is continued until almost the age of man is passed over it!" The town hath indeed three elder sisters in this colony, but it hath wonderfully outgrown them all; and her mother, Old Boston, in England also; yea, within a few years after the first settlement, it grew to be the metropolis of the whole English America. Little was this expected by them that first settled the town, when for a while Boston was proverbially called Lost-town, for the mean and sad circumstances of it. But, O Boston! it is because thou hast obtained help from God, even from the Lord Jesus Christ, who for the sake of his gospel, preached and once prized here, undertook thy patronage. When the world and the church of God had seen twenty-six generations, a psalm was composed, wherein that note occurs with twenty-six repetitions: "His mercy endureth for ever." Truly there has not one year passed over this town, *ab urbe condita*, upon the story whereof we might not make that note our Ebenezer: "His mercy endureth for ever." It has been a town of great experiences. There have been several years wherein the terrible famine hath terribly stared the town in the face; we have been brought sometimes unto the last meal in the barrel; we have cried out with the disciples, "We have not loaves enough to feed a tenth part of us!" but the feared famine has always been kept off; always we have had seasonable and sufficient supplies after a surprizing manner sent in unto us: let the three last years in this thing most eminently proclaim the goodness of our heavenly Shepherd and Feeder. This has been the help of our God; because "his mercy endureth for ever!" The angels of death have often shot the arrows of death into the midst of the town; the small-pox has especially four times been a great plague upon us: how often have there been bills desiring prayers for more than an hundred sick on one day in one of our assemblies? in one twelve-month, about one thousand of our neighbours have one way or other been carried unto their long home; and yet we are, after all, many more than seven thousand souls of us at this hour living on the spot. Why is not a "Lord, have mercy upon us," written on the doors of our abandoned habitations? This hath been the help of our God, because "his mercy endureth for ever."

Never was any town under the cope of heaven more liable to be laid in ashes, either through the carelessness or through the wickedness of them that sleep in it. That such a combustible heap of contiguous houses yet stands, it may be called a standing miracle; it is not because "the watchman keeps the city;" perhaps there may be too much cause of reflection in that thing, and of inspection, too; no, "it is from thy watchful protection, O thou keeper of Boston, who neither slumbers nor sleeps." Ten times has the fire made notable ruins among us, and our good ser vant been almost our master; but the ruins have mostly and quickly been rebuilt. I suppose that many more than a thousand houses are to be seen on this little piece of ground, all filled with the undeserved favours of God. Whence this preservation? This hath been the help of our God; because "his mercy endureth for ever!" But if ever this town saw a year of salvations, transcendently such was the last year unto us. A formidable French squadron hath not shot one bomb into the midst of thee, O thou munition of rocks! our streets have not run with blood and gore, and horrible devouring flames have not raged upon our substance; those are ignorant, and unthinking, and unthankful men, who do not own that we have narrowly escaped as dreadful things as Carthagena, or New-foundland, have suffered. I am sure our more considerate friends beyond-sea were very suspicious, and well nigh despairing, that victorious enemies had swallowed up the town. But "thy soul is escaped, O Boston, as a bird out of the snare of the fowlers." Or, if ye will be insensible of this, ye vain men, yet be sensible that an English squadron hath not brought among us the tremendous pestilence, under which a neighbouring planta-tion hath undergone prodigious desolations. Boston, 'tis a marvellous thing a plague has not laid thee desolate!

MASTER THEOPHILUS EATON HIS GREAT SOUL.

[*From the Same.*]

SO exemplary was he for a Christian, that one who had been a servant unto him, could many years after say, "Whatever difficulty in my daily walk I now meet withal, still something that I either saw or heard in my blessed master Eaton's conversation, helps me through it all; I have reason to bless God that ever I knew him!" It was his custom when he first rose in a morning, to repair unto his study; a study well perfumed with the meditations and supplications of an holy soul. After this, calling his family together, he would then read a portion of the Scripture among them, and after some devout and useful reflections upon it, he would make a prayer, not long, but extraordinarily pertinent and reverent; and in the evening some of the same exercises were again attended. On the Saturday morning he would still take notice of the approaching Sabbath in his prayer, and ask the grace to be remembering of it, and preparing for it; and when the evening arrived, he, besides this, not only repeated a sermon, but also instructed his people, with putting of questions referring to the points of religion, which would oblige them to study for an answer; and if their answer were at any time insufficient, he would wisely and gently enlighten their understandings; all which he concluded with singing of a psalm. When the Lord's day came, he called his family together at the time for the ringing of the first bell, and repeated a sermon, whereunto he added a fervent prayer, especially tending unto the sanctification of the day. At noon he sang a psalm, and at night he retired an hour into his closet; advising those in his house to improve the same time for the good of their own souls. He then called his family together again, and in an obliging manner conferred with them about the things with which they had been entertained in the house of God, shutting up all with a prayer for the blessing of God upon them all. For solemn days of humiliation, or of thanksgiving, he took the same course, and endeavoured still to make those that belonged unto him understand the meaning of the services before them. He seldom used any recreations, but being a great reader, all the time he could spare from company and business, he commonly spent in his beloved study; so that he merited the name which was once given to a learned ruler of the English nation, the name of Beauclerk. In conversing with his friends, he was affable, courteous, and generally pleasant, but grave perpetually; and so cautelous and circumspect in his discourses, and so modest in his expressions, that it became a proverb for incontestable truth, "Governour Eaton said it."

But after all, his humility appeared in having always but low expectations, looking for little regard and reward from any men, after he had merited as highly as possible by his universal serviceableness.

His eldest son he maintained at the college until he proceeded master of arts; and he was indeed the son of his vows, and a son of great hopes. But a severe catarrh diverted this young gentleman from the work of the ministry whereto his father had once devoted him; and a malignant fever then raging in those parts of the country, carried off him with his wife within two or three days of one another. This was counted the sorest of all the trials that ever befell his father in the "days of the years of his pilgrimage;" but he bore it with a patience and composure of spirit which was truly admirable. His dying son looked earnestly on him, and said, "Sir, what shall we do?" Whereto, with a well-ordered countenance, he replied, "Look up to God!" And when he passed by his daughter, drowned in tears on this occasion, to her he said, "Remember the sixth commandment; hurt not yourself with immoderate grief; remember Job, who said, 'The Lord hath given, and the Lord hath taken away; blessed be the name of the Lord!' You may mark what a note the spirit of God put upon it: 'In all this Job sinned not, nor charged God foolishly:' God accounts it a charging of him foolishly, when we don't submit unto his will patiently." Accordingly he now governed himself as one that had attained unto the rule of "weeping as if we wept not;" for it being the Lord's day, he repaired unto the church in the afternoon, as he had been there in the forenoon, though he was never like to see his dearest son alive any more in this world. And though before the first prayer began, a messenger came to prevent Mr. Davenport's praying for the sick person, who was now dead, yet his affectionate father altered not his course, but wrote after the preacher as formerly; and when he came home he held on his former methods of divine worship in his family, not for the excuse of Aaron omitting any thing in the service of God. In like sort, when the people had been at the solemn interment of this his worthy son, he did with a very unpassionate aspect and carriage then say, "Friends, I thank you all for your love and help, and for this testimony of respect unto me and mine: the Lord hath given, and the Lord hath taken; blessed be the name of the Lord!" Nevertheless, retiring hereupon into the chamber where his daughter then lay sick, some tears were observed falling from him while he uttered these words, "There is a difference between a sullen silence or a stupid senselessness under the hand of God, and a child-like submission thereunto."

Thus continually he, for about a score of years, was the glory and pillar of New-Haven colony. He would often say, "Some count it a great matter to die well, but I am sure 'tis a great matter to live well. All our care should be while we have our life to use it well, and so when death puts an end unto that, it will put an end unto all our cares." But having excellently managed his care to live well, God would have him to die well, without any room or time then given to take any care at all; for he enjoyed a death sudden to every one but himself! Having worshipped God with his family after his usual manner, and upon some occasion with much solemnity charged all the family to carry it well unto their mistress who was now confined by sickness, he supped, and then took a turn or two abroad for his meditations. After that he came in to bid his wife good-night, before he left her with her watchers: which when he did, she said, "Methinks you look sad!" Whereto he replyed, "The differences risen in the church of Hartford make me so;" she then added, "Let us even go back to our native country again;" to which he answered, "You may (and so she did), but I shall die here." This was the last word that ever she heard him speak; for, now retiring unto his lodging in another chamber, he was overheard about midnight fetching a groan; and unto one sent in presently to enquire how he did, he answered the enquiry with only saying, "Very ill!" and without saying any more, he fell "asleep in Jesus," in the year 1657, loosing anchor from New-Haven for the better:

——*Sedes, ubi Fata, quietas
Ostendunt.*

Now let his gravestone wear at least the following

EPITAPH.

New-England's glory, full of warmth and light,
Stole away (and said nothing) in the night.

HOW CAPTAIN PHIPS BECAME A KNIGHT OF THE GOLDEN FLEECE.

[*From the Same.*]

HE was of an inclination cutting rather like a hatchet than like a razor; he would propose very considerable matters to himself, and then so cut through them that no difficulties could put by the edge of his resolutions. Being thus of the true temper for doing of great things, he betakes himself to the sea, the right scene for such things; and upon advice of a Spanish wreck about the Bahamas, he took a voyage thither; but with little more success than what just served him a little to furnish him for a voyage to England; whither he went in a vessel, not much unlike that which the Dutchmen stamped on their first coin, with these words about it: *Incertum quo Fata ferant.* Having first informed himself that there was another Spanish wreck, wherein was lost a mighty treasure, hitherto undiscovered, he had a strong impression upon his mind that he must be the discoverer; and he made such representations of his design at White-Hall, that by the year 1683 he became the captain of a king's ship, and arrived at New-England commander of the Algier-Rose, a frigate of eighteen guns and ninety-five men.

To relate all the dangers through which he passed, both by sea and land, and all the tiresome trials of his patience, as well as of his courage, while year after year the most vexing accidents imaginable delayed the success of his design, it would even tire the patience of the reader; for very great was the experiment that Captain Phips made of the Italian observation, "He that cannot suffer both good and evil, will never come to any great preferment." Wherefore I shall supersede all journal of his voyages to and fro, with reciting one incident of his conduct, that showed him to be a person of no contemptible capacity. While he was captain of the Algier-Rose, his men growing weary of their unsuccessful enterprise, made a mutiny, wherein they approached him on the quarter-deck, with drawn swords in their hands, and required him to join with them in running away with the ship, to drive a trade of piracy on the South Seas. Captain Phips, though he had not so much of a weapon as an ox-goad, or a jaw-bone in his hands, yet, like another Shamgar or Samson, with a most undaunted fortitude, he rushed in upon them, and with the blows of his bare hands felled many of them, and quelled all the rest.

But this is not the instance which I intended; that which I intend is, that (as it has been related unto me) one day while his frigate lay careening, at a desolate Spanish island, by the side of a rock, from whence they had laid a bridge to the shore, the men, whereof he had about an hundred, went all but about eight or ten to divert themselves, as they pretended, in the woods; where they all entered into an agreement, which they signed in a ring, that about seven o'clock that evening they would seize the captain, and those eight or ten which they knew to be true unto him, and leave them to perish on this island, and so be gone away unto the South Sea to seek their fortune. Will the reader now imagine that Captain Phips, having advice of this plot but about an hour and a half before it was to be put in execution, yet within two hours brought all these rogues down upon their knees to beg for their lives? But so it was! for these knaves considering that they should want a carpenter with them in their villainous expedition, sent a messenger to fetch unto them the carpenter, who was then at work upon the vessel; and unto him they shewed their articles; telling him what he must look for if he did not subscribe among them. The carpenter, being an honest fellow, did with much importunity prevail for one half hour's time to consider of the matter; and returning to work upon the vessel, with a spy by them set upon him, he feigned himself taken with a fit of the cholick, for the relief whereof he suddenly run unto the captain in the great cabin for a dram; where, when he came, his business was only, in brief, to tell the captain of the horrible distress which he was fallen into; but the captain bid him as briefly return to the rogues in the woods, and sign their articles, and leave him to provide for the rest. The carpenter was no sooner gone but Captain Phips, calling together the few friends (it may be seven or eight) that were left him aboard, whereof the gunner was one, demanded of them, whether they would stand by him in the extremity which he informed them was now come upon him; whereto they replied, "They would stand by him, if he could save them;" and he answered, "By the help of God he did not fear it." All their provisions had been carried ashore to a tent, made for that purpose there; about which they had placed several great guns to defend it, in case of any assault from Spaniards, that might happen to come that way. Wherefore Captain Phips immediately ordered those guns to be silently drawn and turned; and so pulling up the bridge, he charged his great guns aboard, and brought them to bear on every side of the tent. By this time the army of rebels comes out of the woods; but as they drew near to the tent of provisions, they saw such a change of circumstances, that they cried out, "We are betrayed!" And they were soon confirmed in it, when they heard the captain with a stern fury call to them, "Stand off, ye wretches, at your peril!" He quickly saw them cast into a more than ordinary confusion, when they saw him ready to fire his great guns upon them, if they offered one step further than he permitted them; and when he had signified unto them his resolve to abandon them unto all the desolation which they had purposed for him, he caused the bridge to be again laid, and his men begun to take the provisions aboard. When the wretches beheld what was coming upon them, they fell to very humble entreaties; and at last fell down upon their knees, protesting, "That they never had anything against him, except only his unwillingness to go away with the king's ship upon the South-Sea design; but upon all other accounts they would chuse rather to live and die with him than with any man in the world. However, since they saw how much he was dissatisfied at it, they would insist upon it no more, and humbly begged his pardon." And when he judged that he had kept them on their knees long enough, he having first secured their arms, received them aboard; but he immediately weighed anchor, and arriving at Jamaica, he turned them off.

Now, with a small company of other men he sailed from thence to Hispaniola, where, by the policy of his address, he fished out of a very old Spaniard (or Portuguese) a little advice about the true spot where lay the wreck which he had been hitherto seeking, as unprosperously as the chymists have their aurisick stone; that it was upon a reef of shoals, a few leagues to the northward of Port de la Plata, upon Hispaniola, a port so called, it seems, from the landing of some of the shipwrecked company, with a boat full of plate, saved out of their sinking frigate; nevertheless, when he had searched very narrowly the spot, whereof the old Spaniard had advised him, he had not hitherto exactly lit upon it. Such thorns did vex his affairs while he was in the Rose-frigate; but none of all these things could retund the edge of his expectations to find the wreck; with such expectations he returned then into England, that he might there better furnish himself to prosecute a new discovery; for though he judged he might, by proceeding a little further, have come at the right spot; yet he found his present company too ill a crew to be confided in.

So proper was his behaviour, that the best noblemen in the kingdom now admitted him into their conversation; but yet he was opposed by powerful enemies, that clogged his affairs with such demurrages, and such disappointments, as would have wholly discouraged his designs, if his patience had not been invincible. "He who can wait hath what he desireth." Thus his indefatigable patience, with a proportionable diligence, at length overcame the difficulties that had been thrown in his way; and prevailing with the Duke of Albemarle, and some other persons of quality, to fit him out, he set sail for the fishing-ground, which had been so well baited half an hundred years before; and as he had already discovered his capacity for business in many considerable actions, he now added unto those discoveries, by not only providing all, but also by inventing many of the instruments necessary to the prosecution of his intended fishery. Captain Phips arriving with a ship and a tender at Port de la Plata, made a stout canoo of a stately cotton-tree, so large as to carry eight or ten oars, for the making of which periaga (as they call it) he did, with the same industry that he did every thing else, imploy his own hand and adse, and endure no little hardship, lying abroad in the woods many nights together. This periaga, with the tender, being anchored at a place convenient, the periaga kept busking to and again, but could only discover a reef of rising shoals thereabouts, called "The Boilers,"—which, rising to be within two or three foot of the surface of the sea, were yet so steep, that a ship striking on them would immediately sink down, who could say how many fathom, into the ocean? Here they could get no other pay for their long peeping among the boilers, but only such as caused them to think upon returning to their captain with the bad news of their total disappointment. Nevertheless, as they were upon the return, one of the men, looking over the side of the periaga, into the calm water, he spied a sea feather, growing, as he judged, out of a rock; whereupon they bade one of their Indians to dive, and fetch this feather, that they might, however, carry home something with them, and make, at least, as fair a triumph as Caligula's. The diver bringing up the feather, brought therewithal a surprising story, that he perceived a number of great guns in the watery world where he had found his feather; the report of which great guns exceedingly astonished the whole company; and at once turned their despondencies for their ill success into assurances that they had now lit upon the true spot of ground which they had been looking for; and they were further confirmed in these assurances, when, upon further diving, the Indian fetcht up a sow, as they styled it, or a lump of silver worth perhaps two or three hundred pounds. Upon this they prudently buoyed the place, that they might readily find it again; and they went back unto their captain, whom for some while they distressed with nothing but such bad news as they formerly thought they must have carried him. Nevertheless, they so slipt in the sow of silver on one side under the table, where they were now sitting with the captain, and hearing him express his resolutions to wait still patiently upon the providence of God under these disappointments, that when he should look on one side, he might see that odd thing before him. At last he saw it; seeing it, he cried out with some agony, "Why! what is this? whence comes this?" And then, with changed countenances, they told him how and where they got it. "Then," said he, "thanks be to God! we are made;" and so away they went, all hands to work; wherein they had this one further piece of remarkable prosperity, that whereas if they had first fallen upon that part of the Spanish wreck where the pieces of eight had been stowed in bags among the ballast, they had seen a more laborious, and less enriching time of it; now, most happily, they first fell upon that room in the wreck where the bullion had been stored up; and they so prospered in this new fishery, that in a little while they had, without the loss of any man's life, brought up thirty-two tuns of silver; for it was now come to measuring of silver by tuns. Besides which, one Adderly, of Providence, who had formerly been very helpful to Captain Phips in the search of this wreck, did, upon former agreement, meet him now with a little vessel here; and he, with his few hands, took up about six tuns of silver; whereof, nevertheless, he made so little use, that in a year or two he died at Bermudas, and, as I have heard, he ran distracted some while before he died.

Thus did there once again come into the light of the sun a treasure which had been half an hundred years groaning under the waters; and in this time there was grown upon the plate a crust like limestone, to the thickness of several inches; which crust being broken open by iron contrived for that purpose, they knocked out whole bushels of rusty pieces of eight which were grown thereinto. Besides that incredible treasure of plate in various forms, thus fetched up, from seven or eight fathom under water, there were vast riches of gold, and pearls and jewels, which they also lit upon; and, indeed, for a more comprehensive invoice, I must but summarily say, "All that a Spanish frigate uses to be enriched withal." Thus did they continue fishing till, their provisions failing them, 'twas time to be gone; but before they went, Captain Phips caused Adderly and his folk to swear that they would none of them discover the place of the wreck, or come to the place any more till the next year, when he expected again to be there himself. And it was also remarkable that though the sows came up still so fast, that on the very last day of their being there they took up twenty, yet it was afterwards found that they had in a manner wholly cleared that room of the ship where those massy things were stowed.

But there was one extraordinary distress which Captain Phips now found himself plunged into; for his men were come out with him upon seamen's wages, at so much per month; and when they saw such vast litters of silver sows and pigs, as they called them, come on board them at the captain's call, they knew not how to bear it, that they should not share all among themselves, and be gone to lead "a short life and a merry," in a climate where the arrest of those that had hired them should not reach them. In this terrible distress he made his vows unto Almighty God, that if the Lord would carry him safe home to England, with what he had now given him, "to suck of the abundance of the seas, and of the treasures hid in the sands," he would forever devote himself unto the interests of the Lord Jesus Christ and of his people, especially in the country which he did himself originally belong unto. And he then used all the obliging arts imaginable to make his men true unto him, especially by assuring them that, besides their wages, they should have ample requitals made unto them; which if the rest of his employers would not agree unto, he would himself distribute his own share among them. Relying upon the word of one whom they had ever found worthy of their love, and of their trust, they declared themselves content; but still keeping a most careful eye upon them, he hastened back for England with as much money as he thought he could then safely trust his vessel withal; not counting it safe to supply himself with necessary provisions at any nearer port, and so return unto the wreck, by which delays he wisely feared lest all might be lost, more ways than one. Though he also left so much behind him, that many from divers parts made very considerable voyages of gleanings after his harvest; which came to pass by certain Bermudians compelling of Adderly's boy, whom they spirited away with them, to tell them the exact place where the wreck was to be found.

Captain Phips now coming up to London in the year 1687, with near three hundred thousand pounds sterling aboard him, did acquit himself with such an exemplary honesty, that partly by his fulfilling his assurances to the seamen, and partly by his exact and punctual care to have his employers defrauded of nothing that might conscientiously belong unto them, he had less than sixteen thousand pounds left unto himself; as an acknowledgment of which honesty in him, the Duke of Albemarle made unto his wife, whom he never saw, a present of a golden cup, near a thousand pound in value. The character of an honest man he had so merited in the whole course of his life, and especially in this last act of it, that this, in conjunction with his other serviceable qualities, procured him the favours of the greatest persons in the nation; and "he that had been so diligent in his business, must now stand before Kings, and not stand before mean men." There were indeed certain mean men—if base, little, dirty tricks, will entitle men to meanness—who urged the king to seize his whole cargo, instead of the tenths, upon his first arrival; on this pretence, that he had not been rightly informed of the true state of the case when he granted the patent, under the protection whereof these particular men had made themselves masters of all this mighty treasure; but the king replied, that he had been rightly informed by Captain Phips of the whole matter, as it now proved; and that it was the slanders of one then present which had, unto his damage, hindered him from hearkening to the information; wherefore he would give them, he said, no disturbance; they might keep what they had got; but Captain Phips, he saw, was a person of that honesty, fidelity, and ability, that he should not want his countenance. Accordingly the king, in consideration of the service done by him in bringing such a treasure into the nation, conferred upon him the honour of knighthood; and if we now reckon him a knight of the golden fleece, the style might pretend unto some circumstances that would justifie it. Or, call him if you please, "the knight of honesty;" for it was honesty with industry that raised him; and he became a mighty river, without the running in of muddy water to make him so. Reader, now make a pause, and behold one raised by God!

THE LIFE AND DEATH OF MASTER THOMAS HOOKER.

[From the Same.]

WHEN Toxaris met with his countryman Anacharsis in Athens, he gave him this invitation, "Come along with me, and I will shew thee at once all the wonders of Greece;" whereupon he shewed him Solon, as the person in whom there centred all the glories of that city or country. I shall now invite my reader to behold at once the "wonders" of New-England, and it is in one Thomas Hooker that he shall behold them; even in that Hooker, whom a worthy writer would needs call "Saint Hooker," for the same reason (he said), and with the same freedom that Latimer would speak of Saint Bilney, in his commemorations. 'Tis that Hooker, of whom I may venture to say, that the famous Romanist, who wrote a book, *De Tribus Thomis*, or Of Three Thomas's—meaning Thomas the Apostle, Thomas à Becket, and Sir Thomas More—did not a thousandth part so well sort his Thomas's, as a New-Englander might, if he should write a book, *De Duobus Thomis*, or Of Two Thomas's; and with Thomas the Apostle, join our celebrious Thomas Hooker; my one Thomas, even our apostolical Hooker, would in just balances weigh down two of Stapleton's rebellious archbishops or bigoted Lord Chancellors. 'Tis he whom I may call, as Theodoret called Irenæus, "The light of the western churches."

This our Hooker was born at Marfield, in Leicestershire, about the year 1586, of parents that were neither unable nor unwilling to bestow upon him a liberal education; whereto the early and lively sparkles of wit observed in him did very much encourage them. His natural temper was cheerful and courteous; but it was accompanied with such a sensible grandeur of mind, as caused his friends, without the help of astrology, to prognosticate that he was born to be considerable. The influence which he had upon the reformation of some growing abuses, when he was one of the proctors in the university, was a thing that more eminently signalized him, when his more publick appearance in the world was coming on; which was attended with an advancement unto a fellowship in Emanuel College, in Cambridge; the students whereof were originally designed for the study of divinity.

With what ability and fidelity he acquitted himself in his fellowship, it was a thing sensible unto the whole university. And it was while he was in this employment that the more effectual grace of God gave him the experience of a true regeneration. It pleased the spirit of God very powerfully to break into the soul of this person with such a sense of his being exposed unto the just wrath of heaven, as filled him with most unusual degrees of horror and anguish, which broke not only his rest, but his heart also, and caused him to cry out, "While I suffer thy terrors, O Lord, I am distracted!" While he long had a soul harassed with such distresses, he had a singular help in the prudent and piteous carriage of Mr. Ash, who was the sizer that then waited upon him; and attended him with such discreet and proper compassions as made him afterwards to respect him highly all his days. He afterwards gave this account of himself, "That in the time of his agonies, he could reason himself to the rule, and conclude that there was no way but submission to God, and lying at the foot of his mercy in Christ Jesus, and waiting humbly there, till he should please to persuade the soul of his favour; nevertheless, when he came to apply this rule unto himself in his own condition, his reasoning would fail him, he was able to do nothing." Having been a considerable while thus troubled with such impressions for the "spirit of bondage," as were to fit him for the great services and enjoyments which God intended him, at length he received the "spirit of adoption," with well-grounded persuasions of his interest in the new covenant. It became his manner, at his lying down for sleep in the evening, to single out some certain promise of God, which he would repeat and ponder, and keep his heart close unto it, until he found that satisfaction of soul wherewith he could say, "I will lay me down in peace, and sleep; for thou, O Lord, makest me dwell in assurance." And he would afterwards counsel others to take the same course; telling them, "That the promise was the boat which was to carry a perishing sinner over unto the Lord Jesus Christ." .   .   .   .

The conscientious non-conformity of Mr. Hooker to some rites of the church of England, then vigorously pressed, especially upon such able and useful ministers as were most likely to be laid aside by their scrupling of those rites, made it necessary for him to lay down his ministry in Chelmsford, when he had been about four years there employed in it. Hereupon, at the request of several eminent persons, he kept a school in his own hired house, having one Mr. John Eliot for his usher, at little Baddow, not far from Chelmsford; where he managed his charge with such discretion, with such authority, and such efficacy, that, able to do more with a word or a look than most other men could have done by a severer discipline, he did very great service to the church of God, in the education of such as afterwards proved themselves not a little service-able. I have in my hands a manuscript, written by the hands of our blessed Eliot, wherein he gives a very great account of the little academy then maintained in the house of Mr. Hooker; and, among other things, he says: "To this place I was called, through the infinite riches of God's mercy in Christ Jesus to my poor soul; for here the Lord said unto my dead soul, live; and through the grace of Christ, I do live, and I shall live forever! When I came to this blessed family I then saw, and never before, the power of godliness in its lively vigour and efficacy." . . .

Mr. Hooker and Mr. Cotton were, for their different genius, the Luther and Melancthon of New-England; at their arrival unto which country, Mr. Cotton settled with the church of Boston, but Mr. Hooker with the church of New-Town, having Mr. Stone for his assistant. Inexpressible now was the joy of Mr. Hooker, to find himself surrounded with his friends, who were come over the year before, to prepare for his recep-tion; with open arms he embraced them, and uttered these words, "Now I live, if you stand fast in the Lord." But such multitudes flocked over to New-England after them, that the plantation of New-Town became too straight for them; and it was Mr. Hooker's advice that they should not incur the danger of a Sitna, or an Esek, where they might have a Rehoboth. Accordingly, in the month of June, 1636, they removed an hundred miles to the westward, with a purpose to settle upon the de-lightful banks of Connecticut River; and there were about an hundred persons in the first company that made this removal, who not being able to walk above ten miles a day, took up near a fortnight in the journey; having no pillows to take their nightly rest upon, but such as their father Jacob found in the way to Padan-Aram. Here Mr. Hooker was the chief instrument of beginning another colony, as Mr. Cotton, whom he left behind him, was of preserving and perfecting that colony where he left him; for, indeed, each of them were the oracle of their several colonies.

Though Mr. Hooker had thus removed from the Massachuset-bay, yet he sometimes came down to visit the churches in that bay; but when ever he came, he was received with an affection like that which Paul found among the Galatians; yea, 'tis thought that once there seemed some intimation from heaven, as if the good people had overdone in that affection; for on May 26, 1639, Mr. Hooker being here to preach that Lord's day in the afternoon, his great fame had gathered a vast multitude of hearers from several other congregations, and, among the rest, the governour himself, to be made partaker of his ministry. But when he came to preach, he found himself so unaccountably at a loss, that after some shattered and broken attempts to proceed, he made a full stop; saying to the assembly, "That every thing which he would have spoken, was taken both out of his mouth and out of his mind also;" wherefore he desired them to sing a psalm, while he withdrew about half an hour from them; returning then to the congregation, he preached a most admirable sermon, wherein he held them for two hours together in an extraordinary strain both of pertinency and vivacity.

After sermon, when some of his friends were speaking of the Lord's thus withdrawing his assistance from him, he humbly replied, "We daily confess that we have nothing, and can do nothing, without Christ; and what if Christ will make this manifest in us, and on us, before our congregations? What remains, but that we be humbly contented? and what manner of discouragement is there in all of this?" Thus content was he to be nullified, that the Lord might be magnified!

Mr. Hooker, that had been born to serve many, and was of such a publick spirit that I find him occasionally celebrated in the life of Mr. Angier, lately published, for one who would be continually inquisitive how it fared with the church of God, both at home and abroad, on purpose that he might order his prayers and cares accordingly; [which, by the way, makes me think on Mr. Firmin's words: "I look on it, saith he, as an act of a grown Christian, whose interest in Christ is well cleared, and his heart walking close with God, to be really taken up with the publick interest of Christ."] He never took his opportunity to serve himself, but lived a sort of exile all his days, except the last fourteen years of his life, among his own spiritual children at Hartford; however, here also he was an exile. Accordingly, wherever he came, he lived like a stranger in the world! When at the Land's-end he took his last sight of England, he said, "Farewell, England! I expect now no more to see that religious zeal and power of godliness which I have seen among professors in that land!" And he had sagacious and prophetical apprehensions of the declensions which would attend "reforming churches," when they came to enjoy a place of liberty; he said, "That adversity had slain its thousands, but prosperity would slay its ten thousands!" He feared, "That they who had been lively Christians in the fire of persecution, would soon become cold in the midst of universal peace, except some few, whom God by sharp tryals would keep in a faithful, watchful, humble, and praying frame." But under these pre-apprehensions, it was his own endeavour to beware of abating his own first love! and of so watchful, so prayerful, so fruitful a spirit was Mr. Hooker, that the spirit of prophecy itself did seem to grant him some singular afflations. Indeed, every wise man is a prophet; but one so eminently acquainted with Scripture and reason, and church-history, as our Hooker, must needs be a seer, from whom singular prognostications were to be expected. Accordingly, there were many things prognosticated by him, wherein the future state of New-England, particularly of Connecticut, has been so much concerned, that it is pity they should be forgotten. But I will in this history record only two of his predictions. One was, "That God would punish the wanton spirit of the professors in this country, with a sad want of able men in all orders." Another was, "That in certain places of great light here sinned against, there would break forth such horrible sins, as would be the amazement of the world."

He was a man of prayer, which was indeed a ready way to become a man of God. He would say, "That prayer was the principal part of a minister's work; 'twas by this, that he was to carry on the rest." Accordingly, he still devoted one day in a month to private prayer, with fasting, before the Lord, besides the publick fasts, which often occurred unto him. He would say, "That such extraordinary favours as the life of religion, and the power of godliness, must be preserved by the frequent use of such extraordinary means as prayer with fasting; and that if professors grow negligent of these means, iniquity will abound and the love of many wax cold." Nevertheless, in the duty of prayer, he affected strength rather than length; and though he had not so much variety in his publick praying as in his publick preaching, yet he always had a seasonable respect unto present occasions. And it was observed that his prayer was usually like Jacob's ladder, wherein the nearer he came to an end the nearer he drew towards heaven; and he grew into such rapturous pleadings with God, and praisings of God, as made some to say, "That like the master of the feast, he reserved the best wine until the last." Nor was the wonderful success of his prayer, upon special concerns, unobserved by the whole colony; who reckoned him the Moses which turned away the wrath of God from them, and obtained a blast from heaven upon their Indian Amalekites, by his uplifted hands, in those remarkable deliverances which they sometimes experienced. It was very particularly observed, when there was a battle to be fought between the Narraganset and the Monhegin Indians, in the year 1643. The Narraganset Indians had complotted the ruin of the English, but the Monhegin were confederate with us; and a war now being between those two nations, much notice was taken of the prevailing importunity, wherewith Mr. Hooker urged for the accomplishment of that great promise unto the people of God, "I will bless them that bless thee, but I will curse him that curses thee." And the effect of it was, that the Narragansets received a wonderful overthrow from the Monhegins, though the former did three or four to one for number exceed the latter. Such an Israel at prayer was our Hooker! And this praying pastor was blessed, as, indeed, such ministers use to be, with a praying people;

there fell upon his pious people a double portion of the Spirit which they beheld in him.

That reverend and excellent man, Mr. Whitfield, having spent many years in studying of books, did at length take two or three years to study men; and in pursuance of this design, having acquainted himself with the most considerable divines in England, at last he fell into the acquaintance of Mr. Hooker; concerning whom, he afterwards gave this testimony: "That he had not thought there had been such a man on earth; a man in whom there shone so many excellencies, as were in this incomparable Hooker; a man in whom learning and wisdom were so tempered with zeal, holiness, and watchfulness." And the same observer having exactly noted Mr. Hooker, made this remark, and gave this report more particularly of him, "That he had the best command of his own spirit which he ever saw in any man whatever." For though he were a man of a cholerick disposition, and had a mighty vigour and fervour of spirit, which as occasion served was wondrous useful unto him, yet he had ordinarily as much government of his choler as a man has of a mastiff dog in a chain; he "could let out his dog, and pull in his dog, as he pleased." And another that observed the heroical spirit and courage with which this great man fulfilled his ministry, gave this account of him, "He was a person who, while doing his Master's work, would put a king in his pocket."   .   .   .   .

He was indeed of a very condescending spirit, not only towards his brethren in the ministry, but also towards the meanest of any Christians whatsoever. He was very willing to sacrifice his own apprehensions into the convincing reason of another man; and very ready to acknowledge any mistake, or failing in himself. I'll give one example: There happened a damage to be done unto a neighbour, immediately whereupon, Mr. Hooker meeting with an unlucky boy that often had his name up for the doing of such mischiefs, he fell to chiding of that boy as the doer of this. The boy denied it, and Mr. Hooker still went on in an angry manner, charging of him; whereupon said the boy, "Sir, I see you are in a passion, I'll say no more to you;" and so ran away. Mr. Hooker, upon further enquiry, not finding that the boy could be proved guilty, sent for him; and having first by a calm question given the boy opportunity to renew his denial of the fact, he said unto him: "Since I cannot prove the contrary, I am bound to believe; and I do believe what you say;" and then added: "Indeed, I was in a passion when I spake to you before; it was my sin, and it is my shame, and I am truly sorry for it; and I hope in God I shall be more watchful hereafter." So, giving the boy some good counsel, the poor lad went away extremely affected with such a carriage in so good a man; and it proved an occasion of good unto the soul of the lad all his days.   .   .   .   .

He would say, "that he should esteem it a favour from God, if he might live no longer than he should be able to hold up lively in the work of his place; and that when the time of his departure should come, God would shorten the time;" and he had his desire.   Some of his most observant hearers observed an astonishing sort of a cloud in his congregation, the last Lord's day of his publick ministry, when he also administered the Lord's supper among them; and a most unaccountable heaviness and sleepiness, even in the most watchful Christians of the place, not unlike the drowsiness of the disciples when our Lord was going to die; for which one of the elders publickly rebuked them.   When those devout people afterwards perceived that this was the last sermon and sacrament wherein they were to have the presence of the pastor with them, 'tis inexpressible how much they bewailed their unattentiveness unto his farewell dispensations; and some of them could enjoy no peace in their own souls until they had obtained leave of the elders to confess before the whole congregation with many tears, that inadvertency.   But as for Mr. Hooker himself, an epidemical sickness, which had proved mortal to many, though at first small or no danger appeared in it, arrested him.   In the time of his sickness he did not say much to the standers-by; but being asked that he would utter his apprehensions about some important things, especially about the state of New-England, he answered, "I have not that work now to do; I have already declared the counsel of the Lord;" and when one that stood weeping by the bed-side said unto him, "Sir, you are going to receive the reward of all your labours," he replied, "Brother, I am going to receive mercy!"   At last he closed his own eyes with his own hands, and gently stroking his own forehead, with a smile in his countenance, he gave a little groan, and so expired his blessed soul into the arms of his fellow-servants, the holy angels, on July 7, 1647.   In which last hours, the glorious peace of soul, which he had enjoyed without any interruption for nearly thirty years together, so gloriously accompanied him, that a worthy spectator, then writing to Mr. Cotton a relation thereof, made this reflection, "Truly, sir, the sight of his death will make me have more pleasant thoughts of death than ever I yet had in my life!"

Thus lived and thus died one of the first three.   He, of whom the great Mr. Cotton gave this character, that he did, *Agmen ducere et dominari in consionibus, gratia Spiritus Sancti et virtute plenis;* and that he was, *Vir solertis et acerrimi judicii;* and at length he uttered his lamentations in a funeral elegy, whereof some lines were these:

> 'Twas of Geneva's heroes said with wonder,
> (Those worthies three) Farel was wont to thunder,
> Viret like rain on tender grass to show'r,
> But Calvin lively oracles to pour.

All these in Hooker's spirit did remain,
A son of thunder and a show'r of rain ;
A pourer forth of lively oracles,
In saving souls, the sum of miracles.

This was he of whom his pupil, Mr. Ash, gives this testimony : " For his great abilities and glorious services, both in this and in the other England, he deserves a place in the first rank of them whose lives are of late recorded." And this was he of whom his reverend contemporary, Mr. Ezekiel Rogers, tendered this for an epitaph ; in every line whereof methinks the writer deserves a reward equal to what Virgil had, when for every line, referring to Marcellus in the end of his sixth *Æneid*, he received a sum not much less than eighty pounds in money, or as ample a requital as Cardinal Richelieu gave to a poet, when he bestowed upon him two thousand sequins for a witty conceit in one verse of but seven words, upon his coat of arms :

America, although she do not boast
Of all the gold and silver from that coast,
Lent to her sister Europe's need or pride ;
(For that repaid her, with much gain beside,
In one rich pearl, which heaven did thence afford,
As pious Herbert gave his honest word ;)
Yet thinks, she in the catalogue may come
With Europe, Africk, Asia for one tomb.

THE EXQUISITE CHARITY OF MASTER JOHN ELIOT.

[*From the Same.*]

HE that will write of Eliot must write of charity, or say nothing. His charity was a star of the first magnitude in the bright constellation of his vertues, and the rays of it were wonderfully various and extensive.

His liberality to pious uses, whether publick or private, went much beyond the proportions of his little estate in the world. Many hundreds of pounds did he freely bestow upon the poor ; and he would, with a very forcible importunity, press his neighbours to join with him in such beneficences. It was a marvellous alacrity with which he imbraced all opportunities of relieving any that were miserable ; and the good people of Roxbury doubtless cannot remember (but the righteous God will !) how often, and with what ardors, with what arguments, he became a beggar to them for collections in their assemblies, to support such needy objects as had fallen under his observation. The poor counted him their

father, and repaired still unto him with a filial confidence in their neces-
sities; and they were more than seven or eight, or indeed than so many
scores, who received their portions of his bounty. Like that worthy and
famous English general, he could not perswade himself "that he had
anything but what he gave away," but he drove a mighty trade at such
exercises as he thought would furnish him with bills of exchange, which
he hoped "after many days" to find the comfort of; and yet, after all, he
would say, like one of the most charitable souls that ever lived in the
world, "that looking over his accounts he could nowhere find the God of
heaven charged a debtor there." He did not put off his charity to be put
in his last will, as many who therein shew that their charity is against
their will; but he was his own administrator; he made his own hands
his executors, and his own eyes his overseers. It has been remarked that
liberal men are often long-lived men; so do they after many days find
the bread with which they have been willing to keep other men alive.
The great age of our Eliot was but agreeable to this remark; and when
his age had unfitted him for almost all employments, and bereaved him
of those gifts and parts which once he had been accomplished with, being
asked, "How he did?" he would sometimes answer, "Alas, I have lost
everything; my understanding leaves me, my memory fails me, my utter
ance fails me; but, I thank God, my charity holds out still; I find that
rather grows than fails!" And I make no question, that at his death his
happy soul was received and welcomed into the "everlasting habitations,"
by many scores got thither before him, of such as his charity had been
liberal unto.

But besides these more substantial expressions of his charity, he made
the odours of that grace yet more fragrant unto all that were about him,
by that pitifulness and that peaceableness which rendered him yet
further amiable. If any of his neighbourhood were in distress, he was like
a "brother born for their adversity," he would visit them, and comfort
them with a most fraternal sympathy; yea, 'tis not easy to recount how
many whole days of prayer and fasting he has got his neighbours to keep
with him, on the behalf of those whose calamities he found himself
touched withal. It was an extreme satisfaction to him that his wife had attained unto a considerable skill in physick and chirurgery, which enabled
her to dispense many safe, good, and useful medicines unto the poor that
had occasion for them; and some hundreds of sick and weak and maimed
people owed praises to God for the benefit which therein they freely
received of her. The good gentleman her husband would still be casting oil into the flame of that charity, wherein she was of her own accord
abundantly forward thus to be doing of good unto all; and he would
urge her to be serviceable unto the worst enemies that he had in the
world. Never had any man fewer enemies than he! but once having

delivered something in his ministry which displeased one of his hearers, the man did passionately abuse him for it, and this both with speeches and with writings that reviled him. Yet it happening not long after that this man gave himself a very dangerous wound, Mr. Eliot immediately sends his wife to cure him; who did accordingly. When the man was well, he came to thank her, but she took no rewards; and this good man made him-stay and eat with him, taking no notice of all the calumnies with which he had loaded him; but by this carriage he mollified and conquered the stomach of his reviler.

He was also a great enemy to all contention, and would ring aloud courfeu bell wherever he saw the fires of animosity. When he heard any ministers complain that such and such in their flocks were too difficult for them, the strain of his answer still was, "Brother, compass them!" and "Brother, learn the meaning of those three little words, bear, forbear, forgive." Yea, his inclinations for peace, indeed, sometimes almost made him to sacrifice right itself. When there was laid before an assembly of ministers a bundle of papers which contained certain matters of difference and contention between some people which our Eliot thought should rather unite, with an amnesty upon all their former quarrels, he (with some imitation of what Constantine did upon the like occasion) hastily threw the papers into the fire before them all, and, with a zeal for peace as hot as that fire, said immediately, "Brethren, wonder not at what I have done; I did it on my knees this morning before I came among you." Such an excess (if it were one) flowed from his charitable inclinations to be found among those peace-makers which, by following the example of that Man who is our peace, come to be called "the children of God." Very worthily might he be called an Irenæus, as being all for peace; and the commendation which Epiphanius gives unto the ancient of that name, did belong unto our Eliot; he was "a most blessed and a most holy man." He disliked all sorts of bravery; but yet with an ingenious note upon the Greek word in Col. iii. 15, he propounded, "that peace might brave it among us." In short, wherever he came, it was like another old John, with solemn and earnest persuasives to love; and when he could say little else he would give that charge, "My children, love one another!"

Finally, 'twas his charity which disposed him to continual apprecations for, and benedictions on those that he met withal; he had an heart full of good wishes and a mouth full of kind blessings for them. And he often made his expressions very wittily agreeable to the circumstances which he saw the persons in. Sometimes when he came into a family, he would call for all the young people in it, that so he might very distinctly lay his holy hands upon every one of them, and bespeak the mercies of heaven for them all.

THE VOICE OF GOD IN THE THUNDER.

[*From the Same.*]

FIRST, it is to be premised, as herein implied and confessed, that the thunder is the work of the glorious God. It is true, that the thunder is a natural production, and by the common laws of matter and motion it is produced; there is in it a concourse of divers weighty clouds, clashing and breaking one against another, from whence arises a mighty sound, which grows yet more mighty by its resonancies. The subtil and sulphureous vapours among these clouds take fire in this combustion, and lightnings are thence darted forth; which, when they are somewhat grosser, are fulminated with an irresistible violence upon our territories.

This is the Cartesian account; tho' that which I rather choose is, that which the vegetable matter protruded by the subterraneous fire, and exhaled also by the force of the sun, in the vapour that makes our shower a mineral matter of nitre and sulphur, does also ascend into the atmosphere, and there it goes off with fierce explosions.

But, still, who is the author of those laws, according whereunto things are thus moved into thunder? yea, who is the first mover of them? Christians, 'tis our glorious God. There is an intimation somewhere ('tis in Psal. civ. 7,) that there was a most early and wondrous use of the thunder in the first creation of the world: but still the thunder itself, and the tonitruous disposition and generation with which the air is impregnated, was a part of that creation. Well, and whose workmanship is it all? "Ah! Lord, thou hast created all these things; and for thy pleasure they are and were created." It is also true, that angels may be reckoned among the causes of thunders: and for this cause, in the sentence of the Psalms, where they are called "flames of fire," one would have been at a loss whether angels or lightnings were intended, if the apostolical accommodation had not cleared it. But what though angels may have their peculiar influence upon thunders? Is it but the influence of an instrument; they are but instruments directed, ordered, limited by him who is the "God of thunders" and the "Lord of angels." Hence the thunder is ascribed unto our God all the Bible over; in the Scripture of truth, 'tis called the "thunder of God," oftener than I can presently quote unto you. And hence we find the thunder, even now and then, executing the purpose of God. Whose can it be but the "thunder of God," when the pleasure of God has been continually thereby accomplished?   .   .   .

One voice of the glorious God in the thunder, is, "that he is a glorious God, who makes the thunder." There is the marvellous glory of God seen in it, when he "thunders marvellously." Thus do these inferiour and meteorous "heavens declare the glory of God."

The power of God is the glory of God. Now, his thunder does proclaim his power. It is said, " the thunder of his power, who can understand ? " —that is, his powerful thunder ; the thunder gives us to understand that our God is a most powerful one. There is nothing able to stand before those lightnings, which are styled, " the arrows of God : " Castles fall, metals melt ; all flies, when " hot thunder-bolts " are scattered upon them. The very mountains are torn to pieces, when

> ———*Feriunt summos*
> *Fulmina montes.*———

Yea, to speak in the language of the prophets, fulfilled in the thunder storm that routed the Assyrian armies, " the mountains quake, the hills melt, the earth is burnt. Who can stand before his indignation ? and who can abide in the fierceness of his anger ? His fury is poured out like fire, and the rocks are thrown down by him." Suetonius, I think 'tis, who tells us that the haughty and profane Emperour Caligula would yet shrink, and shake, and cover his head at the least thunder, and run to hide himself under a bed. This truly is the voice of the thunder : " Let the proudest sinners tremble to rebel any more against a God who can thus discomfit them with shooting out his lightnings upon them ; sinners, where can you shew your heads, if the Highest give forth his voice with hail stones and coals of fire." Methinks there is that song of Hannah in the thunder (I. Sam. ii. 3, 10), " Talk no more so exceeding proudly ; let not arrogancy come out of your mouth. For the adversaries of the Lord shall be broken to pieces : out of heaven shall he thunder upon them." The omnipotent God in the thunder speaks to those hardy Typhons, that are found fighting against him ; and says, " Oh, do not harden yourselves against such a God ; you are not stronger than he ! " Yea, the great God is proposed as an object for our faith, as well as for our fear in his thunder.

If nothing be too hard for the thunder, we may think surely nothing is too hard for the Lord ! The arm that can wield thunder-bolts is a very mighty arm.

From hence pass on, and admire the other " glorious attributes " of God, which he doth in his thunder display most gloriously : when it thunders, let us adore the wisdom of that God, who thereby many ways does consult the welfare of the universe. Let us adore the justice of that God, who thereby many times has cut off his adversaries ; and let us adore the goodness of that God, who therein preserves us from imminent and impending desolations, and is not so severe as he would be,

> *Si quoties peccant homines sua fulmina mittat.*

A second voice of the glorious God in the thunder, is, " Remember the law of the glorious God that was given in thunder." The people of God were once gathered about a mountain, on which, from his right hand, issued a fiery law for them ; or a law given with lightning. At the promulgation of the ten commandments, we are told in Ex. xx. 18, "All people saw the thunderings, and the lightnings, and the mountain smoaking." Yea, they were such, that the apostle tells us, though Moses himself says nothing of it, they made Moses himself "exceedingly to fear and quake." Well, when it thunders, let us call to mind the commandments, which were once thus thundered unto the world ; and bear in mind that, with a voice of thunder, the Lord still says unto us, " Thou shalt love the Lord thy God with all thy heart, and all thy soul, and all thy strength ; and thou shalt love thy neighbour as thyself." But when the thunder causes us to reflect upon the commandments of our God, let there be a self-examination in that reflection.

Let us now examine ourselves, what is requir'd, and whether we have not omitted it ? what is forbidden, and whether we had not committed it ? and what provocation we have given unto the God of glory to speak unto us in his wrath and vex us in his displeasure. Blessed the thunder that shall thunder-strike us into the acknowledgments of a convinced and a repenting soul.

A third voice of the glorious God in the thunder, is, " Think on the future coming of the glorious God in the thunder, and in great glory." When the day of judgment shall arrive unto us, then "our God shall come, and shall not keep silence ; a fire shall devour before him, and it shall be very tempestuous round about him." The second coming of our Lord will be, as we are advised in II. Thes. i. 7, 8, "with his mighty angels in flaming fire ; " the clouds will be his chariot, but there will be prodigious thunders breaking forth from those clouds.

The redemption of the church, for which the Lord hath long been cried unto, will then be accomplished ; but at what rate ? The Lord will come in the thick clouds of the skies ; at the brightness that shall be before him thick clouds will pass, hail-stones and coals of fire; the Lord also will thunder in the heavens.

I say, then, does it thunder ?—Let us now realize unto ourselves that great and notable day of the Lord, which will be indeed a great and thundering day ! But how far should we now realize it ?—realize it so as to be ready for it ? Oh, count yourselves not safe till you get into such a condition of soul, that your hearts would even leap and spring within you, were you sure that in the very next thunders our precious Lord would make his descent unto us. What if the hour were now turned, wherein the judge of the whole world were going to break in upon us with fierce thunders, and make the mountains to smoke by his coming down upon them, and reign before his ancient people gloriously ? Could you gladly say, "Lo, this is the God of my salvation, and I have waited for him!" I say, let the thunders drive you on to this attainment.

A fourth voice of the glorious God in the thunder, is, "Make your peace with God immediately, lest by the stroke of his thunder he take you away in his wrath." Why is it that persons are usually in such a consternation at the thunder? Indeed, there is a complectional and constitutional weakness in many this way; they have such a disadvantage in a frightful temper, that no considerations can wholly overcome it. But most usually the frights of people at the thunder arise from the terms wherein they may suspect their own souls to stand before an angry God. Their consciences tell them that their sins are yet unpardoned, that their hearts are yet unrenewed, that their title to blessedness is yet unsettled, and that if the next thunder-clap should strike them dead, it had been good for them that they had never been born.

> *Hi sunt qui trepidant, et ad omnia fulgura pallent;*
> *Cum tonat, exanimes primo quoque murmure cœli.*

Here, then, is the voice of God in the thunder: "Art thou ready? Soul, art thou ready? Make ready presently, lest I call for thee before thou art aware." There is in thunder a vehement call unto that regeneration, unto that repenting of sin, that believing on Christ, and that consenting unto the demands of the new covenant, without which no man in his wits can comfortably hold up his face before the thunder. I have now in my house a mariner's compass, whereupon a thunder-clap had this odd effect, that the north point was thereby turned clear about unto the south; and so it will veer and stand ever since unto this day, though the thing happened above thirteen years ago.

I would to God that the next thunder-claps would give as effectual a turn unto all the unconverted souls among us! May the thunder awaken you to turn from every vanity to God in Christ without any delay, lest by the thunder itself it come quickly to be too late. It is a vulgar error, that the thunder never kills any who are asleep: Man, what if the thunder should kill thee in the dead sleep of thy unregeneracy? . . . .

A seventh voice of the glorious God in the thunder, is, "Hear the voice of my word, lest I make you fear the voice of my thunder." When the inhabitants of Egypt persisted in their disobedience to the word of God, it came to that at last, in Ex. ix. 23, "The Lord sent thunder, and the fire ran along upon the ground." Thus the eternal God commands men to let go their sins, and go themselves to serve him; if they are disobedient, they lay themselves open to fiery thunders. This, you may be sure, is the voice of God in the thunder, "Hear my still voice in my ordinances, lest you put me upon speaking to you with more angry thunderbolts." I have known it sometimes remarked that very notorious and resolved sleepers at sermons often have some remarkable suddenness in the circumstances of their death. Truly, if you are scandalously given to sleep under the word of God; and much more, if to sin under it; and most of all, if to scoff under it; it may be, your deaths will be rendered sudden by the other thunders of heaven lighting on you. When it thunders, God saith to all the hearers of his word ordinarily preached, "Consider this, and forget not God, lest he tear you in pieces, and there be none to deliver you."

Finally, And is there not this voice of the glorious God in thunder after all? "O be thankful to the gracious God, that the thunder does no more mischief to you all."

Whatever the witch-advocates may make of it, it is a scriptural and a rational assertion, that in the thunder there is oftentimes, by the permission of God, the agency of the devil. The devil is the prince of the air, and when God gives him leave, he has a vast power in the air, and armies that can make thunders in the air. We are certain that Satan had his efficiency in it, when the fire of God or the lightning fell upon part of Job's estate. How glad would he have been if the good man himself had been in the way, to have been torn in pieces! And perhaps it was the hellish policy of the wicked one, thus to make the good man suspicious that God was become his enemy. Popes that have been conjurors have made fire thus come from heaven, by their confederacies with evil spirits; and we have in our own land known evil spirits, plainly discovering their concurrence in disasters thus occasioned. A great man has therefore noted it, that thunders break oftener on churches than any other houses because the dæmons have a peculiar spite at houses that are set apart for the peculiar service of God.

I say, then, live we thus in the midst of thunders and devils too; and yet live we? Oh! let us be thankful to God for our lives. Are we not smitten by the great ordnance of heaven, discharging every now and then on every side of us? Let us be thankful to the great Lord of heaven, who makes even the wrath of hell to praise him, and the remainder of that wrath does he restrain.

OF ABIGAIL, HIS WIFE.

[An House of Mourning. 1703.]

GO then, my Dove, but now no longer mine!
Leave Earth and now in Heavenly Glory shine.
Bright for thy wisdom, goodness, beauty here;
Now brighter in a more Angelic Sphere.

Jesus, with whom thy soul did long to be,
Into his Ark and Arms has taken thee.
Dear friends with whom thou didst so dearly live
Feel thy one death to them a thousand give.
Thy prayers are done; thy alms are spent; thy pains
Are ended now in endless joys and gains.
The torch that gave my house its pleasant light,
Extinguished, leaves it in how dark a night!
I faint 'till thy last words to mind I call,
Rich words! "Heav'n, Heav'n will make amends for **all.**"

THE LAST DAYS OF INCREASE MATHER.

[*Memoirs of Remarkables in the Life and the Death of the Ever-Memorable Dr. Increase Mather.* 1724.]

AND now the time draws nigh, in which Dr. Mather is to die. He grows old, yet what a green olive-tree in the *proseucha* of his God!—*nec tarda senectus debilitat vires animi, mutatve vigorem.*

Old age came on. But what an one! How bright! How wise! How strong! And in what an uncommon measure serviceable! He had been an old man while he was yet a young man; I can quote a Rabby for it: *Sapiens appellatur senex, etiamsi diebus sit exiguus.* And now he was an old man his public performances had a vigor in them, which 'tis a rare thing to see a young man have any thing equal to.

How did the good people far and near discover even a growth of their appetite for the enjoyment of as much as might be obtained from him! The churches would not permit an ordination to be carried on without him as long as he was able to travel in a coach unto them.

Though in the prefaces of the useful books which he now published he repeated an ungrantable request unto his friends, "no longer to pray for his life," they only prayed the more for it. When he had finished forty-nine years of his public ministry he preached a sermon full of rare and rich thoughts upon "A Jubilee;" and he requested for a dismission from any further public labors. His flock prized them too much to hear of that; but anon, when they saw the proper time for it, that they might render his old age as easy as might be to him, they wisely and kindly voted it, "That the labors of the pulpit should be expected from him only when he should find himself able and inclined for them." It would be no strange thing if while he wanted yet some years to reach fourscore there should be found some little thing that might carry something of senile weakness in it. But he held it unto fourscore in a wonderful exercise of his intellectual powers, and with public ministrations to very great congregations, which his ministry continued still to give the greatest satisfaction to. A treatise which he published about this time, concerning " An Hoary Head found in the Way of Righteousness," notably described what he was himself, and as notably declared, what he was yet able to do. He continued preaching to vast assemblies ; and such well composed sermons that the notes taken by some ready writers after him, when communicated unto the public by the way of the press, found their acceptance in the churches. Among which ready writers we owe our particular thanks to a virtuous gentlewoman, whose exquisite pen helped several of his treatises into the world ; in some sort as the excellent Lady Rich did the most valuable and admirable books of Mr. Strong on " The Covenant." Yea, and even after fourscore the old prophetic strain had not forsaken him.

In September, 1720, he preached an awful sermon (from Amos iii. 7,) on this doctrine : " When God has an holy purpose to visit his people with great judgments, He uses to give them notice and warning of it beforehand." In the conclusion he expressly fortold ; first, " That an heavy judgment was impending over Boston, that would speedily be executed." And then, " That the churches of the country were near to some shocking dispensations." He added : " My brethren, I take no pleasure in testifying unto you of evil days. But when the Word of the Lord is like a fire in a man's bones, there must be something said that may awaken you out of your security." Now within a few months after this the small-pox was brought into Boston, and within as few months more the besom of destruction swept away near a thousand people. And how strangely was way made for the Destroying Angel to do his execution !

But let me not anticipate. I am saying that until fourscore the Doctor held it unto admiration ! And on the day of his attaining to fourscore he preached a sermon full of light and life on those words, Ezek. xvi. 5, " The day when thou wast born." They that wrote after him have printed it. The *mens et ratio et consilium* which are by Cicero mentioned as the prerogatives of " Old Age," were found in him to an uncommon degree. On very many accounts he might have said, as old Georgias did, *Nihil habeo propter quod senectutem meam accusem ;* yea, as a better man, old Drusius did, *Senectus mihi melior quam ipsa juventus.* But that which most of all gave him a comfortable old age, was what Calvin, who did not live to old age, well pitches on as the chiefest comfort of old age : *Tenendum est, præcipuam partem bonæ senectutis, in bona conscientia animoque ; sereno ac tranquillo consistere.* A good heart, filled with the love and peace of God and the soul of an Abraham.

In consideration of this εὐγηρία, it was not amiss for a grandson, upon the birthday on which he entered fourscore, thus to compliment him.

To my most honoured Grandfather, on the day of his entering the eightieth year of his age.

> To my Grandfather in all good so great,
> His nephew does his age congratulate.
> 'Tis not enough, Syr, that you live to see
> Such years ; we hope you'll our true Nestor be.
> We wish the years in which you live and preach,
> To those of a Methuselah may reach.
> 'Tis true, in common reckoning we suppose
> You want eight hundred eighty-six of those,
> But measuring life by works and not by years,
> Your age nine hundred sixty-nine appears.
> Methuselah had a bright father too;
> A "walker with his God ;" Syr, such as you.
> If you and we must have a parting day,
> Death, strike not !—Let him go in Enoch's way.
> And Syr, if prophets mayn't forever live,
> May you in Grandsons left by you survive.

But it is now time for me to tell that after fourscore the report of Moses did no longer want confirmation with him.   He began to be more sensible of those decays which not only caused him to recite the verse of the Roman satirist :

> *O quam continuis, et quantis plena senectus longa malis ! ——.*

but also caused him several times to say to me : " Be sure, you don't pray that you may live beyond fourscore! "   Yet now he preached nobly on " An Old Disciple ; " as well as many other subjects.

And now, he that had wished for " sufferings for the Lord," must be content with sufferings from the Lord.   Even these borne with the faith and patience of the saints have a sort of martyrdom in them, and will add unto the " far more exceeding and eternal weight of glory."

On September 25th, he did with an excellent and pathetic prayer, in a mighty auditory, conclude a " day of prayer" kept by his church, to obtain a good success of the Gospel and the growth of real and vital piety, with plentiful effusions of the good Spirit, especially upon the " Rising Generation."   Within two days after this he fell into an apoplectic sort of deliquium (very much occasioned, as it was thought, by too extreme a concern of his mind on some late occurrences at New Haven), out of which he recovered in a few minutes ; but it so enfeebled him, that he never went abroad any more.

However, his " wisdom yet remained with him."

Robert Calef.

BORN about 1648.　A merchant of Boston.　DIED at Roxbury, Mass., 1719.

A WARNING TO THE MINISTERS.

[More Wonders of the Invisible World. 1700.]

CHRISTIANITY had been but a short time in the world, when there was raised against it, not only open professed enemies, but secret and inbred underminers, who sought thereby to effect that which open force had been so often baffled in.　And notwithstanding that primitive purity and sincerity, which in some good measure was still retained, yet the cunning deceivers and apostate hereticks found opportunity to beguile the unwary, and this in fundamentals.

Among others which then sprung up, with but too much advantage, in the third century, the Maniche did spread his pestiferous sentiments, and taught the existence of two beings, or causes of all things, viz. a good and a bad : but these were soon silenced by the more orthodox doctors, and anathematized by general councils.　And at this day the American Indians, another sort of Maniche, entertaining (thus far) the same belief, hold it their prudence and interest to please that evil being, as well by perpetrating other murders, as by their bloody sacrifices, that so he may not harm them.　The iron teeth of time have now almost devoured the name of the former ; and as to the latter, it is to be hoped that as Christianity prevails among them, they will abhor such abominable belief.

And as those primitive times were not privileged against the spreading of dangerous heresy, so neither can any now pretend to any such immunity, though professing the enjoyment of a primitive purity.

Might a judgment be made from the books of the modern learned divines, or from the practice of courts, or from the faith of many who call themselves Christians, it might be modestly, though sadly, concluded, that the doctrine of the Maniche, at least great part of it, is so far from being forgotten, that 'tis almost everywhere professed.　We in these ends of the earth need not seek far for instances in each respect to demonstrate this.　The books here printed and recommended, not only by the respective authors, but by many of their brethren, do set forth that the devil inflicts plagues, wars, diseases, tempests, and can render the most solid things invisible, and can do things above and against the course of nature, and all natural causes.

Are these the expressions of orthodox believers? or are they not rather expressions becoming a Maniche, or a heathen, as agreeing far better with these than with the sacred oracles, our only rule? the whole current whereof is so diametrically opposite thereto, that it were almost endless to mention all the divine cautions against such abominable belief; he that runs may read, Psal. lxii. 11, and cxxxvi. 4. Lam. iii. 37. Amos iii. 6. Jer. iv. 22. Psal. lxxviii. 26, and clxviii. 6, 8. Job xxxviii. 22 to 34.

These places, with a multitude more, do abundantly testify, that the asserters of such power to be in the evil being, do speak in a dialect different from the Scriptures (laying a firm foundation for the Indians' adorations, which agrees well with what A. Ross sets forth, in his Mistag. Poetic. p. 116, that their ancients did worship the furies and their god *Averinci*, that they might forbear to hurt them).

And have not the courts in some parts of the world, by their practice, testified their concurrence with such belief; prosecuting to death many people upon that notion, of their improving such power of the evil one, to the raising of storms; afflicting and killing of others, though at great distance from them; doing things in their own persons above human strength; destroying cattle, flying in the air, turning themselves into cats or dogs, etc., which by the way must needs imply something of goodness to be in that evil being, who, though he has such power, would not exert it, were it not for this people, or else that they can some way add to this mighty power.

And are the people a whit behind in their beliefs? Is there any thing above mentioned, their strong faith looks upon to be too hard for this evil being to effect?

Here it will be answered, God permits it. Which answer is so far an owning the doctrine, that the devil has in his nature a power to do all these things, and can exert this power, except when he is restrained; which is in effect to say that God has made nature to fight against itself; that he has made a creature who has it in the power of his nature to overthrow nature, and to act above and against it. Which he that can believe may as well believe the greatest contradiction. That being which can do this in the smallest thing, can do it in the greatest. If Moses, with a bare permission, might stretch forth his rod, yet he was not able to bring plagues upon the Egyptians, or to divide the waters, without a commission from the Most High; so neither can that evil being perform any of this without a commission from the same power. The Scripture recites more miracles wrought by men than by angels good and bad. Though this doctrine be so dishonourable to the only Almighty Being, as to ascribe such attributes to the evil one, as are the incommunicable prerogative of him, who is the alone Sovereign Being, yet here is not all; but, as he that steers by a false compass, the further he sails the more he is out of his way; so, though there is in some things a variation from, there is in others a further progression in, or building upon, the said doctrine of the Maniche.

Men in this age are not content barely to believe such an exorbitant power to be in the nature of this evil being; but have imagined that he prevails with many to sign a book, or make a contract with him, whereby they are enabled to perform all the things above mentioned. Another account is given hereof, viz., That by virtue of such a covenant they attain power to commission him. And though the two parties are not agreed which to put it upon, whether the devil empowers the witch, or the witch commissions him; yet both parties are agreed in this, that one way or other the mischief is effected, and so the criminal becomes culpable of death. In the search after such a sort of criminals, how many countries have fallen into such convulsions, that neither the devastations made by a conquering enemy, nor the plague itself, have been so formidable. That not only good persons have thus been blemished in their reputations, but much innocent blood hath been shed, is testified even by those very books: *Cases of Conscience*, p. 33. *Remarkable Provid.* p. 179. *Memor. Provid.* p. 28.

And (to add) what less can be expected, when men, having taken up such a belief, of a covenanting, afflicting and killing witch, and, comparing it with the Scripture, finding no footsteps therein of such a sort of witch, have thereupon desperately concluded that, though the Scripture is full in it, that a witch should not live, yet that it has not at all described the crime, nor means whereby the culpable might be detected?

And hence they are fallen so far as to reckon it necessary to make use of those diabolical and bloody ways, always heretofore practiced, for their discovery; as finding that the rules, given to detect other crimes, are wholly useless for the discovery of such.

This is that which has produced that deluge of blood mentioned, and must certainly do so again, the same belief remaining.

And who can wonder, if Christians that are so easily prevailed with to lay aside their swords as useless, and so have lost their strength, are (with Samson) led blindfold into an idol temple, to make sport for enemies and infidels, and to do abominable actions, not only not Christian, but against even the light of nature and reason? And now, reverend fathers, you who are appointed as guides to the people, and whose lips should preserve knowledge; who are set as shepherds, and as watchmen; this matter appertains to you I did write to you formerly under this head, and acquainted you with my sentiments, requesting that if I erred, you would be pleased to shew it me by Scripture; but from your silence I gather that you approve thereof. For I may reasonably presume that you would have seen it your duty to have informed me better, if you had been sensible of any error. But if in this matter you have acquitted yourselves becoming the titles you are dignified with, you have cause of rejoicing in the midst of calamities that afflict a sinning world.

Particularly, if you have taught the people to fear God, and trust in him, and not to fear a witch or a devil; that the devil has no power to afflict any with diseases, or loss of cattle, etc., without a commission from the Most High; that he is so filled with malice, that whatever commission he may have against any, he will not fail to execute it; that no mortal ever was, or can be, able to commission him, or to lengthen his chain in the least, and that he who can commission him is God; and that the scriptures of truth not only assign the punishment of a witch but give sufficient rules to detect them by; and that, according to Mr. Gaul's fourth head, a witch is one that hates and opposes the word, work and worship of God, and seeks by a sign to seduce therefrom—that they who are guilty according to that head, are guilty of witchcraft, and by the law given by Moses were to be put to death :—If you have taught the people the necessity of charity, and the evil of entertaining so much as a jealousy against their neighbours for such crimes, upon the devil's suggestions to a person pretending to a spectral or diabolical sight; who utter their oracles from malice, frenzy, or a Satanical delusion—that to be inquisitive of such, whose spectres they see, or who it is that afflicts, in order to put the accused person's life in question, is a wickedness beyond what Saul was guilty of in going to the witch—that to consult with the dead, by the help of such as pretend to this spectral sight, and so to get information against the life of any person, is the worst sort of necromancy—that the pretending to drive away spectres, i.e., devils, with the hand, or by striking these to wound a person at a distance, cannot be without witchcraft, as pretending to a sign in order to deceive in matters of so high a nature—that 'tis ridiculous to think, by making laws against feeding, employing or rewarding of evil spirits, thereby to get rid of them.   .   .   .   .

Finally, if you have taught the people what to believe and practice, as to the probation of the accused, by their saying or not saying the Lord's prayer, and as to praying that the afflicted may be able to accuse, and have not shunned in these matters to declare the whole mind of God; you have then well acquitted yourselves (in time of general defection) as faithful watchmen. But if, instead of this, you have, some by word and writing propagated, others recommended, such writings, and abetted the false notions, which are so prevalent in this apostate age, it is high time to consider it. If when authority found themselves almost nonplussed in such prosecutions, and sent to you for your advice what they ought to do, and you have then thanked them for what they had already done (and thereby encouraged them to proceed in those very by-paths already fallen into) it so much the [more] nearly concerns you. Ezek. xxiii. 2 to 8.

To conclude: This whole people are invited and commanded to humble their souls before God, as for other causes, so for the errors that may have been fallen into in these prosecutions on either hand, and to pray that God would teach us what we know not, and help us wherein we have done amiss, that we may do so no more.

This more immediately concerns yourselves; for 'tis not supposed to be intended that God would shew us these things by inspiration; but that such who are called to it should shew the mind of God in these things on both hands, i.e., whether there has been any error in excess or deficiency, or neither in the one nor the other. And if you do not thus far serve the publick, you need not complain of great sufferings and unrighteous discouragements, if people do not applaud your conduct, as you might otherways have expected. But if you altogether hold your peace at such a time as this is, your silence, at least seemingly, will speak this language; that you are not concerned, though men ascribe the power and providence of the Almighty to the worst of his creatures—that if other ages or countries improve the doctrines and examples given them, either to the taking away of the life or reputations of innocents, you are well satisfied. Which, that there may be no shadow of a reason to believe but that your conduct herein may remove all such jealousies, and that God would be with you in declaring his whole mind to the people, is the earnest desire and prayer of, reverend sirs, yours to my utmost,

R. C.

TOUCHING THE SUPPOSED WITCHCRAFT IN NEW ENGLAND.

[*From the Same.*]

MR. PARRIS had been some years a minister in Salem Village, when this sad calamity, as a deluge, overflowed them, spreading itself far and near. He was a gentleman of liberal education; and, not meeting with any great encouragement, or advantage, in merchandising, to which for some time he applied himself, betook himself to the work of the ministry; this village being then vacant, he met with so much encouragement, as to settle in that capacity among them.

After he had been there about two years, he obtained a grant from a part of the town, that the house and land he occupied, and which had been allotted by the whole people to the ministry, should be and remain to him, etc., as his own estate in fee simple. This occasioned great divisions both between the inhabitants themselves, and between a considerable part of them and their said minister; which divisions were but as a beginning, or *prœludium*, to what immediately followed.

It was the latter end of February, 1691, when divers young persons belonging to Mr. Parris's family, and one or more of the neighbourhood, began to act after a strange and unusual manner, viz., as by getting into holes, and creeping under chairs and stools, and to use sundry odd postures and antick gestures, uttering foolish, ridiculous speeches, which neither they themselves nor any others could make sense of. The physicians that were called could assign no reason for this; but it seems one of them, having recourse to the old shift, told them he was afraid they were bewitched. Upon such suggestions, they that were concerned applied themselves to fasting and prayer, which was attended not only in their own private families, but with calling in the help of others. March the 11th, Mr. Parris invited several neighbouring ministers to join with him in keeping a solemn day of prayer at his own house. The time of the exercise, those persons were for the most part silent; but after any one prayer was ended, they would act and speak strangely and ridiculously; yet were such as had been well educated, and of good behaviour; the one, a girl of 11 or 12 years old, would sometimes seem to be in a convulsion fit, her limbs being twisted several ways, and very stiff, but presently her fit would be over. . . . .

Those ill affected or afflicted persons named several that they said they saw, when in their fits, afflicting them.

The first complained of was the said Indian woman, named Tituba: she confessed that the devil urged her to sign a book, which he presented to her, and also to work mischief to the children, etc. She was afterwards committed to prison, and lay there till sold for her fees. The account she since gives of it is, that her master did beat her, and otherways abuse her, to make her confess and accuse (such as he called) her sister-witches; and that whatsoever she said by way of confessing, or accusing others, was the effect of such usage: her master refused to pay her fees, unless she would stand to what she had said.

The children complained likewise of two other women, to be the authors of their hurt, viz., Sarah Good, who had long been counted a melancholy or distracted woman; and one Osborn, an old bed-ridden woman; which two were persons so ill thought of, that the accusation was the more readily believed; and, after examination before two Salem magistrates, were committed. March the 19th, Mr. Lawson (who had been formerly a preacher at the said village) came thither, and hath since set forth, in print, an account of what then passed; about which time, as he saith, they complained of goodwife Cory, and goodwife Nurse, members of churches at the Village and at Salem, many others being by that time accused.

March the 21st. Goodwife Cory was examined before the magistrates of Salem, at the meeting house in the village, a throng of spectators being present to see the novelty. Mr. Noyes, one of the ministers of Salem, began with prayer; after which the prisoner being called, in order to answer to what should be alleged against her, she desired that she might go to prayer; and was answered by the magistrates, that they did not come to hear her pray, but to examine her.

The number of the afflicted were at that time about ten, viz., Mrs. Pope, Mrs. Putman, goodwife Bibber and goodwife Goodall, Mary Wolcott, Mercy Lewes (at Thomas Putman's) and Dr. Grigg's maid, and three girls, viz., Elizabeth Parris, daughter to the minister, Abigail Williams, his niece, and Ann Putman, which last three were not only the beginners, but were also the chief, in these accusations. These ten were most of them present at the examination, and did vehemently accuse her of afflicting them, by biting, pinching, strangling, etc., and they said they did in their fits see her likeness coming to them, and bringing a book for them to sign. Mr. Hathorn, a magistrate of Salem, asked her why she afflicted those children. She said, she did not afflict them. He asked her who did then. She said, "I do not know, how should I know?" She said, they were poor distracted creatures, and no heed to be given to what they said. Mr. Hathorn and Mr. Noyes replied that it was the judgment of all that were there present, that they were bewitched, and only she (the accused) said they were distracted. She was accused by them, that the black man whispered to her in her ear now (while she was upon examination) and that she had a yellow bird, that did use to suck between her fingers, and that the said bird did suck now in the assembly. Order being given to look in that place to see if there were any sign, the girl that pretended to see it said, that it was too late now, for she had removed a pin, and put it on her head; it was upon search found, that a pin was there sticking upright. When the accused had any motion of their body, hands or mouth, the accusers would cry out; as when she bit a lip, they would cry out of being bitten; if she grasped one hand with the other, they would cry out of being pinched by her, and would produce marks; so of the other motions of her body, as complaining of being pressed, when she leaned to the seat next to her; if she stirred her feet, they would stamp, and cry out of pain there. After the hearing, the said Cory was committed to Salem prison, and then their crying out of her abated. .   .   .   .

A child of Sarah Good's was likewise apprehended, being between 4 and 5 years old. The accusers said this child bit them, and would shew such like marks, as those of a small set of teeth, upon their arms: as many of the afflicted as the child cast its eye upon, would complain they were in torment: which child they also committed. .   .   .   .

March 31, 1692, was set apart as a day of solemn humiliation at Salem, upon the account of this business; on which day Abigail Williams said, "that she saw a great number of persons in the village at the administration of a mock sacrament, where they had bread as red as raw flesh, and red drink."

April 1. Mercy Lewis affirmed, "that she saw a man in white, with whom she went into a glorious place," viz., in her fits, "where was no light of the sun, much less of candles, yet was full of light and brightness, with a great multitude in white glittering robes, who sang the song in Rev. v. 9, and the cx. and cxlix. Psalms; and was given that she might tarry no longer in this place." This white man is said to have appeared several times to others of them, and to have given them notice how long it should be before they should have another fit.

April 3. Being sacrament day at the Village, Sarah Cloyce, sister to goodwife Nurse, a member of one of the churches, was (though it seems with difficulty prevailed with to be) present; but being entered the place, and Mr. Parris naming his text, John vi. 70, "Have not I chosen you twelve, and one of you is a devil?" (for what cause may rest as a doubt, whether upon the account of her sister's being committed, or because of the choice of that text) she rose up and went out; the wind shutting the door forcibly, gave occasion to some to suppose she went out in anger, and might occasion a suspicion of her; however, she was soon after complained of, examined and committed.

April 11. By this time the number of the accused and accusers being much increased, there was a publick examination at Salem, six of the magistrates with several ministers being present. There appeared several who complained against others with hideous clamours and screechings. Goodwife Proctor was brought thither, being accused or cried out against; her husband coming to attend and assist her, as there might be need, the accusers cried out of him also, and that with so much earnestness, that he was committed with his wife. About this time, besides the experiment of the afflicted falling at the sight, etc., they put the accused upon saying the Lord's prayer, which one among them performed, except in that petition, "deliver us from evil," she expressed it thus, "deliver us from all evil": this was looked upon as if she prayed against what she was now justly under, and being put upon it again, and repeating those words, "hallowed be thy name" she expressed it, "hollowed be thy name:" this was counted a depraving the words, as signifying to make void, and so a curse rather than a prayer: upon the whole it was concluded that she also could not say it, etc. Proceeding in this work of examination and commitment, many were sent to prison. .   .   .   .

Mrs. Cary, of Charlestown, was examined and committed. Her husband, Mr. Nathaniel Cary, has given account thereof, as also of her escape, to this effect:

"I having heard, some days, that my wife was accused of witchcraft, being much disturbed at it, by advice we went to Salem Village, to see if the afflicted knew her; we arrived there 24th May; it happened to be a day appointed for examination; accordingly, soon after our arrival, Mr. Hathorn and Mr. Curwin, etc., went to the meeting-house, which was the place appointed for that work; the minister began with prayer; and having taken care to get a convenient place, I observed that the afflicted were two girls of about ten years old, and about two or three others, of about eighteen; one of the girls talked most, and could discern more than the rest. The prisoners were called in one by one, and as they came in were cried out of, etc. The prisoners were placed about seven or eight foot from the justices, and the accusers between the justices and them; the prisoners were ordered to stand right before the justices, with an officer appointed to hold each hand, lest they should therewith afflict them; and the prisoners' eyes must be constantly on the justices; for if they looked on the afflicted, they would either fall into their fits, or cry out of being hurt by them. After examination of the prisoners, who it was afflicted these girls, etc., they were put upon saying the Lord's prayer, as a trial of their guilt. After the afflicted seemed to be out of their fits, they would look steadfastly on some one person, and frequently not speak; and then the justices said they were struck dumb, and after a little time would speak again; then the justices said to the accusers, 'Which of you will go and touch the prisoner at the bar?' Then the most courageous would adventure, but before they had made three steps would ordinarily fall down as in a fit. The justices ordered that they should be taken up and carried to the prisoner, that she might touch them; and as soon as they were touched by the accused, the justices would say, 'they are well,' before I could discern any alteration; by which I observed that the justices understood the manner of it. Thus far I was only as a spectator; my wife also was there part of the time, but no notice taken of her by the afflicted, except once or twice they came to her and asked her name.

"But I having an opportunity to discourse Mr. Hale (with whom I had formerly acquaintance) I took his advice what I had best to do, and desired of him that I might have an opportunity to speak with her that accused my wife; which he promised should be, I acquainting him that I reposed my trust in him. Accordingly he came to me after the examination was over, and told me I had now an opportunity to speak with the said accuser, viz., Abigail Williams, a girl of 11 or 12 years old; but that we could not be in private at Mr. Parris's house, as he had promised me; we went therefore into the ale-house, where an Indian man attended us, who it seems was one of the afflicted: to him we gave some cider: he shewed several scars, that seemed as if they had been long there, and shewed them as done by witchcraft, and acquainted us that his wife, who also was a slave, was imprisoned for witchcraft. And now, instead of one accuser, they all came in, who began to tumble down like swine; and then three women were called in to attend them. We in the room were all at a stand, to see who they would cry out of; but in a short time they cried out, 'Cary'; and immediately after a warrant was sent from the justices to bring my wife before them, who were sitting in a chamber near by, waiting for this.

"Being brought before the justices, her chief accusers were two girls. My wife declared to the justices, that she never had any knowledge of them before that day. She was forced to stand with her arms stretched out. I did request that I might hold one of her hands, but it was denied me; then she desired me to wipe the tears from her eyes, and the sweat from her face, which I did; then she desired she might lean herself on me, saying she should faint.

"Justice Hathorn replied, she had strength enough to torment those persons, and she should have strength enough to stand. I speaking something against their cruel proceedings, they commanded me to be silent, or else I should be turned out of the room. The Indian before mentioned was also brought in, to be one of her accusers: being come in he now (when before the justices) fell down and tumbled about like a hog, but said nothing. The justices asked the girls who afflicted the Indian; they answered, she (meaning my wife), and [that she] now lay upon him; the justices ordered her to touch him, in order to his cure, but her head must be turned another way, lest, instead of curing, she should make him worse, by her looking on him, her hand being guided to take hold of his; but the Indian took hold on her hand, and pulled her down on the floor, in a barbarous manner; then his hand was taken off, and her hand put on his, and the cure was quickly wrought. I, being extremely troubled at their inhuman dealings, uttered a hasty speech, 'That God would take vengeance on them, and desired that God would deliver us out of the hands of unmerciful men.' Then her mittimus was writ. I did with difficulty and charge obtain the liberty of a room, but no beds in it; if there had, could have taken but little rest that night. She was committed to Boston prison; but I obtained a habeas corpus to remove her to Cambridge prison, which is in our county of Middlesex. Having been there one night, next morning the jailer put irons on her legs (having received such a command); the weight of them was about eight pounds: these with her other afflictions soon brought her into convulsion fits, so that I thought she would have died that night. I sent to entreat that the irons might be taken off; but all entreaties were in vain, if it would have saved her life, so that in this condition she must continue. The trials at Salem coming on, I went thither, to see how things were managed; and finding that the spectre evidence was there received, together with idle, if not malicious stories, against people's lives, I did easily see which way it would go; for the same evidence that served for one, would serve for all the rest. I acquainted her with her danger; and that if she were carried to Salem to be tried, I feared she would never return. I did my utmost that she might have her trial in our own county, I with several others petitioning the judge for it, and were put in hopes of it; but I soon saw so much, that I understood thereby it was not intended, which put me upon consulting the means of her escape; which through the goodness of God was effected, and she got to Rhode-Island, but soon found herself not safe when there, by reason of the pursuit after her; from thence she went to New York, along with some others that had escaped their cruel hands; where we found his excellency Benjamin Fletcher, Esq, governor, who was very courteous to us. After this, some of my goods were seized in a friend's hands, with whom I had left them, and myself imprisoned by the sheriff, and kept in custody half a day, and then dismissed; but to speak of their usage of the prisoners, and their inhumanity shewn to them at the time of their execution, no sober Christian could bear. They had also trials of cruel mockings; which is the more, considering what a people for religion, I mean the profession of it, we have been; those that suffered being many of them church members, and most of them unspotted in their conversation, till their adversary the devil took up this method for accusing them." . . . .

The 30th of June, the court according to adjournment again sat; five more were tried, viz., Sarah Good and Rebecca Nurse, of Salem Village; Susanna Martin, of Amsbury; Elizabeth How, of Ipswich; and Sarah Wildes, of Topsfield: these were all condemned that sessions, and were all executed on the 19th of July.

At the trial of Sarah Good, one of the afflicted fell in a fit; and after coming out of it she cried out of the prisoner, for stabbing her in the breast with a knife, and that she had broken the knife in stabbing of her; accordingly a piece of the blade of a knife was found about her. Immediately information being given to the court, a young man was called, who produced a haft and part of the blade, which the court having viewed and compared, saw it to be the same; and upon inquiry the young man affirmed, that yesterday he happened to break that knife, and that he cast away the upper part, this afflicted person being then present. The young man was dismissed, and she was bidden by the court not to tell lies; and was improved after (as she had been before) to give evidence against the prisoners.

At execution, Mr. Noyes urged Sarah Good to confess, and told her she was a witch, and she knew she was a witch; to which she replied, "You are a liar; I am no more a witch than you are a wizard; and if you take away my life, God will give you blood to drink."

VOL. II.—12

At the trial of Rebecca Nurse, this was remarkable that the jury brought in their verdict not guilty; immediately all the accusers in the court, and suddenly after all the afflicted out of court, made an hideous outcry, to the amazement not only of the spectators, but the court also seemed strangely surprised: one of the judges expressed himself not satisfied: another of them, as he was going off the bench, said they would have her indicted anew. The chief judge said he would not impose upon the jury; but intimated as if they had not well considered one expression of the prisoner when she was upon trial, viz., that when one Hobbs, who had confessed herself to be a witch, was brought into the court to witness against her, the prisoner, turning her head to her, said, "What, do you bring her? she is one of us," or to that effect; this, together with the clamours of the accusers, induced the jury to go out again, after their verdict, not guilty. But not agreeing, they came into the court; and she being then at the bar, her words were repeated to her, in order to have had her explanation of them; and she making no reply to them, they found the bill, and brought her in guilty; these words being the inducement to it, as the foreman has signified in writing.   .   .   .   .

When goodwife Nurse was informed what use was made of these words, she put in this following declaration into the court:

"These presents do humbly shew to the honoured court and jury, that I being informed that the jury brought me in guilty, upon my saying that goodwife Hobbs and her daughter were of our company; but I intended no otherways, than as they were prisoners with us, and therefore did then, and yet do, judge them not legal evidence against their fellow prisoners. And I being something hard of hearing, and full of grief, none informing me how the court took up my words, and therefore had no opportunity to declare what I intended, when I said they were of our company.

REBECCA NURSE."

After her condemnation she was by one of the ministers of Salem excommunicated; yet the governor saw cause to grant a reprieve; which when known (and some say immediately upon granting) the accusers renewed their dismal outcries against her, insomuch that the governor was by some Salem gentlemen prevailed with to recall the reprieve, and she was executed with the rest.

The testimonials of her Christian behaviour, both in the course of her life and at her death, and her extraordinary care in educating her children, and setting them good examples, etc., under the hands of so many, are so numerous, that for brevity they are here omitted.

It was at the trial of these that one of the accusers cried out publicly of Mr. Willard, minister in Boston, as afflicting of her: she was sent out of the court, and it was told about she was mistaken in the person.

August 5. The court again sitting, six more were tried on the same account, viz., Mr. George Burroughs, sometime minister of Wells, John Proctor, and Elizabeth Proctor his wife, with John Willard, of Salem Village, George Jacobs, Sr., of Salem, and Martha Carrier, of Andover; these were all brought in guilty, and condemned; and were all executed, August 19, except Proctor's wife, who pleaded pregnancy.

Mr. Burroughs was carried in a cart with the others, through the streets of Salem to execution. When he was upon the ladder, he made a speech for the clearing of his innocency, with such solemn and serious expressions, as were to the admiration of all present: his prayer (which he concluded by repeating the Lord's prayer) was so well worded, and uttered with such composedness, and such (at least seeming) fervency of spirit, as was very affecting and drew tears from many, so that it seemed to some that the spectators would hinder the execution. The accusers said the black man stood and dictated to him. As soon as he was turned off, Mr. Cotton Mather, being mounted upon a horse, addressed himself to the people, partly to declare that he [Burroughs] was no ordained minister, and partly to possess the people of his guilt, saying that the devil has often been transformed into an angel of light; and this did somewhat appease the people and the executions went on. When he was cut down, he was dragged by the halter to a hole, or grave, between the rocks, about two foot deep, his shirt and breeches being pulled off, and an old pair of trowsers of one executed put on his lower parts; he was so put in, together with Willard and Carrier, that one of his hands and his chin, and a foot of one of them, were left uncovered.

John Willard had been employed to fetch in several that were accused; but taking dissatisfaction from his being sent to fetch up some that he had better thoughts of, he declined the service; and presently after he himself was accused of the same crime, and that with such vehemency, that they sent after him to apprehend him. He had made his escape as far as Nashawag, about forty miles from Salem; yet 'tis said those accusers did then presently tell the exact time, saying, "Now Willard is taken."

John Proctor and his wife being in prison, the sheriff came to his house and seized all the goods, provisions and cattle that he could come at, and sold some of the cattle at half price, and killed others, and put them up for the West-Indies; threw out the beer out of a barrel, and carried away the barrel; emptied a pot of broth, and took away the pot, and left nothing in the house for the support of the children. No part of the said goods are known to be returned. Proctor earnestly requested Mr. Noyes to pray with and for him; but it was wholly denied, because he would not own himself to be a witch. . . . . He pleaded very hard at execution for a little respite of time, saying that he was not fit to die; but it was not granted.

Old Jacobs being condemned, the sheriff and officers came and seized all he had; his wife had her wedding ring taken from her, but with great difficulty obtained it again. She was forced to buy provisions of the sheriff, such as he had taken, towards her own support, which not being sufficient, the neighbours in charity relieved her.

Margaret Jacobs being one that had confessed her own guilt, and testified against her grandfather Jacobs, Mr. Burroughs and John Willard, she the day before executions came to Mr. Burroughs, acknowledging that she had belied them, and begged Mr. Burroughs's forgiveness; who not only forgave her, but also prayed with and for her.   .   .   .   .

Giles Cory pleaded not guilty to his indictment, but would not put himself on trial by the jury (they having cleared none upon trial) and knowing there would be the same witnesses against him, rather chose to undergo what death they would put him to. In pressing, his tongue being pressed out of his mouth, the sheriff with his cane forced it in again when he was dying. He was the first in New-England that was ever pressed to death.

The cart, going to the hill with these eight to execution, was for some time at a set; the afflicted and others said that the devil hindered it, etc.

Martha Cory, wife to Giles Cory, protesting her innocency, concluded her life with an eminent prayer upon the ladder.

Wardwell, having formerly confessed himself guilty, and after denied it, was soon brought upon his trial; his former confession and spectre testimony was all that appeared against him. At execution, while he was speaking to the people, protesting his innocency, the executioner being at the same time smoking tobacco, the smoke coming in his face interrupted his discourse; those accusers said the devil hindered him with smoke.

Mary Easty, sister also to Rebecca Nurse, when she took her last farewell of her husband, children and friends, was, as is reported by them present, as serious, religious, distinct and affectionate as could well be expressed, drawing tears from the eyes of almost all present.   .   .   .   .

Before her death she put up the following petition:

"To the honourable judge and bench now sitting in judicature in Salem, and the reverend ministers, humbly sheweth, That whereas your humble poor petitioner, being condemned to die, doth humbly beg of you to take it into your judicious and pious consideration, that your poor and humble petitioner, knowing my own innocency (blessed be the Lord for it) and seeing plainly the wiles and subtilty of my accusers, by myself, cannot but judge charitably of others, that are going the same way with myself, if the Lord step not mightly in. I was confined a whole month on the same account that I am now condemned, and then cleared by the afflicted persons, as some of your honours know; and in two days' time I was cried out upon by them, and have been confined, and now am condemned to die. The Lord above knows my innocency then, and likewise doth now, as at the great day will be known to men and angels. I petition to your honours not for my own life, for I know I must die, and my appointed time is set; but the Lord he knows if it be possible that no more innocent blood be shed, which undoubtedly cannot be avoided in the way and course you go in. I question not, but your honours do the utmost of your powers, in the discovery and detecting of witchcraft and witches, and would not be guilty of innocent blood for the world; but by my own innocency I know you are in the wrong way. The Lord in his infinite mercy direct you in this great work, if it be his blessed will, that innocent blood be not shed. I would humbly beg of you that your honours would be pleased to examine some of those confessing witches, I being confident there are several of them have belied themselves and others, as will appear, if not in this world, I am sure in the world to come, whither I am going; and I question not but yourselves will see an alteration in these things. They say, myself and others have made a league with the devil; we cannot confess; I know and the Lord he knows (as will shortly appear) they belie me, and so I question not but they do others; the Lord alone, who is the searcher of all hearts, knows, as I shall answer it at the tribunal seat, that I know not the least thing of witchcraft, therefore I cannot, I durst not, belie my own soul. I beg your honours not to deny this my humble petition, from a poor, dying, innocent person, and I question not but the Lord will give a blessing to your endeavours.　　　　　　　　　　　　　　　　MARY EASTY."

After execution, Mr. Noyes, turning him to the bodies, said, "What a sad thing it is to see eight firebrands of hell hanging there!"

In October, 1692, one of Wenham complained of Mrs. Hale, whose husband, the minister of Beverly, had been very forward in these prosecutions; but being fully satisfied of his wife's sincere Christianity caused him to alter his judgment; for it was come to a stated controversy, among the New-England divines, whether the devil could afflict in a good man's shape; it seems nothing else could convince him, yet when it came so near to himself he was soon convinced, that the devil might so afflict. Which same reason did afterwards prevail with many others, and much influenced to the succeeding change at trials.　　.　　　.　　　.

But before this, the said Bishop's eldest son having married into that family of the Putmans, who were chief prosecutors in this business, he holding a cow to be branded lest it should be seized, and having a push or boil upon his thigh, with his straining it broke; this is that that was pretended to be burnt with the said brand, and is one of the bones thrown to the dogmatical to pick, in "Wonders of the Invisible World," p. 143. The other, of a corner of a sheet, pretended to be taken from a spectre; it is known that it was provided the day before by that afflicted person; and the third bone of a spindle is almost as easily provided, as the piece of the knife; so that Apollo needs not herein be consulted, etc.

Mr. Philip English, and his wife, having made their escape out of prison, Mr. Corwin, the sheriff, seized his estate, to the value of about fifteen hundred pound, which was wholly lost to him, except about three hundred pound value (which was afterwards restored.)

After goodwife Hoar was condemned, her estate was seized, and was also bought again for eight pound.

George Jacobs, son to old Jacobs, being accused, he fled; then the officers came to his house; his wife was a woman crazy in her senses, and had been so several years. She it seems had been also accused. There were in the house with her only four small children, and one of them sucked her eldest daughter, being in prison: the officer persuaded her out of the house, to go along with him, telling her she should speedily return; the children ran a great way after her, crying.

When she came where the afflicted were, being asked, they said they did not know her; at length one said, "Don't you know Jacobs, the old witch?" and then they cried out of her, and fell down in their fits. She was sent to prison, and lay there ten months; the neighbours of pity took care of the children to preserve them from perishing.

About this time a new scene was begun; one Joseph Ballard, of Andover, whose wife was ill (and after died of a fever), sent to Salem for some of those accusers, to tell him who afflicted his wife; others did the like: horse and man were sent from several places to fetch those accusers who had the spectral sight, that they might thereby tell who afflicted those that were any ways ill.

When these came into any place where such were, usually they fell into a fit: after which, being asked who it was that afflicted the person, they would, for the most part, name one whom they said sat on the head, and another that sat on the lower parts, of the afflicted. Soon after Ballard's sending (as above) more than fifty of the people of Andover were complained of, for afflicting their neighbours. Here it was that many accused themselves of riding upon poles through the air; many parents believing their children to be witches, and many husbands their wives, etc. When these accusers came to the house of any upon such account, it was ordinary for other young people to be taken in fits, and to have the same spectral sight.

Mr. Dudley Bradstreet, a justice of peace in Andover, having granted out warrants against and committed thirty or forty to prison, for the supposed witchcrafts, at length saw cause to forbear granting out any more

warrants.   Soon after which, he and his wife were cried out of; himself
was (by them) said to have killed nine persons by witchcraft, and found it
his safest course to make his escape.   .   .   .   .

A worthy gentleman of Boston being about this time accused by those
at Andover, he sent by some particular friends a writ to arrest those accusers in a thousand pound action for defamation, with instructions to
them to inform themselves of the certainty of the proof, in doing which
their business was perceived, and from thenceforward the accusations at
Andover generally ceased.

In October some of these accusers were sent for to Gloucester, and
occasioned four women to be sent to prison; but Salem prison being so
full it could receive no more, two were sent to Ipswich prison.   In November they were sent for again by Lieutenant Stephens, who was told
that a sister of his was bewitched; in their way, passing over Ipswich-
bridge, they met with an old woman, and instantly fell into their fits.
But by this time the validity of such accusations being much questioned,
they found not that encouragement they had done elsewhere, and soon
withdrew.

These accusers swore that they saw three persons sitting upon Lieutenant Stephens's sister till she died; yet bond was accepted for those
three.

And now nineteen persons having been hanged, and one pressed to death,
and eight more condemned, in all twenty and eight, of which above a third
part were members of some of the churches in New-England, and more
than half of them of a good conversation in general, and not one cleared;
about fifty having confessed themselves to be witches, of which not one
executed; above an hundred and fifty in prison, and above two hundred
more accused; the special commission of oyer and terminer comes to a
period, which has no other foundation than the governor's commission;
and had proceeded in the manner of swearing witnesses, viz., by holding
up the hand (and by receiving evidences in writing), according to the
ancient usage of this country; as also having their indictments in English.
In the trials, when any were indicted for afflicting, pining and wasting
the bodies of particular persons by witchcraft, it was usual to hear evidence of matter foreign, and of perhaps twenty or thirty years standing,
about oversetting carts, the death of cattle, unkindness to relations, or
unexpected accidents befalling after some quarrel.   Whether this was
admitted by the law of England, or by what other law, wants to be determined; the executions seemed mixed, in pressing to death for not pleading, which most agrees with the laws of England, and sentencing women
to be hanged for witchcraft, according to the former practice of this country, and not by burning, as is said to have been the law of England.   And
though the confessing witches were many, yet not one of them that

confessed their own guilt, and abode by their confession, was put to death.

Here followeth what account some of those miserable creatures give of their confession under their own hands:

"We, whose names are under written, inhabitants of Andover, when as that horrible and tremendous judgment beginning at Salem Village, in the year 1692, (by some called witchcraft) first breaking forth at Mr. Parris's house, several young persons being seemingly afflicted, did accuse several persons for afflicting them, and many there believing it so to be; we being informed that if a person were sick, the afflicted persons could tell what or who was the cause of that sickness: Joseph Ballard, of Andover (his wife being sick at the same time) he either from himself, or by the advice of others, fetched two of the persons, called the afflicted persons, from Salem Village to Andover: which was the beginning of that dreadful calamity that befell us in Andover. And the authority in Andover, believing the said accusations to be true, sent for the said persons to come together to the meeting-house in Andover (the afflicted persons being there.) After Mr. Barnard had been at prayer, we were blindfolded, and our hands were laid upon the afflicted persons, they being in their fits, and falling into their fits at our coming into their presence (as they said) and some led us and laid our hands upon them, and then they said they were well, and that we were guilty of afflicting of them; whereupon we were all seized as prisoners, by a warrant from a justice of the peace, and forthwith carried to Salem. And by reason of that sudden surprisal, we knowing ourselves altogether innocent of that crime, we were all exceedingly astonished and amazed, and affrighted even out of our reason; and our nearest and dearest relations, seeing us in that dreadful condition, and knowing our great danger, apprehending that there was no other way to save our lives, as the case was then circumstanced, but by our confessing ourselves to be such and such persons, as the afflicted represented us to be, they out of tender love and pity persuaded us to confess what we did confess. And indeed that confession, that it is said we made, was no other than what was suggested to us by some gentlemen; they telling us, that we were witches, and they knew it, and we knew it, and they knew that we knew it, which made us think that it was so; and our understanding, our reason and our faculties almost gone, we were not capable of judging our condition; as also the hard measures they used with us rendered us uncapable of making our defence; but said any thing and every thing which they desired; and most of what we said was but in effect a consenting to what they said. Sometime after, when we were better composed, they telling of us what we had confessed, we did profess that we were innocent, and ignorant of such things. And we hearing that Samuel

Wardwell had renounced his confession, and quickly after was condemned and executed, some of us were told that we were going after Wardwell.

MARY OSGOOD,	ABIGAIL BARKER,
MARY TILER,	SARAH WILSON,
DELIV. DANE,	HANNAH TILER."

It may here be further added, concerning those that did confess, that besides that powerful argument, of life (and freedom from hardships, not only promised, but also performed to all that owned their guilt) there are numerous instances, too many to be here inserted, of the tedious examinations before private persons, many hours together; they all that time urging them to confess (and taking turns to persuade them) till the accused were wearied out by being forced to stand so long, or for want of sleep, etc., and so brought to give an assent to what they said; they then asking them, "Were you at such a witch-meeting?" or "Have you signed the devil's book?" etc., upon their replying, "Yes," the whole was drawn into form, as their confession.

But that which did mightily further such confessions was, their nearest and dearest relations urging them to it. These, seeing no other way of escape for them, thought it the best advice that could be given; hence it was that the husbands of some, by counsel often urging, and utmost earnestness, and children upon their knees intreating, have at length prevailed with them to say they were guilty.   .   .   .

April 25, 1693. The first superior court was held at Boston, for the county of Suffolk; the judges were the lieutenant Governor, Mr. Danforth, Mr. Richards, and Mr. Sewall, esquires; where (besides the acquitting Mr. John Aldin by proclamation) the most remarkable was, what related to Mary Watkins, who had been a servant, and lived about seven miles from Boston, having formerly accused her mistress of witchcraft, and was supposed to be distracted; she was threatened, if she persisted in such accusations, to be punished. This, with the necessary care to recover her health, had that good effect, that she not only had her health restored, but also wholly acquitted her mistress of any such crimes, and continued in health till the return of the year, and then again falling into melancholy humours, she was found strangling herself: her life being hereby prolonged, she immediately accused herself of being a witch; was carried before a magistrate, and committed. At this court a bill of indictment was brought to the grand jury against her, and her confession upon her examination given in as evidence; but these, not wholly satisfied herewith, sent for her, who gave such account of herself, that they (after they had returned into the court to ask some questions) twelve of them agreed to find *ignoramus*, but the court was pleased to send them out again, who again at coming in returned it as before. She was continued for some time in prison, etc., and at length was sold to Virginia. About this time the prisoners in all the prisons were released.

To omit here the mentioning of several wenches in Boston, etc., who pretended to be afflicted, and accused several, the ministers often visiting them, and praying with them, concerning whose affliction narratives are in being, in manuscript; not only these, but the generality of those accusers, may have since convinced the ministers, by their vicious courses, that they might err in extending too much charity to them.

The conclusion of the whole in the Massachusetts colony was, Sir William Phips, governor, being called home, before he went he pardoned such as had been condemned, for which they gave about thirty shillings each to the King's attorney.   .   .   .   .

Before this, the government issued forth the following proclamation:

By the honourable the lieutenant governor, council and assembly of his majesty's province of the Massachusetts-bay, in general court assembled.

Whereas, the anger of God is not yet turned away, but his hand is still stretched out against his people in manifold judgments, particularly in drawing out to such a length the troubles of Europe, by a perplexing war; and more especially respecting ourselves in this province, in that God is pleased still to go on in diminishing our substance, cutting short our harvest, blasting our most promising undertakings more ways than one, unsettling of us, and by his more immediate hand snatching away many out of our embraces by sudden and violent deaths, even at this time when the sword is devouring so many both at home and abroad, and that after many days of public and solemn addressing of him: and although, considering the many sins prevailing in the midst of us, we cannot but wonder at the patience and mercy moderating these rebukes, yet we cannot but also fear that there is something still wanting to accompany our supplications; and doubtless there are some particular sins, which God is angry with our Israel for, that have not been duly seen and resented by us, about which God expects to be sought, if ever He turn again our captivity:

Wherefore it is commanded and appointed, that Thursday, the fourteenth of January next, be observed as a day of prayer, with fasting, throughout this province; strictly forbidding all servile labour thereon; that so all God's people may offer up fervent supplications unto him, for the preservation and prosperity of his majesty's royal person and government, and success to attend his affairs both at home and abroad; that all iniquity may be put away, which hath stirred God's holy jealousy against this land; that He would shew us what we know not, and help us wherein we have done amiss to do so no more; and especially that whatever mis-

takes on either hand have been fallen into, either by the body of this
people, or any orders of men, referring to the late tragedy, raised among
us by Satan and his instruments, through the awful judgment of God, he
would humble us therefore, and pardon all the errors of his servants and
people, that desire to love his name; that he would remove the rod of the
wicked from off the lot of the righteous; that he would bring in the
American heathen, and cause them to hear and obey his voice.

Given at Boston, December 17, 1696, in the eighth year of his Majesty's
reign.

ISAAC ADDINGTON, Secretary.

Upon the day of the fast, in the full assembly at the south meeting-
house in Boston, one of the honourable judges, who had sat in judicature
in Salem, delivered in a paper, and while it was in reading, stood up; but
the copy being not to be obtained at present, it can only be reported by
memory to this effect, viz., It was to desire the prayers of God's people
for him and his; and that God having visited his family, etc., he was
apprehensive that he might have fallen into some errors in the matters at
Salem, and pray that the guilt of such miscarriages may not be imputed
either to the country in general, or to him or his family in particular.

Some, that had been of several juries, have given forth a paper, signed
with their own hands, in these words:

" We whose names are under written, being in the year 1692 called to
serve as jurors in court at Salem on trial of many, who were by some
suspected guilty of doing acts of witchcraft upon the bodies of sundry
persons:

" We confess that we ourselves were not capable to understand, nor
able to withstand, the mysterious delusions of the powers of darkness, and
prince of the air; but were, for want of knowledge in ourselves, and better information from others, prevailed with to take up with such evidence
against the accused, as, on further consideration and better information,
we justly fear was insufficient for the touching the lives of any (Duet.
xvii. 6), whereby we fear we have been instrumental, with others, though
ignorantly and unwittingly, to bring upon ourselves and this people of
the Lord the guilt of innocent blood; which sin the Lord saith, in Scripture, he would not pardon (II. Kings, xxiv. 4), that is, we suppose, in
regard of his temporal judgments. We do therefore hereby signify to all
in general (and to the surviving sufferers in especial) our deep sense of,
and sorrow for, our errors, in acting on such evidence to the condemning
of any person; and do hereby declare, that we justly fear that we were
sadly deluded and mistaken; for which we are much disquieted and distressed in our minds; and do therefore humbly beg forgiveness, first of

God for Christ's sake, for this our error ; and pray that God would not impute the guilt of it to ourselves, nor others ; and we also pray that we may be considered candidly, and aright, by the living sufferers, as being then under the power of a strong and general delusion, utterly unacquainted with, and not experienced in, matters of that nature.

"We do heartily ask forgiveness of you all, whom we have justly offended ; and do declare, according to our present minds, we would none of us do such things again on such grounds for the whole world ; praying you to accept of this in way of satisfaction for our offence, and that you would bless the inheritance of the Lord, that he may be entreated for the land.

Foreman, THOMAS FISK,	THOMAS PEARLY, SEN.,
WILLIAM FISK,	JOHN PEABODY,
JOHN BATCHELER,	THOMAS PERKINS,
THOMAS FISK, JUN.,	SAMUEL SAYER,
JOHN DANE,	ANDREW ELLIOTT,
JOSEPH EVELITH,	HENRY HERRICK, SEN."

Samuel Sewall.

BORN in Bishop-Stoke, England, 1652. DIED in Boston, Mass., 1730.

THE JUDGE'S CONFESSION.

[From the "Sewall Papers," Vol. I., published by the Mass. Hist. Soc. 1878.]

Copy of the Bill I put up on the Fast day ; giving it to Mr. Willard as he pass'd by, and standing up at the reading of it, and bowing when finished ; in the Afternoon.

SAMUEL SEWALL, sensible of the reiterated strokes of God upon himself and family ; and being sensible, that as to the Guilt contracted upon the opening of the late Commission of Oyer and Terminer at Salem (to which the order for this Day relates) he is, upon many accounts, more concerned than any that he knows of, Desires to take the Blame and shame of it, Asking pardon of men, And especially desiring prayers that God, who has an Unlimited Authority, would pardon that sin and all other his sins ; personal and Relative : And according to his infinite Benignity, and Sovereignty, Not Visit the sin of him, or of any other, upon himself or any of his, nor upon the Land : But that He would powerfully defend him against all Temptations to Sin, for the future ; and vouchsafe him the efficacious, saving Conduct of his Word and Spirit.—[Date, *January* 14th, 1697.]

Sam Sewall

AN EARLY ANTI-SLAVERY TRACT.

[*The Selling of Joseph.* 1700.]

For as much as liberty is in real value next unto life : None ought to part with it them
selves, or deprive others of it, but upon most mature consideration.

THE numerousness of slaves at this day in the province, and the uneasiness of them under their slavery, hath put many upon thinking
whether the foundation of it be firmly and well laid ; so as to sustain the
vast weight that is built upon it.   It is most certain that all men, as they
are the sons of Adam, are coheirs ; and have equal right unto liberty,
and all other outward comforts of life.   "God hath given the earth
[with all its commodities] unto the sons of Adam," Psal. cxv. 16.   "And
hath made of one blood, all nations of men, for to dwell on all the face of
the earth, and hath determined the times before appointed, and the bounds
of their habitation : That they should seek the Lord.   Forasmuch then
as we are the offspring of God," etc. Acts xvii. 26, 27, 29.   Now
although the title given by the last Adam doth infinitely better men's
estates, respecting God and themselves ; and grants them a most beneficial and inviolable lease under the broad seal of heaven, who were before
only tenants at will : yet through the indulgence of God to our first
parents after the fall, the outward estate of all and every of their children
remains the same, as to one another.   So that originally and naturally
there is no such thing as slavery.   Joseph was rightfully no more a slave
to his brethren, than they were to him ; and they had no more authority
to sell him than they had to slay him.   And if they had nothing to do
to sell him, the Ishmaelites bargaining with them, and paying down
twenty pieces of silver, could not make a title.   Neither could Potiphar
have any better interest in him than the Ishmaelites had.   Gen. xxxvii.
20, 27, 28. For he that shall in this case plead alteration of property, seems
to have forfeited a great part of his own claim to humanity.   There is
no proportion between twenty pieces of silver and liberty.   The commodity itself is the claimer.   If Arabian gold be imported in any quantities, most are afraid to meddle with it, though they might have it at
easy rates, lest if it should have been wrongfully taken from the owners,
it should kindle a fire to the consumption of their whole estate.   'Tis pity
there should be more caution used in buying a horse, or a little lifeless
dust, than there is in purchasing men and women : whenas they are the
offspring of God, and their liberty is,

——*Auro pretiosior Omni.*

And seeing God hath said, "He that stealeth a man and selleth him,
or if he be found in his hand, he shall surely be put to death."   Exod.

xxi. 16. This law being of everlasting equity, wherein man-stealing is ranked among the most atrocious of capital crimes, what louder cry can there be made of that celebrated warning,

Caveat Emptor!

And all things considered, it would conduce more to the welfare of the province, to have white servants for a term of years, than to have slaves for life. Few can endure to hear of a negro's being made free; and indeed they can seldom use their freedom well; yet their continual aspiring after their forbidden liberty renders them unwilling servants. And there is such a disparity in their conditions, color and hair, that they can never embody with us and grow up into orderly families, to the peopling of the land: but still remain in our body politic as a kind of extravasate blood. As many negro men as there are among us, so many empty places there are in our train bands, and the places taken up of men that might make husbands for our daughters. And the sons and daughters of New England would become more like Jacob and Rachel, if this slavery were thrust quite out of doors. Moreover, it is too well known what temptations masters are under, to connive at the fornication of their slaves; lest they should be obliged to find them wives or pay their fines. It seems to be practically pleaded that they might be lawless; 'tis thought much of, that the law should have satisfaction for their thefts and other immoralities; by which means, holiness to the Lord is more rarely engraven upon this sort of servitude. It is likewise most lamentable to think how, in taking negroes out of Africa and selling of them here, that which God has joined together men do boldly rend asunder; men from their country, husbands from their wives, parents from their children. How horrible is the uncleanness, mortality, if not murder, that the ships are guilty of that bring great crowds of these miserable men and women! Methinks, when we are bemoaning the barbarous usage of our friends and kinsfolk in Africa, it might not be unseasonable to inquire whether we are not culpable in forcing the Africans to become slaves among ourselves. And it may be a question whether all the benefit received by negro slaves will balance the account of cash laid out upon them; and for the redemption of our own enslaved friends out of Africa. Besides all the persons and estates that have perished there.

Obj. 1. These blackamoors are of the posterity of Cham, and therefore are under the curse of slavery. Gen. ix. 25, 26, 27.

Answ. Of all offices, one would not beg this, viz., uncalled for, to be an executioner of the vindictive wrath of God; the extent and duration of which is to us uncertain. If this ever was a commission, how do we know but that it is long since out of date? Many have found it to their cost, that a prophetical denunciation of judgment against a person or people would not warrant them to inflict that evil. If it would, Hazael might justify himself in all he did against his master, and the Israelites, from II. Kings viii. 10, 12.

But it is possible that, by cursory reading, this text may have been mistaken. For Canaan is the person cursed three times over, without the mentioning of Cham. Good expositors suppose the curse entailed on him, and that this prophecy was accomplished in the extirpation of the Canaanites, and in the servitude of the Gibeonites. *Vide pareum.* Whereas the blackamoors are not descended of Canaan, but of Cush. Psal. lxviii. 31. "Princes shall come out of Egypt [Mizraim] Ethiopia [Cush] shall soon stretch out her hands unto God." Under which names, all Africa may be comprehended; and their promised conversion ought to be prayed for. Jer. xiii. 23. "Can the Ethiopian change his skin?" This shows that black men are the posterity of Cush, who time out of mind have been distinguished by their color. And for want of the true, Ovid assigns a fabulous cause of it:

Sanguine tum credunt in corpora summa vocato
Æthiopum populos nigrum traxisse colorem.

Metamorph. lib. 2.

Obj. 2. The *nigers* are brought out of a Pagan country into places where the gospel is preached.

Answ. Evil must not be done, that good may come of it. The extraordinary and comprehensive benefit accruing to the Church of God, and to Joseph personally, did not rectify his brethren's sale of him.

Obj. 3. The Africans have wars one with another: our ships bring lawful captives taken in those wars.

Answ. For aught is known, their wars are much such as were between Jacob's sons and their brother Joseph. If they be between town and town, provincial or national, every war is upon one side unjust. An unlawful war can't make lawful captives. And by receiving, we are in danger to promote and partake in their barbarous cruelties. I am sure, if some gentlemen should go down to the Brewsters to take the air and fish, and a stronger party from Hull should surprise them and sell them for slaves to a ship outward bound, they would think themselves unjustly dealt with; both by sellers and buyers. And yet 'tis to be feared we have no other kind of title to our *nigers.* "Therefore all things whatsoever ye would that men should do to you, do ye even so to them: for this is the law and the prophets." Matt. vii. 12.

Obj. 4. Abraham had servants bought with his money, and born in his house.

Answ. Until the circumstances of Abraham's purchase be recorded, no argument can be drawn from it. In the meantime charity obliges us to conclude that he knew it was lawful and good.

It is observable that the Israelites were strictly forbidden the buying or selling one another for slaves. Levit. xxv. 39, 46. Jer. xxxiv. 8.——22. And God gaged his blessing in lieu of any loss they might conceipt they suffered thereby. Deut. xv. 18. And since the partition wall is broken down, inordinate self love should likewise be demolished. God expects that Christians should be of a more ingenuous and benign frame of spirit. Christians should carry it to all the world, as the Israelites were to carry it one towards another. And for men obstinately to persist in holding their neighbours and brethren under the rigor of perpetual bondage, seems to be no proper way of gaining assurance that God has given them spiritual freedom. Our blessed Saviour has altered the measures of the ancient love-song, and set it to a most excellent new tune, which all ought to be ambitious of learning. Matt. v. 43, 44. John xiii. 34. These Ethiopians, as black as they are, seeing they are the sons and daughters of the first Adam, the brethren and sisters of the last Adam, and the offspring of God, they ought to be treated with a respect agreeable.

HOW JUDGE SEWALL COURTED MADAM WINTHROP.

[From the " Sewall Papers," Vol. III., published by the Mass. Hist. Soc. 1882.]

SEPT.ʳ 5. Mary Hirst goes to Board with Madam Oliver and her Mother Loyd. Going to Son Sewall's I there meet with Madam Winthrop, told her I was glad to meet her there, had not seen her a great while; gave her Mr. Homes's Sermon.   .   .   .   .

7.ʳ 30. Mr. Colman's Lecture: Daughter Sewall acquaints Madam Winthrop that if she pleas'd to be within at 3. p. m. I would wait on her. She answer'd she would be at home.

8.ʳ 1. Satterday, I dine at Mr. Stoddard's: from thence I went to Madam Winthrop's just at 3. Spake to her, saying, my loving wife died so soon and suddenly, 'twas hardly convenient for me to think of marrying again; however I came to this Resolution, that I would not make my Court to any person without first Consulting with her. Had a pleasant discourse about 7 [seven] Single persons sitting in the Fore-seat 7.ʳ 29th, viz. Madᵐ Rebekah Dudley, Catharine Winthrop, Bridget Usher, Deliverance Legg, Rebekah Loyd, Lydia Colman, Elizabeth Bellingham. She propounded one and another for me; but none would do, said Mrs. Loyd was about her Age.

Octobr 3. 2. Waited on Madam Winthrop again; 'twas a little while before she came in. Her daughter Noyes being there alone with me, I said, I hoped my Waiting on her Mother would not be disagreeable to her. She answer'd she should not be against that that might be for her Comfort. I Saluted her, and told her I perceiv'd I must shortly wish her a good Time; (her mother had told me, she was with Child, and within a Moneth or two of her Time). By and by in came Mr. Airs, Chaplain of the Castle, and hang'd up his Hat, which I was a little startled at, it seeming as if he was to lodge there. At last Madam Winthrop came too. After a considerable time, I went up to her and said, if it might not be inconvenient I desired to speak with her. She assented, and spake of going into another Room; but Mr. Airs and Mrs. Noyes presently rose up, and went out, leaving us there alone. Then I usher'd in Discourse from the names in the Fore-seat; at last I pray'd that Katharine [Mrs. Winthrop] might be the person assign'd for me. She instantly took it up in the way of Denyal, as if she had catch'd at an Opportunity to do it, saying she could not do it before she was asked. Said that was her mind unless she should Change it, which she believed she should not; could not leave her Children. I express'd my Sorrow that she should do it so Speedily, pray'd her Consideration, and ask'd her when I should wait on her agen. She setting no time, I mention'd that day Sennight. Gave her Mr. Willard's Fountain open'd with the little print and verses; saying, I hop'd if we did well read that book, we should meet together hereafter, if we did not now. She took the Book, and put it in her Pocket. Took Leave.

8ʳ 5. Midweek, I din'd with the Court; from thence went and visited Cousin Jonathan's wife, Lying in with her little Betty. Gave the Nurse 2ˢ. Although I had appointed to wait upon her, Mᵐ Winthrop, next Monday, yet I went from my Cousin Sewall's thither about 3. p. m. The Nurse told me Madam dined abroad at her daughter Noyes's, they were to go out together. I ask'd for the Maid, who was not within. Gave Katee a penny and a Kiss, and came away. Accompanyed my Son and daughter Cooper in their Remove to their New House. Went to tell Joseph, and Mr. Belcher saw me by the South Meetinghouse though 'twas duskish, and said I had been at House-warming, (he had been at our house). Invited me to drink a Glass of Wine at his house at 7. and eat part of the Pasty provided for the Commissioners voyage to Casco-Bay. His Excellency, Madam Belcher, S. S. Col. Fitch, Mr. D. Oliver, Mr. Anthony Stoddard, Mr. Welsteed, Mr. White, Mr. Belcher sat down. At coming home gave us of the Cake and Ginger Bread to carry away. 'Twas about Ten before we got home; Mr. Oliver and I waited on the Governour to his Gate; and then Mr. Oliver would wait on me home.

8ʳ 6ᵗʰ Lecture-day, Mr. Cutler, President of the Connecticut College, preached in Dr. C. Mather's Turn. He made an excellent Discourse from

Heb. xi. 14. For they that say such things, declare plainly that they seek a Country. Bro^r Odlin, Son Sewall of Brooklin, and Mary Hirst dine with me. I ask'd Mary of Madam Lord, Mr. Oliver and wife, and bid her present my service to them. 8^r 6th A little after 6. p. m. I went to Madam Winthrop's. She was not within. I gave Sarah Chickering the Maid 2^s, Juno, who brought in wood, 1^s. Afterward the Nurse came in, I gave her 18^d, having no other small Bill. After awhile Dr. Noyes came in with his Mother; and quickly after his wife came in: They sat talking, I think, till eight a-clock. I said I fear'd I might be some Interruption to their Business: Dr. Noyes reply'd pleasantly: He fear'd they might be an Interruption to me, and went away. Madam seem'd to harp upon the same string. Must take care of her Children; could not leave that House and Neighbourhood where she had dwelt so long. I told her she might doe her children as much or more good by bestowing what she laid out in Hous-keeping, upon them. Said her Son would be of Age the 7th of August. I said it might be inconvenient for her to dwell with her Daughter-in-Law, who must be Mistress of the House. I gave her a piece of Mr. Belcher's Cake and Ginger-Bread wrapped up in a clean sheet of Paper; told her of her Father's kindness to me when Treasurer, and I Constable. My Daughter Judith was gon from me and I was more lonesom—might help to forward one another in our Journey to Canaan.— Mr. Eyre came within the door; I saluted him, ask'd how Mr. Clark did, and he went away. I took leave about 9 aclock. I told [her] I came now to refresh her Memory as to Monday-night; said she had not forgot it. In discourse with her, I ask'd leave to speak with her Sister; I meant to gain Mad^m Mico's favour to persuade her Sister. She seem'd surpris'd and displeas'd, and said she was in the same condition! . . .

8^r 10th Examin Mr. Briggs his Account; said they could not find Mr. Whittemore. Mr. Willard offer'd to answer for him. But I shew'd the necessity of his being here; and appointed Wednesday 10. a-clock; and order'd notice to be given to the Auditours, to pray their Assistance.

In the Evening I visited Madam Winthrop, who treated me with a great deal of Curtesy; Wine, Marmalade. I gave her a News-Letter about the Thanksgiving; Proposals, for sake of the Verses for David Jeffries. She tells me Dr. Increase Mather visited her this day, in Mr. Hutchinson's Coach.

It seems Dr. Cotton Mather's chimney fell a-fire yesterday, so as to interrupt the Assembly a. m. Mr. Cutler ceased preaching ¼ of an hour.

8^r 11th I writ a few Lines to Madam Winthrop to this purpose: "Madam, These wait on you with Mr. Mayhew's Sermon, and Account of the state of the Indians on Martha's Vinyard. I thank you for your

Unmerited Favours of yesterday; and hope to have the Happiness of Waiting on you to-morrow before Eight a-clock after Noon. I pray GOD to keep you, and give you a joyfull entrance upon the Two Hundred and twenty-ninth year of Christopher Columbus his Discovery; and take Leave, who am, Madam, your humble Serv.ͭ   S. S."

Sent this by Deacon Green, who deliver'd it to Sarah Chickering, her Mistress not being at home.

8.ͬ 12. Give Mr. Whittemore and Willard their Oath to Dr. Mather's Inventory. Visit Mr. Cooper. Go to the Meeting at the Wido Emon's: Mr. Manly pray'd, I read half Mr. Henry's 12ᵗʰ Chapter of the L. Supper. Sung 1, 2, 3, 4, 5, 10, and 12ᵗʰ Verses of the 30ᵗʰ Psalm. Bro.ͬ Franklin concluded with Prayer. At Mad.ͫ Winthrop's Steps I took leave of Capt Hill, &c.

Mrs. Anne Cotton came to door (twas before 8.) said Madam Winthrop was within, directed me into the little Room, where she was full of work behind a Stand; Mrs. Cotton came in and stood. Madam Winthrop pointed to her to set me a Chair. Madam Winthrop's Countenance was much changed from what 'twas on Monday, look'd dark and lowering. At last, the work, (black stuff or Silk) was taken away, I got my Chair in place, had some Converse, but very Cold and indifferent to what 'twas before Ask'd her to acquit me of Rudeness if I drew off her Glove. Enquiring the reason, I told her twas great odds between handling a dead Goat, and a living Lady. Got it off. I told her I had one Petition to ask of her, that was, that she would take off the Negative she laid on me the third of October; She readily answer'd she could not, and enlarg'd upon it; She told me of it so soon as she could; could not leave her house, children, neighbours, business. I told her she might do som Good to help and support me. Mentioning Mrs. Gookin, Nath, the widow Weld was spoken of; said I had visited Mrs. Denison. I told her Yes! Afterward I said, If after a first and second Vagary she would Accept of me returning, Her Victorious Kindness and Good Will would be very Obliging. She thank'd me for my Book, (Mr. Mayhew's Sermon), But said not a word of the Letter. When she insisted on the Negative, I pray'd there might be no more Thunder and Lightening, I should not sleep all night. I gave her Dr. Preston, The Church's Marriage and the Church's Carriage, which cost me 6ˢ at the Sale. The door standing open, Mr. Airs came in, hung up his Hat, and sat down. After awhile, Madam Winthrop moving, he went out. Jnᵒ Eyre look'd in, I said How do ye, or, your servant Mr. Eyre: but heard no word from him. Sarah fill'd a Glass of Wine, she drank to me, I to her, She sent Juno home with me with a good Lantern, I gave her 6.ᵈ and bid her thank her Mistress. In some of our Discourse, I told her I had rather go the Stone-House adjoining to her, than to come to her against her mind. Told her the reason why I came every other night was lest I should drink too deep draughts of Pleasure. She had talk'd of Canary, her Kisses were to me better than the best Canary. Explain'd the expression Concerning Columbus.

8ʳ 13. I tell my Son and daughter Sewall, that the Weather was not so fair as I apprehended. Mr. Sewall preach'd very well in Mr. Wadsworth's Turn. Mr. Williams of Weston and Mr. Odlin dine with us. Text was, the Excellency of the Knowledge of Christ.   .   .   .   .

8ʳ 17. Monday, Give Mr. Danˡ Willard, and Mr. Pelatiah Whittemore their Oaths to their Accounts; and Mr. John Briggs to his, as they are Attornys to Dr. Cotton Mather, Administrator to the estate of Nathan Howell deceased. In the Evening I visited Madam Winthrop, who Treated me Courteously, but not in Clean Linen as somtimes. She said, she did not know whether I would come again, or no. I ask'd her how she could so impute inconstancy to me. (I had not visited her since Wednesday night being unable to get over the Indisposition received by the Treatment received that night, and *I must* in it seem'd to sound like a made piece of Formality.) Gave her this day's Gazett. Heard David Jeffries say the Lord's Prayer, and some other portions of the Scriptures. He came to the door, and ask'd me to go into Chamber, where his Grandmother was tending Little Katee, to whom she had given Physick; but I chose to sit below. Dr. Noyes and his wife came in, and sat a considerable time; had been visiting Son and daughter Cooper. Juno came home with me.

8ʳ 18. Visited Madam Mico, who came to me in a splendid Dress. I said, It may be you have heard of my Visiting Madam Winthrop, her Sister. She answered, Her Sister had told her of it. I ask'd her good Will in the Affair. She answer'd, If her Sister were for it, she should not hinder it. I gave her Mr. Homes's Sermon. She gave me a Glass of Canary, entertain'd me with good Discourse, and a Respectfull Remembrance of my first Wife. I took Leave.

8ʳ 19. Midweek, Visited Madam Winthrop; Sarah told me she was at Mr. Walley's, would not come home till late. I gave her Hannah 3 oranges with her Duty, not knowing whether I should find her or no. Was ready to go home: but said if I knew she was there, I would go thither. Sarah seem'd to speak with pretty good Courage, She would be there. I went and found her there, with Mr. Walley and his wife in the little Room below. At 7 a-clock I mentioned going home; at 8. I put on my Coat, and quickly waited on her home. She found occasion to speak loud to the servant, as if she had a mind to be known. Was Courteous to me; but took occasion to speak pretty earnestly about my keeping a Coach: I said 'twould cost £100. per annum: she said twould cost but £40. Spake much against John Winthrop, his false-heartedness. Mr. Eyre came in and sat awhile; I offer'd him Dr. Incr. Mather's Sermons, whereof Mr. Appleton's Ordination Sermon was one; said he had them already. I said I would give him another. Exit. Came away somewhat late.

8ʳ 20. Mr. Colman preaches from Luke xv. 10. Joy among the Angels: made an Excellent Discourse.

At Council, Col. Townsend spake to me of my Hood: Should get a Wigg. I said twas my chief ornament: I wore it for sake of the Day. Broʳ Odlin, and Sam, Mary, and Jane Hirst dine with us. Promis'd to wait on the Govʳ about 7. Madam Winthrop not being at Lecture, I went thither first; found her very Serene with her daughter Noyes, Mrs. Dering, and the widow Shipreev sitting at a little Table, she in her arm'd Chair. She drank to me, and I to Mrs. Noyes. After awhile pray'd the favour to speak with her. She took one of the Candles, and went into the best Room, clos'd the shutters, sat down upon the Couch. She told me Madam Usher had been there, and said the Coach must be set on Wheels, and not by Rusting. She spake something of my needing a Wigg. Ask'd me what her Sister said to me. I told her, She said, If her Sister were for it, She would not hinder it. But I told her, she did not say she would be glad to have me for her Brother. Said, I shall keep you in the Cold, and asked her if she would be within to morrow night, for we had had but a running Feat. She said she could not tell whether she should, or no. I took Leave. As were drinking at the Governour's, he said: In England the Ladies minded little more than that they might have Money, and Coaches to ride in. I said, And New-England brooks its Name. At which Mr. Dudley smiled. Govʳ said they were not quite so bad here.

8ʳ 21. Friday, My Son, the Minister, came to me p. m. by appointment and we pray one for another in the Old Chamber; more especially respecting my Courtship. About 6. a-clock I go to Madam Winthrop's; Sarah told me her Mistress was gon out, but did not tell me whither she went. She presently order'd me a Fire; so I went in, having Dr. Sibb's Bowels with me to read. I read the two first Sermons, still no body came in: at last about 9. a-clock Mr. Jnᵒ Eyre came in; I took the opportunity to say to him as I had done to Mrs. Noyes before, that I hoped my Visiting his Mother would not be disagreeable to him; He answered me with much Respect. When twas after 9. a-clock He of himself said he would go and call her, she was but at one of his Brothers: A while after I heard Madam Winthrop's voice, enquiring somthing about John. After a good while and Clapping the Garden door twice or thrice, she came in. I mention'd somthing of the lateness; she banter'd me, and said I was later. She receiv'd me Courteously. I ask'd when our proceedings should be made publick: She said They were like to be no more publick than they were already. Offer'd me no Wine that 1 remember. I rose up at 11 a-clock to ccme away, saying I would put on my Coat, She offer'd not to help me. I pray'd her that Juno might light me home, she open'd the Shutter, and said twas pretty light abroad; Juno was weary and gon to bed. So I came home by Star-light as well as I could. At my first coming in, I gave Sarah five Shillings. I writ Mr. Eyre his Name in his book with the date Octobᵣ 21. 1720. It cost me 8ˢ. Jehovah jireh! Madam told me she had visited M. Mico, Wendell, and Wᵐ Clark of the South [Church].

Octobᵣ 22. Daughter Cooper visited me before my going out of Town, staid till about Sun set. I brought her going near as far as the Orange Tree. Coming back, near Leg's Corner, Little David Jeffries saw me, and looking upon me very lovingly, ask'd me if I was going to see his Grandmother? I said, Not to-night. Gave him a peny, and bid him present my Service to his Grandmother.

Octobᵣ 24. I went in the Hackny Coach through the Common, stop'd at Madam Winthrop's (had told her I would take my departure from thence). Sarah came to the door with Katee in her Arms: but I did not think to take notice of the Child. Call'd her Mistress. I told her, being encourag'd by David Jeffries loving eyes, and sweet Words, I was come to enquire whether she could find in her heart to leave that House and Neighbourhood, and go and dwell with me at the South-end; I think she said softly, Not yet. I told her It did not ly in my Lands to keep a Coach. If I should, I should be in danger to be brought to keep company with her Neighbour Brooker, (he was a little before sent to prison for Debt). Told her I had an Antipathy against those who would pretend to give themselves; but nothing of their Estate. I would a proportion of my Estate with my self. And I supposed she would do so. As to a Perriwig, My best and greatest Friend, I could not possibly have a greater, began to find me with Hair before I was born, and had continued to do so ever since; and I could not find in my heart to go to another. She commended the book I gave her, Dr. Preston, the Church Marriage; quoted him saying 'twas inconvenient keeping out of a Fashion commonly used. I said the Time and Tide did circumscribe my Visit. She gave me a Dram of Black-Cherry Brandy, and gave me a lump of the Sugar that was in it. She wish'd me a good Journy. I pray'd God to keep her, and came away. Had a very pleasant Journy to Salem.

8ᵣ 25. Sent a Letter of it to my Son by Wakefield, who delivered it not till Wednesday; so he visited her not till Friday p. m. and then presented my Service to her.   .   .   .   .

31. 2. At night I visited Madam Winthrop about 6. p. m. They told me she was gon to Madam Mico's. I went thither and found she

was gon; so return'd to her house, read the Epistles to the Galatians, Ephesians in Mr. Eyre's Latin Bible. After the clock struck 8. I began to read the 103. Psalm. Mr. Wendell came in from his Warehouse. Ask'd me if I were alone? Spake very kindly to me, offer'd me to call Madam Winthrop. I told him, She would be angry, had been at Mrs. Mico's; he help'd me on with my Coat and I came home: left the Gazett in the Bible, which told Sarah of, bid her present my Service to Mrs. Winthrop, and tell her I had been to wait on her if she had been at home.

Nov.ʳ 1. I was so taken up that I could not go if I would.

Nov.ʳ 2. Midweek, went again, and found Mrs. Alden there, who quickly went out. Gave her about ½ pound of Sugar Almonds, cost 3.ˢ per £. Carried them on Monday. She seem'd pleas'd with them, ask'd what they cost. Spake of giving her a Hundred pounds per annum if I dy'd before her. Ask'd her what sum she would give me, if she should dy first? Said I would give her time to Consider of it. She said she heard as if I had given all to my Children by Deeds of Gift. I told her 'twas a mistake, Point-Judith was mine &c. That in England I own'd, my Father's desire was that it should go to my eldest Son; 'twas 20£ per annum; she thought 'twas forty. I think when I seem'd to excuse pressing this, she seemed to think twas best to speak of it; a long winter was coming on. Gave me a Glass or two of Canary.

Nov.ʳ 4.ᵗʰ Friday, Went again, about 7. a-clock; found there Mr. John Walley and his wife: sat discoursing pleasantly. I shew'd them Isaac Moses's [an Indian] Writing. Madam W. serv'd Comfeits to us. After a-while a Table was spread, and Supper was set. I urg'd Mr. Walley to Crave a Blessing; but he put it upon me. About 9. they went away. I ask'd Madam what fashioned Neck-lace I should present her with, She said, None at all. I ask'd her Whereabout we left off last time; mention'd what I had offer'd to give her; Ask'd her what she would give me; She said she could not Change her Condition: She had said so from the beginning; could not be so far from her Children, the Lecture. Quoted the Apostle Paul affirming that a single Life was better than a Married. I answer'd That was for the present Distress. Said she had not pleasure in things of that nature as formerly: I said, you are the fitter to make me a Wife. If she held in that mind, I must go home and bewail my Rashness in making more haste than good Speed. However, considering the Supper, I desired her to be within next Monday night, if we liv'd so long. Assented. She charg'd me with saying, that she must put away Juno, if she came to me: I utterly deny'd it, it never came in my heart; yet she insisted upon it; saying it came in upon discourse about the Indian woman that obtained her Freedom this Court. About 10. I said I would not disturb the good orders of her House, and came away. She not seeming pleas'd with my Coming away. Spake to her about David Jeffries, had not seen him.

Monday, Nov.r 7th My Son pray'd in the Old Chamber. Our time had been taken up by Son and Daughter Cooper's Visit; so that I only read the 130th and 143. Psalm. Twas on the Account of my Courtship. I went to Mad. Winthrop; found her rocking her little Katee in the Cradle. I excus'd my Coming so late (near Eight). She set me an arm'd Chair and Cusheon; and so the Cradle was between her arm'd Chair and mine. Gave her the remnant of my Almonds; She did not eat of them as before; but laid them away; I said I came to enquire whether she had alter'd her mind since Friday, or remained of the same mind still. She said, Thereabouts. I told her I loved her, and was so fond as to think that she loved me: she said had a great respect for me. I told her, I had made her an offer, without asking any advice; she had so many to advise with, that 'twas an hindrance. The Fire was come to one short Brand besides the Block, which Brand was set up in end; at last it fell to pieces, and no Recruit was made: She gave me a Glass of Wine. I think I repeated again that I would go home and bewail my Rashness in making more haste than good Speed. I would endeavour to contain myself, and not go on to sollicit her to do that which she could not Consent to. Took leave of her. As came down the steps she bid me have a Care. Treated me Courteously. Told her she had enter'd the 4th year of her Widowhood. I had given her the News-Letter before: I did not bid her draw off her Glove as sometime I had done. Her Dress was not so clean as somtime it had been. Jehovah jireh!

Midweek, 9.r 9th Dine at Bro.r Stoddard's: were so kind as to enquire of me if they should invite M.m Winthrop; I answer'd No. Thank'd my Sister Stoddard for her Courtesie; sat down at the Table Simeon Stoddard, esqr, Mad. Stoddard, Samuel Sewall, Mr. Colman, M.m Colman, Mr. Cooper, Mrs. Cooper, Mrs. Hannah Cooper, Mr. Samuel Sewall of Brooklin, Mrs. Sewall, Mr. Joseph Sewall, Mrs. Lydia Walley, Mr. William Stoddard. Had a noble Treat. At night our Meeting was at the Widow Belknap's. Gave each one of the Meeting One of Mr. Homes's Sermons, 12 in all; She sent her servant home with me with a Lantern. Madam Winthrop's Shutters were open as I pass'd by.

Nov.r 10. Mr. Webb preached, Walk as becomes the Gospel. Dined at my Son's with Cousin Holman's Wife.

Nov.r 11th Went not to M.m Winthrop's. This is the 2d Withdraw. . . . .

About the middle of Dec.r Madam Winthrop made a Treat for her Children; Mr. Sewall, Prince, Willoughby: I knew nothing of it; but the same day abode in the Council Chamber for fear of the Rain, and din'd alone upon Kilby's Pyes and good Beer.

𝕹𝖎𝖈𝖍𝖔𝖑𝖆𝖘 𝕹𝖔𝖞𝖊𝖘.

BORN in Newbury, Mass., 1647.   DIED at Salem, Mass., **1717.**

DAMON AND PYTHIAS AT NEWBURY.

[*From Cotton Mather's "Magnalia." 1702.*]

MR. JAMES NOYES was born, 1608, at Choulderton in Wiltshire, of godly and worthy parents. His father was minister of the same town, a very learned man, the schoolmaster of Mr. Thomas Parker. His mother was sister to the learned Mr. Robert Parker, and he had much of his education and tutorage under Mr. Thomas Parker. He was called by him, from Brazen-Nose-College in Oxford, to help him in teaching the free school at Newbury; where they taught school together till the time they came to New England. He was converted in his youth by the ministry of Dr. Twiss and Mr. Thomas Parker, and was admired for his piety and his virtue in his younger years. The reason of his coming to New England was, because he could not comply with the ceremonies of the Church of England. He was married in England to Mrs. Sarah Brown, the eldest daughter of Mr. Joseph Brown of Southampton, not long before he came to New England, which was in the year 1634. In the same ship came Mr. Thomas Parker, Mr. James Noyes, and a younger brother of his, Mr. Nicholas Noyes, who then was a single man: between which three was a more than ordinary endearment of affection, which was never shaken or broken, but by death. Mr. Parker and Mr. James Noyes, and others that came over with them, fasted and prayed together many times before they undertook this voyage; and on the sea Mr. Parker and Mr. Noyes preached or expounded, one in the forenoon, other in the afternoon, every day during the voyage, unless some extraordinary thing intervened, and were abundant in prayer.

When they arrived, Mr. Parker was at first called to preach at Ipswich and Mr. Noyes at Mystic, at which place they continued nigh a year. He had a motion made unto him to be minister at Watertown; but Mr. Parker and others of his brethren and acquaintance settling at Newbury, and gathering the tenth of the churches in the colony, and calling Mr. Noyes to be the teacher of it, he preferred that place; being loath to be separated from Mr. Parker and brethren that had so often fasted and prayed together, both in England and on the Atlantic sea. So he became the teacher of that church, and continued painful and successful in that station something above twenty years without any considerable trouble in the church. Notwithstanding his principles as to discipline were something differing from many of the brethren, there was such condescension on both parts that peace and order was not interrupted. He was very much loved and honored in Newbury; his memory is precious there to this day, and his catechism (which is a public and standing testimony of his understanding and orthodoxy in the principles of religion) is publicly and privately used in that church and town hitherto. He was very well learned in the tongues, and in Greek excelled most. He was much read in the fathers and the schoolmen; and he was much esteemed by his brethren in the ministry. Twice he was called by Mr. Wilson and others to preach, in the time when the Antinomian principles were in danger of prevailing; which he did with good success, and to the satisfaction of those that invited him. Mr. Wilson dearly loved him; and it so happened once at Newbury that he preached in the forenoon about "holiness" so holily and ably, that Mr. Wilson was so affected with it as to change his own text and pitch upon Mr. Noyes' for the afternoon; prefacing his discourse with telling the auditory that his brother Noyes' discourse about holiness in the forenoon had so much impression upon his mind, he knew not how in the afternoon to pursue any other argument. His conversation was so unquestionably godly, that they who differed from him in smaller matters as to discipline held a most amicable correspondence with him and had an high estimation of him.   .   .   .   .

He was as religious at home as abroad, in his family and in secret as he was publicly; and they that best knew him most loved and esteemed him. Mr. Parker and he kept a private fast once a month so long as they lived together, and Mr. Parker after his death till his own departure. Mr. Noyes bitterly lamented the death of K. Charles I., and both he and Mr. Parker too had too great expectations of K. Charles II., but Mr. Parker lived to see his expectations of Charles the second frustrated. He had a long and tedious sickness, which he bore patiently and cheerfully; and he died joyfully in the forty-eighth year of his age, October 22, 1656. He left six sons and two daughters, all of which lived to be married and have children, though since one son and one daughter be dead. He hath now living fifty-six children, grand-children, and great-grand-children. And his brother that came over with him a single man is, through the mercy of God, yet living, and hath of children, grand-children, and great-grand-children, above an hundred: which is an instance of divine favor, in making the "families of his servants in the wilderness like a flock." There was the greatest amity, intimacy, unanimity, yea, unity imaginable between Mr. Parker and Mr. Noyes. So unshaken was their friendship, nothing but death was able to part them. They taught in one school; came over in one ship; were pastor and teacher of one church; and, Mr. Parker continuing always in celibacy, they lived in one house till death separated them for a time; but they are both now together in one Heaven,

as they that best knew them have all possible reason to be persuaded.
Mr. Parker continued in his house as long as he lived; and, as he received a great deal of kindness and respect there, so he showed a great deal of kindness in the educating of his children, and was very liberal to that family during his life and at his death. He never forgot the old friendship, but showed kindness to the dead in showing kindness to the living.

Mr. Parker and Mr. Noyes were excellent singers, both of them; and were extraordinary delighted in singing of psalms. They sang four times a day in the public worship, and always just after evening prayer in the family, where reading the Scripture, expounding, and praying, were the other constant exercises. Mr. Parker and Mr. Noyes were of the same opinion with Dr. Owen about the Sabbath; yet in practice were strict observers of the evening after it. Mr. Parker, whose practice I myself remember, was the strictest observer of the Sabbath that ever I knew. I once asked him, seeing his opinion was otherwise, as to the evening belonging to the Sabbath, why his practice differed from his opinion! He answered me: Because he dare not depart from the footsteps of the flock for his private opinion.

Being got into some passages of Mr. Parker's life before I am aware, I will insert a few more: and you may make what use of them you please. He kept a school, as well as preached, at Newbury in New England. He ordinarily had about twelve or fourteen scholars. He took no pay for his pains, unless any present were freely sent him. He used to say: He lived for the church's sake, and begrudged no pains that were for its benefit; and by his good will he was not free to teach any but such as were designed for the ministry by their parents; for he would say: He could not bestow his time and pains unless it were for the benefit of the church. Though he were blind, yet such was his memory that he could in his old age teach Latin, Greek and Hebrew very artificially. He seldom corrected a scholar, unless for lying and fighting, which were unpardonable crimes in our school. He promoted learning in his scholars by something an unusual way; encouraging them to learn lessons and make verses besides and above their stinted tasks, for which they had pardons in store, that were kept on record in the school, and were for lesser school-faults, such as were not immoralities and sins against God, crossed out; but he always told them, they must not think to escape unpunished for sin against God, by reason of them; though for some lesser defects about their lessons they were accepted.

I heard him tell Mr. Millar, the minister, that the great changes of his life had been signified to him beforehand by dreams. And I heard him say that before a fiery temptation of the devil befell him, he had a very terrible representation, in a dream, of the devil assaulting of him, and he wrestled with him, and had more than once like to have prevailed against him; but that when he was most likely and most near to be overcome, he was afresh animated and strengthened to resist him; till at length the devil seemed to break abroad like a flash of lightning and then disappeared; and that not long after the most dismal temptation of Satan befell him that ever he was sensible of, and that all the passages of that temptation answered the forementioned representation; and that the hazards of it, and his fresh supplies when almost vanquished, and his deliverance was so remarkable, that every day he had lived since that time, he had given thanks to God particularly for his assistance of him in that temptation and his deliverance out of it: though it were twenty years before the time of his now telling me concerning it. Mr. Parker excelled in liberty of speech, in praying, preaching and singing, having a most delicate sweet voice; yet he had all along an impulse upon his spirit, that he should have the palsey in his tongue before he died. His voice held extraordinarily until very old age; and I think the more, because his teeth held sound and good until then; his custom being to wash his mouth and rub his teeth every morning. Some few years before his death, he began to complain of the toothache, and then he quickly began to lose his teeth; and now he said: The daughters of his music began to fail him. And about a year and a half before he died, that which he had long feared befell him, viz., the palsey in his tongue; and so he became speechless, and thus continued until death; having this only help left him, that he could pronounce letters, but not syllables or words. He signified his mind by spelling his words, which was indeed a tedious way, but yet a mercy so far to him and others.

During that time, which was in our first Indian war, when the Indians broke in upon many towns, and committed horrible outrages, and tormented such as they took captives, one night he fell into a dreadful tentation lest the Indians should break in upon Newbury, and the inhabitants might generally escape by fighting or flying, but he being old and blind and grown decrepit, he must of necessity fall into their hands; and that being a minister they would urge him by torture to blaspheme Christ, and that he should not have grace to hold out against the tentation of Indian torture; and with the very fear of this he was for the most part of the night in such agonies of soul, that he was on the very brink of desperation; but at length God helped him by bringing to his mind two places of Scripture: that in Isa. li. 12, 13, "I, even I, am he that comforts thee; who art thou, that thou shouldest be afraid of a man that shall die, and forgettest the Lord thy Maker?" And that in Rom. viii. 35, 36, "Who shall separate us from the love of Christ? Shall tribulation, or distress, or persecution, or famine, or nakedness, or peril, or sword? —— For thy sake we are killed all the day long; —— Nay, in all these things we are more than conquerors through him that hath loved us." Sleep departed from him that night, by reason of the horror of that tentation ; and the joy that came towards morning he was wonderfully affected with ; and in the morning early he pronounced all this to me letter by letter, and glorified God.

Once hearing some of us laughing very freely, while, I suppose, he was better busied in his chamber above us, he came down and gravely said to us : " Cousins, I wonder you can be so merry, unless you are sure of your salvation ! " He was a very holy and heavenly-minded man, and as much mortified to the world as almost any in it. He scarce called any thing his own, but his books and his clothes. When he was urged to vindicate himself to be the author of the *Theses de Traductione Peccatoris ad Vitam,* he utterly refused it, saying, being young at the time when he made them, he was afraid he had not so fully aimed at the glory of God as he ought to have done. But a while after one unbeknown to him in Holland reprinted them, with the name of the author, and set him forth with more advantage than would have been modest or proper for himself to have done ; giving him his parental as well as personal honor ; and saying that his father was *Pater dignus tali Filio,* and that he was *Filius dignus tali Patre.* Thus " he that humbleth himself shall be exalted."

Mr. Wilson once, on occasion of his celibacy, said to him, That if there could be anger in Heaven, his father would chide him, when he came there, because he had not like him a son to follow him. But he had many spiritual children that were the seals of his ministry : he was also a father to the fatherless ; and many scholars were little less beholden to him for their education, than they were to their parents for their generation.

The occasion of his celibacy was this : at the time that he meditated marriage he was assaulted with violent temptations to infidelity, which made him regardless of everything in comparison of confirming his faith about the truth of the scriptures. This occasioned his falling into the study of the prophecies, which proved a means of confirming his faith ; but he fell so in love with that study that he never got out of it until his death ; and the church had doubtless had much benefit by his profound studies in that kind, could the bishops have been persuaded to license his books ; which they refused, because he found the Pope to be prophesied of, where they could not understand it. His whole life, besides what was necessary for the support of it by food and sleep, was prayer, study, preaching, and teaching school. I once heard him say, he felt the whole frame of his nature giving way, which threatened his dissolution to be at hand ; but he thanked God he was not amazed at it.

To conclude all I intend concerning Mr. Parker or Mr. Noyes, I shall give you Mr. Parker's character of Mr. Noyes, who best knew him, and whose testimony of him is very credible.

"Mr. James Noyes, my worthy colleague in the ministry of the gospel, was a man of singular qualifications, in piety excelling, an implacable enemy to all heresy and schism, and a most able warrior against the same. He was of a reaching and ready apprehension, a large invention, a most profound judgment, a rare, and tenacious, and comprehensive memory, fixed and unmovable in his grounded conceptions; sure in words and speech, without rashness; gentle and mild in all expressions, without all passion or provoking language. And as he was a notable disputant, so he never would provoke his adversary, saving by the short knocks and heavy weight of argument. He was of so loving, and compassionate, and humble carriage, that I believe never any were acquainted with him, but did desire the continuance of his society and acquaintance. He was resolute for truth, and in defence thereof had no respect to any persons. He was a most excellent counsellor in doubts, and could strike at an hair's-breadth, like the Benjamites, and expedite the entangled out of the briars. He was courageous in dangers, and still was apt to believe the best, and made fair weather in a storm. He was much honored and esteemed in the country, and his death was much bewailed. I think he may be reckoned among the greatest worthies of this age."

A CONSOLATORY POEM.

[Dedicated unto Mr. Cotton Mather, soon after the Decease of his Excellent and Vertuous Wife, Mrs. Abigail Mather. 1703.]

SIR, after you have wip'd the eyes
  Of thousands in their miseries,
And oft condoled the heavy Fates
Of those that have surviv'd their mates,
It's come at length to your own turn
To be one half within an Urn.
(Your Christ would have it so be done!)
Your other self's torn off and gone.
Gone! said I. Yes, and that's the worst:
Your Wife's but gone to Heaven first.
  You do run fast but she out run,
Hath made herself, not you, undone;
Pray let her wear what she hath won!
Grudge not her happiness above;
You live by Faith, and she by Love.
To live is Christ, to die is gain;
Betwixt you both you have the twain.
She was prepar'd for her release;
And so prepar'd departs in peace.

And who would live that God makes fit
To die, and then gives a permit?
And who would choose a world of fears,
Ready to fall about their ears,
That might get up above the spheres,
And leave the region of dread thunder
To them that love the world that's under;
Where canker'd breasts with envy broil,
And smooth tongues are but dipt in oil;
And Cain's club only doth lie by
For want of opportunity.
Yea, who would live among catarrhs,
Contagions, pains, and strifes, and wars,
That might go up above the stars;
And live in health, and peace, and bliss,
Had in that world, but wish'd in this?

Disturb not then her precious dust
With Threnodies that are unjust.
Let not cross'd Nature now repine.
Sir, Grace hath taught you to resign
To Christ, what Nature called, Mine!
To call for mourners I came not;
There are too many on the spot,
Already all the neighborhood
Have wept as much as weeping's good;
Nor to embalm her Memory;
She did that ere she came to die,
'Tis done to long Eternity!

This phœnix built her nest of spice,
Like to the Birds of Paradise;
Which, when a fever set on-fire,
Her soul took wing and soared higher;
But left choice ashes here behind,
Christ will for resurrection find.

My Muse, pass by her Out Side Grace;
Say nothing of a comely face
Nor what most lovely pleasancies
Dwelt chastely on her charming eyes.
These, and such Lilly-Glories fade,
Absconded all in Death's dark shade.
Yet these again shall rise and shine
Ten thousand times more bright and fine.

Say little of her Inside Grace;
For this world is a spiteful place,
And takes itself for injured,
If saints are prais'd, alive or dead;
And they for wits are in esteem,
That Heaven's Dwellers do blaspheme.
I hate their humor, I profess,
It smells of such rank wickedness.

Yet this saint shall not go her ways,
Without a sprig or two of bays;
Who well deserv'd far greater praise.
　Her maiden virtues render'd her
A meet help for a Minister.
For the best Women, the just Jews
(You know) this proper phrase would use:
"A Woman worthy for to be
Wife to a Priest ;" and such was she.
Good ; studying that her husband too
Nothing but good might always do.
How frugal, yet how generous !
How modest, yet how courteous !
How silent, yet how affable !
How wise, how pure, how peaceable !
As child, her parents' joy; as wife,
Her husband's crown, and heart, and life.
As mother she, a fruitful vine,
Her offspring of an holy line,
By holy nurture made them shine.
　More might be said; but lest I vex
And stir the envy of her sex,
I'll not proceed in commendation,
But leave her to their limitation;
Who having her bright virtue kept
In lustre ; thus at length she slept.
　A sickness full of mysteries,
With violence did on her seize.
She thirty weeks felt Death's attack,
But fervent pray'r still kept her back.
Her Faith and Patience 'twas to try,
And learn us how to live and die.
　At last all thoughts of life were null'd;
For Earth by Heaven was out-pull'd,
And she straight-way must thither go,
Whether her good friends would or no.
So with the Wings of Faith and Love,
And Feathers of an Holy Dove,
She bid this wretched world adieu,
And swiftly up to Heaven flew.
Yet as she flew let this word fall,
" Heav'n, Heav'n will make amends for all."

John Miller.

CHAPLAIN of Fort James, New York, 1692-95.

EVILS AND INCONVENIENCES IN NEW YORK.

[*A Description of the Province and City of New York.* . . . *in the year* 1695.]

THE number of the inhabitants in this province are about three thousand families, whereof almost one-half are naturally Dutch, a great part English, and the rest French; which how they are seated, and what number of families of each nations, what churches, meeting houses, ministers or pretended ministers there are in each county, may be best discerned by the table here inserted. As to their religion, they are very much divided; few of them intelligent and sincere, but the most part ignorant and conceited, fickle and regardless. As to their wealth and disposition thereto, the Dutch are rich and sparing; the English neither very rich, nor too great husbands; the French are poor, and therefore forced to be penurious. As to their way of trade and dealing, they are all generally cunning and crafty, but many of them not so just to their words as they should be. . . . .

Come we now to consider those things which I have said to be either wanting or obstructive to the happiness of New York. . . . .

The first is the wickedness and irreligion of the inhabitants, which abounds in all parts of the province and appears in so many shapes, constituting so many sorts of sin, that I can scarce tell which to begin withal. But, as a great reason of an inlet to the rest, I shall first mention the great negligence of divine things that is generally found in most people, of what sect or party soever they pretend to be; their eternal interests are their least concern, and, as if salvation were not a matter of moment, when they have opportunities of serving God they care not for making use thereof; or, if they go to church, 'tis but too often out of curiosity, and to find out faults in him that preacheth rather than to hear their own, or, what is yet worse, to slight and deride where they should be serious. If they have none of those opportunities, they are well contented, and regard it little if there be any who seem otherwise and discontented. Many of them, when they have them, make appear by their actions 'twas but in show; for though at first they will pretend to have a great regard for God's ordinances, and a high esteem for the ministry, whether real or pretended, a little time will plainly evidence that they were more pleased at the novelty than truly affected with the benefit, when they slight that which they before seemingly so much admired, and speak evil of him who before was the subject of their praise and commendation, and that without any other reason than their own fickle temper and envious humor. In a soil so rank as this, no marvel if the Evil One find a ready entertainment for the seed he is minded to cast in; and from a people so inconstant and regardless of heaven and holy things, no wonder if God withdraw his grace, and give them up a prey to those temptations which they so industriously seek to embrace; hence is it, therefore, that their natural corruption without check or hinderance is, by frequent acts, improved into habits most evil in the practice and difficult in the correction.

One of which, and the first I am minded to speak of, is drunkenness, which, though of itself a great sin, is yet aggravated in that it is an occasion of many others. 'Tis in this country a common thing, even for the meanest persons, so soon as the bounty of God has furnished them with a plentiful crop, to turn what they can as soon as may be into money, and that money into drink, at the same time when their family at home have nothing but rags to protect their bodies from the winter's cold; nay, if the fruits of their plantations be such as are by their own immediate labor convertible into liquor, such as cider, perry, etc., they have scarce the patience to stay till it is fit for drinking, but, inviting their pot-companions, they all of them, neglecting whatsoever work they are about, set to it together, and give not over till they have drunk it off. And to these sottish engagements they will make nothing to ride ten or twenty miles, and at the conclusion of one debauch another generally is appointed, except their stock of liquor fail them. Nor are the mean and country people only guilty of this vice, but they are equaled, nay surpassed, by many in the city of New York, whose daily practice is to frequent the taverns, and to carouse and game their night employment.

This course is the ruin and destruction of many merchants, especially those of the younger sort, who, carrying over with them a stock, whether as factors, or on their own account, spend even to prodigality, till they find themselves bankrupt ere they are aware.

Gabriel Thomas.

Quaker Emigrant with Penn. Resident in Philadelphia and West-New-Jersey, 1682-97.

PENNSYLVANIA AND THE CITY OF BROTHERLY LOVE.

[Account of the Province and Country of Pensilvania. 1698.]

PENNSYLVANIA lies between the latitude of forty and forty-five degrees; West Jersey on the east, Virginia on the west, Maryland south, and Canada on the north. In length three hundred, and in breadth one hundred and eighty miles.

The natives, or first inhabitants of this country in their original, are supposed by most people to have been of the Ten Scattered Tribes, for they resemble the Jews very much in the make of their persons, and tincture of their complexions. They observe new moons, they offer their first fruits to a Maneto, or supposed Deity, whereof they have two, one, as they fancy, above (good), another below (bad); and have a kind of Feast of Tabernacles, laying their altars upon twelve stones, observe a sort of mourning twelve months, customs of women, and many other rites to be touched (here) rather than dwelt upon. . . . They are very charitable to one another, the lame and the blind (among them) living as well as the best; they are also very kind and obliging to the Christians.

The next that came there, were the Dutch (who called the country New Netherlands) between fifty and sixty years ago, and were the first planters in those parts; but they made little or no improvement (applying themselves wholly to traffic in skins and furs, which the Indians or natives furnished them with, and which they bartered for rum, strong liquors, and sugar, with others, thereby gaining great profit) till near the time of the wars between England and them, about thirty or forty years ago.

Soon after them came the Swedes and Fins, who applied themselves to husbandry, and were the first Christian people that made any considerable improvement there.

There were some disputes between these two nations some years, the Dutch looking upon the Swedes as intruders upon their purchase and possession, which was absolutely terminated in the surrender made by John Rizeing, the Swedes' governor, to Peter Stuyvesant, governor for the Dutch, in 1655. In the Holland war about the year 1655, Sir Robert Carr took the country from the Dutch for the English, and left his cousin, Captain Carr, governor of that place; but in a short time after, the Dutch re-took the country from the English, and kept it in their possession till the peace was concluded between the English and them, when the Dutch surrendered that country with East and West Jersey, New York (with the whole countries belonging to that government) to the English again. But it remained with very little improvement till the year 1681, in which William Penn, Esq., had the country given him by King Charles the Second, in lieu of money that was due to (and signal service done by) his father, Sir William Penn, and from him bore the name of Pennsylvania.

Since that time the industrious (nay indefatigable) inhabitants have built a noble and beautiful city, and called it Philadelphia, which contains above two thousand houses, all inhabited; and most of them stately, and of brick, generally three stories high, after the mode in London, and as many several families in each. There are very many lanes and alleys, as first, Huttons Lane, Morris Lane, Jones's Lane, wherein are very good buildings; Shorters Alley, Towers Alley, Wallers Alley, Turners Lane, Sikes Alley, and Flowers Alley. All these alleys and lanes extend from the Front Street to the Second Street. There is another alley in the Second Street, called Carters Alley. There are, also, besides these alleys and lanes several fine squares and courts within this magnificent city (for so I may justly call it). As for the particular names of the several streets contained therein, the principal are as follows, viz., Walnut Street, Vine Street, Mulberry Street, Chestnut Street, Sassafras Street, taking their names from the abundance of those trees that formerly grew there; High Street, Broad Street, Delaware Street, Front Street, with several of less note, too tedious to insert here.

The air here is very delicate, pleasant, and wholesome; the heavens serene, rarely overcast, bearing mighty resemblance to the better part of France; after rain they have commonly a very clear sky; the climate is something colder in the depth of winter, and hotter in the height of summer (the cause of which is its being a main land or continent; the days also are two hours longer in the shortest day in winter, and shorter by two hours in the longest day of summer) than here in England, which makes the fruit so good, and the earth so fertile.

There are among other various sorts of frogs, the Bull Frog, which makes a roaring noise, hardly to be distinguished from that well known of the beast from whom it takes its name. There is another sort of frog, that crawls up to the tops of trees, there seeming to imitate the notes of several birds, with many other strange and various creatures, which would take up too much room here to mention.

And now for their lots and lands in city and country, in their great advancement since they were first laid out, which was within the compass of about twelve years, that which might have been bought for fifteen or eighteen shillings, is now sold for fourscore pounds in ready silver; and some other lots that might have been then purchased for three pounds within the space of two years, were sold for a hundred pounds apiece, and likewise some land that lies near the city, that sixteen years ago might have been purchased for six or eight pounds the hundred acres, cannot now be bought under one hundred and fifty or two hundred pounds.

Now the true reason why this fruitful country and flourishing city advance so considerably in the purchase of lands both in the one and the other, is their great and extended traffic and commerce both by sea and land, viz., to New York, New England, Virginia, Maryland, Carolina, Jamaica, Barbadoes, Nevis, Monserat, Antego, St. Christophers, Barmudas, Newfoundland, Maderas, Saltetudeous, and Old England; besides several other places. Their merchandise chiefly consists in horses, pipe-staves, pork and beef salted and barrelled up, bread and flour, all sorts of grain, peas, beans, skins, furs, tobacco, or potashes, wax, etc., which are bartered for rum, sugar, molasses, silver, negroes, salt, wine, linen, household goods, etc.

However, there still remain lots of land, both in the aforesaid city and country, that any may purchase almost as cheap as they could at the first laying out or parcelling of either city or country; which is (in the judgment of most people) the likeliest to turn to account to those that lay their money out upon it, and in a shorter time than the aforementioned lots and lands that are already improved, and for several reasons. In the first place, the country is now well inhabited by the Christians, who have great stocks of all sorts of cattle, that increase extraordinarily, and upon that account they are obliged to go farther up into the country, because there is the chiefest and best place for their stocks, and for them that go back into the country, they get the richest land, for the best lies thereabouts.

Secondly, farther into the country is the principal place to trade with the Indians for all sorts of pelt, as skins and furs, and also fat venison, of whom people may purchase cheaper by three parts in four than they can at the city of Philadelphia.

Thirdly, backwards in the country lies the mines where is copper and iron, besides other metals and minerals, of which there is some improvement made already in order to bring them to greater perfection; and that will be a means to erect more inland market-towns, which exceedingly promote traffic.

.   .   .   .

I must needs say, even the present encouragements are very great and inviting, for poor people (both men and women) of all kinds, can here get three times the wages for their labor they can in England or Wales.

I shall instance in a few which may serve; nay, and will hold in all the rest. The first was a blacksmith (my next neighbor), who himself and one negro man he had, got fifty shillings in one day, by working up a hundred pound weight of iron, which at sixpence per pound (and that is the common price in that country) amounts to that sum.

And for carpenters, both house and ship, bricklayers, masons, either of these tradesmen will get between five and six shillings every day constantly. As to journeymen shoemakers, they have two shillings per pair both for men and women's shoes; and journeymen tailors have twelve shillings per week and their diet. Sawyers get between six and seven shillings the hundred for cutting of pine boards. And for weavers, they have ten or twelve pence the yard for weaving of that which is little more than half a yard in breadth. Wool combers have for combing twelve pence per pound. Potters have sixteen pence for an earthen pot which may be bought in England for four pence. Tanners may buy their hides green for three half pence per pound, and sell their leather for twelve pence per pound. And curriers have three shillings and four pence per hide for dressing it; they buy their oil at twenty pence per gallon. Brickmakers have twenty shillings per thousand for their bricks at the kiln. Felt makers will have for their hats seven shillings apiece, such as may be bought in England for two shillings apiece; yet they buy their wool commonly for twelve or fifteen pence per pound. And as to the glaziers, they will have five pence a quarry for their glass. The rule for the coopers I have almost forgot; but this I can affirm of some who went from Bristol (as their neighbors report) that could hardly get their livelihoods there, are now reckoned in Pennsylvania, by a modest computation, to be worth some hundreds (if not thousands) of pounds. The bakers make as white bread as any in London, and as for their rule, it is the same in all parts of the world that I have been in. The butchers for killing a beast, have five shillings and their diet; and they may buy a good fat, large cow for three pounds or thereabouts. The brewers sell such beer as is equal in strength to that in London, half ale and half stout for fifteen shillings per barrel; and their beer hath a better name, that is, is in more esteem than English beer in Barbadoes, and is sold for a higher price there. And for silversmiths, they have between half a crown and three shillings an ounce for working their silver, and for gold equivalent. Plasterers have commonly eighteen pence per yard for plastering. Lastmakers have sixteen shillings per dozen for their lasts. And heelmakers have two shillings a dozen for their heels. Wheel and millwrights, joiners, braziers, pewterers, dyers, fullers, combmakers, wire-drawers, cagemakers, cardmakers, painters, cutlers, ropemakers, carvers, blockmakers, turners, buttonmakers, hair and wood sievemakers, bodicemakers, gunsmiths, locksmiths, nailers, file-cutters, skinners, furriers, glovers, pattenmakers, watchmakers, clockmakers, sadlers, collarmakers, barbers, printers, bookbinders, and all other tradesmen, their gains and wages are about the same proportions as the forementioned trades in their advancements, as to what they have in England.

Of lawyers and physicians I shall say nothing, because this country is very peaceable and healthy; long may it so continue and never have occasion for the tongue of the one nor the pen of the other, both equally destructive to men's estates and lives; besides forsooth, they, hangman-like, have a license to murder and make mischief. Laboring men have commonly here between 14 and 15 pounds a year, and their meat, drink, washing and lodging; and by the day their wages is generally between eighteen pence and half a crown, and diet also. But in harvest they have usually between three and four shillings each day, and diet. The maidservants' wages is commonly betwixt six and ten pounds per annum, with very good accommodation. And for the women who get their livelihood by their own industry, their labor is very dear, for I can buy in London a cheese-cake for two pence, bigger than theirs at that price, when at the same time their milk is as cheap as we can buy it in London, and their flour cheaper by one-half.

Corn and flesh, and what else serves man for drink, food and raiment, is much cheaper here than in England or elsewhere; but the chief reason why wages of servants of all sorts is much higher here than there, arises from the great fertility and produce of the place; besides, if these large stipends were refused them they would quickly set up for themselves, for they can have provision very cheap, and land for a very small matter, or next to nothing in comparison of the purchase of lands in England; and the farmers there can better afford to give that great wages than the farmers in England can, for several reasons very obvious.

It is now time to return to the City of Brotherly Love (for so much the Greek word or name Philadelphia imports) which, though at present so obscure, that neither the mapmakers nor geographers have taken the least notice of her, though she far exceeds her namesake of Lydia (having above two thousand noble houses for her five hundred ordinary) or Celisia, or Cælesyria; yet in a very short space of time she will, in all probability, make a fine figure in the world, and be a most celebrated emporium. Here is lately built a noble town house or guild hall, also a handsome market house, and a convenient prison. The number of Christians both old and young inhabiting in that country, are, by a modest computation, adjudged to amount to above twenty thousand.

In the said city are several good schools of learning for youth, in order to the attainment of arts and sciences, as also reading, writing, etc. Here is to be had on any day in the week, tarts, pies, cakes, etc. We have also several cook shops, both roasting and boiling, as in the city of London; bread, beer, beef, and pork are sold at any time much cheaper than in England (which arises from their plenty); our wheat is very white and clear from tares, making as good and white bread as any in Europe. Happy blessings, for which we owe the highest gratitude to our plentiful Provider, the great Creator of heaven and earth. The water-mills far exceed those in England, both for quickness and grinding good meal, there being great choice of good timber, and earlier corn than in the aforesaid place, they are made by one Peter Deal, a famous and ingenious workman, especially for inventing such like machines.

All sorts of very good paper are made in the German-town; as also very fine German linen, such as no person of quality need be ashamed to wear; and in several places they make very good druggets, crapes, camblets, and serges, besides other woolen clothes, the manufacture of all which daily improves. And in most parts of the country there are many curious and spacious buildings, which several of the gentry have erected for their country houses. As for the fruit trees they plant, they arrive at such perfection, that they bear in a little more than half the time that they commonly do in England.

The Christian children born here are generally well-favored and beautiful to behold; I never knew any come into the world with the least blemish on any part of its body, being in the general observed to be better natured, milder, and more tender-hearted than those born in England.

There are very fine and delightful gardens and orchards in most parts of this country; but Edward Shippey (who lives near the capital city) has an orchard and gardens adjoining to his great house that equalizes (if not exceeds) any I have ever seen, having a very famous and pleasant summer house erected in the middle of his extraordinary fine and large garden, abounding with tulips, pinks, carnations, roses (of several sorts), lilies, not to mention those that grow wild in the fields.

Reader, what I have here written is not a fiction, flam, whim, or any sinister design, either to impose upon the ignorant or credulous, or to curry favor with the rich and mighty, but in mere pity and pure compassion to the numbers of poor laboring men, women, and children in England, half starved, visible in their meagre looks, that are continually wandering up and down looking for employment without finding any, who here need not lie idle a moment, nor want due encouragement or reward for their work, much less vagabond or drone it about. Here are no beggars to be seen (it is a shame and disgrace to the State that there are so many in England), nor indeed have any here the least occasion or temptation to take up that scandalous lazy life.

Jealousy among men is here very rare, and barrenness among women hardly to be heard of, nor are old maids to be met with; for all commonly marry before they are twenty years of age, and seldom any young married woman but hath a child upon her lap.

What I have delivered concerning this Province is indisputably true. I was an eye-witness to it all, for I went in the first ship that was bound from England for that country, since it received the name of Pennsylvania, which was in the year 1681. The ship's name was the "John and Sarah" of London, Henry Smith, Commander. I have declined giving any account of several things which I have only heard others speak of, because I did not see them myself, for I never held that way infallible, to make reports from hearsay. I saw the first cellar when it was digging for the use of our Governor, Will. Penn.

GEORGE KEITH'S NEW RELIGION.

[*From the Same.*]

THE way of worship the Swedes use in this country is the Lutheran; the English have four sorts of assemblies or religious meetings here: as first, the Church of England, who built a very fine church in the city of Philadelphia in the year 1695. Secondly, the Anabaptists; thirdly, the Presbyterians, and two sorts of Quakers (of all the most numerous by much), one party holding with George Keith; but whether both parties will join together again in one I cannot tell, for that gentleman hath altered his judgment since he came to England, concerning his church-orders in Pennsylvania, by telling and showing them precepts that were lawful in the time of the law, but forbidden under the gospel to pay tithes, or ministers to preach for hire, etc., as also to sprinkle infants; and he tells the Presbyterian minister, That he must go to the Pope of Rome for his call, for he had no Scripture for it, and that water-baptism and the outward Supper are not of the nature of the everlasting gospel; nor essential parts of it, as see his "Truth Advanced," page 173. He gives likewise a strict charge concerning plain language and plain habit, and that they should not be concerned in the compelling part of the worldly government, and that they should set their negroes at liberty after some reasonable time of service; likewise, they should not take the advantage of the law against one another, as to procure them any corporeal punishment. These orders, he tells his followers, would make distinction between them and Jews and moral heathens. This was in the year 1693, in Pennsylvania. But now, the year 1697, since he came to England, his judgment is changed, for he tells his disciples that water-baptism is come in the room of circumcision; and by so doing, they would distinguish themselves from either Jews, Pagans, or moral heathens. He keeps his meeting once a week at Turners Hall in Fill-Pot-Lane, London, on Sundays in the afternoon; he begins between two and three of the clock and commonly ends between four and five.

Friendly Reader, by this thou mayest see how wavering and mutable men of great outward learning are. If the truth of this be by anybody questioned, let them look in the Creed, and the Paper against Christians

being concerned in Worldly Government, and the Paper concerning Ne-
groes, that was given forth by the appointment of the Meeting held by
George Keith at Philip James's house in the city of Philadelphia, in
Pennsylvania; and his Letter also in Maryland against the Presbyterian
Catechism, printed at Boston in New England in 1695, with the Answer
to it bound up together in one Book, and in "Truth Advanced," page 173.
And, for what relates to him since in England, let them look into the
"Quakers' Argument Refuted, Concerning Water-Baptism and the Lord's
Supper," page 70.   And now, Reader, I shall take my leave of thee,
recommending thee with my own self to the directions of the Spirit of
God in our conscience, and that will agree with all the Holy Scriptures
in its right place; and when we find ourselves so, we have no need to
take any thought or care what anybody shall say of us.

Jonathan Dickinson.

A Merchant of Philadelphia, Pa. Wrecked on the Florida Coast, in a Voyage from Jamaica to
Philadelphia, Sept., 1696. DIED in Philadelphia, 1722.

THE CAPTURE OF THE CASTAWAYS.

[*God's Protecting Providence.* 1699.]

ABOUT the eighth or ninth hour came two Indian men . . . .
from the southward, running fiercely and foaming at the mouth,
having no weapons except their knives; and forthwith, not making any
stop, violently seized the two first of our men they met with, who were
carrying corn from the vessel to the top of the bank where I stood to
receive it and put it into a cask.   They used no violence, for the men
resisted not, but taking them under the arm brought them towards me.
Their countenance was very furious and bloody.   They had their hair tied
in a roll behind, in which stuck two bones shaped, one like a broad arrow,
the other a spear head.   The rest of our men followed from the vessel,
asking me what they should do, whether they should get their guns to
kill these two; but I persuaded them otherwise, desiring them to be quiet,
showing their inability to defend us from what would follow; but to put
our trust in the Lord, who was able to defend to the uttermost.   I walked
towards the place where our sick and lame were; the two Indian men
following me.   I told them the Indians were come and coming upon us;
and whilst these two (letting the men loose) stood with a wild furious
countenance, looking upon us, I bethought myself to give them some

tobacco and pipes, which they greedily snatched from me, and, making a snuffing noise like a wild beast, turned their backs upon us and run away.

We communed together and considered our condition, being amongst a barbarous people, such as were generally accounted man-eaters, believing those two were gone to alarum their people. We sat ourselves down, expecting cruelty and hard death, except it should please the Almighty God to work wonderfully for our deliverance. In this deep concernment some of us were not left without hopes ; blessed be the name of the Lord in whom we trusted.

As we were under a deep exercise and concernment, a motion arose from one of us that, if we should put ourselves under the denomination of Spaniards (it being known that that nation had some influence on them, and one of us named Solomon Cresson speaking the Spanish language well), it was hoped this might be a means for our delivery ; to which the most of the company assented.

Within two or three hours after the departure of the two Indians, some of our people being near the beach or strand returned and said the Indians were coming in a very great number, all running and shouting. About this time the storm was much abated, the rain ceased, and the sun appeared, which had been hid from us many days. The Indians went all to the vessel, taking forth whatever they could lay hold on, except rum, sugar, molasses, beef and pork.

But their Casseekey (for so they call their king) with about thirty more came down to us in a furious manner, having a dismal aspect and foaming at the mouth. Their weapons were large Spanish knives, except their Casseekey's, who had a bagganett that belonged to the master of our vessel. They rushed in upon us and cried, " *Nickaleez, Nickaleez.*" We understood them not at first, they repeating it over unto us often. At last they cried, " *Espainia* " or " Spaniard "; by which we understood them that at first they meant " English "; but they were answered to the latter in Spanish, " Yea," to which they replied, " No *Spainia*, no," but all cried out " *Nickaleez, Nickaleez.*" We sitting on our chests, boxes and trunks, and some on the ground, the Indians surrounded us. We stirred nor moved not, but sat all, or most of us, very calm and still, some of us in a good frame of spirit, being freely given up to the Will of God.

Whilst we were thus sitting, as a people almost unconcerned, these bloody-minded creatures placed themselves, each behind one, kicking and throwing away the bushes that were nigh or under their feet. The Casseekey had placed himself behind me, standing on the chest which I sat upon, they all having their arms extended with their knives in their hands, ready to execute their bloody design, some taking hold of some of us by the heads, with their knees set against our shoulders. In this

posture they seemed to wait for the Casseekey to begin.   They were high
in words which we understood not.   But on a sudden it pleased the Lord
to work wonderfully for our preservation, and instantly all these savage
men were struck dumb and like men amazed the space of a quarter of an
hour, in which time their countenances fell and they looked like another
people.   They quitted their places they had taken behind us and came
in amongst us, requiring to have all our chests, trunks and boxes un-
locked; which being done, they divided all that was in them.   Our
money the Casseekey took unto himself, privately hiding in the bushes.
Then they went to pulling off our clothes, leaving each of us only a pair
of breeches or an old coat, except my wife and child, Robert Barrow and
our master, from whom they took but little this day.

Having thus done, they asked us again, " *Nickaleez, Nickaleez?* "   But
we answered by saying " Pennsylvania."

We began to inquire after St. Augusteen, also would talk of Sta.
Lucea, which was a town that lay about a degree to the northward; but
they cunningly would seem to persuade us that they both lay to the
southward.   We signified to them that they lay to the northward, and
we would talk of the Havana that lay to the southward.   These places
they had heard of, and knew which way they lay.

At length the Casseekey told us how long it was to Sta. Lucea by
days' travel; but cared not to hear us mention St. Augusteen.   They
would signify by signs, we should go to the southward.   We answered,
That we must go the northward for Augusteen.   When they found they
could not otherwise persuade us, they signified that we should go to the
southward for the Havana, and that it was but a little way.

We gave them to understand that we came that way and were for the
northward; all which took place with them.   We perceived that the
Casseekey's heart was tendered towards us; for he kept mostly with us
and would the remaining part of this day keep off the petty robbers, which
would have had our few rags from us.   Sometime before night we had a
shower of rain, whereupon the Casseekey made signs for us to build some
shelter; upon which we got our tent up and some leaves to lie upon.

About this time our vessel lay dry on shore and the Indians gathered
themselves together, men and women, some hundreds in numbers.   Having got all the goods out of the vessel and covered the bay for a large
distance. opened all the stuffs and linens and spread them to dry.   They
would touch no sort of strong drink, sugar nor molasses, but left it in
the vessel.   They shouted and made great noises in the time of plunder.
Night coming on, the Casseekey put those chests and trunks which he
had reserved for himself into our tent; which pleased us and gave an
expectation of his company, for he was now become a defender of us
from the rage of others.   The Casseekey went down to the waterside

amongst his people and returned with three old coats that were wet and torn, which he gave us; one whereof I had. We made a fire at each end of our tent and laid ourselves down, it being dark; but hearing hideous noises and fearing that they were not satisfied, we expected them upon us. The chief Indian (or Casseekey) lay in the tent upon his chests; and about midnight we heard a company of Indians coming from the vessel towards us, making terrible shouts and coming fiercely up to the tent; the Casseekey called to them, which caused them to stand. It seemed they had killed a hog and brought him; so the Casseekey asked us if we would eat the hog? Solomon Cresson, by our desire, answered him that we used not to eat at that time of the night; whereupon they threw the hog down before the tent, and the Casseekey sent them away. They went shouting to the seashore, where there were some hundreds of them revelling about our wrack.

THE PAINFUL JOURNEY TO ST. AUGUSTINE.

[*From the Same.*]

THE 9 month 11. We embarked in our two boats, and those of our people that were at the other town were to have a large canoe to carry them thence, and were to meet us in the Sound. We rowed several leagues and did not meet them; being then about ten o'clock; the Spaniard would go on shore and travel back by land to see after them. We being by an inlet of the sea which was a mile over, the Spaniard ordered us to go on the other side and there stay for him; which we did many hours. . . . At length the canoe with our people came, but our Spaniard was not come, but in about half an hour's time he came with a small canoe. . . . .

We set forward in our two boats and the two canoes, and rowed till night, being nigh a place of thicketty wood, which we made choice of to lodge at for this night. Here was wood enough. We made large fires, were pleased with the place, and lay down to rest. About midnight I had a great loss. Having about a quart of berries whole, and as much pounded to mix with water to feed our child with, the fire being disturbed, the cloth which we had our food in was burnt. All was lost, and nothing to be had until we could get to the Spaniards, which was two days' march at least. About an hour after this the wind rose at northwest and it began to rain. . . . .

In this shower of rain the four Indians got from amongst us, took their canoes, and away they went back again. When day appeared, we missed them, upon which we went to the waterside, where we found the two canoes gone. And now we were in a great strait; but the Spaniard said, those that could travel best must go by land. The persons pitched upon were Richard Limpeney, Andrew Murray, Cornelius Toker, Joseph Kirle's boy, John Hilliard, and Penelope, with seven negroes, named Peter, Jack, Cæsar, Sarah, Bell, Susanna and Quenza. The Spaniard and the Indian Wan-Antonia went with them to direct them, the way carrying them over land to the seashore, and then directing to keep the seashore along to the northward.

. They returned to us, and we with our two boats rowed all day without ceasing till sunsetting; and when we put on shore, the place was an old Indian field on a high bleak hill, where had been a large Indian house, but it was tumbled down. Of the ruins of this house we made a shelter against the northwest wind, which began to blow very bleak. The Spaniard went to the sea, which was not two miles off, to see if our people had passed, and at his return he said, they were gone by. We asked if they could reach to any house or Indian town for shelter; for we supposed, should they be without fire this night, they could not live. He said, they must travel all night. Night came on. We had fire and wood enough, and had gathered a great heap of grass to lie in, hoping to have got some rest; but the northwest increased, and the cold was so violent, that we were in a lamentable condition, not able to rest; for as we lay or stood so close to the fire that it would scorch us, that side from it was ready to freeze. We had no other way but to stand and keep turning for the most part of the night. We all thought that we never felt the like. The Spaniard that was clothed was as bad to bear it as we that were naked. At length day appeared and we must go.

The 9 month 13. This morning we were loath to part with our fires; but to stay here it could not be. So we went to our boats; wading in the water was ready to benumb us. But we put forward, and rowing about two leagues came to an old house, where the Spaniard told us we must leave the boats and travel by land. We had a boggy marsh to wade through for a mile to get to the seashore, and had about five or six leagues along the bay or strand to the Spanish sentinel's house. The northwest wind was violent, and the cold such that the strongest of us thought we should not outlive that day. Having got through the boggy marsh and on the seashore, our people, black and white, made all speed, one not staying for another that could not travel so fast; none but I with my wife and child, Robert Barrow, my kinsman Benjamin Allen and my negro London, whom I kept to help carry my child, keeping together. The rest of our company had left us, expecting not to see some of us again, especially Robert Barrow, my wife and child. We travelled after as well as we could; having gone about two miles, the cold so seized on my kinsman Benjamin Allen that he began to be stiff in his limbs, and staggered and fell, grievously complaining that the cold would kill him. Our negro having our young child, I and my wife took our kinsman under each arm and helped him along; but at length his limbs were quite stiff, his speech almost gone, and he began to foam at the mouth. In this strait we knew not what to do; to stay with him we must perish also, and we were willing to strive as long as we could. We carried our kinsman and laid him under the bank, not being dead. I resolved to run after our people, some of them not being out of sight; which I did, and left my wife and child with the negro to follow as fast as they could. I ran about two miles, making signs to them, thinking, if they should look behind and see me running, they would stop till I got up with them. I was in hopes that if I could have accomplished this my design, to have got help to have carried my kinsman along. But they stopped not, and I ran until the wind pierced me so that my limbs failed, and I fell; yet still I strove and getting up walked backwards to meet my wife. As I was going, I met with the Spaniard coming out of the sand-hills, and Joseph Kirle's negro Ben. I made my complaint to the Spaniard, but he, not being able to understand me well, went forward. I then applied myself to the negro, making large promises, if he would fetch my kinsman; he offered to go back and use his endeavor, which he did. At length my wife and child came up with me. She was almost overcome with grief, expressing in what manner we were forced to part with our kinsman, and expecting that she and the child should go next.

Poor Robert Barrow was a great way behind us. I feared we should never see him again. I used my endeavor to comfort and cheer my wife, entreating her not to let grief overcome her. I had hopes that the Lord would help us in this strait, as He hath done in many since we were in this land. . . . .

I took my child from the negro and carried him. I had an Indian mat with a split in it, through which I put my head, hanging over my breast unto my waist. Under this I carried my child, which helped to break the wind off it; but the poor babe was black with cold from head to foot, and its flesh as cold as a stone; yet it was not froward. Its mother would take it now and then, and give it the breast, but little could it get at it; besides, we dared not stop in the least, for if we did, we should perceive our limbs to fail. About two o'clock in the afternoon we came up with our negro woman Hagar, with her child at her back almost dead; and a little further we came up with our negro girl Quenza, being dead as we thought, for she was as stiff as a dead body could be, and her eyes set; but at length we perceived her breathe; but she had no sense, nor motion. We carried her from the waterside under the bank.

This increased my wife's sorrow, and she began to doubt she should not be able to travel much further; but I endeavored to encourage her not to leave striving as long as any ability was left. . . . .

The sun was nigh setting, and we began to look out for the sentinel's post; and my negro at times got upon several of the highest sand-hills to look out, but could not see any house nor the smoke of fire. This was terrible to us all, for the day being so cold, the night much more, and we not able to travel without rest, being a starved people both within our bodies and without, and if we ceased from travelling, we should instantly be numbed and move no further. In the midst of these reasonings and doubtings we were got into, I espied a man, as I thought, standing on the bank, but at great distance. I was afraid to speak, lest it should prove otherwise; but he was soon seen by the whole company, and at length we espied him walking towards the land. This confirmed us, and so we took to the hills again to look out, yet could not see the house from thence; but on the next hill we saw it. This was joy unto us, though we began to have a sense of our tiredness, for our resolution abated after we had got sight of the house.

When we got to the house, we found four sentinels and the Spaniard our guide, with the three of our men, viz., Joseph Buckley, Nathaniel Randall, and John Shires. The Spaniard bid us welcome and made room for us to sit down by the fire. The chiefest man of the sentinels took a kersey coat and gave my wife to cover her, and gave each of us a piece of bread made of Indian corn, which was pleasant unto us; after it we had plenty of hot casseena drink. It was dark, and we endeavored to prevail with the Spaniards to go seek for Robert Barrow and my kinsman, offering them considerable; but they seemed not fully to understand me, yet I could make them sensible that my kinsman was almost dead, if not quite, and that the old man was in a bad condition. They made me to understand that the weather was not fit to go out, but they would watch if Robert should pass by. About an hour or two after, one of the Spaniards being walking out of the bay met with Robert and brought him into the house. We rejoiced to see him, and inquired concerning our kinsman and negro Ben. He said our kinsman was striving to get up and could not; he came to him and spake unto him; he could not answer, but cried, and he could not help him; but coming along at some considerable distance met negro Ben, who said he was going for Benjamin Allen, so he past him; and some miles further he saw negro Jack drawing himself down from the bank, his lower parts being dead, and crying out for some fire that he might save his life; but he did not see the negro girl whom we hauled out of the way. We were under a great concern for our kinsman; the Spaniards we could not prevail upon to go and fetch him, or go and carry wherewith to make a fire; which had they done and found them living, it might have preserved them; but we hoped negro Ben would bring our kinsman.

The Spaniards would have had most of us to have gone to the next sentinel's house, which was a league further; but we all begged hard of them to let us lie in their house in any place on the ground for we were not able to travel further: besides, the cold would kill us; for we were in such a trembling, shaking condition, and so full of pain from head to foot, that it's not to be expressed. At length the Spaniards 'consented that Robert Barrow, I, my wife and child, and John Smith should lie in the house; but to Joseph Buckley, Nathaniel Randall, John Shires and my negro London they would not grant that favor. So one of the Spaniards taking a firebrand bid those four go with him. He directed them to a small thicket of trees and showed them to gather wood and make large fires and sleep there. These poor creatures lay out, and it proved a hard, frosty night. The Spaniard returned and said they were got into a wood and had fire enough. We were silent, but feared they would hardly live till morning.

After they were gone, the Spaniards took a pint of Indian corn and parched it and gave part to us, which we accepted cheerfully; also they gave us some casseena drink. We were in extraordinary pain, so that we could not rest, and our feet were extremely bruised; the skin was off, and the sand caked with the blood that we could hardly set our feet to the ground after we had been some time in the house. The night was extreme cold though we were in the house; and by the fire we could not be warm, for one side did scorch whilst the other was ready to freeze: and thus we passed the night.

The 9 month 14. This morning we looked out, and there was a very hard frost on the ground, so it was terrible to go out of doors. Our people returned from the wood, but complained heavily of their hardship in the night. They had not been an hour in the house before the Spaniards gave us all a charge to be gone to the next sentinel's house. This was grievous to us all, but more especially to my wife, who could not raise herself when down; but go we must, for, though we entreated hard for my wife and Robert Barrow, we could not prevail that they might stay till we could get a canoe. As we were all going one Spaniard made a sign for me and my wife to stay, which we did; and it was to have a handful of parched corn. As soon as we had received it they bid us be gone to the next sentinel's, where was victuals enough for us. The sun was a great height, but we could not feel any warmth it gave, the northwester beginning to blow as hard as it did the day before; and having deep sand to travel through, which made our travelling this one league very hard, especially to my wife and Robert. The Spaniards sent my wife a blanket, to be left at the next sentinel's house.

At length we came to an inlet of the sea; on the other side was the look-out and sentinel's house. Here were all our people sitting, waiting to be carried over, and in a little time came one of the sentinels with a canoe and carried us over.

This sentinel would not suffer us to come into his house, but caused us to kindle a fire under the lee of his house and there sit down. About half an hour after he bid us be gone to the next sentinel's, which was a league further, giving us a cup of casseena and two quarts of Indian corn for us all, bidding us go to our company at next house and have our corn dressed there.

I understood that our negro woman Hagar got hither late last night having her child dead at her back, which the Spaniards buried.

One of the Spaniards went with us to the next inlet, carrying a stick of fire to set fire of some trash to make a signal for them on the other side to fetch us over, the inlet being very wide. When the canoe came over for us, our guide took the blanket from my wife; but the negro which brought over the canoe lent my wife one of his coats; so we got over, but before we got to the house we had a shower of hail. At this house we were kindly received, having such a mess of victuals as we had not had in a long time before, which was very pleasant to our hunger-starved stomachs. Our people went hence this morning for Augusteen, having a guide with them; but John Hoster and Penelope were left here, not being able to travel. We remained here till the morrow, but the night was so extreme cold that we could not rest.

The 9 month 15. This morning the Spaniards bid us prepare to travel, for they were not able to maintain us. We understood that it was five or six leagues to Augusteen, and we could not travel so far, being all of us lamed and stiff. We entreated them to let us go in a canoe, but they denied us. We entreated for the two women and Robert Barrow. At length we prevailed that they should go up in a canoe, for the canoe was to go whether we went or not.

While all this discourse was, came in a couple of Spaniards, one being the sentinel that went with our people the day before; the other was a person the Governor had sent with a canoe and four Spaniards to fetch us. This was cheerful news; for had we gone to have travelled without a guide, we should have perished. The man that came for us brought two blankets, one for my wife, the other for Penelope. He desired us to be going. About a league distance from the place he left the canoe, which we parted with very unwillingly; for some of our people, had they had a mile further to have gone, could not have gone it. The wind still continued at northwest and blowed very fiercely; and extreme cold it was. We had such a continual shivering and pain in our bones that we were in violent anguish.

Our poor child was quiet, but so black with cold and shaking that it was admirable how it lived. We got to Augusteen about two hours before night. Being put on shore, we were directed to the Governor's house; being got thither we were led up a pair of stairs, at the head whereof stood the Governor, who ordered my wife to be conducted to his wife's apartment. I and John Smith went into a room where the Governor asked us a few questions; but seeing how extreme cold we were, he gave us a cup of Spanish wine and sent us into his kitchen to warm ourselves at the fire. About half an hour afterwards the Governor sent for John Smith and me and gave us a shirt and sliders, a hat and a pair of silk stockings, telling us he had no woolen clothes as yet, but would have some made. We put on the linen and made all haste into the kitchen to the fire. Robert Barrow was quartered at another house. The persons came to the Governor's house and took such as they were minded to quarter in their houses; so that Joseph Kirle, John Smith, I, my wife and child lodged at the Governor's house. All our people that came up with Joseph Kirle came to see us. We perceived the people's great kindness; for they were all well clothed from head to foot with the best the people had.   .   .   .   .

We had a plentiful supper, and we fed like people that had been half starved, for we ate not knowing when we had enough; and we found our palates so changed by eating of berries, that we could not relish the taste of salt any more than if it had no saltness in it. We had lodging provided.

William Penn.

BORN in London, England, 1644. DIED at Ruscombe, Berkshire, England, **1718.**

A LETTER TO THE INDIANS.

[Select Works of William Penn. 1782.]

MY FRIENDS, There is a Great God and Power, that hath made the world and all things therein, to whom you and I and all people owe their being and well-being; and to whom you and I must one day give an account for all that we do in the world. This Great God hath written his Law in our hearts, by which we are taught and commanded to love and help, and do good to one another, and not to do harm and mischief unto one another. Now this Great God hath been pleased to make me concerned in your part of the world, and the king of the country where I live hath given me a great province therein; but I desire to enjoy it with your love and consent, that we may always live together as neighbors and friends; else what would the Great God do to us? who hath made us not to devour and destroy one another, but to live soberly and kindly together in the world.   Now I would have you well observe that I am very sensible of the unkindness and injustice that hath been too much exercised towards you by the people of these parts of the world, who have sought themselves, and to make great advantages by you, rather than to be examples of justice and goodness unto you, which I hear hath been matter of trouble unto you, and caused great grudgings and animosities, sometimes to the shedding of blood, which hath made the Great God angry.   But I am not such a man, as is well known in my own country.   I have great love and regard towards you, and I desire to win and gain your love and friendship by a kind, just, and peaceable life, and the people I send are of the same mind, and shall in all things behave themselves accordingly; and if in any thing any shall offend you or your people, you shall have a full and speedy satisfaction for the same, by an equal number of just men on both sides, that by no means you may have just occasion of being offended against them.

I shall shortly come to you myself, at what time we may more largely and freely confer and discourse of these matters; in the mean time I have sent my commissioners to treat with you about land, and a firm league of peace.—Let me desire you to be kind to them and the people, and receive these presents and tokens which I have sent you, as a testimony of my good-will to you, and my resolution to live justly, peaceably, and friendly with you.

I am your loving friend,

W. PENN

ON HIS DEPARTURE FROM AMERICA.

[Written from aboard the ketch " Endeavor," the Sixth month, 1684.]

TO THOMAS LLOYD, J. CLAYPOLE, J. SIMCOCK, C. TAYLOR, AND J. HARRISON, to be communicated in Meetings in Pennsylvania and the Territories thereunto belonging, among friends.

My love and my life is to you, and with you, and no water can quench it, nor distance wear it out, or bring it to an end.   I have been with you, cared over you, and served you with unfeigned love; and you are beloved of me, and near to me beyond utterance. I bless you in the name and power of the Lord, and may God bless you with his righteousness, peace, and plenty all the land over! O that you would eye him in all, through all, and above all the labor of your hands, and let it be your first care how you may glorify him in your undertakings; for to a blessed end are you brought hither; and if you see and keep but in the sense of that providence, your coming, staying, and improving will be sanctified; but if any forget him, and call not upon his name in truth, He will pour out his plagues upon them, and they shall know who it is judgeth the children of men.

O, you are now come to a quiet land! And now that liberty and authority are with you and in your hands, let the government be upon His shoulders in all your spirits, that you may rule for him under whom the princes of this world will one day esteem it their honor to govern and serve in their places. I cannot but say, when these things come mightily upon my mind, as the Apostle said of old, "What manner of persons ought we to be in all godly conversation!" Truly the name and honor of the Lord are deeply concerned in you as to the discharge of yourselves in your present station, many eyes being upon you; and remember that, as we have been belied about disowning the true religion, so, of all government, to behold us exemplary and Christian in the use of it will not only stop our enemies, but minister conviction to many on that account prejudiced. O that you may see and know that service, and do it for the Lord in this your day!

And thou, Philadelphia, the virgin settlement of this province, named before thou wert born, what love, what care, what service, and what travail hast here been to bring thee forth and preserve thee from such as would abuse and defile thee!

O that thou mayest be kept from the evil that would overwhelm thee; that, faithful to the God of thy mercies, in the life of righteousness, thou mayest be preserved to the end! My soul prays to God for thee, that thou mayest stand in the day of trial, that thy children may be blessed of the Lord, and thy people saved by his power. My love to thee has been great, and the remembrance of thee affects my heart and mine eye.—The God of eternal strength keep and preserve thee to his glory and thy peace!

So, dear friends, my love again salutes you all, wishing that grace, mercy and peace, with all temporal blessings, may abound richly amongst you! so says, so prays your friend and lover in the truth,

WILLIAM PENN.

John Wise.

BORN in Roxbury, Mass., 1652. DIED at Ipswich, Mass., 1725.

THE ANGLO-SAXON HATRED OF ARBITRARY POWER.

[*The Churches' Quarrel Espoused*. 1710.]

ENGLISHMEN hate an arbitrary power (politically considered) as they hate the devil.

For that they have, through immemorial ages, been the owners of very fair enfranchisements and liberties, that the sense, favor or high esteem of them are (as it were) *extraduce*, transmitted with the elemental materials of their essence from generation to generation, and so ingenate and mixed with their frame, that no artifice, craft or force used can root it out. *Naturam expellas furca licet usque recurrit.* And though many of their incautelous princes have endeavored to null all their charter rights and immunities, and aggrandize themselves in the servile state of the subjects, by setting up their own separate will for the great standard of government over the nations, yet they have all along paid dear for their attempts, both in the ruin of the nation, and in interrupting the increase of their own grandeur, and their foreign settlements and conquests.

Had the late reigns, before the accession of the great William and Mary to the throne of England, but taken the measures of them, and her present majesty, in depressing vice, and advancing the union and wealth, and encouraging the prowess and bravery of the nation, they might by this time have been capable to have given laws to any monarch on earth ; but spending their time in the pursuit of an absolute monarchy (contrary to the temper of the nation, and the ancient constitution of the government) through all the meanders of state craft, it has apparently kept back the glory and dampened all the most noble affairs of the nation. And when under the midwifery of Machiavelian art, and cunning of a daring prince, this monster, tyranny, and arbitrary government, was at last just born, upon the holding up of a finger ! or upon the least signal given, on the whole nation goes upon this hydra.

The very name of an arbitrary government is ready to put an Englishman's blood into a fermentation ; but when it really comes, and shakes its whip over their ears, and tells them it is their master, it makes them stark mad ; and being of a mimical genius, and inclined to follow the court mode, they turn arbitrary too.

That some writers, who have observed the governments and humors of nations, thus distinguish the English :

The emperor (say they) is the king of kings, the king of Spain is the king of men, the king of France the king of asses, and the king of England the king of devils; for that the English nation can never be bridled and rid by an arbitrary prince. Neither can any chains put on by despotic and arbitrary measures hold these legions.

Thomas Bridge.

BORN near London, England, 1657. DIED in Boston, Mass., 1715.

THE CHOICE OF CIVIL OFFICERS.

[Jethro's Advice recommended to the Inhabitants of Boston in N. E. 1710.]

MANIFEST your value for your privileges by choosing men hating covetousness into all such public offices and stations as are at your dispose. Consider:—There is no security for any privilege or trust committed to a covetous man. They are usually timorous and fearful, they are flatterers and time-servers, and their greediness after riches will influence them to accept a good proffer when presented by them that know how to make the advantage. It is impossible to conceive the mischiefs done by the covetous. How many cities, towns and countries have been bought and sold by the covetous! Whence had the French their glory, but by pensioners in the several neighboring countries, who exposed privileges to sale whereby he had the opportunity to seize the effects? And is not this one great end of this long and expensive war (which hath cost many millions of treasure and hundreds of thousand lives), to make him refund that which he purchased so clandestinely?

Men hating covetousness will do much service. I intend not this qualification, exclusive of others, but in conjunction; even able men, men fearing God, men of truth, hating covetousness; this generous principle will dispose them to employ all their talents and interests to serve the public. They will have a watchful eye over the covetous, they know their narrow selfish souls are always contriving by subtle artifices to gull the public; and therefore will endeavor to prevent them. Whereas the public good lying near the hearts of these, they will be always projecting and contriving something to promote it, viz., To reform the manners of the town; to prevent nuisances and inconveniences; to strengthen and defend it; to regulate and increase the trade of it; to relieve and supply the poor; and to punish the disorderly as far as their power extends. And besides all this, will be examples of a ready, cheerful contribution of their proportion to the public charge.

Men hating covetousness will not only do most service for the public, but with least expense. Here we may observe : There are indeed divers offices in the town, which qualified men ought to attend out of pure regard to the public good (as members of the body politic) without expecting a salary. Men hating covetousness will serve the town in such capacities, readily, cheerfully and impartially, and ought to be treated with respect, loved and valued for their fidelity. It is lamentable to consider what ill-usage such have sometimes met with.

There are other officers in the town, who justly expect a support suitable to their stations and work; I advise to choose men hating covetousness into such stations and employment: — on this account, that they will do most good with least charge; which will appear if we consider, (1.) That those who choose persons into public offices, whether ecclesiastical or civil, ought to provide for their subsistence to such a degree, that they may diligently and cheerfully attend on that service to which they call them : this is their due by the laws of God and man; to deny or withhold it, is to contradict one of the first dictates of the law of nature, therefore such may and ought to expect it, and depend upon it. (2.) Men hating covetousness will be content with a competency; there is a bound and limit to their desires in this respect. As they pray that God would feed them with food convenient, so they expect no more from man, but what is suitable to their station and circumstance. But here I must observe, that for this their temper, they are often horribly abused and neglected; for which God will judge. But then consider, if covetous greedy men be put in such stations, what will follow. They will thus argue : "There is a suitable supply for the support of me and mine due to me by all laws divine and human. If I provide not for my own, especially for those of my own house, I deny the faith, i. e., the Christian faith, and am worse than an infidel. I have no other way to subsist while I live, nor leave to mine when I die. These people deny me what is just and equal; it is not for want, they have enough, they have plenty. I see it in their costly and extravagant garbs, their stately fabrics, their rich furniture; in their shops, ships, in their fields and barns. Therefore having an opportunity in my hand, I will improve it, and employ all the methods and agents I can, to get that which they unjustly detain from me." And thus oftentimes covetous men squeeze more treasure from them, than would support many others ; and they have no remedy; but may sit down bewailing their folly, in withholding more than was meet. I beseech you to consider what mischief covetous men may do in their several offices and stations ; some by false entries, defacing or altering of records; by wasting of treasure ; by unjust rates and cruel exactions, by denying to vote or selling of votes ; and by innumerable methods and subtle devices; and you will perceive they are dangerous men and to be avoided ; they are often (as we term them) sober men, and nothing to be objected, save only in the matter of covetousness ; they will pretend to save charges, but are of all men most profuse and lavish, will lose opportunities for doing of service, and part with rich advantages for the public, rather than stay a few hours from their own interest.

The Saybrook Platform.

ASSENTED to by the United Ministers of Connecticut in 1708.

CAUSE AND MANNER OF ITS ADOPTION.

[*The Heads of Agreement.* 1710.]

OUR difficulties having been of a long time troublesome, for the healing our wounds a more explicate asserting the rules of government sufficiently provided in the holy word hath been thought highly expedient—Wherefore,

The Honorable, the General Assembly of this Colony, out of a tender regard to the welfare of the Churches within the limits of their government, were pleased to appoint the several elders of each county, with messengers from their Churches, to meet in council ; in which they should endeavor to agree in some general rules conformable to the Word of God for a method of discipline to be practised in our Churches. These several councils having met and drawn up some rules for Church government, did by their delegates meet and constitute one General Assembly of the Churches of this colony, at Saybrook, September 9th, 1708. Who, after a full consent and agreement unto the Confession of Faith assented unto by the Synod of Boston, did, being studious of keeping "the unity of the Spirit in the bond of peace," Eph. iv. 3, agree that the Heads of Agreement assented to by the united brethren formerly called Presbyterian and Congregational in England, be observed by the Churches throughout this colony ; which are herewith published : and, after consideration of the several draughts of the county councils, did, with a Christian condescension and fraternal amicableness, unanimously agree to the Articles for the Administration of Church Discipline now offered to public view, all which being presented were allowed of and established by the General Assembly of this colony, as by their acts appears. . . . The aforesaid articles consist in two heads, *The one holding forth the power of particular Churches in the management of Discipline confirmed by scriptures annexed.*

The other *serves to preserve, promote, or recover the peace and edification of the Churches by the means of a consociation of the Elders and Churches, or of an association of the Elders.*

THE HEADS OF AGREEMENT.

[*From the Same.*]

I. OF CHURCHES AND CHURCH MEMBERS.

WE acknowledge our Lord Jesus Christ to have one Catholic Church or Kingdom, comprehending all that are united to him, whether in heaven or earth. And do conceive the whole multitude of visible believers, and their infant seed (commonly called the Catholic visible Church), to belong to Christ's spiritual kingdom in this world. But, for the notion of a Catholic visible Church here, as it signifies its having been collected into any formed society under a visible common head on earth, whether one person singly or many collectively, we, with the rest of Protestants, unanimously disclaim it.

2. We agree that particular societies of visible saints who, under Christ their head, are statedly joined together for ordinary communion with one another in all the ordinances of Christ, are particular churches, and are to be owned by each other as instituted churches of Christ, though differing in apprehensions and practice in some lesser things.

3. That none shall be admitted as members, in order to communion in all the special ordinances of the Gospel, but such persons as are knowing and sound in the fundamental doctrine of the Christian religion; without scandal in their lives; and, to a judgment regulated by the word of God, are persons of visible holiness and honesty, credibly professing cordial subjection to Jesus Christ.

4. A competent number of such visible saints (as before described) do become the capable subjects of stated communion in all the special ordinances of Christ, upon their mutual declared consent and agreement to walk together therein according to Gospel rule. In which declaration different degrees of explicitness shall no ways hinder such churches from owning each other as instituted churches.

5. Though parochial bounds be not of divine right, yet for common edification the members of a particular church ought (as much as conveniently may be) to live near one another.

6. That each particular church hath right to choose their own officers, and, being furnished with such as are duly qualified and ordained according to the Gospel rule, hath authority from Christ for exercising

government and of enjoying all the ordinances of worship within itself.

7. In the administration of church power it belongs to the Pastors and other Elders of every particular church, if such there be, to rule and govern ; and to the brotherhood to consent, according to the rule of the Gospel.

8. That all professors as before described are bound in duty, as they have opportunity, to join themselves as fixed members of some particular church ; their thus joining being part of their professed subjection to the Gospel of Christ, and an instituted means of their establishment and edification ; whereby they are under the pastoral care and, in case of scandalous or offensive walking, may be authoritatively admonished or censured for their recovery, and for vindication of the truth and the church professing it.

9. That a visible professor, thus joined to a particular church, ought to continue steadfast with the said church ; and not forsake the ministry, and ordinances there dispensed, without an orderly seeking a recommendation unto another church ; which ought to be given, when the case of the person apparently requires it.

II. OF THE MINISTRY.

1. We agree that the ministerial office is instituted by Jesus Christ for the gathering, guiding, edifying and governing of his church ; and to continue to the end of the world.

2. They who are called to this office ought to be endued with competent learning and ministerial gifts, as also with the grace of God, sound in judgment, not novices in the faith and knowledge of the Gospel ; without scandal, of holy conversation, and such as devote themselves to the work and service thereof.

3. That ordinarily none shall be ordained to the work of this ministry but such as are called and chosen thereunto by a particular church.

4. That in so great and weighty a matter as the calling and choosing a pastor, we judge it ordinarily requisite that every such church consult and advise with the pastors of neighboring congregations.

5. That after such advice the person consulted about, being chosen by the brotherhood of that particular church over which he is to be set, and he accepting, be duly ordained and set apart to his office over them ; wherein 'tis ordinarily requisite that the pastors of neighboring congregations concur with the preaching Elder or Elders, if such there be.

6. That, whereas such ordination only is intended for such as never before had been ordained to the ministerial office ; if any judge that, in case also of the removal of one formerly ordained to a new station or

pastoral charge, there ought to be a like solemn recommending him and his labors to the grace and blessing of God, no different sentiments or practice herein shall be any occasion of contention, or breach of communion among us.

7. It is expedient that they who enter on the work of preaching the Gospel be not only qualified for the communion of saints, but also that, except in case extraordinary, they give proof of their gifts and fitness for the said work, unto the Pastors of churches, of known abilities, to discern and judge of their qualifications; that they may be sent forth with solemn approbation and prayer; which we judge needful, that no doubt may remain concerning their being called unto the work; and for preventing (as much as in us lieth) ignorant and rash intruders.

III. OF CENSURES.

1. As it can not be avoided but that. in the purest churches on earth, there will sometimes offences and scandals arise by reason of hypocrisy and prevailing corruption: so Christ hath made it the duty of every church to reform itself by spiritual remedies, appointed by him, to be applied in all such cases, viz.: Admonition and Excommunication.

2. Admonition, being the rebuking of an offending member in order to conviction, is in case of private offences to be performed according to the rule in Matt. xviii. 15, 16, 17; and in case of public offences openly before the church, as the honor of the Gospel and the nature of the scandal shall require; and if either of the Admonitions take place for the recovery of the fallen person, all further proceedings in a way of censure are thereon to cease, and satisfaction to be declared accordingly.

3. When all due means are used, according to the order of the Gospel, for the restoring an offending and scandalous brother, and he, notwithstanding, remains impenitent, the censure of Excommunication is to be proceeded unto; wherein the Pastor and other Elders (if there be such) are to lead and go before the church: and the brotherhood to give their consent in a way of obedience unto Christ, and to the Elders, as over them in the Lord.

4. It may sometimes come to pass that a church member, not otherwise scandalous, may fully withdraw and divide himself from the communion of the church to which he belongeth. In which case, when all due means for the reducing him prove ineffectual, he having thereby cut himself off from that church's communion, the church may justly esteem and declare itself discharged of any further inspection over him.

IV. OF COMMUNION OF CHURCHES.

1. We agree that particular churches ought not to walk so distinct and separate with each other, as not to have care and tenderness towards one another. But their Pastors ought to have frequent meetings together that by mutual advice, support, encouragement, and brotherly intercourse, they may strengthen the hearts and hands of each other in the ways of the Lord.

2. That none of our particular churches shall be subordinate to one another, each being endued with equality of power from Jesus Christ. And that none of the said particular churches, their officer or officers, shall exercise any power or have any superiority over any other church or their officers.

3. That known members of particular churches constituted as aforesaid may have occasional communion with one another in the ordinances of the Gospel, viz.: the Word, Prayer, Sacraments, Singing of Psalms, dispensed according to the mind of Christ: unless that church with which they desire communion hath any just exception against them.

4. That we ought not to admit any one to be a member of our respective congregations, that hath joined himself to another, without endeavors of mutual satisfaction of the congregation concerned.

5. That one church ought not to blame the proceedings of another until it hath heard what that church charged, its elders or messengers, can say in vindication of themselves from any charge of irregular or injurious proceedings.

6. That we are most willing and ready to give an account of our church proceedings to each other, when desired, for preventing or removing any offences that may arise among us. Likewise we shall be ready to give the right hand of fellowship and walk together according to the Gospel rules of communion of churches.

V. OF DEACONS AND RULING ELDERS.

We agree, the office of a Deacon is of divine appointment, and that it belongs to their office to receive, lay out, and distribute the church's stock to its proper uses, by the direction of the Pastor and brethren, if need be. And, whereas divers are of opinion that there is also the office of Ruling Elders, who labor not in word and doctrine, and others think otherwise, we agree that this difference make no breach among us.

VI. OF OCCASIONAL MEETING OF MINISTERS, ETC.

1. We agree that in order to concord, and in other weighty and difficult cases, it is needful and according to the mind of Christ that the

Ministers of the several churches be consulted and advised with about such matters.

2. That such meetings may consist of smaller or greater numbers, as the matters shall require.

3. That particular churches, their respective elders and members, ought to have a reverential regard to their judgment so given, and not dissent therefrom without apparent ground from the word of God.

VII. OF OUR DEMEANOR TOWARDS THE CIVIL MAGISTRATE.

1. We do reckon ourselves obliged continually to pray for God's protection, guidance and blessing upon the rulers set over us.

2. That we ought to yield unto them not only subjection in the Lord, but support, according to our station and abilities.

3. That, if at any time it shall be their pleasure to call together any number of us, to require an account of our affairs and the state of our congregations, we shall most readily express all dutiful regard to them herein.

VIII. OF A CONFESSION OF FAITH.

As to what appertains to soundness of judgment in matters of faith, we esteem it sufficient that a church acknowledge the Scriptures to be the word of God, the perfect and only rule of faith and practice, and own either the doctrinal part of those commonly called the Articles of the Church of England, or the Confession or Catechisms, shorter or longer, compiled by the Assembly at Westminster, or the Confession agreed on at the Savoy, to be agreeable to the said rule.

IX. OF OUR DUTY AND DEPORTMENT TOWARDS THEM THAT ARE NOT IN COMMUNION WITH US.

1. We judge it our duty to bear a Christian respect to all Christians, according to their several ranks and stations, that are not of our persuasion or communion.

2. As for such as may be ignorant of the principles of the Christian Religion, or of vicious conversation, we shall in our respective places, as they give opportunity, endeavor to explain to them the doctrine of life and salvation, and to our utmost persuade them to be reconciled to God.

3. That such who appear to have the essential requisites to Church-communion, we shall willingly receive them in the Lord, not troubling them with disputes about lesser matters.

As we assent to the fore-mentioned Heads of Agreement, so we unanimously resolve, as the Lord shall enable us, to practice according to them.

Benjamin Wadsworth.

BORN in Milton, Mass., 1669.   DIED at Cambridge, Mass., 1737.

THE CHARACTER OF WILLIAM III.

[King William Lamented in America. 1702.]

OUR late King William was a great blessing to his people with respect to his example in general.   He was by his example an encourager of virtue and discourager of vice.   I am not able to give his character and therefore dare not undertake it, unless in repeating the words of one who has attempted it.

"A Prince the best qualified for a throne, being great without pride, true to his word, wise in his deliberations, secret in his councils, generous in his attempts, undaunted in dangers, valiant without cruelty. Who loves justice with moderation, government without tyranny, religion without persecution, and devotion without hypocrisy or superstition. A Prince unchanged under all events, never puffed up with success or disheartened with hardships and misfortunes; always the same though under various circumstances, which is the true symptom of a great soul."   .   .   .   .

Some persons when advanced to highest power and authority, have given up themselves to the most sluggish ease, the most shameful licentiousness, and the most brutish pleasures: they have lived as though their chief business was to employ all their power in satisfying their cursed lusts; they have been guilty of greater cruelty, oppression and tyranny than can easily be expressed.   Such were several of the Roman Emperors; one of which was so vile as to wish, "That all the Roman people had but one neck, that so he might destroy them all at once."   Such are ordinarily, some of the sorest plagues, the greatest curses that a people meet withal.   But our deceased, bewailed Sovereign was quite contrary. He was ever ready to deny himself even of lawful, allowable recreations and pleasures for the good of his people, and that from his very youth. He was born at the Hague in Holland, November 4, 1650.   And before he was seventeen years old, he did wonderful things indeed in delivering Holland, his native country, from the unjust assaults, ravages, and insults of the French power.   He frequently and eminently exposed his person in dangerous battles to recover liberty for his country.   Like another Nehemiah he sought the welfare of his people.   Neither did he seek the welfare of any one Nation only, but the welfare of all Protestant people. When England, Scotland, and Ireland were in languishing circumstances, almost quite deprived of liberty and property; having their religion, laws, and lives in utmost hazard; sinking under arbitrary power and tyranny; almost overwhelmed with Popery and slavery (or at least in eminent danger of being so),—I say, when they were in this woful case, this illustrious and noble Prince, with great generosity, valor, and courage, did venture his person for their relief, and came over the sea to help them. He landed in England November 5, 1688, and never ceased his prudent applications till the kingdom was quietly possessed of those precious things, which were before so much endangered. The greatness of his spirit and action in this affair is not easily to be described. 'Twas a pious and noble undertaking that has but few (if any) parallels in history. Neither did he seek himself in this affair, but the good of our nation and the Protestants in general, declaring himself in these words: "We have nothing before our eyes in this our undertaking, but the preservation of the Protestant religion, the covering of all men from persecution for their consciences, and the securing the whole nation the free enjoyment of all their laws, rights, and liberties under a just and legal government."

Indeed, this declaration was noble and generous, and his following practice was truly answerable to it. Thus he was, under God, the deliverer of England from Popery and slavery, which they were so eminently in danger of. In this thing, God did that which was wonderful in the eyes and rejoicing to the hearts of his faithful children. Hereupon he was within a little while, viz., Feb. 13, 1688, proclaimed and soon after, viz., April 11, 1688, crowned King of England. And when he had done all this for our nation, he was yet willing to do more. He carried it towards them as their protector, defender, and nursing father; he led their armies, fought their battles, and frequently exposed and jeoparded his royal person in the high places of the field, for their good and welfare. He exposed himself to dangers by sea and land for their sakes. The Protestant interest lay near to his royal heart; his desire and ambition was to suppress Popery and slavery as much as possible and to advance the contrary; and never spared to venture his royal life in the most hazardous enterprises for that end. While he thus fought the battles of the Lord, Divine Protection was a shield unto him; though he was several times wounded in battle, yet not dangerously. Once when a bullet slanted upon his right shoulder, took out a piece of his coat, and tore the skin and flesh, he said upon it: "There was no necessity the bullet should have come nearer." He put himself under Divine Protection, and though there were many Popish, hellish plots and conspiracies against his sacred life, yet merciful Divine Providence rendered them abortive and fruitless. In his great undertakings for God's People, he put not his confidence in men, but trusted in the Lord. When he was coming to save England he said in his Declaration, "We hope that all people will judge rightly of us, and approve of these, our proceedings, but we chiefly rely on the blessing of God for the success of this, our undertaking, in which we place our whole and only confidence."

And in the morning before he designed a terrible battle with his enemies, he has retired to his coach with his chaplain, to have his person and affairs seriously and suitably recommended to the protection and blessing of Heaven.

Neither did our courageous and religious King count it enough to expose his person in time of war for the good of his people, but when he had obtained peace for them he did his utmost to make them happy.

John Williams.

BORN in Roxbury, Mass., 1664.   DIED at Deerfield, Mass., **1729.**

THE DESOLATIONS OF DEERFIELD.

[*The Redeemed Captive Returning to Zion.* 1707.]

ON Tuesday, the 29th of February, 1703–4, not long before break of day, the enemy came in like a flood upon us ; our watch being unfaithful ;—an evil, the awful effects of which, in the surprisal of our fort, should bespeak all watchmen to avoid, as they would not bring the charge of blood upon themselves.   They came to my house in the beginning of the onset, and by their violent endeavors to break open doors and windows, with axes and hatchets, awaked me out of sleep ; on which I leaped out of bed, and, running towards the door, perceived the enemy making their entrance into the house.   I called to awaken two soldiers in the chamber, and returning toward my bedside for my arms, the enemy immediately broke into the room, I judge to the number of twenty, with painted faces, and hideous acclamations.   I reached up my hands to the bed-tester for my pistol, uttering a short petition to God, for everlasting mercies for me and mine, on account of the merits of our glorified Redeemer ; expecting a present passage through the valley of the shadow of death ; saying in myself, as Isa. xxxviii. 10, 11, "I said, in the cutting off of my days, I shall go to the gates of the grave : I am deprived of the residue of my years.   I said, I shall not see the Lord, even the Lord, in the land of the living : I shall behold man no more with the inhabitants of the world."   Taking down my pistol, I cocked it, and put it to the breast of the first Indian that came up ; but my pistol missing fire, I was seized by three Indians who disarmed me, and bound me naked, as I was in my shirt, and so I stood for near the space of an hour. Binding me, they told me they would carry me to Quebec. My pistol missing fire was an occasion of my life's being preserved; since which I have also found it profitable to be crossed in my own will. The judgment of God did not long slumber against one of the three which took me, who was a captain, for by sunrising he received a mortal shot from my next neighbor's house; who opposed so great a number of French and Indians as three hundred, and yet were no more than seven men in an ungarrisoned house.

I cannot relate the distressing care I had for my dear wife, who had lain in but a few weeks before; and for my poor children, family, and Christian neighbors. The enemy fell to rifling the house, and entered in great numbers into every room. I begged of God to remember mercy in the midst of judgment; that he would so far restrain their wrath, as to prevent their murdering of us; that we might have grace to glorify his name, whether in life or death; and, as I was able, committed our state to God. The enemies who entered the house, were all of them Indians and Macquas, and insulted over me awhile, holding up hatchets over my head, threatening to burn all I had; but yet God, beyond expectation, made us in a great measure to be pitied; for, though some were so cruel and barbarous as to take and carry to the door two of my children and murder them, as also a negro woman; yet they gave me liberty to put on my clothes, keeping me bound with a cord on one arm, till I put on my clothes to the other; and then changing my cord, they let me dress myself, and then pinioned me again. Gave liberty to my dear wife to dress herself and our remaining children. About sun an hour high, we were all carried out of the house, for a march, and saw many of the houses of my neighbors in flames, perceiving the whole fort, one house excepted, to be taken. Who can tell what sorrows pierced our souls, when we saw ourselves carried away from God's sanctuary, to go into a strange land, exposed to so many trials; the journey being at least three hundred miles we were to travel; the snow up to the knees, and we never inured to such hardships and fatigues; the place we were to be carried to, a Popish country. Upon my parting from the town, they fired my house and barn. We were carried over the river, to the foot of the mountain, about a mile from my house, where we found a great number of our Christian neighbors, men, women, and children, to the number of an hundred, nineteen of which were afterward murdered by the way, and two starved to death, near Cowass, in a time of great scarcity or famine the savages underwent there. When we came to the foot of the mountain, they took away our shoes, and gave us in the room of them Indian shoes, to prepare us for our travel. Whilst we were there, the English beat out a company that remained in the town, and pursued them to the river, killing and wounding many of them; but the body of the army being alarmed, they repulsed those few English that pursued them.

I am not able to give you an account of the number of the enemy slain, but I observed after this fight no great, insulting mirth, as I expected; and saw many wounded persons, and for several days together they buried of their party, and one of chief note among the Macquas. The Governor of Canada told me, his army had that success with the loss of but eleven men; three Frenchmen, one of which was the lieutenant of the army, five Macquas, and three Indians. But after my arrival at Quebec, I spake with an Englishman, who was taken in the last war, and of their religion; who told me, they lost above forty, and that many were wounded. I replied, "The Governor of Canada said they lost but eleven men." He answered, "'Tis true that there were but eleven killed outright at the taking of the fort, but many others were wounded, among whom was the ensign of the French; but," said he, "they had a fight in the meadow, and in both engagements they lost more than forty. Some of the soldiers, both French and Indians, then present, told me so," said he, adding, that the French always endeavor to conceal the number of their slain.

After this, we went up the mountain, and saw the smoke of the fires in the town, and beheld the awful desolations of Deerfield. And before we marched any farther, they killed a sucking child belonging to one of the English. There were slain by the enemy of the inhabitants of Deerfield, to the number of thirty-eight, besides nine of the neighboring towns. We travelled not far the first day; God made the heathen so to pity our children, that, though they had several wounded persons of their own to carry upon their shoulders, for thirty miles, before they came to the river, yet they carried our children, incapable of travelling, in their arms, and upon their shoulders. When we came to our lodging place, the first night, they dug away the snow, and made some wigwams, cut down some small branches of the spruce-tree to lie down on, and gave the prisoners somewhat to eat; but we had but little appetite. I was pinioned and bound down that night, and so I was every night whilst I was with the army. Some of the enemy who brought drink with them from the town fell to drinking, and in their drunken fit they killed my negro man, the only dead person I either saw at the town, or in the way.

In the night an Englishman made his escape: in the morning (March 1), I was called for, and ordered by the general to tell the English, that if any more made their escape, they would burn the rest of the prisoners. He that took me was unwilling to let me speak with any of the prisoners, as we marched; but on the morning of the second day, he being appointed to guard the rear, I was put into the hands of my other master, who permitted me to speak to my wife, when I overtook her, and to walk with her to help her in her journey. On the way we discoursed of the happi-

ness of those who had a right to an house not made with hands, eternal
in the heavens; and God for a father and friend; as also, that it was our
reasonable duty quietly to submit to the will of God, and to say, "The
will of the Lord be done." My wife told me her strength of body began
to fail, and that I must expect to part with her; saying, she hoped God
would preserve my life, and the life of some, if not of all our children
with us; and commended to me, under God, the care of them. She never
spake any discontented word as to what had befallen us, but with suitable expressions justified God in what had happened. We soon made a
halt, in which time my chief surviving master came up, upon which I
was put upon marching with the foremost, and so made my last farewell
of my dear wife, the desire of my eyes, and companion in many mercies
and afflictions. Upon our separation from each other, we asked for each
other grace sufficient for what God should call us to. After our being
parted from one another, she spent the few remaining minutes of her stay
in reading the Holy Scriptures; which she was wont personally every
day to delight her soul in reading, praying, meditating on, by herself, in
her closet, over and above what she heard out of them in our family worship. I was made to wade over a small river, and so were all the English, the water above knee deep, the stream very swift; and after that to
travel up a small mountain;—my strength was almost spent, before I
came to the top of it. No sooner had I overcome the difficulty of that
ascent, but I was permitted to sit down, and be unburdened of my pack.
I sat pitying those who were behind, and entreated my master to let me
go down and help my wife; but he refused, and would not let me stir
from him. I asked each of the prisoners (as they passed by me) after
her, and heard that, passing through the above-said river, she fell down,
and was plunged over head and ears in the water; after which she travelled not far, for, at the foot of that mountain, the cruel and bloodthirsty
savage who took her slew her with his hatchet at one stroke, the tidings
of which were very awful. And yet such was the hard-heartedness of the
adversary, that my tears were reckoned to me as a reproach. My loss
and the loss of my children was great; our hearts were so filled with sorrow, that nothing but the comfortable hopes of her being taken away, in
mercy to herself, from the evils we were to see, feel, and suffer under,
(and joined to the assembly of the spirits of just men made perfect, to
rest in peace, and joy unspeakable and full of glory, and the good pleasure of God thus to exercise us,) could have kept us from sinking under,
at that time. That Scripture, "Naked came I out of my mother's womb,
and naked shall I return thither: the Lord gave, and the Lord hath
taken away; blessed be the name of the Lord,"—was brought to my
mind, and from it, that an afflicting God was to be glorified; with some
other places of Scripture, to persuade to a patient bearing my afflictions.

FAVORS IN THE MIDST OF AFFLICTIONS.

[From the Same.]

MY march on the French river was very sore, for, fearing a thaw, we travelled a very great pace; my feet were so bruised, and my joints so distorted by my travelling in snow-shoes, that I thought it impossible to hold out. One morning a little before break of day my master came and awaked me out of sleep, saying, "Arise, pray to God, and eat your breakfast, for we must go a great way to-day." After prayer I arose from my knees, but my feet were so tender, swollen, bruised, and full of pain, that I could scarce stand upon them without holding by the wigwam. And when the Indians said, "You must run to-day," I answered I could not run. My master pointed out his hatchet; said to me, "Then I must dash out your brains and take off your scalp." I said, "I suppose, then, you will do so, for I am not able to travel with speed." He sent me away alone, on the ice. About sun half an hour high he overtook me, for I had gone very slowly, not thinking it possible to travel five miles. When he came up, he called me to run; I told him I could go no faster. He passed by without saying one word more: so that sometimes I scarce saw anything of him for an hour together. I travelled from about break of day till dark, and never so much as sat down at noon to eat warm victuals,—eating frozen meat, which I had in my coat-pocket, as I travelled. We went that day two of their days' journey as they came down. I judge we went forty or forty-five miles that day. God wonderfully supported me, and so far renewed my strength, that in the afternoon I was stronger to travel than in the forenoon. My strength was restored and renewed to admiration. We should never distrust the care and compassion of God, who can give strength to them who have no might, and power to them who are ready to faint.

When we entered on the lake, the ice was rough and uneven, which was very grievous to my feet, that could scarce bear to be set down on the smooth ice on the river. I lifted up my cry to God in ejaculatory requests, that he would take notice of my state, and some way or other relieve me. I had not marched above half a mile before there fell a moist snow, about an inch and a half deep, that made it very soft for my feet to pass over the lake to the place where my master's family was. Wonderful favors in the midst of trying afflictions!

AMONG THE FRENCH AND INDIANS.

[*From the Same.*]

THE next morning the bell rang for mass. My master bid me go to church; I refused; he threatened me and went away in a rage. At noon the Jesuits sent for me to dine with them, for I ate at their table all the time I was at the fort; and after dinner they told me the Indians would not allow of any of their captives staying in their wigwams whilst they were at church, and were resolved by force and violence to bring us all to church if we would not go without. I told them it was highly unreasonable so to impose upon those who were of a contrary religion, and to force us to be present at such a service as we abhorred, was nothing becoming Christianity. They replied, they were savages, and would not hearken to reason, but would have their wills. Said also, if they were in New England themselves, they would go into their churches and see their ways of worship. I answered, the case was far different, for there was nothing (themselves being judges) as to matter or manner of worship but what was according to the word of God in our churches, and therefore it could not be an offence to any man's conscience. But among them there were idolatrous superstitions in worship. They said, "Come and see, and offer us conviction of what is superstitious in worship." To which I answered, that I was not to do evil that good might come of it, and that forcing in matters of religion was hateful. They answered, "The Indians are resolved to have it so, and they could not pacify them without my coming; and they would engage they should offer no force or violence to cause any compliance with their ceremonies." The next mass, my master bid me go to church. I objected; he rose and forcibly pulled me by my head and shoulders out of the wigwam to the church, which was nigh the door. So I went in and sat down behind the door: and there saw a great confusion, instead of any Gospel order; for one of the Jesuits was at the altar saying mass in a tongue unknown to the savages, and the other, between the altar and the door, saying and singing prayers among the Indians at the same time; and many others were at the same time saying over their Pater-nosters and Ave Mary by tale from their chaplet, or beads on a string. At our going out we smiled at their devotion so managed, which was offensive to them, for they said we made a derision of their worship. When I was here a certain savagess died. One of the Jesuits told me she was a very holy woman, who had not committed one sin in twelve years. After a day or two the Jesuits asked me what I thought of their way now I saw it. I told them I thought Christ said of it, "Howbeit, in vain do they worship me, teaching for doctrines the commandments of men. For, laying aside the commandment of God, ye hold the tradition of men, as the washing of pots and cups; and many other such like things ye do. And he said unto them, Full well ye reject the commandment of God, that ye may keep your own tradition." They told me they were not the commandments of men, but apostolical traditions, of equal authority with the Holy Scriptures; and that after my death I would bewail my not praying to the Virgin Mary, and that I should find the want of her intercession for me with her Son; judging me to hell for asserting the Scriptures to be a perfect rule of faith; and said I abounded in my own sense, entertaining explications contrary to the sense of the Pope, regularly sitting with a General Council, explaining Scripture and making articles of faith. I told them it was my comfort that Christ was to be my judge, and not they, at the great day; and as for their censuring and judging me, I was not moved with it.

One day a certain savagess taken prisoner in Philip's war, who had lived at Mr. Bulkley's at Weathersfield, called Ruth, who could speak English very well and who had been often at my house, being now proselyted to the Romish faith, came into the wigwam, and with her an English maid who was taken in the last war. She was dressed in Indian apparel, and was unable to speak one word of English. She could neither tell her own name nor the name of the place from whence she was taken. These two talked in the Indian dialect with my master a long time; after which my master bade me cross myself; I told him I would not; he commanded me several times, and I as often refused. Ruth said, " Mr. Williams, you know the Scripture, and therefore act against your own light; for you know the Scripture saith, 'Servants, obey your masters'; he is your master and you his servant." I told her she was ignorant and knew not the meaning of the Scripture; telling her I was not to disobey the great God to obey my master, and that I was ready to die and suffer for God if called thereto. On which she talked with my master: I suppose she interpreted what I said. My master took hold of my hand to force me to cross myself, but I struggled with him, and would not suffer him to guide my hand. Upon this he pulled off a crucifix from off his own neck, and bade me kiss it; but I refused once and again. He told me he would dash out my brains with his hatchet if I refused. I told him I should sooner choose death than to sin against God. Then he ran and took up his hatchet and acted as though he would have dashed out my brains. Seeing I was not moved, he threw down his hatchet, saying he would bite off all my nails if I still refused. I gave him my hand and told him I was ready to suffer: he set his teeth in my thumb-nail and gave a gripe, and then said, " No good minister, no love God, as bad as the Devil," and so left off. I have reason to bless God, who strengthened me to withstand. By this he was so discouraged, as never more to meddle with me about my religion. I asked leave of the Jesuits to pray with those English of our town that were with me; but they absolutely refused to give us any permission to pray one with another, and did what they could to prevent our having any discourse together.

𝔖𝔞𝔯𝔞𝔥 𝔎𝔢𝔪𝔟𝔩𝔢 𝔎𝔫𝔦𝔤𝔥𝔱.

BORN in Boston, Mass., 1666. DIED at New London, Conn., 1727.

FROM BOSTON TO NEW YORK IN 1704.

[The Journals of Madam Knight, etc., from the Original Manuscripts. 1825.]

MONDAY, October the second, 1704.—About three o'clock afternoon, I began my journey from Boston to New Haven; being about two hundred mile. My kinsman, Captain Robert Luist, waited on me as far as Dedham, where I was to meet the western post.

I visited the Rev. Mr. Belcher, the minister of the town, and tarried there till evening, in hopes the post would come along. But he not coming, I resolved to go to Billings's where he used to lodge, being twelve miles further. But being ignorant of the way, Madam Belcher, seeing no persuasions of her good spouse's or hers could prevail with me to lodge there that night, very kindly went with me to the tavern, where I hoped to get my guide, and desired the hostess to inquire of her guests whether any of them would go with me. But they being tied by the lips to a pewter engine, scarcely allowed themselves time to say what clownish. . . . . [*MS. incomplete.*] Pieces of eight, I told her no, I would not be accessory to such extortion.

"Then John shan't go," says she. "No, indeed, shan't he;" and held forth at that rate a long time, that I began to fear I was got among the quaking tribe, believing not a limber-tongued sister among them could outdo Madam Hostess.

Upon this, to my no small surprise, son John arose, and gravely demanded what I would give him to go with me? "Give you?" says I, "are you John?" "Yes," says he, "for want of a better;" and behold! this John looked as old as my host, and perhaps had been a man in the last century. "Well, Mr. John," says I, "make your demands." "Why, half a piece of eight and a dram," says John. I agreed, and gave him a dram (now) in hand to bind the bargain.

My hostess catechised John for going so cheap, saying his poor wife would break her heart. . . . [*MS. incomplete.*]

His shade on his horse resembled a globe on a gate post. His habit, horse and furniture, its looks and goings incomparably answered the rest.

Thus jogging on with an easy pace, my guide telling me it was danger-ous to ride hard in the night (which his horse had the sense to avoid), he entertained me with the adventures he had passed by late riding, and imminent dangers he had escaped, so that, remembering the heroes in "Parismus" and the "Knight of the Oracle," I didn't know but I had met with a prince disguised.

When we had ridden about an hour, we came into a thick swamp, which by reason of a great fog, very much startled me, it being now very dark. But nothing dismayed John: he had encountered a thou-sand and a thousand such swamps, having a universal knowledge in the woods; and readily answered all my inquiries which were not a few.

In about an hour, or something more, after we left the swamp, we came to Billings's, where I was to lodge. My guide dismounted and very complacently helped me down and showed the door, signing to me with his hand to go in; which I gladly did—but had not gone many steps into the room, ere I was interrogated by a young lady I understood afterwards was the eldest daughter of the family, with these, or words to this purpose; viz., "Law for me!—what in the world brings you here at this time of night? I never see a woman on the road so dreadful late in all the days of my versal life. Who are you? Where are you going? I'm scared out of my wits!"—with much more of the same kind. I stood aghast, preparing to reply, when in comes my guide—to him madam turned, roaring out: "Lawful heart, John, is it you?—how de do! Where in the world are you going with this woman? Who is she?" John made no answer, but sat down in the corner, fumbled out his black junk, and saluted that instead of Deb; she then turned again to me and fell anew into her silly questions, without asking me to sit down.

I told her she treated me very rudely, and I did not think it my duty to answer her unmannerly questions. But to get rid of them, I told her I came there to have the post's company with me to-morrow on my jour-ney, etc. Miss stared awhile, drew a chair, bade me sit, and then ran up stairs and put on two or three rings (or else I had not seen them before), and returning, set herself just before me, showing the way to Reding, that I might see her ornaments, perhaps to gain the more respect. But her granam's new rung sow, had it appeared, would have affected me as much. I paid honest John with money and dram according to contract, and dismissed him, and prayed Miss to show me where I must lodge. She conducted me to a parlor in a little back lean-to, which was almost filled with the bedstead, which was so high that I was forced to climb on a chair to get up to the wretched bed that lay on it; on which having stretched my tired limbs, and laid my head on a sad-colored pillow, I began to think on the transactions of the past day.

Tuesday, October the third, about 8 in the morning, I with the post proceeded forward without observing any thing remarkable; and about two, afternoon, arrived at the post's second stage, where the western post met him and exchanged letters. Here, having called for something to eat, the woman brought in a twisted thing like a cable, but something whiter; and, laying it on the board, tugged for life to bring it into a capacity to spread; which having with great pains accomplished, she served in a dish of pork and cabbage, I suppose the remains of dinner. The sauce was of a deep purple, which I thought was boiled in her dye kettle; the bread was Indian, and everything on the table service agreeable to these. I, being hungry got a little down; but my stomach was soon cloyed, and what cabbage I swallowed served me for a cud the whole day after.

Having here discharged the ordinary for self and guide (as I understood was the custom), about three afternoon went on with my third guide, who rode very hard; and having crossed Providence ferry, we came to a river which they generally ride through. But I dare not venture; so the post got a lad and canoe to carry me to t'other side, and he rode through and led my horse. The canoe was very small and shallow, so that when we were in she seemed ready to take in water, which greatly terrified me, and caused me to be very circumspect, sitting with my hands fast on each side, my eyes steady, not daring so much as to lodge my tongue a hair's breadth more on one side of my mouth than t'other, nor so much as think on Lot's wife, for a wry thought would have overset our wherry; but was soon put out of this pain, by feeling the canoe on shore, which I as soon almost saluted with my feet; and rewarding my sculler, again mounted and made the best of our way forwards. The road here was very even and the day pleasant, it being now near sunset. But the post told me we had near fourteen miles to ride to the next stage (where we were to lodge). I asked him of the rest of the road, foreseeing we must travel in the night. He told me there was a bad river we were to ride through, which was so very fierce a horse could sometimes hardly stem it; but it was but narrow, and we should soon be over. I cannot express the concern of mind this relation set me in: no thoughts but those of the dangerous river could entertain my imagination, and they were as formidable as various, still tormenting me with blackest ideas of my approaching fate—sometimes seeing myself drowning, otherwhiles drowned, and at the best like a holy sister just come out of a spiritual bath in dripping garments.

Now was the glorious luminary, with his swift coursers, arrived at his stage, leaving poor me with the rest of this part of the lower world in darkness, with which *we* were soon surrounded. The only glimmering we now had was from the spangled skies, whose imperfect reflections rendered every object formidable. Each lifeless trunk, with its shattered limbs, appeared an armed enemy; and every little stump like a ravenous devourer. Nor could I so much as discern my guide, when at any distance, which added to the terror.

Thus, absolutely lost in thought and dying with the very thoughts of drowning, I came up with the post, whom I did not see till even with his horse: he told me he stopped for me, and we rode on very deliberately a few paces, when we entered a thicket of trees and shrubs, and I perceived by the horse's going we were on the descent of a hill, which, as we came nearer the bottom, was totally dark with the trees that surrounded it. But I knew by the going of the horse we had entered the water, which my guide told me was the hazardous river he had told me of; and he, riding up close to my side, bid me not fear—we should be over immediately. I now rallied all the courage I was mistress of, knowing that I must either venture my fate of drowning, or be left like the children in the wood. So, as the post bid me, I gave reins to my nag; and sitting as steady as just before in the canoe, in a few minutes got safe to the other side, which he told me was the Narragansett country.

Here we found great difficulty in travelling, the way being very narrow, and on each side the trees and bushes gave us very unpleasant welcomes with their branches and boughs, which we could not avoid, it being so exceeding dark. My guide, as before, so now, put on harder than I, with my weary bones, could follow; so left me and the way behind him. Now returned my distressed apprehensions of the place where I was: the dolesome woods, my company next to none, going I knew not whither, and encompassed with terrifying darkness; the least of which was enough to startle a more masculine courage. Added to which the reflections, as in the afternoon of the day, that my call was very questionable, which till then I had not so prudently as I ought considered. Now, coming to the foot of a hill, I found great difficulty in ascending; but being got to the top, was there amply recompensed with the friendly appearance of the kind Conductress of the night, just then advancing above the horizontal line. The raptures which the sight of that fair planet produced in me, caused me for the moment to forget my present weariness and past toils; and inspired me for most of the remaining way with very diverting thoughts, some of which, with the other occurrences of the day, I reserved to note down when I should come to my stage. My thoughts on the sight of the moon were to this purpose:

Fair Cynthia, all the homage that I may
Unto a creature, unto thee I pay ;
In lonesome woods to meet so kind a guide,
To me's more worth than all the world beside.
Some joy I felt just now, when safe got o'er
Yon surly river to this rugged shore,
Deeming rough welcomes from these clownish trees,
Better than lodgings with Nereidees.
Yet swelling fears surprise ; all dark appears—
Nothing but light can dissipate those fears.
My fainting vitals can't lend strength to say,
But softly whisper, O I wish 'twere day.
The murmur hardly warmed the ambient air,
Ere thy bright aspect rescues from despair :
Makes the old Hag her sable mantle loose,
And a bright joy does through my soul diffuse.
The boisterous trees now lend a passage free,
And pleasant prospects thou givest light to see.

From hence we kept on, with more ease than before: the way being smooth and even, the night warm and serene, and the tall and thick trees at a distance, especially when the moon glared light through the branches, filled my imagination with the pleasant delusions of a sumptuous city, filled with famous buildings and churches, with their spiring steeples, balconies, galleries and I know not what: grandeurs which I had heard of, and which the stories of foreign countries had given me the idea of.

Here stood a lofty church—there is a steeple,
And there the grand parade—O see the people !
That famous castle there, were I but nigh,
To see the moat and bridge and walls so high—
They're very fine ! says my deluded eye.

Being thus agreeably entertained without a thought of any thing but thoughts themselves, I on a sudden was roused from these pleasing imaginations by the post's sounding his horn, which assured me he was arrived at the stage where we were to lodge ; and that music was then most musical and agreeable to me.

Being come to Mr. Haven's, I was very civilly received, and courteously entertained, in a clean, comfortable house ; and the good woman was very active in helping off my riding clothes, and then asked what I would eat. I told her I had some chocolate, if she would prepare it; which with the help of some milk, and a little clean brass kettle, she soon effected to my satisfaction. I then betook me to my apartment, which was a little room parted from the kitchen by a single board partition ; where, after I had noted the occurrences of the past day, I went to bed, which, though pretty hard, yet neat and handsome. But I could

get no sleep, because of the clamor of some of the town topers in next
room, who were entered into a strong debate concerning the signification
of the name of their country; viz. *Narragansett.* One said it was named
so by the Indians, because there grew a brier there, of a prodigious
height and bigness, the like hardly ever known, called by the Indians
Narragansett; and quotes an Indian of so barbarous a name for his
author, that I could not write it. His antagonist replied no—it was
from a spring it had its name, which he well knew where it was, which
was extreme cold in summer, and as hot as could be imagined in the
winter, which was much resorted to by the natives, and by them called
Narragansett (hot and cold), and that was the original of their place's
name—with a thousand impertinences not worth notice, which he uttered
with such a roaring voice and thundering blows with the fist of wickedness on the table, that it pierced my very head. I heartily fretted, and
wished them tongue tied; but with as little success as a friend of mine
once, who was (as she said) kept a whole night awake, on a journey, by
a country lieutenant and a sergeant, ensign and a deacon, contriving how
to bring a triangle into a square. They kept calling for t'other gill,
which, while they were swallowing, was some intermission; but, presently, like oil to fire, increased the flame. I set my candle on a chest by
the bedside, and sitting up, fell to my old way of composing my resentments, in the following manner:

> I ask thy aid, O potent Rum!
> To charm these wrangling topers dumb.
> Thou hast their giddy brains possest—
> The man confounded with the beast—
> And I, poor I, can get no rest.
> Intoxicate them with thy fumes:
> O still their tongues till morning comes!

And I know not but my wishes took effect; for the dispute soon ended
with t'other dram; and so good night!

Wednesday, October 4th. About four in the morning we set out for
Kingston (for so was the town called) with a French doctor in our company. He and the post put on very furiously, so that I could not keep
up with them, only as now and then they would stop till they saw me.
This road was poorly furnished with accommodations for travellers, so
that we were forced to ride twenty-two miles by the post's account, but
nearer thirty by mine, before we could bait so much as our horses, which
I exceedingly complained of. But the post encouraged me, by saying
we should be well accommodated anon at Mr. Devil's, a few miles further.
But I questioned whether we ought to go to the devil to be helped out
of affliction. However, like the rest of deluded souls that post to the
infernal den, we made all possible speed to this devil's habitation; where

alighting, in full assurance of good accommodation, we were going in. But meeting his two daughters, as I supposed twins,—they so nearly resembled each other, both in features and habit, and looked as old as the devil himself, and quite as ugly,—we desired entertainment, but could hardly get a word out of them, till with our importunity, telling them our necessity, etc., they called the old sophister, who was as sparing of his words as his daughters had been, and no, or none, were the replies he made us to our demands. He differed only in this from the old fellow in t'other country : he let us depart. However, I thought it proper to warn poor travellers to endeavor to avoid falling into circumstances like ours, which at our next stage I sat down and did as followeth :

> May all that dread the cruel fiend of night
> Keep on, and not at this cursed mansion light.
> 'Tis hell ; 'tis hell ! and devils here do dwell :
> Here dwells the Devil—surely this is hell.
> Nothing but wants : a drop to cool your tongue
> Can't be procured these cruel fiends among.
> Plenty of horrid grins and looks severe,
> Hunger and thirst, but pity's banished here—
> The right hand keep, if hell on earth you fear !

Thus leaving this habitation of cruelty, we went forward ; and arriving at an ordinary about two miles further, found tolerable accommodation. But our hostess, being a pretty full mouthed old creature, entertained our fellow traveller, the French doctor, with innumerable complaints of her bodily infirmities ; and whispered to him so loud that all the house had as full a hearing as he : which was very diverting to the company (of which there was a great many), as one might see by their sneering. But poor weary I slipped out to enter my mind in my Journal, and left my great landlady with her talkative guests to themselves.

From hence we proceeded (about ten forenoon) through the Narragansett country, pretty leisurely ; and about one afternoon came to Paukataug River, which was about two hundred paces over, and now very high, and no way over to t'other side but this. I dared not venture to ride through, my courage at best in such cases but small, and now at the lowest ebb, by reason of my weary, very weary, hungry and uneasy circumstances. So taking leave of my company, though with no little reluctance that I could not proceed with them on my journey, stopped at a little cottage just by the river, to wait the water's falling, which the old man that lived there said would be in a little time, and he would conduct me safe over. This little hut was one of the wretchedest I ever saw a habitation for human creatures. It was supported with shores enclosed with clapboards, laid on lengthways, and so much asunder that the light came through everywhere ; the door tied on with a cord in the

place of hinges; the floor the bare earth; no windows but such as the
thin covering afforded, nor any furniture but a bed with a glass bottle
hanging at the head on't; an earthen cup, a small pewter basin, a board
with sticks to stand on, instead of a table, and a block or two in the
corner instead of chairs. The family were the old man, his wife and two
children; all and every part being the picture of poverty. Notwithstanding both the hut and its inhabitants were very clean and tidy: to
the crossing the old proverb, that bare walls make giddy housewives.

I blessed myself that I was not one of this miserable crew; and the
impressions their wretchedness formed in me caused me on the very spot
to say:

> Though ill at ease, a stranger and alone,
> All my fatigues shall not extort a groan.
> These indigents have hunger with their ease;
> Their best is worse behalf than my disease.
> Their miserable hut which heat and cold
> Alternately without repulse do hold;
> Their lodgings thin and hard, their Indian fare,
> The mean apparel which the wretches wear,
> And their ten thousand ills which can't be told,
> Makes nature ere 'tis middle aged look old.
> When I reflect, my late fatigues do seem
> Only a notion or forgotten dream.

I had scarce done thinking, when an Indian-like animal came to the door,
on a creature very much like himself, in mien and feature, as well as
ragged clothing; and having lit, makes an awkward scratch with his
Indian shoe, and a nod, sits on the block, fumbles out his black junk,
dips it in the ashes, and presents it piping hot to his muscheetoes, and
fell to sucking like a calf, without speaking, for near a quarter of an
hour. At length the old man said, "How does Sarah do?" who I understood was the wretch's wife and daughter to the old man: he replied,
"As well as can be expected," etc. So I remembered the old saying, and
supposed I knew Sarah's case. But he being, as I understood, going
over the river, as ugly as he was, I was glad to ask him to show me the way
to Saxton's, at Stonington; which he promising, I ventured over with
the old man's assistance; who having rewarded to content, with my
tattertailed guide, I rid on very slowly through Stonington, where the
road was very stony and uneven. I asked the fellow, as we went, divers
questions of the place and way, etc. I being arrived at my country,
to Saxton's, at Stonington, was very well accommodated both as to victuals and lodging, the only good of both I had found since my setting
out. Here I heard there was an old man and his daughter to come that
way, bound to New London; and, being now destitute of a guide, gladly
waited for them, being in so good a harbor, and accordingly, Thursday,
October the fifth, about 3 in the afternoon, I set forward with neighbor

Polly and Jemima, a girl about eighteen years old, who he said he had been to fetch out of the Narragansetts, and said they had rode thirty miles that day, on a sorry lean jade, with only a bag under her for a pillion, which the poor girl often complained was very uneasy.

We made good speed along, which made poor Jemima make many a sour face, the mare being a very hard trotter; and after many a hearty and bitter "Oh," she at length lowed out: "Lawful heart, father! This bare mare hurts me dingeely; I'm direful sore, I vow;" with many words to that purpose. "Poor child," says Gaffer, "she used to serve your mother so." "I don't care how mother used to do," quoth Jemima, in a passionate tone. At which the old man laughed, and kicked his jade o' the side, which made her jolt ten times harder.

About seven that evening we came to New London ferry: here, by reason of a very high wind, we met with great difficulty in getting over —the boat tossed exceedingly, and our horses capered at a very surprising rate, and set us all in a fright; especially poor Jemima, who desired her father to say "So Jack" to the jade, to make her stand. But the careless parent, taking no notice of her repeated desires, she roared out in a passionate manner: "Pray sooth, father; are you deaf? Say 'So Jack' to the jade, I tell you." The dutiful parent obeys, saying "So Jack, so Jack," as gravely as if he'd been to saying Catechise after young Miss, who with her fright looked of all colors in the rainbow.

Being safely arrived at the house of Mrs. Prentice's in New London, I treated neighbor Polly and daughter for their diverting company, and bade them farewell; and between nine and ten at night waited on the Rev. Mr. Gurdon Saltonstall, minister of the town, who kindly invited me to stay that night at his house, where I was very handsomely and plentifully treated and lodged; and made good the great character I had before heard concerning him, viz., that he was the most affable, courteous, generous and best of men.

Friday, October 6th. I got up very early, in order to hire somebody to go with me to New Haven, being in great perplexity at the thoughts of proceeding alone; which my most hospitable entertainer observing, himself went and soon returned with a young gentleman of the town, whom he could confide in to go with me; and about eight this morning, with Mr. Joshua Wheeler, my new guide, taking leave of this worthy gentleman, we advanced on towards Seabrook. The roads all along this way are very bad, encumbered with rocks and mountainous passages, which were very disagreeable to my tired carcass; but we went on with a moderate pace which made the journey more pleasant. But after about eight miles riding, in going over a bridge under which the river ran very swift, my horse stumbled and very narrowly 'scaped falling over into the water, which extremely frightened me. But through God's goodness I met with no harm, and mounting again, in about half a mile's riding, came to an ordinary, was well entertained by a woman of about seventy and vantage, but of as sound intellectuals as one of seventeen. She entertained Mr. Wheeler with some passages of a wedding awhile ago at a place hard by, the bridegroom being about her age or something above, saying his children were dreadfully against their father's marrying, which she condemned them extremely for. . . . . .

Saturday, October 7th, we set out early in the morning, and being something unacquainted with the way, having asked it of some we met, they told us we must ride a mile or two and turn down a lane on the right hand; and by their direction we rode on, but not yet coming to the turning, we met a young fellow and asked him how far it was to the lane which turned down towards Guilford. He said we must ride a little further, and turn down by the corner of Uncle Sam's lot. My guide vented his spleen at the lubber; and we soon after came into the road, and keeping still on, without anything further remarkable, about two o'clock afternoon we arrived at New Haven, where I was received with all possible respects and civility. Here I discharged Mr. Wheeler with a reward to his satisfaction, and took some time to rest after so long and toilsome a journey; and informed myself of the manners and customs of the place, and at the same time employed myself in the affair I went there upon.

They are governed by the same laws as we in Boston (or little differing), throughout this whole colony of Connecticut, and much the same way of Church government, and many of them good, sociable people, and I hope religious too: but a little too much independent in their principles, and, as I have been told, were formerly in their zeal very rigid in their administrations towards such as their laws made offenders, even to a harmless kiss or innocent merriment among young people. Whipping being a frequent and counted an easy punishment, about which as other crimes, the Judges were absolute in their sentences. They told me a pleasant story about a pair of justices in those parts, which I may not omit the relation of.

A negro slave belonging to a man in the town, stole a hog's head from his master, and gave or sold it to an Indian, native of the place. The Indian sold it in the neighborhood, and so the theft was found out. Thereupon the heathen was seized, and carried to the Justice's house to be examined. But his worship (it seems) was gone into the field, with a brother in office, to gather in his pompions; whither the malefactor is hurried, and complaint made, and satisfaction in the name of justice demanded. Their worships can't proceed in form without a bench: whereupon they order one to be immediately erected, which, for want of fitter materials, they made with pompions—which being finished, down sit their worships, and the malefactor called, and by the senior justice interrogated after the following manner: "You Indian, why did you steal from this man? You shouldn't do so—it's a grandy wicked thing to steal." "Hol't, Hol't," cries justice junior, "Brother, you speak negro to him; I'll ask him. You, sirrah, why did you steal this man's hog's head?" "Hog's head?" replies the Indian, "me no stomany." "No?" says his worship; and, pulling off his hat, patted his own head with his hand, says, "Tatapa—you, Tatapa—you; all one this. Hog's head all one this." "Hah!" says Netop, "now me stomany that." Whereupon the company fell into a great fit of laughter, even to roaring. Silence is commanded, but to no effect: for they continued perfectly shouting. "Nay," says his worship, in an angry tone, "if it be so, *take me off the bench.*"

Their diversions in this part of the country are on lecture days and training days mostly: on the former there is riding from town to town.

And on training days the youth divert themselves by shooting at the target, as they call it (but it very much resembles a pillory), where he that hits nearest the white has some yards of red ribbon presented him, which being tied to his hat-band, the two ends streaming down his back, he is led away in triumph, with great applause, as the winners of the Olympic games. They generally marry very young: the males oftener, as I am told, under twenty than above: they generally make public weddings, and have a way something singular (as they say) in some of them, viz., just before joining hands the bridegroom quits the place, who is soon followed by the bridesmen, and as it were dragged back to duty—being the reverse to the former practice among us, to steal mistress bride.

There are great plenty of oysters all along by the sea side, as far as I rode in the colony, and those very good. And they generally lived very well and comfortably in their families. But too indulgent (especially the farmers) to their slaves: suffering too great familiarity from them, permitting them to sit at the table and eat with them (as they say to save time), and into the dish goes the black hoof as freely as the white hand. They told me that there was a farmer lived near the town where I lodged who had some difference with his slave, concerning something the master had promised him and did not punctually perform; which caused some hard words between them; but at length they put the matter to arbitration and bound themselves to stand to the award of such as they named—which done, the arbitrators, having heard the allegations of both parties, ordered the master to pay forty shillings to black face, and acknowledge his fault. And so the matter ended: the poor master very honestly standing to the award.

There are everywhere, in the towns as I passed, a number of Indians the natives of the country, and are the most salvage of all the salvages of that kind that I had ever seen: little or no care taken (as I heard upon enquiry) to make them otherwise. They have in some places lands of their own, and governed by laws of their own making;—they marry many wives and at pleasure put them away, and on the least dislike or fickle humor, on either side, saying "Stand away," to one another is a sufficient divorce. And indeed those uncomely "Stand aways" are too much in vogue among the English in this (indulgent) colony, as their records plentifully prove, and that on very trivial matters, of which some have been told me, but are not proper to be related by a female pen, though some of that foolish sex have had too large a share in the story.   .   .   .   .

They give the title of merchant to every trader; who rate their goods according to the time and specie they pay in, viz., "Pay," "Money," "Pay as money," and "Trusting." "Pay" is grain, pork, beef, etc., at the prices set by the General Court that year; "Money" is pieces of eight, reals, or Boston or bay shillings (as they call them), or "good hard money," as sometimes silver coin is termed by them; also "Wampum," viz., Indian beads, which serves for change. "Pay as money" is provisions, as aforesaid, one-third cheaper than as the Assembly or General Court sets it; and "Trust" as they and the merchant agree for time.

Now, when the buyer comes to ask for a commodity, sometimes before the merchant answers that he has it, he says, "Is your pay ready?" Perhaps the chap replies, "Yes." "What do you pay in?" says the merchant. The buyer having answered, then the price is set; as suppose he wants a sixpenny knife, in pay it is twelve pence—in pay as money, eight pence, and hard money, its own price, viz., six pence. It seems a very intricate way of trade and what *lex mercatoria* had not thought of.

Being at a merchant's house, in comes a tall country fellow, with his alfogeos full of tobacco; for they seldom loose their cud, but keep chewing and spitting as long as their eyes are open,—he advanced to the middle of the room, makes an awkward nod, and spitting a large deal of aromatic tincture, he gave a scrape with his shovel-like shoe, leaving a small shovel full of dirt on the floor, made a full stop, hugging his own pretty body with his hands under his arms, stood staring round him, like a cat let out of a basket. At last, like the creature Balaam rode on, he opened his mouth and said: "Have you any ribinen for hat-bands to sell, I pray?" The questions and answers about the pay being past, the ribbon is brought and opened. Bumpkin Simpers cries, "It's confounded gay, I vow;" and beckoning to the door, in comes Joan Tawdry, dropping about fifty curtsies, and stands by him: he shows her the ribbon. "Law, you," says she, "it's right gent, do you take it, 'tis dreadful pretty." Then she enquires, "Have you any hood silk, I pray?" which being brought and bought, "Have you any thread silk to sew it with?" says she; which being accommodated with they departed. They generally stand after they come in a great while speechless, and sometimes don't say a word till they are asked what they want, which I impute to the awe they stand in of the merchants, who they are constantly almost indebted to; and must take what they bring without liberty to choose for themselves; but they serve them as well, making the merchants stay long enough for their pay.

We may observe here the great necessity and benefit both of education and conversation; for these people have as large a portion of mother wit, and sometimes a larger, than those who have been brought up in cities; but, for want of improvements, render themselves almost ridiculous, as above. I should be glad if they would leave such follies, and am sure all that love clean houses (at least) would be glad on't too.

They are generally very plain in their dress, throughout all the colony, as I saw, and follow one another in their modes; that you may know where they belong, especially the women, meet them where you will.

Their chief red letter day is St. Election, which is annually observed according to charter, to choose their governor—a blessing they can never be thankful enough for, as they will find, if ever it be their hard fortune to lose it. The present governor in Connecticut is the Hon. John Winthrop, Esq., a gentleman of an ancient and honorable family, whose father was governor here sometime before, and his grandfather had been governor of the Massachusetts. This gentlemen is a very courteous and affable person, much given to hospitality, and has by his good services gained the affections of the people as much as any who had been before him in that post.

December 6th. Being by this time well recruited and rested after my journey, my business lying unfinished by some concerns at New York depending thereupon, my kinsman, Mr. Thomas Trowbridge, of New Haven, must needs take a journey there before it could be accomplished, I resolved to go there in company with him and a man of the town which I engaged to wait on me there. Accordingly, December 6th, we set out from New Haven, and about eleven same morning came to Stratford ferry; which crossing, about two miles on the other side baited our horses and would have eat a morsel ourselves, but the pumpkin and Indian mixed bread had such an aspect, and the bare-legged punch so awkward or rather awful a sound, that we left both, and proceeded forward, and about seven at night came to Fairfield, where we met with good entertainment and lodged; and early next morning set forward to Norrowalk, from its half Indian name "North-walk," where about twelve at noon we arrived, and had a dinner of fried venison, very savory. Landlady, wanting some pepper in the seasoning, bid the girl hand her the spice in the little " gay " cup on the shelf.   From hence we hastened towards Rye, walking and leading our horses near a mile together, up a prodigious high hill; and so riding till about nine at night, and there arrived and took up our lodgings at an ordinary, which a French family kept.   Here being very hungry, I desired a fricassee, which the French-man, undertaking, managed so contrary to my notion of cookery, that I hastened to bed supperless; and being shown the way up a pair of stairs which had such a narrow passage that I had almost stopped by the bulk of my body; but arriving at my apartment found it to be a little lean-to chamber, furnished among other rubbish with a high bed and a low one, a long table, a bench and a bottomless chair.   Little Miss went to scratch up my kennel, which rustled as if she had been in the barn among the husks, and suppose such was the contents of the ticking.   Nevertheless, being exceeding weary, down I laid my poor carcass (never more tired), and found my covering as scanty as my bed was hard.   Anon I heard another rustling noise in the room—called to know the matter—little Miss said she was making a bed for the men; who, when they were in bed, complained their legs lay out of it by reason of its shortness.   My poor bones complained bitterly, not being used to such lodgings, and so did the man who was with us; and poor I made but one groan, which was from the time I went to bed to the time I rose, which was about three in the morning, sitting up by the fire till light, and, having dis-charged our ordinary—which was as dear as if we had had far better fare, —we took our leave of Monsieur and about seven in the morning came to New Rochelle, a French town, where we had a good breakfast.   And on the strength of that about an hour before sunset got to York. . . . .

The City of New York is a pleasant, well compacted place, situated on a commodious river which is a fine harbor for shipping.   The buildings, brick generally, very stately and high, though not altogether like ours in Boston.   The bricks in some of the houses are of divers colors and laid in checkers, being glazed looked very agreeable.   The inside of them are neat to admiration, the wooden work, for only the walls are plastered, and the summers and joists are plained and kept very white scoured, as so are all the partitions if made of boards.   The fire-places have no jambs (as ours have) but the backs run flush with the walls, and the hearth is of tiles and is as far out into the room at the ends as before the fire, which is generally five foot in the lower rooms, and the piece over where the mantle tree should be is made as ours with joiners' work, and as I sup-pose is fastened to iron rods inside. . . . .

They are generally of the Church of England and have a New Eng-land gentleman for their minister, and a very fine church set out with all customary requisites.   There are also Dutch and divers conventicles, as they call them, viz., Baptist, Quakers, etc.   They are not strict in keeping the Sabbath, as in Boston and other places where I had been, but seem to deal with great exactness, as far as I see or deal with. They are sociable to one another and courteous and civil to strangers, and fare well in their houses. The English go very fashionable in their dress. But the Dutch, especially the middling sort, differ from our women, in their habit go loose, wear French muches, which are like a cap and a head band in one, leaving their ears bare, which are set out with jewels of a large size and many in number; and their fingers hooped with rings, some with large stones in them of many colors, as were their pendants in their ears, which you should see very old women wear as well as young.

They have vendues very frequently and make their earnings very well by them, for they treat with good liquor liberally, and the customers drink as liberally and generally pay for't as well, by paying for that which they bid up briskly for, after the sack has gone plentifully about, though sometimes good pennyworths are got there. Their diversion in the winter is riding sleighs about three or four miles out of town, where they have houses of entertainment at a place called the Bowery, and some go to friends' houses, who handsomely treat them. Mr. Burroughs carried his spouse and daughter and myself out to one Madame Dowes, a gentlewoman that lived at a farmhouse, who gave us a handsome entertainment of five or six dishes and choice beer and metheglin, cider, etc., all which she said was the produce of her farm. I believe we met fifty or sixty sleighs that day; they fly with great swiftness, and some are so furious that they will turn out of the path for none except a loaded cart. Nor do they spare for any diversion the place affords, and sociable to a degree, their tables being as free to their neighbors as to themselves.

Having here transacted the affair I went upon and some other that fell in the way, after about a fortnight's stay there, I left New York with no little regret, and Thursday, December 21st, set out for New Haven with my kinsman Trowbridge, and the man that waited on me. . . . .

Being got to Milford, it being late in the night, I could go no further; my fellow traveller going forward, I was invited to lodge at Mrs. ——, a very kind and civil gentlewoman, by whom I was handsomely and kindly entertained till the next night. The people here go very plain in their apparel (more plain than I had observed in the towns I had passed), and seem to be very grave and serious. They told me there was a singing Quaker lived there, or at least had a strong inclination to be so, his spouse not at all affected that way. Some of the singing crew came there one day to visit him, who being then abroad, they sat down (to the woman's no small vexation), humming and singing and groaning after their conjuring way—says the woman: "Are you singing Quakers?" "Yea," say they. "Then take my squalling brat of a child here and sing to it," says she, "for I have almost split my throat with singing to him, and can't get the rogue to sleep." They took this as a great indignity, and immediately departed. Shaking the dust from their heels, left the good woman and her child among the number of the wicked.

This is a seaport place and accommodated with a good harbor, but I had not opportunity to make particular observations, because it was Sabbath day—this evening.

December 24th. I set out with the gentlewoman's son, whom she very civilly offered to go with me when she saw no persuasions would cause me to stay, which she pressingly desired, and crossing a ferry, having but nine miles to New Haven, in a short time arrived there and was kindly received and well accommodated amongst my friends and relations.

The government of Connecticut colony begins westward toward York at Stamford (as I am told) and so runs Eastward toward Boston (I mean in my range, because I don't intend to extend my description beyond my own travels), and ends that way at Stonington, and has a great many large towns lying more northerly. It is a plentiful country for provisions of all sorts and it's generally healthy. No one that can and will be diligent in this place need fear poverty nor the want of food and raiment.

January 6th. Being now well recruited and fit for business, I discoursed the persons I was concerned with, that we might finish in order to my return to Boston. They delayed as they had hitherto done, hoping to tire my patience. But I was resolute to stay and see an end of the matter, let it be never so much to my disadvantage; so, January 9th, they came again and promised the Wednesday following to go through with the distribution of the estate, which they delayed till Thursday, and then came with new amusements. But at length, by the mediation of that holy good gentleman, the Rev. Mr. James Pierpont, the minister of New Haven, and with the advice and assistance of other our good friends, we came to an accommodation and distribution, which having finished, though not till February, the man that waited on me to York taking charge of me, I set out for Boston. We went from New Haven upon the ice (the ferry being not passable thereby), and the Rev. Mr. Pierpont, with Madam Prout, cousin Trowbridge, and divers others, were taking leave, we went onward without anything remarkable till we come to New London, and lodged again at Mr. Saltonstall's; and here I dismissed my guide, and my generous entertainer provided me Mr. Samuel Rogers of that place to go home with me. I stayed a day here longer than I intended by the commands of the Hon. Governor Winthrop to stay and take a supper with him, whose wonderful civility I may not omit. The next morning I crossed the ferry to Groton, having had the honor of the company of Madam Livingston (who is the governor's daughter) and Mary Christophers and divers others to the boat;

and that night lodged at Stonington, and had roast beef and pumpkin sauce for supper. The next night at Haven's, and had roast fowl, and the next day we came to a river, which, by reason of the freshets coming down, was swelled so high, we feared it impassable, and the rapid stream was very terrifying; however, we must over, and that in a small canoe. Mr. Rogers assuring me of his good conduct, I, after a stay of near an hour on the shore for consultation, went into the canoe, and Mr. Rogers paddled about one hundred yards up the creek by the shore side, turned into the swift stream and dexterously steering her, in a moment we came to the other side, as swiftly passing as an arrow shot out of the bow by a strong arm. I stayed on the shore till he returned to fetch our horses, which he caused to swim over, himself bringing the furniture in the canoe. But it is past my skill to express the exceeding fright all these transactions formed in me. We were now in the colony of the Massachusetts, and, taking lodgings at the first inn we came to, had a pretty difficult passage the next day, which was the second of March, by reason of the sloughy ways then thawed by the sun. Here I met Capt. John Richards of Boston, who was going home, so being very glad of his company we rode something harder than hitherto, and, missing my way in going up a very steep hill, my horse dropped down under me as dead; this new surprise no little hurt me, meeting it just at the entrance into Dedham, from whence we intended to reach home that night. But was now obliged to get another horse there, and leave my own, resolving for Boston that night if possible. But in going over the causeway at Dedham, the bridge being overflowed by the high waters coming down, I very narrowly escaped falling over into the river, horse and all, which 'twas almost a miracle I did not. Now it grew late in the afternoon, and the people having very much discouraged us about the sloughy way, which they said we should find very difficult and hazardous, it so wrought on me, being tired and dispirited and disappointed of my desires of going home, that I agreed to lodge there that night, which we did at the house of one Draper, and the next day being March 3d we got safe home to Boston, where I found my aged and tender mother and my dear and only child in good health, with open arms, ready to receive me, and my kind relations and friends flocking in to welcome me and hear the story of my transactions and travels, I having this day been five months from home; and now I cannot fully express my joy and satisfaction, but desire sincerely to adore my Great Benefactor for thus graciously carrying forth and returning in safety his unworthy handmaid.

———————

Robert Beverly.

BORN in Virginia, about 1670. DIED there, about 1735.

A ROYALIST GOVERNOR IN VIRGINIA.

[*The History and Present State of Virginia.* 1705.]

IN November, 1698, Francis Nicholson, Esq., was removed from Maryland, to be Governor of Virginia. But he went not then with that smoothness on his brow he had carried with him, when he was appointed Lieutenant-Governor. He talked then no more of improving of manufactures, towns, and trade. Neither was he pleased to make the acts of assembly the rule of his judgments, as formerly, but his own all-sufficient will and pleasure. Instead of encouraging the manufactures, he sent over inhuman memorials against them, which were so opposite to all reason, that they refuted themselves. In one of these, he remonstrates, "That the tobacco of that country often bears so low a price, that it will not yield clothes to the people that make it;" and yet presently after, in the same memorial, he recommends it to the parliament "to pass an act, forbidding the plantations to make their own clothing;" which, in other words, is desiring a charitable law that the planters shall go naked. In a late memorial concerted between him and his creature, Col. Quarrey, 'tis most humbly proposed, "That all the English colonies on the continent of North America be reduced under one government and under one Viceroy; and that a standing army be there kept on foot, to subdue the Queen's enemies;" which, in plain English, is imploring her majesty to put the plantations under martial law, and in the consequence, to give the Viceroy a fair opportunity of shaking off his dependence upon England.

He began his government with a pompous show of zeal for the Church; though his practice was not of a piece with his pious pretensions. It must be confessed that he has bestowed some liberalities upon the clergy, but always upon condition, that they should proclaim his charity, either by signing addresses dictated by himself, in his own commendation, or at least by writing letters of it to the bishops in England. And he would ever be so careful to hinder these representations from miscarrying, that he constantly took copies of them, and sent them with his own letters.

He likewise gave himself airs of encouraging the college, but he used this pretext for so many by-ends, that at last the promoters of that good work grew weary of the mockery. They perceived his view was to gain himself a character, and if he could but raise that, the college might sink. And in truth he has been so far from advancing it, that now after the six years of his government, the scholars are fewer than at his arrival.

Soon after his accession to the government, he caused the assembly, and courts of judicature, to be removed from Jamestown, where there were good accommodations for people, to Middle Plantation, where there were none. There he flattered himself with the fond imagination of being the founder of a new city. He marked out the streets in many places, so as that they might represent the figures of a *W*, in memory of his late Majesty King William, after whose name the town was called Williamsburg. There he procured a stately fabric to be erected, which he placed opposite to the college, and graced it with the magnificent name of the "Capitol."

This imaginary city is yet advanced no further than only to have a few public houses, and a store-house, more than were built upon the place before. And by the frequency of public meetings, and the misfortune of his residence, the students are interrupted in their study, and make less advances than formerly.

To defray the charge of building the Capitol, he suggested the pernicious duty of fifteen shillings for each Christian servant imported, except English, and twenty shillings for each negro. I call this a pernicious duty, because 'tis a great hindrance to the increase of that young colony, as well as a very unequal tax upon their labor.

It has been the constant maxim of this gentleman to set the people at variance as much as possible among themselves. Whether this proceed from his great fondness to the Machiavelian principle, *divide et impera*, or from his exceeding good nature, I will not pretend to determine. But it is very certain that, by his management, he has divided the most friendly and most united people in the world into very unhappy factions. And, what is still worse, he has been heard to declare publicly to the populace, "That the gentlemen imposed upon them, and that the servants had been all kidnapped, and had a lawful action against their masters."

And that these things may make the more effectual impression, he takes care to vilify the gentlemen of the council in public places, by the grossest and most injurious language. He is frequently pleased to send vexatious commands, to summon people in her Majesty's name, to attend him at some general meeting, and when they come, all the business perhaps he has with them, is to affront them before all the company.

In the General Court, of which he is chief judge, he has often behaved himself in that boisterous manner, that neither the rest of the judges on the bench, nor the lawyers at the bar, could use their just freedom. There 'tis usual with him to fall into excessive passion, and utter the most abusive language against those that presume to oppose his arbitrary proceedings. If the Attorney-General be so scrupulous as to excuse himself from executing his illegal commands, he runs a great risk of being ill used. For in the year 1700, Mr. Fowler, who was then the King's attorney, declining some hard piece of service, as being against law, his Excellency in a fury took him by the collar, and swore that he knew of no law they had, and that his commands should be obeyed without hesitation or reserve. He often commits gentlemen to jail, without the least shadow of complaint against them, and that without bail or mainprise, to the great oppression of the Queen's loyal subjects. Some of those have taken the liberty to tell him that such proceedings were illegal, and not to be justified in any country that had the happiness to be governed by the laws of England. To whom he has been heard to reply, "That they had no right at all to the liberties of English subjects, and that he would hang up those that should presume to oppose him, with Magna Charta about their necks."

He often mentions the absolute government of Fez and Morocco with great pleasure, and extols the inhuman cruelties of that prince toward his subjects. And particularly one day at a meeting of the governors of the college, upon some opposition they made against one of his violent proceedings, he vouchsafed to tell them, "That they were dogs　.　.　. that he knew how to govern the Moors, and would beat them into better manners."

Neither does this gentleman treat the assemblies with more gentleness than particular people; for he has said very publicly, "That he knew how to govern the country without assemblies; and if they should deny him any thing, after he had obtained a standing army, he would bring them to reason, with halters about their necks."

But no wonder that he deals so freely with the people there, since neither Her Majesty's instructions, nor the laws of that country can restrain him. Thus he takes upon him to transact matters of the greatest moment, without advice of the Council; as for example, he has appointed several officers, without their advice, which he ought not to do. Sometimes he has brought his orders in his hand into the Council, and signed them at the board, without so much as acquainting the Council what they were, though at the same time they ought not to pass without their advice; and after he had done this, he ordered the clerk to enter them into the minutes, as if they had been acted by the consent of the Council.

If any of the council happen to argue, or vote any thing contrary to this gentleman's inclinations, he instantly flies out into the most outrageous passions, and treats them with terms very unbecoming his station. By this means he takes away all freedom of debate, and makes the Council of no other use than to palliate his arbitrary practices. Sometimes, when he finds he cannot carry matters as he desires, he makes no scruple of entering them in the council-books by his own authority; he likewise causes many things to be razed out, and others put in, by his own absolute will and pleasure. Nay, sometimes, too, he has caused an abstract of the journals to be sent to England, instead of the journals themselves; by which artifice he leaves out, or puts in, just as much as he thinks fit.

He is very sensible how unwarrantable and unjust these proceedings are, and therefore has been always jealous, lest some of the many that have been injured, should send over their complaints to England. This has put him upon a practice most destructive to all trade and correspondence, which is, the intercepting and breaking open of letters. His method was to give directions to some of his creatures dwelling near the mouths of the rivers, to send on board the several ships, that happened to arrive, and in the Governor's name demand the letters. Thus he used to get them, and open as many as he thought fit, after which sometimes he would cause them to be sent where they were directed, and sometimes keep them. By this management many people have not only suffered the loss of their letters, and of their accounts, invoices, etc., but likewise have missed great advantages, for want of timely advice, occasioned by the stopping of their letters.

Another effect of his jealousy was to set spies upon such people as he suspected. These were to give him an account of all the words and actions of those which were most likely to complain. Nay, his Excellency has condescended to act the low part of an eves-dropper himself, and to stand under a window to listen for secrets, that would certainly displease him. This practice has made every man afraid of his neighbor, and destroyed the mutual confidence of the dearest friends.

But the most extraordinary method of learning secrets, that ever was used in an English government, was a kind of inquisition, which this gentleman has been pleased to erect frequently in that country. He would call courts at unusual times, to inquire into the life and conversation of those persons that had the misfortune to be out of his favor; though there was not the least public accusation against them. To these courts he summoned all the neighbors of the party he intended to expose, especially those that he knew were most intimate with him. Upon their appearance, he administered an oath to them, to answer truly to all such interrogatories as he should propose. Then he would ask them endless questions, concerning the particular discourse and behavior of the party, in order to find out something that might be the ground of an accusation.

In the second year of this gentleman's government, there happened an adventure very fortunate for him, which gave him much credit with those who relied on his own account of the matter; and that was the taking of a pirate within the Capes of that country.

It fell out that several merchant ships were got ready, and fallen down to Lynhaven Bay, near the mouth of James River, in order for sailing. A pirate being informed of this, and hearing that there was no man-of-war there, except a sixth rate, ventured within the Capes, and took several of the merchant ships; but a small vessel happened to come down the bay, and, seeing an engagement between the pirate and a merchant-man, made a shift to get into the mouth of James River, where the Shoram, a fifth rate man-of-war, was newly arrived. The sixth rate, commanded by Capt. John Aldred, was then on the Carine in Elizabeth River, in order for her return to England.

The Governor happened to be at that time at Kiquotan, sealing up his letters, and Captain Passenger, commander of the Shoram, went ashore to pay his respects to him. In the meanwhile news was brought that a pirate was got within the Capes; upon which the captain was in haste to go aboard his ship: but the Governor would have stayed him, promising to go along with him. The captain soon after asked his excuse, and went off, leaving him another boat, if he pleased to follow. It was about one o'clock in the afternoon, when the news was brought; but 'twas within night, before his Excellency went aboard, staying all that while ashore, upon some weighty pretences. However, at last he followed, and by break of day the man-of-war was fairly out between the Capes and the pirate; where, after ten hours' sharp engagement, the pirate was obliged to strike and surrender upon the terms of being left to the King's mercy.

Now it happened that three men of this pirate's gang were not on board their own ship at the time of the surrender, and so were not included in the articles of capitulation, but were tried in that country. In summing up the charge against them (the Governor being present), the Attorney-General extolled his Excellency's mighty courage and conduct, as if the honor of taking the pirate had been due to him. Upon this, Capt. Passenger took the freedom to interrupt Mr. Attorney in open court, and said that he was commander of the Shoram; that the pirates were his prisoners; and that nobody had pretended to command in that engagement but himself. He further desired that the Governor would do him the justice to confess whether he had given the least word of command all that day, or directed any one thing during the whole fight. Upon this, his Excellency tamely acknowledged that what the captain said was true, and so fairly yielded him all the honor of that exploit.

THE PASTIMES OF COLONIAL VIRGINIA.

[From the Same.]

FOR their recreation, the plantations, orchards, and gardens constantly afford them fragrant and delightful walks. In their woods and fields, they have an unknown variety of vegetables, and other rarities of nature to discover and observe. They have hunting, fishing, and fowling, with which they entertain themselves an hundred ways. Here is the most good-nature and hospitality practised in the world, both toward friends and strangers; but the worst of it is, this generosity is attended now and then with a little too much intemperance. The neighborhood is at much the same distance as in the country in England; but with this advantage, that all the better sort of people have been abroad, and seen the world, by which means they are free from that stiffness and formality, which discover more civility than kindness. And besides, the goodness of the roads and the fairness of the weather bring people oftener together.

The Indians, as I have already observed, had in their hunting a way of concealing themselves, and coming up to the deer, under the blind of a stalking-head, in imitation of which many people have taught their horses to stalk it, that is, to walk gently by the huntsman's side, to cover him from the sight of the deer. Others cut down trees for the deer to browse upon, and lie in wait behind them. Others again set stakes at a certain distance within their fences, where the deer have been used to leap over into a field of peas, which they love extremely; these stakes they so place, as to run into the body of the deer, when he pitches, by which means they impale him.

They hunt their hares (which are very numerous) a-foot, with mongrels or swift dogs, which either catch them quickly, or force them to hole in a hollow tree, whither all their hares generally tend, when they are closely pursued. As soon as they are thus holed, and have crawled up into the body of a tree, the business is to kindle a fire and smother them with smoke, till they let go their hold and fall to the bottom stifled; from whence they take them. If they have a mind to spare their lives, upon turning them loose they will be as fit as ever to hunt at another time: for the mischief done them by the smoke immediately wears off again.

They have another sort of hunting, which is very diverting, and that they call vermin-hunting; it is performed a-foot, with small dogs in the night, by the light of the moon or stars. Thus in summer time they find abundance of raccoons, opossums, and foxes in the corn-fields, and about their plantations; but at other times they must go into the woods for them. The method is to go out with three or four dogs, and, as soon as they come to the place, they bid the dogs seek out, and all the company follow immediately. Wherever a dog barks, you may depend upon finding the game; and this alarm draws both men and dogs that way. If this sport be in the woods, the game by that time you come near it is perhaps mounted to the top of an high tree, and then they detach a nimble fellow up after it, who must have a scuffle with the beast, before he can throw it down to the dogs; and then the sport increases, to see the vermin encounter those little curs. In this sort of hunting, they also carry their great dogs out with them, because wolves, bears, panthers, wild cats, and all other beasts of prey, are abroad in the night.

For wolves they make traps, and set guns baited in the woods, so that, when he offers to seize the bait, he pulls the trigger, and the gun discharges upon him. What Elian and Pliny write of the horses being benumbed in their legs, if they tread in the track of a wolf, does not hold good here; for I myself, and many others, have rid full speed after wolves in the woods, and have seen live ones taken out of a trap, and dragged at a horse's tail; and yet those that followed on horse-back have not perceived any of their horses to falter in their pace. . . . .

There is yet another kind of sport, which the young people take great delight in, and that is, the hunting of wild horses; which they pursue sometimes with dogs, and sometimes without. You must know they have many horses foaled in the woods of the uplands, that never were in hand, and are as shy as any savage creature. These having no mark upon them belong to him that first takes them. However, the captor commonly purchases these horses very dear, by spoiling better in the pursuit; in which case he has little to make himself amends, besides the pleasure of the chase. And very often this is all he has for it, for the wild horses are so swift, that 'tis difficult to catch them; and when they are taken, 'tis odds but their grease is melted, or else, being old, they are so sullen that they can't be tamed.

The inhabitants are very courteous to travellers, who need no other recommendation, but the being human creatures. A stranger has no more to do, but to inquire upon the road where any gentleman or good housekeeper lives, and there he may depend upon being received with hospitality. This good nature is so general among their people, that the gentry, when they go abroad, order their principal servant to entertain all visitors with everything the plantation affords. And the poor planters, who have but one bed, will very often sit up, or lie upon a form or couch all night, to make room for a weary traveller to repose himself after his journey.

If there happen to be a churl, that either out of covetousness, or ill-nature, would not comply with this generous custom, he has a mark of infamy set upon him, and is abhorred by all.   But I must confess (and am heartily sorry for the occasion), that this good neighborhood has of late been much depraved by the present Governor, who practises the detestable politics of governing by parties; by which feuds and heart-burnings have been kindled in the minds of the people, and friend-ship, hospitality, and good-neighborhood have been extremely dis-couraged.

Ebenezer Cook.

NOTHING is known of this Satirist.

OF MEETING A GODLY KNAVE IN MARYLAND.

[*The Sot-Weed Factor*. 1708.]

WITH Cockerouse as I was sitting,
   I felt a fever intermitting;
A fiery pulse beat in my veins,
From cold I felt resembling pains.
This cursed seasoning, I remember,
Lasted from March to cold December;
Nor would it then its quarters shift
Until by Cardus turn'd adrift,
And had my doctress wanted skill,
Or kitchen physic at her will,
My father's son had lost his lands,
And never seen the Goodwin sands.
But thanks to fortune and a nurse
Whose care depended on my purse,
I saw myself in good condition,
Without the help of a physician.
At length the shivering ill relieved,
Which long my head and heart had grieved;
I then began to think with care,
How I might sell my British ware,
That with my freight I might comply,
Did on my charter party lie.
To this intent, with guide before,
I tript it to the eastern shore;
While riding near a sandy bay,
I met a Quaker, " Yea " and " Nay; "
A pious conscientious rogue,
As e'er wore bonnet or a brogue,
Who neither swore nor kept his word
But cheated in the fear of God;

And when his debts he would not **pay,**
By light within he ran away.
With this sly zealot soon I struck
A bargain for my English truck,
Agreeing for ten thousand weight
Of Sot-weed good and fit for freight,
Broad Oronooko bright and sound,
The growth and product of his ground;
In cask that should contain complete,
Five hundred of tobacco neat.
The contract thus betwixt us made,
Not well acquainted with the trade,
My goods I trusted to the cheat,
Whose crop was then aboard the fleet;
And, going to receive my own,
I found the bird was newly flown.
Cursing this execrable slave,
This damned pretended godly knave;
On dire revenge and justice bent,
I instantly to council went,
Unto an ambidexter Quack,
Who learnedly had got the knack
Of giving glisters, making pills,
Of filling bonds, and forging wills;
And with a stock of impudence
Supplied his want of wit and sense;
With looks demure, amazing people,
No wiser than a Daw in steeple.
My anger flushing in my face,
I stated the preceding case;
And of my money was so lavish,
That he'd have poisoned half the parish,
And hanged his father on a tree
For such another tempting fee.
Smiling, said he, "The cause is clear,
I'll manage him you need not fear;
The case is judged, good sir, but look
In Galen, No—in my Lord Cook,
I vow to God I was mistook:
I'll take out a provincial writ,
And trounce him for his knavish **wit;**
Upon my life we'll win the cause,
With all the ease I cure the yaws."
Resolved to plague the holy brother,
I set one rogue to catch another.
To try the cause then fully bent,
Up to Annapolis I went,
A city situate on a plain,
Where scarce a house will keep out **rain;**

But stranger here will scarcely meet
With market-place, exchange, or street,
And if truth I may report,
'Tis not so large as Tottenham court.
St. Mary's once was in repute,   ⎫
Now here the judges try the suit   ⎬
And lawyers twice a year dispute.   ⎭
As oft the bench most gravely meet, ⎫
Some to get drunk and some to eat   ⎬
A swingeing share of country treat. ⎭
But as for justice right or wrong,
Not one among the numerous throng
Knows what they mean, or has the heart
To give his verdict on a stranger's part.

.   .   .   .

The biassed court, without delay,
Adjudged my debt in country pay;
In pipe-staves, corn, or flesh of boar,
Rare cargo for the English shore;
Raging with grief, full speed I ran
To join the fleet at *Kicketan ;*
Embarked and waiting for a wind
I left this dreadful curse behind.

John Lawson.

BORN in Scotland.   CAPTURED and burned by Indians in North Carolina, 1712

REVELS OF THE CAROLINA INDIANS.

[*The History of Carolina.* 1714.]

THE king and war captain invited us to see their masquerade. This feast was held in commemoration of the plentiful harvest of corn they had reaped the summer before, with an united supplication for the like plentiful produce the year ensuing. These revels are carried on in a house made for that purpose, it being done round with white benches of fine canes, joining along the wall; and a place for the door being left, which is so low that a man must stoop very much to enter therein. This edifice resembles a large hayrick, its top being pyramidal, and much bigger than their other dwellings, and at the building whereof, every one assists till it is finished. All their dwelling houses are covered with bark, but this differs very much; for it is very artificially thatched with sedge and rushes. As soon as finished, they place some one of

their chiefest men to dwell therein, charging him with the diligent preservation thereof, as a prince commits the charge and government of a
fort or castle to some subject he thinks worthy of that trust. In these
state houses is transacted all public and private business relating to the
affairs of the government, as the audience of foreign ambassadors from
other Indian rulers, consultation of waging and making war, proposals of
their trade with neighboring Indians, or the English who happen to come
amongst them. In this theatre, the most aged and wisest meet, determin-
ing what to act, and what may be most convenient to omit.   .   .   .   .

As soon as we came into it, they placed our Englishmen near the
king, it being my fortune to sit next him, having his great general or
war captain on my other hand. The house is as dark as a dungeon, and
as hot as one of the Dutch stoves in Holland. They had made a circular
fire of split canes in the middle of the house ; it was one man's employment to add more split reeds to the one end as it consumed at the other,
there being a small vacancy left to supply it with fuel. They brought in
great store of loblolly and other medleys, made of Indian grain, stewed
peaches, bear, venison, etc., every one bringing some offering to enlarge
the banquet, according to his degree and quality. When all the viands
were brought in, the first figure began with kicking out the dogs, which
are seemingly wolves made tame with starving and beating, they being
the worst dog masters in the world ; so that it is an infallible cure for
sore eyes, ever to see an Indian's dog fat. They are of quite a contrary
disposition to horses ; some of their kings having gotten by great chance
a jade, stolen by some neighboring Indian, and transported farther into
the country and sold, or bought sometimes of a Christian that trades
amongst them. These creatures they continually cram and feed with
maize, and what the horse will eat, till he is as fat as a hog—never making any further use of him than to fetch a deer home that is killed somewhere near the Indian's plantation.

After the dogs had fled the room, the company was summoned by beat
of drum ; the music being made of a dressed deer's skin, tied hard upon
an earthern porridge pot. Presently in came fine men dressed up with
feathers, their faces being covered with vizards made of gourds ; round
their ankles and knees were hung bells of several sorts ; having wooden
falchions in their hands (such as stage fencers commonly use) ; in this
dress they danced about an hour, showing many strange gestures, and
brandishing their wooden weapons as if they were going to fight each
other ; oftentimes walking very nimbly round the room, without making
the least noise with their bells, a thing I much admired at ; again turning their bodies, arms and legs into such frightful postures that you
would have guessed that they had been quite raving mad : at last they cut
two or three high capers and left the room. In their stead came in a

parcel of women and girls, to the number of thirty odd, every one taking place according to her degree of stature—the tallest leading the dance and the least of all being placed last; with these they made a circular dance, like a ring representing the shape of the fire they danced about. Many of these had great horse bells about their legs, and small hawk bells about their necks. They had musicians, who were two old men, one of whom beat a drum, while the other rattled with a gourd that had corn in it to make a noise withal. To these instruments they both sung a mournful ditty; the burthen of their song was in remembrance of their former greatness and numbers of their nation, the famous exploits of their renowned ancestors, and all actions of moment that had in former days been performed by their forefathers.   .   .   .   .

Their way of dancing is nothing but a sort of stamping motion, much like the treading upon founder's bellows. This female gang held their dance for above six hours, being all of them of a white lather, like a running horse that has just come in from his race. My landlady was the ringleader of the Amazons, who, when in her own house, behaved herself very discreetly and wearily in her domestic affairs; yet custom had so infatuated her as to almost break her heart with dancing amongst such a confused rabble. During this dancing, the spectators do not neglect their business in working the loblolly-pots and the other meat that was brought thither; more or less of them being continually eating, whilst the others were dancing.

"HUSQUENAWING."

[*From the Same.*]

THERE is one most abominable custom amongst them, which they call husquenawing their young men, which I have not made any mention of as yet, so will give you an account of it here. You must know, that most commonly once a year, at farthest once in two years, these people take up so many of their young men as they think are able to undergo it, and husquenaugh them, which is to make them obedient and respective to their superiors, and, as they say, is the same to them as it is to us to send our children to school, to be taught good breeding and letters. This house of correction is a large, strong cabin, made on purpose for the reception of the young men and boys that have not passed the graduation already; and it is always at Christmas that they husquenaugh their youth, which is by bringing them into this house and keeping them dark all the time, where they more than half starve them.

Besides, they give them pellitory bark, and several intoxicating plants, that make them go raving mad as ever were any people in the world; and you may hear them make the most dismal and hellish cries and howlings that ever human creatures expressed; all which continues about five or six weeks, and the little meat they eat is the nastiest, loathsome stuff, and mixed with all manner of filth it is possible to get. After the time is expired, they are brought out of the cabin, which never is in the town, but always a distance off, and guarded by a jailor or two, who watch by turn. Now when they first come out, they are as poor as ever any creatures were; for you must know several die under this diabolical purgation. Moreover, they either really are, or pretend to be dumb, and do not speak for several days, I think twenty or thirty, and look so ghastly, and are so changed, that it is next to an impossibility to know them again, although you were never so well acquainted with them before. I would fain have gone into the mad house, and have seen them in their time of purgatory, but the king would not suffer it, because, he told me, they would do me or any other white man an injury, that ventured in amongst them, so I desisted. They play this prank with girls as well as boys, and I believe it a miserable life they endure, because I have known several of them run away at that time to avoid it. Now the savages say if it were not for this, they could never keep their youth in subjection, besides that it hardens them ever after to the fatigues of war, hunting, and all manner of hardship, which their way of living exposes them to. Beside, they add, that it carries off those infirm, weak bodies, that would have been only a burden and disgrace to their nation, and saves the victuals and clothing for better people, that would have been expended on such useless creatures.

Francis Yonge.

Surveyor-General of South Carolina in 1719.

AN EARLY REBELLION IN SOUTH CAROLINA.

[*A Narrative of the Proceedings, etc.* 1726.]

ON Monday the 21st of December, 1719, Mr. Johnson came to town from his plantation, being informed they designed to proclaim their governor in the king's name, and wrote circular letters to his council to meet him, but they did not come; he had talked to Colonel Paris, the commanding officer of the militia of the town, and engaged him in his interest, as he thought; and, as he had ordered the town companies to be reviewed the 21st of December, on account of the advice he had received from the Havanah, as before related—and finding they pitched on that day to proclaim their governor, that they might have the better opportunity to draw them, when together, in arms, to forward their purposes (for they could not well be in arms, but by some authority)—he, on the Saturday before, ordered that they should not muster, but wait for farther orders; and had given particular orders to Colonel Paris, that he should not suffer a drum to beat in the town; and had assurances from him, his orders should be obeyed. Notwithstanding which, when he came early on the Monday morning, he found the militia drawn up in the market-place, with colors flying at the forts, and on board all the ships in the harbor, and great solemnity preparing for their proclaiming their governor. It would be tedious to the reader, to enumerate all that he did at this juncture to oppose their proceedings; some he menaced, and handled more roughly, and some spoke fair to, to persuade them from what they were doing; and, going to the commanding officer, he asked him, how he durst appear in arms, contrary to his orders? and commanded him in the king's name to disperse his men. But he answered, he was obeying the orders of the convention. And the governor approaching him, he commanded his men to present their muskets at him, and bade him stand off, at his peril. Mr. Johnson was in hopes some gentlemen and others might have joined him; but the defection was so general, that hardly a man but was in arms; and only one of his council and Mr. John Lloyd walked with him; and it appeared the latter of these was sent under pretence of being his friend, by the other party, to prevent any hot action he might have been provoked to do, for that was his business all the day; and two days afterwards he was sworn into their new council.

Col. Rhett, who had always pretended to be very popular, and to have great power with the people, and to be extremely in the interest of the Lords' proprietors, did not appear in the Lords' behalf to assist Mr. Johnson. And indeed this whole affair was owing to his and Mr. Trott's councils, who did, as usual in such cases, leave their masters in the lurch; as will appear by their future transactions. In short, they proceeded to proclaim their governor, which they did in spite of all the opposition Mr. Johnson could give them; which could not be much, he being, as I have said, left entirely alone; although he did, in their march, stop the militia that attended them, and had almost persuaded them to alter their opinion; which if he could have effected, he might have been able to have given a great deal of trouble to the opposite party: but Sir Hovendine Walker was with them, and put them in mind to keep up the spirits of the people; which occasioned their turning back and haranguing their men, who thereupon marched on as they formerly intended.

Surely, after this, no one will say but Mr. Johnson did all that was possible to prevent the defection of the people. And these minute circumstances we have been the more particular in, because their Lordships have been made believe, that he was himself in the design, and connived at their transactions, which he might have prevented if he would. A thing very improbable, that he should join with the people to divest himself of his government, and, when he had done so, refuse to govern them in their own way as they desired: which, it is plain, he might have done, but that he thought it was inconsistent with his honor, and the trust reposed in him by the Lords Proprietors; and that his so doing might have been resented by his majesty as a presumptuous act he had no authority for.

The people, having thus overcome all the little opposition could be made, proceeded to choose a council of twelve, after the manner of the king's governments. Of these, Sir Hovendine Walker was chosen president; so they had now their governor, council, and convention (as they called themselves); but they soon after voted themselves an assembly, and, as such, made laws, appointed officers, especially a new chief justice in the place of Mr. Trott, a secretary, a provost-marshal, and voted, that no one should be capable of bearing an office in the province that owned the authority of the Lords Proprietors, except such as related to their own particular revenue, which were Mr. Rhett and Mr. Yonge, their receiver and surveyor-general. They also passed a new duty law, and several laws for raising money to defray the expense of the government, to pay agents whom they sent to represent their affairs to his majesty, and for other uses.

Hugh Jones.

BORN in England, 1669. Came to America, 1696. DIED in Cecil Co., Md., 1760.

VIRGINIA IN 1722.

[*The Present State of Virginia.* 1724.]

THE habits, life, customs, computations, etc., of the Virginians are much the same as about London, which they esteem their home; and for the most part have contemptible notions of England, and wrong sentiments of Bristol and the other outports, which they entertain from seeing and hearing the common dealers, sailors and servants that come from those towns, and the country places in England and Scotland, whose language and manners are strange to them; for the planters and even the native negroes generally talk good English without idiom or tone, and can discourse handsomely upon most common subjects; and conversing with persons belonging to trade and navigation from London, for the most part they are much civilized, and wear the best of clothes according to their station; nay, sometimes too good for their circumstances, being for the generality comely, handsome persons, of good features and fine complexions (if they take care), of good manners and address. The climate makes them bright, and of excellent sense, and sharp in trade; an idiot or deformed native being almost a miracle.

Thus they have good natural notions and will soon learn arts and sciences; but are generally diverted by business or inclination from profound study and prying into the depth of things; being ripe for management of their affairs before they have laid so good a foundation of learning, and had such instructions, and acquired such accomplishments as might be instilled into such good natural capacities. Nevertheless, through their quick apprehension they have a sufficiency of knowledge and fluency of tongue, though their learning for the most part be but superficial.

They are more inclinable to read men by business and conversation than to dive into books, and are for the most part only desirous of learning what is absolutely necessary in the shortest and best method.

Having this knowledge of their capacities and inclination from sufficient experience, I have composed on purpose some short treatises adapted with my best judgment to a course of education for the gentlemen of the plantations: consisting in a short English grammar; an accidence to Christianity; an accidence to the mathematics, especially to arithmetic in all its parts and applications, algebra, geometry, surveying of land and navigation.

These are the most useful branches of learning for them, and such as they willingly and readily master, if taught in a plain and short method, truly applicable to their genius; which I have endeavored to do for the use of them and all others of their temper and parts.

They are not very easily persuaded to the improvement of useful inventions (except a few, such as sawing mills), neither are they great encouragers of manufactures, because of the trouble and certain expense in attempts of this kind, with uncertain prospect of gain; whereas by their staple commodity, tobacco, they are in hopes to get a plentiful provision; nay, often very great estates.

Upon this account they think it folly to take off their hands (or negroes) and employ their care and time about anything that may make them lessen their crop of tobacco.

So that though they are apt to learn, yet they are fond of, and will follow their own ways, humors and notions, being not easily brought to new projects and schemes; so that I question if they would have been imposed upon by the Mississippi or South Sea or any other such monstrous bubbles.

In their computations of time, weights and measures, both of length, superficies and solidity, they strictly adhere to what is legal; not running into precarious customs as they do in England. Thus their quart is the true Winchester; their hundred is 100, not 112, and they survey land by statute measure.

Indeed, what English coin is there is advanced in value, so that a shilling passes for 14*d.*, and a guinea goes by tale for 26*s.;* but the current money is the Spanish, which in reality is about 15*l.* per cent. inferior to our English coin, as settled by law: but frequently the value of this varies in respect of sterling bills according to the circumstances of trade; currency and sterling being sometimes at a par; but for the generality 10 per cent. discount is allowed for sterling bills.

As for education, several are sent to England for it; though the Virginians being naturally of good parts (as I have already hinted) neither require nor admire as much learning as we do in Britain; yet more would be sent over, were they not afraid of the small-pox, which most commonly proves fatal to them.

But, indeed, when they come to England, they are generally put to learn to persons that know little of their temper, who keep them drudging on in what is of least use to them, in pedantic methods too tedious for their volatile genius.

For grammar learning, taught after the common roundabout way, is not much beneficial nor delightful to them; so that they are noted to be more apt to spoil their school fellows than improve themselves; because they are imprisoned and enslaved to what they hate and think useless, and have not peculiar management proper for their humor and occasion.

A civil treatment with some liberty, if permitted with discretion, is most proper for them, and they have most need of, and readily take polite and mathematical learning; and in English may be conveyed to them (without going directly to Rome and Athens) all the arts, sciences and learned accomplishments of the ancients and moderns, without the fatigue and expense of another language, for which most of them have little use or necessity, since (without another) they may understand their own speech, and all other things requisite to be learned by them, sooner and better.

Thus the youth might as well be instructed there as here by proper methods, without the expense and danger of coming hither; especially if they make use of the great advantage of the college at Williamsburg, where they may (and many do) imbibe the principles of all human and divine literature, both in English and in the learned languages.

By the happy opportunity of this college may they be advanced to religious and learned education, according to the discipline and doctrine of the established Church of England ; in which respect this college may prove of singular service, and be an advantageous and laudable nursery and strong bulwark against the contagious dissensions in Virginia; which is the most ancient and loyal, the most plentiful and flourishing, the most extensive and beneficial colony belonging to the Crown of Great Britain, upon which it is most directly dependent; wherein is established the Church of England, free from faction and sects, being ruled by the laws, customs and constitutions of Great Britain, which it strictly observes, only where the circumstances and occasion of the country by an absolute necessity require some small alterations; which nevertheless must not be contrary (though different from and subservient) to the laws of England.

Though the violence of neither whig nor Tory reigns there, yet have they parties; for the very best administration must expect to meet with some opposition in all places, especially where there is a mixture of people of different countries concerned, whose education and interest may propose to them notions and views different from each other.

Most other plantations, especially they that are granted away to proprietors, are inferior to Virginia; where the seeming interest and humor of the owners often divert them from pursuit of the most proper methods; besides, they cannot have such a right claim to the favor of the Crown, nor demand its best protection, since they may often interfere with its interest; whereas Virginia is esteemed one of the most valuable gems in the Crown of Great Britain.

Thus Virginia, having to itself, with Maryland, the staple commodity of tobacco, has a great advantage of all other plantations on the continent for the encouragement of the Crown; whereas others belonging to gentlemen, or having no peculiar trade, cannot expect such power to advance and improve their interest.

To this add that Virginia equals, if not exceeds, all others in goodness of climate, soil, health, rivers, plenty and all necessaries and conveniences of life.   Besides, she has, among others, these particular advantages of her younger sister Maryland, viz., freedom from Popery and the direction of proprietors; not but that part of Virginia which is between the rivers Potomac and Rappahannock belongs to proprietors, as to the quit rent, yet the government of these counties (called the northern neck) is under the same regulation with the other parts of the country.

If New England be called a receptacle of Dissenters, and an Amsterdam of religion, Pennsylvania the nursery of Quakers, Maryland the retirement of Roman Catholics, North Carolina the refuge of runaways, and South Carolina the delight of buccaneers and pirates, Virginia may be justly esteemed the happy retreat of true Britons and true Churchmen for the most part; neither soaring too high nor drooping too low, consequently should merit the greater esteem and encouragement.

The common planters, leading easy lives, do not much admire labor, or any manly exercise, except horse-racing, nor diversion, except cock-fighting, in which some greatly delight. This easy way of living, and the heat of the summer, make some very lazy, who are then said to be climate-struck.

The saddle horses, though not very large, are hardy, strong and fleet, and will pace naturally and pleasantly at a prodigious rate.

They are such lovers of riding that almost every ordinary person keeps a horse ; and I have known some spend the morning in ranging several miles in the woods to find and catch their horses only to ride two or three miles to church, to the court-house, or to a horse race, where they generally appoint to meet upon business, and are more certain of finding those that they want to speak or deal with, than at their home.

No people can entertain their friends with better cheer and welcome ; and strangers and travellers are here treated in the most free, plentiful and hospitable manner ; so that a few inns or ordinaries on the road are sufficient.

As to the weather, the spring and fall are not unlike those seasons in England, only the air is never long foggy nor very cloudy ; but clear, sometimes of a bluish color, occasioned by the thin smoke dispersed in the air from the flames of the woods and leaves, which are fired in hunting, to drive the beasts from their lurking places, or in the spring to burn the old leaves and grass, that there may be the better pasture the next summer.

The months of December, January and February are generally much colder, and June, July, and August are much hotter than in England ; though sometimes it is on a sudden very cool in summer and pretty warm in winter, the weather being governed by the winds, which, with sudden storms from the northwest and sometimes from the west and southwest, bring violent gusts or tempests, with thunder, lightning, and rain, very terrible but soon over.

The northwest winds are exquisitely sharp and cold, proceeding from clouds arising from the vast lakes and prodigious snowy mountains that lie to that quarter ; but the southerly winds and others are very warm.

The days and nights are there always much nearer the equality of twelve hours than in the latitude of England.

At the sudden changes of the weather from heat to cold, people are apt to take cold, often neglecting to shift their clothes with the weather, which, with abundance of damps and mists from the water, and by eating too plentifully of some delicious fruits, makes the people subject to fevers and agues, which is the country distemper, a severe fit of which (called a seasoning) most expect sometime after their arrival in that climate ; but the goodness of God has furnished us with a perfect catholicon for that sickness, viz., "the bark," which, being taken and repeated in a right manner, seldom fails of a cure, unless the morbific matter comes to a head again from fresh causes and so returns with mastery; upon which recourse must be had to the same specific remedy; besides which there are several ways of cure, but none so universal and sure as that.

Some, for want of timely care, through ignorance or obstinacy, will permit the distemper to lurk about them so long, till at last it has reduced them to an irrecoverable, lingering, ill habit of body, especially if they live meanly, drinking too much water and eating too much salt meat; and this cachexy generally ends their lives with a dropsy, consumption, the jaundice, or some such illness.

Besides this, some are troubled with the dry gripes, proceeding from colds, I suppose, which take away for a long time the use of the limbs of some, especially hard drinkers of rum; some that have lain out in mighty cold weather have been frost-bitten and lost their fingers or toes.

There is no danger of wild beasts in travelling; for the wolves and bears which are up the country never attack any, unless they be first assaulted and hurt; and the wolves of late are much destroyed by virtue of a law which allows good rewards for their heads with the ears on, to prevent imposition and cheating the public; for the ears are cropped when a head is produced.

The bears are also much destroyed by the out-planters, etc., for the sake of their flesh and skins.

As for rattlesnakes, etc., they make off from you, unless you, by carelessness, chance to tread on them; and then their bite is found now not to be mortal, if remedies can be applied in time.

The worst inconvenience in travelling across the country is the circuit that must be taken to head creeks, etc., for the main roads wind along the rising ground between the rivers, though now they much shorten their passage by mending the swamps and building of bridges in several places; and there are established ferries at convenient places over the great rivers; but in them is often much danger from sudden storms, bad boats, or unskilful or wilful ferrymen; especially if one passes in a boat with horses, of which I have great reason to be most sensible by the loss of a dear brother at Chickahominy Ferry, in February, 1723-4.

As for their drink, good springs of excellent water abound everywhere almost, which is very cooling and pleasant in summer, and the general drink of abundance, not so much out of necessity as choice.

Some planters, etc., make good small drink with cakes of persimmons, a kind of plums which grow there in great plenty; but the common small beer is made of molasses, which makes extraordinary brisk good-tasted liquor at a cheap rate, with little trouble in brewing; so that they have it brisk and fresh as they want it in winter and summer. And as they brew, so do they bake daily bread or cakes, eating too much hot and new bread, which cannot be wholesome, though it be pleasanter than what has been baked a day or two.

Some raise barley and make malt there, and others have malt from England, with which those that understand it brew as good beer as in England, at proper seasons of the year; but the common strong malt drink mostly used is Bristol beer, of which is consumed vast quantities there yearly; which, being well brewed and improved by crossing the sea, drinks exceedingly fine and smooth; but malt liquor is not so much regarded as wine, rack, brandy, and rum punch, with drams of rum or brandy for the common sort, when they drink in a hurry.

The common wine comes from Madeira or Fayal, which, moderately drunk, is fittest to cheer the fainting spirits in the heat of summer, and to warm the chilled blood in the bitter colds of winter, and seems most peculiarly adapted for this climate. Besides this, are plentifully drunk with the better sort, of late years, all kinds of French and other European wine, especially claret and port.

Here is likewise used a great deal of chocolate, tea and coffee, which, with several sorts of apparel, they have as cheap or cheaper than in England, because of the debenture of such goods upon their exportation thither. Besides, they are allowed to have wines directly from Madeira, and other commodities are brought from the West Indies and the Continent, which cannot be brought to England without spoiling.

As for grinding corn, etc., they have good mills upon the runs and creeks; besides hand-mills, wind-mills, and the Indian invention of pounding hominy in mortars burned in the stump of a tree, with a log for a pestle hanging at the end of a pole, fixed like the pole of a lave.

Though they are permitted to trade to no parts but Great Britain, except these places, yet have they in many respects better and cheaper commodities than we in England, especially of late years; for the country may be said to be altered and improved in wealth and polite living within these few years, since the beginning of Col. Spotswood's government, more than in all the scores of years before that, from its first discovery. The country is yearly supplied with vast quantities of goods from Great Britain, chiefly from London, Bristol, Liverpool, Whitehaven, and from Scotland.

The ships that transport these things often call at Ireland to victual, and bring over frequently white servants, which are of three kinds: 1. Such as come upon certain wages by agreement for a certain time. 2. Such as come bound by indenture, commonly called kids, who are usually to serve four or five years. 3. Those convicts or felons that are transported, whose room they had much rather have than their company; for abundance of them do great mischiefs, commit robbery and murder, and spoil servants that were before very good. But they frequently there meet with the end they deserved at home, though indeed some of them prove indifferent good. Their being sent thither to work as slaves for punishment is but a mere notion, for few of them ever lived so well and so easy before, especially if they are good for anything. These are to serve seven, and sometimes fourteen years, and they, and servants by indentures, have an allowance of corn and clothes when they are out of their time, that they may be therewith supported till they can be provided with service or otherwise settled. With these three sorts of servants are they supplied from England, Wales, Scotland, and Ireland, among which they that have a mind to it may serve their time with ease and satisfaction to themselves and their masters, especially if they fall into good hands. Except the last sort, for the most part who are loose villains, made tame by Wild and then enslaved by his forward namesake. To prevent too great a stock of which servants and negroes, many attempts and laws have been in vain made.

These, if they forsake their roguery, together with the other kids of the later Jonathan, when they are free, may work day labor, or else rent a small plantation for a trifle almost; or else turn overseers, if they are expert, industrious, and careful, or follow their trade, if they have been brought up to any, especially smiths, carpenters, tailors, sawyers, coopers, bricklayers, etc. The plenty of the country and the good wages given to workfolks occasion very few poor, who are supported by the parish, being such as are lame, sick, or decrepit through age, distempers, accidents or some infirmities; for where there is a numerous family of poor children, the vestry takes care to bind them out apprentices till they are able to maintain themselves by their own labor; by which means they are never tormented with vagrant and vagabond beggars, there being a reward for taking up runaways that are at a small distance from their home, if they are not known or are without a pass from their master, and can give no good account of themselves, especially negroes.

In all convenient places are kept stores or warehouses of all sorts of goods, managed by storekeepers or factors, either for themselves or others in the country or in Great Britain.

This trade is carried on in the fairest and genteelest way of merchandise by a great number of gentlemen of worth and fortune, who, with the commanders of their ships, and several Virginians (who come over through business or curiosity, or often to take possession of estates which every year fall here to some or other of them), make as considerable and handsome a figure, and drive as great and advantageous a trade for the advancement of the public good, as most merchants upon the Royal Exchange.

At the stores in Virginia, the planters, etc., may be supplied with what English commodities they want.

The merchants, factors, or storekeepers in Virginia buy up the tobacco of the planters, either for goods or current Spanish money, or with sterling bills payable in Great Britain.   .   .   .   .

The tobacco purchased by the factors or storekeepers is sent home to their employers, or consigned to their correspondent merchants in Great Britain.

But most gentlemen, and such as are beforehand in the world, lodge money in their merchant's hands here, to whom they send their crop of tobacco, or the greatest part of it.

This money is employed according to the planter's orders, chiefly in sending over yearly such goods, apparel, liquors, etc., as they write for, for the use of themselves, their families, slaves, and plantations; by which means they have every thing at the best hand and the best of its kind.

Samuel Penhallow.

BORN in Cornwall, England, 1665. DIED at Portsmouth, N. H., 1726.

THE STRANGE END OF A GREAT EXPEDITION.

[*The History of the Wars of New-England with the Eastern Indians.* 1726.]

COLONEL NICHOLSON, by the reduction of Port Royal (which from that time bears the name of Annapolis Royal), was but the more inflamed with the desire of the conquest of Canada. Wherefore, upon his return to England, he so effectually represented to the queen and ministry, the great advantage that would accrue unto the crown thereby, that he obtained orders for a sufficient force, both by sea and land, with the assistance of the several colonies. And, for the better expediting the same, he set sail the latter end of April, some time before the fleet, with express orders unto the several governors of New England, New York, the Jerseys, and Philadelphia, to get their quotas of men in readiness. He arrived at Boston on June the eighth, 1711, to the great joy and satisfaction of the country. A Congress hereupon was appointed at New London, being nearest the centre, where the several governors met, with a firm resolution of carrying on the important affairs. On the 25th, the castle gave a signal of ships in the bay, which proved to be the fleet: upon which the troops of guards and regiment of foot were under arms to receive them, and, as his Excellency was not yet returned, the gentlemen of the Council, and others of distinction, went to congratulate them.

Brigadier Hill was Commander in Chief of these her Majesty's troops, and Sir Hovenden Walker, Admiral of the fleet, which consisted of fifteen men of war, forty transports, a battalion of marines, and several regiments under Colonel Kirk, Colonel Segmore, Brigadier Hill, Colonel Disnee, Colonel Windress, Colonel Clayton and Colonel Kaine, with upwards of five thousand men, who arrived safe in health, and encamped on Noddle's Island, where the General invited the Governor to view them under arms. They made the finest appearance that was ever yet seen or known in America. Her Majesty, out of her royal favor, was also pleased to send six ships, with all manner of warlike stores, and a fine train of artillery, with forty horses to draw the same.

It is surprising to think how vigorously this expedition was forwarded, while at Boston, although a town but of eighty years standing, out of a howling wilderness; yet scarce any town in the kingdom (but where stores are laid up before) could have effected the same in so short a time. For in less than a month the whole army was supplied with ten weeks' provision, and all other necessaries that were wanted, besides two regiments of our New England forces, under the command of Colonel Vetch and Colonel Walton, who embarked at the same time, in transports of our own. On the day that the fleet sailed, Colonel Nicholson set out for New York, and from thence for Albany, having ordered batteaux before, and everything else on the inland frontiers to be in readiness for passing the lake with utmost application. The assembly of New York raised ten thousand pounds, besides their proportion of men, the Jerseys five, and although Pennsylvania was not so free of their persons, because of their persuasion, yet were as generous in their purse as any of the other colonies in carrying on the expedition.

Every thing now looked with a smiling aspect of success, considering the powerful strength by land and sea, the former being as fine regimental troops as any that belonged to the Duke of Marlborough's army; and the latter as serviceable ships as any in the whole navy. . . . .

The first harbor they made after they sailed from Nantasket, was Cape Gaspé, from thence they sailed up St. Lawrence river, until they got up off the Virgin Mountains; the weather then proving foggy, and the wind freshening, the Admiral asked the pilots what was best to do? who advised that, as the fleet was on the north shore, it would be best to bring to, with their heads unto the southward, but he, obstinately refusing, acted the reverse, and ordered their heads unto the north, which was so astonishing unto the pilots that one and another foretold their fear (unto the officers) and the destiny that would attend them before the morning; which accordingly fell out. For at one of the clock, nine ships, with fifteen hundred men, were all cast ashore, and most of the rest in as eminent danger; but so soon as the former struck they fired their guns, which gave caution to the rest, some of which wore, and stood off; others were so encompassed by the breakers that they were obliged to bring to their anchors, which was their last refuge; but before the day approached the wind happily shifted to W. N. W., upon which they cut their cables, and came to sail. Soon after, a council of war was called, but the result not known until the evening, and then the flag bore away to Spanish River, without giving the usual signal; on which many of the windward ships were left behind; but a small man of war was ordered to cruise the next day for those that were left, and to take up such as might be alive among the dead, who were about six hundred. After this, they made towards the fleet, but were eight days in getting down; during which time the wind was eastwardly, and had our fleet proceeded (as it were to be wished they had) might easily have got unto Quebec in forty-eight hours.

Upon this disaster, the whole country (and indeed the nation) was alarmed, and many censures and jealousies arose, some imputing it to cowardice, but most to treachery, and the secret influence of some malcontents then at helm; otherwise, why would a matter of such vast importance to the British kingdom be hushed up in silence, and the principal officers not summoned to appear? If the Admiral was in fault, wherefore was he not called to an account? Or why did not the General, to vindicate himself, lay a remonstrance before the council board? And the pilots (who were ordered from hence at so great a charge to the country, to represent matters in a true light) been examined? But instead thereof, dismissed without being asked one question! However, one thing is remarkable, that among those that were shipwrecked, and lost their lives, there was but one single person that belonged to New England among them.

Colonel Nicholson at this juncture was industriously engaged in getting the batteaux ready for passing the lake with a considerable number of friend Indians, as well as English, for the attack of Montreal, which, next to Quebec, was the place of greatest importance in all the French territories. But just as he was ready to embark, an express came and gave an account of the miserable disaster that befell the fleet: whereas, if he had proceeded, his whole army would probably have been cut off; for, upon advice of our fleet's misfortune, the French drew off all their auxiliaries, and most of their militia, to reinforce Montreal, being advised of the descent that was making on them. So great was our loss in this enterprise, that it affected the whole country seven years after; as the advance and expense of so much money and provisions might well do. And it as much flushed the enemy: for out of the ruins of our vessels they not only got much plunder, but fortified their castle and out-door batteries, with a considerable number of cannon. They moreover stirred up the French and Indians about Annapolis Royal to revolt from their allegiance to the crown.

Thomas Symmes.

BORN 1678.   Minister of Bradford, Mass.   DIED, 1725.

THE ENGAGEMENT AT PIGWACKET.

[Lovewell Lamented. 1725.]

IT was about the 16th of April, 1725, that the brave and intrepid Captain John Lovewell began the arduous and perilous undertaking of marching from Dunstable to Pigwacket, with forty-six men under his command.   .   .   .   .

From the Thursday before the battle, the company were apprehensive they were discovered and dogged by the enemy ; and on Friday night the watch heard the Indians about the camp and alarmed the company, but, it being very dark, they could make no further discovery.

On Saturday, the eight of May, while they were at prayers, very early in the morning, they heard a gun ; and some little time after they espied an Indian on a point, that ran into Saco pond.

They now concluded that the design of the gun, and the Indian's discovering himself, was to draw them that way.—They expected now without fail to be attacked, and it was proposed and consulted, whether it would be prudent to venture an engagement with the enemy (who they perceived were now sufficiently alarmed), or endeavor a speedy retreat. The men generally and boldly answered : "We came to see the enemy ; we have all along prayed God we might find them ; and we had rather trust Providence with our lives, yea, die for our country, than try to return without seeing them, if we might, and be called cowards for our pains."

The captain readily complied to lead them on, though not without manifesting some apprehensions, and, supposing the enemy were ahead of them (when, as it proved, they were in the rear ordered the men to lay down their packs, and march with the greatest caution, and in the utmost readiness.

When they had marched about a mile and a half or two miles, Ensign Wyman espied an Indian coming towards them, whereupon he gave a signal, and they all squatted and let the Indian come on. In a short time several guns were fired at him, upon which the Indian fired upon Capt. Lovewell, with beaver-shot, and wounded him mortally (as is supposed), though he made but little complaint and was still able to travel, and at the same time wounded Mr. Samuel Whitney.—Ensign Wyman immediately fired at and killed the Indian, and Mr. Frye and another scalped him.

They then marched back towards their packs (which the enemy had found in the mean time and seized), and about ten of the clock, when they came pretty near to where they had laid them, at the northeast end of Saco Pond, on a plain where there were few trees and but little brush, the Indians rose up in front and rear, in two parties, and ran towards the English, three or four deep, with their guns presented : the English also instantly presented their guns, and rushed on to meet them.

When they had advanced to within a few yards of each other, they fired on both sides, and the Indians fell in considerable numbers, but the English, most, if not all of them, escaped the first shot, and drove the Indians several rods.   Three or four rounds were fired on both sides ; but the Indians being more than double in number to our men, and having already killed Captain Lovewell, Mr. Fullam (only son of Major Fullam of Weston), Ensign Harwood, John Jefts, Jonathan Kittridge, Daniel Woods, Ichabod Johnson, Thomas Woods, and Josiah Davis, and wounded Lieutenants Farwell and Robbins, and Robert Usher, in the place where the fight began, and striving to surround the rest, the word was given to retreat to the pond, which was done with a great deal of good conduct, and proved a great service to the English (the pond covering their rear), though the Indians got the ground where the dead of our party lay.

The fight continued very furious and obstinate, till towards night,— the Indians roaring and yelling and howling like wolves, barking like dogs, and making all sorts of hideous noises,—the English frequently shouting and huzzaing, as they did after the first round.   At one time, Captain Wyman is confident, the Indians were diverting themselves in powowing, by their striking upon the ground, and other odd motions,—but Wyman, creeping up and shooting their chief actor, broke up their meeting.

Some of the Indians, holding up ropes, asked the English if they would take quarter ; but were briskly answered, that they would have no quarter but at the muzzles of their guns.

About the middle of the afternoon, the ingenious Mr. Jonathan Frye (only son of Capt. James Frye of Andover), a young gentleman of a liberal education, who took his degree at Harvard College, 1723, and was chaplain to the company, and greatly beloved by them for his excellent performances and good behavior, and who fought with undaunted courage till that time of day, was mortally wounded.   But when he could fight no longer, he prayed audibly several times for the preservation and success of the residue of the company.

Some time after sunset, the enemy drew off, and left the field to our men. It was supposed and believed, that not more than twenty of the enemy went off well. About midnight, the English assembled themselves, and, upon examining into their situation, they found Jacob Farrar just expiring by the pond, and Lieutenant Robbins and Robert Usher unable to travel.

Lieutenant Robbins desired his companions to charge his gun and leave it with him, which they did; he declaring that, "As the Indians will come in the morning to scalp me, I will kill one more of them if I can."   .   .   .   .

Four of the wounded men, viz., Farwell, Frye, Davis and Jones, after they had travelled about a mile and a half, found themselves unable to go any further, and with their free consent the rest kept on their march, hoping to find a recruit at the fort, and to return with fresh hands to relieve them.

As they proceeded on, they divided into three companies one morning, as they were passing a thick wood, for fear of making a track by which the enemy might follow them. One of the companies came upon three Indians, who pursued them some time; meanwhile Elias Barron, one of this party, strayed from the others, and got over Ossapy river, by the side of which his gun case was found, and he was not heard of afterwards. Eleven, in another party, reached the fort at Ossapy, but to their great surprise found it deserted. The coward who fled in the beginning of the battle ran directly to the fort, and gave the men posted there such a frightful account of what had happened, that they all fled from the fort, and made the best of their way home.

Solomon Keyes also came to the fort. When he had fought in the battle till he had received three wounds, and had become so weak by the loss of blood that he could not stand, he crawled up to Ensign Wyman, in the heat of the battle, and told him he was a dead man; "but," said he, "if it be possible, I will get out of the way of the Indians, that they may not get my scalp." Keyes then crept off to the side of the pond to where he providentially found a canoe, when he rolled himself into it, and was driven by the wind several miles towards the fort; he gained strength fast, and reached the fort as soon as the eleven before mentioned; and they all arrived at Dunstable on the 13th of May, at night.

On the 15th of May, Ensign Wyman and three others arrived at Dunstable. They suffered greatly for want of provisions. They informed, that they were wholly destitute of all kinds of food, from a Saturday morning till the Wednesday following; when they caught two mouse squirrels, which they roasted whole, and found to be a sweet morsel. They afterwards killed some partridges and other game, and were comfortably supplied till they got home.

Eleazer Davis arrived at Berwick, and reported that he and the other three who were left with him waited some days for the return of the men from the fort, and, at length, despairing of their return, though their wounds were putrefied and stank, and they were almost dead with famine, yet they all travelled on several miles together, till Mr. Frye desired Davis and Farwell not to hinder themselves any longer on his account, for he found himself dying, and he laid himself down, telling them he should never rise more, and charged Davis, if it should please God to bring him home, to go to his father and tell him, that he expected in a few hours to be in eternity, and that he was not afraid to die. —They left him, and this amiable and promising young gentleman, who had the journal of the march in his pocket, was not heard of again.

Lieutenant Farwell, who was greatly and no doubt deservedly applauded and lamented, was also left by Davis within a few miles of the fort, and was not afterwards heard of. But Davis, getting to the fort and finding provision there, tarried and refreshed himself, and recovered strength to travel to Berwick.   .   .   .   .

Several of the Indians, particularly Paugus, their Chief, were well known to Lovewell's men, and frequently conversed with each other during the engagement. In the course of the battle, Paugus and John Chamberlain discoursed familiarly with each other; their guns had become foul, from frequent firing; they washed their guns at the pond, and the latter assured Paugus that he should kill him; Paugus also menaced him, and bid defiance to his insinuation. When they had prepared their guns, they loaded and discharged them, and Paugus fell.

A son of Paugus, after it had become a time of peace, went to Dunstable, to revenge his father's death with the death of Chamberlain. He did not go directly to Chamberlain's, but to the house of a neighbor, where he tarried several days upon some pretended business, that his design might not be discovered; his errand was, however, suspected, and a hint given to Chamberlain,—who cut a port-hole above his door, through which he very early one morning discovered an Indian behind his woodpile, lying with his gun pointing directly to the door; and it was supposed that the same musket which had conveyed the mean of death to the bosom of the great Paugus, also proved fatal to his son, as he was not afterwards heard of.

It is also reported of this Chamberlain (who was a stout and a courageous man, and who used to say that he was not to be killed by an Indian), that he was once fired at by an Indian, as he was at work in a sawmill, at night; he was in a stooping position, and did not discover the Indian till he fired, who was so near him that he immediately knocked him down with a crowbar, with which he was setting his log. . . . .

Ensign Wyman was rewarded with a captain's commission after his return, and every man was crowned with the grateful thanks of their countrymen, for this heavy blow given to a plundering savage foe, the common enemy of their country.

Anonymous.

LOVEWELL'S FIGHT.

[A Popular Ballad.   Written shortly after the Battle of May 8th, 1725.]

OF worthy Captain LOVEWELL, I purpose now to sing,
  How valiantly he served his country and his King;
He and his valiant soldiers did range the woods full wide,
And hardships they endured to quell the Indian's pride.

'Twas nigh unto Pigwacket, on the eighth day of May,
They spied a rebel Indian soon after break of day;
He on a bank was walking, upon a neck of land,
Which leads into a pond as we're made to understand.

Our men resolved to have him, and travelled two miles round,
Until they met the Indian, who boldly stood his ground;
Then up speaks Captain LOVEWELL, "Take you good heed," says he,
"This rogue is to decoy us, I very plainly see.

"The Indians lie in ambush, in some place nigh at hand,
In order to surround us upon this neck of land;
Therefore we'll march in order, and each man leave his pack;
That we may briskly fight them when they make their attack."

They came unto this Indian, who did them thus defy,
As soon as they came nigh him, two guns he did let fly,
Which wounded Captain LOVEWELL, and likewise one man more,
But when this rogue was running, they laid him in his gore.

Then having scalped the Indian, they went back to the spot,
Where they had laid their packs down, but there they found them not,
For the Indians having spied them, when they them down did lay,
Did seize them for their plunder, and carry them away.

These rebels lay in ambush, this very place hard by,
So that an English soldier did one of them espy,

And cried out, "Here's an Indian;" with that they started out,
As fiercely as old lions, and hideously did shout.

With that our valiant English all gave a loud huzza,
To show the rebel Indians they feared them not a straw:
So now the fight began, and as fiercely as could be,
The Indians ran up to them, but soon were forced to flee.

Then spake up Captain LOVEWELL, when first the fight began,
"Fight on my valiant heroes! you see they fall like rain."
For as we are informed, the Indians were so thick,
A man could scarcely fire a gun and not some of them hit.

Then did the rebels try their best our soldiers to surround,
But they could not accomplish it, because there was a pond,
To which our men retreated and covered all the rear,
The rogues were forced to flee them, although they skulked for fear.

Two logs there were behind them that close together lay,
Without being discovered, they could not get away;
Therefore our valiant English they travelled in a row,
And at a handsome distance as they were wont to go.

'Twas ten o'clock in the morning when first the fight begun,
And fiercely did continue until the setting sun;
Excepting that the Indians some hours before 'twas night,
Drew off into the bushes and ceased a while to fight.

But soon again returned, in fierce and furious mood,
Shouting as in the morning, but yet not half so loud;
For as we are informed, so thick and fast they fell,
Scarce twenty of their number at night did get home well.

And that our valiant English till midnight there did stay,
To see whether the rebels would have another fray;
But they no more returning, they made off towards their home,
And brought away their wounded as far as they could come.

Of all our valiant English there were but thirty-four,
And of the rebel Indians there were about fourscore.
And sixteen of our English did safely home return,
The rest were killed and wounded, for which we all must mourn.

Our worthy Captain LOVEWELL among them there did die,
They killed Lieut. ROBBINS, and wounded good young FRYE,
Who was our English Chaplain; he many Indians slew,
And some of them he scalped when bullets round him flew.

Young FULLAM too I'll mention, because he fought so well,
Endeavoring to save a man, a sacrifice he fell:
But yet our valiant Englishmen in fight were ne'er dismayed,
But still they kept their motion, and WYMAN's Captain made,

Who shot the old chief PAUGUS, which did the foe defeat,
Then set his men in order, and brought off the retreat ;
And braving many dangers and hardships in the way,
They safe arrived at Dunstable, the thirteenth day of May.

Benjamin Colman.

BORN in Boston, Mass., 1673. DIED there, 1747.

A QUARREL WITH FORTUNE.

[*The Life and Character of the Reverend Benjamin Colman, D.D. By E. Turell.* 1749.]

[The Daughter with Mr. Colman used to range over the Manor in the Afternoons. She asked a poem from him : He told her it would lead into a Quarrel. She promised it should not on her Part. So the next Day he wrote one with this Title, "A Quarrel with Fortune :" Because (forsooth) he was not equal to her in Rank and Riches—In it was the following Simile. E. T.]

SO have I seen a little silly fly
    Upon a blazing taper dart and die.
The foolish insect ravish'd with so bright
And fair a glory, would devour the light.
At first he wheels about the threatening fire,
With a career as fleet as his desire :
This ceremony past, he joins the same
In hopes to be transform'd himself to flame.
The fiery, circumambient sparkles glow,
And vainly warn him of his overthrow,
But resolute he'll to destruction go.
So mean-born mortals, such as I, aspire,
And injure with unhallowed desire,
The glory we ought only to admire.
We little think of the intense fierce flame,
That gold alone is proof against the same ;
And that such trash as we, like drossy lead,
Consume before it, and it strikes us dead.

THE ASCENT OF THE SAINT.

[*A Poem on Elijah's Translation.* 1707.]

'TWAS at high noon, the day serene and fair,
    Mountains of lum'nous clouds roll'd in the air,

Benjamin Colman

When on a sudden, from the radiant skies,
Superior light flasht in Elisha's eyes.
The Heav'ns were cleft, and from the imperial **throne**
A stream of glory, dazzling splendor, shone ;
Beams of ten thousand suns shot round about,
The sun and every blazon'd cloud went out ;
Bright hosts of angels lin'd the heavenly way,
To guard the saint up to eternal day.
Then down the steep descent a chariot bright,
And steeds of fire, swift as the beams of light.
Wing'd seraphs ready stood, bow'd low to greet
The fav'rite saint, and hand him to his seat.
Enthron'd he sat, transformed with joys his mien,
Calm his gay soul, and, like his face, serene.
His eye and burning wishes to his God,
Forward he bow'd, and on the triumph rode.

A TALE OF PIRACY.

[*It is a Fearful Thing to Fall into the Hands of the Living God.* 1726.]

THE miserable persons to whom, and at whose desire, the foregoing sermon was preached, were Samuel Cole and Henry Greenvill. There
was also present with them George Condick. The captain of the pirates
William Fly, refused to come into public. I moved the others for his
sake, to let me preach to them in private. But they said it was the last
Sabbath they had to live, and they earnestly desired to be in an assembly
of worshippers, that they might have the prayers of many together over
them, and that others might take the more warning by them.

The story of these wretched men is short and tragical. They sailed
from Jamaica on board a snow, John Green, Commander, bound to
Guinea. They had not been long at sea before they conspired to seize
the captain and mate and then go a pirating. On the 27th of May, 1726,
they put in execution their wicked design, in a most cruel and barbarous
manner. About one o'clock in the morning, William Fly, then boatswain
of the snow " Elizabeth," after he had been for some time forward with
several of the sailors, came aft with Alexander Mitchel and others, and said
to Morrice Cunden (gunner of the ship), then at helm, " D——n you, you
dog, if you stir hand or foot, or speak a word, I'll blow your brains out!"

And immediately thereupon he went into the cabin where Captain
Green was in bed, and Alexander Mitchel followed him ; and while they
were there Morrice Cunden heard the captain cry out: " What's the matter?" But they soon hauled him upon deck, and were about to throw

him into the sea; when the poor man begged of them to spare his life, saying, "For God's sake, Boatswain, don't throw me overboard, for if you do I shall go to hell!" But though in the anguish and amazement of his soul he thus pleaded with them, that they would not send him down quick into hell, for that he was not fit to die; yet his plea made no impression at all upon their hardened hearts. Fly bid him say after him these words, "Lord, have mercy upon my soul!" and away they hurried the poor surprised and astonished man overboard. It is affirmed that he caught hold of a rope and held for his life, which when one of these wretches saw he cut off his hand with an ax; and so he dropped into eternity.

At the same time some others of this bloody crew surprised the mate of the ship, Thomas Jenkins. And Thomas Streaton (the carpenter of the ship) deposed that he heard Samuel Cole say to Jenkins, "Come out of your cabin, you dog!" and presently he was hauled out, and told that he should go overboard after his captain. When he was in the sea he was heard calling earnestly to the doctor to hand him a rope. But the doctor was by this time himself putting into irons.

Thus bloodily these inhuman creatures began their piracy, but vengeance followed them and suffered them not to live.

William Fly, the chief and worst (we may suppose) of these barbarous rogues, took on him the command, and named the snow the "Fame's Revenge." They were well stored with powder, and rum and provisions, but wanted a better vessel; and in quest of this it is likely they bent their course, first to Carolina, and from thence to New England. On the third of June they took a sloop at anchor off North Carolina, on board of which was Mr. William Atkinson, a passenger; who was afterwards the happy instrument in the hand of God for their destruction. They very much needed one so well skilled as Atkinson was both as a mariner and pilot, and Fly treated him well on that account, but kept a strict eye upon him, forbidding him to have any conversation with the forced men; and, lest he should, he had a hammock given him in the cabin.

They commanded him to carry them to Martha's Vineyard in order to wood and water there, and in hopes to meet with some sloop fitting for their purpose. But he resolved to run the venture of carrying them past the Vineyard, and run them up into or near the bay before they were aware of it. When they perceived it they began to look upon him with an evil eye, and spake of throwing him overboard. But as Fly was uttering his rage at him the next morning on this account, and telling him what death he should die if anything ill befell them through his conduct, a schooner came in sight, which put an end to Fly's rage, for the joy of a good prize. They found it a schooner of Marblehead, George Girdler, Master.

Mr. Atkinson had some time before this meditated the seizing on Fly and company, and found means secretly to communicate his mind to some on board, whom he thought he might trust; particularly to Samuel Walker, and Thomas Streaton; and Walker had spoken of it to James Benbrook; who all consented if a fair opportunity should offer.

It was very necessary to his design to ingratiate himself, as far as he honestly and with a good conscience could, with Fly and his pirates. Yet in doing this he ran a risk both of his innocence and his life; of his innocence, for " with a furious man thou shalt not go, lest thou learn his ways and get a snare to thy soul; " and of his life, for as some of the pirates, the captain especially, began to think friendly of him and to hearken to his advice (they all depending on him to navigate the ship), so if a ship of war had taken them it is to be feared that he had in vain pleaded his innocence and good intentions. But the good God who preserved, has also pleaded his innocence. And we ought to praise his virtue, conduct and courage, and give God the glory of it.

Fly had no sooner taken the schooner of Marblehead, but they discovered another at a distance from them. Whereupon he put three men on board the schooner, and purposed to bear down on the new sail with both his vessels. But Mr. Atkinson with a ready thought advised him to put six men into the schooner, and send her down on the fishing vessels, being herself one of their company but a day before, and so there would be no likelihood of their flying from her : " but," said he, " if the snow and the schooner now bear down together, they'll take you for what you are, and make away from you." Fly came into his advice and put three men more into the schooner, and parted with her, standing a course wide from her.

Now Atkinson's thoughts were hard at work how to draw Fly away from his arms on the quarter-deck. For there he kept alone, nor would suffer Atkinson to step up, so much as to set down the bowl of punch after he had drank to him. And probably a message which he received from a chief pirate on board the schooner, by the boat, " To have a special care of his friend," did increase his jealousy ; though he seemed only to laugh at it.

Within a little while Atkinson spied a sail ahead to the leeward, and informed Fly of it. And presently after he pretended to discover two or three more sail, and told him he would have a fleet of prizes. But Fly with his glass could see but one. " Why," said Atkinson, " If you were but here, sir, with your glass, ahead, you would easily see them all." On a sudden Fly forgot his caution, and comes off the quarter-deck, where his arms lay, and sits him down ahead to spy the sails spoken of. Then Atkinson gave the sign to his friends, and Walker followed by Benbrook came up, pretending at first to direct the captain to look a point or two on such a side, while Atkinson (a spare and slender man) passed aft toward the arms, and in the instant that Walker laid hold of Fly he took the fire-arms, and returned pointing the gun to the pirate's breast, and telling him " He was a dead man if he did not immediately submit himself his prisoner." The wicked Fly earnestly begged for his life, and now found that mercy which he had so barbarously denied to his innocent captain.

In the midst of this struggle the pirate Greenvill put up his head from between decks : for there as Providence ordered it he and Condick were at this instant ; and as for the pirate Cole he had been in irons for two days before, by Fly's order, for some mutiny he had made. This it was that rendered the subduing them so easy to Atkinson and his three companions ; for now Streaton had fallen in, and guarded one place, while Atkinson did the other, keeping the pirates down. The action was so surprising to the other forced men, that for a time they stood astonished and like men amazed, not capable of acting for their own deliverance ; although vehemently called upon and threatened by Atkinson. But in a little time they came to themselves and joyfully fell in with their deliverers.

When Fly found himself chained down and effectually secured, he fell at times into the most desperate ragings, cursing himself and her that bare him, and the day wherein he was born ; cursing the very heavens and in effect the God that judged him ; cursing all rovers that should ever give quarter again to an Englishman ; and wishing all the devils of hell would come and fly away with the ship ; the same blasphemer now in his furious despair, or worse than he ever was before in his jollity and pride ; when he would sometimes even dare to ridicule the noise of God's thunder, as it rattled over him, saying, " That they were playing bowls in the air," etc., and as the lightnings sometimes flashed upon them, he would say—" Who fires now ? Stand by," etc.—So he dared the dreadful vengeance, which pursued him swift as the lightnings and suddenly struck him.

But Capt. Atkinson and his brave mates are much to be praised, that they dealt so mercifully with these bloody men ; and neither " blew their brains out " (their own phrase) nor threw them overboard.

Blessed be God that kept them that day from shedding blood, and from avenging themselves with their own hands. It was much better to reserve the murderers to the judgment of the law, in the proper course of it. Hereby the guilty Miserables had a space granted them for repentance, and were brought under the happy means of it; means happy, we hope, to two of them, namely Greenvill and Cole.

Capt. Atkinson and company now made the best of their way for the Port of Boston.

THE CITIZEN'S OBLIGATIONS.

[The Religious Regards we Owe to our Country. 1718.]

NO man is made only for himself, and his own private affairs, but to serve, profit, and benefit others. We are manifestly formed for society, and designed by our great Creator for a mutual dependance on and serviceableness unto each other here in the body. Both the safety and the pleasure of life depend upon our joint proposing and pursuing this design.

As soon as we read but of two men in the world, we find that God expected the one should be the other's keeper. It were yet a Cainish temper to doubt or deny this obligation. He was both a murderer and a liar that first denied this, and 'tis pity that he has left any children behind him in his cursed image. Cain flew in the face of God, and did violence to nature, did outrage to his own conscience, when he asked, " Am I my brother's keeper? " Ignorant and impudent man! Did he not feel that within himself, that he ought to be so? As Cain was of that wicked one, so is he of Cain who thinks himself not born for the welfare of others, but merely for himself and his own petty, private, and temporal concerns. And like Cain he deserves to be cursed from the earth, and driven from the face of men, as well as hid from the face of God; a fugitive and a vagabond, and afraid of every one he sees. This is a due punishment of so barbarous a principle. For as the man renounces others, so must they him; and while he declares that others must look for no good from him, they may well apprehend all imaginable evil and mischief from him, and he from them again. For his principle runs him into all manner of injustice and injury, barbarity and bloodiness, as it did Cain; and the earth cannot bear the monster, but cries for vengeance against him.

A man's private and domestic affairs are too *petite* to engross his noble soul; they are too small and narrow a compass for him to confine himself within. He is endowed for much greater things, and he much debases himself if he do not think so.

But our country, and the particular places where we dwell, are ordinarily the bounds of our influence. Especially is it so as to common and ordinary people, who are known only in their own neighborhood, and find enough near home to keep them employed. And here prudence as well as charity teaches us to begin.

William Byrd.

Born in Westover, Va., 1674.　Died in Virginia, 1744.

THE FIRST SURVEY IN THE DISMAL SWAMP.

[The History of the Dividing Line: Run in the Year 1729.]

SOME borderers, too, had a great mind to know where the line would come out, being for the most part apprehensive lest their lands should be taken into Virginia.　In that case they must have submitted to some sort of order and government; whereas, in North Carolina, every one does what seems best in his own eyes.　There were some good women that brought their children to be baptized, but brought no capons along with them to make the solemnity cheerful.　In the mean time it was strange that none came to be married in such a multitude, if it had only been for the novelty of having their hands joined by one in holy orders. Yet so it was, that though our chaplain christened above an hundred, he did not marry so much as one couple during the whole expedition.　But marriage is reckoned a lay contract in Carolina, as I said before, and a country justice can tie the fatal knot there, as fast as an archbishop.

None of our visitors could, however, tell us any news of the surveyors, nor indeed was it possible any of them should at that time, they being still laboring in the midst of the Dismal.

It seems they were able to carry the line this day no further than one mile and sixty-one poles, and that whole distance was through a miry cedar bog, where the ground trembled under their feet most frightfully. In many places, too, their passage was retarded by a great number of fallen trees, that lay horsing upon one another.

Though many circumstances concurred to make this an unwholesome situation, yet the poor men had no time to be sick, nor can one conceive a more calamitous case than it would have been to be laid up in that uncomfortable quagmire.　Never were patients more tractable, or willing to take physic, than these honest fellows; but it was from a dread of laying their bones in a bog that would spew them up again.　That consideration also put them upon more caution about their lodging.

They first covered the ground with square pieces of cypress bark, which now, in the spring, they could easily slip off the tree for that purpose.　On this they spread their bedding; but unhappily the weight and warmth of their bodies made the water rise up betwixt the joints of the bark, to their great inconvenience.　Thus they lay not only moist, but also exceedingly cold, because their fires were continually going out. For no sooner was the trash upon the surface burnt away, but immedi-

WILLIAM BYRD

ately the fire was extinguished by the moisture of the soil, insomuch that it was great part of the sentinel's business to rekindle it again in a fresh place, every quarter of an hour. Nor could they indeed do their duty better, because cold was the only enemy they had to guard against in a miserable morass, where nothing can inhabit.

We could get no tidings yet of our brave adventurers, notwithstanding we dispatched men to the likeliest stations to inquire after them. They were still scuffling in the mire, and could not possibly forward the line this whole day more than one mile and sixty-four chains. Every step of this day's work was through a cedar bog, where the trees were somewhat smaller and grew more into a thicket. It was now a great misfortune to the men to find their provisions grow less as their labor grew greater; they were all forced to come to short allowance, and consequently to work hard without filling their bellies. Though this was very severe upon English stomachs, yet the people were so far from being discomfited at it, that they still kept up their good-humor, and merrily told a young fellow in the company, who looked very plump and wholesome, that he must expect to go first to pot, if matters should come to extremity.

This was only said by way of jest, yet it made him thoughtful in earnest. However, for the present he returned them a very civil answer, letting them know that, dead or alive, he should be glad to be useful to such worthy good friends. But, after all, this humorous saying had one very good effect, for that younker, who before was a little inclined by his constitution to be lazy, grew on a sudden extremely industrious, that so there might be less occasion to carbonade him for the good of his fellow-travellers.   .   .   .   .

The surveyors and their attendants began now in good earnest to be alarmed with apprehensions of famine, nor could they forbear looking with some sort of appetite upon a dog that had been the faithful companion of their travels.

Their provisions were now near exhausted. They had this morning made the last distribution, that so each might husband his small pittance as he pleased. Now it was that the fresh colored young man began to tremble every joint of him, having dreamed, the night before, that the Indians were about to barbecue him over live coals.

The prospect of famine determined the people, at last, with one consent, to abandon the line for the present, which advanced but slowly, and make the best of their way to firm land. Accordingly they sat off very early, and, by the help of the compass which they carried along with them, steered a direct westerly course. They marched from morning till night, and computed their journey to amount to about four miles, which was a great way, considering the difficulties of the ground. It was all along a cedar-swamp, so dirty and perplexed, that if they had not travelled for their lives, they could not have reached so far.

On their way they espied a turkey-buzzard, that flew prodigeously high to get above the noisome exhalations that ascend from that filthy place. This they were willing to understand as a good omen, according to the superstition of the ancients, who had great faith in the flight of vultures. However, after all this tedious journey, they could yet discover no end of their toil, which made them very pensive, especially after they had eat the last morsel of their provisions. But to their unspeakable comfort, when all was hushed in the evening, they heard the cattle low, and the dogs bark, very distinctly, which, to men in that distress, was more delightful music than Faustina or Farinelli could have made. In the mean time the commissioners could get no news of them from any of their visitors, who assembled from every point of the compass. . .

However long we might think the time, yet we were cautious of showing our uneasiness, for fear of mortifying our landlord. He had done his best for us, and therefore we were unwilling he should think us dissatisfied with our entertainment. In the midst of our concern, we were most agreeably surprised, just after dinner, with the news that the Dismalites were all safe. These blessed tidings were brought to us by Mr. Swan, the Carolina surveyor, who came to us in a very tattered condition.

After very short salutations, we got about him as if he had been a Hottentot, and began to inquire into his adventures. He gave us a detail of their uncomfortable voyage through the Dismal, and told us, particularly, they had pursued their journey early that morning, encouraged by the good omen of seeing the crows fly over their heads; that, after an hour's march over very rotten ground, they, on a sudden, began to find themselves among tall pines, that grew in the water, which in many places was knee-deep. This pine swamp, into which that of Coropeak drained itself, extended near a mile in breadth; and though it was exceedingly wet, yet it was much harder at bottom than the rest of the swamp; that about ten in the morning they recovered firm land, which they embraced with as much pleasure as shipwrecked wretches do the shore.

After these honest adventurers had congratulated each other's deliverance, their first inquiry was for a good house, where they might satisfy the importunity of their stomachs. Their good genius directed them to Mr. Brinkley's, who dwells a little to the southward of the line. This man began immediately to be very inquisitive, but they declared they had no spirits to answer questions till after dinner.

"But pray, gentlemen," said he, "answer me one question, at least: what shall we get for your dinner?" To which they replied, "No matter what, provided it be but enough." He kindly supplied their wants as soon as possible, and by the strength of that refreshment they made a shift to come to us in the evening, to tell their own story. They all looked very thin, and as ragged as the Gibeonite ambassadors did in the days of yore. Our surveyors told us they had measured ten miles in the Dismal, and computed the distance they had marched since to amount to about five more, so they made the whole breadth to be fifteen miles in all.

A PROFITABLE DAY.

[*A Journey to the Land of Eden: Anno* 1733.]

MAJOR MAYO'S survey being no more than half done, we were obliged to amuse ourselves another day in this place. And that the time might not be quite lost, we put our garments and baggage into good repair. I for my part never spent a day so well during the whole voyage. I had an impertinent tooth in my upper jaw, that had been loose for some time, and made me chew with great caution. Particularly I could not grind a biscuit but with much deliberation and presence of mind. Toothdrawers we had none amongst us, nor any of the instruments they make use of. However, invention supplied this want very happily, and I contrived to get rid of this troublesome companion by cutting a caper. I caused a twine to be fastened round the root of my tooth, about a fathom in length, and then tied the other end to the snag of a log that lay upon the ground, in such a manner that I could just stand upright. Having adjusted my string in this manner, I bent my knees enough to enable me to spring vigorously off the ground, as perpendicularly as I could. The force of the leap drew out the tooth with so much ease that I felt nothing of it, nor should have believed it was come away, unless I had seen it dangling at the end of the string. An under tooth may be fetched out by standing off the ground and fastening your string at due distance above you. And having so fixed your gear, jump off your standing, and the weight of your body, added to the force of the spring, will poise out your tooth with less pain than any operator upon earth could draw it.

This new way of tooth-drawing, being so silently and deliberately performed, both surprised and delighted all that were present, who could not guess what I was going about. I immediately found the benefit of getting rid of this troublesome companion, by eating my supper with more comfort than I had done during the whole expedition.

A VISIT TO COLONEL SPOTSWOOD.

[*A Progress to the Mines, in the Year* 1732.]

SEPT., 1732. This famous town consists of Colonel Spotswood's enchanted castle on one side of the street, and a baker's dozen of ruinous tenements on the other, where so many German families had dwelt some years ago; but are now removed ten miles higher, in the Fork of Rappahannock, to land of their own. There had also been a chapel about a bow-shot from the colonel's house, at the end of an avenue of cherry trees, but some pious people had lately burnt it down, with intent to get another built nearer to their own homes. Here I arrived about three o'clock, and found only Mrs. Spotswood at home, who received her old acquaintance with many a gracious smile. I was carried into a room elegantly set off with pier glasses, the largest of which came soon after to an odd misfortune. Amongst other favorite animals that cheered this lady's solitude, a brace of tame deer ran familiarly about the house, and one of them came to stare at me as a stranger. But unluckily spying his own figure in the glass, he made a spring over the tea-table that stood under it, and shattered the glass to pieces, and falling back upon the tea-table made a terrible fracas among the china. This exploit was so sudden, and accompanied with such a noise, that it surprised me, and perfectly frightened Mrs. Spotswood. But 'twas worth all the damage to show the moderation and good humor with which she bore this disaster. In the evening the noble colonel came home from his mines, who saluted me very civilly, and Mrs. Spotswood's sister, Miss Theky, who had been to meet him *en cavalier*, was so kind too as to bid me welcome. We talked over a legend of old stories, supped about 9, and then prattled with the ladies, till it was time for a traveller to retire. In the mean time I observed my old friend to be very uxorious, and exceedingly fond of his children. This was so opposite to the maxims he used to preach up before he was married, that I could not forbear rubbing up the memory of them. But he gave a very good-natured turn to his change of sentiments, by alleging that whoever brings a poor gentlewoman into so solitary a place, from all her friends and acquaintance, would be ungrateful not to use her and all that belongs to her with all possible tenderness.

We all kept snug in our several apartments till nine, except Miss Theky, who was the housewife of the family. At that hour we met over a pot of coffee, which was not quite strong enough to give us the palsy. After breakfast the colonel and I left the ladies to their domestic affairs, and took a turn in the garden, which has nothing beautiful but three terrace walks that fall in slopes one below another. I let him understand, that besides the pleasure of paying him a visit, I came to be instructed by so great a master in the mystery of making of iron, wherein he had led the way, and was the Tubal Cain of Virginia. He corrected me a little there, by assuring me he was not only the first in this country, but the first in North America, who had erected a regular furnace. That they ran altogether upon bloomeries in New England and Pennsylvania, till his example had made them attempt greater works. But in this last colony, they have so few ships to carry their iron to Great Britain, that they must be content to make it only for their own use, and must be obliged to manufacture it when they have done. That he hoped he had done the country very great service by setting so good an example.   .   .   .   .

Our conversation on this subject continued till dinner, which was both elegant and plentiful. The afternoon was devoted to the ladies, who showed me one of their most beautiful walks. They conducted me through a shady lane to the landing, and by the way made me drink some very fine water that issued from a marble fountain, and ran incessantly. Just behind it was a covered bench, where Miss Theky often sat and bewailed her virginity. Then we proceeded to the river, which is the south branch of Rappahannock, about fifty yards wide, and so rapid that the ferry boat is drawn over by a chain, and therefore called the Rapidan. At night we drank prosperity to all the colonel's projects in a bowl of rack punch, and then retired to our devotions.

Having employed about two hours in retirement, I sallied out at the first summons to breakfast, where our conversation with the ladies, like whip syllabub, was very pretty, but had nothing in it. This, it seems, was Miss Theky's birthday, upon which I made her my compliments, and wished she might live twice as long a married woman as she had lived a maid. I did not presume to pry into the secret of her age, nor was she forward to disclose it, for this humble reason, lest I should think her wisdom fell short of her years.   .   .   .   .

We had a Michaelmas goose for dinner, of Miss Theky's own raising, who was now good-natured enough to forget the jeopardy of her dog. In the afternoon we walked in a meadow by the river side, which winds in the form of a horseshoe about Germanna, making it a peninsula, containing about four hundred acres. Rappahannock forks about fourteen miles below this place, the northern branch being the larger, and consequently must be the river that bounds my Lord Fairfax's grant of the northern neck.

The sun rose clear this morning, and so did I, and finished all my little affairs by breakfast. It was then resolved to wait on the ladies on horseback, since the bright sun, the fine air, and the wholesome exercise, all invited us to it. We forded the river a little above the ferry, and rode six miles up the neck to a fine level piece of rich land, where we found about twenty plants of ginseng, with the scarlet berries growing on the top of the middle stalk. The root of this is of wonderful virtue in many cases, particularly to raise the spirits and promote perspiration, which makes it a specific in colds and coughs. The colonel complimented me with all we found, in return for my telling him the virtues of it. We were all pleased to find so much of this king of plants so near the colonel's habitation, and growing too upon his own land; but were, however, surprised to find it upon level ground, after we had been told it grew only upon the north side of Stony Mountains. I carried home this treasure with as much joy as if every root had been a graft of the Tree of Life, and washed and dried it carefully. This airing made us as hungry as so many hawks, so that between appetite and a very good dinner, 'twas difficult to eat like a philosopher. In the afternoon the ladies walked me about amongst all their little animals, with which they amuse themselves, and furnish the table; the worst of it is, they are so tender-hearted they shed a silent tear every time any of them are killed. At night the colonel and I quitted the threadbare subject of iron, and changed the scene to politics. He told me the ministry had receded from their demand upon New England, to raise a standing salary for all succeeding governors, for fear some curious members of the House of Commons should inquire how the money was disposed of that had been raised in the other American colonies for the support of their governors. . . . .

Our conversation was interrupted by a summons to supper, for the ladies, to show their power, had by this time brought us tamely to go to bed with our bellies full, though we both at first declared positively against it. So very pliable a thing is frail man, when women have the bending of him.

Oct. 1, 1732. Our ladies overslept themselves this morning, so that we did not break our fast till ten. We drank tea made of the leaves of ginseng, which has the virtues of the root in a weaker degree, and is not disagreeable. So soon as we could force our inclinations to quit the ladies, we took a turn on the terrace walk, and discoursed upon quite a new subject. The colonel explained to me the difference between the galleons and the flota, which very few people know. The galleons, it seems, are the ships which bring the treasure and other rich merchandise to Cartagena from Portobello, to which place it is brought overland from Panama and Peru. And the flota is the squadron that brings the treasure, etc., from Mexico and New Spain, which make up at La Vera Cruz. Both these squadrons rendezvous at the Havanna, from hence they shoot the Gulf of Florida, in their return to Old Spain. That this important port of the Havanna is very poorly fortified, and worse garrisoned and provided, for which reason it may be easily taken. Besides, both the galleons and flota, being confined to sail through the gulf, might be intercepted by our stationing a squadron of men-of-war at the most convenient of the Bahama Islands. And that those islands are of vast consequence for that purpose. He told me also that the assogue ships are they that carry quicksilver to Portobello and La Vera Cruz to refine the silver, and that, in Spanish, assogue signifies quicksilver. Then my friend unriddled to me the great mystery, why we have endured all the late insolences of the Spaniards so tamely. The Assiento contract, and the liberty of sending a ship every year to the Spanish West Indies, make it very necessary for the South Sea Company to have effects of great value in that part of the world. Now these being always in the power of the Spaniards, make the directors of that company very fearful of a breach, and consequently very generous in their offers to the ministry to prevent it. For fear these worthy gentlemen should suffer, the English squadron, under Admiral Hosier, lay idle at the Bastimentos, till the ships' bottoms were eaten out by the worm, and the officers and men, to the number of 5,000, died like rotten sheep, without being suffered, by the strictest orders, to strike one stroke, though they might have taken both the flota and galleons, and made themselves master of the Havanna into the bargain, if they had not been chained up from doing it. All this moderation our peaceable ministry showed even at a time when the Spaniards were furiously attacking Gibraltar, and taking all the English ships they could, both in Europe and America, to the great and everlasting reproach of the British nation. That some of the ministry, being tired out with the clamors of the merchants, declared their opinion for war, and while they entertained those sentiments they pitched upon him, Colonel Spotswood, to be Governor of Jamaica, that by his skill and experience in the art military, they might be the better able to execute their design of taking the Havanna. But the courage of these worthy patriots soon cooled, and the arguments used by the South Sea directors persuaded them once again into more pacific measures. When the scheme was dropped, his government of Jamaica was dropped at the same time, and then General Hunter was judged fit enough to rule that island in time of peace. After this the colonel endeavored to convince me that he came fairly by his place of postmaster-general, notwithstanding the report of some evil-disposed persons to the contrary. The case was this. Mr. Hamilton, of New Jersey, who had formerly had that post, wrote to Colonel Spotswood, in England, to favor him with his interest to get it restored to him. But the colonel considering wisely that charity began at home, instead of getting the place for Hamilton, secured it for a better friend · though, as he tells the story, that gentleman was absolutely refused, before he spoke the least good word for himself.

John Thompson.

Born near Belfast, Ireland.   Minister of St. Mark's Parish, Culpeper Co., Va.

AN ARGUMENT FOR MARRYING A CLERGYMAN.

[A Letter to Lady Spotswood. Written, May, 1742.]

MADAM: By diligently perusing your letter, I perceive there is a material argument, which I ought to have answered; upon which your strongest objection against completing my happiness would seem to depend, viz., that you would incur the censures of the world for marrying a person of my station and character.   By which I understand that you think it a diminution to your honor and the dignity of your family to marry a person in the station of a clergyman.   Now, if I can make it appear that the ministerial office is an employment, in its nature the most honorable and in its effects the most beneficial to mankind, I hope your objections will immediately vanish, that you will keep me no longer in suspense and misery, but consummate my happiness.

I make no doubt, Madam, but that you will readily grant that no man can be employed in any work more honorable than what immediately relates to the King of Kings and Lord of Lords, and to the salvation of souls, immortal in their nature and redeemed by the Blood of the Son of God.   The powers committed to their care cannot be exercised by the Heb. i. 14.   greatest prince of earth, and it is the same work in kind, and is the same in the design of it, with that of the blessed angels, who are ministering spirits for those who shall be heirs of salvation.   It is the same business that the Son of God discharged when he condescended to dwell amongst men, which engages men in the greatest acts of doing good, in turning sinners from the error of their ways, and, by all wise and prudent means, in gaining souls unto God; and the faithful and diligent discharge of this holy function gives a title to the highest de-Dan. xii. 3.   gree of glory in the next world; for they that be wise shall shine as the brightness of the firmament, and they that turn many to righteousness as the stars for ever and ever.

All nations, whether learned or ignorant, whether civil or barbarous, have agreed in this as a dictate of natural reason, to express their reverence for the Deity, and their affection to religion, by bestowing extraordinary privileges of honor upon such as administer in holy things, and by providing liberally for their maintenance.   And that the honor due to the holy function flows from the law of nature, appears from hence: that in the earliest times the civil and sacred authority were united in the same person.   Thus Melchisedeck was King and Priest of Salem; and

among the Egyptians the priesthood was joined with the crown. The
Greeks accounted the priesthood of equal dignity with king- Æn. 3.
ship; which is taken notice of by Aristotle in several places of his
"Politics."   And among the Latins we have a testimony from Virgil,
that at the same time Anias was both priest and king. Nay, Moses
himself, who was Prince of Israel, before Aaron was conse- Ex. xxiv. 6.
crated, officiated as priest in that solemn sacrifice by which the covenant
with Israel was confirmed.

And the primitive Christians always expressed a mighty value and
esteem for their clergy, as plainly appears by ecclesiastical history. And
even in our days, as bad as the world is, those of the clergy who live up
to the dignity of their profession, are generally reverenced and esteemed
by all religious and well disposed men.

From all which, it evidently appears that in all ages and nations of
the world, whether Jews, heathens, or Christians, great honor and dignity has been always conferred upon the clergy. And, therefore, dear
Madam, from hence you may infer how absurd and ridiculous those
gentlemen's notions are, who would fain persuade you that marrying
with the clergy would derogate from the honor and dignity of your
family. Whereas, in strict reasoning, the contrary thereof would rather
appear, and that it would very much tend to support the honor and
dignity of it. Of this, I hope you'll be better convinced, when you consider the titles of honor and respect that are given to those who are
invested with the ministerial function amply displayed in the Scriptures.
Those invested with that character are called the Ministers of Christ,
Stewards of the Mysteries of God, to whom they have committed the
Word of Reconciliation, the Glory of Christ, Ambassadors for Christ, in
Christ's stead, Co-workers with him, Angels of the Churches. And
when it is moreover declared that whosoever despiseth them, despiseth
not man, but God. All which titles show that upon many accounts they
stand called, appropriated and devoted to God himself. And, therefore,
if a Gentleman of this sacred and honorable character should be married
to a Lady, though of the greatest extraction and most excellent personal
qualities (which I'm sensible you're endowed with), can be no disgrace
to her, nor her family, nor draw the censure of the world upon either,
for such an action. And, therefore, dear Madam, your argument being
refuted, you can no longer consistently refuse to consummate my happiness.

JOHN THOMPSON.

Thomas Chalkley.

BORN in London, England, 1675.   DIED at the Friendly Islands, 1749.

THE DOCTOR'S DREAM.

[*A Journal of the Life, Labours, Travels, etc., of Thomas Chalkley.* 1749.]

AFTER we had been almost seven weeks at sea, we thought that we
were near the land, but we sounded several days and found no bottom, although we let out abundance of line, I think above three hundred
yards.   About this time our Doctor dreamed a dream which was to
this effect, himself relating it to me.   He said: " He dreamed that
he went on shore at a great and spacious town, the buildings whereof
were high, and the streets broad, and as he went up the street he saw a
large sign on which was written in great golden letters ' Shame.'   At the
door of the house (to which the sign belonged) stood a woman with a can
in her hand, who said unto him :   ' Doctor will you drink ? '   He replied,
' With all my heart, for I have not drank anything but water a great
while ' (our wine and cyder being all spent, having had a long passage);
and he drank a hearty draught which he said made him merry.   So he
went up the street reeling to and fro, when a grim fellow, coming behind
him, clapped him on the shoulder and told him ' That he arrested him in
the name of the Governor of the place ! '   He asked him for what, and
said, ' What have I done ? '   He answered, ' For stealing the woman's
can.'   The can he had indeed, and so he was led before the Governor,
which was a mighty black dog, the biggest and grimmest that ever he saw
in his life ; and witness was brought in against him by an old companion
of his, and he was found guilty, and his sentence was to go to prison and
there lay forever."

He told me this dream so punctually and with such an emphasis that
it affected me with serious sadness, and caused my heart to move within
me (for to me the dream seemed true and the interpretation sure).   I then
told him he was an ingenious man and might clearly see the interpretation
of that dream, which exactly answered to his state and condition, which
I thus interpreted to him: " This great and spacious place, wherein the
buildings were high and the streets broad, is thy great and high profession.   The sign on which was written ' Shame,' which thou sawest, and
the woman at the door with the can in her hand, truly represents that
great, crying and shameful sin of drunkenness, which thou knowest to be
thy great weakness, which the woman with the can did truly represent to
thee.   The grim fellow who arrested thee in the Devil's territories is
Death who will assuredly arrest all mortals.   The Governor whom

thou sawest representing a great black dog is certainly the Devil, who after his servants have served him to the full will torment them eternally in Hell."

So he got up as it were in haste and said, "God forbid! It is nothing but a dream." But I told him it was a very significant one and a warning to him from the Almighty, who sometimes speaks to men by dreams.

In seven weeks after we left sight of the land of America, we saw the Scilly Islands and next day saw the land of England, which was a comfortable sight to us; in that God Almighty had preserved us hitherto and that we were so far got on our way. We drove about the Channel's mouth for several days for want of wind; after which, for two days the wind came up, and we got as far up the Channel as Limebay, and then an easterly wind blew fresh for several days, and we turned to windward, but rather lost than got on our way, which was tiresome and tedious to some of us.

Now about this time, being some days after the doctor's dream, a grievous accident happened to us. We, meeting with a Dutch vessel in Limebay a little above the Start, hailed her, and she us. They said they came from Lisbon, and were bound for Holland. She was loaded with wine, brandy, fruit, and such like commodities, and we having little but water to drink, by reason our passage was longer than we expected, therefore we sent our boat on board, in order to buy us a little wine to drink with our water. Our doctor, and a merchant that was a passenger, and one sailor, went on board, where they staid until some of them were overcome with wine, although they were desired to beware thereof; so that, when they came back, a rope being handed to them, they being filled with wine unto excess were not capable of using it dexterously, insomuch that they overset the boat, and she turned bottom upwards, having the doctor under her. The merchant caught hold of a rope called the main-sheet, whereby his life was saved. The sailor, not getting so much drink as the other two, got nimbly on the bottom of the boat, and floated on the water till such time as our other boat was hoisted out, which was done with great speed, and we took him in; but the doctor was drowned before the boat came. The seaman that sat upon the boat saw him sink, but could not help him. This was the greatest exercise that we met with in all our voyage: and much the more so, as the doctor was of an evil life and conversation, and much given to excess in drinking. When he got on board the aforesaid ship, the master sent for a can of wine, and said: "Doctor, will you drink?" He replied: "Yes, with all my heart, for I have drank no wine a great while." Upon which he drank a hearty draught, that made him merry (as he said in his dream); and, notwithstanding the admonition which was so clearly manifested to him but three days before, and the many promises he had made to

Almighty God, some of which I was a witness of, when strong convictions were upon him, yet now he was unhappily overcome, and in drink when he was drowned. This is, I think, a lively representation of the tender mercy and just judgment of the Almighty to poor mortals; and I thought it worthy to be recorded to posterity, as a warning to all great lovers of wine and strong liquors.

John Gyles.

In Military Service of the Province of Massachusetts, 1698–1736.

THE ADVENTURES OF A CAPTIVE.

[*Memoirs of Odd Adventures, Strange Deliverances, etc.* 1736.]

ON the second spring of my captivity my Indian master and his squaw went to Canada; but sent me down the river with several Indians to the Fort, in order to plant corn. The day before we came to the planting field we met two young Indian men, who seemed to be in great haste. After they had passed us I understood that they were going with an express to Canada, and that there was an English vessel at the mouth of the river. I, not perfect in the language, nor knowing that English vessels traded with them in time of war, supposed a peace was concluded on, and that the captives would be released; and was so transported with the fancy, that I slept but little, if at all, that night. Early the next morning we came to the village, where the ecstasy ended, for I had no sooner landed, but three or four Indians dragged me to the great wigwam, where they were yelling and dancing round James Alexander, a Jerseyman, who was taken from Falmouth, in Casco Bay. This was occasioned by two families of Cape Sable Indians, who having lost some friends by a number of English fishermen, came some hundred of miles to revenge themselves on the poor captives! They soon came to me, and tossed me about till I was almost breathless, and then threw me into the ring to my fellow captive, and took him out again, and repeated their barbarities to him. And then I was hauled out again by three Indians, by the hair of my head, and held down by it, till one beat me on the back and shoulders so long that my breath was almost beat out of my body. And then others put a tomahawk into my hand, and ordered me to get up and dance and sing Indian, which I performed with the greatest reluctance, and in the act seemed resolute to purchase my death, by killing two or three of those monsters of cruelty, thinking it impossible to survive their bloody treatment. But it was impressed on my mind, "'Tis not in their power to take away your life;" so I desisted.

Then those Cape Sable Indians came to me again like bears bereaved of their whelps, saying, "Shall we who have lost relations by the English, suffer an English voice to be heard among us?" etc. Then they beat me again with the axe. Then I repented that I had not sent two or three of them out of the world before me, for I thought that I had much rather die than suffer any longer. They left me the second time, and the other Indians put the tomahawk into my hand again, and compelled me to sing. And then I seemed more resolute than before to destroy some of them; but a strange and strong impulse that I should return to my own place and people, suppressed it as often as such a motion rose in my breast. Not one of the Indians showed the least compassion; but I saw the tears run down plentifully on the cheeks of a Frenchman that sat behind; which did not alleviate the tortures that poor James and I were forced to endure for the most part of this tedious day; for they were continued till the evening; and were the most severe that ever I met with in the whole six years that I was captive with the Indians.

After they had thus inhumanly abused us, two Indians took us up and threw us out of the wigwam, and we crawled away on our hands and feet, and were scarce able to walk, etc., for several days. Some time after they again concluded on a merry dance, when I was at some distance from the wigwam dressing leather, and an Indian was so kind as to tell me that they had got James Alexander, and were in search of me. My Indian master and his squaw bid me run as for my life into a swamp and hide, and not to discover myself, unless they both came to me, for then I might be assured the dance was over. I was now master of their language, and a word or a wink was enough to excite me to take care of one. I ran to the swamp, and hid in the thickest place that I could find. I heard hollowing and whooping all around me; sometimes they passed very near, and I could hear some threaten, and others flatter me, but I was not disposed to dance; and if they had come upon me, I resolved to show them a pair of heels, and they must have had good luck to have catched me.

I heard no more of them till about evening (for I think I slept), when they came again, calling "Chon, Chon," but John would not trust them. After they were gone, my master and his squaw came where they told me to hide, but could not find me; and when I heard them say with some concern, that they believed that the other Indians had frightened me into the woods, and that I was lost, I came out, and they seemed well pleased, and told me that James had had a bad day of it; that as soon as he was released he ran away into the woods, and they believed he was gone to the Mohawks. James soon returned and gave me a melancholy account of his sufferings; and the Indians' fright concerning the Mohawks passed over.

They often had terrible apprehension of the incursion of the Mohawks. One very hot season a great number gathered together at the village; and, being a very droughty people, they kept James and myself night and day fetching water from a cold spring that ran out of a rocky hill about three-quarters of a mile from the fort. In going thither, we crossed a large interval—corn-field—and then a descent to a lower interval before we ascended the hill to the spring. James being almost dead as well as I, with this continual fatigue, contrived to fright the Indians. He told me of it, but conjured me to secrecy, yet said he knew that I could keep counsel. The next dark night James, going for water, set his kettle on the descent to the lowest interval, and ran back to the fort, puffing and blowing, as in the utmost surprise, and told his master that he saw something near the spring, that looked like Mohawks (which he said were only stumps—aside). His master, being a most courageous warrior, went with James to make discovery, and when they came to the brow of the hill, James pointed to the stumps, and withal touched his kettle with his toe, which gave it motion down hill, and at every turn of the kettle the bail clattered; upon which James and his master could see a Mohawk in every stump in motion, and turned tail to, and he was the best man that could run fastest. This alarmed all the Indians in the village. They, though about thirty or forty in number, packed off, bag and baggage, some up the river and others down, and did not return under fifteen days; and the heat of the weather being finely over, our hard service abated for this season. I never heard that the Indians understood the occasion of the fright, but James and I had many a private laugh about it.

But my most intimate and dear companion was one John Evans, a young man taken from Quochecho. We, as often as we could, met together, and made known our grievances to each other, which seemed to ease our minds; but when it was known by the Indians, we were strictly examined apart, and falsely accused, that we were contriving to desert. But we were too far from the sea to have any thought of that; and when they found that our story agreed, we received no punishment. An English captive girl about this time (who was taken by Medocawando) would often falsely accuse us of plotting to desert, but we made the truth so plainly appear, that she was checked and we released. But the third winter of my captivity he went into the country, and the Indians imposed a heavy burden on him, though he was extreme weak with long fasting; and as he was going off the upland over a place of ice which was very hollow, he broke through, fell down, and cut his knee very much, notwithstanding he travelled for some time. But the wind and cold were so forcible, that they soon overcame him, and he sat or fell down, and all the Indians passed by him. Some of them went back the next day after him, or his pack, and found him, with a dog in his arms, both froze as stiff as a stake. And all my fellow-captives were dispersed and dead; but through infinite and unmerited goodness I was supported under, and carried through, all difficulties.

SUPERSTITIONS OF THE WOODS.

[From the Same.]

THE Indians are very often surprised with the appearance of ghosts and demons; and sometimes encouraged by the Devil, for they go to him for success in hunting, etc. I was once hunting with Indians who were not brought over to the Romish faith, and after several days' hunting they proposed to inquire, according to their custom, what success they should have. They accordingly prepared many hot stones, and laid them in a heap, and made a small hut covered with skins and mats, and then in the dark night two of the Powaws went into this hot-house with a large vessel of water, which at times they poured on those hot rocks, which raised a thick steam; so that a third Indian was obliged to stand without, and lift up a mat, to give it vent when they were almost suffocated. There was an old squaw who was kind to captives, and never joined with them in their powawing, to whom I manifested an earnest desire to see their management. She told me, that if they knew of my being there, they would kill me, and that when she was a girl, she had known young persons to be taken away by an hairy man; and therefore she would not advise me to go, lest the hairy man should carry me away. I told her I was not afraid of that hairy man, nor could he hurt me if she would not discover me to the Powaws. At length she promised that she would not, but charged me to be careful of myself.

I went within three or four feet of the hot-house, for it was very dark, and heard strange noises and yellings, such as I never heard before. At times the Indian who tended without would lift up the mat, and a steam rise up, which looked like fire in the dark. I lay there two or three hours, but saw none of their hairy men or demons, and when I found that they had finished their ceremony, I went to the wigwam, and told the squaw what had passed; who was glad that I returned without hurt; and never discovered what I had done. After some time, inquiry was made, what success we were like to have in our hunting? The Powaws said, that they had very likely signs of success, but no real, visible appearance as at other times. A few days after, we moved up the river, and had pretty good success.

One afternoon as I was in a canoe with one of the Powaws, the dog barked and presently a moose passed by, within a few rods of us, so that the waves which he made by wading rolled our canoe. The Indian shot at him, but the moose took very little notice of it, and went into the woods to the southward. The fellow said, "I'll try if I can't fetch you back, for all your haste." The evening following, we built our two wigwams on a sandy point on the upper end of an island in the river, north-west of the place where the moose went into the woods; and the Indian powawed the greatest part of the night following, and in the morning we had the fair track of a moose, round our wigwams, though we did not see or taste of it.—I am of opinion, that the Devil was permitted to humor those unhappy wretches sometimes, in some things.

An Indian being some miles from his wigwam, and the weather being warm, he supposed the hedge-hogs would come out of their den. He waylaid the mouth of it till late at night. They not coming out as usual, he was going home, but had not passed far, before he saw a light like a blaze, at a little distance before him, and darting his spear at it, it disappeared. Then on the bank of the river, he heard a loud laughter, with a noise like a rattling in a man's throat. The Indian railed at the demon whom he supposed made the noise, calling it a rotten spirit of no substance, etc. He continued to hear the noise and see the light till he came into the wigwam, which he entered, in his hunting habit, with snow-shoes and all on, so frightened, that it was some time before he could speak to relate what had happened.

That it may further appear how much they were deluded, or under the influence of Satan, read two stories which were related and believed by the Indians.

The first of a boy who was carried away by a large bird called a Gulluoa, who buildeth her nest on a high rock or mountain. A boy was hunting with his bow and arrow at the foot of a rocky mountain, when the Gulluoa came diving through the air, grasped the boy in her talons, and though he was eight or ten years of age, she soared aloft, and laid him in her nest, a prey for her young; where the boy lay constantly on his face, but would look sometimes under his arms and saw two young ones with much fish and flesh in the nest, and the old bird constantly bringing more. So that the young ones not touching him, the old one clawed him up and set him where she found him; who returned, and related the odd event to his friends. As I have, in a canoe, passed near the mountain, the Indians have said to me, "There is the nest of the great bird that carried the boy away." And there seemed to be a great number of sticks put together in form of a nest on the top of the mountain. At another time they said : "There is the bird, but he is now, as a boy to a giant, to what he was in former days." The bird which they pointed to, was a large speckled bird, like an Eagle, though somewhat larger.

The other notion is, that a young Indian in his hunting was belated and lost his way, and on a sudden he was introduced to a large wigwam full of dried eels, which proved to be a beaver's house, in which he lived till the spring of the year, when he was turned out of the house, and set upon a beaver-dam, and went home, and related the affair to his friends at large.

Roger Wolcott.

BORN in Windsor, Conn., 1679. DIED there, 1767.

THE LESSON OF LIFE.

[Poetical Meditations; Being the Improvement of some Vacant Hours. 1725.]

AND is our life a life wherein we borrow,
　No, not the smallest respite from our sorrow?
Our profits are they but some yellow dust,
Subject to loss, to canker-eat and rust ;
Whose very image breedeth ceaseless cares
In every mind where it dominion bears?
And are our pleasures mainly in excess,
Which genders gilt and ends in bitterness ?
Are honors fickle and dependent stuff,
Oft-times blown furthest from us by a puff ?
Doth pale-fac'd envy wait at every stage,
To bite and wound us in our pilgrimage ?
Is all we have, or hope, but adventure ?
Then here's naught worth our stay, let us encounter
The King of Terrors bravely, undismay'd,
As gallant Aria to her Pætus said.

And so might be my choice, but that I see
Hell's flashes folding through eternity ;
And hear damn'd company, that there remain,
For very anguish, gnaw their tongues in twain.

Then him for happy I will never praise,
That's filled with honor, wealth, or length of days;
But happy he, though in a dying hour,
O'er whom the Second Death obtains no power.

A STORM AT SEA.

[A Brief Account of the Agency of the Honorable John Winthrop. From the Same.]

THEIR ancient homes they leave to come no more;
 Their weeping friends and kindred on the shore
They bid adieu, and with an aching heart
Shake hands; 'tis hard when dearest friends must part,
But here they part, and leave their parent isle,
Their whilome happy seat.   The winds awhile
Are courteous and conduct them on their way,
To near the midst of the Atlantic Sea,
When suddenly their pleasant gales they change
For dismal storms that on the ocean range;
For faithless Æolus meditating harms
Breaks up the peace, and, priding much in arms,
Unbars the great artillery of Heaven;
And, at the fatal signal by him given,
The cloudy chariots threat'ning take the plains,
Drawn by wing'd steeds, hard pressing on their reins.
These vest battalions, in dire aspect rais'd,
Start from the barriers-night with lightning blaz'd,
Whilst clashing wheels, resounding thunder cracks
Struck mortals deaf, and Heaven astonished shakes.

Here the ship captain in the midnight watch
Stamps on the deck and thunders up the hatch;
And to the mariners aloud he cries,
" Now all from safe recumbency arise !
All hands aloft and stand well to your tack,
Engend'ring storms have clothed the sky with black;
Big tempests threaten to undo the world:
Down top-sail, let the main-sail soon be furled;
Haste to the fore-sail, there take up a reef;
'Tis time, boys, now if ever to be brief :
Aloof for life, lets try to stem the tide,
The ship's much water, thus we may not ride.
Stand roomer, then, let's run before the sea,
That so the ship may feel her steerage way.
Steady at helm!"   Swiftly along she scuds
Before the wind and cuts the foaming suds,
Sometimes aloft she lifts her prow so high,
As if she'd run her bowsprit through the sky.
Then from the summit ebbs and hurries down,
As if her way were to the Centre shown.

Meanwhile our founders in the cabin sate,
Reflecting on their true and sad estate;
Whilst holy Warham's sacred lips did treat
About God's promises and mercies great.

Still more gigantic births spring from the clouds,
Which tore the tatter'd canvas from the shrouds,
And dreadful balls of lightning fill the air,
Shot from the hand of the Great Thunderer.

And now a mighty sea the ship o'er rakes,
Which falling on the deck the bulkhead breaks;
The sailors cling to ropes and frighted cry:
"The ship is foundered! we die! we die!"

IN THE FIELDS.

[From the Same.]

THE grassy banks are like a verdant bed,
  With choicest flowers all enameled,
O'er which the winged choristers do fly,
And wound th' air with wonderous melody.
Here Philomel high percht upon a thorn
Sings cheerful hymns to the approaching morn.
The song once set, each bird tunes up his lyre,
Responding heavenly music through the choir.
Within these fields fair banks of violets grows,
And near them stand the air-perfuming rose,
And yellow lilies fair enameled
With ruddy spots, here, blushing hang the head.

George Berkeley.

Born in Kilkenny, Ireland, 1684.   Died at Oxford, England, 1753.

A GLIMPSE OF HIS COUNTRY HOUSE NEAR NEWPORT.

[Alciphron, or the Minute Philosopher. 1732.]

AFTER dinner we took our walk to Crito's, which lay through half a dozen pleasant fields planted round with plane-trees, that are very common in this part of the country. We walked under the delicious shade of these trees for about an hour before we came to Crito's house, which stands in the middle of a small park, beautified with two fine groves of oak and walnut, and a winding stream of sweet and clear water. We met a servant at the door with a small basket of fruit which he was carrying into a grove, where he said his master was with the two strangers. We found them all three sitting under a shade. And, after the usual forms at first meeting, Euphranor and I sat down by them. Our conversation began upon the beauty of this rural scene, the fine season of the year, and some late improvements which had been made in the adjacent country by new methods of agriculture. Whence Alciphron took occasion to observe that the most valuable improvements came latest. I should have small temptation, said he, to live where men have neither polished manners, nor improved minds, though the face of the country were ever so well improved. But I have long observed that there is a gradual progress in human affairs. The first care of mankind is to supply the cravings of nature; in the next place they study the conveniences and comforts of life. But the subduing prejudices and acquiring true knowledge, that Herculean labor, is the last, being what demands the most perfect abilities, and to which all other advantages are preparative. Right, said Euphranor, Alciphron hath touched our true defect. It was always my opinion that, as soon as we had provided subsistence for the body, our next care should be to improve the mind. But the desire of wealth steps between and engrosseth men's thoughts.

THE VIEW FROM HONEYMAN'S HILL.

[From the Same.]

WE amused ourselves next day, every one to his fancy, till nine of the clock, when word was brought that the tea-table was set in the library: which is a gallery on the ground floor, with an arched door at one end, opening into a walk of limes; where, as soon as we had drank tea, we were tempted by fine weather to take a walk, which led us to a small mount, of easy ascent, on the top whereof we found a seat under a spreading tree. Here we had a prospect, on one hand, of a narrow bay, or creek, of the sea, inclosed on either side by a coast beautified with rocks and woods, and green banks and farm-houses. At the end of the bay was a small town, placed upon the slope of a hill, which, from the advantage of its situation, made a considerable figure. Several fishing boats and lighters, gliding up and down on a surface as smooth and bright as glass, enlivened the prospect. On the other hand, we looked down on green pastures, flocks, and herds, basking beneath in sunshine, while we, in our superior situation, enjoyed the freshness of air and shade. Here we felt that sort of joyful instinct which a rural scene and fine weather inspire; and proposed no small pleasure in resuming and

George Berkeley

continuing our conference, without interruption, till dinner: but we had hardly seated ourselves, and looked about us, when we saw a fox run by the foot of our mount into an adjacent thicket. A few minutes after, we heard a confused noise of the opening of hounds, the winding of horns, and the roaring of country squires. While our attention was suspended by this event, a servant came running out of breath, and told Crito that his neighbor, Ctesippus, a squire of note, was fallen from his horse attempting to leap over a hedge, and brought into the hall, where he lay for dead. Upon which we all rose, and walked hastily to the house, where we found Ctesippus just come to himself, in the midst of half a dozen sun-burnt squires, in frocks and short wigs, and jockey-boots. Being asked how he did, he answered, it was only a broken rib. With some difficulty Crito persuaded him to lie on a bed till the chirurgeon came. These fox-hunters, having been up early at their sport, were eager for dinner, which was accordingly hastened. They passed the afternoon in a loud rustic mirth, gave proof of their religion and loyalty by the healths they drank, talked of hounds and horses, and elections, and country affairs, till the chirurgeon, who had been employed about Ctesippus, desired he might be put into Crito's coach and sent home, having refused to stay all night. Our guests being gone, we reposed ourselves after the fatigue of this tumultuous visit, and next morning assembled again at the seat of the mount.

THE IDEAL PHILOSOPHY IN BRIEF.

[*From the Same.*]

ALCIPHRON—EUPHRANOR.

ALC.—What am I to think then. Do we see anything at all, or is it altogether fancy and illusion?

EUPH.—Upon the whole, it seems the proper objects of sight are light and colors, with their several shades and degrees; all which, being infinitely diversified and combined, form a language wonderfully adapted to suggest and exhibit to us the distances, figures, situations, dimensions, and various qualities of tangible objects: not by similitude, nor yet by inference of necessary connection, but by the arbitrary imposition of Providence: just as words suggest the things signified by them.

ALC.—How! Do we not, strictly speaking, perceive by sight such things as trees, houses, men, rivers, and the like?

EUPH.—We do, indeed, perceive or apprehend those things by the faculty of sight. But will it follow from thence that they are the proper and immediate objects of sight, any more than that all those things are the proper and immediate objects of hearing, which are signified by the help of words or sounds?

ALC.—You would have us think then, that light, shades, and colors, variously combined, answer to the several articulations of sound in language; and that, by means thereof, all sorts of objects are suggested to the mind through the eye, in the same manner as they are suggested, by words or sounds, through the ear: that is, neither from necessary deduction to the judgment, nor from similitude to the fancy, but purely and solely from experience, custom, and habit.

EUPH.—I would not have you think any thing, more than the nature of things obligeth you to think, nor submit in the least to my judgment, but only to the force of truth; which is an imposition that I suppose the freest thinkers will not pretend to be exempt from.

ALC.—You have led me, it seems, step by step, till I am got I know not where. But I shall try to get out again, if not by the way I came, yet by some other of my own finding. Here Alciphron, having made a short pause, proceeded as follows:

Answer me, Euphranor, should it not follow, from these principles, that a man, born blind, and made to see, would at first sight not only not perceive their distance, but also not so much as know the very things themselves which he saw, for instance, men or trees? which surely to support must be absurd.

EUPH.—I grant, in consequence of those principles which both you and I have admitted, that such a one would never think of men, trees, or any other objects that he had been accustomed to perceive by touch, upon having his mind filled with new sensations of light and colors, whose various combinations he doth not yet understand, or know the meaning of; no more than a Chinese, upon first hearing the words man and tree, would think of the things signified by them. In both cases, there must be time and experience, by repeated acts, to acquire a habit of knowing the connection between the signs and things signified; that is to say, of understanding the language, whether of the eyes or of the ears. And I conceive no absurdity in this.

ALC.—I see, therefore, in strict philosophical truth, that rock only in the same sense that I may be said to hear it, when the word rock is pronounced.

EUPH.—In the very same.

ALC.—How comes it to pass then, that every one shall say he sees, for instance, a rock, or a house, when those things are before his eyes; but nobody will say, he hears a rock, or a house, but only the words or sounds themselves, by which those things are said to be signified or suggested but not heard? Besides, if vision be only a language, speaking to the eyes, it may be asked, when did men learn this language? To acquire the knowledge of so many signs, as go to the making up a language, is a work of some difficulty. But will any man say, he hath spent time, or been at pains, to learn this language of vision?

Euph.—No wonder, we cannot assign a time beyond our remotest memory. If we have been all practising this language, ever since our first entrance into the world; if the Author of nature constantly speaks to the eyes of all mankind, even in their earliest infancy, whenever the eyes are open in the light, whether alone or in company; it doth not seem to me at all strange, that men should not be aware they had ever learned a language, begun so early, and practiced so constantly, as this of vision. And, if we also consider that it is the same throughout the whole world, and not, like other languages, differing in different places; it will not seem unaccountable, that men should mistake the connection between the proper objects of sight, and the things signified by them, to be founded in necessary relation or likeness: or, that they should even take them for the same things. Hence it seems easy to conceive why men, who do not think, should confound, in this language of vision, the signs with the things signified, otherwise than they are wont to do in the various particular languages formed by the several nations of men.

It may be also worth while to observe, that signs being little considered in themselves, or for their own sake, but only in their relative capacity, and for the sake of those things whereof they are signs, it comes to pass that the mind often overlooks them, so as to carry its attention immediately on to the things signified. Thus, for example, in reading, we run over the characters with the slightest regard, and pass on to the meaning. Hence it is frequent for men to say they see words, and notions, and things, in reading a book: whereas, in strictness, they see only the characters which suggest words, notions, and things. And, by parity of reason, may we not suppose that men, not resting in but overlooking the immediate and proper objects of sight, as in their own nature of small moment, carry their attention onward to the very thing signified, and talk as if they saw the secondary objects? which, in truth and strictness, are not seen, but only suggested and apprehended by means of the proper objects of sight, which alone are seen.

Alc.—To speak my mind freely, this dissertation grows tedious, and runs into points too dry and minute for a gentleman's attention.

I thought, said Crito, we had been told, the minute philosophers loved to consider things closely and minutely.

Alc.—That is true, but in so polite an age who would be a mere philosopher? There is a certain scholastic accuracy, which ill suits the freedom and ease of a well-bred man. But, to cut short this chicane, I propound it fairly to your own conscience, whether you really think that God himself speaks every day, and in every place, to the eyes of all men?

EUPH.—That is really, and in truth, my opinion: and it should be yours too, if you are consistent with yourself and abide by your own definition of language. Since you cannot deny that the great mover and author of nature constantly explaineth himself to the eyes of men, by the sensible intervention of arbitrary signs, which have no similitude or connection with the things signified; so as by compounding and disposing them, to suggest and exhibit an endless variety of objects, differing in nature, time, and place, thereby informing and directing men how to act with respect to things distant and future, as well as near and present. In consequence, I say, of your own sentiments and concessions, you have as much reason to think the Universal Agent, or God, speaks to your eyes, as you can have for thinking any particular person speaks to your ears.

ALC.—I cannot help thinking that some fallacy runs throughout this whole ratiocination, though perhaps I may not readily point it out. It seems to me, that every other sense may as well be deemed a language as that of vision. Smells and taste, for instance, are signs that inform us of other qualities, to which they have neither likeness nor necessary connection.

EUPH.—That they are signs is certain, as also that language and all other signs agree in the general nature of sign, or so far forth as signs. But it is as certain that all signs are not language; not even all significant sounds, such as the natural cries of animals, or the inarticulate sounds and interjections of men. It is the articulation, combination, variety, copiousness, extensive and general use, and easy application of signs (all which are commonly found in vision) that constitute the true nature of language. Other senses may indeed furnish signs; and yet those signs have no more right than inarticulate sounds to be thought a language.

ALC.—Hold! let me see! In language, the signs are arbitrary, are they not?

EUPH.—They are.

ALC.—And, consequently, they do not always suggest real matters of fact. Whereas, this natural language, as you call it, or these visible signs, do always suggest things in the same uniform way, and have the same constant regular connection with matters of fact: whence it should seem, the connection was necessary, and therefore, according to the definition premised, it can be no language. How do you solve this objection?

Euph.—You may solve it yourself, by the help of a picture or looking-glass.

Alc.—You are in the right. I see there is nothing in it. I know not what else to say to this opinion, more than that it is so odd and contrary to my way of thinking, that I shall never assent to it.

GREATNESS OF PLATO AND THE ANCIENT SCHOOLS.

[*Siris : a Chain of Philosophical Reflections and Inquiries concerning the Virtues of Tar-Water. 1744.*]

PREVAILING studies are of no small consequence to a state, the religion, manners, and civil government of a country ever taking some bias from its philosophy, which affects not only the minds of its professors and students, but also the opinions of all the better sort and the practice of the whole people, remotely and consequentially indeed, though not inconsiderably. Have not the polemic and scholastic philosophy been observed to produce controversies in law and religion? And have not Fatalism and Sadducism gained ground, during the general passion for the corpuscularian and mechanical philosophy, which hath prevailed for about a century? This, indeed, might usefully enough have employed some share of the leisure and curiosity of inquisitive persons. But when it entered the seminaries of learning as a necessary accomplishment, and most important part of education, by engrossing men's thoughts, and fixing their minds so much on corporeal objects and the laws of motion, it hath, however undesignedly, indirectly, and by accident, yet not a little indisposed them for spiritual, moral, and intellectual matters. Certainly, had the philosophy of Socrates and Pythagoras prevailed in this age, among those who think themselves too wise to receive the dictates of the Gospel, we should not have seen interest take so general and fast hold on the minds of men, nor public spirit reputed to be γενναῖαν εὐήθειαν, a generous folly, among those who are reckoned to be the most knowing as well as the most getting part of mankind.

It might very well be thought serious trifling to tell my readers that the greatest men had ever a high esteem for Plato ; whose writings are the touchstone of a hasty and shallow mind ; whose philosophy has been the admiration of ages ; which supplied patriots, magistrates, and law-givers to the most flourishing states, as well as fathers to the Church and doctors to the schools. Albeit in these days the depths of that old learning are rarely fathomed ; and yet it were happy for these lands if our young nobility and gentry, instead of modern maxims, would imbibe the notions of the great men of antiquity. But, in these free-thinking times, many an empty head is shook at Aristotle and Plato, as well as at the Holy Scriptures. And the writings of those celebrated ancients are by most men treated on a foot with the dry and barbarous lucubrations of the schoolmen. It may be modestly presumed there are not many among us, even of those who are called the better sort, who have more sense, virtue, and love of their country than Cicero, who in a Letter to Atticus could not forbear exclaiming, *O Socrates et Socratici viri! nunquam vobis gratiam referam.* Would to God many of our countrymen had the same obligations to those Socratic writers! Certainly, where the people are well educated, the art of piloting a state is best learned from the writings of Plato. But among bad men, void of discipline and education, Plato, Pythagoras, and Aristotle, themselves, were they living, could do but little good. Plato hath drawn a very humorous and instructive picture of such a state; which I shall not transcribe for certain reasons. But whoever has a mind may see it, in the seventy-eighth page of the second tome of Aldus's edition of Plato's works.

Thomas Prince.

BORN in Sandwich, Mass., 1687. DIED in Boston, Mass., 1758.

THE GREAT EARTHQUAKE IN JAMAICA.

[*An Improvement of the Doctrine of Earthquakes.* 1755.]

THERE are many in this country that well remember the fearful tidings of that earthquake in Jamaica, on June 7th, 1692. It came on between 11 and 12 at noon in a clear, calm, and sunshine day. It began with a small trembling, so as to make some think of an earthquake; which thought was confirmed by a second shake something stronger, accompanied with a hollow rumbling noise almost like thunder, which made them begin to run out of their houses. But alas! This was but short warning for them to provide for their safety; for at the heels of the second came the third and most violent shake, which threw down and drowned nine-tenths of Port Royal, their capital town, in two minutes, and all the houses by the wharf in less than one.

The streets rose like the waves of the sea; lifting up all that were in them, and immediately dropping down into pits. The shake was so fierce, that it threw the people on their knees and faces, as they ran in

Your most respectfull
humble Servant
T Prince

the streets to seek for safety. In several places the ground would crack and open and shut quick and fast in a wonderful manner. Some have seen two or three hundred of these openings at one time; in some of which many of the people were swallowed up. Some the earth caught by the middle and squeezed to death. The heads, arms, or legs of others only appeared above ground. At the same time a flood of water gushed out and rolled over others. Some caught hold of beams and rafters; others were afterwards found dead and almost covered with sand. Some who were swallowed quite down, rose again in other streets, being cast up with great quantities of water, and some into the midst of the harbor: and yet some of these through the wonderful goodness of God were saved; while others that went down quick, were never seen more.

These were the smaller openings. The larger swallowed great houses; and out of some there issued whole rivers spouting to a vast height in the air, with ill stenches that were very offensive. All the wharves and some of the houses sunk at once; and the most so soon, that the people had no time to get out; those who were in the upper chambers meeting the waters at the garret stairs as they were running down for safety. While some of the houses were quite swallowed up in the earth, others were thrown on heaps; and even the best streets in the town, full of stately buildings, sunk so deep as to be near thirty feet under water.

Several sloops and ships were overset and lost in the harbor. The sea, suddenly rising and swelling with a strange emotion, came rolling with such a force as to drive the ships from their anchors, breaking their cables in an instant, and dashing them against the tops of the sunken houses.

While the earth was laboring in these convulsions, the people ran up and down, pale and trembling with horror, like so many ghosts; as if the dissolution of the whole frame of the world were at hand.

And yet the shake was stronger in the country than in the town, where it left more houses standing than in all the rest of the island: though it be more than one hundred and sixty miles long and about fifty broad. They were almost all either thrown down or swallowed up. And my author says it is not to be doubted, if there had been five thousand towns in Jamaica, but every one of them had been ruined.

The waters of wells above thirty foot deep flew out at the top. In several places the earth gaped prodigiously with great spoutings of water. The sky, which before was clear and blue, became in a minute dull and reddish, like a red-hot oven. Amazing noises were made by the fall of the mountains and the rumblings that were heard under ground.

In the mountains were the most violent shakings. Some falling down stopped up the roads and rivers; and many were thrown in heaps upon others. A great mountain split, and tumbling drove all the trees before it, and overwhelmed several settlements with their inhabitants, a mile off. Another large high mountain sunk and was quite devoured; and in the place thereof arose a lake twelve or fifteen miles over.

In a certain ground on the north side of the island the planters' houses, with the greatest part of their plantations, were swallowed up, houses, people, trees and all, in one great opening. In the room of which arose at first a lake of a thousand acres extent; but afterwards it dried away, and left not the least appearance of house, tree, or anything else that was there before.

In fine: The earth continued shaking for two months after; and all the while the mountains tottering, and bellowing most loud and hideous noises. About two thousand people perished in town, a thousand more in the other parts of the island; and 'tis thought, if the shakes had fell out in the night, but very few had been left alive. Great numbers of dead bodies were floating from one side of the harbor to the other; sometimes one or two hundred in a heap, as the winds and seas drove them. And such a general sickness presently followed which few escaped, and was very fatal. Half the people saved from the earthquake at Port Royal are said to have died of the sickness at Kingston; where five hundred graves were dug in one month's time, two or three buried in one grave. About two thousand swept away; and in the rest of the island a thousand more.

And thus I have mentioned something of God's amazing execution of this sort of judgments in other places.

Cadwallader Colden.

BORN in Ireland, 1688.   DIED at Spring Hill, L. I., 1776.

THE STORY OF PISKARET.

[*The History of the Five Indian Nations. 1727.*]

IT has been a constant maxim with the Five Nations to save the children and young men of the people they conquer, to adopt them into their own nation, and to educate them as their own children without distinction. These young people soon forget their own country and nation; and by this policy the Five Nations make up the losses which their nation suffers by the people they lose in war. The wisest and best soldiers of the Adirondacks, when it was too late, discovered that they must imitate and learn the art of war from those enemies that they at first despised. Now, five of their chief captains endeavor to perform by them-

selves singly, with art and by stratagem, what they could not perform by force at the head of their armies; but, they having no longer any hopes of conquering their enemies, their thoughts were only set on revenge.

The Five Nations had taken one of the chief captains of the Adirondacks, and had burnt him alive. This gave Piskaret, who was the chief captain of the Adirondacks, so deep a resentment, that the difficulty or danger of the most desperate attempt made no impression upon his spirit where he had the hope of revenge.

I shall give the particulars of this from the French accounts; for by it the nature of the Indians, and the manner of their making war, may be more easily understood.

Piskaret, with four other captains, set out from Trois Rivieres in one canoe, each being provided with three fuzees. In two days they reached Sorel River, where they perceived five canoes of the Five Nations with ten men in each. At first those of the Five Nations believed that this canoe was the van of some considerable party, and therefore went from it with all the force of their paddles. When they saw that after a considerable time no others followed, they returned, and, as soon as they came within call, they raised their war shout, which they call "*Sassakue,*" and bid Piskaret and his fellows surrender. He answered, That he was their prisoner, and that he could no longer survive the captain they had burnt; but that he might not be accused of surrendering cowardly, he bid them advance to the middle of the river, which they did with surprising swiftness. Piskaret had beforehand loaded all his arms with two bullets each, which he joined together with a small wire ten inches in length with design to tear the canoes in pieces (which it could not fail to do, they being made only of birch bark) and gave his companions direction, each to choose a canoe, and level his shot between wind and water.

As the canoes approached, he made as if he designed to escape; and to prevent him, those of the Five Nations separated from each other with too much precipitation, and surrounded him. The Adirondacks, the better to amuse the enemy, sung their death song, as ready to surrender themselves, when every one suddenly took his piece and fired upon the canoes, which they reiterated three times, with the arms that lay ready. Those of the Five Nations were extremely surprised; for firearms were still terrible to them, and they tumbled out of their canoes, which immediately sunk. The Adirondacks knocked them all on the head in the water, except some of the chiefs that they made prisoners, whose fate was as cruel as that of the Adirondack captain, who had been burnt alive.

Piskaret was so far from having his revenge glutted with this slaughter, and the cruel torments with which he made his prisoners die, that it seemed rather to give a keener edge to it; for he soon after attempted another enterprise in which the boldest of his countrymen durst not accompany him.

He was well acquainted with the country of the Five Nations; he set out alone about the time that the snow began to melt, with the precaution of putting the hinder part of his snow shoes forward, that if any should happen upon his footsteps they might think he was gone the contrary way; and for further security went along a ridge, where the snow was melted, and where his footsteps could not be discovered but in a few places. When he found himself near one of the villages of the Five Nations he hid himself in a hollow tree. In the night he found out a place nearer at hand, and more proper to retire into, for the execution of any enterprise. He found four piles of wood standing close together, which the Indians had provided against the winter and their busy times, in the middle of which was a hollow place, in which he thought he could safely hide. The whole village was fast asleep when he entered a cabin, killed four persons and took off their scalps, being all that were in the house, and then returned quietly into his hole. In the morning the whole village was in an alarm, as soon as the murder was discovered, and the young men made all possible haste to follow the murderer. They discovered Piskaret's footsteps, which appeared to them to be the footsteps of some person that fled; this encouraged them in their pursuit. Sometimes they lost the track, and sometimes found it again, till at last they entirely lost it, where the snow was melted, and they were forced to return, after much useless fatigue. Piskaret quiet in the midst of his enemies waited with impatience for the night. As soon as he saw that it was time to act (viz., in the first part of the night, when the Indians are observed to sleep very fast) he entered into another cabin, where he killed every person in it, and immediately retired into his wood pile.

In the morning there was a greater outcry than before, nothing was seen but wailing, tears, and a general consternation. Everyone runs in quest of the murderer, but no track to be seen besides the track which they saw the day before. They searched the woods, swamps, and clifts of the rocks, but no murderer to be found. They began to suspect Piskaret, whose boldness and cunning was too well known to them. They agreed that two men next night should watch in every cabin. All day long he was contriving some new stratagem; he bundles up his scalps, and in the night he slips out of his lurking place. He approaches one of the cabins as quietly as possible, and peeps through a hole to see what could be done; there he perceived guards on the watch; he went to another, where he found the same care. When he discovered that they were everywhere upon their guard, he resolved to strike his last blow, and opened a door, where he found a sentinel nodding with his pipe in his mouth; Piskaret split his skull with his hatchet, but had not time to take his scalp, for another man, who watched at the other end of the cabin, raised the cry, and Piskaret fled. The whole village immediately was in an uproar, while he got off as fast as he could; many pursued him, but as he was so swift as to run down the wild cows and the deer, the pursuit gave him no great uneasiness. When he perceived they came near him, he would holloa to them, to quicken their pace, then spring from them like a buck. When he gained any distance he would loiter till they came near, then holloa, and fly. Thus he continued all day, with design to tire them out with the hopes of overtaking him.

As they pursued only a single man, five or six of the nimblest young men continued the chase, till being tired they were forced to rest in the night, which when Piskaret observed, he hid himself near them in a hollow tree. They had not time to take victuals with them, and being wearied and hungry, and not apprehending any attack from a single person that fled, they all soon fell asleep. Piskaret observed them, fell upon them, killed them all, and carried away their scalps.

These stories may seem incredible to many, but will not appear to be improbable to those who know how extremely revengeful the Indians naturally are. That they every day undertake the greatest fatigues, the longest journeys, and the greatest dangers, to gratify that devouring passion, which seems to gnaw their souls, and gives them no ease till it is satisfied. All barbarous nations have been observed to be revengeful and cruel, the certain consequences of an unbounded revenge, as the curbing of these passions is the happy effect of being civilized. . . . .

The Five Nations gave out that they intended next winter to visit Yonnondio (the name they give to the Governor of Canada). These visits are always made with much show. They gathered together 1,000 or 1,200 men, and, passing over Corlear's Lake, they fell in with Nicolet River, where it falls into the south side of Lake St. Pierre, in St. Lawrence River, eight leagues above Trois Rivieres; six scouts marched three leagues before the army, who met with Piskaret, as he returned from hunting, loaded with the tongues of wild cows. As they came near him, they sung their song of peace, and Piskaret, taking them for ambassadors, stopped and sung his. It is probable that he having glutted his private revenge, and his nation having been long harassed with a cruel war, he too greedily swallowed the bait: peace being what he and all his nation earnestly desired. He invited them therefore to go along with him to his village, which was but two or three leagues further: and, as he went, he told them that the Adirondacks were divided into two bodies, one of which hunted on the north side of St. Lawrence River at Wabmache, three leagues above Trois Rivieres, and the other at Nicolet. One of the scouts had on purpose stayed behind; this man followed Piskaret, and coming up behind him knocked him on the head with his hatchet. Then they all returned to their army with Piskaret's head. The Five Nations immediately divided likewise into two bodies, they surprised the Adirondacks, and cut them in pieces.

Anonymous.

ON A LADY, SINGING.

[The Boston "Weekly Rehearsal." 1731.]

WHILST Celia sings, let no intruding breath
      Deform the air; ye winds, grow calm as death.
On silken wings, ye whispering zephyrs fly,
And in soft murmurs steal along the sky,
Soft as the murmurs of a virgin's sigh.
Close in the deep recesses of my breast,
Those deep recesses, where she reigns confest,
Let every traitor passion lie confined;
Let Love himself seem banished from my mind.
Let every sigh be hushed; for should my sighs
Burst forth, and in rebellious murmurs rise,
My sighs with noise the solemn scene would fill
And breathe a storm, though all the winds were still.
In vain, ye gales, your silken plumes display,
In silence rise, in silence melt away,
Soft as the voice, and gentle as the lay.
Strange power of harmony! whose silver sound
Can charm so sweetly, and so sweetly wound.
Transported with the notes, that pierce our ear,
Our raptured souls exulting spring to hear.
My raptured soul would soar with every strain,
But that thy eyes command it back again.
To raise our powers with heavenly notes is thine,
To bid our grosser parts to soul refine;
'Tis thine, fair Maid, with gentle warbling airs,
To soothe our passions, and beguile all cares.
All—but the cares of love; these still arise,
Heave in our breasts, and wanton in our eyes.
Assisted by thy breath, the flames aspire,
Glow with new rage, and blaze with double fire.
Thus darts in venom steeped with barbarous skill,
Wing certain fate, with two-fold anguish kill.

None but the Father of the gods, and you,
Could dart a flame so bright and killing too.
Swift as Jove's lightning flies each fatal sound,
And, like Jove's lightning, kills without a wound.
The muse invoked in elegiac strains,
Soft warbling, strings the lyre to ease our pains.
Flow soft, ye strains! and soothe her savage mind;
O learn to charm the nymph, who charms mankind.
In vain, alas! the muse and treacherous lyre
Torment our flames and face the raging fire:
Whilst you, like Echo, with so sweet a sound,
Repeat our strains.——Our strains increase the wound.
Think, then, thou Fairest of the fairer train!
What fatal beauties arm thy face and mien;
Whose very voice can lasting flame inspire,
We think 'tis *air*, but ah! we feel 'tis *fire*.

Ⓦilliam Stith.

BORN in Virginia, 1689. DIED at Williamsburg, Va., 1755.

THE UN-SOLOMONIZED JAMES I.

[*The History of the First Discovery and Settlement of Virginia.* 1747.]

IF more than a century is not enough to un-solomonize that silly monarch, I must give up all my notions of things.   A king's character, whilst he lives, is, and ought to be sacred, because his authority depends upon it.   But when his authority, the reason of it's being sacred, determines, the inviolableness of his character is also at an end.   And I take it to be the main part of the duty and office of an historian, to paint men and things in their true and lively colors; and to do that justice to the vices and follies of princes and great men, after their death, which it is not safe or proper to do, whilst they are alive.   And herein, as I judge, chiefly consist the strength and excellency of Tacitus and Suetonius. Their style and manner are far inferior to Livy's, and the writers of the Julian and Augustan ages.   But they have more than painted, and exposed alive to view, the greatest train of monsters that ever disgraced a throne, or did dishonor to human nature; and thereby have obtained to themselves a rank among the best and most valuable writers.

King James I. fell indeed far short of the Cæsar's superlative wickedness and supremacy in vice.   He was, at best, only very simple and injudicious, without any steady principle of justice and honor; which was rendered the more odious and ridiculous, by his large and constant pretensions to wisdom and virtue. And he had, in truth, all the forms of wisdom; forever erring very learnedly, with a wise saw, or Latin sentence, in his mouth. For he had been bred up under Buchanan, one of the brightest geniuses and most accomplished scholars of that age, who had given him Greek and Latin in great waste and profusion, but it was not in his power to give him good sense. That is the gift of God and nature alone, and it is not to be taught; and Greek and Latin without it, only cumber and overload a weak head, and often render the fool more abundantly foolish. I must therefore confess, that I have ever had, from my first acquaintance with history, a most contemptible opinion of this monarch; which has perhaps been much heightened and increased, by my long studying and conning over the materials of this history. For he appears, in his dealings with the company, to have acted with such mean arts and fraud, and such little tricking, as highly misbecome majesty. And I am much mistaken, if his arbitrary proceedings and unjust designs will appear from any part of his history more fully, than from these transactions with the company and colony; which have been thus far unknown to the English historians, and will perhaps be still thought too insignificant for their notice. However, I hope my speaking my mind thus sincerely and impartially will give no umbrage or offence to any man, or party of men. For I declare myself to be of no party; but have labored solely with a view to find out and relate the truth.

RICHARD GRENVILLE'S LAST FIGHT.

[From the Same.]

THE following year, 1591, Sir Richard Grenville was sent, by the Queen, Vice-Admiral to the Lord Thomas Howard, with seven ships of war, and a few other small vessels, to intercept the Spanish plate-fleet. At the Azores, this small squadron was surprised by fifty-three capital ships, purposely sent from Spain; and Sir Richard Grenville, who was unwilling to leave a great part of his men, then on shore for water and other necessaries, to the insolence and barbarity of the islanders, staid so long in getting them off, that he was hemmed in between the enemy's fleet and the island of Flores. In this dangerous situation he scorned to show any signs of fear, or to owe his safety to flight; but he bravely bore down upon the enemy, and endeavored to break through them, in which attempt he maintained a gallant and obstinate fight with the best of the Spanish ships, for fifteen hours together. He was at once laid aboard by the St. Philip, a ship of fifteen hundred tons and seventy-eight large pieces of ordnance, and four other of the stoutest ships in the Spanish fleet, full of men—in some two hundred, in some five hundred, and in others eight hundred soldiers, besides mariners; and he never had less than two large galleons by his side, which, from time to time, were relieved by fresh ships, men, and ammunition. Yet he behaved himself with such uncommon bravery and conduct, that he disabled some, sunk others, and obliged them all to retire. Neither did he ever leave the deck, though wounded in the beginning of the close fight, till he received a dangerous wound in the body by a musket bullet. When he went down to have it dressed, he received another shot in the head, and his surgeon was killed by his side. By this time also most of his bravest men were slain, his ship much disabled, his deck covered with dead and wounded, and scattered limbs, and his powder spent to the very last barrel. Yet in this condition he ordered the vessel to be sunk, but it was prevented by the rest of the officers; though many of the crew joined with him, and the master-gunner, if he had not been restrained, would have killed himself, sooner than fall into the hands of the Spaniards.

When the ship, or rather wreck, was surrendered, Sir Richard was carried on board the Spanish Admiral, where he died within two days, highly admired by the very enemy, for his extraordinary courage and resolution. And when he found the pangs of death approach, he said to the officers, that stood round him, in the Spanish tongue: "Here die I, Richard Grenville, with a joyful and quiet mind, having ended my life like a true soldier, that fought for his country, Queen, religion, and honor;" thus summing up, in short, all the generous motives that fire the breasts of the truly brave and great, to exert themselves beyond the common pitch of humanity.

And such was the gallant end of this noble gentleman, who, next to Sir Walter Raleigh, was the principal person concerned in this first adventure of Virginia.

THE HISTORY OF CAPTAIN JOHN SMITH.

[From the Same.]

HE was born a gentleman, to a competent fortune, at Willoughby in Lincolnshire, in the year 1579. From his very childhood, he had a roving and romantic fancy, and was strangely set upon performing some brave and adventurous achievement. Accordingly, being about thirteen years of age at school, he sold his satchel and books, and all he had, to raise money, in order to go secretly beyond sea. But his father dying just at that time, he was stopped for the present, and fell into the hands of guardians, more intent on improving his estate, than him. However, at fifteen, in the year 1594, he was bound to a merchant at Lynne, the most considerable trader in those parts. But because he would not send him immediately to sea, he found means in the train of Mr. Peregrine Berty, second son to the Lord Willoughby, to pass into France. Here, and in the low-countries, he first learned the rudiments of war; to which profession he was led by a strong propensity of genius. He was afterwards carried into Scotland, with delusive hopes, from a Scottish gentleman, of being effectually recommended to King James. But soon finding himself baffled in his expectations, he returned to Willoughby, his native place; where, meeting with no company agreeable to his way of thinking, he retired into a wood, at a good distance from any town, and there built himself a pavilion of boughs, and was wholly employed in studying some treatises of the art of war, and in the exercise of his horse and lance. But his friends, being concerned at such a whimsical turn of mind, prevailed with an Italian gentleman, rider to the Earl of Lincoln, to insinuate himself into his acquaintance; and, as he was an expert horseman, and his talent and studies lay the same way with Mr. Smith's, he drew him from his sylvan retirement, to spend some time with him at Tattersall.

But Smith's genius soon hurried him again into Flanders; where, lamenting to see such effusion of Christian blood, he resolved to try his fortune against the Turks. In order to this, he passed through France, with variety of adventure and misfortune, in which he always showed a high and martial spirit. At Marseilles he embarked for Italy. But the ship meeting with much foul weather, a rabble of pilgrims on board hourly cursed him for a Huguenot, railed at Queen Elizabeth and his whole nation, and swore they should never have fair weather, as long as he was in the ship. At last, the passions of these pious Christians rose so high, that they threw him overboard; trusting, we may suppose, in the merit and supererogation of that holy pilgrimage, to expiate the trifling offence and peccadillo of murder. However, Smith, by the Divine assistance, got safe to a small uninhabited island, against Nice in Savoy. From thence he was, the next day, taken off by a French Rover, who treated him very kindly, and with whom he therefore made the tour of the whole Mediterranean, both on the Mahometan and the Christian coasts. At length, after a desperate battle, having taken a very rich Venetian ship, the generous Frenchman set him ashore, with his share of the prize: amounting to five hundred sequins in specie, and a box of rich commodities, worth near as much more. And now out of curiosity ranging all the regions and principalities of Italy, he at last went to Vienna, and entered himself a gentleman volunteer, in Count Meldritch's regiment, against the Turk.

He had not been long in the Christian army, before he was distinguished for a man of great personal bravery; and in the sieges of Olumpagh and Alba-Regalis, he was the author of some stratagems, which showed a happy talent for war, and did signal service to the Christian cause. He was thereupon immediately advanced to the command of a troop of horse; and was, soon after, made sergeant-major of the regiment, a post, at that time, next to the lieutenant-colonel. But Count Meldritch, a Transylvanian nobleman by birth, afterwards passed with his regiment out of the imperial service into that of his natural prince, Sigismond Bathori, Duke of Transylvania. And here, endeavoring to recover some patrimonial lordships, then in the possession of the Turk, he laid siege to a strong town, chiefly inhabited by renegados and banditti. Whilst their works were advancing slowly, and with great difficulty, a Turkish officer issued forth of the town, and challenged any Christian, of the dignity of a captain, to a single combat. Many were eager of the honor of humbling this haughty Musselman; but it was at last decided, by lot, in favor of Captain Smith. Accordingly, the ramparts of the town being filled with fair dames and men in arms, and the Christian army drawn up in battalia, the combatants entered the field, well mounted and richly armed, to the sound of hautboys and trumpets; where, at the first encounter, Smith bore the Turk dead to the ground, and went off triumphantly with his head. But the infidel garrison being enraged at this he afterwards engaged two other officers; and, being a great master of his arms and the management of his horse, he carried off their heads, in the same manner. After which being attended with a guard of six thousand men, with the three Turkish horses led before him, and before each a Turk's head upon a spear, he was conducted to the General's pavilion; who received him with open arms, and presented him with a fine horse, richly caparisoned, and with a scimitar and belt, worth three hundred ducats. Soon after, the Duke himself, coming to view his army, gave him his picture, set in gold; settled three hundred ducats upon him, as a yearly pension; and issued his letters patent of noblesse, giving him three Turk heads, in a shield, for his arms; which coat he ever afterwards bore, and it was admitted and recorded in the Herald's office in England, by Sir William Segar, garter, principal king at arms.

But, soon after, the duke of Transylvania was deprived of his dominions by the emperor; and Smith, at the fatal battle of Rottenton, in the year 1602, was left upon the field, among the dreadful carnage of Christians, as dead. But the pillagers, perceiving life in him, and judging, by the richness of his habit and armor, that his ransom might be considerable, took great pains to recover him. After that, he was publicly sold, among the other prisoners; and was bought by a Bashaw, who sent him to Constantinople, as a present to his mistress, Charatza Tragabigzanda, a beautiful young Tartarian lady. Smith was then twenty-three years of age, in the bloom of life, and, as it seems, of a very handsome person. For this young lady was so moved with compassion, or rather love, for him, that she treated him with the utmost tenderness and regard. And, to prevent his being ill used or sold by her mother, she sent him into Tartary, to her brother, who was Timor Bashaw of Nalbrits, on the Palus Mœotis. Here she intended he should stay, to learn the language, together with the manners and religion of the Turks, till time should make her mistress of herself.

But the Bashaw, suspecting something of the matter, from the affectionate expressions with which she recommended and pressed his good usage, only treated Smith with the greater cruelty and inhumanity. Smith's high spirit, raised also by a consciousness of Tragabigzanda's passion, could but ill brook his harsh treatment. At last, being one day threshing alone at a grange above a league from the house, the Timor came, and took occasion to kick, spurn and revile him, that, forgetting all reason, Smith beat out his brains with his threshing bat. Then reflecting upon his desperate state, he hid the body under the straw, filled his knapsack with corn, put on the Timor's clothes, and, mounting his horse, fled into the deserts of Circassia. After two or three days' fearful wandering, he happened, providentially, on the castragan, or great road, that leads into Muscovy. Following this for sixteen days, with infinite dread and fatigue, he at last arrived at a Muscovite garrison on the frontiers. Here he was kindly entertained and presented, as also at all the places through which he passed. Having travelled through Siberia, Muscovy, Transylvania, and the midst of Europe, he at length found his old friend and gracious patron, the Duke of Transylvania, at Leipsic, together with Count Meldritch, his colonel. Having spent some time with them, the duke at his departure gave him a pass, intimating the services he had done, and the honors he had received ; presenting him, at the same time, with fifteen hundred ducats of gold, to repair his losses. And, although he was now intent on returning to his native country, yet, being furnished with this money, he spent some time in travelling through the principal cities and provinces of Germany, France, and Spain. From the last, being led by the rumor of wars, he passed over into Africa, and visited the court of Morocco. Having viewed many of the places and curiosities of Barbary, he at last returned, through France, to England ; and, in his passage in a French galley, they had a most desperate engagement, for two or three days together, with two Spanish men-of-war. In England all things were still, and in the most profound peace ; so that there was no room or prospect for a person of his active and warlike genius. And therefore, having spent some time in an idle and uneasy state, he willingly embarked himself with Captain Gosnold, in the project of settling colonies in America, and came to Virginia.

His conduct here has been sufficiently related, and I shall finish his character, with the testimonies of some of his soldiers and fellow adventurers. They own him to have made justice his first guide, and experience his second : That he was ever fruitful in expedients, to provide for the people under his command, whom he would never suffer to want any thing, he either had, or could procure : That he rather choose to lead, than send his soldiers into danger ; and, upon all hazardous or fatiguing expeditions, always shared everything equally with his company and never desired any of them to do or undergo anything, that he was not ready to do or undergo himself : That he hated baseness, sloth, pride, and indignity, more than any danger : That he would suffer want, rather than borrow ; and starve, sooner than not pay : That he loved action more than words ; and hated falsehood and covetousness worse than death : and that his adventures gave life and subsistency to the colony, and his loss was their ruin and destruction. They confess, that there were many captains in that age (as there are indeed in all ages) who were no soldiers ; but that Captain Smith was a soldier, of the true old English stamp, who fought, not for gain or empty praise, but for his country's honor and the public good : That his wit, courage, and success here, were worthy of eternal memory : That by the mere force of his virtue and courage, he awed the Indian kings, and made them submit, and bring presents : That, notwithstanding such a stern and invincible resolution, there was seldom seen a milder and more tender heart than his was : That he had nothing in him counterfeit or sly, but was open, honest, and sincere : and that they never knew a soldier, before him, so free from those military vices of wine, tobacco, debts, dice, and oaths.

Sir John Randolph.

BORN about 1693.   Attorney-General of Virginia.   DIED at Williamsburg, Va., 1737.

TWO COLONIAL LAWYERS.

[From Randolph's Breviate Book.   In the Virginia Historical Register, Vol. I. 1848.]

ON the 14th of December, 1734, died suddenly of a fit, John Holloway, Esq., after having languished about ten months with a sort of epilepsy at certain times of the moon, which had much impaired his memory and understanding. He had practised in this court upwards of thirty years, with great reputation for diligence and learning; and was so much in the good opinion of the court, that I have upon many occasions known him prevail for his clients against reasons and arguments much stronger and better than his. His opinions were by most people looked upon as decisive, and were very frequently acquiesced in by both parties, those against whom he pronounced being discouraged from disputing against so great authority. He practised with much artifice and cunning, being thoroughly skilled in attorneyship; but when his causes came to a hearing, he reasoned little, was tedious in reading long reports of some cases, and little abridgments of others, out of which he would collect short aphorisms and obiter sayings of judges, and rely upon them, without regarding the main point in question; and arbitrarily affirm or deny a matter of law, which had often too much weight against the reason and difference of things. By this method he gained many causes, which always gave him great joy, but was as impatient if he lost one as if it tended to a diminution of his credit. He was blameable for one singular practice, in drawing notes for special verdicts; he would state naked circumstances of facts only, and leave to the court to collect the matter of fact out of them; so that upon such verdicts we have had many tedious debates about what the fact was. Whereas, if that had been found positively as it should be, there would have been no need of a special verdict. But against this I could never prevail.

His greatest excellence was his diligence and industry; but for learning, I never thought he had any, nor could it be expected he should. He had served a clerkship; went a youth afterwards into the army in Ireland in the beginning of King William's reign; after that betook himself to business, having got to be one of the attorneys of the Marshalsea court; but not being contented with his income from that, turned Projector and ruined himself, which brought him first into Maryland, and afterwards hither.   .   .   .   .

His reputation was such, that he was universally courted, and most people thought themselves obliged to him, if he would engage of their side upon any terms; and he really thought so himself. This gave him great opportunities of exacting excessive fees, which I have heard he always did where the value of the thing in question would allow it; and covered great blemishes in one part of his private life, besides many imperfections of his mind, which anybody might observe who knew any thing of him. He was of a haughty, insolent nature; passionate and peevish to the last degree. He had a stiffness in his carriage which was ridiculous and often offensive; and was an utter stranger to hospitality. He was sincere in his friendship where he professed any,—but not constant, apt to change upon small provocations, and to contract new friendship upon very slight grounds, in which he would be very warm and ready to do all good offices. One of his greatest defects was that he would always bring his opinion and friendship to agree. But what he wanted in virtue and learning to recommend him was abundantly supplied by fortunate accidents. He was fourteen years Speaker of the House of Burgesses, and eleven years Public Treasurer. But in those he acted with little applause and less abilities, though he was three times chosen, and once unanimously. His management of the Treasury contributed to his ruin, and brought him to the grave with much disgrace. I was always his friend, and had a great deal of reason to believe him mine. Yet it was impossible to be blind to some imperfections. He died little lamented in the 69th year of his age.

In a few days afterwards in London died William Hopkins, Esq., who had practised in this court about twelve years, and in that time, by hard study and observation, he made a surprising progress; became a very ingenious lawyer and a good pleader, though at his first coming he was raw and much despised. But he had a carelessness in his nature, which preserved him from being discouraged, and carried him on till he came to be admired. He had a good foundation in school learning, understood Latin and French well, had a strong memory, a good judgment, a quickness that was very visible, and a handsome person,—all mighty advantages. But his manner was awkward, his temper sour, if it was to be judged by the action of his muscles ; and was given, was too much given, to laugh at his own discourses.

When he had brought himself into good business, he almost totally neglected it, which I believe was owing to a desire of dipping into all kinds of knowledge, wherein he had a great deal of vanity, and prevented his digesting what he had so well as he would have done otherwise. He had many good qualities in his practice; was moderate in his fees; ingenious and earnest ; never disputed plain points, but was a candid, fair arguer. Yet he had a failing which brought him to a quarrel with me. It was an odd sort of pride, that would not suffer him to keep an equilibrium in his own conceits. He could not see himself admired, without thinking it an injury to him to stand upon a level with any other. And therefore, though I was always his friend, had done him many kindnesses, and he himself thought himself obliged to me, he came into so ill a temper, as not to allow me either learning or honesty ; which broke our acquaintance, and after that I thought I discovered some seeds·of malice in him. He died in the flower of his age, and may be justly reckoned a loss to this poor country, which is not like to abound (at present at least) in great geniuses.

Aquila Rose.

BORN in England, about 1795. Clerk of the Pennsylvania Assembly. DIED, 1728.

TO HIS COMPANION AT SEA.

[Poems on Several Occasions. 1740.]

DEBARRED, my friend, of all the joys
 The land, and charming sex can give,
Nor wind, nor wave, our peace destroys;
 We'll laugh, and drink, and nobly live.

The generous wine imparts a heat
 To raise and quicken every sense.
No thoughts of death our bliss defeat,
 Nor steal away our innocence.

Secure, should earth in ruins lie,
 Should seas and skies in rage combine;
Unmoved, all dangers we'll defy,
 And feast our souls with generous wine.

For, should a fear each sense possess,
 Of chilly death and endless fate,
Our sorrow ne'er can make it less;
 But wine alone can dissipate.

Then fill the glass; nay, fill a bowl,
 And fill it up with sparkling wine;
It shall the strongest grief control,
 And make soft wit with pleasure join.

THE MUCH-LOVED CHILD.

[From the Same.]

THOU mournful muse, bewail the lovely boy,
 The parents' hope, and near relations' joy;
In notes that suit my sorrow, guide my quill,
And tear the cypress from the sacred hill.
 Aurelius, lovely boy! how soon thou'rt fled,
To silent mansions of the peaceful dead!
So nipping frosts the tender buds decay,
And make the finest flowers to fade away:
So death's sharp scythe all human things destroys,
Mars our chief hopes, and spoils our greatest joys:

The youth but came, and saw, and passed away,
Snatched in the morning of the flowery day.
    Mourn, all ye loves, beneath the sacred shade,
    Aurelius in his bloom of youth is dead.

His lisping tongue a future wit declared,
And every accent was with pleasure heard:
His actions gave a presage to the sense
Of pious love, with graceful negligence.
No affectation in his humor passed,
He seemed a child with manly virtues graced;
Yet him, nor grace, nor wit, nor beauty save,
Too soon he leaves us for the darksome grave.
    Mourn, all ye youths, the fair Aurelius lies,
    In death's cold arms, a mournful sacrifice.

Mean were our joys, too worthless, and too vile,
That would his truth and innocence beguile;
Tired with the sight, his spirit left the earth,
For those immortal realms that gave him birth;
Whilst all his friends lament his absence here,
And spend in every thought of him a tear;
Their memories paint his image still in view,
And the dear shade their care and griefs renew:
The halcyons so, in briny grief complain
To the deaf billows and relentless main;
With new-made wings their feathered breasts they beat,
And Œnus' death in mournful notes repeat.
Clymene so, and so her daughters, mourn
The generous youth from Phœbus' chariot borne.
So Philomel bewailed sad Isis' fate,
And mournful accents still her woes relate.
    So mourn the youth, adorned with wit and grace,
    Who breathless lies in chilly death's embrace.

But mourning 's vain: no tears will control,
Or stop one moment the departing soul:
What mortal dares with Providence contend;
He ruled the birth, and will command the end?
Can we a life, to death-struck plants, supply,
Or save the meanest flower that 's doomed to die?
Our skill 's too weak to ward off potent death,
No physick's aid can call the flying breath;
Our lengthened years are measured by a span,
And fleeting shuttles show the state of man.
We're poor and helpless at our infant breath,
And old-age-childhood terminates in death:
Whilst death at once can set the spirit free,
To find a state that shall forever be.
    No longer mourn, Aurelius happy reigns,
    Himself a cherub in th' etherial plains.

No more, my friends, let sorrow thus arise,
Nor pierce with your complaints the distant skies:
Let holy David mitigate your grief,
David will sure at once afford relief;
Whilst his dear child in deadly sickness lay,
That heaven might spare the boy he'd sigh and pray;
But when the will of heaven at once he found,
And his soul fled through death's capacious wound,
He dried his eyes, bedewed with briny tears,
Left off his sorrows, and dispelled his fears;
Then quiet rests: "I shall to him," said he,
"Return in peace, he cannot come to me."
No longer mourn, ye friends, no longer mourn,
All heavenly forms must sure to heaven return.

Samuel Mather.

Born in Boston, Mass., 1706. Died there, 1785.

THE HOME LIFE OF COTTON MATHER.

[The Life of the Very Reverend and Learned Cotton Mather. 1729.]

I MUST here mention it for the glory of God as well as the honor of his servant, that, although he met with so many bereavements in his family (as well as sorrows on other accounts), yet he never "fainted in the day of adversity." He thought his sorrows should rather animate than hinder his numerous "essays to do good;" and therefore, when the desires of his eyes were taken away, and when he was deprived of his children, none of these things moved him so far as to hinder him from his duty. No! He ever preached after their deaths, every one of their deaths, and printed the sermons, that so others might be the better for his griefs. .   .   .   .

I will conclude section 4 with reciting some special rules which he observed in the education of his children.

He poured out continual prayers to the God of all grace for them, that he would be a father to them, bestow his Son and grace upon them, guide them by his counsel, and bring them to glory. And in this action he mentioned them distinctly, every one by name, to the Lord.

He began betimes to entertain them with delightful stories, especially Scriptural ones; and he would ever conclude with some lesson of piety, bidding them to learn that lesson from the story.

And thus every day at the table he used himself to tell some entertaining tale before he rose; and endeavor to make it useful to the olive-plants about the table.

When his children accidentally at any time came in his way, it was his custom to let fall some sentence or other, that might be monitory or profitable to them. This matter occasioned labor, study and contrivance.

He betimes tried to engage his children in exercises of piety; and especially secret prayer. For while he gave them very plain and brief directions, and would suggest unto them the petitions which he would have them make before the Lord, and which he would therefore explain to their apprehension and capacity. And he would often call upon them: "Child, don't you forget every day to go alone and pray as I have directed you."

He betimes endeavored to form in his children a temper of benignity. He would put them upon doing services and kindnesses for one another and for other children. He would applaud them when he saw them delight in it. He would upbraid all aversion to it. He would caution them exquisitely against all revenges of injuries, and would instruct them to return good offices for evil ones. He would show them how they would by this goodness become like the good God and the blessed Jesus. He would let them discern he was not satisfied, except when they had a sweetness of temper shining in them.

As soon as possible he would make the children learn to write; and, when they had the use of the pen, he would employ them in writing out the most instructive and profitable things he could invent for them. In this way he proposed to fill their minds with excellent things, which he hoped would make a deep impression upon their minds.

He incessantly endeavored that his children might betimes be acted by principles of reason and honor.

He would first beget in them an high opinion of their Father's love to them, and of his being best able to judge what shall be good for them.

Then he would make them sensible it was folly for them to pretend to any wit or will of their own. They must resign all to him, who would be sure to do what is best; his Word must be their Law.

He would cause them to understand that it is an hurtful and shameful thing to do amiss. He would aggravate this on all occasions, and let them see how amiable they will render themselves by well-doing.

The first chastisement which he would inflict for any ordinary fault, was to let the child see and hear him in an astonishment, and hardly able to believe that the child could do so base a thing; but believing that they would never do it again.

He would never come to give the child a blow, except in case of obstinacy or something that is very criminal.

To be chased for a while out of his presence, he would make to be looked upon as the sorest punishment in his family.

He would with all possible insinuations come upon them to gain this point, that "to learn all great things was the noblest thing in the world." He was not fond of proposing play to them as a reward of any diligent application to learn what is good; lest they should think diversion to be a better and nobler thing than diligence. He would have them to propound and expect at this rate: "I have done well; and now I will go to my father, who will teach me something curious for it." He would have his children account it a privilege to be taught; and would sometimes manage the matter so, that refusing to teach them something should be looked upon as a punishment. The strain of his threatenings therefore was: "You shall not be allowed to read, or to write, or to learn such a thing, if you do not as I have bidden you."

The slavish way of education, carried on with raving and kicking and scourging (in schools as well as families) he looked upon as a dreadful judgment of God on the world; he thought the practice abominable and expressed a mortal aversion to it.

Though he found a vast, a wonderful advantage in having his children strongly biassed by the principles of reason and honor (which he observed that children will feel and understand sooner than is commonly thought for), yet he would not neglect any means and endeavors to have higher principles infused into them.

He would therefore betimes awe them with the sense of the eye of God upon them in the ways which they take. He would show them how they must love our Lord Jesus Christ, and how they must demonstrate it by doing what their parents require of them. He would often tell them of the good angels, who love them, help them, guard them from evil, and do many good offices for them; who likewise take a very diligent notice of them, and ought not in any measure to be disobliged.

He would not say much to them of the evil angels; because he would not have them entertain any frightful fancies about the apparitions of devils. But yet he would briefly let them know that there are devils, who tempt them to wickedness, who are glad when they do wickedly, and who may get leave of God to kill them for it. Heaven and hell he set before them clearly and faithfully, as the consequences of their good or bad behavior here.

When the children were capable of it, he would take them alone one by one; and, after many affectionate, loving, strong charges unto them to fear God, to serve Christ and shun sin, he would pray with them in his study, and make them the witnesses of the agonies and strong cries with which he, on their behalf, addressed the Throne of Grace.

He found much benefit by a particular method, as of catechising the children, so of carrying on the repetition of the public sermons unto them. The answers of the catechism he would explain with abundance of brief questions which make them to take in the whole meaning; and he found by this way that they did so. And when the sermons were to be repeated, he chose to put every truth into a question, to be answered with "Yes," or "No." In this way he would awaken the attention as well as enlighten the understanding of his children. And in this way he would take the opportunity to ask : " Do you desire such or such a grace of God ? " and the like. And in this way he had opportunity to demand, and perhaps to obtain, their early and frequent (and why not sincere?) consent unto the glorious Articles of the New Covenant.   .   .   .   .

It is a saying of Gerson's, *Qui bene vivit semper orat,* He that lives well, prays without ceasing. Mr. Mather was one of those "good livers." He prayed always, at least six times a day every day.   .   .   .   .

His conversation he endeavored to render extremely entertaining, and it was so; for he produced such a variety of useful discourse as made him welcome wherever there was any relish for learning, politeness, and ingenuity. He had the *Je ne scay quoi* of conversation in perfection. As for his friends when in company with him, when his speech dropped upon them, after his words they spake not again ; they waited for him, as for the rain, and they opened their mouth wide as for the latter rain. If he laughed on them, they believed it not. And as for his enemies,— even they confessed his excellent and profitably pleasing conversation, and in society with him they were filled with silent wonder. Happy the conversation and happy the sharers in it !

I shall here give you the rules he observed in conversing. They may be ranked under three heads :

First, he would not affect loquacity in his discourses, but, on the contrary, much deliberation. The gravity and discretion accompanying such a caution, he beheld as of greater consequence to one in all companies than the reputation of wit, which by a greater volubility of tongue might easily be acquired ; and, besides, he remembered "in many words there wants not sin."

Secondly, he would studiously decline to utter anything that he foresaw might be useless ; and much more, everything that might be hurtful and sinful to be uttered. It was his ambition everywhere to speak usefully, and say only those things that one or other might be the wiser or better for.

Thirdly, he would, with all the nice contrivance imaginable, improve opportunities to say something or other that might particularly set off some glories of his Lord. He would everywhere contrive, if it were possible, to let fall some sentence or other, by which high thoughts of Christ might be raised in those that heard him.

Thinking his charitable disbursements may most suitably be reserved for the next chapter, I shall only here give you his private sentiments of charitableness in his own words :

"I am not unable with a little study to write in seven languages. I feast myself with the sweets of all the sciences which the more polite part of mankind ordinarily pretend unto. I am entertained with all kinds of histories, ancient and modern. I am no stranger to the curiosities, which by all sorts of learning are brought unto the curious. These intellectual pleasures are far beyond any sensual ones. Nevertheless, all this affords me not so much delight as it does to relieve the distresses of any one poor, mean, miserable neighbor; and much more to do any extensive service for the redress of those epidemical miseries under which mankind in general is languishing, and to advance the kingdom of God in the world." His private conduct was consonant with his sentiments.

It was his watchful desire and study, never to maintain a personal quarrel with any man breathing; but rather deny himself of his humor, his esteem, or anything in the world. His reason was, because no man can manage a personal quarrel without losing abundance of precious time, which may be laid out infinitely better in the service of Christ and his Church; besides a deal of inevitable sin, which will insinuate itself into every personal quarrel by which one's internal peace is broken. And further, since we have but a short time to live in the world, he thought it foolish to throw away any of it in squabbles.

Considering that for men, even good men, to speak evil one of another, is a very evil thing, he thought it would be a considerable service to seek the suppression of that vice or any vergencies to it in himself. Wherefore, after flights to his Jesus for strength to will and perform, he made these resolutions.

That he would never speak falsely of any man; and that if he spake evil of any man, it should be under these limitations and regulations:

First, that he would keep a charity for the person of whom he spoke, wishing most heartily that all good might be spoken of him; and he would from charity speak to those when with them; always thinking, "Whether what he said might be for the benefit of the hearers?"

Secondly, if he spoke what was evil of any person, he would carefully watch over his heart, that he did not utter it with delight. He would manage it with brevity and aversion, as a very ungrateful subject.

Thirdly, when he must or was obliged to speak what is evil of any man, if he knew of any good that could be spoken of him, he would be sure to balance the evil with the mention of the good.

Fourthly, before he would speak evil of a man, he would consider whether he should not first speak to him; and, be it how it will, he would ordinarily speak nothing, but what he should cheerfully and contentedly say in the hearing of the man of whom he is talking.

And, fifthly, he would aggravate nothing; and when he spoke of an evil would not make it worse than it was.

These rules he conscientiously observed. Would to God, others were so careful as to take a due notice of them!

Because he did not love to be disturbed with tedious and impertinent visitors, and because his friends (*amici temporis fures*) might sometimes unseasonably interrupt him, he wrote over his study door in capitals, BE SHORT. And yet, let him be ever so busy when a friend came to see him, he threw all by, he was perfectly easy, with pleasure communicated the observations he had lately met with, and was so very obliging that, although his friends knew his hurry and great business, they knew not how to leave him.

He would rarely see a torn leaf of a Bible in the street, but would take it up with some particular mark of respect; not knowing but he might find some special admonition. This he found a very profitable practice.

When he rode abroad, he would most commonly take some young gentleman with him, with whom he used to pray in private at their lodging in inns and gentlemen's houses, and unto whom he would endeavor in all possible ways to recommend religion with the sweet and easy, but strong charms of it.

When he went into any considerable towns, he would for the most part beg play-days for the boys; and, as a condition for their being excused from school, he would enjoin some religious task upon them.

If he heard that any person had done him wrong in word or deed, he would seldom let him know that he had any knowledge of it. The best way he thought was to forgive the wrong and bury it in silence. For, besides the consideration due to the internal advantage reaped by such Christianity, there is this to be considered: Such is the malignity in the most of men, that they will hate you only because they know they have wronged you. They will, as far as they can, justify the wrong they have done you; and because they imagine you owe them a like wrong, they will bear a confirmed spite to you. But he found the best way was patience and silence: the consequence of which has been, those who wronged him became his best friends afterwards. . . . .

In the observation of one whole year of his Diary, I take notice of it:

That he had preached about seventy-two public sermons and many private ones; perhaps near half as many.

That not one day passed without some contrivance to do good invented and registered; besides, I suppose, many never entered his memorials.

That no one day had passed without being able to say at night, that some of his revenues, though small, had been dealt out to pious uses.

That he had prepared and published about fourteen books.

That he had kept sixty fasts and twenty-two vigils.

A vast variety of other things I find recorded, which I shall omit; I bring this only as a specimen of his Diary, how it was replenished and what pains he took not to spend his life in vain.

But, notwithstanding he took such care of spending his time, yet I often in his books find him complaining of his "deficiencies," etc. His first years he calls "time so misspent as to render it unworthy to be called a life." After he was grown in years, he chose rather to say, such a "year of his age" than his "life." On one of his books I read, such a "year of a forfeited life;" on another year, of "my sinning against my precious Redeemer;" on another, "Alas, of my unfruitfulness!" On a fourth, "A year sweel'd away in sin and sloth." So that it might be said of him, as was said of one that was very "exact in his walk," that his life was *perpetua censura*, a continual censure of himself.

John Seccomb.

BORN in Medford, Mass., 1708.   DIED at Chester, Nova Scotia, 1793.

FATHER ABBEY'S WILL.

To which is now added, a letter of Courtship to his virtuous and amiable Widow.

CAMBRIDGE, *December*, 1730.

Some time since died here, Mr. Matthew Abbey, in a very advanced age : He had for a great number of years served the College in quality of Bedmaker and Sweeper : Having no child, his wife inherits his whole estate, which he bequeathed to her by his last will and testament, as follows, viz. :

TO my dear wife,
　My joy and life
I freely now do give her
　My whole estate,
　With all my plate,
Being just about to leave her.

　My tub of soap,
　A long cart rope,
A frying pan and kettle,
　An ashes pail,
　A threshing flail,
An iron wedge and beetle.

Two painted chairs,
Nine warden pears,
A large old dripping platter,
This bed of hay,
On which I lay,
An old saucepan for butter.

A little mug,
A two-quart jug,
A bottle full of brandy,
A looking glass,
To see your face
You'll find it very handy.

A musket true
As ever flew,
A pound of shot and wallet,
A leather sash,
My calabash,
My powder horn and bullet.

An old sword blade,
A garden spade,
A hoe, a rake, a ladder,
A wooden can,
A close-stool pan,
A clyster-pipe and bladder.

A greasy hat,
My old ram cat,
A yard and half of linen,
A woolen fleece,
A pot of grease,
In order for your spinning.

A small tooth comb,
An ashen broom,
A candlestick and hatchet,
A coverlid
Striped down with red,
A bag of rags to patch it.

A ragged mat,
A tub of fat,
A book put out by Bunyan,
Another book
By Robin Cook,
A skein or two of spunyarn,

An old black muff,
Some garden stuff,

A quantity of borage,
　　Some devil's weed
　　And burdock seed,
To season well your porridge.

　　A chafing dish,
　　With one salt fish,
If I am not mistaken,
　　A leg of pork,
　　A broken fork,
And half a flitch of bacon.

　　A spinning wheel,
　　One peck of meal,
A knife without a handle,
　　A rusty lamp,
　　Two quarts of samp,
And half a tallow candle.

　　My pouch and pipes,
　　Two oxen tripes,
An oaken dish well carved,
　　My little dog
　　And spotted hog,
With two young pigs just starved.

　　This is my store,
　　I have no more,
I heartily do give it,
　　My years are spun,
　　My days are done,
And so I think to leave it.

Thus father Abbey left his spouse,
As rich as church or college mouse,
Which is sufficient invitation
To serve the college in his station.

NEW HAVEN, *January* 2, 1731.

Our sweeper having lately buried his spouse, and accidentally hearing of the death and will of his deceased Cambridge brother, has conceived a violent passion for the relict. As love softens the mind and disposes to poetry, he has eased himself in the following strains, which he transmits to the charming widow, as the first essay of his love and courtship:

MISTRESS Abbey
　　To you I fly,
You only can relieve me
　　To you I turn,
　　For you I burn,
If you will but believe me.

Then gentle dame
Admit my flame,
And grant me my petition;
If you deny,
Alas ! I die,
In pitiful condition.

Before the news
Of your dear spouse
Had reached us at New Haven,
My dear wife died,
Who was my bride,
In anno eighty-seven.

Thus being free,
Let's both agree
To join our hands, for I do
Boldly aver
A widower
Is fittest for a widow.

You may be sure
'Tis not your dower
I make this flowing verse on;
In these smooth lays
I only praise
The glories of your person.

For the whole that
Was left by Mat.
Fortune to me has granted
In equal store,
I've one thing more
Which Matthew long had wanted.

No teeth, 'tis true
You have to show,
The young think teeth inviting.
But, silly youths!
I love those mouths
Where there's no fear of biting.

A leaky eye,
That's never dry,
These woful times is fitting.
A wrinkled face
Adds solemn grace
To folks devout at meeting.

A furrowed brow,
Where corn might grow,

Such fertile soil is seen in 't,
   A long hook nose,
   Though scorned by foes,
For spectacles convenient.

Thus to go on
   I would put down
Your charms from head to foot,
   Set all your glory
   In verse before ye,
But I've no mind to do 't.

Then haste away,
   And make no stay;
For, soon as you come hither,
   We'll eat and sleep,
   Make beds and sweep
And talk and smoke together.

But if, my dear,
   I must move there,
Towards Cambridge straight I'll set **me**
   To touse the hay
   On which you lay,
If age and you will let me.

Ebenezer and Jane Turell.

E. T. BORN in Boston, Mass., 1702. DIED at Medford, Mass., 1778.—J. T. BORN in Boston,
Mass., 1708. DIED at Medford, Mass., 1735.

A FAIR PURITAN AND HER POETRY.

[*Memoirs of the Life and Death of the Pious and Ingenious Mrs. Jane Turell.* By
E. Turell. 1735.]

THE buddings of reason and religion appeared on her sooner than
usual. Before her second year was completed she could speak distinctly, knew her letters, and could relate many stories out of the Scriptures to the satisfaction and pleasure of the most judicious. I have
heard that Governor Dudley, with other wise and polite gentlemen,
have placed her on a table, and sitting round it, owned themselves
diverted with her stories. Before she was four years old (so strong and
tenacious was her memory), she could say the greater part of the As-

sembly's Catechism, many of the Psalms, some hundred lines of the best poetry, read distinctly, and make pertinent remarks on many things she read. .   .   .   .

Even at the age of four, five, and six she asked many astonishing questions about divine mysteries, and carefully laid up and hid the answers she received to them in her heart. Throughout her childhood she discovered a very serious spirit. Her heart was tender, and her conscience a well-informed faithful guide and monitor.

The most that I am able to collect of her life from six to ten is general (and from her), viz., that her father daily instructed her, and enriched her mind with the best knowledge; and excited her to the due performance of all duty. And that her tender, gracious mother (who died about four years before her) often prayed for, and over her, and gave her the wisest counsels, and most faithful warnings; and that she was thankful and grew in knowledge and (she hoped) in grace under them. That she loved the school and the exercises of it, and made a laudable progress in the various kinds of learning proper to her age and sex.

At nine or ten (if not before) she was able to write; for in the year 1718, I find a letter of her honored father's to her, wrote in answer to one of hers, dated Brookline——which he expresses himself well pleased with. A copy of it follows:

"MY DEAR CHILD: I have this morning your letter, which pleases me very well, and gives me hopes of many a pleasant line from you in time to come; if God spare you to me, and me to you.

"I very much long to see your mother, but doubt whether the weather will permit me to-day. I pray God to bless you and make you one of his children. I charge you to pray daily, and read your Bible, and fear to sin. Be very dutiful to your mother, and respectful to everybody. Be very humble and modest, womanly and discreet. Take care of your health, and as you love me do not eat green apples. Drink sparingly of the waters, except the day be warm. When I last saw you, you were too shame-faced; look people in the face, speak freely and behave decently. I hope to bring Nabby in her grandfather's chariot to see you. The meanwhile I kiss your dear mother, and commend her health to the gracious care of God, and you with her to his grace. Give my service to Mr. A—— and family: also to Mr. S—— and madame; and be sure you never forget the respect they have honored you with.

"Your loving father.

"BOSTON, *Aug. 4th,* 1718."

In this her eleventh year I find an hymn fairly written by her, dated January 4, 1718, which I give you verbatim:

> I fear the great Eternal One above,
> The God of Grace, the God of Love :
> He to whom seraphims hallelujahs sing,
> And angels do their songs and praises bring.
> Happy the soul that does in heaven rest,
> Where with his Saviour he is ever blest;
> With heavenly joys and rapture is possest,
> No thoughts but of his God inspire his breast.
> Happy are they that walk in wisdom's ways,
> That tread her paths, and shine in all her rays.

Her father was pleased to encourage her in this feeble essay she made at verse: he condescended to return her rhymes like her own, level to her present capacity, with a special aim to keep and fix her mind on God and heavenly things, with which she had begun.   .   .   .   .

These condescensions of her father were no doubt of great use to her, and had in some measure the effect proposed, to put her on thinking and writing more and better, and to gain more of his esteem for ingenuity and piety, which she was wisely ambitious of; but above all to approve her heart before God, her heavenly Father who sees in secret.   .   .

Between these and her eighteenth year there are to be seen among her composures many things considerable both in verse and prose.

In poetry (among others), there are the following :

"To her honored father, on his being chosen President of Harvard College," a poem of thirty lines, dated December 27, 1724, which begins thus :

> SIR,
>
> An infant muse begs leave beneath your feet,
> To lay the first essays of her poetic wit;
> That under your protection she may raise
> Her song to some exalted pitch of praise.
> You who among the bards are found the chief, etc.

But I am not allowed to insert the other lines, and but a small part of the next poem to her friend, on her return to Boston, which begins after this manner :

> Thrice welcome home, thou glory of our isle,
> On whom indulgent heaven delights to smile;
> Whose face the graces make their chosen seat,
> In whom the charms of wit and beauty meet.
> O, with what wond'ring eyes I on you gaze,
> And can't recover from the sweet amaze !
> This lovely form, those sweet but sparkling eyes
> Have made the noble Polydore their prize, etc.

ON READING THE WARNING BY MRS. SINGER.

Surprised I view, wrote by a female pen,
Such a grave warning to the sons of men.
Bold was the attempt and worthy of your lays,
To strike at vice, and sinking virtue raise.
Each noble line a pleasing terror gives,
A secret force in every sentence lives.
Inspired by virtue you could safely stand
The fair reprover of a guilty land.
You vie with the famed prophetess of old,
Burn with her fire, in the same cause grow bold.
Dauntless you undertake th' unequal strife,
And raise dead virtue by your verse to life.
A woman's pen strikes the cursed serpent's head,
And lays the monster gasping, if not dead.

TO MY MUSE, DECEMBER 29, 1752.

Come, gentle muse, and once more lend thine aid,
O bring thy succor to a humble maid!
How often dost thou liberally dispense
To our dull breast thy quick'ning influence!
By thee inspired, I'll cheerful tune my voice,
And love and sacred friendship make my choice.
In my pleased bosom you can freely pour
A greater treasure than Jove's golden shower.
Come now, fair muse, and fill my empty mind,
With rich ideas, great and unconfined.
Instruct me in those secret arts that lie
Unseen to all but to a poet's eye.
O let me burn with Sappho's noble fire,
But not like her for faithless man expire.
And let me rival great Orinda's fame,
Or like sweet Philomela's be my name.
Go lead the way, my muse, nor must you stop,
'Till we have gained Parnassus' shady top :
'Till I have viewed those fragrant soft retreats,
Those fields of bliss, the muses' sacred seats.
I'll then devote thee to fair virtue's fame,
And so be worthy of a poet's name.

In prose there are also many things:

Some essay to write her own life, which begins with thanksgivings to God for distinguishing her from most in the world by the blessings of nature, Providence, and grace.

Her thoughts on matrimony, with the rules whereby she resolved to guide herself in that important affair of life.

She writes of the wisdom and goodness of God in making man a sociable creature; of the institution of marriage in paradisaical state, and the happiness of the first couple; and what alone will render persons happy in our fallen state; namely, a faithful discharge of all the duties of that relation; and then particularizes the duties, and treats of the mischiefs that follow upon the neglect of them; shows at large what their duty is who are about to enter into that state, namely, to seek to God by humble prayer for his direction and conduct, and that he would overrule all the circumstances of that momentous affair in mercy, on which so much of the comfort and pleasure of life depends.—She carries her thoughts to the afflictions and temptations of that condition, and prays for sufficient grace to carry aright under all. And for her assistance in making a right choice she laid down a number of rules, from which she resolves never to start. Some of them are the following:

(1) "I would admit the addresses of no person who is not descended of pious and credible parents.

(2) "Who has not the character of a strict moralist, sober, temperate, just and honest.

(3) "Diligent in his business, and prudent in matters.

(4) "Fixed in his religion, a constant attender on the public worship, and who appears not in God's house with the gravity becoming a Christian.

(5) "Of a sweet and agreeable temper; for if he be owner of all the former good qualifications, and fails here, my life will be still uncomfortable."

Before she had seen eighteen, she had read, and (in some measure) digested all the English poetry and polite pieces in prose, printed and manuscripts, in her father's well furnished library, and much she borrowed of her friends and acquaintance. She had indeed such a thirst after knowledge that the leisure of the day did not suffice, but she spent whole nights in reading.

I find she was sometimes fired with a laudable ambition of raising the honor of her sex, who are therefore under obligations to her; and all will be ready to own she had a fine genius, and is to be placed among those who have excelled.

When I was first inclined (by the motions of God's providence and spirit) to seek her acquaintance (which was about the time she entered in her nineteenth year) I was surprised and charmed to find her so accomplished. I found her in a good measure mistress of the politest writers and their works; could point out the beauties in them, and had made many of their best thoughts her own: And as she went into more free conversation, she discoursed how admirably on many subjects!

I grew by degrees into such an opinion of her good taste, that when she put me upon translating a psalm or two, I was ready to excuse myself, and if I had not feared to displease her should have denied her request.

After her marriage, which was on August 11th, 1726, her custom was, once in a month or two, to make some new essay in verse or prose, and to read from day to day as much as a faithful discharge of the duties of her new condition gave leisure for: and I think I may with truth say that she made the writing of poetry a recreation and not a business.

What greatly contributed to increase her knowledge in divinity, history, physic, controversy, as well as poetry, was her attentive hearing most that I read upon those heads through the long evenings of the winters as we sat together.   .   .   .   .

When she had read Mr. Waller's poems, it appears that she was struck with the pleasing admiration of him also; as for the beauty of his thoughts, so more especially for the purity of his style and delicacy of language. It was he that taught us the simplicity and easiness of expression, which has ever since been the character of our best writers.

ON THE INCOMPARABLE MR. WALLER.

Hail, chaste Urania! thy assistance bring,
And fire my breast while I attempt to sing,
In artless lays, Waller, the poets' king.
Waller, the tuneful name my soul inspires,
And kindles in thy breast poetic fires.

Hail, mighty genius! Favorite of the nine!
Thy merits in four reigns distinguished shine.
Country and court, alternate, you enjoy,
One claims thy nobler thoughts, and one thy muse employ.

Chaste is thy muse, and lofty is her song,
Softer than Ovid and like Virgil strong.
Much thee thy county, more its language owe,
All that adorns it, it received from you.
What sterling lines are in thy poems found!
In sweetest numbers you your thoughts express,
The justest standard of our English verse.
A tender passion every bosom warms,
Whene'er you sing of Sacharissa's charms,
O lovely maid! mild as the morning light,
When first its beams salute our longing sight.
As virgin fountains in their basins roll,
So calm, so bright is Sacharissa's soul.

> As the fierce sun, by his meridian rays,
> Exhales the moisture from this lower earth ;
> Again at night by dews the fields repays,
> That nature labors with a double birth :
> So you engross in your capacious soul
> All that the world polite and learned call ;
> But in your works you do repay the whole,
> With large additions of your own to all.
> O happy isle that bare a son so bright,
> Of whom the ages since have learned to write.

．　　．　　．　　．　　．　　．　　．　　．　　．

In her diary she takes notice of God's judgments and mercies to the land, particularly his visitations by earthquakes, thunders, lightnings, storms, drought, etc. ．　　．　　．　　．

Some unhappy affairs of Medford in the years 1729 and '30, produced many prayers and tears from her, with the following poem in imitation of the 133 psalm, which I publish as a monument for and motive to my own people, to continue in love and peace :

> Behold how good, how sweet, their joy does prove,
> Where brethren dwell in unity and love !
> When no contention, strife or fatal jar
> Disturb the peace and raise the noisy war.
> 'Tis like the ointment, which of old was poured
> On Aaron's head, and down his garments showered ;
> Through all the air perfuming odor spreads,
> Diffusing sweetness to the neighboring meads.
> Or like the dew on Hermon's lofty head
> Which on the mounts of Zion moisture spread.
> 'Circled with peace, they shall within the land
> As shining patterns, and examples stand.
> If sinners wrangle, let the saints agree ;
> The gospel breathes out naught but unity.
> To such the blessing from the Lord is given,
> Even life eternal, in the highest heaven.

Having related these things, you will not wonder if I now declare myself a witness of her daily close walk with God during her married state, and of her retirements for reading, self-examination and devotion.

It was her practice to read the Bible out in course once a year, the book of psalms much oftener, besides many chapters and a multitude of verses which she kept turned down in a Bible, which she had been the owner and reader of more than twenty years. If I should only present my readers with a catalogue of these texts, I doubt not but that they would admire the collection, be gratified with the entertainment; and easily conjecture many of her holy frames and tempers from them. I must own, considering her tender make and often infirmities she exceeded in devotion. And I have thought myself obliged sometimes (in compassion to her) to call her off, and put her in mind of God's delighting in mercy more than in sacrifice.

How often has she lain whole nights by me mourning for sin, calling upon God, and praising him, or discoursing of Christ and heaven! And when under doubts entreating me to help her (as far as I could) to a full assurance of God's love.   Sometimes she would say, "Well, I am content if you will show me that I have the truth of grace."   And I often satisfied her with one of Mr. Baxter's marks of love to Christ, namely, lamenting and panting after him; for this kind of love she was sure she exercised in the most cloudy hours of her life.

I may not forget to mention the strong and constant guard she placed at the door of her lips.   Who ever heard her call an ill name? or detract from anybody? When she apprehended she received injuries, silence and tears were her highest resentments. But I have often heard her reprove others for rash and angry speeches.

In every relation she sustained, she was truly exemplary, sensible how much of the life and power of religion consists in the conscientious practice and performance of relative duties.

No child had a greater love to and reverence for her parents; she even exceeded in fear and reverence of her father, notwithstanding all his condescensions to her, and vast freedoms with her.

As a wife she was dutiful, prudent and diligent, not only content but joyful in her circumstances. She submitted as is fit in the Lord, looked well to the ways of her household, and her own works praise her in the gates.

Her very apparel discovered modesty and chastity. She loved to appear neat and clean, but never gay and fine.   .   .   .   .

She honored all men and loved everybody. "Love and goodness was natural to her," as her father expresses it in a letter years ago.

Her tender love to her only sister, has been already seen; and was on all occasions manifested, and grew exceedingly to her death. A few days before it, I heard her speak to her particularly of preparing for another world. "Improve (said she) the time of health, 'tis the only time for doing the great work in."

And in return for her love and amiable carriage, she had the love and esteem of all that knew her. Those that knew her best loved her best, and praise her most.

Her humility was so great, that she could well bear (without being elated) such praises as are often found in her father's letters to us, viz.:

" I greatly esteem as well as highly love you. The best of children deserves all that a child can of a father. My soul rejoices in you. My joy, my crown. I give thanks to God for you daily. I am honored in being the father of such a daughter." Her husband also, and he praiseth her as a meet help both in spirituals and temporals. . . . .

The people, among whom she lived the last eight years of her life, both old and young, had a love and veneration for her, as a person of the strictest virtue and undefiled religion. Her innocence, modesty, ingenuity, and devotion charmed all into an admiration of her. And I question whether there has been more grief and sorrow shown at the death of any private person, by people of all ranks, to whom her virtues were known; mourning, for the loss sustained by ourselves, not for her, nor as others who have no hope. For it is beyond doubt that she died in the Lord, and is blessed.

John Osborn.

BORN in Sandwich, Mass., 1713. DIED at Middletown, Conn., 1753.

A WHALING SONG.

[Preserved in Kettell's " Specimens of American Poetry." 1829.]

WHEN spring returns with western gales,
  And gentle breezes sweep
The ruffling seas, we spread our sails
  To plough the watery deep.

For killing northern whales prepared,
  Our nimble boats on board,
With craft and rum (our chief regard)
  And good provisions stored.

Cape Cod, our dearest native land,
  We leave astern, and lose
Its sinking cliffs and lessening sands
  While Zephyr gently blows.

Bold, hardy men, with blooming age,
  Our sandy shores produce;
With monstrous fish they dare engage,
  And dangerous callings choose.

Now towards the early dawning east
  We speed our course away,
With eager minds and joyful hearts,
  To meet the rising day.

Then as we turn our wandering eyes,
    We view one constant show;
Above, around, the circling skies,
    The rolling seas below.

When eastward, clear of Newfoundland,
    We stem the frozen pole,
We see the icy islands stand,
    The northern billows roll.

As to the north we make our way,
    Surprising scenes we find;
We lengthen out the tedious day,
    And leave the night behind.

Now see the northern regions, where
    Eternal winter reigns:
One day and night fills up the year,
    And endless cold maintains.

We view the monsters of the deep,
    Great whales in numerous swarms;
And creatures there, that play and leap,
    Of strange, unusual forms.

When in our station we are placed,
    And whales around us play,
We launch our boats into the main,
    And swiftly chase our prey.

In haste we ply our nimble oars,
    For an assault designed;
The sea beneath us foams and roars,
    And leaves a wake behind.

A mighty whale we rush upon,
    And in our irons throw:
She sinks her monstrous body down
    Among the waves below.

And when she rises out again,
    We soon renew the fight;
Thrust our sharp lances in amain,
    And all her rage excite.

Enraged, she makes a mighty bound;
    Thick foams the whitened sea;
The waves in circles rise around,
    And widening roll away.

She thrashes with her tail around,
   And blows her reddening breath;
She breaks the air, a deafening sound,
   While ocean groans beneath.

From numerous wounds, with crimson flood,
   She stains the frothy seas,
And gasps, and blows her latest blood,
   While quivering life decays.

With joyful hearts we see her die,
   And on the surface lay;
While all with eager haste apply,
   To save our deathful prey.

John Adams.

BORN in Nova Scotia, 1704. Minister of Newport, R. I. DIED at Cambridge, Mass., 1740.

THE CONTENTED MAN.

[Poems on Several Occasions. 1745.]

HAPPY the man, who, in a calm of soul,
   Can all his warring passions' waves control;—
Who stands unmoved, and hears the rustling wind
Of malice strive to shake his steadfast mind;
From whose clear breast full satisfaction boils,
While in his cheeks rejoice the cheerful smiles.
In vain would Envy with her harpy claws
His peace destroy, or prey upon his joys.
He feels, he feels perpetual rivulets run,
Of joys immortal, in his breast begun:
Looking to future bliss, his ravished eyes
Behold the blushing dawn of glories rise.
He sees the mansions ever clear and bright,
The fields all purpled with distinguished light;
For these his panting breast with ardor heaves,
For these the world in his desires he leaves:—
The glittering tinsel of its gaudy shows,
And wealth which in a golden current flows.
The lofty seats to which the great aspire,
And pleasures which the madding youth admire,—
All wear no charms in his discerning eyes,
Whose high affection dwells above the skies.
In Scythian realms, where hoary winter reigns,
And binds the running streams with icy chains,

A heavenly fervor ever burns within,
Warms his cool thoughts, and gives him peace unseen.
If under Phœbus' piercing beams he dwells,
A cooling spring of inward ease he feels.
No riches swell to vanity his soul,
Who knows the fount from whence those riches roll.
No want contracts the largeness of his thoughts,
And nothing grieves him but his conscious faults;
He makes his God his everlasting tower,
And in his firm munition stands secure.

OF LOVE AND BEAUTY.

[*From the Same.*]

BUT now, the muse in softer measures flows,
   And gayer scenes and fairer landskips shows;
The reign of fancy, when the sliding hours
Are passed with lovely *Nymph* in woven bowers;
Where coolly shades, and lawns forever green,
And streams, and warbling birds adorn the scene:
Where smiles, and graces, and the wanton train
Of *Cytherea*, crown the flowery plain.
What can their charms in equal numbers tell?
The glow of roses, and the lily pale;
The waving ringlets of their flowing hair,
Their snowy bosom, and their killing air;
Their sable brows in beauteous arches bent,
The darts which from their vivid eyes are sent,
And, fixing in our easy-wounded hearts,
Can never be removed by all our arts?
'Tis then with love, and love alone, possest,
Reason has fled, and passion claims our breast.
How many evils then will fancy form?
A frown will gather, and discharge a storm:
Her smile more soft and cooling breezes brings,
Than zephyrs fanning with their silken wings.
But tedious absence is the lover's night,
And then what cruel shades oppress his sight!
Lingering, the moments tedious roll away,
And ages lengthen out the lonely day.
'Tis then our fancy paints the scenes of love,
And we in fields of our ideas rove:
Ten thousand times of former joys repeat,
To make them lasting as they once were great.
The shady picture mocks our hopes with air,
Nor fills them with the substance of the fair.

AS GLIDES THE PICTURED DREAM.

[*" To the Rev. Mr. Turell on the Death of his Virtuous Consort." From the Same.*]

THE darts of death within her bosom deep
   Have urged the fatal wound, and fixed the lasting sleep.
The impartial tyrant round his arrows throws,
Nor heeds our prayers nor melts before our vows.
The charms of beauty wither from his hands,
As fades a flower, and to a tempest bends.
Nor eloquence can soothe, nor virtue awe,
Nor force repel the power of nature's law.
To limits fixed, our destined course we bend,
And with resistless haste to death's pale empire tend.
From scene to scene our shifting moments go,
And then return the ground the dust we owe.
As glides the pictured dream before our sight,
Winged with the fleeting shadows of the night,
So borne upon the quick succeeding hours
We drop in death, and drink surviving showers.
Adown our cheeks th' unwearied currents shed
Can ne'er revive, but may increase the dead.
Had you the lyre of Orpheus, which could move
The quickened stones, and each attentive grove;
Or could you flow in such a moving strain
As Turell warbled to the listening plain;
In vain the tender plaints would charm her ears,
Bound to the breathing consort of the spheres.
Who would the doubtful maze of life repeat,
Where fleeting scenes the gilded fancy cheat?
Where cares and sorrows circle through our years,
While future evils rise before our fears?
And feel the fires of heavenly rapture die,
And blot with tears the vision of the sky?

David Brainerd.

BORN in Haddam, Conn., 1718. DIED at Northampton, Mass., 1747.

HOW BRAINERD FOUND THE EXCELLENT WAY OF SALVATION.

[*From Dwight's Revision of the Memoirs by Jonathan Edwards.* 1822.]

SOME GLOOMY AND DESPONDING THOUGHTS OF A SOUL UNDER CON-
VICTIONS OF SIN, AND CONCERN FOR ITS ETERNAL SALVATION.

I BELIEVE my case is singular, that none ever had so many strange
and different thoughts and feelings as I.

2. I have been concerned much longer than many others I have known, or concerning whom I have read, who have been savingly converted, and yet I am left.

3. I have withstood the power of convictions a long time; and there-fore I fear I shall be finally left of God.

4. I never shall be converted without stronger convictions and greater terrors of conscience.

5. I do not aim at the glory of God in anything I do, and therefore I cannot hope for mercy.

6. I do not see the evil nature of sin, nor the sin of my nature; and therefore I am discouraged.

7. The more I strive, the more blind and hard my heart is, and the worse I grow continually.

8. I fear that God never showed mercy to one so vile as I.

9. I fear that I am not elected, and therefore must perish.

10. I fear that the day of grace is past with me.

11. I fear that I have committed the unpardonable sin.

12. I am an old sinner; and if God had designed mercy for me, He would have called me home to himself before now.

After a considerable time spent in similar exercises and distresses, one morning, while I was walking in a solitary place, as usual, I at once saw that all my contrivances and projects to effect or procure deliverance and salvation for myself, were utterly in vain; I was brought quite to a stand, as finding myself totally lost. I had thought many times before, that the difficulties in my way were very great; but now I saw, in another and very different light, that it was forever impossible for me to do anything towards helping or delivering myself. I then thought of blaming myself, that I had not done more, and been more engaged, while I had opportunity—for it seemed now as if the season of doing was for-ever over and gone—but I instantly saw, that, let me have done what I would, it would no more have tended to my helping myself, than what I had done; that I had made all the pleas I ever could have made to all eternity; and that all my pleas were vain. The tumult that had been before in my mind, was now quieted; and I was somewhat eased of that distress which I felt while struggling against a sight of myself, and of the divine sovereignty. I had the greatest certainty, that my state was for-ever miserable, for all that I could do; and wondered that I had never been sensible of it before.

While I remained in this state, my notions respecting my duties were quite different from what I had ever entertained in times past. Before this, the more I did in duty, the more hard I thought it would be for God to cast me off; though at the same time I confessed, and thought I saw, that there was no goodness or merit in my duties; but now, the more I did in prayer or any other duty, the more I saw that I was indebted to God for allowing me to ask for mercy; for I saw that self-interest had led me to pray, and that I had never once prayed from any respect to the glory of God. Now I saw that there was no necessary connection between my prayers and the bestowment of divine mercy; that they laid not the least obligation upon God to bestow his grace upon me; and that there was no more virtue or goodness in them, than there would be in my paddling with my hand in the water (which was the comparison I had then in my mind); and this because they were not performed from any love or regard to God. I saw that I had been heaping up my devotions before God, fasting, praying, etc., pretending, and indeed really thinking sometimes, that I was aiming at the glory of God; whereas I never once truly intended it, but only my own happiness. I saw that as I had never done anything for God, I had no claim on anything from him, but perdition, on account of my hypocrisy and mockery. Oh, how different did my duties now appear from what they used to do! I used to charge them with sin and imperfection; but this was only on account of the wanderings and vain thoughts attending them, and not because I had no regard to God in them; for this I thought I had. But when I saw evidently that I had regard to nothing but self-interest; then they appeared a vile mockery of God, self-worship, and a continual course of lies. I saw that something worse had attended my duties than barely a few wanderings; for the whole was nothing but self-worship, and an horrid abuse of God.

I continued, as I remember, in this state of mind, from Friday morning till the Sabbath evening following (July 12, 1739), when I was walking again in the same solitary place, where I was brought to see myself lost and helpless, as before mentioned. Here, in a mournful melancholy state, I was attempting to pray; but found no heart to engage in that or any other duty; my former concern, exercise, and religious affections were now gone. I thought that the spirit of God had quite left me; but still was not distressed; yet disconsolate, as if there was nothing in heaven or earth could make me happy. Having been thus endeavoring to pray —though, as I thought, very stupid and senseless—for near half an hour; then, as I was walking in a dark thick grove, unspeakable glory seemed to open to the view and apprehension of my soul. I do not mean any external brightness, for I saw no such thing; nor do I intend any imagination of a body of light, somewhere in the third heavens, or anything of that nature; but it was a new inward apprehension or view that I had of God, such as I never had before, nor anything which had the least resemblance of it. I stood still; wondered; and admired! I knew that I never had seen before anything comparable to it for excellency and beauty; it was widely different from all the conceptions that ever I had of God, or things divine. I had no particular apprehension of any one person in the Trinity, either the Father, the Son, or the Holy Ghost; but it appeared to be Divine glory. My soul rejoiced with joy unspeakable, to see such a God, such a glorious divine Being; and I was inwardly pleased and satisfied, that he should be God over all forever and ever. My soul was so captivated and delighted with the excellency, loveliness, greatness, and other perfections of God, that I was even swallowed up in him; at least to that degree, that I had no thought (as I remember) at first, about my own salvation, and scarce reflected that there was such a creature as myself.

Thus God, I trust, brought me to a hearty disposition to exalt him, and set him on the throne, and principally and ultimately to aim at his honor and glory, as king of the universe. I continued in this state of inward joy, peace, and astonishment, till near dark, without any sensible abatement; and then began to think and examine what I had seen; and felt sweetly composed in my mind all the evening following. I felt myself in a new world, and everything about me appeared with a different aspect from what it was wont to do. At this time, the way of salvation opened to me with such infinite wisdom, suitableness, and excellency, that I wondered I should ever think of any other way of salvation; was amazed that I had not dropped my own contrivances, and complied with this lovely, blessed, and excellent way before. If I could have been saved by my own duties, or any other way that I had formerly contrived, my whole soul would now have refused it. I wondered that all the world did not see and comply with this way of salvation, entirely by the righteousness of Christ.

The sweet relish of what I then felt, continued with me for several days, almost constantly, in a greater or less degree.—I could not but sweetly rejoice in God, lying down and rising up. The next Lord's day I felt something of the same kind, though not so powerful as before. But not long after I was again involved in thick darkness, and under great distress; yet not of the same kind with my distress under convictions. I was guilty, afraid, and ashamed to come before God; was exceedingly pressed with a sense of guilt: but it was not long before I felt, I trust, true repentance and joy in God.—About the latter end of August, I again fell under great darkness; it seemed as if the presence of God was clean gone forever; though I was not so much distressed about my spiritual state, as I was at my being shut out from God's presence, as I then sensibly was. But it pleased the Lord to return graciously to me not long after. —[Written about 1739.]

A SAVAGE REFORMER.

[*From the Same.*]

OF all the sights I ever saw among them, or indeed anywhere else, none appeared so frightful, or so near akin to what is usually imagined of infernal powers, none ever excited such images of terror in my mind, as the appearance of one who was a devout and zealous reformer, or rather, restorer of what he supposed was the ancient religion of the Indians. He made his appearance in his pontifical garb, which was a coat of bear skins, dressed with the hair on, and hanging down to his toes ; a pair of bear-skin stockings ; and a great wooden face, painted, the one half black, the other half tawny, about the color of an Indian's skin, with an extravagant mouth, cut very much awry ; the face fastened to a bear-skin cap, which was drawn over his head. He advanced toward me with the instrument in his hand, which he used for music in his idolatrous worship ; which was a dry tortoise shell with some corn in it, and the neck of it drawn on to a piece of wood, which made a very convenient handle. As he came forward he beat his tune with the rattle, and danced with all his might, but did not suffer any part of his body, not so much as his fingers, to be seen. No one would have imagined from his appearance or actions, that he could have been a human creature, if they had not had some intimation of it otherwise. When he came near me, I could not but shrink away from him, although it was then noon day, and I knew who it was ; his appearance and gestures were so prodigiously frightful. He had a house consecrated to religious uses, with divers images cut upon the several parts of it. I went in, and found the ground beat almost as hard as a rock, with their frequent dancing upon it.

I discoursed with him about Christianity. Some of my discourse he seemed to like, but some of it he disliked extremely. He told me that God had taught him his religion, and that he never would turn from it ; but wanted to find some who would join heartily with him in it ; for the Indians, he said, were grown very degenerate and corrupt. He had thoughts, he said, of leaving all his friends, and travelling abroad, in order to find some who would join with him ; for he believed that God had some good people somewhere, who felt as he did. He had not always, he said, felt as he now did ; but had formerly been like the rest of the Indians, until about four or five years before that time. Then, he said, his heart was very much distressed, so that he could not live among the Indians, but got away into the woods, and lived alone for some months. At length, he says, God comforted his heart, and showed him what he should do ; and since that time he had known God, and tried to serve him : and loved all men, be they who they would, so as he never did before.   He treated me with uncommon courtesy, and seemed to be hearty in it.   I was told by the Indians that he opposed their drinking strong liquor with all his power; and that, if at any time he could not dissuade them from it by all he could say, he would leave them, and go crying into the woods.   It was manifest that he had a set of religious notions which he had examined for himself, and not taken for granted, upon bare tradition; and he relished or disrelished whatever was spoken of a religious nature, as it either agreed or disagreed with his standard.

While I was discoursing, he would sometimes say, " Now that I like; so God has taught me," etc., and some of his sentiments seemed very just. Yet he utterly denied the existence of a devil, and declared there was no such creature known among the Indians of old times, whose religion he supposed he was attempting to revive.   He likewise told me, that departed souls all went southward, and that the difference between the good and the bad, was this: that the former were admitted into a beautiful town with spiritual walls; and that the latter would forever hover around these walls, in vain attempts to get in.   He seemed to be sincere, honest, and conscientious in his own way, and according to his own religious notions; which was more than I ever saw in any other Pagan.   I perceived that he was looked upon and derided among most of the Indians, as a precise zealot, who made a needless noise about religious matters; but I must say that there was something in his temper and disposition, which looked more like true religion, than anything I ever observed among other heathens.

Jonathan Edwards.

Born in East Windsor, Conn., 1703.   Died at Princeton, N. J., 1758.

HIS EARLY AND RAPTUROUS SENSE OF DIVINE THINGS.

[From the Personal Narrative Found among his MSS.]

FROM about that time, I began to have a new kind of apprehensions and ideas of Christ, and the work of redemption, and the glorious way of salvation by him.   An inward, sweet sense of these things, at times, came into my heart; and my soul was led away in pleasant views and contemplations of them.   And my mind was greatly engaged to spend my time in reading and meditating on Christ, on the beauty and excellency of his person, and the lovely way of salvation by free grace in him.   I found no books so delightful to me, as those that treated of these subjects.   Those words Cant. ii. 1. used to be abundantly with me, "I am the Rose of Sharon, and the Lily of the valleys." The words seemed to me sweetly to represent the loveliness and beauty of Jesus Christ. The whole book of Canticles used to be pleasant to me, and I used to be much in reading it, about that time; and found, from time to time, an inward sweetness, that would carry me away, in my contemplations. This I know not how to express otherwise than by a calm, sweet abstraction of soul from all the concerns of this world; and sometimes a kind of vision, or fixed ideas and imaginations, of being alone in the mountains, or some solitary wilderness, far from all mankind, sweetly conversing with Christ, and wrapt and swallowed up in God. The sense I had of divine things would often of a sudden kindle up, as it were, a sweet burning in my heart; an ardor of soul, that I know not how to express.

Not long after I first began to experience these things, I gave an account to my father of some things that had passed in my mind. I was pretty much affected by the discourse we had together; and when the discourse was ended, I walked abroad alone, in a solitary place in my father's pasture, for contemplation. And as I was walking there, and looking upon the sky and clouds, there came into my mind so sweet a sense of the glorious majesty and grace of God, as I know not how to express. I seemed to see them both in a sweet conjunction; majesty and meekness joined together: it was a sweet, and gentle, and holy majesty; and also a majestic meekness; an awful sweetness; a high, and great, and holy gentleness.

After this my sense of divine things gradually increased, and became more and more lively, and had more of that inward sweetness. The appearance of everything was altered: there seemed to be, as it were, a calm, sweet cast or appearance of divine glory in almost everything. God's excellency, his wisdom, his purity and love, seemed to appear in everything; in the sun, moon, and stars; in the clouds and blue sky; in the grass, flowers, trees; in the water and all nature; which used greatly to fix my mind. I often used to sit and view the moon for a long time; and in the day spent much time in viewing the clouds and sky, to behold the sweet glory of God in these things: in the mean time, singing forth, with a low voice, my contemplations of the Creator and Redeemer. And scarce anything, among all the works of nature, was so sweet to me as thunder and lightning; formerly nothing had been so terrible to me. Before, I used to be uncommonly terrified with thunder, and to be struck with terror when I saw a thunder-storm rising; but now, on the contrary, it rejoiced me. I felt God, if I may so speak, at the first appearance of a thunder-storm; and used to take the opportunity, at such times, to fix myself in order to view the clouds, and see the lightnings play, and hear the majestic and awful voice of God's thunder, which oftentimes was ex-

Eng.^d by H.B.Hall's Sons. New York.

Jonathan Edwards

ceedingly entertaining, leading me to sweet contemplations of my great and glorious God. While thus engaged, it always seemed natural for me to sing, or chant forth my meditations; or to speak my thoughts in soliloquies with a singing voice.

.   .   .   .

The heaven I desired was a heaven of holiness; to be with God, and to spend my eternity in divine love, and holy communion with Christ. My mind was very much taken up with contemplations on heaven, and the enjoyments there; and on living there in perfect holiness, humility and love; and it used at that time to appear a great part of the happiness of heaven that there the saints could express their love to Christ. It appeared to me a great clog and burden, that what I felt within, I could not express as I desired. The inward ardor of my soul seemed to be hindered and pent up, and could not freely flame out as it would. I used often to think how in heaven this principle should freely and fully vent and express itself. Heaven appeared exceedingly delightful, as a world of love; and that all happiness consisted in living in pure, humble, heavenly, divine love.

I remember the thoughts I used then to have of holiness; and said sometimes to myself, "I do certainly know that I love holiness, such as the gospel prescribes." It appeared to me, that there was nothing in it but what was ravishingly lovely; the highest beauty and amiableness—a *divine* beauty; far purer than anything here upon earth; and that everything else was like mire and defilement in comparison of it.

Holiness, as I then wrote down some of my contemplations on it, appeared to me to be of a sweet, pleasant, charming, serene, calm nature; which brought an inexpressible purity, brightness, peacefulness and ravishment to the soul. In other words, that it made the soul like a field or garden of God, with all manner of pleasant flowers; enjoying a sweet calm, and the gently vivifying beams of the sun. The soul of a true Christian, as I then wrote my meditations, appeared like such a little white flower as we see in the spring of the year; low and humble on the ground, opening its bosom to receive the pleasant beams of the sun's glory; rejoicing, as it were, in a calm rapture; diffusing around a sweet fragrancy; standing peacefully and lovingly, in the midst of other flowers round about; all in like manner opening their bosoms, to drink in the light of the sun. There was no part of creature-holiness that I had so great a sense of its loveliness, as humility, brokenness of heart and poverty of spirit; and there was nothing that I so earnestly longed for. My heart panted after this—to lie low before God, as in the dust; that I might be nothing, and that God might be ALL; that I might become as a little child.

THAT MATERIAL EXISTENCE IS MERELY IDEAL.

[From " The Mind." Written while a Youth at College.]

THE whole of what we any way observe, whereby we get the idea of Solidity, or Solid Body, are certain parts of Space, from whence we receive the ideas of light and colors ; and certain sensations by the sense of feeling; and we observe that the places, whence we receive these sensations, are not constantly the same, but are successively different, and this light and colors are communicated from one part of space to another. And we observe that these parts of Space, from whence we receive these sensations, resist and stop other bodies, which we observe communicated successively through the parts of Space adjacent; and that those that there were before at rest, or existing constantly in one and the same part of Space, after this exist successively in different parts of Space, and these observations are according to certain stated rules. I appeal to any one that takes notice and asks himself; whether this be not all, that ever he experienced in the world, whereby he got these ideas; and that this is all that we have or can have any idea of in relation to bodies. All that we observe of Solidity is, that certain parts of Space, from whence we receive the ideas of light and colors, and a few other sensations, do likewise resist anything coming within them. It therefore follows, that if we suppose there be anything else than what we thus observe, it is but only by way of Inference.

I know that it is nothing but the Imagination will oppose me in this: I will therefore endeavor to help the Imagination thus. Suppose that we received none of the sensible qualities of light, colors, etc., from the resisting parts of Space (we will suppose it possible for resistance to be without them), and they were, to appearance, clear and pure; and all that we could possibly observe, was only and merely Resistance; we simply observed that Motion was resisted and stopped, here and there, in particular parts of Infinite Space. Should we not then think it less unreasonable to suppose that such effects should be produced by some Agent present in those parts of Space, though Invisible. If we, when walking upon the face of the Earth, were stopped at certain limits, and could not possibly enter into such a part of Space, nor make anybody enter into it; and we could observe no other difference, no way, nor at any time, between that and other parts of clear space; should we not be ready to say, What is it stops us; What is it hinders all entrance into that place ?

The reason, why it is so exceedingly natural to men, to suppose that there is some Latent *Substance*, or Something that is altogether hid, that upholds the properties of bodies, is, because all see at first sight, that the properties of bodies are such as need some Cause, that shall every moment have influence to their continuance, as well as a Cause of their first existence. All therefore agree, that there is Something that is there, and upholds these properties. And it is most true, there undoubtedly is; but men are wont to content themselves in saying merely, that it is Something; but that Something is He, " by whom all things consist."

The distribution of the objects of our thoughts, into Substances and Modes, may be proper; if, by Substance, we understand, a complexion of such ideas, which we conceive of as subsisting together, and by them-selves; and, by Modes, those simple ideas which cannot be by them-selves, or subsist in our mind alone.

A SELF-TRAINED BERKELEIAN.

[" Notes on Natural Science." Written in his Sixteenth Year.]

AND how doth it grate upon the mind, to think that Something should be from all eternity, and yet Nothing all the while be conscious of it. To illustrate this: Let us suppose that the World had a being from all eternity, and had many great changes, and wonderful revolutions, and all the while Nothing knew it, there was no knowledge in the Universe of any such thing. How is it possible to bring the mind to imagine this? Yea, it is really impossible it should be, that anything should exist, and Nothing know it. Then you will say, If it be so, it is, because Nothing has any existence but in consciousness: No, certainly, nowhere else, but either in created or uncreated consciousness.

Suppose there were another Universe, merely of .bodies, created at a great distance from this; created in excellent order, harmonious motions, and a beautiful variety; and there was no created intelligence in it, nothing but senseless bodies, and nothing but God knew anything of it, I demand where else that Universe would have a being, but only in the Divine consciousness? Certainly, in no other respect. There would be figures, and magnitudes, and motions, and proportions; but where, where else, except in the Almighty's knowledge? How is it possible there should?—But then you will say, For the same reason, in a room closely shut up, which nobody sees, there is nothing, except in God's knowledge. —I answer, Created beings are conscious of the effects of what is in the room; for, perhaps, there is not one leaf of a tree, nor a spear of grass, but what produces effects, all over the Universe, and will produce them, to the end of eternity. But any otherwise, there is nothing in a room so shut up, but only in God's consciousness. How can anything be there, any other way? This will appear to be truly so, to any one who thinks of it, with the whole united strength of his mind. Let us suppose, for illustration, this impossibility, that all the spirits in the Universe were, for a time, deprived of their consciousness, and that God's consciousness, at the same time, were to be intermitted. I say the Universe, for that time, would cease to be, of itself; and this not merely, as we speak, because the Almighty could not attend to uphold it; but because God could know nothing of it. It is our foolish imagination, that will not suffer us to see it. We fancy there may be figures and magnitudes, relations and properties, without any one knowing of it. But it is our imagination hurts us. We do not know what figures and properties are.

Our imagination makes us fancy that we see shapes, and colors, and magnitudes, though nobody is there to behold it. But to help our imagination, let us thus state the case: Let us suppose the creation deprived of every ray of light, so that there should not be the least glimmering of light in the Universe. Now all will own, that, in such case, the Universe would really be immediately deprived of all its colors. No one part of the Universe is any more red, or blue, or green, or yellow, or black, or white, or light, or dark, or transparent, or opaque. There would be no visible distinction between the Universe and the rest of the incomprehensible void: yea, there would be no difference, in these respects, between the Universe and the infinite void; so that any part of that void would really be as light and as dark, as white and as black, as red and as green, as blue and as brown, as transparent and as opaque, as any part of the Universe: so that, in such case, there would be no difference, in these respects, between the Universe and Nothing. So also, there would be no difference between one part of the Universe and another: all, in these respects, is alike confounded with, and undistinguished from, infinite emptiness.

At the same time, also, let us suppose the Universe to be altogether deprived of motion, and all parts of it to be at perfect rest. Then, the Universe would not differ from the void, in this respect: there would be no more motion in the one, than in the other. Then, also, solidity would cease. All that we mean, or can be meant, by solidity, is resistance: resistance to touch, the resistance of some parts of space. This is all the knowledge we get of solidity, by our senses, and, I am sure, all that we can get, any other way. But solidity shall be shown to be nothing else, more fully, hereafter. But there can be no resistance, if there is no motion. One body cannot resist another, when there is perfect rest among them. But, you will say, Though there is no actual resistance, yet there is potential resistance: that is, such and such parts of space would resist upon occasion. But this is all that I would have, that there is no solidity now; not but that God could cause there to be, on occasion. And if there is no solidity, there is no extension, for extension is the extendedness of solidity. Then, all figure, and magnitude, and proportion, immediately cease. Put, then, both these suppositions together: that is, deprive the Universe of light, and motion, and the case would stand thus, with the Universe: There would be neither white nor black, neither blue nor brown, neither bright nor shaded, pellucid nor opaque, no noise nor sound, neither heat nor cold, neither fluid nor solid, neither wet nor dry, neither hard nor soft, nor solidity, nor extension, nor figure, nor magnitude, nor proportion, nor body, nor spirit. What, then, is to become of the Universe? Certainly, it exists nowhere, but in the Divine mind. This will be abundantly clearer to one, after having read what I have further to say of solidity, etc.: so that we see that a Universe, without motion, can exist nowhere else, but in the mind—either infinite or finite.

Corollary. It follows from hence, that those beings, which have knowledge and consciousness, are the only proper, and real, and substantial beings: inasmuch as the being of other things is only by these. From hence, we may see the gross mistake of those who think material things the most substantial beings, and spirits more like a shadow; whereas, spirits only are properly substance.

LAPLACE ANTICIPATED.

[*From the Same.*]

IT is certain that, when God first created Matter, or the various Chaoses of Atoms, besides creating the Atoms and giving the whole Chaos its motion, he designed the figure and shape of every Atom, and likewise their places; which doubtless was done with infinite wisdom, and with an eye to what should follow from the particular bulk, figure and place of every Atom; and this be so ordered that, without doing anything more, the Chaoses of themselves, according to the established Laws of Matter, were brought into these various and excellent forms, adapted to every of God's ends, excepting the more excellent works of plants and animals, which it was proper and fit God should have an immediate hand in. So the Atoms of one Chaos were created in such places, of such magnitudes and figures, that the Laws of Nature brought them into this form, fit, in every regard, for them who were to be the inhabitants.

A YOUNG CHRISTIAN'S DIRECTORY.

[From the Seventy Resolutions formed in his Twentieth Year. 1722-23.]

BEING sensible that I am unable to do anything without God's help, I do humbly entreat him by his grace, to enable me to keep these resolutions, so far as they are agreeable to his will, for Christ's sake.

Resolved, That I will do whatsoever I think to be most to the glory of God and my own good, profit and pleasure, in the whole of my duration; without any consideration of the time, whether now, or never so many myriads of ages hence. Resolved to do whatever I think to be my duty, and most for the good and advantage of mankind in general. Resolved, so to do, whatever difficulties I meet with, how many soever, and how great soever.

To be continually endeavoring to find out some new contrivance, and invention, to promote the forementioned things.

Never *to do* any manner of thing, whether in soul or body, less or more, but what tends to the glory of God, nor *be*, nor *suffer* it, if I can possibly avoid it.

To live with all my might, while I do live.

Never to do anything, which I should be afraid to do, if it were the last hour of my life.

To think much, on all occasions, of my own dying, and of the common circumstances which attend death.

When I feel pain, to think of the pains of martyrdom, and of hell.

When I think of any theorem in divinity to be solved, immediately to do what I can toward solving it, if circumstances do not hinder.

If I take delight in it as a gratification of pride, or vanity, or on any such account, immediately to throw it by.

Never to do anything out of revenge.

Never to suffer the least motions of anger toward irrational beings.

Never to speak evil of any one, so that it shall tend to his dishonor, more or less, upon no account except for some real good.

To live so, at all times, as I think is best in my most devout frames, and when I have the clearest notions of the things of the Gospel, and another world.

Never to do anything, which, if I should see in another, I should count a just occasion to despise him for, or to think any way the more meanly of him.

Whenever I do any conspicuously evil action, to trace it back, till I come to the original cause; and then, both carefully endeavor to do so no more, and to fight and pray with all my might against the original of it.

Never to count that a prayer, nor to let that pass as a prayer, nor that as a petition of a prayer, which is so made, that I cannot hope that God will answer it; nor that as a confession, which I cannot hope God will accept.

In narrations, never to speak anything but the pure and simple verity.

Never, henceforward, till I die, to act as if I were any way my own, but entirely and altogether God's.

That no other end but religion shall have any influence at all on any of my actions; and that no action shall be, in the least circumstance, any otherwise than the religious end will carry it.

Never to allow any pleasure or grief, joy or sorrow, nor any affection at all, nor any degree of affection, nor any circumstance relating to it, but what helps religion.

That I will act so, as I think I shall judge would have been best, and most prudent, when I come into the future world.

That I will act so, in every respect, as I think I shall wish I had done, if I should at last be damned.

I frequently hear persons in old age, say how they would live, if they were to live their lives over again: Resolved, That I will live just so as I can think I shall wish I had done, supposing I live to old age.

To endeavor, to my utmost, so to act, as I can think I should do, if I had already seen the happiness of heaven, and hell torments.

On the supposition, that there never was to be but one individual in the world, at any one time, who was properly a complete Christian, in all respects of a right stamp, having Christianity always shining in its true lustre, and appearing excellent and lovely, from whatever part and under whatever character viewed: Resolved, To act just as I would do, if I strove with all my might to be that one, who should live in my time.

Always to do that which I shall wish I had done when I see others do it.

Let there be something of benevolence in all that I speak.

OF SARAH PIERREPONT, WHO AFTERWARD BECAME HIS WIFE.

[*Written on a Blank Leaf, in* 1723.]

THEY say there is a young lady in New Haven who is beloved of that Great Being, who made and rules the world, and that there are certain seasons in which this Great Being, in some way or other invisible, comes to her and fills her mind with exceeding sweet delight, and that she hardly cares for anything, except to meditate on him—that she expects after a while to be received up where he is, to be raised up out of the world and caught up into heaven; being assured that he loves her too well to let her remain at a distance from him always. There she is to dwell with him, and to be ravished with his love and delight forever. Therefore, if you present all the world before her, with the richest of its treasures, she disregards it and cares not for it, and is unmindful of any pain or affliction. She has a strange sweetness in her mind and singular purity in her affections; is most just and conscientious in all her conduct; and you could not persuade her to do anything wrong or sinful, if you would give her all the world, lest she should offend this Great Being. She is of a wonderful sweetness, calmness and universal benevolence of mind; especially after this Great God has manifested himself to her mind. She will sometimes go about from place to place, singing sweetly; and seems to be always full of joy and pleasure; and no one knows for what. She loves to be alone, walking in the fields and groves, and seems to have some one invisible always conversing with her.

A CHILD OF THE COVENANT.

[*Narrative of Surprising Conversions.* 1736.]

I NOW proceed to the other instance that I would give an account of, which is of the little child forementioned. Her name is Phebe Bartlet, daughter of William Bartlet. I shall give the account as I took it from the mouths of her parents, whose veracity none that know them doubt of.

She was born in March, in the year 1731. About the latter end of April, or beginning of May, 1735, she was greatly affected by the talk of her brother, who had been hopefully converted a little before, at about eleven years of age, and then seriously talked to her about the great things of religion. Her parents did not know of it at that time, and were not wont, in the counsels they gave to their children, particularly to direct themselves to her, by reason of her being so young, and, as they supposed, not capable of understanding; but, after her brother had talked to her, they observed her very earnestly to listen to the advice they gave to the other children, and she was observed very constantly to retire, several times in a day, as was concluded, for secret prayer, and grew more and more engaged in religion, and was more frequently in her closet, till at last she was wont to visit it five or six times in a day, and was so engaged in it, that nothing would, at any time, divert her from her stated closet exercises. Her mother often observed and watched her, when such things occurred, as she thought most likely to divert her, either by putting it out of her thoughts, or otherwise engaging her in-clinations, but never could observe her to fail. She mentioned some very remarkable instances.

She once, of her own accord, spake of her unsuccessfulness, in that she could not find God, or to that purpose. But on Thursday, the last day of July, about the middle of the day, the child being in the closet, where it used to retire, its mother heard it speaking aloud, which was unusual, and never had been observed before; and her voice seemed to be as of one exceeding importunate and engaged, but her mother could distinctly hear only these words (spoken in her childish manner, but seemed to be spoken with extraordinary earnestness, and out of distress of soul), "Pray bessed Lord give me salvation! I pray, beg pardon all my sins!" When the child had done prayer, she came out of the closet, and came and sat down by her mother, and cried out aloud. Her mother very earnestly asked her several times, what the matter was, before she would make any answer, but she continued exceedingly crying, and writhing her body to and fro, like one in anguish of spirit. Her mother then asked her whether she was afraid that God would not give her salvation. She then answered, "Yes, I am afraid I shall go to hell!" Her mother then endeavored to quiet her, and told her she would not have her cry—she must be a good girl, and pray every day, and she hoped God would give her salvation. But this did not quiet her at all—but she continued thus earnestly crying and taking on for some time, till at length she suddenly ceased crying and began to smile, and presently said with a smiling countenance, "Mother, the kingdom of heaven is come to me!" Her mother was surprised at the sudden alteration, and at the speech, and knew not what to make of it, but at first said nothing to her. The child presently spake again, and said, "There is another come to me, and there is another—there is three;" and being asked what she meant, she answered, "One is, thy will be done, and there is another—enjoy him for ever;" by which it seems that when the child said, "There is three come to me," she meant three passages of her catechism that came to her mind.

After the child had said this, she retired again into her closet; and her mother went over to her brother's, who was next neighbor; and when she came back, the child, being come out of the closet, meets her mother with this cheerful speech, "I can find God now!" Referring to what she had before complained of, that she could not find God. Then the child spoke again, and said, "I love God!" Her mother asked her how well she loved God, whether she loved God better than her father and mother, she said, "Yes." Then she asked her whether she loved God better than her little sister Rachel, she answered, "Yes, better than anything!" Then her eldest sister, referring to her saying she could find God now, asked her where she could find God; she answered, "In heaven." "Why," said she, "have you been in heaven?" "No," said the child. By this it seems not to have been any imagination of any thing seen with bodily eyes that she called God, when she said I can find God now. Her mother asked her whether she was afraid of going to hell, and that had made her cry. She answered, "Yes, I was; but now I shall not." Her mother asked her whether she thought that God had given her salvation; she answered, "Yes." Her mother asked her when; she answered, "To-day." She appeared all that afternoon exceeding cheerful and joyful. One of the neighbors asked her how she felt herself? She answered, "I feel better than I did." The neighbor asked her what made her feel better; she answered, "God makes me." That evening as she lay abed, she called one of her little cousins to her, that was present in the room, as having something to say to him; and when he came, she told him that heaven was better than earth. The next day being Friday, her mother, asking her her catechism, asked her what God made her for; she answered, "To serve him;" and added, "Everybody should serve God, and get an interest in Christ."   .   .   .   .

She has manifested great love to her minister; particularly when I returned from my long journey for my health last fall, when she heard of it, she appeared very joyful at the news, and told the children of it with an elevated voice, as the most joyful tidings, repeating it over and over, "Mr. Edwards is come home! Mr. Edwards is come home!" She still continues very constant in secret prayer, so far as can be observed (for she seems to have no desire that others should observe her when she retires, but seems to be a child of a reserved temper), and every night before she goes to bed will say her catechism, and will by no means miss of it; she never forgot it but once, and then after she was abed, thought of it, and cried out in tears, "I have not said my catechism!" And would not be quieted till her mother asked her the catechism as she lay in bed. She sometimes appears to be in doubt about the condition of her soul, and when asked whether she thinks that she is prepared for death, speaks something doubtfully about it; at other times seems to have no doubt, but when asked, replies "Yes," without hesitation.

SINNERS IN THE HANDS OF AN ANGRY GOD.

[*Sermon Preached at Enfield, Conn., July 8, 1741.*]

DEUTERONOMY, xxxii. 35.—" Their foot shall slide in due time."

IN this verse is threatened the vengeance of God on the wicked unbelieving Israelites, that were God's visible people and lived under means of grace; and that notwithstanding all God's wonderful works that He had wrought toward that people, yet remained as is expressed in v. 28, void of counsel, having no understanding in them; and that, under all the cultivations of heaven, brought forth bitter and poisonous fruit; as in the two verses next preceding the text.

The expression that I have chosen for my text, *their foot shall slide in due time*, seems to imply the following things relating to the punishment and destruction that these wicked Israelites were exposed to.

1. That they were always exposed to destruction; as one that stands or walks in slippery places is always exposed to fall. This is implied in the manner of their destruction's coming upon them, being represented by their foot's sliding. The same is expressed, Psalm lxxiii. 18: "Surely thou didst set them in slippery places; thou castedst them down into destruction."

2. It implies that they were always exposed to sudden, unexpected destruction. As he that walks in slippery places is every moment liable to fall, he cannot foresee one moment whether he shall stand or fall the next; and, when he does fall, he falls at once, without warning, which is also expressed in that Psalm lxxiii. 18, 19: "Surely thou didst set them in slippery places; thou castedst them down into destruction: how are they brought into desolation as in a moment."

3. Another thing implied is, that they are liable to fall of themselves, without being thrown down by the hand of another; as he that stands or walks on slippery ground needs nothing but his own weight to throw him down.

4. That the reason why they are not fallen already, and do not fall now, is only that God's appointed time is not come. For it is said that, when that due time, or appointed time, comes, *their feet shall slide.* Then they shall be left to fall, as they are inclined by their own weight. God will not hold them up in these slippery places any longer, but will let them go; and then, at that very instant, they shall fall into destruction; as he that stands in such slippery declining ground on the edge of a pit that he cannot stand alone, when he is let go he immediately falls and is lost.

The observation from the words that I would now insist upon is this.

There is nothing that keeps wicked men at any one moment out of hell, but the mere pleasure of God.

By the mere pleasure of God, I mean his sovereign pleasure, his arbitrary will, restrained by no obligation, hindered by no manner of difficulty, any more than if nothing else but God's mere will had in the least degree, or in any respect whatsoever, any hand in the preservation of wicked men one moment.

The truth of this observation may appear by the following considerations.

1. There is no want of power in God to cast wicked men into hell at any moment. Men's hands cannot be strong when God rises up: the strongest have no power to resist him, nor can any deliver out of his hands.

He is not only able to cast wicked men into hell, but he can most easily do it. Sometimes an earthly prince meets with a great deal of difficulty to subdue a rebel, that has found means to fortify himself, and has made himself strong by the number of his followers. But it is not so with God. There is no fortress that is any defence against the power of God. Though hand join in hand, and vast multitudes of God's enemies combine and associate themselves, they are easily broken in pieces: they are as great heaps of light chaff before the whirlwind; or large quantities of dry stubble before devouring flames. We find it easy to tread on and crush a worm that we see crawling on the earth; so it is easy for us to cut or singe a slender thread that anything hangs by; thus easy is it for God, when he pleases, to cast his enemies down to hell. What are we, that we should think to stand before him, at whose rebuke the earth trembles, and before whom the rocks are thrown down!

2. They deserve to be cast into hell; so that divine justice never stands in the way, it makes no objection against God's using his power at any moment to destroy them. Yea, on the contrary, justice calls aloud for an infinite punishment of their sins. Divine justice says of the tree that brings forth such grapes of Sodom, "Cut it down, why cumbreth it the ground?" The sword of divine justice is every moment brandished over their heads, and it is nothing but the hand of arbitrary mercy, and God's mere will, that holds it back.

3. They are already under a sentence of condemnation to hell. They do not only justly deserve to be cast down thither, but the sentence of the law of God, that eternal and immutable rule of righteousness that God has fixed between him and mankind, is gone out against them; and stands against them; so that they are bound over already to hell: "He that believeth not is condemned already." So that every unconverted man properly belongs to hell: that is his place; from thence he is; "Ye are from beneath:" and thither he is bound; it is the place that justice, and God's word, and the sentence of his unchangeable law, assign to him.

4. They are now the objects of that very same anger and wrath of God, that is expressed in the torments of hell: and the reason why they do not go down to hell at each moment, is not because God, in whose power they are, is not then very angry with them; as angry, as He is with many of those miserable creatures that He is now tormenting in hell, and do there feel and bear the fierceness of his wrath. Yea, God is a great deal more angry with great numbers that are now on earth; yea, doubtless, with many that are now in this congregation, that, it may be, are at ease

and quiet, than He is with many of those that are now in the flames of hell.

So that it is not because God is unmindful of their wickedness, and does not resent it, that He does not let loose his hand and cut them off. God is not altogether such an one as themselves, though they may imagine him to be so. The wrath of God burns against them; their damnation does not slumber; the pit is prepared; the fire is made ready; the furnace is now hot; ready to receive them; the flames do now rage and glow. The glittering sword is whet and held over them, and the pit hath opened her mouth under them.

5. The devil stands ready to fall upon them, and seize them as his own, at what moment God shall permit him. They belong to him; he has their souls in his possession, and under his dominion. The Scripture represents them as his goods, Luke xi. 21. The devils watch them; they are ever by them, at their right hand; they stand waiting for them, like greedy hungry lions that see their prey, and expect to have it, but are for the present kept back; if God should withdraw his hand by which they are restrained, they would in one moment fly upon their poor souls. The old serpent is gaping for them; hell opens its mouth wide to receive them; and, if God should permit it, they would be hastily swallowed up and lost.

6. There are in the souls of wicked men those hellish principles reigning, that would presently kindle and flame out into hell-fire, if it were not for God's restraints. There is laid in the very nature of carnal men a foundation for the torments of hell: there are those corrupt principles in reigning power in them, and in full possession of them, that are the beginnings of hell-fire. These principles are active and powerful, exceeding violent in their nature, and, if were not for the restraining hand of God upon them, they would soon break out, they would flame out after the same manner as the same corruptions, the same enmity does in the hearts of damned souls, and would beget the same torments in them as they do in them.   .   .   .   .

7. It is no security to wicked men for one moment, that there are no visible means of death at hand. It is no security to a natural man, that he is now in health, and that he does not see which way he should now immediately go out of the world by any accident, and that there is no visible danger in any respect in his circumstances. The manifold and continual experience of the world in all ages, shows that this is no evidence that a man is not on the very brink of eternity, and that the next step will not be into another world. The unseen, unthought-of ways and means of persons going suddenly out of the world are innumerable and inconceivable. Unconverted men walk over the pit of hell on a rotten covering, and there are innumerable places in this covering so weak that

they will not bear their weight, and these places are not seen. The
arrows of death fly unseen at noonday ; the sharpest sight cannot discern
them. God has so many different, unsearchable ways of taking wicked
men out of the world and sending them to hell, that there is nothing to
make it appear that God had need to be at the expense of a miracle, or go
out of the ordinary course of his providence, to destroy any wicked man,
at any moment. All the means that there are of sinners going out of
the world, are so in God's hands, and so absolutely subject to his power
and determination, that it does not depend at all less on the mere will of
God, whether sinners shall at any moment go to hell, than if means were
never made use of, or at all concerned in the case.

8. Natural men's prudence and care to preserve their own lives, or the
care of others to preserve them, do not secure them a moment. This,
divine providence and universal experience do also bear testimony to.
There is this clear evidence that men's own wisdom is no security to them
from death ; that if it were otherwise we should see some difference between the wise and politic men of the world, and others, with regard to
their liableness to early and unexpected death ; but how is it in fact?
"How dieth the wise man? As the fool."

9. All wicked men's pains and contrivance, they use to escape hell,
while they continue to reject Christ and so remain wicked men, do not
secure them from hell one moment. Almost every natural man that
hears of hell, flatters himself that he shall escape it ; he depends upon
himself for his own security, he flatters himself in what he has done, in
what he is now doing, or what he intends to do ; every one lays out matters in his own mind how he shall avoid damnation, and flatters himself
that he contrives well for himself, and that his schemes will not fail.
They hear indeed that there are but few saved, and that the bigger part
of men that have died heretofore are gone to hell ; but each one imag-
ines that he lays out matters better for his own escape than others have
done: he does not intend to come to that place of torment ; he says
within himself, that he intends to take care that shall be effectual, and to
order matters so for himself as not to fail.

But the foolish children of men do miserably delude themselves in their
own schemes, and, in their confidence in their own strength and wisdom,
they trust to nothing but a shadow. The bigger part of those that heretofore have lived under the same means of grace, and are now dead, are
undoubtedly gone to hell ; and it was not because they were not as wise
as those that are now alive ; it was not because they did not lay out
matters as well for themselves to secure their own escape. If it were so
that we could come to speak with them, and could inquire of them, one
by one, whether they expected, when alive, and when they used to hear
about hell, ever to be subjects of that misery, we, doubtless, should hear

one and another reply, " No, I never intended to come here : I had laid out matters otherwise in my mind ; I thought I should contrive well for my-self : I thought my scheme good : I intended to take effectual care ; but it came upon me unexpectedly ; I did not look for it at that time, and in that manner ; it came as a thief ; death outwitted me : God's wrath was too quick for me : O my cursed foolishness ! I was flattering myself and pleasing myself with vain dreams of what I would do hereafter ; and when I was saying peace and safety, then sudden destruction came upon me."

10. God has laid himself under no obligation, by any promise, to keep any natural man out of hell one moment : God certainly has made no promises either of eternal life, or of any deliverance or preservation from eternal death, but what are contained in the covenant of grace, the promises that are given in Christ, in whom all the promises are yea and amen. But surely they have no interest in the promises of the covenant of grace that are not the children of the covenant, and that do not believe in any of the promises of the covenant, and have no interest in the Mediator of the covenant.

So that, whatever some have imagined and pretended about promises made to natural men's earnest seeking and knocking, it is plain and mani-fest that, whatever pains a natural man takes in religion, whatever pray-ers he makes, till he believes in Christ, God is under no manner of obli-gation to keep him a moment from eternal destruction.

So that thus it is, that natural men are held in the hand of God over the pit of hell ; they have deserved the fiery pit and are already sentenced to it ; and God is dreadfully provoked, his anger is as great toward them as to those that are actually suffering the executions of the fierceness of his wrath in hell, and they have done nothing in the least to appease or abate that anger, neither is God in the least bound by any promise to hold them up one moment ; the devil is waiting for them, hell is gaping for them, the flames gather and flash about them, and would fain lay hold on them and swallow them up ; the fire pent up in their own hearts is struggling to break out ; and they have no interest in any Mediator, there are no means within reach that can be any security to them. In short, they have no refuge, nothing to take hold of ; all that preserves them every moment is the mere arbitrary will, and uncovenanted, unobliged forbearance of an incensed God.

APPLICATION.

The use may be of awakening to unconverted persons in this congre-gation. This that you have heard is the case of every one of you that are out of Christ. That world of misery, that lake of burning brimstone, is extended abroad under you. There is the dreadful pit of the glowing flames of the wrath of God; there is hell's wide gaping mouth open; and you have nothing to stand upon, nor anything to take hold of. There is nothing between you and hell but the air; it is only the power and mere pleasure of God that holds you up.

You probably are not sensible of this; you find you are kept out of hell, but do not see the hand of God in it; but look at other things, as the good state of your bodily constitution, your care of your own life, and the means you use for your own preservation. But indeed these things are nothing; if God should withdraw his hand, they would avail no more to keep you from falling than the thin air to hold up a person that is suspended in it.

Your wickedness makes you as it were heavy as lead and to tend downwards with great weight and pressure towards hell; and, if God should let you go, you would immediately sink and swiftly descend and plunge into the bottomless gulf, and your healthy constitution, and your own care and prudence, and best contrivance, and all your righteousness, would have no more influence to uphold you and keep you out of hell, than a spider's web would have to stop a falling rock. Were it not that so is the sovereign pleasure of God, the earth would not bear you one moment; for you are a burden to it; the creation groans with you; the creature is made subject to the bondage of your corruption, not willingly; the sun does not willingly shine upon you to give you light to serve sin and Satan; the earth does not willingly yield her increase to satisfy your lusts; nor is it willingly a stage for your wickedness to be acted upon; the air does not willingly serve you for breath to maintain the flame of life in your vitals, while you spend your life in the service of God's enemies. God's creatures are good, and were made for men to serve God with, and do not willingly subserve to any other purpose, and groan when they are abused to purposes so directly contrary to their nature and end. And the world would spew you out, were it not for the sovereign hand of him who hath subjected it in hope. There are the black clouds of God's wrath now hanging directly over your heads, full of the dreadful storm and big with thunder; and were it not for the restraining hand of God, it would immediately burst forth upon you. The sovereign pleasure of God, for the present, stays his rough wind; otherwise it would come with fury, and your destruction would come like a whirlwind, and you would be like the chaff of the summer threshing floor.

The wrath of God is like great waters that are dammed for the present; they increase more and more, and rise higher and higher, till an outlet is given; and, the longer the stream is stopped, the more rapid and mighty is its course when once it is let loose. It is true that judgment against your evil work has not been executed hitherto; the floods of God's vengeance have been withheld; but your guilt in the meantime is constantly increasing, and you are every day treasuring up more wrath; the waters are continually rising and waxing more and more mighty; and there is nothing but the mere pleasure of God that holds the waters back, that are unwilling to be stopped and press hard to go forward. If God should only withdraw his hand from the floodgate, it would immediately fly open, and the fiery floods of the fierceness and wrath of God would rush forth with inconceivable fury, and would come upon you with omnipotent power; and, if your strength were ten thousand times greater than it is, yea, ten thousand times greater than the strength of the stoutest, sturdiest devil in hell, it would be nothing to withstand or endure it.

The bow of God's wrath is bent, and the arrow made ready on the string, and justice bends the arrow at your heart and strains the bow, and it is nothing but the mere pleasure of God, and that of an angry God, without any promise or obligation at all, that keeps the arrow one moment from being made drunk with your blood.

Thus are all you that never passed under a great change of heart by the mighty power of the Spirit of God upon your souls; all that were never born again, and made new creatures, and raised from being dead in sin to a state of new, and before altogether unexperienced, light and life (however you may have reformed your life in many things, and may have had religious affections, and may keep up a form of religion in your families and closets, and in the houses of God, and may be strict in it), you are thus in the hands of an angry God; it is nothing but his mere pleasure that keeps you from being this moment swallowed up in everlasting destruction.

However unconvinced you may now be of the truth of what you hear, by-and-by you will be fully convinced of it. Those that are gone from being in the like circumstances with you, see that it was so with them: for destruction came suddenly upon most of them; when they expected nothing of it, and while they were saying, Peace and safety: now they see that those things that they depended on for peace and safety were nothing but thin air and empty shadows.

The God that holds you over the pit of hell, much as one holds a spider, or some loathsome insect, over the fire, abhors you and is dreadfully provoked; his wrath towards you burns like fire; he looks upon you as worthy of nothing else but to be cast into the fire; he is of purer eyes than to bear to have you in his sight; you are ten thousand times so abominable in his eyes, as the most hateful and venomous serpent is in ours. You have offended him infinitely more than ever a stubborn rebel did his prince: and yet it is nothing but his hand that holds you from falling into the fire every moment: it is ascribed to nothing else that you did not go to hell the last night; that you was suffered to awake again in this world, after you closed your eyes to sleep; and there is no other reason to be given why you have not dropped into hell since you arose in the morning, but that God's hand has held you up: there is no other reason to be given why you have not gone to hell, since you have sat here in the house of God, provoking his pure eyes by your sinful wicked manner of attending his solemn worship: yea, there is nothing else that is to be given as a reason why you do not this very moment drop down into hell.

O sinner! consider the fearful danger you are in: it is a great furnace of wrath, a wide and bottomless pit, full of the fire of wrath, that you are held over in the hand of that God, whose wrath is provoked and incensed as much against you, as against many of the damned in hell: you hang by a slender thread, with the flames of divine wrath flashing about it, and ready every moment to singe it and burn it asunder; and you have no interest in any Mediator, and nothing to lay hold of to save yourself, nothing to keep off the flames of wrath, nothing of your own, nothing that you ever have done, nothing that you can do, to induce God to spare you one moment.   .   .   .   .

Thus it will be with you that are in an unconverted state, if you continue in it; the infinite might, and majesty, and terribleness, of the Omnipotent God shall be magnified upon you in the ineffable strength of your torments: you shall be tormented in the presence of the holy angels, and in the presence of the Lamb; and, when you shall be in this state of suffering, the glorious inhabitants of heaven shall go forth and look on the awful spectacle, that they may see what the wrath and fierceness of the Almighty is; and when they have seen it, they will fall down and adore that great power and majesty. "And it shall come to pass, that from one moon to another, and from one Sabbath to another, shall all flesh come to worship before me, saith the Lord. And they shall go forth and look upon the carcasses of the men that have transgressed against me; for their worm shall not die, neither shall their fire be quenched, and they shall be an abhorring unto all flesh."

It is everlasting wrath. It would be dreadful to suffer this fierceness and wrath of Almighty God one moment; but you must suffer it to all eternity: there will be no end to this exquisite, horrible misery: when you look forward you shall see a long forever, a boundless duration before you, which will swallow up your thoughts and amaze your soul; and you will absolutely despair of ever having any deliverance, any end, any mitigation, any rest at all; you will know certainly that you must wear out long ages, millions of millions of ages, in wrestling and conflicting with this Almighty merciless vengeance; and then, when you have so done, when so many ages have actually been spent by you in this manner, you will know that all is but a point to what remains. So that your punishment will indeed be infinite. Oh, who can express what the state of a soul in such circumstances is! All that we can possibly say about it gives but a very feeble, faint representation of it; it is inexpressible and inconceivable: for "who knows the power of God's anger?"

How dreadful is the state of those that are daily and hourly in danger of this great wrath and infinite misery! But this is the dismal case of every soul in this congregation that has not been born again, however moral and strict, sober and religious, they may otherwise be. Oh, that you would consider it, whether you be young or old! There is reason to think that there are many in this congregation, now hearing this discourse, that will actually be the subjects of this very misery to all eternity. We know not who they are, or in what seats they sit, or what thoughts they now have. It may be they are now at ease, and hear all these things without much disturbance, and are now flattering themselves that they are not the persons; promising themselves that they shall escape. If we knew that there was one person, and but one, in the whole congregration, that was to be the subject of this misery, what an awful thing it would be to think of! If we knew who it was, what an awful sight would it be to see such a person! How might all the rest of the congregation lift up a lamentable and bitter cry over him! But alas! Instead of one, how many is it likely will remember this discourse in hell! And it would be a wonder, if some that are now present should not be in hell in a very short time, before this year is out. And it would be no wonder if some persons, that now sit here in some seats of this meeting-house in health, and quiet and secure, should be there before to-morrow morning.

THE ETERNITY OF HELL TORMENTS.

[From the Sermon bearing that title.]

I SHALL improve this subject in a use of exhortation to sinners, to take care to escape these eternal torments. If they be eternal, one would think that would be enough to awaken your concern and excite your diligence. If the punishment be eternal, it is infinite, as we said before; and therefore no other evil, no death, no temporary torment that ever you heard of, or that you can imagine, is anything in comparison with it, but is as much less and less considerable, not only as a grain of sand is less than the whole universe, but as it is less than the boundless space which encompasses the universe. Therefore here,

(1.) Be entreated to consider attentively how great and awful a thing eternity is. Although you cannot comprehend it the more by considering, yet you may be made more sensible that it is not a thing to be disregarded. Do but consider what it is to suffer extreme torment forever and ever; to suffer it day and night, from one day to another, from one year to another, from one age to another, from one thousand ages to another, and so, adding age to age, and thousands to thousands, in pain, in wailing and lamenting, groaning and shrieking, and gnashing your teeth; with your souls full of dreadful grief and amazement, with your bodies and every member full of racking torture, without any possibility of getting ease; without any possibility of moving God to pity by your cries; without any possibility of hiding yourselves from him; without any possibility of diverting your thoughts from your pain; without any possibility of obtaining any manner of mitigation, or help, or change for the better any way.

(2.) Do but consider how dreadful despair will be in such torment. How dismal will it be, when you are under these racking torments, to know assuredly that you never, never shall be delivered from them; to have no hope; when you shall wish that you might but be turned into nothing, but shall have no hope of it; when you shall wish that you might be turned into a toad or a serpent, but shall have no hope of it; when you would rejoice, if you might but have any relief, after you shall have endured these torments millions of ages, but shall have no hope of it; when after you shall have worn out the age of the sun, moon, and stars, in your dolorous groans and lamentations, without any rest day or night, or one minute's ease, yet you shall have no hope of ever being delivered; when after you shall have worn out a thousand more such ages, yet you shall have no hope, but shall know that you are not one whit nearer to the end of your torments; but that still there are the same groans, the same shrieks, the same doleful cries, incessantly to be made by you, and that the smoke of your torment shall still ascend up, forever and ever; and that your souls, which shall have been agitated with the wrath of God all this while, yet will still exist to bear more wrath; your bodies, which shall have been burning and roasting all this while in these glowing flames, yet shall not have been consumed, but will remain to roast through an eternity yet, which will not have been at all shortened by what shall have been past.

You may by considering make yourselves more sensible than you ordinarily are; but it is a little you can conceive of what it is to have no hope in such torments.

How sinking would it be to you to endure such pain as you have felt in this world, without any hopes, and to know that you never should be delivered from it, nor have one minute's rest! You can now scarcely conceive how doleful that would be. How much more to endure the vast weight of the wrath of God without hope! The more the damned in hell think of the eternity of their torments, the more amazing will it appear to them; and alas! they are not able to avoid thinking of it, they will not be able to keep it out of their minds. Their tortures will not divert them from it, but will fix their attention to it. O how dreadful will eternity appear to them after they shall have been thinking on it for ages together, and shall have had so long an experience of their torments!— The damned in hell will have two infinites perpetually to amaze them and swallow them up: one is an infinite God, whose wrath they will bear, and whom they will behold their perfect and irreconcilable enemy. The other is the infinite duration of their torment.

WHY SAINTS IN GLORY WILL REJOICE TO SEE THE TORMENTS OF THE DAMNED.

[Sermon: The end of the Wicked contemplated by the Righteous.]

NEGATIVELY: it will not be because the saints in heaven are the subjects of any ill disposition; but, on the contrary, this rejoicing of theirs will be the fruit of an amiable and excellent disposition: it will be the fruit of a perfect holiness and conformity to Christ, the holy Lamb of God. The devil delights in the misery of men from cruelty, and from envy and revenge, and because he delights in misery, for its own sake, from a malicious disposition.

But it will be from exceedingly different principles, and for quite other reasons, that the just damnation of the wicked will be an occasion of rejoicing to the saints in glory. It will not be because they delight in seeing the misery of others absolutely considered. The damned suffering divine vengeance will be no occasion of joy to the saints merely as it is the misery of others, or because it is pleasant to them to behold the misery of others merely for its own sake. The rejoicing of the saints on this occasion is no argument that they are not of a most amiable and excellent spirit, or that there is any defect on that account, that there is anything wanting, which would render them of a more amiable disposition. It is no argument that they have not a spirit of goodness and love reigning in them in absolute perfection, or that herein they do not excel the greatest instances of it on earth, as much as the stars are higher than the earth, or the sun brighter than a glow-worm.

And whereas the heavenly inhabitants are in the text called upon to rejoice over Babylon, because God had avenged them on her; it is not to be understood that they are to rejoice in having their revenge glutted, but to rejoice in seeing the justice of God executed, and in seeing his love to them in executing it on his enemies.

2. Positively: the sufferings of the damned will be no occasion of grief to the heavenly inhabitants, as they will have *no love nor pity* to the damned as such. It will be no argument of want of a spirit of love in them, that they do not love the damned; for the heavenly inhabitants will know that it is not fit that they should love them, because they will know then that God has no love to them, nor pity for them; but that they are the objects of God's eternal hatred. And they will then be perfectly conformed to God in their wills and affections. They will love what God loves, and that only. However the saints in heaven may have loved the damned while here, especially those of them who were near and dear to them in this world, they will have no love to them hereafter.

It will be an occasion of their rejoicing, as the glory of God will appear in it. The glory of God appears in all his works: and therefore there is no work of God which the saints in glory shall behold and contemplate but what will be an occasion of rejoicing to them. God glorifies himself in the eternal damnation of the ungodly men. God glorifies himself in all that he doth; but he glorifies himself principally in his eternal disposal of his intelligent creatures: some are appointed to everlasting life, and others left to everlasting death.

The saints in heaven will be perfect in their love to God: their hearts will be all a flame of love to God, and therefore they will greatly value the glory of God, and will exceedingly delight in seeing him glorified. The saints highly value the glory of God here in this, but how much more will they so do in the world to come. They will therefore greatly rejoice in all that contributes to that glory. The glory of God will in their esteem be of greater consequence than the welfare of thousands and millions of souls.—Particularly,

They will rejoice in seeing the *justice* of God glorified in the sufferings of the damned. The misery of the damned, dreadful as it is, is but what justice requires. They in heaven will see and know it much more clearly than any of us do here. They will see how perfectly just and righteous their punishment is, and therefore how properly inflicted by the supreme Governor of the world. They will greatly rejoice to see justice take place, to see that all the sin and wickedness that have been committed in the world is remembered of God and has its due punishment. The sight of this strict and immutable justice of God will render him amiable and adorable, in their eyes. They will rejoice when they see him who is their Father and eternal portion so glorious in his justice.

Then there will be no remaining difficulties about the justice of God, about the absolute decrees of God, or anything pertaining to the dispensations of God towards men. But divine justice in the destruction of the wicked will then appear as light without darkness, and will shine as the sun without clouds, and on this account will they sing joyful songs of praise to God, as we see the saints and angels do, when God pours the vials of his wrath upon antichrist.　　.　　.　　.　　.

It will occasion rejoicing in them, as they will have the greater sense of *their own happiness,* by seeing the contrary misery.　It is the nature of pleasure and pain, of happiness and misery, greatly to heighten the sense of each other.　Thus the seeing of the happiness of others tends to make men more sensible of their own calamities ; and the seeing of the calamities of others tends to heighten the sense of our own enjoyments.

When the saints in glory, therefore, shall see the doleful state of the damned, how will this heighten their sense of the blessedness of their own state, so exceedingly different from it !　When they shall see how miserable others of their fellow-creatures are, who were naturally in the same circumstances with themselves; when they shall see the smoke of their torment, and the raging of the flames of their burning, and hear their dolorous shrieks and cries, and consider that they in the meantime are in the most blissful state, and shall surely be in it to all eternity ; how will they rejoice !

This will give them a joyful sense of the grace and love of God to them, because hereby they will see how great a benefit they have by it. When they shall see the dreadful miseries of the damned, and consider that they deserved the same misery, and that it was sovereign grace, and nothing else, which made them so much to differ from the damned, that, if it had not been for that, they would have been in the same condition ; but that God from all eternity was pleased to set his love upon them, that Christ hath laid down his life for them, and hath made them thus gloriously happy forever, O how will they admire that dying love of Christ, which has redeemed them from so great a misery, and purchased for them so great happiness, and has so distinguished them from others of their fellow-creatures !　How joyfully will they sing to God and the Lamb, when they behold this !

THAT THE DEVIL CAN CITE SCRIPTURE FOR HIS PURPOSE.

[*Treatise on Religious Affections.* 1746.]

IT is no sign that religious affections are truly holy and spiritual, or that they are not, that they come with texts of Scripture, remarkably brought to the mind.　　.　　.　　.　　.

What evidence is there that the devil cannot bring texts of Scripture to the mind, and misapply them to deceive persons ?　There seems to be nothing in this which exceeds the power of Satan.　It is no work of such mighty power, to bring sounds or letters to persons' minds, that we have any reason to suppose nothing short of Omnipotence can be sufficient for it. If Satan has power to bring any words or sounds at all to persons' minds, he may have power to bring words contained in the Bible. There is no higher sort of power required in men, to make the sounds which express the words of a text of Scripture than to make the sounds which express the words of an idle story or song. And so the same power in Satan, which is sufficient to renew one of those kinds of sounds in the mind, is sufficient to renew the other: the different signification, which depends wholly on custom, alters not the case, as to ability to make or revive the sounds or letters. Or will any suppose, that texts or Scriptures are such sacred things, that the devil durst not abuse them, nor touch them? In this also they are mistaken. He who was bold enough to lay hold on Christ himself, and carry him hither and thither, into the wilderness, and into a high mountain, and to a pinnacle of the temple, is not afraid to touch the Scripture, and abuse that for his own purpose; as he showed at the same time that he was so bold with Christ, he then brought one Scripture and another, to deceive and tempt him. And if Satan did presume, and was permitted to put Christ himself in mind of texts of Scripture to tempt *him*, what reason have we to determine that he dare not, or will not be permitted, to put wicked men in the mind of texts of Scripture, to tempt and deceive *them?* And if Satan may thus abuse one text of Scripture, so he may another. Its being a very excellent place of Scripture, a comfortable and precious promise, alters not the case, as to his courage or ability. And if he can bring one comfortable text to the mind, so he may a thousand; and may choose out such Scriptures as tend most to serve his purpose; and may heap up Scripture promises, tending, according to the perverse application he makes of them, wonderfully to remove the rising doubts, and to confirm the false joy and confidence of a poor deluded sinner.

We know the devil's instruments, corrupt and heretical teachers, can and do pervert the Scripture, to their own and others' damnation (II. Pet. iii. 16). We see they have the free use of Scripture, in every part of it; there is no text so precious and sacred, but they are permitted to abuse it, to the eternal ruin of multitudes of souls; and there are no weapons they make use of with which they do more execution. And there is no manner of reason to determine, that the devil is not permitted thus to use the Scripture, as well as his instruments. For when the latter do it, they do it as his instruments and servants, and through his instigation and influence; and doubtless he does the same he instigates others to do; the devil's servants do but follow their master, and do the same work that he does himself.

And as the devil can abuse the Scripture, to deceive and destroy men, so may men's own folly and corruptions as well. The sin which is in men, acts like its father. Men's own hearts are deceitful like the devil, and use the same means to deceive.

So that it is evident, that any person may have high affections of hope and joy, arising on occasion of texts of Scripture, yea, precious promises of Scripture coming suddenly and remarkably to their minds, as though they were spoken to them, yea, a great multitude of such texts, following one another in a wonderful manner; and yet all this be no argument that these affections are divine, or that they are any other than the effects of Satan's delusions.

CHARACTER OF DAVID BRAINERD.

[Sermon Preached on the day of Brainerd's Funeral. 1747.]

THUS God sanctified, and made meet for his use, that vessel that He intended to make eminently a vessel of honor in his house, and which he had made of large capacity, having endowed him with very uncommon abilities and gifts of nature. He was a singular instance of a ready invention, natural eloquence, easy flowing expression, sprightly apprehension, quick discerning, and a very strong memory; and yet of a very penetrating genius, close and clear thought, and piercing judgment. He had an exact taste: his understanding was (if I may so express it) of a quick, strong and distinguishing scent.

His learning was very considerable; he had a great taste for learning; and applied himself to his studies in so close a manner when he was at college, that he much injured his health; and was obliged on that account for a while to leave the college, throw by his studies and return home. He was esteemed one that excelled in learning in that society.

He had an extraordinary knowledge of men, as well as things. Had a great insight into human nature, and excelled most that ever I knew in a communicative faculty; he had a peculiar talent at accommodating himself to the capacities, tempers, and circumstances, of those that he would instruct or counsel.

He had extraordinary gifts for the pulpit; I never had opportunity to hear him preach, but have often heard him pray; and I think his manner of addressing himself to God, and expressing himself before him, in that duty, almost inimitable; such (so far as I may judge) as I have very rarely known equalled. He expressed himself with that exact propriety and pertinency, in such significant, weighty, pungent expressions; with that decent appearance of sincerity, reverence, and solemnity, and great distance from all affectation, as forgetting the presence of men, and as being in the immediate presence of a great and holy God, that I have scarcely ever known paralleled. And his manner of preaching, by what I have often heard of it from good judges, was no less excellent; being clear and instructive, natural, nervous, forcible, and moving, and very searching and convincing. He nauseated an affected noisiness, and violent boisterousness in the pulpit; and yet much disrelished a flat, cold delivery, when the subject of discourse, and matter delivered, required affection and earnestness.

Not only had he excellent talents for the study and the pulpit, but also for conversation. He was of a sociable disposition; and was remarkably free, entertaining, and profitable in his ordinary discourse; and had much of a faculty of disputing, defending truth and confuting error.

As he excelled in his judgment and knowledge of things in general, so especially in divinity. He was truly, for one of his standing, an extraordinary divine. But above all, in matters relating to experimental religion. In this I know I have the concurring opinion of some that have had a name for persons of the best judgment. And according to what ability I have to judge of things of this nature, and according to my opportunities, which of late have been very great, I never knew his equal, of his age and standing, for clear, accurate notions of the nature and essence of true religion, and its distinctions from its various false appearances; which I suppose to be owing to these three things meeting together in him;—the strength of his natural genius, and the great opportunities he had of observation of others, in various parts, both white people and Indians, and his own great experience.

His experiences of the holy influences of God's Spirit were not only great at his first conversion, but they were so, in a continued course, from that time forward; as appears by a record, or private journal, he kept of his daily inward exercises, from the time of his conversion until he was disabled by the failing of his strength a few days before his death. The change which he looked upon as his conversion, was not only a great change of the present views, affections, and frame of his mind; but was evidently the beginning of that work of God on his heart which God carried on, in a very wonderful manner, from that time to his dying day. He greatly abhorred the way of such as live on their first work, as though they had now got through their work, and are thenceforward, by degrees, settled in a cold, lifeless, negligent, worldly frame; he had an ill opinion of such persons' religion.

Oh that the things that were seen and heard in this extraordinary person, his holiness, heavenliness, labor and self-denial in life, his so remarkably devoting himself and his all, in heart and practice, to the glory of God, and the wonderful frame of mind manifested, in so steadfast a manner, under the expectation of death, and the pains and agonies that brought it on, may excite in us all, both ministers and people, a due sense of the greatness of the work we have to do in the world, the excellency and amiableness of thorough religion in experience and practice, and the blessedness of the end of such, whose death finishes such a life, and the infinite value of their eternal reward, when absent from the body and present with the Lord; and effectually stir us up to endeavors, that in the way of such a holy life we may at least come to so blessed an end. AMEN.

CONCERNING THE NOTION OF LIBERTY, AND OF MORAL AGENCY.

[*Freedom of the Will.* 1754.]

THE plain and obvious meaning of the words *Freedom* and *Liberty*, in common speech, is *power, opportunity, or advantage, that any one has, to do as he pleases.* Or, in other words, his being free from hindrance or impediment in the way of doing, or conducting in any respect, as he wills. (I say not only doing, but conducting; because a voluntary forbearing to do, sitting still, keeping silence, etc., are instances of persons' conduct, about which Liberty is exercised; though they are not so properly called doing.) And the contrary to Liberty, whatever name we call that by, is a person's being hindered or unable to conduct as he will, or being necessitated to do otherwise.

If this which I have mentioned be the meaning of the word Liberty, in the ordinary use of language; as I trust that none that has ever learned to talk, and is unprejudiced, will deny: then it will follow that in propriety of speech neither Liberty, nor its contrary, can properly be ascribed to any being or thing, but that which has such a faculty, power or property, as is called will. For that which is possessed of no such thing as will, cannot have any power or opportunity of doing according to its will, nor be necessitated to act contrary to its will, nor be restrained from acting agreeably to it. And therefore to talk of Liberty, or the contrary, as belonging to the very will itself, is not to speak good sense; if we judge of sense, and nonsense, by the original and proper signification of words. For the will itself is not an agent that has a will: the power of choosing itself, has not a power of choosing. That which has the power of volition or choice is the man or the soul, and not the power of volition itself. And he that has the Liberty of doing according to his will, is the agent or doer who is possessed of the will; and not the will which he is possessed of. We say with propriety, that a bird let loose has power and Liberty to fly; but not that the bird's power of flying has a power and Liberty of flying. To be free is the property of an agent, who is possessed of powers and faculties, as much as to be cunning, valiant, bountiful, or zealous. But these qualities are the properties of men or persons and not the properties of properties.

There are two things that are contrary to this which is called Liberty in common speech. One is constraint; the same is otherwise called force, compulsion, and coaction; which is a person's being necessitated to do a thing contrary to his will. The other is restraint; which is his being hindered, and not having power to do according to his will. But that which has no will, cannot be the subject of these things. I need say the less on this head, Mr. Locke having set the same thing forth, with so great clearness, in his *Essay on the Human Understanding.*

But one thing more I would observe concerning what is vulgarly called Liberty; namely, that power and opportunity for one to do and conduct as he will, or according to his choice, is all that is meant by it; without taking into the meaning of the word anything of the cause or original of that choice; or at all considering how the person came to have such a volition; whether it was caused by some external motive or internal habitual bias; whether it was determined by some internal antecedent volition, or whether it happened without a cause; whether it was necessarily connected with something foregoing, or not connected. Let the person come by his volition or choice how he will, yet, if he is able, and there is nothing in the way to hinder his pursuing and executing his will, the man is fully and perfectly free, according to the primary and common notion of freedom.

What has been said may be sufficient to show what is meant by Liberty, according to the common notions of mankind, and in the usual and primary acceptation of the word: but the word, as used by Arminians, Pelagians and others, who oppose the Calvinists, has an entirely different signification. These several things belong to their notion of Liberty. 1. That it consists in a self-determining power in the will, or a certain sovereignty the will has over itself, and its own acts, whereby it determines its own volitions; so as not to be dependent, in its determinations, on any cause without itself, nor determined by anything prior to its own acts. 2. Indifference belongs to Liberty in their notion of it, or that the mind, previous to the act of volition, be in equilibrio. 3. Contingence is another thing that belongs and is essential to it; not in the common acceptation of the word, as that has been already explained, but as opposed to all necessity, or any fixed and certain connection with some previous ground or reason of its existence. They suppose the essence of Liberty so much to consist in these things, that unless the will of man be free in this sense, he has no real freedom, how much soever he may be at Liberty to act according to his will.

A moral Agent is a being that is capable of those actions that have a moral quality, and which can properly be denominated good or evil in a moral sense, virtuous or vicious, commendable or faulty. To moral Agency belongs a moral faculty, or sense of moral good and evil, or of such a thing as desert or worthiness, of praise or blame, reward or punishment; and a capacity which an agent has of being influenced in his actions by moral inducements or motives, exhibited to the view of understanding and reason, to engage to a conduct agreeable to the moral faculty.

The sun is very excellent and beneficial in its action and influence on the earth, in warming it, and causing it to bring forth its fruits; but it is not a moral Agent. Its action, though good, is not virtuous or meritorious. Fire that breaks out in a city, and consumes great part of it, is very mischievous in its operation; but is not a moral Agent. What it does is not faulty or sinful, or deserving of any punishment. The brute creatures are not moral Agents. The actions of some of them are very profitable and pleasant; others are very hurtful; yet, seeing they have no moral faculty, or sense of desert, and do not act from choice guided by understanding, or with a capacity of reasoning and reflecting, but only from instinct, and are not capable of being influenced by moral inducements, their actions are not properly sinful or virtuous; nor are they properly the subjects of any such moral treatment for what they do, as moral Agents are for their faults or good deeds.

Here it may be noted, that there is a circumstantial difference between the moral Agency of a ruler and a subject. I call it circumstantial, because it lies only in the difference of moral inducements they are capable of being influenced by, arising from the difference of circumstances. A ruler, acting, in that capacity only, is not capable of being influenced by a moral law, and its sanctions of threatenings and promises, rewards and punishments, as the subject is; though both may be influenced by a knowledge of moral good and evil. And therefore the moral agency of the Supreme Being, who acts only in the capacity of a ruler toward his creatures, and never as a subject, differs in that respect from the moral Agency of created intelligent beings. God's actions, and particularly those which are to be attributed to him as moral governor, are morally good in the highest degree. They are most perfectly holy and righteous; and we must conceive of him as influenced in the highest degree, by that which, above all others, is properly a moral inducement, viz., the moral good which He sees in such and such things: and therefore He is, in the most proper sense, a moral Agent, the source of all moral ability and Agency, the fountain and rule of all virtue and moral good; though by reason of his being supreme over all, it is not possible He should be under the influence of law or command, promises or threatenings, rewards or punishments, counsels or warnings. The essential qualities of a moral

Agent are in God, in the greatest possible perfection; such as understanding, to perceive the difference between moral good and evil; a
capacity of discerning that moral worthiness and demerit, by which some
things are praiseworthy, others deserving of blame and punishment; and
also a capacity of choice, and choice guided by understanding, and a
power of acting according to his choice or pleasure, and being capable
of doing those things which are in the highest sense praiseworthy. And
herein does very much consist that image of God wherein He made man
(which we read of Gen. i. 26, 27, and chapter ix. 6), by which God dis-
tinguishes man from the beasts, viz., in those faculties and principles of
nature, whereby he is capable of moral Agency. Herein very much consists the natural image of God; as his spiritual and moral image, wherein
man was made at first, consisted in that moral excellency, that he was
endowed with.

WHETHER ANY EVENT, OR VOLITION, CAN COME TO PASS WITHOUT A CAUSE.

[From the Same.]

I ASSERT that nothing ever comes to pass without a Cause. What
is self-existent must be from eternity, and must be unchangeable; but
as to all things that begin to be, they are not self-existent, and therefore
must have some foundation of their existence without themselves; that
whatsoever begins to be which before was not, must have a Cause why it
then begins to exist, seems to be the first dictate of the common and natural sense which God hath implanted in the minds of all mankind, and
the main foundation of all our reasonings about the existence of things,
past, present, or to come.

And this dictate of common sense equally respects substances and
modes, or things and the manner and circumstances of things. Thus, if
we see a body which has hitherto been at rest, start out of a state of rest,
and begin to move, we do as naturally and necessarily suppose there is
some Cause or reason of this new mode of existence, as of the existence
of a body itself which had hitherto not existed. And so if a body,
which had hitherto moved in a certain direction, should suddenly change
the direction of its motion; or if it should put off its old figure, and take
a new one; or change its color: the beginning of these new modes is a
new Event, and the mind of mankind necessarily supposes that there is
some Cause or reason of them.

If this grand principle of common sense be taken away, all arguing from
effects to Causes ceaseth, and so all knowledge of any existence, besides

what we have by the most direct and immediate intuition. Particularly all our proof of the being of God ceases : we argue his being from our own being and the being of other things, which we are sensible once were not, but have begun to be ; and from the being of the world, with all its constituent parts, and the manner of their existence ; all which we see plainly are not necessary in their own nature, and so not self-existent, and therefore must have a Cause. But if things, not in themselves necessary, may begin to be without a Cause, all this arguing is vain. . . . .

But if once this grand principle of common sense be given up, that what is not necessary in itself, must have a Cause ; and we begin to maintain, that things may come into existence, and begin to be, which heretofore have not been, of themselves without any Cause ; all our means of ascending in our arguing from the creature to the Creator, and all our evidence of the Being of God, is cut off at one blow. In this case, we cannot prove that there is a God, either from the Being of the world, and the creatures in it, or from the manner of their being, their order, beauty and use. For if things may come into existence without any Cause at all, then they doubtless may without any Cause answerable to the effect. Our minds do alike naturally suppose and determine both these things ; namely, that what begins to be has a Cause, and also that it has a Cause proportionable and agreeable to the effect. The same principle which leads us to determine that there cannot be anything coming to pass without a Cause, leads us to determine that there cannot be more in the effect than in the Cause.

Yea, if once it should be allowed, that things may come to pass without a Cause. we should not only have no proof of the Being of God, but we should be without evidence of the existence of anything whatsoever, but our own immediately present ideas and consciousness. For we have no way to prove any thing else, but by arguing from effects to causes ; from the ideas now immediately in view, we argue other things not immediately in view : from sensations now excited in us, we infer the existence of things without us, as the Causes of these sensations ; and from the existence of these things, we argue other things, which they depend on, as effects on Causes. We infer the past existence of ourselves, or anything else, by memory ; only as we argue that the ideas. which are now in our minds, are the consequences of past ideas and sensations. We immediately perceive nothing else but the ideas which are this moment extant in our minds. We perceive or know other things only by means of these, as necessarily connected with others, and dependent on them. But if things may be without Causes, all this necessary connection and dependence is dissolved, and so all means of our knowledge is gone. If there be no absurdity nor difficulty in supposing one thing to start out of non-existence into being, of itself without a Cause ; then there is no absurdity nor difficulty in supposing the same of millions of millions. For nothing, or no difficulty multiplied, still is nothing, or no difficulty, nothing multiplied by nothing, does not increase the sum.

And indeed, according to the hypothesis I am opposing, of the acts of the Will coming to pass without a Cause, it is the case in fact, that millions of millions of Events are continually coming into existence contingently, without any cause or reason why they do so, all over the world, every day and hour, through all ages. So it is in a constant succession, in every moral agent. This contingency, this efficient nothing, this effectual No Cause, is always ready at hand, to produce this sort of effects, as long as the agent exists, and as often as he has occasion.

If it were so, that things only of one kind, viz., acts of the Will, seemed to come to pass of themselves; but those of this sort in general came into being thus; and it were an event that was continual, and that happened in a course, wherever were capable subjects of such events; this very thing would demonstrate that there was some Cause of them, which made such a difference between this Event and others, and that they did not really happen contingently. For contingence is blind, and does not pick and choose for a particular sort of events. Nothing has no choice. This No Cause, which causes no existence, cannot cause the existence which comes to pass, to be of one particular sort only, distinguished from all others. Thus, that only one sort of matter drops out of the heavens, even water, and that this comes so often, so constantly and plentifully, all over the world. in all ages, shows that there is some Cause or reason of the falling of water out of the heavens; and that something besides mere contingence has a hand in the matter.

If we should suppose nonentity to be about to bring forth; and things were coming into existence, without any Cause or antecedent, on which the existence, or kind, or manner of existence depends; or which could at all determine whether the things should be stones, or stars, or beasts, or angels, or human bodies. or souls, or only some new motion or figure in natural bodies, or some new sensations in animals, or new ideas in the human understanding, or new volitions in the Will; or anything else of all the infinite number of possibles; then certainly it would not be expected, although many millions of millions of things are coming into existence in this manner, all over the face of the earth, that they should all be only of one particular kind, and that it should be thus in all ages, and that this sort of existences should never fail to come to pass where there is room for them, or a subject capable of them, and that constantly whenever there is occasion for them.

If any should imagine, there is something in the sort of Event that renders it possible for it to come into existence without a Cause, and should say, that the free acts of the Will are existences of an exceeding different nature from other things; by reason of which they may come into existence without any previous ground or reason of it, though other things cannot; if they make this objection in good earnest, it would be an evidence of their strangely forgetting themselves; for they would be giving an account of some ground of the existence of a thing, when at the same time they would maintain there is no ground of its existence. Therefore I would observe, that the particular nature of existence, be it ever so diverse from others, can lay no foundation for that thing's coming into existence without a Cause; because to suppose this, would be to suppose the particular nature of existence to be a thing prior to the existence; and so a thing which makes way for existence, with such a circumstance, namely, without a cause or reason of existence. But that which in any respect makes way for a thing's coming into being, or for any manner or circumstance of its first existence, must be prior to the existence. The distinguished nature of the effect, which is something belonging to the effect, cannot have influence backward, to act before it is. The peculiar nature of that thing called volition, can do nothing, can have no influence, while it is not. And afterwards it is too late for its influence; for then the thing has made sure of existence already, without its help.

So that it is indeed as repugnant to reason, to suppose that an act of the Will should come into existence without a Cause, as to suppose the human soul, or an angel, or the globe of the earth, or the whole universe, should come into existence without a Cause. And if once we allow, that such a sort of effect as a Volition may come to pass without a Cause, how do we know but that many other sorts of effects may do so too? It is not the particular kind of effect that makes the absurdity of supposing it has been without a Cause, but something which is common to all things that ever begin to be, viz., that they are not self-existent, or necessary in the nature of things.

THE SECONDARY AND INFERIOR KIND OF BEAUTY.

[*A Dissertation, concerning the Nature of True Virtue. Written,* 1754-58.]

THAT consent, agreement, or union of Being to Being, which has been spoken of, viz., the union or propensity of *minds* to mental or spiritual existence, may be called the highest, and first, or primary beauty that is to be found among things that exist: being the proper and peculiar beauty of spiritual and moral Beings, which are the highest and first part of the universal system, for whose sake all the rest has existence.

Yet there is another inferior, secondary beauty, which is some image of this, and which is not peculiar to spiritual Beings, but is found even in inanimate things; which consists in a mutual consent and agreement of different things in form, manner, quantity, and visible end or design; called by the various names of regularity, order, uniformity, symmetry, proportion, harmony. Such is the mutual agreement of the various sides of a square, or equilateral triangle, or of a regular polygon. Such is, as it were, the mutual consent of the different parts of the periphery of a circle, or surface of a sphere, and of the corresponding parts of an ellipsis. Such is the agreement of the colors, figures, dimensions and distances of the different spots on the chess board. Such is the beauty of the figures on a piece of chintz or brocade. Such is the beautiful proportion of the various parts of a human body, or countenance. And such is the sweet mutual consent and agreement of the various notes of a melodious tune. This is the same that Mr. Hutcheson, in his treatise on beauty, expresses by uniformity in the midst of variety. Which is no other than the consent or agreement of different things, in form, quantity, etc. He observes, that the greater the variety is, in equal uniformity, the greater the beauty. Which is no more than to say, the more there are of different mutually agreeing things, the greater is the beauty. And the reason of that is, because it is more considerable to have many things consent one with another, than a few only.

The beauty which consists in the visible fitness of a thing to its use and unity of design, is not a distinct sort of beauty from this. For it is to be observed, that one thing which contributes to the beauty of the agreement and proportion of various things, is their relation one to another; which connects them, and introduces them together into view and consideration, and whereby one suggests the other to the mind, and the mind is led to compare them, and so to expect and desire agreement. Thus the uniformity of two or more pillars, as they may happen to be found in different places, is not an equal degree of beauty as that uniformity in so many pillars in the corresponding parts of the same building. So means and an intended effect are related one to another. The answerableness of a thing to its use is only the proportion, fitness, and agreeing of a cause or means to a visibly designed effect, and so an effect suggested to the mind by the idea of the means. This kind of beauty is not entirely different from that beauty which there is in fitting a mortise to its tenon. Only when the beauty consists in unity of design, or the adaptedness of a variety of things to promote one intended effect, in which all conspire, as the various parts of an ingenious complicated machine, there is a double beauty, as there is a two-fold agreement and conformity. First, there is the agreement of the various parts to the designed end. Secondly, through this, viz., the designed end or effect, all the various particulars agree one with another, as the general medium of their union, whereby they being united in this third, they thereby are all united one to another.

The reason, or at least one reason why God has made this kind of mutual consent and agreement of things beautiful and grateful to those intelligent Beings that perceive it, probably is, that there is in it some image of the true, spiritual, original beauty which has been spoken of; consisting in Being's consent to Being, or the union of minds or spiritual Beings in a mutual propensity and affection of heart. The other is an image of this, because by that uniformity, diverse things become as it were one, as it is in this cordial union. And it pleases God to observe analogy in his works, as is manifest in fact in innumerable instances; and especially to establish inferior things in an analogy to superior. Thus, in how many instances has he formed brutes in analogy to the nature of mankind? And plants in analogy to animals with respect to the manner of their generation and nutrition. And so he has constituted the external world in an analogy to things in the spiritual world, in numberless instances; as might be shown, if it were necessary, and here were proper place and room for it.—Why such analogy in God's works pleases him, it is not needful now to inquire. It is sufficient that He makes an agreement or consent of different things, in their form, manner, measure, to appear beautiful, because here is some image of a higher kind of agreement and consent of spiritual Beings. It has pleased him to establish a law of nature, by virtue of which the uniformity and mutual correspondence of a beautiful plant, and the respect which the various parts of a regular building seem to have one to another, and their agreement and union, and the consent or concord of the various notes of a melodious tune, should appear beautiful; because therein is some image of the consent of mind, of the different members of a society or system of intelligent Beings sweetly united in a benevolent agreement of heart—And here, by the way, I would further observe, probably it is with regard to this image or resemblance, which secondary beauty has of true spiritual beauty, that God has so constituted nature, that the presenting of this inferior beauty, especially in those kinds of it which have the greatest resemblance of the primary beauty, as the harmony of sounds, and the beauties of nature, have a tendency to assist those whose hearts are under the influence of a truly virtuous temper, to dispose them to the exercises of divine love, and enliven in them a sense of spiritual beauty.   .   .

This secondary kind of beauty, consisting in uniformity and proportion, not only takes place in material and external things, but also in things immaterial; and is, in very many things, plain and sensible in the latter, as well as the former; and when it is so, there is no reason why it should not be grateful to them that behold it, in these as well as the other, by virtue of the same sense, or the same determination of mind to be gratified with uniformity and proportion. If uniformity and proportion be the things that affect, and appear agreeable to, this sense of beauty, then why should not uniformity and proportion affect the same sense in immaterial things as well as material, if there be equal capacity of discerning it in both? And indeed *more* in spiritual things (*cœteris paribus*), as these are more important than things merely external and material.

This is not only reasonable to be supposed, but it is evident in fact, in numberless instances. There is a beauty of order in society, besides what consists in benevolence, or can be referred to it, which is of the secondary kind. As, when the different members of society have all their appointed office, place and station, according to their several capacities and talents, and every one keeps his place, and continues in his proper business. In this there is a beauty, not of a different kind from the regularity of a beautiful building, or piece of skilful architecture, where the strong pillars are set in their proper place, the pilasters in a place fit for them, the square pieces of marble in the pavement, in a place suitable for them, the panels in the walls and partitions in their proper places, the cornices in places proper for them, etc. As the agreement of a variety in one common design, of the parts of a building, or complicated machine, is one instance of that regularity, which belongs to the secondary kind of beauty, so there is the same kind of beauty in immaterial things, in what is called *wisdom*, consisting in the united tendency of thoughts, ideas, and particular volitions, to one general purpose: which is a distinct thing from the goodness of that general purpose, as being useful and benevolent.

So there is a beauty in the virtue called *justice*, which consists in the agreement of different things, that have relation to one another, in nature, manner and measure: and therefore is the very same sort of beauty with that uniformity and proportion, which is observable in those external and material things that are esteemed beautiful. There is a natural agreement and adaptedness of things that have relation one to another, and a harmonious corresponding of one thing to another: that he who from his will *does* evil to others, should *receive* evil from the will of others, or from the will of him or them whose business it is to take care of the injured, and to act in their behalf: and that he should suffer evil in *proportion* to the evil of his doings. Things are in natural regularity and mutual agreement, not in a metaphorical but literal sense, when he whose heart opposes the general system, should have the hearts of that system, or the heart of the head and ruler of the system, against him: and that in consequence, he should receive evil in proportion to the evil tendency of the opposition of his heart.—So, there is a like agreement in nature and measure, when he that loves, has the proper returns of love, when he that from his heart promotes the good of another, has his good promoted by the other; as there is a kind of justice in a becoming gratitude.   .   .   .   .

From all that has been observed concerning this secondary kind of beauty, it appears that that disposition or sense of the mind, which consists in determination of mind to approve and be pleased with this beauty, considered simply and by itself, has nothing of the nature of true virtue, and is entirely a different thing from a truly virtuous taste. For it has been shown, that this kind of beauty is entirely diverse from the beauty of true virtue, whether it takes place in material or immaterial things. And therefore it will follow, that a taste of this kind of beauty is entirely a different thing from a taste of true virtue. Who will affirm, that a disposition to approve of the harmony of good music, or the beauty of a square, or equilateral triangle, is the same with true holiness, or a truly virtuous disposition of mind! It is a relish of uniformity and proportion, that determines the mind to approve these things. And if this be all, there is no need of anything higher, or of anything in any respect diverse, to determine the mind to approve and be pleased with equal uniformity and proportion among spiritual things which are equally discerned. It is virtuous to love true virtue, as that denotes an agreement of the heart with virtue. But it argues no virtue, for the heart to be pleased with that which is entirely distinct from it.

Though it be true, there is some analogy in it to spiritual and virtuous beauty, as much as material things can have analogy to things spiritual (on which they can have no more than a shadow), yet, as has been observed, men do not approve it because of any such analogy perceived.

And not only reason, but experience plainly shows, that men's approbation of this sort of beauty, does not spring from any virtuous temper, and has no connection with virtue. For, otherwise, men's delight in the beauty of squares, and cubes, and regular polygons, in the regularity of buildings, and the beautiful figures in a piece of embroidery, would increase in proportion to men's virtue; and would be raised to a great height in some eminently virtuous or holy men; but would be almost wholly lost in some others that are very vicious and lewd. It is evident in fact, that a relish of these things does not depend on general benevolence, or any benevolence at all to any Being whatsoever, any more than a man's loving the taste of honey, or his being pleased with the smell of a rose. A taste of this inferior beauty in things immaterial, is one thing which has been mistaken by some moralists, for a true virtuous principle, implanted naturally in the hearts of all mankind.

John Callender.

BORN in Boston, Mass., 1706.   Minister at Newport, R. I.   DIED, 1748.

LIBERTY OF CONSCIENCE IN RHODE ISLAND.

[An Historical Discourse. 1739.]

IT is a pity we cannot entirely confute all the opprobrious things which some have written of some of the inhabitants. I am satisfied a great many of them were wholly groundless, many others very much aggravated and misrepresented, and some things made to be reproaches which in reality were praiseworthy.

I take it to have been no dishonor to the colony, that Christians of every denomination were suffered to lead quiet and peaceable lives, without any fines or punishments for their speculative opinions, or for using those external forms of worship they believed God had appointed, and would accept. Bigots may call this confusion and disorder, and it may be so, according to their poor worldly notions of religion and the kingdom of Christ. But the pretended order of human authority assuming the place and prerogatives of Jesus Christ, and trampling on the consciences of his subjects, is, as Mr. R. Williams most justly calls it, "monstrous disorder."

Though it be very certain, that a public worship of God is very necessary, even to civilize mankind, who would be likely to lose all sense of religion without it ; yet it will not follow, that the civil magistrate, as such, has authority to appoint the rites of worship, and constrain all his subjects to use them, much less to punish them for using any other. What has been forever the consequences of his pretending to such authority, and using his power to support it ? What glory doth it bring to God, and what good can it do to men, to force them to attend a worship they disapprove ? It can only make them hypocrites, and God abhors such worshippers.

Notwithstanding our constitution left every one to his own liberty, and his conscience ; and notwithstanding the variety of opinions that were entertained, and notwithstanding some may have contracted too great an indifference to any social worship, yet I am well assured there scarce ever was a time, the hundred years past, in which there was not a weekly public worship of God, attended by Christians, on this island and in the other first towns of the colony.

It is no ways unlikely, some odd and whimsical opinions may have been broached ; the liberty enjoined here would tempt persons distressed for their opinions in the neighboring governments, to retire to this colony as an asylum. It is no ways unlikely, that some persons of a very different genius and spirit from the first settlers, might intrude themselves, and use this liberty as an occasion to the flesh ; but the first set of men who came here, were a pious generation, men of virtue and godliness, notwithstanding their tincture of enthusiasm, which was not peculiar to them, and notwithstanding their peculiar opinions of justification, and the nature and rights of the Christian church. They had not so many great and wise men among them, perhaps, as were in some of the other colonies ; but their whole number was very small, in comparison with the other colonies. Nevertheless, they had some very considerable men, and of superior merit. It is true, likewise, their form of government was too feeble; their first Patent left them without sufficient authority in their civil officers, to check any popular humors ; but yet, they did, and that as early as the Massachusetts colony, form a body of good laws, by which all vice, and every immorality, was discouraged or punished. And throughout the whole history of the island and colony, there is manifestly an aim and endeavor to prevent or suppress all disorders and immoralities, and to promote universal peace, virtue, godliness, and charity. . . . .

It must be a mean, contracted way of thinking, to confine the favor of God and the power of godliness to one set of speculative opinions, or any particular external forms of worship. How hard must it be, to imagine all other Christians but ourselves must be formal and hypocritical, and destitute of the grace of God, because their education or capacity differs from ours, or that God has given them more or less light than to us, though we cannot deny, they give the proper evidence of their fearing God, by their working righteousness ; and show their love to him, by keeping what they understand He has commanded ; and though their faith in Christ Jesus purifies their hearts, and works by love, and over-comes the world, it would be hard to show why liberty of conscience, mutual forbearance and good will, why brotherly kindness and charity, is not as good a centre of unity, as a constrained uniformity in external ceremonies, or a forced subscription to ambiguous articles. Experience has dearly convinced the world, that unanimity in judgment and affec-tion cannot be secured by penal laws. Who can tell why the unity of the spirit in the bonds of peace, is not enough for Christians to aim at ? And who can assign a reason why they may not love one another, though abounding in their own several senses ? And why, if they live in peace, the God of love and peace may not be with them ?

Indulgence to tender consciences might be a reproach to the colony an hundred years ago, but a better way of thinking prevails in the Prot-estant part of the Christian church at present. It is now a glory to the colony, to have avowed such sentiments so long ago, while blindness in this article happened in other places, and to have led the way as an example to others, and to have first put the theory into practice.

Liberty of conscience is more fully established and enjoyed now, in the other New-English colonies ; and our mother kingdom grants a legal toleration to all peaceable and conscientious dissenters from the parliamentary establishment. Greater light breaking into the world and the church, and especially all parties by turns experiencing and complaining aloud of the hardships of constraint, they are come to allow as reasonable to all others, what they want and challenge for themselves. And there is no other bottom but this to rest upon, to leave others the liberty we should desire ourselves, the liberty wherewith Christ hath made them . free. This is doing as we would be done by, the grand rule of justice and equity ; this is leaving the government of the church to Jesus Christ, the King and head over all things, and suffering his subjects to obey and serve him.

William Stephens.

BORN on the Isle of Wight, 1671.   President of the Georgia Colony.   DIED in Georgia, 1753.

POLITICS AND RACING IN COLONIAL GEORGIA.

[A Journal of the Proceedings in Georgia. 1742.]

AN odd humor being lately sprung up among some of our people for horse-racing, several days successively, it gave me a jealousy of some farther latent design, when I observed it was promoted by that desperate crew, whose whole study and employment was to disturb the quiet of the place, and keep the spirits of the well-meaning in a continual flutter.

The horses were ordinarily mean and low-priced, such as are mostly adapted to common uses, for hire, etc. ; the riders also ready, for payment in drink, to contribute to the diversion. The race a little more than a quarter of a mile, from the gate of the public garden, to the midst of Johnson's Square. This answered the purpose of the betters (Dr. Tailfer and his associates) very well, and occasioned a gathering together of a number of people, idling ; among whom, a great number of children, in the way of danger (as I thought).

After the race was over, it was very remarkable that, instead of going to Jenkins's, Tailfer directed the bets to be spent at another public house ; for this reason only, as I could find ; because he could there find more people to talk to, than at their club ; several not scrupling to go here, who would have thought it a scandal on themselves to be seen in their company at the usual place of their meeting.

Seeing matters thus carried on, I had the curiosity to try if we could not penetrate farther into what they were doing. Wherefore, Mr. Jones and I went in the evening to the same house (Mr. Parker being out of town at his plantation) and, taking a little room adjoining to this assembly, we called for a glass of wine, sitting to observe what passed; where we soon discovered what I guessed to be their business, and could hear distinctly their prolocutor displaying his parts most vehemently to his audience, in a long harangue, to show how grievously ill-used this poor colony had been, for a great while past, through the arbitrary proceedings of those who had the government of it: and now at last, after all, they could imagine, that people were to be sweetened by some trifling amendments which they thought fit to make, in relation to the inheritance of their lands. But he would make it appear it was the basest tenure in Christendom; and that it was not in the power of any man living to be safe in what he held, it being liable to such a multitude of forfeitures, which the grantors would, at their pleasure, take advantage of. But he hoped in a few months to see a new leaf turned over, and that justice would be done by a superior power; and as for those tools who worked under them here (meaning, without doubt, such as had the execution of the Trust's commands) it was in vain for them to conceal their instructions; for all must now very soon come to light, etc., with abundance more such like ribaldry, too long to dwell upon here; all tending to inflame his hearers, and excite disturbances.

I could not find, however, with all this connivance, that any person of good character had joined their company; only two or three loose, idle fellows were got among them, who had more regard for their share of drink in the wagers lost, than to the doctor's eloquence. But the staunch members of the club stuck together, as at other times. After about an hour's stay, my companion having no longer patience to bear such roasting among others, we walked off, and left them to make what they pleased of it.

THE OLD GOVERNOR'S SORROW.

[A Letter to his Son in England. Written from Savannah, Ga., Sept. 20, 1740.]

DEAR SON: I received yours of the 25th of April, intimating that the mournful event was come to pass, which a former letter bade me expect, of the final separation of your mother from us all; which has made such an impression, as words cannot utter, on the weakness of a man already pressed down with sorrow, troubles, and the infirmities of age. Endeavoring to recollect what little faculty of reason I had left, during that pungent grief which oppresses my heart, I remembered it was my duty to lay my hand upon my mouth; and without repining to improve the short time I have left, that I may make sure of entering that place of rest, where I may find her a saint; though from me so many years by the divine permission, for my chastisement and better instruction. To what end is grief? Or what does lamentation avail? Nevertheless 'tis a debt which nature demands, and tears are now the only token of that affection which all the crosses in life could never extinguish.

When I return my thoughts towards her offspring, there also sorrow overwhelms me; many of them toiling in an unkind world, and hardly attaining to a sufficient competency of living with comfort; and here you, to whom I am writing, stand first in my thoughts, who have partaken in a large measure of the bitter draught, whereof the dregs, I fear, yet remain to my share.

More and more anxious do I grow to learn how it fares with all that are left of my family; who now, I fear, are become dispersed, without any certain place of resort, where to meet sometimes, and take council together how best to withstand all adversities. Pray let me have the relief my heart stands in need of, in this particular more especially.

Before I shut up, as I am left here for a short while, who (from a miserable inability to do any good among you) scarce deserve the name of a father; fain would I offer somewhat of advice, by what means your future attainment to the most perfect happiness in this life, is to be sought; and, most undoubtedly, nothing can so well conduce to it, as unity among yourselves, and keeping alive that sincere affection one towards another, which I ever thought (and it has been one of the most comfortable thoughts in my life) was subsisting in the heart of each of you. 'Tis this divine remedy that will cure all the anguish which arises from the bitter crosses in this life; sticking together in all conflicts of adversity, when a threefold cord is not easily broken; lovingly assisting, *but not depending upon,* one another; and what can hurt you? Others may attain to grandeur and a richer state of life; but what harm does that do you? You'll surely find peace of mind here, and happiness, beyond the power of devils to take from you, hereafter.

Tell them all that their poor, aged father entreats them, by the tender mercies of Christ, to embrace this his most ardent advice, the last of the sort I may ever give; and recommending you all to the protection of the good God, who is the Fountain of Love, I remain,

Your very affectionate father,

Will. Stephens.

Charles Chauncy.

Born in Boston, Mass., 1705.   Died there, 1787.

SOME ODDITIES OF BELIEF.

[*Seasonable Thoughts on the State of Religion in New-England.* 1743.]

THE way in which these fears have been excited, in many places is not, in my opinion, the best evidence in favor of them.   People have been too much applied to, as though the preacher rather aimed at putting their passions into a ferment, than filling them with such a reasonable solicitude as is the effect of a just exhibition of the truths of God to their understandings.   I have myself been present, when an air of seriousness reigned visibly through a whole congregation.   They were all silence and attention, having their eye fastened on the minister, as though they would catch every word that came from his mouth.   And yet, because they did not cry out or swoon away, they were upbraided with their hardness of heart and ranked among those who were sermon-proof, gospel-glutted; and every topic made use of, with all the voice and action the speaker was master of, to bring forward a general shriek in the assembly.   Nay, in order to give the people a plain intimation of what he wanted, this same preacher sometimes told them of the wonderful effects wrought by the sermon he was then preaching; how in such a congregation, they were all melted and dissolved, and in another so overpowered, that they could not help screaming out or falling down, as though they had been struck dead.   Nay, one of the preachers in this new way, was so open some months ago, as in plain words to call upon the people to cry out, and plead with them to do so.   This he did three several times in one sermon, and had upon it so many loud cries.   And 'tis too well known to need much to be said upon it, that the gentlemen, whose preaching has been most remarkably accompanied with these extraordinaries, not only use in their addresses to the people, all the terrible words they can get together, but in such a manner, as naturally tends to put weaker minds out of possession of themselves.   A friend in the country, in a letter to me upon these matters, expresses himself in these words, " Under the preaching and exhortations of these itinerants and exhorters (the manner of which is frequently very boisterous and shocking, and adapted to the best of their skill to alarm and surprise the imagination and passions), it is no unusual thing for persons to be plunged into the utmost anxiety and distress, which is often attended with a trembling of the body, fainting, falling down, etc.   The preacher now frequently grows more tempestuous, and dreadful in his manner of address and seems to endeavor all he can to increase, and spread the rising consternation, and terror of their souls : which, by this means, is sometimes spread over a great part of an assembly in a few minutes from its first appearance. I have seen the "struck" (as they are called) and distressed brought together, from the several parts of the assembly, into the square body by themselves, and two or three persons at work upon them at once, smiting, stamping and crying out to them with a mighty voice, in the most terrible manner and language ;—the poor creatures fainting, screeching and bitterly crying out under them. You may easily think what terrors of imagination, distraction of passions, and perplexity of thoughts they endured. I was last summer at an evening lecture at a neighboring parish, at which one of the most famous preachers in the new method carried on. He had entered but a little way in his sermon (which was delivered in a manner sufficiently terrible) when there began to be some commotion among the young women. This inspired him with new life. He lifted up his voice like a trumpet, plentifully poured down terrors upon them. About half a score of young women were presently thrown into violent hysteric fits. I carefully observed them. When he grew calm and moderate in his manner, though the things delivered were equally awakening, they by degrees grew calm and still ; when he again assumed the terrible and spake like thunder, the like violent strugglings immediately returned upon them from time to time. Sometimes he put a mighty emphasis upon little unmeaning words and delivered a sentence of no importance with a mighty energy, yet the sensible effect was as great as when the most awful truth was brought to view." This account may be relied on. For it is given by one capable of making observation, and who bears as unblemished a character as most ministers in the country.

Agreeable whereto is the account we have printed in the Boston Post-Boy ; in which the writer, speaking of the itinerant preachers, among other things, observes : " Their main design in preaching seems not so much to inform men's judgments, as to terrify and affright their imagination ; by awful words and frightful representations to set the congregation into hideous shrieks and out-cries. And to this end in every place where they come, they represent that God is doing extraordinary things in other places, and that they are some of the last hardened wretches that stand out ; that this is the last call that ever they are likely to have ; that they are now hanging over the pit of destruction, and just ready this moment to fall into it ; that hell-fire now flashes in their faces ; and that the devil now stands ready to seize upon them, and carry them to hell : and they will oftentimes repeat the awful words, ' damned ! ' ' damned ! ' ' damned ! ' three or four times over."

It is well known, no preacher in the new way has been more noted for his instrumentality in producing these shriekings and faintings and trem-

Charles Chauncy

blings, than the Rev. Mr. James Davenport of Southhold; and yet, one of the ministers of this town (who has always been a great friend to that which he esteemed the good work of God going on in the land) having been, one night, a witness to this inexpressible management among the people, and the terrible effects consequent thereupon in their screaming and crying out, and the like, thought himself obliged in conscience to go to him the next day, and declare against such a method of acting : And accordingly went, and told him to his face (as he himself informed me) that in the appearance of the last night, he was persuaded, there was no hand of the spirit of God ; and that it was no other than might have been expected, if a man raving mad from Bedlam had gone among the people, and behaved as he had done. And one of the charges exhibited and proved against this Mr. Davenport, when brought before the General Assembly of Connecticut, was, " That he endeavored by unwarrantable means to terrify, and affect his hearers." And that,

1. " By pretending some extraordinary discovery and assurance of the very near approach of the end of the world ; and that though he did not assign the very day, yet that he then lately had it clearly opened to him and strongly impressed upon his mind, that in a very short time all these things would be involved in devouring flames." (N. B. This same impression, he told the people at Boston, he had lately had upon his mind, and was as sure the day of judgment was at the door, as of the things he then saw with his eyes ; and made use of this accordingly, as an argument to work upon their passions.)

2. " By an indecent and affected imitation of the agony and passion of our blessed Saviour ; and also by voice and gesture, of the surprise, horror, and amazement, of persons supposed to be sentenced to eternal misery, and,

3. " By a too peremptory and unconditioned denouncing damnation against such of his auditory, as he looked upon as opposers ; vehemently crying out, that he saw hell-flames flashing in their faces, and they were now ! now ! dropping down to hell ! And also added, Lord thou knowest, that there are many in that gallery, and in these seats, that are now dropping down to hell ! "

An account of Mr. Davenport's preaching, not altogether unlike this, a gentleman in Connecticut wrote to one of the ministers in this town, upon his own knowledge, in these words : " At length he turned his discourse to others, and with the utmost strength of his lungs addressed himself to the congregation, under these and such like expressions, viz.: ' You poor unconverted creatures, in the seats, in the pews, in the galleries, I wonder you don't drop into hell ! It would not surprise me, I should not wonder at it, if I should see you drop down now, this minute, into hell. You Pharisees, hypocrites, now, now, now, you are going right into the bottom of hell. I wonder you don't drop into hell by scores, and hundreds,' etc. And in this terrible manner he ended the sermon." 'Tis then added: "After a short prayer, he called for all the distressed persons (which were near twenty) into the foremost seats. Then he came out of the pulpit, and stripped off his upper garments, and got up into the seats, and leaped up and down for some time, and clapped his hands, and cried out in those words: 'The war goes on, the fight goes on, the devil goes down, the devil goes down!' and then betook himself to stamping and screaming most dreadfully."

And what is it more than might be expected, to see people so affrightened as to fall into shrieks and fits, under such methods as these? Especially when they have first been possessed of the notion that the persons who make use of them are men of God in an extraordinary sense; as being sent immediately, as it were, to deliver his messages to them. The mind is now prepared to receive almost any impression from this kind of persons; and it is no wonder if, by their terrifying voice and action, people are thrown into agitations and convulsions.

I doubt not but the Divine Spirit often accompanies the preached Word, so as that, by his influence, sinners are awakened to a sense of sin, and filled with deep distress of soul. But the blessed Spirit must not, at random, be made the author of all those surprises, operating in strange effects upon the body, which may be seen among people. They may be produced other ways; yea, I trust, that has been already said, which makes it evident they have actually been produced, even by the wild and extravagant conduct of some overheated preachers.

CLERICAL EPITHETS IN THE EIGHTEENTH CENTURY.

[*From the Same.*]

A SURPRISING instance of this, we have in Mr. Tennent, notwithstanding his character by Mr. Whitefield, as a mighty charitable man. Perhaps there cannot be produced, out of any author, a greater number of more slanderous names than he has freely bestowed upon the body of the clergy of this generation. I shall here present the reader with a list of them, as they have been collected out of his sermon at Nottingham, and published by the Synod at Philadelphia. They are therein represented as hirelings; caterpillars; letter-learned-Pharisees; men that have the craft of foxes, and the cruelty of wolves; plastered hypocrites; varlets; the seed of the serpent; foolish builders, whom the devil drives into the ministry; dry nurses; dead dogs that cannot bark; blind men;

dead men; men possessed with the devil; rebels and enemies to God; guides that are stone-blind, and stone-dead; children of Satan, that, like their father, may do good to men's souls by chance-medley; daubers with untempered mortar; moral negroes; salt without savor; that stink in the nostrils of God and man; Judases, whose chief desire is to finger the penny, and to carry the bag; murderous hypocrites, that are to take care less they feel the force of a halter in this world, or an aggravated damnation in the next; subtle selfish hypocrites, that would not let one honest man come into the ministry if they could help it; swarms of locusts, crowds of Pharisees, that have as coveteously, as cruelly, crept into the ministry, in this adulterous generation, who as nearly resemble the character given of the old Pharisees, as one crow's egg does another, whose hearers are as blind as moles, and dead as stones; successors of Nicodemus; blind leaders of the blind; formalists; dead drones; sons of Sceva, with a fine long string of prayers; false apostles; deceitful workers, ministers of Satan, etc.

James Ralph.

BORN, probably, in Philadelphia, Penn.   DIED at Chiswick, England, 1762.

THE PRINCE'S VISION.

[Zeuma, or the Love of Liberty. 1729.]

ONCE, as with ardent zeal he urged the chase,
    And pressed, with matchless swiftness, to secure
His frighted prey, through the thick wood, from far
He spied, low bending o'er the limpid stream,
An aged hermit; who seemed wrapped in thought
And solitary muse; behind him, arched
By nature in the hollow rock, appeared
A gloomy cave, o'ergrown with moss, his calm
Abode; above, with difficult ascent,
Arose the hill, with vivid verdure crowned;
Around, the forest spread its grateful shade,
And gently murmured to the gale; beneath,
Spontaneous flowers adorned the grassy turf,
And sweetened every breeze: long gazed the king
On the enchanting scene, and wondered much
It had till then escaped his haunt; when, waked
By his approaching step, the father rose,
And with meek reverence thus began: "'Tis not,
Great prince, by accident you've strayed to this
Sequestered place, but by divine decree;

That you may know what instant dangers threat
Your rule, what miseries your realms;
That no surprise enervate your resolves
When war alarms you to the field; no dread
Of stranger nations, or unusual arms
Confuse the combat, and in foul retreat
Disperse your routed squadrons o'er the plain."
He said, and led him, by a winding way,
To the high brow of that delightful hill,
And bid him view the prospect round. He looked,
And lo! the whole world's globe seemed stretched along
Before his view, so far the landscape reached,
So many objects crowded on the eye;
On this side cities stand, and forests wave,
Green fields extend, and gentle rivers glide;
O'erhanging precipices frown, and hills
Ascend on high: on this the white sea foams,
And on the nearer shores, with speedy roll,
Breaks wide its hasty billows. Zeuma starts
At the surprising roar, yet still intent,
Beholds the restless wave, when, new and strange!
High tossing on the angry surge appear
Vast floating piles, that with capacious wings
Collect the breathing gale, and by degrees
Approach the strand; with thundering voice discharge
Huge streams of ruddy flame, in cloudy smoke
Involved, and fright the nations round. Again
The monarch starts, astonished at the noise,
While, down their steepy sides, descend a throng
Of bearded men, of foreign look and mien;
That brightened o'er the plain with shining arms,
And all the pomp of war. To them succeeds
An herd of creatures, fierce and active, trained
To battle, and the din of arms; on which
The warriors mounting, all proceed, in firm
And regular array, across the field;
Then sound a charge; and o'er the tranquil glebe
Let loose destruction, and with slaughter glut
The sword; with dire oppressive force, and stern
Dominion fix their barbarous rule, and lord
It o'er the groaning tribes. With horror struck,
Sad Zeuma overlooked the scene, and mourned
The dire event: when thus the hoary sage
His lore renewed. "These are the foes that now
Are marching to invade your land; and such
The ills that must afflict your tribes; see o'er
Yon ridge of hills, contemning all the force
Of freezing cold, and wintry gales, they pass
Unwearied with the toil: then haste away,
Alarm your people, and with princely care

Draw all your squadrons to the field. If aught
Of doubt yet hangs upon your mind,
Again survey the landscape, and believe
My mission from above." He looked and all
The illusive prospect vanished from the view,
And naught remained, but one vast length of wood,
That murmuring bowed before the wanton gale.
   So, where the setting sun, with upward ray
Adorns the evening clouds in fleecy gold,
And purple deeply dyed, the attentive eye,
With wonder, views a maze of objects dawn
In bright confusion o'er the blue sky's edge,
And with a round of never-ceasing change
Perplex the doubtful scene, till night's deep shade,
Ascending swiftly, darkens o'er the heavens,
And in gray vapors sweeps the whole away.

THE GRIEFS OF AUTHORS.

[*The Case of Authors by Profession or Trade Stated.* 1758.]

THERE is hardly a page in the annals of the world which does not seem to show, that Wit and Money have been always at war, and always treated one another with reciprocal contempt.

Perhaps for this only reason, that the man of money could acquire everything but ideas, and the man of wits—ideas could never acquire him money.

But, whatever the cause may be, such is the fact; and, as if the bulk of mankind derived some kind of gratification from the quarrel, they have each in his way contributed all they could to render it perpetual.

Thus, a man may plead for money, prescribe or quack for money, preach and pray for money, marry for money, fight for money, do anything within the law for money, provided the expedient answers, without any the least imputation.

But if he writes like one inspired from heaven, and writes for money, the man of touch, in the right of Midas his great ancestor, enters his caveat against him as a man of taste; declares the two provinces to be incompatible; that he who aims at praise ought to be starved; and that there ought to be so much drawback upon character for every acquisition in coin. .   .   .   .

And yet the art of writing is as much an art, as the art of painting or the art of war. The pen, as a tool, is of as much importance, at least, as the pencil; and, as a weapon offensive or defensive, has its power, and can do some sort of execution, as well as a sword. .   .   .   .

Supposing the writer by trade and the volunteer to have equal abilities and equal accomplishments, the former, as the current of the times now sets, has the best chance to be the best writer of the two.

And first, I make a difference in times, for this reason,—Bacon, etc., were always in action; and, when out of place, had always the pen in their hands; consequently, were habitual writers, or possessed of all the advantages that a habit of writing could give them.

But the volunteer-writers of our times are holiday-writers indeed. That is to say,—they write just enough to show they can read, and, having so done, throw away the pen. Whereas, by the very malice of his stars, the writer by trade is forever obliged to write on; and thereby obtains that mastery in matter, method, style and manner, which is hardly to be obtained in any other way.

Nathaniel Ames.

BORN in Bridgewater, Mass., 1708.   DIED at Dedham, Mass., 1764.

THE WAKING OF THE SUN.

[An Astronomical Diary, or an Almanac for the Year of our Lord Christ, 1739.]

THE winds, disturbed, with horrid murmurs rise,
    And mix the foamy billows with the skies;
The earth, as dead, no fruit nor comfort yields,
Wrinkled and fled 's the beauty of the fields:
But when proud Aries ushers in the spring,
And Sol returns to comfort us again,

The earth revives, and clothes herself with green,
And rich embroideries on the meads are seen.
His gentle rays Orion's bands despoil;
And genial warmth makes jocund Nature smile,
Unlocks the virgin bosom of the flowers,
And bread and wine distil in April showers.

The winged musicians welcome him with notes,
As Orpheus' lyre were tuned in their throats,
So charmed are we their harmony to hear,
That all our very soul gets in the ear.
When for repose he yields to shady night,
And in his ebon box locks up the light;

And darkness with her sable mantle covers,
Sweet stolen sports of joyful meeting lovers;
His starry parliament, those twinkling fires,
That sit in council whilst their Lord retires,

Adorn the ample canopy with light,
And sparkle on the gloomy brow of night.

Ere this bright prince uplifts his golden head,
From the soft pillow of his sea-green bed,
Aurora in her blooming splendor dressed,
Comes blushing from her chamber in the east;
Her rosy hand the dusky cloud adorns,
That Iris' painted bow she almost scorns.

Enfringed with gold, and rich embroideries laid;
Whence mingling lights reflect a beauteous shade.
All this refulgent glory o'er his head
Prepared against, he 's pleased to quit his bed.
His pale faced queen, who wore his silver-light
And handed down his glories all the night,

When he comes forth, declares her social dread,
And at his glorious presence hides her head.
The lesser orbs, that nightly set and rise,
Yield up their light when he ascends the skies.
Nor needs their light, with glory all his own,
Rides through the heavens unrivalled on his throne.

Meanwhile his eye, our rolling world surveys,
And gilds its mountains with his golden rays,
Fattening with grass and vines each fruitful vale,
To feed the brute, and cheerful man regale.
Expels the horrors of the dreary night,
Gladdening the dumpish soul with beamy light,
And courts with beauteous objects the admiring sight.

He clothes material nature with his rays;
Thus blest our hemisphere, the whilst he stays,
Until the proud, ambitious, envious West,
Too eager to enjoy this princely guest,
Calls him to bed; where, ravished from our sight,
He leaves us to the solemn frowns of night.

AN ESSAY UPON THE MICROSCOPE.

[Almanac for 1744.]

ARTIFICER, go make a watch,
        In which no seeming imperfection lurks,
Whose wheels with time exact do onward roll,
And one small spring maintains the motion of the whole,
        'Tis all an artless homely botch
Compared with the least of Nature's works.

If through an optic glass
You view a spire of grass
That in the road is trod,
With admiration you may gaze
On veins that branch a thousand ways,
In nice proportion wrought,
Which truly to the assisted eyes are brought,
That he who is not void of common sense
Or filled with daring impudence,
Must own its maker truly to be God.
Pray let your brethren, men,
Use but the optic glass again,
Thy rarest piece to scan;
In thy so well contrived machine,
Those boasted beauties that are seen
After thou hast laid the hammer by,
And done thy best to cheat the naked eye,
We view such large unsightly flaws
Not marked by just proportion's laws
Which shows thou wert a clumsy fingered man.
Urania's sons who view the sky,
Erect long tubes to assist the eye;
May we believe the intelligence they give,
They tell us many a star
That we behold is bigger far
Than the small world on which we live.
These massy globes their maker's skill display,
But the minutest creatures do their part,
The grovelling worm that under foot is trod
And smallest mite proclaims a God:
And butterflies as well as they,
The feathers on whose painted wings
Outdo the ornaments of kings
And all their costly workmanship of art.
Behold! ye whalers who go forth,
Coasting along the icy north
Under the feeble influence of day,
Where huge leviathan does play;
'Gainst whose impenetrable sides the billows roar
Foaming and broke as from some rocky shore;
Tell me, brave lads, tell me when you
The unwieldy tumblings of that watery monarch view,
When all your darts, and strength, and numbers fail,
When with the sportive glances of his tail,
Keen as a knife he cuts in twain,
Or oars, or boats, or men,—
Do not your brethren then,
When any of their crew are slain,
Stand off awhile and gaze,
With wonder and with vast amaze ?

This optic glass creates a thought in me,
As wonderful as what you see:
Being not deceived, nor mad, nor frantic,
But with my eyes do really view,
    Crossing their wide Atlantic
Of but a drop of vinegar or two,
Ten thousand little fish, and here and there a whale,
      Whose bulky size
        By far outvies
    All other tribes that therein sail,
With more perhaps invisible to sight,
Whose numerous species fall below,
What any glass could ever show;
Small as the beams of light.
At this amazed, Oh! wonderful, said I,
Who made the earth, who rules the sky,
    When He his own idea first surveyed,
    Before his beauteous works were made,
    Then formed the wondrous plan,
    And took an atom for a space
    To minute down the universe.
      Both things inert,
      Things animate,
Our rolling world, and every lofty sphere,
    The unerring hand divine
    In characters immensely fine,
Most truly hath delineated there:
There all his works in true proportion stand.

A PROPHECY FOR NORTH AMERICA.

[*Almanac for* 1758.]

THIRDLY, of the future state of North America.—Here we find a vast stock of proper materials for the art and ingenuity of man to work upon:—Treasures of immense worth; concealed from the poor ignorant aboriginal natives! The curious have observed that the progress of human literature (like the sun) is from the east to the west; thus has it travelled through Asia and Europe, and now is arrived at the eastern shore of America.

As the celestial light of the Gospel was directed here by the finger of God, it will doubtless finally drive the long, long night of heathenish darkness from America. So arts and sciences will change the face of nature in their tour from hence over the Appalachian Mountains to the western ocean; and as they march through the vast desert, the residence of wild beasts will be broken up, and the obscene howl cease forever; instead of which the stones and trees will dance together in the music of Orpheus,—the rocks will disclose their hidden gems,—and the inestimable treasures of gold and silver be broken up. Huge mountains of iron ore are already discovered; and vast stores are reserved for future gen erations.

This metal, more useful than gold and silver, will employ millions of hands, not only to form the martial sword and peaceful share alternately, but an infinity of utensils improved in the exercise of art and handicraft among men. Nature through all her works has stamped authority on this law, namely, "That all fit matter shall be improved to its best purpose." Shall not then those vast quarries that teem with mechanic stone,—those for structure be piled into great cities,—and those for sculpture into statues to perpetuate the honor of renowned heroes; even those who shall now save their country? O! ye unborn inhabitants of America! should this page escape its destined conflagra tion at the year's end, and these alphabetical letters remain legible,— when your eyes behold the sun after he has rolled the seasons round for two or three centuries more, you will know that in Anno Domini 1758, we dreamed of your times.

Mather Byles.

BORN in Boston, Mass., 1706. DIED there, 1788.

THE TEACHING OF THE GRAVE.

[*To his Excellency Governor Belcher, on the Death of his Lady.* 1736.]

AH! what avail the sable velvet spread
   And golden ornaments, amidst the dead?
No beam smiles there, no eye can there discern
The vulgar coffin from the marble urn:
The costly honors, preaching, seem to say,
"Magnificence must mingle with the clay."

Learn here, ye Fair, the frailty of your face,
Ravished by death, or nature's slow decays:
Ye great, must so resign your transient power,
Heroes of dust, and monarchs of an hour!
So must each pleasing air, each gentle fire,
And all that's soft, and all that's sweet expire.

Mather Byles

THE DELIGHTS OF THE NEXT WORLD.

[*The Glorious Rest of Heaven: A Sermon.* 1745.]

THE employment of heaven is glorious employment. As the company is so excellent and illustrious, so no less is the conversation with which they gratify and entertain one another, in those delightful habitations. Doubtless those happy spirits will discourse together, on the actions of their past lives; the blessings they were favored with, the miseries they escaped from, and glory that they now possess. Those that knew one another upon earth, will be much better acquainted there; and where any have been instrumental in forwarding and helping on one another in their way to heaven, they will be mutual joys to one another when they meet together.

How blessed and pleasing an intercourse must it be, for friends to congratulate the arrival of friends to that holy world; to talk over the prayers they have perhaps formerly made together; the pious conversation they have carried on upon earth; and the serious religion they promoted in each other's minds, by their word and their examples. It will certainly be no little satisfaction, for them there to renew to one another, the thoughts and discourses they once entertained concerning the glory and happiness of the kingdom where they will then reign. They will say one to another, How dark and obscure were our conceptions of this felicity! How low and mean the talk we formerly had about it! How inadequate and trifling the most exalted strokes of our mortal discourses to these sublime enjoyments!

And as the conversation we shall have with those which we were familiar with on earth, will be so pleasant and happy, so no less will that delight us, which we shall have with those who have gone to heaven before us. To mix in the divine and sinless companies there, to hear the improving expressions of their tongues, and attend to the soft persuasion that sits upon their lips, this will be a very noble entertainment. How glad shall we be, to hear Paul give us an account of his conversion with his own mouth; or Noah himself be the relator of the flood which bore him up in his ark, over the tops of the mountains! To hear Moses, in an improved sublimity of style, tell of the wonders of the creation, and relate the pomp and terror of Mount Sinai, when its summit blazed with fire unto the midst of heaven, and the black smoke arose like the smoke of a furnace, and rolled away through the air; while the voice of the trumpet echoed louder and louder, and the whole mountain shook to its foundations.

THE LAST TEMPEST.

[*"The Conflagration." Poems on Several Occasions.* 1736.]

IN some calm midnight, when no whispering breeze
    Waves the tall woods, or curls the undimpled seas,
Lulled on their oozy beds, the rivers seem
Softly to murmur in a pleasing dream;
The shaded fields confess a still repose,
And on each hand the dewy mountains drowse:
Meantime the moon, fair empress of the night!
In solemn silence sheds her silver light,
While twinkling stars their glimmering beauties show,
And wink perpetual o'er the heavenly blue ;
Sleep, nodding, consecrates the deep serene,
And spreads her brooding wings o'er all the dusky scene;
Through the fine ether moves no single breath;
But all is hushed as in the arms of death.
    At once, great God ! thy dire command is given,
That the last tempest shake the frame of heaven.

.   .   .   .

Eternal mountains totter on their base,
And strong convulsions work the valley's face ;
Fierce hurricanes on sounding pinions soar,
Rush o'er the land, on the tossed billows roar,
And dreadful in resistless eddies driven,
Shake all the crystal battlements of heaven.
See the wild winds, big blustering in the air,
Drive through the forests, down the mountains tear,
Sweep o'er the valleys in their rapid course,
And nature bends beneath the impetuous force.
Storms rush at storms, at tempests tempests roar,
Dash waves on waves, and thunder to the shore.
Columns of smoke on heavy wings ascend,
And dancing sparkles fly before the wind.
Devouring flames, wide-waving, roar aloud,
And melted mountains flow a fiery flood :
Then, all at once, immense the fires arise,
A bright destruction wraps the crackling skies ;
While all the elements to melt conspire,
And the world blazes in the final fire.
    Yet shall ye, flames, the wasting globe refine,
And bid the skies with purer splendor shine,
The earth, which the prolific fires consume,
To beauty burns, and withers into bloom ;
Improving in the fertile flame it lies,
Fades into form, and into vigor dies :
Fresh-dawning glories blush amidst the blaze,
And nature all renews her flowery face.

With endless charms the everlasting year
Rolls round the seasons in a full career;
Spring, ever-blooming, bids the fields rejoice,
And warbling birds try their melodious voice;
Where'er she treads, lilies unbidden blow,
Quick tulips rise, and sudden roses glow:
Her pencil paints a thousand beauteous scenes,
Where blossoms bud amid immortal greens;
Each stream, in mazes, murmurs as it flows,
And floating forests gently bend their boughs.
Thou, autumn, too, sitt'st in the fragrant shade,
While the ripe fruits blush all around thy head:
And lavish nature, with luxuriant hands,
All the soft months in gay confusion blends.

TO THE GREAT MR. POPE.

[Letter to Alexander Pope. Written in 1727.]

SIR:—You are doubtless wondering at the novelty of an epistle from the remote shores where this dates its origin; as well as from so obscure a hand as that which subscribes it. But what corner of the earth so secret, as not to have heard the fame of Mr. Pope? Or who so retired as not to be acquainted with his admirable compositions, or so stupid as not to be ravished with them?

Fame, after a man is dead, has been by some ingenious writers compared to an applause in some distant region. If this be a just similitude, you may take the pleasure of an admired name in America, and of spreading a transport over the face of a new world: By which you may, in some measure, imagine the renown in which your name will flourish many ages to come, and anticipate a thousand years of futurity.

To let you see a little of the reputation which you bear in these unknown climates, and the improvements we are making under your auspicious influences, in the polite studies of the Muses, I transmit to you the enclosed Poems: Assuring myself, though not of the approbation of your judgment, yet of the excuse and lenity of that candor which is forever inseparable from a great genius. But notwithstanding all these representations of your goodness, which my imagination is able to form, I find it very difficult to suppress the struggle of passions which swells my breast, while I am writing a letter to so great a man. I am at once urged by a generous ambition to be known to you; and forbid by a trembling consciousness of my own unworthiness and obscurity. Prompted by desire, flushed with hope, or appalled with concern, I add to the incorrectness which I would now most of all wish to escape. In short, Sir, when I approach you it is with a real awe and reverence, like that, which you have so humorously described in the Guardian upon dedications.

How often have I been soothed and charmed with the ever-blooming landscapes of your Windsor Forest? And how does my very soul melt away, at the soft complaint of the laughing Eloisa? How frequently has the Rape of the Lock commanded the various passions of my mind: provoked laughter; breathed a tranquillity; or inspired a transport! And how often have I been raised, and borne away by the resistless fire of the Iliad, as it glows in your immortal translation!

Permit me, Sir, to conclude my letter with asking the favor of a few lines from the hand which has blest the world with such divine productions. If you thus honor me, assure yourself the joys you will produce in me, will be inferior to none but the poetic rapture of your own breast. Perhaps you will be disposed to write, when I confess, that I have a more superstitious ardor to see a word written by your pen, than ever Tom Folio in the Tattler, to see a simile of Virgil with that advantage.

I am, Sir, your great admirer, and

most obedient humble Servant,

MATHER BYLES.

NEW ENGLAND, BOSTON, *Oct.* 7, 1727.

HYMN WRITTEN DURING A VOYAGE.

[Poems on Several Occasions. 1736.]

GREAT God thy works our wonder raise;
  To thee our swelling notes belong;
While skies and winds, and rocks and seas,
  Around shall echo to our song.

Thy power produced this mighty frame,
  Aloud to thee the tempests roar,
Or softer breezes tune thy name
  Gently along the shelly shore.

Round thee the scaly nation roves,
  Thy opening hands their joys bestow,
Through all the blushing coral groves,
  These silent gay retreats below.

See the broad sun forsake the skies,
  Glow on the waves and downward glide,
Anon heaven opens all its eyes,
  And star-beams tremble o'er the tide.

Each various scene, or day or night,
  Lord! points to thee our nourished soul;
Thy glories fix our whole delight;
  So the touched needle courts the pole.

Joseph Green.

Born in Boston, Mass., 1706.   Died in England, 1780.

THE PARSON'S PSALM.

[A Parody on Mather Byles's Stanzas written at Sea.]

IN David's Psalms an oversight
  Byles found one morning at his tea,
Alas! that he should never write
  A proper song to sing at sea.

Thus ruminating on his seat,
  Ambitious thoughts at length prevailed.
The bard determined to complete
  The part wherein the prophet failed.

He sat awhile and stroked his Muse,*
  Then taking up his tuneful pen,
Wrote a few stanzas for the use
  Of his seafaring brethren.

The task performed, the bard content,
  Well chosen was each flowing word;
On a short voyage himself he went,
  To hear it read and sung on board.

Most serious Christians do aver,
  (Their credit sure we may rely on,)
In former times that after prayer,
  They used to sing a song of Zion.

Our modern parson having prayed,
  Unless loud fame or faith beguiles,
Sat down, took out his book and said,
  "Let's sing a psalm of Mather Byles."

* Byles's favorite cat, so named by his friends.

At first, when he began to read,
 Their heads the assembly downward hung,
But he with boldness did proceed,
 And thus he read, and thus they sung.

THE PSALM.

With vast amazement we survey
 The wonders of the deep,
Where mackerel swim, and porpoise play,
 And crabs and lobsters creep.

Fish of all kinds inhabit here,
 And throng the dark abode.
Here haddock, hake, and flounders are,
 And eels, and perch, and cod.

From raging winds and tempests free,
 So smoothly as we pass,
The shining surface seems to be
 A piece of Bristol glass.

But when the winds and tempests rise,
 And foaming billows swell,
The vessel mounts above the skies,
 And lower sinks than hell.

Our heads the tottering motion feel,
 And quickly we become
Giddy as new-dropped calves, and reel
 Like Indians drunk with rum.

What praises then are due that we
 Thus far have safely got,
Amarescoggin tribe to see,
 And tribe of Penobscot.

OF DR. BYLES'S CAT.

[The Poet's Lamentations for the Loss of his Cat, which he used to call his Muse.]

OPPRESSED with grief in heavy strains I mourn
 The partner of my studies from me torn.
How shall I sing? what numbers shall I choose?
For in my favorite cat I've lost my muse.
No more I feel my mind with raptures fired,
I want those airs that Puss so oft inspired;

No crowding thoughts my ready fancy fill,
Nor words run fluent from my easy quill;
Yet shall my verse deplore her cruel fate,
And celebrate the virtues of my cat.
   In acts obscene she never took delight;
No caterwauls disturbed our sleep by night;
Chaste as a virgin, free from every stain,
And neighboring cats mewed for her love in **vain.**
   She never thirsted for the chicken's blood;
Her teeth she only used to chew her food;
Harmless as satires which her master writes,
A foe to scratching, and unused to bites,
She in the study was my constant mate;
There we together many evenings sate.
Whene'er I felt my towering fancy fail,
I stroked her head, her ears, her back, and tail;
And as I stroked improved my dying song
From the sweet notes of her melodious tongue:
Her purrs and mews so evenly kept time,
She purred in metre, and she mewed in rhyme.
But when my dulness has too stubborn proved,
Nor could by Puss's music be removed,
Oft to the well-known volumes have I gone,
And stole a line from Pope or Addison.
   Ofttimes when lost amidst poetic heat,
She leaping on my knee has took her seat;
There saw the throes that rocked my laboring brain,
And licked and clawed me to myself again.
   Then, friends, indulge my grief, and let me mourn,
My cat is gone, ah! never to return.
Now in my study, all the tedious night,
Alone I sit, and unassisted write;
Look often round (O greatest cause of pain),
And view the numerous labors of my brain;
Those quires of words arrayed in pompous rhyme,
Which braved the jaws of all-devouring time,
Now undefended and unwatched by cats,
Are doomed a victim to the teeth of rats.

A LAMENTATION FOR OLD TENOR CURRENCY.

[*A Mournful Lamentation for the Sad and Deplorable Death of Mr. Old Tenor.*]

A DOLEFUL tale prepare to hear,
   As ever yet was told:
The like, perhaps, ne'er reach'd the ear
   Of either young or old.

'Tis of the sad and woful death
   Of one of mighty fame,
Who lately hath resigned his breath;
   Old Tenor was his name.

In vain ten thousands intercede,
   To keep him from the grave;
In vain, his many good works plead;
   Alas! they cannot save.
The powers decree and die he must,
   It is the common lot,
But his good deeds, when he's in dust,
   Shall never be forgot.

He made our wives and daughters fine,
   And pleased everybody;
He gave the rich their costly wine,
   The poor their flip and toddy.
The laborer he set to work;
   In ease maintained the great:
He found us mutton, beef, and pork,
   And everything we eat.

To fruitful fields by swift degrees,
   He turned our desert land:
Where once naught stood but rocks and trees,
   Now spacious cities stand.
He built us houses strong and high,
   Of wood, and brick, and stone;
The furniture he did supply;
   But now, alas! he's gone.

The merchants, too, those topping folks,
   To him owe all their riches;
Their ruffles, lace, and scarlet cloaks,
   And eke their velvet breeches.
He launched their ships into the main,
   To visit distant shores;
And brought them back, full fraught with gain,
   Which much increased their stores.

Led on by him, our soldiers bold
   Against the foe advance;
And took, in spite of wet and cold,
   Strong Cape Breton from France.
Who from that fort the French did drive,
   Shall he so soon be slain?
While they, alas! remain alive,
   Who gave it back again?

From house to house, and place to place,
   In paper doublet clad,

He passed and where he showed his face,
    He made the heart full glad.
But cruel death, that spareth none,
    Hath robbed us of him too;
Who through the land so long hath gone,
    No longer now must go.

In senate he, like Cæsar, fell,
    Pierced through with many a wound,
He sunk, ah, doleful tale to tell!
    The members sitting round:
And ever since that fatal day
    O! had it never been,
Closely confined at home he lay,
    And scarce was ever seen,

Until the last of March, when he
    Submitted unto fate;
In anno regis twenty-three,
    Ætatis forty-eight.
Forever gloomy be that day,
    When he gave up the ghost;
For by his death, oh! who can say,
    What hath New England lost?

Then, good Old Tenor, fare thee well,
    Since thou art dead and gone;
We mourn thy fate, e'en while we tell
    The good things thou hast done,
Since the bright beams of yonder sun,
    Did on New England shine,
In all the land, there ne'er was known
    A death so mourned as thine.

Of every rank are many seen,
    Thy downfall to deplore;
For 'tis well known that thou hast been
    A friend to rich and poor.
We'll o'er thee raise a silver tomb,
    Long may that tomb remain,
To bless our eyes for years to come,
    But wishes, ah! are vain.

And so God bless our noble state,
    And save us all from harm,
And grant us food enough to eat,
    And clothes to keep us warm.
Send us a lasting peace, and keep
    The times from growing worse;
And let us all in safety sleep,
    With silver in our purse.

John Winthrop.

BORN in Boston, Mass., 1714.   DIED at Cambridge, Mass., 1779.

THE EFFECTS OF THE EARTHQUAKE.

[A Lecture on Earthquakes.   Read at Harvard, 1755.]

IMAGINE, then, the earth trembling with a huge thundering noise, or heaving and swelling like a rolling sea:—now gaping in chasms of various sizes, and then immediately closing again; either swallowing up the unhappy persons who chanced to be over them, or crushing them to death by the middle:—from some, spouting up prodigious quantities of water to a vast height, or belching out hot, offensive and suffocating exhalations; while others are streaming with torrents of melted minerals.   Some houses moving out of their places; others cracking and tumbling into heaps of rubbish; and others again, not barely by whole streets, but by whole cities at a time, sinking downright to a great depth in the earth, or under water.   On the shore, the sea roaring and rising in billows; or else retiring to a great distance from the land, and then violently returning like a flood to overwhelm it; vessels driven from their anchors; some overset and lost, others thrown up on the land.   In one place, vast rocks flung down from mountains, and choking up rivers, which, being then forced to find themselves new channels, sweep away such trees, houses, etc., as had escaped the fury of the shock; in another, mountains themselves sinking in a moment, and their places possessed by pools of water.   Some people running about, pale with fear, trembling for the event, and ignorant whither to fly for shelter; others thrown with violence down on the ground, not being able to keep on their feet; and others shrieking or groaning in the agonies of death—even the brute creation manifesting all the signs of consternation and astonishment.

Imagine these things to yourselves, and you will then have a view, though but an imperfect one, of some of those images of horror and desolation, which accompany the more violent earthquakes.   .   .   .   .

Though these explosions, and consequent concussions of the earth, have indeed occasioned most terrible desolations, and in this light may justly be regarded as the tokens of an incensed Deity, yet it can by no means be concluded from hence, that they are not of real and standing advantage to the globe in general.   Multitudes, it is true, have at different times suffered by them; multitudes have been destroyed by them; but much greater multitudes may have every day been benefited by them.

The all-wise Creator could not but foresee all the effects of all the powers he implanted in matter; and, as we find in innumerable instances (and the more we know of his works, the more such instances we discover) that He has established such laws for the government of the world, as tend to promote the good of the whole, we may reasonably presume that He has done it in this case as well as others. To me, at least, the argument on this side the question, drawn from the general analogy of nature, appears to have more force, than any that I have seen offered on the other. For there is nothing, however useful, however necessary, but what is capable of producing, and in fact has produced, damage, in single instances. It were endless to particularize here; I shall therefore only mention one or two things by way of specimen.

The power of gravity—a power of such indispensable importance, that without it the system of nature could not subsist a moment,—has yet proved the destruction of multitudes. The wind, so necessary for the purposes of navigation, as well as to purge the air, which would otherwise stagnate and putrefy—how often has it risen to such a pitch, as to overthrow houses, and wreck vessels, by which means thousands have perished!

Even thunder and lightning, which, next to earthquakes, are the most terrible phenomena of nature, are yet universally allowed to be necessary to free the atmosphere from a certain unwholesome sultriness which often infects it. Other instances of the like sort I leave to your own reflections: and would rather observe, that the world is governed by general laws; and general laws must, from the nature of them, be liable sometimes to do hurt.

However, laws of this sort are sufficiently vindicated, not only as wise, but as good, if upon the whole they produce a maximum of good (to borrow an expression from the mathematicians); and this, it is in the highest degree probable, all the laws of nature do. It may be added, that as in the animal body, the evacuations, which are of absolute necessity to maintain life and health, do yet sometimes run to such extremes as to prove mortal; so in like manner, these explosions of subterraneous vapor, whose effects have sometimes been so fatal, may, notwithstanding this, be highly conducive, and even indispensably necessary, to the good of this globe in general. The explosions themselves, as well as the laws in consequence of which they are produced, may be necessary on various accounts; and particularly to the carrying on the more secret and noble works of nature within the entrails of the earth. Let me dilate a little on this matter.

By the incessant action of gravity and other attractive powers, and by the perpetual consumption of fluids, the earth becomes continually more and more hard, compact, and dense. Now an openness or looseness of contexture, to a certain degree, in the earth, is necessary to carry on the operations of nature within it. So that on the supposition that mineral, metalline, and other subterraneous bodies grow within the earth, it should seem that the earth must become gradually less and less fit for the production of them. Since, then, the direct, immediate, and most general effect of earthquakes is, by shaking, to loosen and disunite the parts of the earth, and to open its pores, it seems agreeable to reason to infer, that this is the end primarily aimed at in these concussions.

But you will take notice, that I speak here only of physical or natural ends. For, though I make no doubt that the laws of nature were established, and that the operations of nature are conducted with a view, ultimately, to moral purposes; and that there is the most perfect coincidence, at all times, between God's government of the natural and of the moral world; yet it would be improper for me to enter into these disquisitions at this time, since my province limits me to consider this subject only in the relation which it bears to natural philosophy. It is in the physical sense alone that I say the disjoining the parts of the earth, and opening its pores, may be the end primarily aimed at in earthquakes, as such mutations in the earth may from time to time become necessary to the production of subterraneous bodies; and perhaps this end could not be effectually answered by less forcible methods. This point may receive some light, if not proof, from the operations of agriculture. We find it necessary, by ploughing, digging, etc., to break the clods of the ground, to comminute and even pulverize it, in order to fit it for the purposes of vegetation ; and we find it necessary to renew these labors every year.

Now, the use and tendency of these artificial operations may bear some analogy to those of the greater operations of nature, which we are speaking of. And, indeed, it is not in the least degree improbable, that such a loosening of the parts of the earth may promote even the growth of vegetables on its surface, as well as of minerals in its bowels ; it being now well known, that all vegetables, the smaller as well as the larger, shoot some fibres of their roots to vastly greater depths, than those to which any of our instruments of tillage ever penetrate. This, it is likely, may be one reason of the wonderful fertility, for which Ætna and Vesuvio have been so generally and so highly celebrated. Again : it may be necessary now and then, to have such subterraneous vapors, as are generated by fermentation, discharged up into the air ; as their continuance below, in the caverns of the earth, might be an impediment to those important processes which are there carrying on. But those very vapors, which might obstruct some sorts of natural processes while below the surface of the earth, may as much advance others when above it. We know that in many cases of the fermentation of bodies, especially of such dense ones as salts and minerals, air is plentifully absorbed ; and that in many others it is as plentifully generated: so that great part of the exhalations thrown out by earthquakes may be true, permanent air, and designed to recruit what has been absorbed by bodies here on the surface.

And perhaps the grounds on which the great Newton founded his "suspicion, that the finest, the most subtile, and most spirituous parts of our air, and those which are most necessary to maintain the life of all things, come chiefly from the comets," may equally support another suspicion, that some such particles of air may be derived also from subterraneous eruptions. For among the almost infinite variety of particles which are thrown out of the earth in these eruptions, it is most likely that, if some are noxious, others will be salutary. It may also be necessary from time to time to have the subterraneous streams diverted from their former courses into new ones: partly, that different places in the lower regions may be watered by them; and partly, that the waters themselves, by passing through different beds or channels, may alter their properties, and convey new tinctures to different places.

Joseph Bellamy.

BORN in Cheshire, Conn., 1719. DIED at Bethlem, Conn., 1790.

THE SUM OF ALL VIRTUE.

[*To a Correspondent, who had written to ask him, "What is the Nature of Virtue?"*]

BETHLEM, *Oct.* 20, 1764.

DEAR SIR: *Love* is the sum of all virtue—love to being in general, to God the great Being, and to all other beings in due proportion, those only excepted who stand excommunicated by the great Judge of all, as irreclaimable enemies to God, and to all good. Our neighbors, although our personal enemies, are to be loved as ourselves, for they are our flesh and blood, as good by nature as we, and as capable and desirous of happiness. Their faults we are never to speak, unless in duty we are called to it. Though they belie us, we are to return good for evil, blessing for cursing. The example of God, and of his Son, ought always to fill our minds, and be our pattern; but the ways of the world we are not to imitate. There is more pleasure in it, and it is a more gentlemanlike thing to be like God, than like the devil. This is the sum of the matter.   J. BELLAMY.

A PICTURE OF THE MILLENNIUM.

[*An Election Sermon.* 1762.]

LET us stop here, a few minutes, and think what the consequences would be, should righteousness, which is the glory of the Deity, and the very beauty of heaven, should that holy and divine temper, which reigns there in perfection, descend on crowned heads, and fill the courts of princes, and spread down through every rank, even down to the meanest cottager, and to the poorest beggar; what would the consequences be? Heaven would soon begin on earth.

Princes, even the most haughty monarchs of the earth, who, to gratify their pride and ambition, do often now, in the present state of things, summon mighty armies, spread war, devastation, and ruin through whole countries, would be at once turned into other men, " be converted and become as little children," as harmless as doves, as meek as lambs. Such would be their humility, their self-abhorrence, their penitence, their reverence toward the Deity, and love to the human kind, that they would speedily, and with the utmost sincerity, begin to concert measures for a universal, perpetual peace. Ambassadors for that end would be sent from, and to every monarch, prince, and court; and orders be soon dispatched to fleets and armies to stop the effusion of human blood. The thundering cannons would cease to roar; peace, universal peace, be soon proclaimed; for every monarch, from the heart, would soon begin to say to each other, " Take your right, my brother, and let me have mine, and let us live in love and peace, and seek the true happiness of our subjects, and, no longer go on sacrificing thousands of precious lives in quarrels which honest men might settle with the utmost ease." And so now the "nations would beat their swords into ploughshares, and their spears into pruning-hooks, neither would they learn war any more."

And should righteousness, should all right affections, should supreme love to God and Jesus Christ, love to our holy religion, brotherly love, meekness, gentleness, fidelity, temperance, chastity, and all the Christian graces, not only take possession of the hearts of kings, but spread through all their royal families, among their privy counsellors, through their parliaments, and to all their courts of justice, and should the sacred flame fly from city to city, from town to town, through all their dominions, and into all their distant colonies, into what a glorious and happy state would things be immediately brought! Look round upon all ranks and orders of men, and behold the glorious change. Go to the clergy, and view them in their studies, or in their pulpits: behold, they are clothed with righteousness; they are inflamed with every holy, pious, benevolent, heavenly affection; they love their master, they love their people, they love their work; they "delight in the law of the Lord, and in his law do they meditate day and night." They are like trees planted by the rivers of water, whose leaf never falls, and which bring forth fruit in their season; and out of their "treasure" from time to time they "bring forth things new and old;" while their public prayers and their sermons are animated with the humblest, purest, warmest devotion. And, O, behold, how they love one another! Look through a province; they are united in the same faith, and love and live as brethren. Yea, look through a kingdom, yea, look from kingdom to kingdom; there are no sects, no parties, no divisions. They all, ministers and people, make up one great family, united in faith and love; united in one and the same belief, and in the most cordial affection to one another. And ministers, of choice, give themselves wholly to their work; and their people, from their own inclination, unite as one to give them an honorable support, not as their burden, but as their delight; they even take pleasure in it.

Go to the merchant's shop, and you will find not only just weights and just measures, but also piety toward God and love to the human kind, diligence and industry, prudence in their calling, frugality in their expenses, generosity to the poor, charmingly mingled in their characters. And while wealth flows in upon them from every quarter, they are clothed with humility; and they, their children, and all they have, bear this inscription in great capitals, HOLINESS TO THE LORD.

Go to the house, the happy house, of the industrious farmer. In early morning he and all his arise, and assemble to worship the Great Eternal. Devoutly they read God's holy word, and offer up prayer and praises, in the name of Jesus Christ, with penitent, humble, and grateful hearts. With alacrity and joy they go forth to their labors, and enjoy the delights of heaven in their fields; love and harmony reign within doors; the parents happy in God, in one another, and in their offspring; while their children grow up in piety toward God, reverence toward their parents, and in the most cordial affection to one another. And hearken, and hear the wise maxims of the household where righteousness reigns: "Let us be industrious and frugal, that we may be able to render to all men their dues; tribute to whom tribute, custom to whom custom; yea, let us be industrious and frugal, that we may have wherewith to give to the poor, and to make the widow's heart sing for joy. And let all we have be consecrated to God; and while we live upon his bounty, let us live to his glory, and prepare for his heavenly kingdom."

Go into neighborhoods. Malice and envy are gone; tattling and backbiting are no more heard. Love, undissembled love, and good-will, reign. Go to courts of justice, and, behold, they are unfrequented; for the people are become righteous, and live in love. And, while they do as they would be done by, there seldom happens any affair that needs to be disputed at the bar.

Go to the house of the governor, who, as he was advanced to his high station merely on account of his merit, so he is the wisest man in the province, and a father to all his subjects. Every morning and evening he makes King Solomon's prayer for a wise and understanding heart; for it is his great concern to fill his station well. He is loved, revered, and obeyed by all his people, who live under him as one united, happy family conscientiously concerned, by their good behaviour, to render his government as easy and happy to him as possible. All the influence his high station, superior wisdom, and goodness give him over their hearts, is wholly consecrated to make them a still holier and happier people. For he feels toward them all the good-will and tenderness which are wont to reside in the heart of a nursing father or nursing mother toward an infant child.

Go to the taverns, and even they are houses of piety and good order. No rioting or drunkenness, no chambering or wantonness to be found there; no town dwellers assembled for drinking and debauchery. No; for there are no such people to be found in towns where righteousness universally prevails. At these houses the stranger and the traveller may call, refresh themselves in quiet, or take lodging in peace, and in the morning go their ways, rejoicing to see good order and religion reign everywhere.

Go to the cottages of the poor, if you can find them, for their number will be but small in such a state of things; none rendered poor by a course of excessive drinking, or by gay dressing, or by high living, or by idleness, or by any dishonest practices. A few, perhaps, you may find rendered poor through some natural infirmity of body or mind, or by some adversity which it was not in their power to foresee and prevent, and these are as humble as they are poor. They quietly submit to Providence, they are thankful for the little they have, they are industrious and prudent according to their abilities; and instead of envying their neighbors, they rejoice in their prosperity. They are beloved by every one; and their neighbors feel a peculiar pleasure in granting them relief from time to time; so that, in the midst of their poverty, they are really happy, and want none of the necessaries of life, and enjoy many of its conveniences.

Go to the schools of the prophets, to the seminaries of learning, and see a little picture of heaven. The whole society in perfect love and harmony, making swift advances in all knowledge divine and human, growing up in love to God and to the human kind, and ripening for public service, under the indefatigable labors of their wise and learned instructors, whom they love and honor as dutiful children do their pa-

rents. Meanwhile, peace and plenty, universal love and harmony, reign
from town to town, through all the province, through all the kingdom,
yea, through all the kingdoms of the earth where righteousness thus
prevails, and heaven looks down propitious, and declares, "Blessed shalt
thou be in thy basket and in thy store, blessed shalt thou be in the house
and in the field." Nor let any think this a description of a fictitious
state of things; rather let every one know, that all this, and more than
all this, shall be accomplished, when once that petition, so often put up
by the true followers of Jesus, by his special direction,—"Thy kingdom
come, thy will be done on earth as it is in heaven,"—is answered, and his
holy religion comes to take place among mankind, when once "the stone
cut out without hands becomes a great mountain, and fills the whole
earth."

Eliza Lucas.

Born about 1721.   Daughter of Lt. Col. Lucas, Governor of Antigua.   Wife of Chief-Justice
Charles Pinckney.   Died, 1792.

A LOVE-LETTER OF THE LAST CENTURY.

[*To the Hon. Charles Pinckney.   Written in* 1741.]

SIR:—The penance you have enjoined is equal to an Egyptian task;
for I take it to be full as hard for me to repeat Doctor Parnell's "Hermit" to you, having never read it more than twice, as it was to them
to make brick without straw; but if you will be so good as to lend me
the book, I'll promise to repeat it to you some time in September next,
which is the soonest I can promise myself the pleasure of waiting on Mrs.
P. We are much obliged to Mr. Dart for the mocking birds; my papa
will be very much pleased with them. To secure them from their mortal foe, the cat, I have put them in my own closet, where they afford me
a thousand useful reflections. Here the niggard that eats his morsel
alone, and the mean, suspicious wretch whose bolted door ne'er moved in
pity to the wandering poor, may learn a lesson of hospitality from the
birds of the air.

The little chirpers have drawn to the window an old bird that has a
nest in a tree in the garden, with three young ones in it. These six employ her morning in providing for and feeding them. I was one day sitting in the room viewing them perched, and as I supposed expecting their
warbling benefactress, when she came to the window, from whence I imagined the sight of me must soon fright her (it was impossible for me to

move); but even that could not prevent her generous purpose to the lit-tle strangers, but she flew close by me, and perching on the cage dropped in what her bounty had before provided.

This thing pleased me more than you can imagine; I communicated it to some of my neighbors, and begged their company next day to be wit-ness of the fact, for I really thought it would appear incredible. They were so obliging as to say they could never doubt my veracity upon any subject whatever, though what I attested might appear extremely im-probable; but in this case there was nothing extraordinary, for it was very common to hang a cage of young mocking birds in the garden, to be raised by the old one, if there was one near; but this I was a stranger to.

I see you smile while you have been reading this to Mrs. Pinckney, and she replies, "The dear girl forgot she was not writing to little Polly when she indulged her descriptive vein, and that the subject of her birds is too trifling a one to engage your attention." Be it so, but it is your own fault; you will have me write, and as my ideas are trifling my subject must be conformable to them.

AN ESSAY IN CRITICISM.

[To Miss Bartlett. Written, May 2, 1742.]

DEAR MISS BARTLETT: I send by the bearer my compliments to Mrs. Pinckney, and the last volume of "Pamela." She is a good girl, and as such I love her dearly; but I must think her very de-fective, and even blush for her, while she allows herself that disgusting liberty of praising herself, or what is very like it, repeating all the fine speeches made to her by others,—when a person distinguished for modesty in every other respect should have chosen rather to conceal them, or at least let them come from some other hand; especially as she might have considered those high compliments might have proceeded from the partiality of her friends, or with a view to encourage her and make her aspire after those qualifications which are ascribed to her, which I know experimentally to be often the case. But then you answer, she was a young country girl, had seen nothing of life, and it was natural for her to be pleased with praise; and she had not art enough to conceal it. True, before she was Mrs. B——, it be excusable, when only wrote to her father and mother; but after she had the advantage of Mr. B.'s conver-sation, and others of sense and distinction, I must be of another opinion. But here arises a difficulty,—we are to be made acquainted by the author of all particulars; how then is it to be done? I think by Miss Darnford, or some other lady very intimate with Mrs. B. How you smile at my presumption for instructing one so far above my own level as the author of "Pamela" (whom I esteem much for the regard he pays to virtue and religion throughout his whole piece); but, my dear Miss Bartlett, contract your smile into a mortified look, for I acquit the author. He designed to paint no more than a woman; and he certainly designed it as a reflection upon the vanity of our sex, that a character, so complete in every other instance, should be so greatly defective in this. Defective indeed, for when she mentions that poor creature, Mr. H.'s applauses, it puts me in mind of the observation in "Don Quixote," how grateful is praise, even from a madman.

I have run thus far before I was aware, for I have neither capacity nor inclination for criticism; though Pamela sets me the example by criticising Mr. Locke, and has taken the liberty to dissent from that admirable author. One word more, and I have done; and that is, I think the author has kept up to nature (one of the greatest beauties in the whole piece), for, had his heroine no defect, the character must be unnatural,— as it would be in me to forget my respects to your worthy Uncle and Aunt Pinckney, and that I am, Yours, etc.,

E. Lucas.

Samuel Davies.

BORN in Newcastle Co., Del., 1724. DIED at Princeton, N. J., 1761.

A PARSON'S CALL TO ARMS.

[*The Curse of Cowardice. A Sermon Preached to the Militia of Hanover county in Virginia, May 8, 1758.*]

CAN Indian revenge and thirst for blood be glutted? or can French ambition and avarice be satisfied? No, we have no method left, but to repel force with force, and give them blood to drink in their turn, who have drunk ours. If we sit still and do nothing, or content ourselves, as, alas, we have hitherto, with feeble, dilatory efforts, we may expect these barbarities will not only continue, but that the Indians, headed by the French, those eternal enemies of peace, liberty, and Britons, will carry their inroads still farther into the country, and reach even to us. By the desertion of our remote settlements, the frontiers are approaching every day nearer and nearer to us: and if we cannot stand our ground now,—when we have above an hundred miles of a thick settled country between us and the enemy,—much less shall we be able, when our strength is weakened by so vast a loss of men, arms, and riches, and we lie exposed to their immediate incursions. Some cry, "Let the enemy come down to us, and then we will fight them." But this is the trifling excuse of cowardice or security, and not the language of prudence and fortitude. Those who make this plea, if the enemy should take them at their word, and make them so near a visit, would be as forward in flight as they are now backward to take up arms.

Such, my brethren, such, alas! is the present state of our country: it bleeds in a thousand veins; and without a timely remedy, the wound will prove mortal. And in such circumstances, is it not our duty in the sight of God, is it not a work to which the Lord loudly calls us, to take up arms for the defence of our country? Certainly it is: and " cursed is he," who having no ties sufficiently strong to confine him at home, "keepeth his sword from blood." The mean, sneaking wretch, that can desert the cause of his country in such an exigency; his country, in the blessings of which he shared, while in peace and prosperity; and which is therefore entitled to his sympathy and assistance in the day of its distress; that cowardly ungrateful wretch sins against God and his country, and deserves the curse of both. Such a conduct in such a conjuncture, is a moral evil, a gross weakness; and exposes the wretch to the heavy curse of God both in this and the eternal world.

And here I cannot but observe, that among the various and numberless sins under which our country groans, and which must be looked upon as the causes of our public calamities, by every one that believes a divine providence (a doctrine so comfortable, and so essential both in nature and revealed religion; an article in the creed of heathens and Mahometans, as well as Jews and Christians), I say, among these various sins, cowardice and security are none of the least. He that hath determined the bounds of our habitation, hath planted us in a land of liberty and plenty; a land, till lately, unalarmed with the terrors of war, and unstained with human blood. Indeed, all things considered, there are but few such happy spots upon our globe. And must it not highly provoke our divine Benefactor, to see a people thus distinguished with blessings, so insensible of their worth, so ungrateful for them and so unacquainted with their own unworthiness to receive them? What can be more evidential of their undue apprehensions of the worth of these blessings, than their being so little concerned to secure and recover them? The generality among us have acted as if their interests at stake were so trifling, that it would not be worth while to take pains, or encounter dangers, to preserve them. What greater evidence can be given of ingratitude, than a supine neglect of these blessings, and such a stupidly tame and irresisting resignation of them into bloody and rapacious hands?

And what can be more evidential of a proud insensibility of our unworthiness of such blessings, than our being so inapprehensive of losing them, even in the most threatening and dangerous circumstances? Our countrymen in general have acted as if beings of their importance and merit might certainly rest in the quiet, unmolested possession of their liberty and property, without any one daring to disturb them, and without their doing anything for their own defence; or as if neither God nor man could strip them of their enjoyments. What vain, self-confident presumption, what intolerable insolence is this, in a sinful nation, a people laden with iniquity, who have forfeited every blessing, even the ground they tread upon, and the air they breathe in; and who live merely by the unmerited grace and bounty of God! Is not cowardice and security, or an unwillingness to engage with all our might in the defence of our country, in such a situation, an enormous wickedness in the sight of God, and worthy of his curse, as well as a scandalous, dastardly meanness in the sight of men, and worthy of public shame and indignation? Is it not fit, that those who so contemptuously depreciate the rich and undeserved bounties of heaven, and who swell so insolently with a vain conceit of their own importance and worth, should be punished with the loss of these blessings? What discipline can be more seasonable or congruous? May we not suppose that divine Providence has permitted our body politic to suffer wound after wound, and baffled all our languid efforts, in order to give it sensibility, and rouse us to exert our strength in more vigorous efforts? Has not the curse of God lain heavy upon our country, because we have done the work of the Lord deceitfully, and kept back our swords from blood?

And shall this guilt increase from year to year, till we are entirely crushed with the enormous load? Shall neither the fear of Jehovah's curse, nor the love of our country, nor even the love of ourselves, and our own personal interest, constrain us at length to relieve our ravaged country, and defend the blessings which God has entrusted to our custody, as well as lent us to enjoy?   .   .   .   .

Oh! for the all-prevailing force of Demosthenes's oratory—but I recall my wish, that I may correct it—Oh! for the influence of the Lord of armies, the God of battles, the Author of true courage and every heroic virtue, to fire you into patriots this moment and soldiers!—Ye young and hardy men, whose very faces seem to speak that God and nature formed you for soldiers, who are free from the incumbrance of families depending upon you for subsistence, and who are perhaps but of little service to society, while at home, may I not speak for you, and declare as your mouth, "Here we are, all ready to abandon our ease, and rush into the glorious dangers of the field, in defence of our country?" Ye that love your country, enlist; for honor will follow you in life or death in such a cause.

William Livingston.

BORN in Albany, N. Y., 1723.   DIED at Elizabethtown, N. J., 1790.

THE WIFE.

[Philosophic Solitude. 1747.]

BY love directed, I would choose a wife,
    To improve my bliss, and ease the load of life.
Hail, wedlock! hail, inviolable tie!
Perpetual fountain of domestic joy!
Love, friendship, honor, truth, and pure delight
Harmonious mingle in the nuptial rite.
In Eden, first the holy state began,
When perfect innocence distinguished man;
The human pair, the Almighty pontiff led,
Gay as the morning, to the bridal bed;
A dread solemnity the espousals graced,
Angels the witnesses, and God the priest!
All earth exulted on the nuptial hour,
And voluntary roses decked the bower,
The joyous birds on every blossomed spray,
Sung hymeneans to the important day,
While Philomela swelled the spousal song,
And Paradise with gratulation rung.

  Relate, inspiring muse! where shall I find
A blooming virgin with an angel mind?
Unblemished as the white-robed virgin quire
That fed, O Rome! thy consecrated fire?
By reason awed, ambitious to be good,
Averse to vice, and zealous for her God?
Relate, in what blest region can I find
Such bright perfections in a female mind?
What phœnix-woman breathes the vital air
So greatly good, and so divinely fair?
Sure not the gay and fashionable train,
Licentious, proud, immoral, and profane;
Who spend their golden hours in antic dress,
Malicious whispers, and inglorious ease.

  Lo! round the board a shining train appears
In rosy beauty, and in prime of years!
This hates a flounce, and this a flounce approves,
This shows the trophies of her former loves;
Polly avers that Sylvia dressed in green,
When last at church the gaudy nymph was seen;
Chloe condemns her optics; and will lay
'Twas azure satin, interstreaked with gray;

Wel. Liv eington

Lucy, invested with judicial power,
Awards 'twas neither—and the strife is o'er.
Then parrots, lapdogs, monkeys, squirrels, beaux,
Fans, ribbons, tuckers, patches, furbelows,
In quick succession, through their fancies run,
And dance incessant on the flippant tongue.
And when, fatigued with every other sport,
The belles prepare to grace the sacred court,
They marshal all their forces in array,
To kill with glances, and destroy in play.
Two skilful maids, with reverential fear,
In wanton wreaths collect their silken hair;
Two paint their cheeks, and round their temples pour
The fragrant unguent, and the ambrosial shower;
One pulls the shape-creating stays; and one
Encircles round her waist the golden zone;
Not with more toil to improve immortal charms,
Strove Juno, Venus, and the queen of arms,
When Priam's son adjudged the golden prize,
To the resistless beauty of the skies.
At length, equipped in Love's enticing arms,
With all that glitters, and with all that charms,
The ideal goddesses to church repair,
Peep through the fan, and mutter o'er a prayer,
Or listen to the organ's pompous sound,
Or eye the gilded images around;
Or, deeply studied in coquettish rules,
Aim wily glances at unthinking fools;
Or show the lily hand with graceful air,
Or wound the fopling with a lock of hair:
And when the hated discipline is o'er,
And misses tortured with repent, no more,
They mount the pictured coach; and, to the play,
The celebrated idols hie away.

Not so the lass that should my joys improve,
With solid friendship, and connubial love:
A native bloom, with intermingled white,
Should set her features in a pleasing light;
Like Helen flushing with unrivalled charms,
When raptured Paris darted in her arms.
But what, alas! avails a ruby cheek,
A downy bosom, or a snowy neck!
Charms ill supply the want of innocence,
Nor beauty forms intrinsic excellence,
But in her breast let moral beauties shine,
Supernal grace and purity divine:
Sublime her reason, and her native wit
Unstrained with pedantry, and low conceit:
Her fancy lively, and her judgment free
From female prejudice and bigotry:

Averse to idle pomp and outward show,
The flattering coxcomb, and fantastic beau.
The fop's impertinence she should despise,
Though sorely wounded by her radiant eyes;
But pay due reverence to the exalted mind,
By learning polished, and by wit refined,
Who all her virtues, without guile, commends,
And all her faults as freely reprehends.
Soft Hymen's rites her passion should approve,
And in her bosom glow the flames of love:
To me her soul, by sacred friendship, turn,
And I, for her, with equal friendship burn:
In every stage of life afford relief,
Partake my joys, and sympathize my grief;
Unshaken, walk in Virtue's peaceful road,
Nor bribe her Reason to pursue the mode;
Mild as the saint whose errors are forgiven,
Calm as a vestal, and composed as heaven.
This be the partner, this the lovely wife,
That should embellish and prolong my life,
A nymph! who might a second fall inspire,
And fill a glowing cherub with desire!
With her I'd spend the pleasurable day,
While fleeting minutes gaily danced away:
With her I'd walk, delighted, o'er the green,
Through every blooming mead, and rural scene;
Or sit in open fields damasked with flowers,
Or where cool shades imbrown the noon-tide bowers.
Imparadised within my eager arms.
I'd reign the happy monarch of her charms;
Oft on her panting bosom would I lay,
And in dissolving raptures melt away;
Then lulled, by nightingales, to balmy rest,
My blooming fair should slumber at my breast.

THE CAREER OF A COLONIAL DICTATOR.

[*A Review of the Military Operations in North America.* 1757.]

AS the Lieutenant-Governor will appear, in the course of this letter, to bear a principal part in our public transactions, it will be necessary, before I proceed any farther, to present your Lordship with his picture at full length. Without an intimate knowledge of that gentleman's history and genius, it will be impossible to comprehend his conduct, or trace his actions to their genuine source.

He is the eldest branch of one of the first families in the province.

His father, a French refugee, a gentleman of distinguished rank in this city, and who here acquired a large fortune, sent him for his education to the University of Cambridge. He was a youth of prompt parts, and made a considerable progress in learning, especially in the classics. In the year 1729 he was, by Governor Montgomery's recommendation, created one of his Majesty's Council of New York; but never engaged the public attention till the time of Mr. Cosby. He became then very famous. With this governor he took part in most or all of his measures —measures extremely arbitrary, and productive of an administration odious and turbulent. Cosby, in return for his ministerial services, loaded him with favors. Deposing Chief-Justice Morris (the main obstacle to his perilous projects) he raised him to the first seat on the bench. But though his Excellency had the disposition of offices, he could by no means delegate the affections of the people. Accordingly, our politician was equally honored and despised. He enjoyed the smiles of the Governor, which loaded him with the curses of the people; was caressed by the former, and by the latter abhorred. Cosby leaving a successor capable of governing without a prompter, the Chief-Justice found it necessary to deface the memory of his former conduct, by cultivating the arts of popularity. Mr. Clarke, who succeeded, being perfectly master of our constitution, a gentleman of experience and penetration, and intimately acquainted with the temper of the people, in a short time reconciled all parties; and by restoring the public tranquillity, rendered Mr. De Lancey's plodding abilities utterly useless. Hence he was at full leisure to court the populace. Suddenly he became transformed into a patriot; and strange to relate without a single act of patriotism. His uncommon vivacity with the semblance of affability and ease; his adroitness at a jest, with a show of condescension to his inferiors, wonderfully facilitated his progress. These plausible arts, together with his influence as Chief-Justice, and a vast personal estate at use, all conspired to secure his popular triumph. To establish such an undue power and amazing influence would, in a Grecian commonwealth, have exposed a man of less ambition and better principles to the ostracism.

Mr. Clarke being superseded by Governor Clinton, Mr. De Lancey was presented with a fresh opportunity for the exhibition of his political genius. Mr. Clinton, a gentleman of but indifferent parts, wholly resigned himself into his hands. Contenting himself with the title and salary of Governor, he left the sole direction of affairs to his minister, who, by reason of his late acquired omnipotence with the assembly, carried all his points, and even endeared him to the people. This intimacy subsisted no longer than it was found conducive to his designs. Having obtained from Mr. Clinton a new commission for his office of Chief-Justice during good behavior; and flattering himself with the hopes of another appointing him Lieutenant-Governor, through the interest of his friends in England, he cared not how soon his Excellency abdicated the province, nor how tempestuous he rendered his administration; and was therefore prepared for an open rupture. He no sooner thought himself capable of acting independently of the Governor, than, like Sixtus Quintus, who threw aside his crutches the moment of his exaltation to the popedom, he put off all that humble devotion by which he had so fatally deceived his too credulous master, and openly set himself at defiance against him. Now he began to dictate rather than advise; and instead of Sejanus, chose to be Tiberius himself. Dining one day with Mr. Clinton and insisting upon some favorite point with great imperiousness, the Governor, who had hitherto very cordially suffered himself to be led, refused on this occasion to be driven. The Chief-Justice then arose and left him; declaring with an oath, he "would make his administration uneasy for the future." His Excellency replied "he might do his worst." Thus they parted; nor were ever afterwards reconciled.

This breach gave rise to the contentions which so unhappily imbroiled our provincial affairs during the remainder of his administration. The assembly were instantly inflamed. He who before had been able to make them connive at very unjustifiable steps, could at once stir up an opposition to the most unexceptionable measures. Remonstrances, warm and virulent, were now drawn up; unworthy their own dignity to offer, and replete with the grossest language to his Majesty's representative. Thus was formed against Mr. Clinton a powerful party, which ceased not, while he continued at the helm, to harass and perplex him. To such an exorbitant length did they carry their opposition, as to throw off the restraint of humanity; they had even recourse to force and violence. Nay, a partisan of the Chief-Justice, in defiance of the sacred rights of the magistracy and the law—to show his resentment against Mr. Clinton and his adherents—assaulted the mayor; whipped the sheriff; damned the Governor; and stabbed his physician. My Lord, we became the sport and contempt of our neighbors; and it is beyond contradiction that Mr. De Lancey, by blowing up the coals of contention, did the province more injury than he will ever be able to repair. Nor is there any reason to doubt that the enormous power of this gentleman, and the ferment raised against Mr. Clinton, occasioned the 39th article of the King's instructions to Sir Danvers Osborn; which appears purposely calculated to render our future Governors independent on his influence over the assembly. For a law indefinite, making provision for the salary allowed by the King to his Governors, and competent salaries to all judges, justices, and other necessary officers and ministers of government—such a law, I say, would effectually render a Governor independent of the assembly, and consequently of any undue influence in it.

Not without such independence, or an abridgment of Mr. De Lancey's power, by reducing him to his primitive private station, do I see any probability of the extinction of that party-spirit which hath so long disturbed the tranquillity and injured the public weal of the colony.

Mr. Clinton being superseded by Sir Danvers Osborn, a gentleman of a most amiable moral character, retired into the country; from whence he proposed to embark for Great Britain. The Chief-Justice, notwithstanding his long declared enmity, and unwearied industry to embarrass his administration, had now—the humility, shall I call it?—to dispatch a messenger to him, with design if possible to procure an accommodation, in order to secure his favor in England, when he could no longer distress him in America. It were difficult to determine whether this required a higher degree of assurance or servility. But it is no uncommon thing to behold the same person fastidious and fawning, supercilious and sycophantic. Mr. Clinton, far from an implacable enemy, began to be softened; when his lady (who, if born among the Scythians, had been the Thalestris of antiquity) unravelling the secret, frustrated at once all expectations of a composition; and gave the plenipotentiary such a volley of invective against his constituent, as rendered all future overtures entirely hopeless. On the death of Sir Danvers Osborn, equally unexpected and deplored, Mr. De Lancey published the commission he had just received, appointing him Lieutenant-Governor.

He was now to act a part entirely new, and demanding the full exertion of his political dexterity. In the first place he had to convince the ministry of his utmost efforts to carry the King's instructions in the house of representatives; and in the next, in order to preserve his popularity with the assembly, and not in the most flagrant manner counteract his avowed principles, he was to satisfy them that in reality he by no means expected their compliance with them. To execute the former part of this plan—in his speech of the 31st of October, 1753, to the Council and General Assembly, he says, " You will perceive by the 39th article of his Majesty's instructions to Sir Danvers Osborn (copies of which I shall herewith deliver you) how highly his Majesty is displeased at the neglect of, and contempt shown to his royal commission and instructions, by your passing laws of so extraordinary nature, and by such your unwarrantable proceedings, particularly set forth in this instruction. Hence also his Majesty's royal pleasure as to these matters will appear, and what he expects from you. On this head, I must observe to you, that by our excellent constitution the executive power is lodged in the crown: That all government is founded on a confidence, that every person will discharge the duty of his station; and if there should be any abuse of power, that the legal and regular course is to make application to his Majesty, who having a paternal tenderness for

all his subjects, is always ready to hear and redress their grievances."
And then addressing himself to the assembly in particular:—"I must
earnestly press it upon you, that in preparing your bill for the support
of government, and other public services, you pay a due regard to his
Majesty's pleasure signified in his instructions, and frame them in such a
manner as when laid before me for my assent, I may give it consistent
with my duty to his Majesty."

What think you, my Lord? could your favorite Garrick have personated Richard the Third in a livelier manner, than this gentleman the
real advocate for the royal instruction? Could the man, who but a day
or two before had intrigued with the members how to elude that very
instruction, preserve his gravity while acting such a tragi-comical farce?
for that, my Lord, was the method in which he performed the second
part of his plan. As his Majesty's representative, he was obliged to urge
their compliance with seeming sincerity and warmth—but as James De
Lancey, Esq., their old friend and best adviser, it was his real senti-
ment, that never ought they to submit.

Matters being thus previously adjusted, the assembly in their address
studiously avoid a categorical answer with respect to the indefinite support; but to gratify his honor, and blacken the memory of Mr. Clinton,
that he might not prejudice him in England, they make use of this
memorable evasion:—"On reading the 39th article of his Majesty's
instructions to Sir Danvers Osborn, your honor's immediate predecessor,
we are extremely surprised to find that the public transactions of this
colony have been so maliciously misrepresented to our most gracious
sovereign. We can, sir, with truth and justice, affirm that his Majesty
has not in his dominions a people more firmly, and that from principles
of real affection, devoted to his person, family, and government, than
the inhabitants of this colony, and we are greatly at a loss to discover
in what instances the peace and tranquillity of the colony have been disturbed, or wherein order and government have been subverted. If the
course of justice has been obstructed, or in any case perverted, it has
been by the direction, or through the means of Mr. Clinton, late Governor of this province, who sent peremptory orders to the judges, clerk,
and sheriff of Duchess county, to stay process, and stop the proceedings
in several cases of private property, depending in that court; and who
did in other counties commissionate judges and justices of known ill
characters and extreme ignorance. One stood even presented for perjury
in the Supreme Court of this province, whom he rewarded with the
office of assistant judge; and others were so shamefully ignorant and
illiterate, as to be unable to write their own names. From whence we
greatly fear that justice has in many cases been partially, or very unduly
administered."

I shall not trouble your Lordship with a vindication of Mr. Clinton; but only observe that the suits commenced in Duchess county were by deserters against their captains; that the Governor, who was no lawyer, assured the house, his letters to the justices were written unadvisedly, and with precipitation; and that, if any man was injured, he would readily compensate his damages. And as to the charge of appointing ignorant justices, it lies with equal truth against all our governors (Mr. De Lancey himself not excepted) who, to influence elections, have gone into an unjustifiable practice of intrusting blank commissions with certain favorites in the respective counties, empowered to place and displace civil and military officers at their pleasure. These election jobbers are generally the court members in assembly; and decency, my Lord, should have induced them to stifle the ridiculous assertion that Mr. Clinton rewarded a man for being perjured, as well as the more pertinent invective against the dangerous usage just mentioned, for corrupting the house of representatives. But to disgrace Mr. Clinton was expedient to the Lieut.-Governor, and hence this attack upon the former.

Upon his honor's advancement to the government, the press labored with addresses; and the incense offered upon the occasion might have perfumed the whole temple of Delphos. It was not enough, that, agreeable to ancient usage, he was presented with the compliments of public bodies alone. It was necessary, from the number of addresses, to display his extensive influence and the universal joy, thereby, if possible, to lay the foundation of his continuance in the administration. Accordingly, the very militia officers and supervisors of Queen's county (a motley assemblage) were made to groan out their aspirations for this auspicious event—"Oh! that his gracious Majesty would be pleased to confirm and fix for you, for a long time, in this exalted station!" Never have I seen an insignificant interjection more insignificantly employed. To so extravagant a pitch, my Lord, did this exuberant ardor arrive, that we at length found him clothed with an incommunicable attribute of the Deity himself—even his immutable moral rectitude. "These things in you," say they, "are not so properly called virtues, as natural endowments. You will not, you cannot, act otherwise than you do." With such fustian can some men be regaled; and by such fustian is sometimes a whole nation deluded.

To proceed in the character of this remarkable American; he is a person of quick apprehension and extensive acquaintance with the law, which he acquired with incredible application, to obliterate the indifferent figure he made when first elevated to the chief seat on the bench, to serve the purposes of Governor Cosby. Without the talents, he has all the ambition of a Ripperda. His thirst after popularity, which in him is a mere engine of state, hath almost banished all public spirit; and the triumphs of power occasioned the exile of common sense. Apprehensive of the diminution of his own lustre, his jealousy will not admit a competitor; but sets him at mortal odds with a rising independent spirit, lest it be rewarded with popular favor, and thence result into popular interest—in derogation of his own sovereign influence. Hence, whoever would accomplish a patriot measure must either obtain his leave; and then he arrogates *to* himself the merit due to its author; or carry it by mere stratagem, without which he may be sure of a disappointment. In the latter case, he has generally address enough to be revenged on the projector, by rendering both him and his project universally odious. Some among us see these arts; many suspect them; few dare mention them; and fewer still oppose them. Thus a people who would by no means be forcibly deprived of their liberties, post into voluntary bondage; and they who would scorn a vassalage to the greatest monarch, become dupes to a dictator of their own creation. Of all provincial affairs he is the uncontrolled director.

As Chief-Justice, great is his interest in the counties; with that interest he commands elections; with his sway in elections he rules the assembly; and with his sovereignty over the house controls a governor. His influence with the members of the assembly being the main source of his exorbitant power, never will he serve the Crown at the risk of a dissension with the house. He will only stand by a governor while at his devotion and standing fair with the people; but in case of a rupture instantly sacrifice prerogative on the altar of popularity. His own interest is his idol, and everything else made subservient to procure it veneration and esteem. The men who are his greatest tools are generally by himself the most despised; and sometimes treated with despite and insult. If they discover the least freedom of resentment (which few of them dare discover), he can with a smile, or a joke, or a promise, or a bottle, at once dissipate the struggling resolution, and reduce them to their primitive obsequiousness. By hints, by threats and blandishments, by emissaries, by dark insinuations, and private cabals, he is able to render any measure hateful or popular—to put down, or raise up, whom, when, and what he pleases. Nay, my Lord, I will venture to affirm— and every man in the province must bear me testimony—that while his influence continues to be supported with his office of Chief-Justice, no operation, in which this colony is concerned, can promise success, should this monopolizer of power be determined to obstruct it.

Should it now be inquired, must not a man so extremely popular be necessarily possessed of eminent virtue, and warmly devoted to the weal of the people, who thus cordially resound his fame, submit to his control, and agree to adorn his triumph? The question can only come from a novice in history and a stranger to mankind. In the judgment of your

Lordship, who is deeply read in both, I am confident that popularity is no indication of merit. With the deluded multitude the best men are often unpopular—the most pernicious extolled and adored. The people are ever ready to be bewitched, cheated, and enslaved by a powerful, crafty seducer; and, what is worse, ever ready to sacrifice whoever would disabuse and release them. The same people who could without emotion behold a Sidney bleeding in defence of public liberty, could commit a riot in rescuing a Sacheverell for preaching sedition and subverting the nation. Your Lordship remembers that Masaniello, in the short space of ten days, was a poor fisherman,—a popular incendiary,—a sovereign viceroy,—stripped of his honors,—treated like a malefactor,—knocked on the head,—and thrown into a ditch. Who, in fine, was more popular than the pestilent Claudius, except perhaps the more pestilent Catiline? 'Twas, therefore, well observed by the Protector Cromwell that the very men who followed him with acclamations and torrents of flattery, would with the same demonstrations of joy accompany him to the gallows. Thus, my Lord, I have presented you with a faithful portrait of the Lieut.-Governor of New York, who is to bear no small share in the public affairs, of which I have the honor to transmit your Lordship an account—a portrait under which there had been no need of fixing a name, to direct to the original those who have the least knowledge of that gentleman's character.

THE STORY OF BRADDOCK'S DEFEAT.

[*From the Same.*]

ABOUT this time the colonies were filled with universal joy, on the agreeable news that the New England troops were become masters of Beau Sejour and Bay Verte, on the isthmus of Nova Scotia, whereby a new province was added to the British empire in America; and that a strong fleet, under Admiral Boscawen, lay before Louisburgh, to intercept the French supplies—and which had also seized two of their capital ships, the Lys and Alcide, and sent them into Halifax. General Braddock was now on his march toward the Ohio, at the head of about 2,200 men, in order to invest Fort Du Quesne, and drive the French from their encroachments on the frontiers of Virginia and Pennsylvania. From Fort Cumberland to Fort Du Quesne the distance is not less than 130 miles. Mr. Braddock began his march from the former on the 10th of June, leaving the garrison under the command of Col. Innes. Innumerable were the difficulties he had to surmount, in a country rugged, pathless, and unknown, across the Alleghany mountains, through unfrequented woods, and dangerous defiles. From the little meadows the army proceeded in two divisions. At the head of the first, consisting of 1,400 men, was the General himself with the greatest part of the ammunition and artillery. The second, with the provisions, stores, and heavy baggage, was led by Col. Dunbar. Never was man more confident of success, than this brave though unfortunate officer. Being advised at the great meadows that the enemy expected a reinforcement of 500 regular troops, he pushed on by forced marches with so much dispatch, that he fatigued the soldiers, weakened his horses, and left his second division near forty miles in the rear.

The enemy, being not more than 200 strong at their fort on the Ohio, gave no obstruction to the march of our forces till the memorable 9th of July—a day never to be forgotten in the annals of North America. About noon our troops passed the Monongahela, and were then within seven miles of Fort Du Quesne. Unapprehensive of the approach of an enemy, at once was the alarm given by a quick and heavy fire upon the vanguard under Lieut.-Col. Gage. Immediately the main body, in good order and high spirits, advanced to sustain them. Orders were then given to halt, and form into battalia.

At this juncture the van falling back upon them in great confusion a general panic seized the whole body of the soldiery; and all attempts to rally them proved utterly ineffectual. The General and all the officers exerted their utmost activity to recover them from the universal surprise and disorder; but equally deaf were they to entreaties and commands. During this scene of confusion they expended their ammunition in the wildest and most unmeaning fire, some discharging their pieces on our own parties, who were advanced from the main body for the recovery of the cannon. After three hours spent in this melancholy situation, enduring a terrible slaughter, from (it may be said) an invisible foe, orders were given to sound a retreat, that the men might be brought to cover the wagons. These they surrounded but a short space of time; for, the enemy's fire being again warmly renewed from the front and left flank, the whole army took to immediate flight, leaving behind them all the artillery, provisions, ammunitions, baggage, military chest, together with the General's cabinet, containing his instructions and other papers of consequence. So great was the consternation of the soldiers that it was impossible to stop their career,—flying with the utmost precipitation three miles from the field of action; where only one hundred began to make a more orderly retreat.

What was the strength of the enemy has hitherto remained to us uncertain. According to Indian accounts, they exceeded not 400, chiefly Indians; and whether any were slain is still to be doubted, for few were seen by our men, being covered by stumps and fallen trees. Great indeed was the destruction on our side. Numbers of officers sacrificed their lives through singular bravery. Extremely unfortunate was the whole staff. The General, after having five horses shot under him, received a wound in his lungs, through his right arm, of which he died in four days. His secretary, eldest son of Major-General Shirley, a gentleman of great accomplishments, by a shot through the head was killed upon the spot. Mr. Orme and Capt. Morris, aid-de-camps, were all wounded. Of the 44th regiment, Sir Peter Halket, Colonel, was slain, with several other officers; and Lieut.-Col. Gage wounded. Lieut.-Col. Burton, of the 48th regiment, was among the wounded; and many gallant officers perished in the field. Our whole loss was about seven hundred killed and wounded.

To what causes this unhappy catastrophe is to be ascribed, has been matter of much inquiry and animated debate. The officers charged the defeat to the cowardice of the men ; but, in a representation they made to Mr. Shirley by order of the Crown, they in some measure apologize for their behaviour—alleging that they were harassed by duties unequal to their numbers, and dispirited through want of provisions; that time was not allowed them to dress their food ; that their water (the only liquor, too, they had) was both scarce and of a bad quality ;—in fine, that the provincials had disheartened them, by repeated suggestions of their fears of a defeat, should they be attacked by Indians, in which case the European method of fighting would be entirely unavailing. But, my Lord, however censurable the conduct of the soldiery may be thought, Mr. Braddock, too sanguine in his prospects, was generally blamed for neglecting to cultivate the friendship of the Indians, who offered their assistance, and who, it is certain, had a number of them preceded the army, would have seasonably discovered the enemy's ambuscade. The Virginian rangers also, instead of being made to serve as regulars in the ranks with the English troops, should have been employed as out-scouts. But this step, so necessary to guard against surprise, was too unhappily omitted, the whole army, according to the representation above mentioned, following only three or four guides. When the routed party joined the second division, forty miles short of the place of action, the terror diffused itself through the whole army. Your Lordship might naturally expect to hear that Col. Dunbar then intrenched himself, and called on the neighboring colonies for immediate reinforcements ;—as by such a step the enemy might have been detained at Fort Du Quesne, prevented from ravaging the frontiers, or throwing succors into Niagara. But alas! my Lord, an infatuation seemed to accompany all our measures on the southern quarter. Fearful of an unpursuing foe, all the ammunition, and so much of the provisions were destroyed, for accelerating their flight, that Dunbar was actually obliged to send for thirty horse-loads of the latter, before he reached Fort Cumberland—where he arrived a very few days after, with the shattered remains of the English troops.

Nicholas Scull.

BORN near Philadelphia, Penn., 1687.　DIED in Philadelphia, 1762.

A WAR OF KINGS.

[*Kawanio Che Keeteru: A true Relation of a Bloody Battle Fought between George and Lewis. 1756.*]

THERE lived a man not long ago,
　And yet may live for ought I know,
A patriot bold of honest fame,
A Briton true, and "George" his name.
His generous breast contained a heart
That dared to act an honest part;
He loved the cause of liberty,
And scorned a life that was not free;
His country's cause he would defend,
And venture all to serve a friend;
No man more bold in time of danger,
To fear, as well as vice, a stranger.
Thus, long our hero lived at ease
With all the world, in love and peace,
Till Lewis, whose ambitious mind,
Nor law, nor justice, e'er could bind,
Seized on a part of George's land,
And held possession, sword in hand.
Our hero, though averse to war,
Could not this daring insult bear,
But soon resolved his foe to fight,
And by the sword regain his right.

　　·　　·　　·　　·　　·　　·

　No sooner had the king of day
　Bedecked the Eastern sky with gray,
　When both the champions, well prepared,
　In the decisive field appeared.

　Quoth George, "I joy to meet you here;
　Now to defend yourself prepare!"
　Lewis returned, "Yourself defend,
　Your life or mine the strife must end!"

This said, they instantly engage
With manly strength and martial rage;
A bloody combat long they held,
Each side unknowing how to yield.
They fought as brave, some authors tell us,
As did famed Hector and Achilles:
And asking both these heroes' pardon,
They laid each other full as hard on.
At length our warrior, filled with shame,
Unto a close engagement came,
And soon let Lewis understand
What 'twas to fight him hand to hand.
For, now, alas! the crimson tide
Flowed freely from the aggressor's side;
And, though he scarce his sword could wield,
His pride forbade his heart to yield.

When George, perceiving his distress,
His haughty foe did thus address:
"Lewis," quoth he, "let 's end the strife;
Restore my land, and take thy life."
Quoth Lewis: "Know, that still I live,
And scorn the life that thou can'st give.
No; one of us must die this day,
For death alone shall end the fray."
Thus he, when at our warrior's head
With both his hands a blow he made;
But George, who kept a watchful eye,
Perceived the stroke, and put it by,
And at this usage quite enraged,
His foe with double force engaged.

Now, Lewis, when it was too late,
Saw plainly his approaching fate;
Yet, dauntless, bravely played his part
'Till George's sword had pierced his heart:
At which he fell; and, falling, cried,
"My punishment is just;" and died.

Now from the multitude around,
Loud acclamations shake the ground;
Crying, "Now all our fears are fled,
For, lo! the lawless tyrant 's dead;
May heaven its choicest gifts bestow
Upon the man that gave the blow."

Samuel Niles.

BORN on Block Island, 1674. Minister at Braintree, Mass. DIED, 1762.

THE FRENCH ON BLOCK ISLAND.

[*A Summary Historical Narrative of the Wars in New-England. Completed*, 1760.]

SOME time in July, 1689, three French privateer vessels came to Block Island; upon which the people were alarmed, not then knowing whether they were English or French. The vessels were a large bark, a barge, a large sloop, and a lesser one. They had an Englishman with them, one William Trimming, who was wont treacherously to decoy and betray those they met with at sea, pretending they were Englishmen, as he had the perfect use of the English tongue. Him they sent on shore with some men in a periauger, which lay off at a small distance; while he took the advantage of stepping from one rock to another, and came alone to the islanders who were standing on the shore in arms,—who inquired of him who they were, and from whence they came, and whither they were bound, and their captain, or commodore's name. To which he answered, their commodore was George Astin (of whom they had often heard as a noted privateer, that had done great exploits against the French and Spaniards in the West Indies), and that they were Englishmen (when they were a mixed company, mostly French, with some Spaniards and Mestizos, and their captain's name was Pekar, a Frenchman); that they came from Jamaica, and were bound into Newport on Rhode Island (which was so far true, that their design was to take and rifle that town); that they wanted a pilot to conduct them into the harbor; and that they wanted to be supplied with some wood and water, and fresh provisions for their money. This was a plausible and very pleasing account to the inhabitants, though perfidiously false in the articles of greatest importance. What farther confirmed their credit in the case was, there happened to be a stranger on the island at that time, and then among the people, who pretended a particular acquaintance with Captain Astin, and also sent his compliments to him; so that, upon the whole, the islanders were very well satisfied, and fearless of danger.

Upon having thus told his story, Trimming, doubtless much pleased, went off to the periauger that waited for him. He having made a motion for a pilot to Newport, which was about ten leagues distant from them, several that had sailed to and from thence, in hopes of some great reward, went on board. They no sooner were got there, but they were immediately clapped down under the hatches and examined on the strength of Newport and of Block Island; and finding this last not able to resist them, they resolved to play their game in plundering the people of this island. Accordingly, manning their three periaugers, with about fifty men in each of them, they made to the harbor, having their guns all lying in the bottom of their boats out of sight,—where the people met them, and were something amused at their great number. But being well satisfied, as they thought, that there was no monkery in the case, therefore in a very friendly manner directed them to shun some sunken rocks that lay at the entrance into the harbor; and to requite their kindness, as they laid to the wharf, every one of them started up with his gun presented, and told the people if they stirred from the place, or made resistance, they were dead men. Thus tamely and unexpectedly, to their great surprise, they were all taken and made prisoners of war.

As for their coming in such great numbers, as before is noted, which at first gave the people some ground of suspicion, to this they were soon reconciled, supposing that they were willing to walk and divert themselves on the land, as they had been a long time at sea. So that all circumstances seemed to concur, by the treachery of this Trimming, to make them an easy prey to their enemies. As they were thus become masters of the island, they disarmed the men and stove their guns to pieces on the rocks, and carried the people and confined them in the house of Captain James Sands, before mentioned, which was large and accommodable for their purpose, and not far from the harbor. This they made their prison and place of rendezvous, and soon set upon plundering houses, and killing cattle, sheep and hogs, some to feed on, others for waste and spoil, and to impoverish the inhabitants.   .   .   .   .

However, news quickly reached to the main, that Block Island was taken by the French; upon which the country was alarmed; and bonfires made from Pawcatuck Point, which is the utmost extent of Rhode Island government next to Connecticut, and from thence round on Rhode Island to Seconet Point, which then was the farthest part of the Massachusetts government, but is now taken into the government of Rhode Island, upon a late overture of that affair—whether justly or not it is neither my province nor purpose now to determine.

They continued about a week on the island, plundering houses, stripping the people of their clothing, ripping up beds, throwing out the feathers, and carrying away the ticking. In this time they offered great abuses to Simon Ray, Esq., an aged gentleman who lived somewhat remote in the island, and had not removed his money nor choicest part of his goods out of his house until they saw a company of the enemy at a distance coming thither. He and his son (who was of the same name, and after bore the like distinguishing characters of honor and usefulness that his father had done before, who is now lately deceased also) as there was no minister in the place, were wont in succession, in a truly Christian, laudable manner, to keep a meeting in their own house on Lord's days, to pray, sing a suitable portion of the Psalms, and read in good sermon books, and, as they found occasion, to let drop some words of exhortation in a religious manner on such as attended their meeting. Upon the sight of the French coming, the son (then a young man) with the servants carried out some chests and what they could most readily convey out of the house, and hid them, and themselves also. When the Frenchmen came into the house, they found only the old gentleman and his wife; all the rest of the family were fled. The French demanded his money. He told them he had none at his command. They observed by the signs on the floor, that chests and other things were lately removed, and the money, which they principally aimed at,—asked him where they were. He told them he did not know, for his people had carried them out, and he could not tell where they put them. They bid him call his folks, that they might bring them again; which he did, but had no answer, for they were all fled out of hearing. They being thus disappointed, one of them, in a violent rage, got a piece of a rail and struck him on his head therewith, and in such fury that the blood instantly gushed out and ran on the floor. Upon which his wife took courage, and sharply reprehended them for killing her husband, which she then supposed they had done. Upon this they went off, without the game they expected. After the flow of blood was over, he recovered his health; and lived many years in his former religious usefulness, as before is noted.

Another man they used barbarously, by tricing him up and whipping him in an unmerciful manner, to make him confess where his money was, and bring it to them; when at the same time, as he declared to them, he had none or next to none. The case was this, as I understood it. They inquired of some one or more of the people, "Who were the likeliest among them to have money?" They told them of John Rathbun, who was the most likely. This poor man bearing his father's name (they supposing him to be the person) suffered this cruelty in the room of his father, who escaped by that means with his money. .   .   .   .

While they remained riding in the bay they took two vessels bound up the Sound, one laden with steel mostly, which they sunk; the other was laden with wine and spirituous liquors, which they purposed to carry off with them, but were prevented, as we shall find afterwards. The privateers perceiving, by the bonfires before spoken of, that the country was alarmed, and perhaps, by those that had gone on board them with hopes of becoming their pilots, before mentioned, being informed of the strength and numbers of men on Rhode Island, were discouraged making an attempt on Newport; therefore determined to attack New London. Accordingly they sailed thither, and up into the harbor. The country being before alarmed, as was said, and having had intelligence of their approach, the men in the bordering towns came down in great numbers; and the fort with their great guns firing on them, they found the harbor too hot for them. They therefore drew off and concluded to return to Block Island, and renew their spoils and plunder there. Some of their company went on an island called Fisher's Island, lying near New London, and among others this treacherous fellow, Trimming, before spoken of, of which they had some intelligence at Stonington. Upon which seventeen men went from thence over to the island, which is not far distant in the easternmost end. There was but one house on the island, though about nine miles in length, where this party of Frenchmen were at that time. The English got near the house before they were discovered; upon which Trimming came out to them, in a pretended friendly manner, drawing his gun behind him. They demanded "who and from whence they were." He replied, they were cast-away men. One of the Englishmen replied: "If you are friends, lay down your gun, and come behind us." Immediately Mr. Stephen Richardson, as was supposed through surprise, shot him dead on the spot, for which act he was much blamed. Thus he that delighted in falsehood in his life died with a lie in his mouth and received, it seems, the just reward of his perfidious, villainous and multiplied treacheries.

While these French privateers were making an attempt at New London, the people at Newport fitted out two vessels from thence with volunteers to engage them, supposing they were still at Block Island. These vessels were sloops under the command of Captain and Commodore Paine, who had some years before followed the privateering design, and Captain John Godfrey, his second; and inquiring for the French, they were told that when they left the island they shaped their course westward toward New London; upon which our English vessels stretched off to the southward, and soon made a discovery of a small fleet standing eastward. Supposing them to be the French they were in quest of, they tacked and came in as near the shore as they could with safety, carrying one anchor to wear and another to seaboard, to prevent the French boarding them on each side at once, and to bring their guns and men all on one side, the better to defend themselves and annoy the enemy. The French probably discovered them also, and made all the sail they could, expecting to make prizes of them. Accordingly they sent a periauger before them, full of men, with design to pour in their small arms on them and take them, as their manner was, supposing they were unarmed vessels and only bound up on trade. Captain Paine's gunner urged to fire on them. The Captain denied, alleging it more advisable to let the enemy come nearer under their command. But the gunner still urging it, being certain, as he said, he should rake fore and aft, thus with much importunity at length the Captain gave him liberty. He fired on them but the bullet went wide of them, and I saw it skip on the surface of the water several times, and finally lodge in a bank, as they were not very far distant from the shore. This brought them to a stand, and to row off as fast as they could and wait until their vessels came up.

When they came, they bore down on the English, and there ensued a very hot sea-fight for several hours, though under the land, the great bark foremost, pouring in a broadside with small arms. Ours bravely answered them in the same manner, with their huzzas and shouting. Then followed the larger sloop, the captain whereof was a very violent, resolute fellow. He took a glass of wine to drink, and wished it might be his damnation if he did not board them immediately. But as he was drinking, a bullet struck him in his neck, with which he instantly fell down dead, as the prisoners, before spoken of, afterward reported. However, the large sloop proceeded as the foremost vessel had done, and the lesser sloop likewise. Thus they passed by in course and then tacked and brought their other broadside to bear. In this manner they continued the fight until the night came on and prevented their farther conflict. Our men as valiantly paid them back in their own coin, and bravely repulsed them, and killed several of them. The Captain, before spoken of, with one or more were after driven on the shore. In this action the continued fire was so sharp and violent, that the echo in the woods made a noise as though the limbs of the trees were rent and tore off from their bodies (as I have observed); yet they killed but one man, an Indian fellow of the English party, and wounded six white men, who after recovered. They overshot our men, so that many of their bullets, both great and small, were picked up on the adjacent shore.

Our men expected a second encounter in the morning, and, their ammunition being much spent, sent in the night for the island's stock, as the French lay off at anchor but a small distance from them all the night.—But having found the engagement too hot for them, they hoisted their sails and stood off to sea ; and one reason might be this, as was reported, that their Commodore understood by some means that it was Captain Paine he had encountered, [and] said, " He would as soon choose to fight with the devil as with him." Such was their dialect. Now this Captain Paine and Pekar, the French Commodore, had sailed together a-privateering, Paine captain, and Pekar his lieutenant, in some former wars. The French standing off to sea, Captain Paine and Captain Godfrey, and their soldiers, with the valor and spirit of true Englishmen, pursued them, but the privateers, being choice sailers, were too light of foot for them. The French, finding that they hauled on the vessel before spoken of, loaded with wines and brandy, which was not so good a sailer as the others, and fearing the English would make a prey of her, fired a great shot through her bottom, so that when our men came to her she was sunk under water in her fore part, the stern only buoyed up by a long boat fastened to it; and as she was standing right up and down in the water, they could not get anything out of her. They no sooner cut the painter, but she instantly sunk to the bottom. They brought the boat with them in their return, which was the only prize and trophy of their victory; only as the enemy were vanquished, and that they had so courageously chased them off the New England coast. When Pekar heard that Trimming was killed, he greatly lamented, and said he had rather have lost thirty of his men.

Before the year was expired, some of the same company, with others, landed in the night and surprised the people in their beds, and proceeded in like manner as before, plundering houses, stripping the people of their clothing, killing creatures and making great waste and spoil; but killed no person. I suppose I was the greatest sufferer of any under their hands at this time; for before I had dressed myself, one of their company rushed into the chamber where I lodged. After some free and seemingly familiar questions he asked me, which I answered with like freedom; but being alone, without any of his company, not knowing what danger might befall him (as I after apprehended) on a sudden, and with a different air, he says to me, "Go down, you dog." To which I replied, "Presently; as soon as I have put on my stockings and shoes." At which, with the muzzle of his gun he gave such a violent thrust at the pit of my stomach, that it threw me backward on the bed, as I was sitting on the bedside, so that it was some time before I could recover my breath. As soon as I could, I gathered them up. He drew his cutlass and beat me, smiting with all his power, to the head of the stairs, and it was a very large chamber. He followed me down the stairs, and then bound my hands behind me with a sharp small line, which soon made my hands swell and become painful. How I managed after with my stockings and shoes I have now forgot. However, after this I met with no abuse from them the whole time of their stay on the island.

The first time the island was taken, of which I have given a narrative before, I took the first opportunity to make my escape, and some others did the like; and though we camped in a small piece of upland in a great swamp, yet every leaf that stirred with the wind made me with surprise conclude the French were come upon us. This made me determine with myself, that if ever it were my lot in providence to be taken by them again, I would continue in and see the worst of my bondage, until it pleased God to send me deliverance. This resolution I held, though I had a fair opportunity to make an escape, and notwithstanding the ill treatment I met with at first, as before is related.

The French came a third time while I was on the island, and came to anchor in the bay on Saturday, some time before night; and acquainted us who they were and what they intended, by hoisting up their white colors. None of the people appearing to oppose them, and having, at this time, my aged grandparents, Mr. James Sands and his wife, before mentioned, to take the care of, with whom I then dwelt; knowing also that if they landed they would make his house the chief seat of their rendezvous, as they had done twice before, and not knowing what insults or outrage they might commit on them, I advised to the leaving their house and betaking themselves to the woods for shelter, till they might return under prospects of safety; which they consented to. Accordingly we took our flight into the woods, which were at a considerable distance, where we encamped that night as well as the place and circumstances would allow, with some others, that for the like reasons fell into our company. The next morning, being Lord's day morning, I expressed my desire to go occultly and see the conduct of the French, and their proceedings. One of the company offered to go with me. We went together, and placed ourselves on the top of a hill, where were small bushes and a large swamp behind us; but in fair sight of the house I went from, viz., my grandfather's house. It seems the French had not landed till that morning, for we had not long been seated there before we saw them coming from the water-side in two files (which made a long train) with their colors flying, and, if I mistake not, their trumpet sounding. I did not then think of counting their number. Thus they came in triumph, and as absolute lords of the soil and all belonging thereto— as indeed they were for the time; but their reign was but short, as the sequel will prove. (My companion in this discovery was Mr. Thomas Mitchell who then, and many years after, was an inhabitant on Block Island, alias New Shoreham.)

In this manner they went to the house, and immediately set up their standard on a hill on the back side of it, and directly shot and killed three hogs fatted with whey in a sty, and then killed the geese, as there were many there. Having had but little sleep the night before, I proposed to Mr. Mitchell to keep a good look-out, and watch their motions, till I endeavored to sleep a little, and thus to proceed interchangeably; when I made the hard ground my lodging for the time, which was long. Upon my awaking, he lay down; and as he lay and slept, the French fired many guns at the house, and I heard several bullets whistling over my head. Suspecting they had made some discovery of us, I awakened him, telling him what I had observed; therefore that it was advisable to shift our quarters. Accordingly, as we were moving from the place, we espied a large ship about a league to leeward of the township, riding at anchor (the fog at sea had been very thick till then), which happened to be Captain Dobbins, in The Nonesuch man-of-war, stationed in those seas, which we at first sight supposed. This ship appearing put the

Frenchmen into a great surprise, by their motions, by running up to their standard on the hill, then down again, and others doing the like. The man-of-war still making all sail possible, there being but a small breeze of wind at south-west, and right ahead, according to the sailor's phrase, they soon left the house and with all speed and seeming confusion hastened to their vessel.   .   .   .   .

Soon after these privateers took to their heels, hoping to get out of the man-of-war's reach, the fog thickened, and the wind rose and blew hard at south-west, so that we quickly lost sight of them both. The French kept close upon the wind, in hopes to weather a place called No Man's Land, lying southward of Martha's Vineyard ; but the wind scanting on them, and blowing hard, they ran into a place (if I mistake not) called Buzzard's Bay, which emphatically proved so to them. There they were land-locked, and could not get out, although the French vessel was quickly out of sight by reason of the thick fog which continued. Yet as if the Nonesuch had tracked them by the print of their heels in the ocean, or had followed them in their wake, she came in upon them, Providence so ordering, and took them. When they saw, to their astonishment, the man-of-war so unexpectedly overtaking them, about forty of their men went on shore and were disarmed and seized by the people that dwelt near the place, and sent prisoners to Boston. The others on board Captain Dobbins took and made prisoners of war, and their ship became a rich prize, which we saw about three days after following him into Newport, where she was condemned.

These French privateers, or some others, came a fourth time and landed on Block Island, in the former war with France ; but the people on the island took courage, and encountered them in an open pitched battle, and drove them off from the shore, without any hurt to the English, except one man slightly wounded in his finger. They never after that troubled the people any more. The great spoil made on the island by the French, in their repeated visits, and particularly on my father's interest, occasioned my staying from school six years, when I intended only a short visit to my friends. In this time I turned my hand to husbandry, and sometimes to handicraft. I helped to build a vessel, among other things, for the West India trade, and caulked one side and the master-workman the other ; and she proved very tight and answerable to the design. After the space of six years thus employed, I returned again to school, so that, by reason of this delay, I was near two-and-twenty years old when I entered into the college at Cambridge, the Rev. Dr. Increase Mather then being President,—and Mr. John Leverett, afterward President, and Mr. William Brattle, after the reverend pastor of Cambridge Church, were the only fellows. The kindness of these worthy gentlemen I hope not to forget, who, I conclude, favored me the more, as I was the first that came to college from Rhode Island government.

THE FALL OF QUEBEC.

[*From the Same.*]

A S the people in Quebec and the inhabitants of the several settlements
and villages on the River St. Lawrence refused to accept of the
offers made them by General Wolfe in manifesto, four large parties were
sent out to destroy the country. Two of them proceeded by land, and
the other two by water, down the river. And, while they lay at [Isle]
Madame, they saw two villages, which were large, on fire; for the rangers
made great havoc through the country. A man-of-war was sent down to
a place called the Straits of Belleisle, to destroy a village there; where
they lost twelve men, and some were wounded. On the 28th of August,
two ships, the "Lowestoffe" and "Hunter," went by the town, in the
evening, to join Captain Rous in the "Sunderland." The French fired
smartly on them, killed one man and wounded two.

Some short time before the 13th of September, General Wolfe crossed
the river, and got above Quebec, with his small Prussian army as it was
called (I suppose, for their courage and remarkable success), consisting
of about 4,000 men; and, in about two hours after, General Montcalm,
that headed the French army of twelve thousand,—some said more,—with
a troop of five hundred horse in their front, [advanced] to give General
Wolfe battle in the Plain of Abraham, as it was called by the French.
The French kept a continued fire as they advanced toward our army; but
General Wolfe's order to his men was, not to fire until the enemy came
within about twenty rods of them, and, was said, in a manner within
the reach of their bayonets; but to squat, and secure themselves as much
as possible from the fury of the fire on them. His orders were punctually
obeyed; and when the enemy advanced to the distance before mentioned,
when his men had sustained three fires from the adversary, the word of
command was to fire; which was performed in such a manner as broke
the order of the horse, and threw them into the utmost confusion,—
probably by the wounding some and killing others of the horses, their
riders falling from them, and stumbling one on another, and on slain
men under their feet. It may easily be conceived what a consternation
they must suddenly [have been] thrown into; so that under a surprise,
and panic fear of what would follow, [they] soon began to retreat, and
soon after made their flight. Our men pursued them, and made havoc
in their pursuit,—beating them out of their trenches, and following them,
as was said, to their sally-ports,—so that the action lasted but about
fifteen minutes. However, in this time, the brave and renowned General
Wolfe received two balls, as was said, through his body, that ended his
days with his conquest; yet survived so long as to ask how the affair

stood; and when he heard that the enemy were defeated and [had] fled, he said he could then die in peace; and, accordingly, soon expired. Thus died a courageous and successful British hero; greatly and very deservedly lamented in the land, as an instrument in the hand of God, that had wrought such a wonderful deliverance, never to be forgotten, for the poor people in the country, in reducing Quebec into subjection to the Crown of Great Britain,—Quebec, I say, that had so long been the source and sink of all the barbarous cruelties that had been committed by the French, and Indians in their interest, at times of peace as well as in times of war, almost from the first settling of the English in this country. May God have glory, and the people, in our frontier settlements especially, reap the comfort of living quietly in their dwellings, free from the fear of the enemy, and be excited to fear God, and set up his worship, and maintain it in its gospel purity,—lamentably neglected in such places, for the most part: for which, and the growing corruptions of the land, we may conclude God has put the weapons of war, slaughter, and bloodshed, into our heathen and other enemies' hands, and given them commission to make the miserable havoc and spoils which they have done in the country; which we now hope, in the mercy of God, to be freed from. To return. In this action, Montcalm, the French general, was slain, and the second in command under him; the third wounded and taken prisoner; and the fourth killed. General Wolfe being killed, and General Monckton wounded in his lungs, the command of the army devolved on General Townsend, who, being advanced to the walls of Quebec, sent in a summons for a surrender of the city; acquainting them withal, that if they refused, and he was put upon storming the town, he would put all he found in it to the sword,—and those also, as it was said, that were their prisoners, taken in their flight, which were about two hundred in number: which they soon complied with. Upon their swearing allegiance to the King of Great Britain, and approving themselves accordingly, then they should be protected, and freely enjoy their own religion, estates, and properties, without any molestation; agreeably to demands made at first by General Wolfe in his manifesto, before any acts of hostility were begun. . . . .

The Governor of Quebec, Vaudreuil, stole out of the town in the time of the battle, and escaped; so that the city was surrendered by Monsieur Ramsey, then in chief command. It was reported by a person of veracity, as was said, who had been a prisoner with the French two years, that in that time, as he was in Canada, this Vaudreuil, then Governor, invited him one day to dine with him. He accordingly went; and, when he came thither, the Governor conducted him into a fine and large apartment, hung all round the room with Englishmen's scalps: showing him that such an one was a colonel's, and another a lieutenant-colonel's scalp; such a captain's; and such and such were the scalps of under English officers. It was also said he had a vault, prepared and improved for that purpose, where the scalps of English people were stowed in bulk.   .   .   .   .

The body of General Wolfe was carried home in the "Lowestoffe" man-of-war, to [be] enshrined in a cabinet of honor with the laurels of victories he had won in America; whose magnanimity and warlike prowess induced his Britannic Majesty to confer on him the honor and trust of a commander over his troops in two important enterprises,—in the first, [as] second in command under the brave General Amherst, in the reduction of Cape Breton, and territories thereto belonging, as has been briefly related; and then as chief of the land forces in recovering Quebec (the King of France's chief strength and glory in this land); who sacrificed his life in the conquest, and died victorious. It was said, that —under and together with the agreeable news of the surrender of Quebec —when it first reached the garrison at Crown Point, the death of General Wolfe was so affecting to the British forces there, that scarce any of them were able to refrain from shedding tears, as it was an alloy to the joy and satisfaction which otherwise doubtless would have run through the country and nation, with the tokens and marks of a laudable triumph, not in our own strength or desert, but in thankful praises to God, that had so wonderfully wrought our deliverance from the insulting cruelties of the French and Indians, that had not only destroyed great numbers of our people, but prevented the enlargement of settlements in the inland parts of the several Governments.

.   .   .   .

It was very remarkable, among many other instances in the siege of Quebec, that when the troops were passing by the city to the assistance of General Wolfe, in boats and transports, though the enemy's fire was so hot and violent from their several batteries, yet their red-hot balls and others were so directed, in Providence, that [while] some fell short, and many in the midst of them, they, notwithstanding, got up safely, with little or no damage. It was also remarkable, as was reported, that, in the time of the siege, the English prisoners desired to be released out of the prison, but were denied; and though bombs and cannon-balls fell and destroyed the houses round about and on every side, yet the prison escaped, and none in it were hurt. The deliverance of the poor prisoners, at the surrender of Quebec, must be as life from the dead—to escape out of that loathsome stinking cell where so many English people had successively perished under French tyranny and cruelty, in the most miserable manner, according to all accounts had from thence, from one time to another, especially in ruptures between the English and French crowns, to all of our people that are so miserable as to fall into their hands; for as it is the French maxim, that no faith is to be kept with heretics; so, in consequence, no favor is to be shown them when they fall within the reach of their inhuman barbarities.

. . . .

When the command of the army, by General Wolfe's death, devolved on General Townsend, he observed an old Highlander in the front of the army, laying about him with the most surprising strength and agility,— bearing down all before him,—till, almost spent with the fatigue, he retired behind a breastwork of dead bodies, most of which, as was said, he had slain with the force of his own sword; where he drew breath for a short time, and then, casting off his upper coat as too cumbersome, he returned again to the charge, and at every blow brought a Frenchman to the ground. The General, admiring his intrepid behavior, after the engagement was over sent for him; and, after he had bestowed on him the proper encomiums his gallant behavior deserved, he asked him how he could leave his native country, in such an advanced age, to follow the fortunes of war. The Highlander replied, his hatred to the French, on account of their perfidious behavior on many occasions, had made him leave his family now, when he was seventy years old, as a volunteer, in order to take revenge upon them before his death. General Townsend was so highly pleased with the magnanimity of this old soldier, that he took him home when he returned from Quebec, and presented him to Mr. Pitt, by whom he was introduced to his Majesty; who was graciously pleased to give him a lieutenant's commission, with the liberty of serving in any corps or in any country he chose; or, if he had rather return to his family, to have a lieutenant's full pay during life. He had made himself, together with the honors conferred on him by the King, so remarkable, that as he walked the streets in London, it was told, they that saw him cried, "There goes the brave old Highlander! Long live the gallant old boy." This soldier's sword,—with which he so valiantly distinguished himself,—as he said, has descended down from father to son, in succession, for three hundred years, as a particular legacy. It was an excellent weapon; and he was so extremely fond of it that he always took it to bed with him. He said his promotion flowed so fast on him, that he hoped to be a colonel, though then near seventy-three years of age. His name was Malcolm Macpherson, of Phones in Badenoch. He after returned to this country.

Verse of the French and Indian War.

SONG OF BRADDOCK'S MEN.

[The History of an Expedition against Fort Du Quesne in 1755.]

TO arms, to arms! my jolly grenadiers!
 Hark how the drums do roll it along!
To horse, to horse, with valiant good cheer;
 We'll meet our proud foe before it is long.
  Let not your courage fail you;
   Be valiant, stout, and bold;
  And it will soon avail you,
   My loyal hearts of gold.
Huzzah, my valiant countrymen!—again I say huzzah!
'Tis nobly done—the day's our own—huzzah, huzzah!

March on, march on, brave Braddock leads the foremost;
 The battle is begun as you may fairly see.
Stand firm, be bold, and it will soon be over;
 We'll soon gain the field from our proud enemy.
  A squadron now appears, my boys;
   If that they do but stand!
  Boys, never fear, be sure you mind
   The word of command!
Huzzah, my valiant countrymen! again I say huzzah!
'Tis nobly done—the day's our own—huzzah, huzzah!

See how, see how, they break and fly before us!
 See how they are scattered all over the plain!
Now, now—now, now, our country will adore us!
 In peace and in triumph, boys, when we return again!
  Then laurels shall our glory crown
   For all our actions told:
  The hills shall echo all around,
   My loyal hearts of gold.
Huzzah, my valiant countrymen!—again I say huzzah!
'Tis nobly done—the day's our own—huzzah, huzzah!

AN EPITAPH FOR BRADDOCK.

*[Braddock's Fate, with an Incitement to Revenge. Composed, by one Tilden,
August 20, 1755.]*

BENEATH this stone brave Braddock lies,
　Who always hated cowardice,
But fell a savage sacrifice;
　Amidst his Indian foes.
I charge you, heroes, of the ground,
To guard his dark pavilion round,
And keep off all obtruding sound,
　And cherish his repose.

Sleep, sleep, I say, brave, valiant man,
Bold death, at last, has bid thee stand,
And to resign thy great demand,
　And cancel thy commission:
Altho' thou didst not much incline,
Thy post and honors to resign;
Now iron slumber doth confine;
　None envies thy condition.

THE DEATH OF WOLFE.

[Pennsylvania Gazette, Nov. 8, 1759.]

THY merits, Wolfe, transcend all human praise,
　The breathing marble or the muses' lays.
Art is but vain—the force of language weak,
To paint thy virtues, or thy actions speak.
Had I Duché's or Godfrey's magic skill,
Each line to raise, and animate at will—
To rouse each passion dormant in the soul,
Point out its object, or its rage control—
Then, Wolfe, some faint resemblance should we find
Of those great virtues that adorned thy mind.
Like Britain's genius shouldst thou then appear,
Hurling destruction on the Gallic rear—
While France, astonished, trembled at thy sight,
And placed her safety in ignoble flight.
Thy last great scene should melt each Briton's heart,
And rage and grief alternately impart.
　With foes surrounded, midst the shades of death,
These were the words that closed the warrior's breath—
"My eyesight fails!—but does the foe retreat?
If they retire, I'm happy in my fate!"

A generous chief, to whom the hero spoke,
Cried, "Sir, they fly!—their ranks entirely broke:
Whilst thy bold troops o'er slaughtered heaps advance,
And deal due vengeance on the sons of France."
The pleasing truth recalls his parting soul,
And from his lips these dying accents stole:—
"I'm satisfied!" he said, then winged his way,
Guarded by angels, to celestial day.
　　An awful band!—Britannia's mighty dead,
Receives to glory his immortal shade.
Marlborough and Talbot hail the warlike chief—
Halket and Howe, late objects of our grief,
With joyful song conduct their welcome guest
To the bright mansions of eternal rest—
For those prepared who merit just applause
By bravely dying in their country's cause.

William Smith.

BORN in New York, N. Y., 1728.   DIED in Quebec, Canada, 1793.

THE RULE OF JACOB LEISLER; AND HIS FATE.

[*The History of the Province of New-York.* 1757.   *Completed from the Author's MS.,
and republished by the N. Y. Hist. Soc., 1826–29.*]

A GENERAL disaffection to the government prevailed among the
people. Papists began to settle in the colony under the smiles of
the Governor. The collector of the revenues, and several principal officers, threw off the mask, and openly avowed their attachment to the doctrines of Rome. A Latin school was set up, and the teacher strongly
suspected for a Jesuit. The people of Long Island, who were disappointed
in their expectation of mighty boons promised by the Governor on his
arrival, were become his personal enemies; and, in a word, the whole
body of the people trembled for the Protestant cause. Here the leaven
of opposition first began to work. Their intelligence from England, of
the designs there in favor of the Prince of Orange, blew up the coals of
discontent, and elevated the hopes of the disaffected. But no man dared
to spring into action till after the rupture in Boston. Sir Edmund Andros, who was perfectly devoted to the arbitrary measures of King James,
by his tyranny in New England had drawn upon himself the universal
odium of a people animated with the love of liberty, and in the defence
of it resolute and courageous; and, therefore, when they could no longer

endure his despotic rule they seized and imprisoned him, and afterwards sent him to England.

The government, in the mean time, was vested in the hands of a committee for the safety of the people, of which Mr. Bradstreet was chosen president. Upon the news of this event, several captains of our militia convened themselves to concert measures in favor of the Prince of Orange. Among these Jacob Leisler was the most active. He was a man in tolerable esteem among the people, and of a moderate fortune, but destitute of every qualification necessary for the enterprise. Milborne, his son-in-law, an Englishman, directed all his councils, while Leisler as absolutely influenced the other officers.

The first thing they contrived, was to seize the garrison in New York; and the custom, at that time, of guarding it every night by the militia, gave Leisler a fine opportunity of executing the design. He entered it with forty-nine men, and determined to hold it till the whole militia should join him. Colonel Dongan, who was about to leave the province, then lay embarked in the bay, having a little before resigned the government to Francis Nicholson, the Lieutenant-Governor. The council, civil officers, and magistrates of the city, were against Leisler, and therefore many of his friends were at first fearful of openly espousing a cause disapproved by the gentlemen of figure. For this reason, Leisler's first declaration in favor of the Prince of Orange was subscribed only by a few, among several companies of the trained bands. While the people, for four days successively, were in the utmost perplexity to determine what part to choose,—being solicited by Leisler on the one hand, and threatened by the Lieutenant-Governor on the other,—the town was alarmed with a report that three ships were coming up with orders from the Prince of Orange. This falsehood was very seasonably propagated to serve the interest of Leisler; for on that day, the 3d of June, 1689, his party was augmented by the addition of six captains and four hundred men in New York, and a company of seventy men from East Chester, who all subscribed a second declaration, mutually covenanting to hold the fort for the Prince. Colonel Dongan continued till this time in the harbor, waiting the issue of these commotions; and Nicholson's party, being now unable to contend with their opponents, were totally dispersed, the Lieutenant-Governor himself absconding the very night after the last declaration was signed.

Leisler, being now in complete possession of the fort, sent home an address to King William and Queen Mary, as soon as he received the news of their accession to the throne. It is a tedious, incorrect, ill-drawn narrative of the grievances which the people had endured, and the methods lately taken to secure themselves, ending with a recognition of the sovereignty of the King and Queen over the whole English dominions.

This address was soon followed by a private letter from Leisler to King William, which, in very broken English, informs his Majesty of the state of the garrison, the repairs he had made to it, and the temper of the people, and concludes with strong protestations of his sincerity, loyalty, and zeal. Jost Stoll, an ensign, on the delivery of this letter to the King, had the honor to kiss his Majesty's hand, but Nicholson, the Lieutenant-Governor, and one Ennis, an Episcopal clergyman, arrived in England before him ; and by falsely representing the late measures in New York, as proceeding rather from their aversion to the Church of England, than zeal for the Prince of Orange, Leisler and his party missed the rewards and notice, which their activity for the revolution justly deserved. For though the King made Stoll the bearer of his thanks to the people for their fidelity, he so little regarded Leisler's complaints against Nicholson, that he was soon after preferred to the government of Virginia. Dongan returned to Ireland, and it is said succeeded to the earldom of Limerick.

Leisler's sudden investiture with supreme power over the province, and the probable prospects of King William's approbation of his conduct, could not but excite the envy and jealousy of the late council and magistrates, who had refused to join in the glorious work of the revolution ; and hence the spring of all their aversion, both to the man and his measures.

Colonel Bayard, and Courtland, the mayor of the city, were at the head of his opponents, and finding it impossible to raise a party against him in the city they very early retired to Albany and there endeavored to foment the opposition.

Leisler, on the other hand, fearful of their influence, and to extinguish the jealousy of the people, thought it prudent to admit several trusty persons to a participation of that power which the militia, on the 1st of July, had committed solely to himself. In conjunction with these (who, after the Boston example, were called The Committee of Safety), he exercised the government, assuming to himself only the honor of being president in their councils. This model continued till the month of December, when a packet arrived with a letter from the Lords Carmarthen, Halifax, and others, directed " To Francis Nicholson, Esq., or, in his absence, to such as for the time being take care for preserving the peace and administering the laws in their Majesties' province of New York, in America."

This letter was dated the 29th of July, and was accompanied with another from Lord Nottingham, dated the next day, which after empowering Nicholson to take upon him the chief command, and to appoint for his assistance as many of the principal freeholders and inhabitants as he should think fit, requiring also " to do everything appertaining to the office of Lieutenant-Governor, according to the laws and customs of New York, until further orders."

Nicholson being absconded when this packet came to hand, Leisler considered the letter as directed to himself and from this time issued all kinds of commissions in his own name, assuming the title, as well as authority, of Lieutenant-Governor.   .   .   .   .

Except the eastern inhabitants of Long Island, all the southern part of the colony cheerfully submitted to Leisler's command.   The principal freeholders, however, by respectful letters, gave him hopes of their sub-mission, and thereby prevented his betaking himself to arms, while they were privately soliciting the colony of Connecticut to take them under its jurisdiction.   They had, indeed, no aversion to Leisler's authority, in favor of any other party in the province, but were willing to be incor-porated with a people from whence they had originally colonized; and, therefore, as soon as Connecticut declined their request, they openly ap-peared to be advocates for Leisler.   .   .   .   .

The people of Albany, in the mean time, were determined to hold the garrison and city for King William, independent of Leisler, and on the 26th of October, which was before the packet arrived from Lord Notting-ham, formed themselves into a convention for that purpose.   .   .   .   .

Taking it for granted that Leisler at New York, and the convention at Albany, were equally affected to the revolution, nothing could be more egregiously foolish than the conduct of both parties, who by their intes-tine divisions threw the province into convulsions, and sowed the seeds of mutual hatred and animosity, which for a long time after greatly em-barrassed the public affairs of the colony.

When Albany declared for the Prince of Orange, there was nothing else that Leisler could properly require; and, rather than sacrifice the public peace of the province to the trifling honor of resisting a man who had no evil designs, Albany ought, in prudence, to have delivered the garrison into his hands, till the King's definitive orders should arrive.   But while Leisler, on the one hand, was inebriated with his new-gotten power, so on the other, Bayard, Courtland, Schuyler and others, could not brook a sub-mission to the authority of a man, mean in his abilities, and inferior in his degree.   Animated by these principles, both parties prepared, the one to reduce, if I may use the expression, the other to retain, the garrison of Albany.

Mr. Livingston, a principal agent for the convention, retired into Con-necticut to solicit the aid of that colony for the protection of the frontiers against the French.

Leisler, suspecting that they were to be used against him, endeavored not only to prevent these supplies, but wrote letters to have Livingston apprehended as an enemy to the reigning powers, and to procure succors from Boston, falsely represented the convention as in the interest of the French and King James.

Jacob Milborne was commissioned for the reduction of Albany. Upon his arrival there, a great number of the inhabitants armed themselves and repaired to the fort, then commanded by Mr. Schuyler, while many others followed the other members of the convention to a conference with him at the City Hall.   Milborne, to proselyte the crowd, declaimed much against King James, popery, and arbitrary power ; but his oratory was lost upon the hearers, who after several meetings still adhered to the convention.

Milborne then advanced with a few men up to the fort, and Mr. Schuyler had the utmost difficulty to prevent both his own men, and the Mohawks, who were then in Albany and perfectly devoted to his service, from firing upon Milborne's party, which consisted of an inconsiderable number.   In these circumstances, he thought proper to retreat, and soon after departed from Albany.   In the Spring, he commanded another party upon the same errand, and the distress of the country on an Indian irruption gave him all the desired success.   No sooner was he possessed of the garrison than most of the principal members of the convention absconded.   Upon which, their effects were arbitrarily seized and confiscated, which so highly exasperated the sufferers, that their posterity, to this day, cannot speak of these troubles, without the bitterest invectives against Leisler and all his adherents.   .   .   .   .

While our allies were faithfully exerting themselves against the common enemy, Colonel Henry Sloughter who had a commission to be Governor of this Province, dated the 4th of January, 1689, arrived here, and published it on the 19th of March, 1691.   Never was a Governor more necessary to the province than at this critical conjuncture ; as well for reconciling a divided people, as for defending them against the wiles of a cunning adversary.   But either through the hurry of the King's affairs, or the powerful interest of a favorite, a man was sent over, utterly destitute of every qualification for government, licentious in his morals, avaricious and poor.   .   .   .   .

If Leisler had delivered the garrison to Colonel Sloughter, as he ought to have done, upon his first landing, besides extinguishing in a great degree the animosities then subsisting, he would doubtless have attracted the favorable notice, both of the Governor and the Crown.

But being a weak man he was so intoxicated with the love of power, that though he had been well informed of Sloughter's appointment to the government, he not only shut himself up in the fort with Bayard and Nichols, whom he had before that time imprisoned, but refused to deliver them up or to surrender the garrison.   From this moment he lost all credit with the Governor who joined the other party against him.   On the second demand of the fort, Milborne and Delanoy came out, under pretence of conferring with his Excellency, but in reality to discover his designs. Sloughter, who considered them as rebels, threw them both into gaol. Leisler, upon this event, thought proper to abandon the fort, which Colonel Sloughter immediately entered.

Bayard and Nichols were now released from their confinement and sworn of the Privy Council. Leisler, having thus ruined his cause, was apprehended with many of his adherents, and a commission of oyer and terminer issued to Sir Thomas Robinson, Colonel Smith, and others, for their trials.

In vain did they plead the merit of their zeal for King William, since they had so lately opposed his Governor. Leisler, in particular, endeavored to justify his conduct, insisting that Lord Nottingham's letter entitled him to act in the quality of Lieutenant-Governor. Whether it was through ignorance or sycophancy, I know not: but the judges instead of pronouncing their own sentiments upon this part of the prisoner's defence, referred it to the Governor and council, praying their opinion, whether that letter "or any other letters, or papers, in the packet from White-Hall, can be understood, or interpreted, to be and contain any power or direction to Captain Leisler, to take the government of this province upon himself, or that the administration thereupon be holden good in law." The answer was, as might have been expected, in the negative; and Leisler and his son were condemned to death for high treason. These violent measures drove many of the inhabitants, who were fearful of being apprehended, into the neighboring colonies, which shortly after occasioned the passing an act of general indemnity.   .   .   .   .

Colonel Sloughter proposed, immediately after the session, to set out to Albany, but as Leisler's party were enraged at his imprisonment and the late sentence against him, his enemies were afraid new troubles would spring up in the absence of the Governor. For this reason, both the assembly and council advised that the prisoners should be immediately executed. The sufferers under their government stated their oppressions to the assembly, who unanimously resolved on the 17th April, 1691, that their services were tumultuous and illegal and against the rights of the new King and Queen; that they had illegally and arbitrarily thrown divers Protestant subjects into doleful nauseous prisons; proscribed and forced others out of the colony; that the depredation upon Schenectady was imputable to their usurpations. That they had ruined merchants and others by seizures of their effects; levied money and rebelliously raised forces; and that their refusal to surrender the fort was rebellion.

The council concurred with the resolves on the next day. The assembly at first waived an answer to the Governor's question, respecting the propriety of reprisoning the convicts; he urged them again for an explicit answer three weeks after (11th May) whether they ought, or ought not to be executed ; and within eight days after this the council consented to the execution, and the assembly declared their approbation. Sloughter, who had no inclination to favor them in this request, chose rather to delay such a violent step, being fearful of cutting off two men who had vigorously appeared for the King and so signally contributed to the revolution. Nothing could be more disagreeable to their enemies, whose interest was deeply concerned in their destruction ; and, therefore, when no other measures could prevail with the Governor, tradition informs us that a sumptuous feast was prepared, to which Colonel Sloughter was invited. When his Excellency's reason was drowned in his cups, the entreaties of the company prevailed with him to sign the death-warrant, and before he recovered his senses the prisoners were executed.

Leisler's son afterwards carried home a complaint to King William, against the Governor. His petition was referred, according to the common course of plantation affairs, to the lords commissioners of trade, who, after hearing the whole matter, reported on the 11th of March, 1692, "That they were humbly of opinion, that Jacob Leisler and Jacob Milborne, deceased, were condemned and had suffered according to law."

Their lordships, however, interceded for their families as fit objects of mercy, and this induced Queen Mary, who approved the report on the 17th of March, to declare, "That upon the humble application of the relations of the said Jacob Leisler and Jacob Milborne, deceased, her Majesty will order the estates of Jacob Leisler and Jacob Milborne to be restored to their families, as objects of her Majesty's mercy."

The bodies of these unhappy sufferers were afterwards taken up, and interred with great pomp in the old Dutch church in the city of New York. Their estates were restored to their families, and Leisler's children, in the public estimation, are rather dignified, than disgraced, by the fall of their ancestor.

MANNERS AND CUSTOMS OF COLONIAL NEW YORK.

[From the Same.]

MANY have been the discouragements to the settlement of this colony. The French and Indian irruptions, to which we have always been exposed, have driven many families into New Jersey. At home, the British acts for the transportation of felons have brought all the American colonies into discredit with the industrious and honest poor, both in the kingdoms of Great Britain and Ireland. . . . .

The bigotry and tyranny of some of our governors, together with the great extent of their grants, may also be considered among the discouragements against the full settlement of the province. Most of these gentlemen, coming over with no other view than to raise their own fortunes, issued extravagant patents, charged with small quit-rents, to such as were able to serve them in the assembly; and these patentees, being generally men of estates, have rated their lands so exorbitantly high that very few poor persons could either purchase or lease them. Add to all these, that the New England planters have always been disaffected to the Dutch; nor was there, after the surrender, any foreign accession from the Netherlands. The province being thus poorly inhabited, the price of labor became so enormously enhanced, that we have been constrained to import negroes from Africa, who are employed in all kinds of servitude and trades.

English is the most prevailing language among us, but not a little corrupted by the Dutch dialect, which is still so much used in some counties, that the sheriffs find it difficult to obtain persons sufficiently acquainted with the English tongue, to serve as jurors in the courts of law.

The manners of the people differ as well as their language. In Suffolk and Queens county, the first settlers of which were either natives of England, or the immediate descendants of such as begun the plantations in the eastern colonies, their customs are similar to those prevailing in the English counties from whence they originally sprang.

In the city of New York, through our intercourse with the Europeans, we follow the London fashions; though, by the time we adopt them, they become disused in England. Our affluence, during the late war, introduced a degree of luxury in tables, dress, and furniture, with which we were before unacquainted. But still we are not so gay a people as our neighbors in Boston and several of the Southern colonies. The Dutch counties, in some measure, follow the example of New York, but still retain many modes peculiar to the Hollanders.

The city of New York consists principally of merchants, shopkeepers, and tradesmen, who sustain the reputation of honest, punctual, and fair dealers.

With respect to riches, there is not so great an inequality among us as is common in Boston and some other places. Every man of industry and integrity has it in his power to live well, and many are the instances of persons who came here distressed by their poverty, who now enjoy easy and plentiful fortunes.

New York is one of the most social places on the continent. The men collect themselves into weekly evening clubs. The ladies, in winter, are frequently entertained either at concerts of music or assemblies, and make a very good appearance. They are comely and dress well, and scarce any of them have distorted shapes.

Tinctured with a Dutch education, they manage their families with becoming parsimony, good providence, and singular neatness. The practice of extravagant gaming, common to the fashionable part of the fair sex in some places, is a vice with which my countrywomen cannot justly be charged. There is nothing they so generally neglect as reading, and indeed all the arts for the improvement of the mind,—in which, I confess, we have set them the example. They are modest, temperate, and charitable; naturally sprightly, sensible, and good-humored; and, by the helps of a more elevated education, would possess all the accomplishments desirable in the sex. Our schools are in the lowest order—the instructors want instruction; and, through a long, shameful neglect of all the arts and sciences, our common speech is extremely corrupt, and the evidences of a bad taste, both as to thought and language, are visible in all our proceedings, public and private.

The people, both in town and country, are sober, industrious, and hospitable, though intent upon gain. The richer sort keep very plentiful tables, abounding with great varieties of flesh, fish, fowl, and all kinds of vegetables. The common drinks are beer, cider, weak punch, and Madeira wine. For dessert, we have fruits in vast plenty, of different kinds and various species.

Gentlemen of estates rarely reside in the country, and hence few or no experiments have yet been made in agriculture. The farms being large, our husbandmen, for that reason, have little recourse to art for manuring and improving their lands; but it is said that nature has furnished us with sufficient helps, whenever necessity calls us to use them. It is much owing to the disproportion between the number of our inhabitants, and the vast tracts remaining still to be settled, that we have not, as yet, entered upon scarce any other manufactures than such as are indispensably necessary for our home convenience. Felt-making, which is perhaps the most natural of any we could fall upon, was begun some years ago, and hats were exported to the West Indies with great success, till lately prohibited by an act of parliament.

The inhabitants of this colony are in general healthy and robust, taller, but shorter lived, than Europeans, and, both with respect to their minds and bodies, arrive sooner to an age of maturity.

Breathing a serene, dry air, they are more sprightly in their natural tempers than the people of England, and hence instances of suicide are here very uncommon. The history of our diseases belongs to a profession with which I am very little acquainted. Few physicians among us are eminent for their skill. Quacks abound like locusts in Egypt, and too many have recommended themselves to a full practice and profitable subsistence. This is the less to be wondered at, as the profession is under no kind of regulation. Loud as the call is, to our shame be it remembered, we have no law to protect the lives of the King's subjects from the malpractice of pretenders. Any man at his pleasure sets up for physician, apothecary, and chirurgeon. No candidates are either examined or licensed, or even sworn to fair practice.

The natural history of this province would of itself furnish a small volume; and, therefore, I leave this also to such as have capacity and leisure to make useful observations in that curious and entertaining branch of natural philosophy.

AN ANTI-SEMITIC EXCITEMENT IN NEW YORK.

[*From the Same.*]

THE old party had made some efforts at the election, but with little success. Their most strenuous exertions were in the city during the session to introduce Adolph Philipse, the late Speaker, in the place of Gerrit Van Horne, a deceased member, whose son offered himself in the place of his father.

Before Cosby, the Sheriff, had made a return of Mr. Philipse, petitions were preferred by the other candidate and his electors, complaining of partiality; upon which the House ordered, that neither of them should sit till the conduct of the sheriff had been examined and considered.

Mr. Smith appeared as counsel for Van Horne and insisted that Philipse should distinguish which of the allegations of his client he denied or confessed, that time might be saved in the exhibition of the proofs. His antagonist, more consistent with the usage of Parliament, moved and carried a majority for a scrutiny of the votes. . . . .

In the debates between the candidates, Mr. Smith made a question, whether the Jews were qualified for electors, some of them having voted for Mr. Philipse. The cavil was taken up hastily in one day, and referred for argument on the next; and a resolve carried against the Hebrews by the mere dint of eloquence.

The auditors of this memorable debate of the 23d September never mention it without the highest encomiums upon the art of the orator.

Mr. Murray, as counsel for Mr. Philipse, drily urged the authority of the election law giving a vote to all freeholders of competent estates, without excepting the descendants of Abraham according to the flesh; and with astonishment heard a reply which captivated the audience into an opinion that the exception must be implied for the honor of Christianity and the preservation of the constitution. The whole history of the conduct of England against the Jews was displayed on this occasion, and arguments thence artfully deduced against their claims to the civil rights of citizenship. After expressing the emotions of pity naturally arising upon a detail of their sufferings under the avaricious and barbarous policy of ancient times, he turned the attention of his hearers to that mystery of love and terror manifested in the sacrifice of Christ; and so pathetically described the bloody tragedy at Mount Calvary, that a member cried out with agony and in tears, beseeching him to desist, and declaring his conviction. Many others wept; and the unfortunate Israelites were content to lose their votes could they escape with their lives; for some auditors of weak nerves and strong zeal were so inflamed by this oratory, that but for the interposition of their demagogues, and the votes of the House in their favor, the whole tribe in this dispersion would have been massacred that very day for the sin of their ancestors in crucifying Jesus of Nazareth, and imprecating his innocent blood upon themselves and their children.

It is at such moments that the arts of persuasion show their power, and few men were more eminently possessed of them than Van Horne's counsellor. He had the natural advantages of figure, voice, vivacity, memory, imagination, promptness, strong passions, volubility, invention, and a taste for ornament. These talents were improved by the assiduous industry of a robust constitution, with uninterrupted health and temperance, in the pursuit of various branches of science, and particularly in the law and theology. His progress in the latter was the more extensive, from an early turn to a life of piety and devotion. He studied the Scriptures in their originals, when young, and in advanced life they were so familiar to him that he often read them to his family in English from the Hebrew or Greek, without the least hesitation. He was bred a Dissenter in Buckinghamshire, and attached to the doctrines of Calvin; a great part of his time was spent in the works, French, English, and Latin, of the most celebrated divines of that stamp. He was for some time in suspense about entering into the service of the church. Dr. Colman of Boston, upon the perusal of a letter of his penning, in the name of the Presbyterian Church of New York, requesting a minister to take the care of it, declared that no man could be more fit than he who had so well described the character of a proper subject for that vacancy. These things are mentioned, to account for that surprise of his auditors at that *copia* and oratory which Mr. Smith indulged, when he laid aside his law books and took up the Bible in the debate I have mentioned. He imagined that the House would reject the votes of all the non-resident freeholders, and if the Jewish voices were struck out of the poll-lists, that his client would prevail. His religious and political creed were both inflamed by the heat of the times. It was natural for a mind trembling several years past for the liberties of the colony, and himself then under the rod of oppression for asserting them, to take fire at the prospect of the most distant inlet of mischief. And perhaps he was not himself conscious at that time, of the length to which his transition, from the impolicy of a Jewish interposition in the legislation of a Christian community, to the severity of exercising it, would carry him. That severity was then to be justified, and to this he reconciled his judges by an affecting representation of the agonies of the Cross. He prepared no notes for this memorable speech; it was delivered within a few hours after the thought of an implicative exception in the election act was first conceived; and the astonishment of the audience rose the higher, by the rare instance of so much pulpit eloquence from a law character at the bar of the House.

But though the Israelites were rejected, the non-resident voices were accepted, and Mr. Philipse, with his nephew the second Justice, admitted to a share in councils which they would neither sway nor control. And yet this act of justice to the old Speaker gave great offence within doors, the majority adopting Mr. Alexander's erroneous opinion, contrary to legal exposition and parliamentary usage, that a personal residence was as requisite in the elector, as communion of interests by a competent freehold.

The Judges, too, about this time grew not only impatient under the reproaches incurred by the order for silencing Zenger's counsel, but fearful of its consequences. The populace wishing for an opportunity, by action for damages, to repay them the losses they had sustained, their resentment rose the higher, as Mr. Smith, who had lately visited Virginia, was importuned to remove to that colony. To effect a reconciliation, the Lieutenant-Governor and Mr. Murray were employed to feel the pulses of the two popular lawyers, and testify the wishes of the Judges that they would return to the bar. After some punctilios, *honore servando*, the Judges agreed to cancel their injurious order, upon the promise of the latter to release all actions and damages, under the pretext of gratifying the timidity of their wives, who were said to be in constant anxiety from the apprehension of prosecutions and outrages, and in the October Term this year, Mr. Alexander and Mr. Smith appeared again at the bar, without any further condescensions on either side.

Anthony Benezet.

Born in St. Quentin's, France, 1713.　A Philadelphia Quaker.　Died, 1784.

AN EARLY PROTEST AGAINST THE SLAVE-TRADE.

[*A Caution and Warning to Great Britain and her Colonies.* 1766.]

A T a time when the general rights and liberties of mankind, and the preservation of those valuable privileges transmitted to us from our ancestors, are become so much the subjects of universal consideration, can it be an inquiry indifferent to any, how many of those who distinguish themselves as the advocates of liberty, remain insensible and inattentive to the treatment of thousands and tens of thousands of our fellow men who from motives of avarice, and the inexorable decree of tyrant custom, are at this very time kept in the most deplorable state of slavery, in many parts of the British Dominions?

The intent of publishing the following sheets is more fully to make known the aggravated iniquity attending the practice of the Slave-Trade; whereby many thousands of our fellow-creatures, as free as ourselves by nature, and equally with us the subjects of Christ's redeeming Grace, are yearly brought into inextricable and barbarous bondage; and many, very many, to miserable and untimely ends.

The truth of this lamentable complaint is so obvious to persons of candor, under whose notice it hath fallen, that several have lately published their sentiments thereon, as a matter which calls for the most serious consideration of all who are concerned for the civil or religious welfare of their country.　How an evil of so deep a dye hath so long, not only passed uninterrupted by those in power, but hath even had their countenance, is indeed surprising, and, charity would suppose, must in a great measure have arisen from this,—that many persons in government, both of the clergy and laity, in whose power it hath been to put a stop to the Trade, have been unacquainted with the corrupt motives which give life to it, and the groans, the dying groans, which daily ascend to God, the common Father of mankind, from the broken hearts of those his deeply oppressed creatures.　Otherwise the powers of the earth would not,—I think I may venture to say, could not,—have so long authorized a practice so inconsistent with every idea of liberty and justice, which, as the learned James Foster says, "bids that God which is the God and Father of the Gentiles unconverted to Christianity, most daring and bold defiance; and spurns at all the principles both of natural and revealed Religion."　.　.　.　.

Some who have only seen negroes in an abject state of slavery, broken-spirited and dejected, knowing nothing of their situation in their native country, may apprehend that they are naturally insensible of the benefits of liberty, being destitute and miserable in every respect, and that our suffering them to live amongst us (as the Gibeonites of old were permitted to live with the Israelites), though even on more oppressive terms, is to them a favor; but these are certainly erroneous opinions, with respect to far the greatest part of them: although it is highly probable that in a country which is more than three thousand miles in extent from north to south, and as much from east to west, there will be barren parts, and many inhabitants more uncivilized and barbarous than others; as is the case in all other countries. Yet from the most authentic accounts, the inhabitants of Guinea appear, generally speaking, to be an industrious, humane, sociable people, whose capacities are naturally as enlarged, and as open to improvement, as those of the Europeans; and that their country is fruitful, and in many places well improved, abounding in cattle, grain and fruits. And, as the earth yields all the year round a fresh supply of food, and but little clothing is requisite, by reason of the continual warmth of the climate, the necessaries of life are much easier procured in most parts of Africa, than in our more northern climes. This is confirmed by many authors of note, who have resided there.   .   .   .   .

Those, who are acquainted with the Trade, agree that many negroes on the sea-coast, who have been corrupted by their intercourse and converse with the European factors, have learnt to stick at no act of cruelty for gain. These make it a practice to steal abundance of little blacks of both sexes, when found on the roads or in the fields, where their parents keep them all day to watch the corn, etc. Some authors say the negro factors go six or seven hundred miles up the country, with goods bought from the Europeans, where markets of men are kept in the same manner as those of beasts with us. . . . They are put on board the vessels, the men being shackled with irons two and two together. Reader, bring the matter home, and consider whether any situation in life can be more completely miserable than that of those distressed captives. When we reflect that each individual of this number had some tender attachment which was broken by this cruel separation; some parent or wife, who had not an opportunity of mingling tears in a parting embrace; perhaps some infant or aged parent whom his labor was to feed, and vigilance protect; themselves under the dreadful apprehension of an unknown perpetual slavery; pent up within the narrow confines of a vessel, sometimes six or seven hundred together, where they lie as close as possible. Under these complicated distresses they are often reduced to a state of desperation, wherein many have leaped into the sea, and have kept themselves under water till they were drowned; others have starved themselves to death, for the prevention whereof some masters of vessels have cut off the legs and arms of a number of those poor desperate creatures, to terrify the rest. Great numbers have also frequently been killed, and some deliberately put to death under the greatest torture, when they have attempted to rise, in order to free themselves from their present misery and the slavery designed them. An instance of the last kind appears particularly in an account given by the master of a vessel, who brought a cargo of slaves to Barbadoes; indeed it appears so irreconcilable to the common dictates of humanity, that one would doubt the truth of it, had it not been related by a serious person of undoubted credit, who had it from the captain's own mouth.   .   .   .   .

Britons boast themselves to be a generous, humane people, who have a true sense of the importance of liberty; but is this a true character, whilst that barbarous, savage Slave-Trade, with all its attendant horrors, receives countenance and protection from the legislature, whereby so many thousand lives are yearly sacrificed? Do we indeed believe the truth declared in the Gospel? Are we persuaded that the threatenings, as well as the promises therein contained, will have their accomplishment? If indeed we do, must we not tremble to think what a load of guilt lies upon our nation generally and individually, so far as we in any degree abet or countenance this aggravated iniquity?

Thomas Godfrey.

BORN in Philadelphia, Penn., 1736. DIED in North Carolina, **1763.**

THE PATRIOT.

[Juvenile Poems on Various Subjects. 1765.]

A PARAPHRASE ON THE FIRST PSALM.

BLEST is the man who never lent
   To bold designing men his ear,
Who, on his Country's good intent,
   From bribing offices is clear;

But ever constant will remain,
   Supporter of her lawful right;—
Will firm her liberty maintain
   Against oppressors day and night.

Like a fair tree he shall appear,
  Which, planted by some river's side,
Its fruit does in due season bear,
  And blooms in vernal nature's pride.

Thus shall it flourish, thus shall rise;
  Its verdant leaf shall never fade;
Its beauties still shall glad our eyes,
  And pleasure dwell beneath its shade.

But men of dark, base treachery,
  Like chaff before the active wind,
By giddy factions tossed shall be,
  Till left the scorn of all mankind.

Where justice reigns they shun the place,
  Or where the open way doth shine,
Or where bright truth our Senates grace;
  But, veiled by night, they then design.

To all, the virtuous Patriot, known,
  Shall ever live in endless fame,
Whilst they (their deep laid schemes o'erthrown)
  Shall die, and with them die their name.

A DITHYRAMBIC ON WINE.

[*From the Same.*]

COME ! let Mirth our hours employ,
  The jolly God inspires;
The rosy juice our bosom fires,
And tunes our souls to joy.
See, great Bacchus now descending,
Gay, with blushing honors crowned;
Sprightly Mirth and Love, attending,
        Around him wait,
        In smiling state—
        Let Echo resound,
        Let Echo resound
The joyful news all around.

Fond Mortals, come; if love perplex,
In wine relief you'll find;
Who'd whine for women's giddy sex
More fickle than the wind?
If beauty's bloom thy fancy warms,
Here see her shine,
Clothed in superior charms;

More lovely than the blushing morn,
When first the opening day
Bedecks the thorn,
And makes the meadows gay.
Here see her in her crystal shrine;
See and adore; confess her all divine,
The Queen of Love and Joy.
Heed not thy Chloe's scorn—
  This sparkling glass,
  With winning grace,
Shall ever meet thy fond embrace,
And never, never, never cloy,
  No never, never cloy.

Here, Poet! see, Castalia's spring—
Come, give me a bumper, I'll mount to the skies,
Another, another—'Tis done!   I arise;
  On fancy's wing,
  I mount, I sing,
  And now, sublime,
Parnassus' lofty top I climb—
But hark! what sounds are these I hear,
Soft as the dream of her in love,
Or Zephyrs whispering through the grove?
And now, more solemn far than funeral woe,
The heavy numbers flow!
  And now again,
  The varied strain,
Grown louder and bolder, strikes quick on the ear,
And thrills through every vein.

'Tis Pindar's song!
His softer notes the fanning gales
Waft across the spicy vales,
  While, through the air,
  Loud whirlwinds bear
The harsher notes along.
  Inspired by wine,
He leaves the lazy crowd below,
Who never dared to peep abroad,
And, mounting to his native sky,
Forever there shall shine.
  No more I'll plod
  The beaten road;
Like him inspired, like him I'll mount on high;
  Like his my strain shall flow.

Haste, ye Mortals! leave your sorrow;
Let pleasure crown to-day—to-morrow
  Yield to fate.

Join the universal chorus,
          Bacchus reigns,
               Ever great;
          Bacchus reigns,
               Ever glorious—
Hark ! the joyful groves rebound,
Sporting breezes catch the sound,
And tell to hill and dale around—
          "Bacchus reigns"—
          While far away
The busy echoes die away.

THE WISH.

[*From the Same.*]

I ONLY ask a moderate fate,
   And, thcugh not in obscurity,
I would not, yet, be placed too high;
Between the two extremes I'd be,
Not meanly low, nor yet too great,
From both contempt and envy free.

   If no glittering wealth I have,
Content of bounteous heaven I crave,
For that is more
Than all the India's shining store,
To be unto the dust a slave.
With heart, my little I will use,
Nor let pain my life devour,
Or for a griping heir refuse
Myself one pleasant hour.

   No stately edifice to rear;
My wish would bound a small retreat,
In temperate air, and furnished neat;
No ornaments would I prepare,
No costly labors of the loom
Should e'er adorn my humble room;
To gild my roof I naught require
But the stern Winter's friendly fire.

   Free from tumultuous cares and noise,
If gracious Heaven my wish would give,
While sweet content augments my joys,
Thus my remaining hours I'd live.
By arts ignoble never rise,
The miser's ill-got wealth despise;
But blest my leisure hours I'd spend,
The Muse enjoying, and my friend.

AMYNTOR.

[From the Same.]

LONG had Amyntor free from love remained;
The God, enraged to see his power disdained,
Bent his best bow, and, aiming at his breast
The fatal shaft, he thus the swain addrest:

"Hear me, hear me, senseless rover,—
Soon thou now shalt be a lover,
Cupid will his power maintain;
Haughty Delia shall enslave thee,
Thou, who thus insulting brav'st me,
Shall, unpitied, drag the chain."

He ceased, and quick he shot the pointed dart;
Far short it fell, nor reached Amyntor's heart;
The angry God was filled with vast surprise;
Abashed he stood, while thus the swain replies:

"Think not, Cupid, vain deceiver,
I will own thy power ever,
Guarded from thy arts by wine;
Haughty Beauty ne'er shall grieve me,
Bacchus still shall e'er relieve me,
All his rosy joys are mine;
All his rosy joys are mine."

THE DEATHS OF EVANTHE AND ARSACES.

[The Prince of Parthia: A Tragedy. 1765.]

EVANTHE.

LEAD me, oh! lead me to my loved Arsaces,
Where is he?

ARSACES.

Ha! What's this?   Just heavens!—my fears—

EVANTHE.

Arsaces, oh! thus circled in thy arms,
I die without a pang.

ARSACES.

Ha! die?—why stare ye,
Ye lifeless ghosts?   Have none of ye a tongue
To tell me I'm undone?

GOTARZES.

Soon, my brother,
Too soon, you'll know it by the sad effects;
And if my grief will yet permit my tongue
To do its office, thou shalt hear the tale.
Cleone, from the turret, viewed the battle,
And on Phraates fixed her erring sight.
Thy brave unhappy friend she took for thee,
By his garb deceived, which like to thine he wore.
Still with her eye she followed him, where'er
He pierced the foe, and to Vardanes' sword
She saw him fall a hapless victim, then,
In agonies of grief, flew to Evanthe,
And told the dreadful tale—the fatal bowl
I saw—

ARSACES.

Be dumb, nor ever give again
Fear to the heart, with thy ill-boding voice.

EVANTHE.

Here, I'll rest, till death, on thy loved bosom,
Here let me sigh my—Oh! the poison works.

ARSACES.

Oh! horror!

EVANTHE.

Cease—this sorrow pains me more
Than all the wringing agonies of death,
The dreadful parting of the soul from this,
Its wedded clay—Ah! there—that pang shot through
My throbbing heart.

ARSACES.

Save her, ye Gods!—oh! save her!
And I will bribe you with clouds of incense;
Such numerous sacrifices, that your altars
Shall even sink beneath the mighty load.

EVANTHE.

When I am dead, dissolved to native dust,
Yet let me live in thy dear memory—
One tear will not be much to give Evanthe.

ARSACES.

My eyes shall e'er two running fountains be,
And wet thy urn with overflowing tears;
Joy ne'er again within my breast shall find
A residence—Oh! speak, once more.

EVANTHE.

Life's just out—
My father—Oh! protect his honored age,
And give him shelter from the storms of fate,
He's long been fortune's sport—support me—ah!—
I can no more—my glass is spent—farewell—
Forever—Arsaces!—oh!   [*Dies.*]

ARSACES.

Stay, oh! stay,
Or take me with thee—dead! she's cold and dead!
Her eyes are closed, and all my joys are flown
Now burst ye elements, from your restraint,
Let order cease, and chaos be again,
Break! break, tough heart!—Oh! torture—life dissolve—
Why stand ye idle? Have I not one friend
To kindly free me from this pain? One blow,
One friendly blow would give me ease.

BARZAPHERNES.

The Gods
Forefend!—Pardon me, Royal Sir, if I
Dare, seemingly disloyal, seize your sword.
Despair may urge you far—

ARSACES.

Ha! traitors! rebels!—
Hoary, reverend villain! what, disarm me?
Give me my sword—what, stand ye by, and see
Your Prince insulted? Are ye rebels all?—

BARZAPHERNES.

Be calm, my gracious Lord!

GOTARZES.

Oh! my loved brother!

ARSACES.

Gotarzes, too! all! all! conspired against me?
Still, are ye all resolved that I must live,
And feel the momentary pangs of death?—
Ha!—this shall make a passage for my soul—
                    [*Snatches Barzaphernes' sword.*]

Out, out, vile cares, from your distressed abode—
                    [*Stabs himself.*]

BARZAPHERNES.

Oh! ye eternal Gods!

GOTARZES.

Distraction! heavens!
I shall run mad.

ARSACES.

Ah! 'tis in vain to grieve—
The steel has done its part, and I'm at rest.—
Gotarzes, wear my crown, and be thou blest.
Cherish Barzaphernes, my trusty chief—
I faint, oh! lay me by Evanthe's side—
Still wedded in our deaths—Bethas—

BARZAPHERNES.

Despair,
My Lord, has broke his heart. I saw him stretched
Along the flinty pavement in his gaol—
Cold, lifeless—

ARSACES.

He's happy then—had he heard
This tale, he'd—Ah! Evanthe chides my soul
For lingering here so long—another pang
And all the world, adieu—oh! adieu—

[*Dies.*]

GOTARZES.

Oh!—
Fix me, heaven, immovable, a statue,
And free me from o'erwhelming tides of grief,

BARZAPHERNES.

Oh! my loved Prince, I soon shall follow thee;
Thy laurelled glories whither are they fled?—
Would I had died before this fatal day!—
Triumphant garlands pride my soul no more,
No more the lofty voice of war can charm—
And why then am I here? Thus then—

[*Offers to stab himself.*]

GOTARZES.

Ah! hold,
Nor rashly urge the blow—think of me, and
Live—My heart is wrung with streaming anguish,
Tore with the smarting pangs of woe, yet will I
Dare to live, and stem misfortune's billows.
Live then, and be the guardian of my youth,
And lead me on through virtue's rugged path.

BARZAPHERNES.

O, glorious youth, thy words have roused the
Drooping genius of my soul; thus let me

Clasp thee in my aged arms; yes, I will live—
Live to support thee in thy kingly rights,
And when thou'rt firmly fixed, my task's performed,
My honorable task—then I'll retire,
Petition gracious Heaven to bless my work,
And in the silent grave forget my cares.

GOTARZES.

Now to the Temple let us onward move,
And strive to appease the angry powers above.
Fate yet may have some ills reserved in store,
Continued curses, to torment us more.
Though, in their district, Monarchs rule alone,
Jove sways the mighty Monarch on his throne;
Nor can the shining honors which they wear,
Purchase one joy, or save them from one care.

Elizabeth Graeme Ferguson.

BORN at "Graeme Park," near Philadelphia, Penn., 1739.   DIED near her birthplace, 1801.

THE COUNTRY PARSON.

[Parody on Pope's Lines. Printed in a Collection of Poems by Nathaniel Evans. 1772.]

HOW happy is the country parson's lot !
    Forgetting bishops, as by them forgot;
Tranquil of spirit, with an easy mind,
To all his vestry's votes he sits resigned:
Of manners gentle, and of temper even,
He jogs his flocks, with easy pace, to heaven.
In Greek and Latin, pious books he keeps;
And, while his clerk sings psalms, he—soundly sleeps.
His garden fronts the sun's sweet orient beams,
And fat church-wardens prompt his golden dreams.
The earliest fruit, in his fair orchard, blooms;
And cleanly pipes pour out tobacco's fumes.
From rustic bridegroom oft he takes the ring;
And hears the milkmaid plaintive ballads sing.
Back-gammon cheats whole winter nights away,
And Pilgrim's Progress helps a rainy day.

Nathaniel Evans.

BORN in Philadelphia, Penn., 1742.   DIED in Gloucester Co., N. J., 1767.

TO MAY.

[Poems on Several Occasions. 1772.]

NOW had the beam of Titan gay
   Ushered in the blissful May,
Scattering from his pearly bed,
Fresh dew on every mountain's head;
Nature mild and debonair,
To thee, fair maid, yields up her care.
May, with gentle plastic hand,
Clothes in flowery robe the land;
O'er the vales the cowslip spreads,
And eglantine beneath the shades;
Violets blue befringe each fountain,
Woodbines lace each steepy mountain;
Hyacinths their sweets diffuse,
And the rose its blush renews;
With the rest of Flora's train,
Decking lowly dale or plain.

   Through creation's range, sweet May!
Nature's children own thy sway—
Whether in the crystal flood,
Amorous, sport the finny brood;
Or the feathered tribes declare
That they breathe thy genial air,
While they warble in each grove
Sweetest notes of artless love;
Or their wound the beasts proclaim,
Smitten with a fiercer flame;
Or the passions higher rise,
Sparing none beneath the skies,
But swaying soft the human mind
With feelings of ecstatic kind—
Through wide creation's range, sweet May!
All nature's children own thy sway.

   Oft will I, (e'er Phosphor's light
Quits the glimmering skirts of night)
Meet thee in the clover field,
Where thy beauties thou shalt yield
To my fancy, quick and warm,
Listening to the dawn's alarm,
Sounded loud by Chanticleer,
In peals that sharply pierce the ear.

And, as Sol his flaming car
Urges up the vaulted air,
Shunning quick the scorching ray,
I will to some covert stray,
Coolly bowers or latent dells,
Where light-footed Silence dwells.
And whispers to my heaven-born dream,
Fair Schuylkill, by thy winding stream!
There I'll devote full many an hour,
To the still-fingered Morphean power,
And entertain my thirsty soul
With draughts from Fancy's fairy bowl;
Or mount her orb of varied hue,
And scenes of heaven and earth review.

   Nor in milder eve's decline,
As the sun forgets to shine,
And sloping down the ethereal plain,
Plunges in the western main,
Will I forbear due strain to pay
To the song-inspiring May;
But as Hesper 'gins to move
Round the radiant court of Jove,
(Leading through the azure sky
All the starry progeny,
Emitting prone their silver light,
To re-illume the shades of night)
Then, the dewy lawn along,
I 'll carol forth my grateful song,
Viewing with transported eye
The blazing orbs that roll on high,
Beaming lustre, bright and clear,
O'er the glowing hemisphere.
Thus from the early blushing morn,
Till the dappled eve's return,
Will I, in free unlabored lay,
Sweetly sing the charming May !

         END OF VOL. II.

INDEX OF AUTHORS, ETC., IN VOL. II.

A General Index of Authors and Selections will be found in the Closing Volume.

ACKNOWLEDGMENTS.

The Editors and the Publishers of this work are under obligations to various learned Societies, and especially to many Publishing Houses, without whose generous coöperation the LIBRARY OF AMERICAN LITERATURE could not be completed upon its design.

Indebtedness to friends and institutions rendering assistance will be acknowledged in a Supplementary Preface (Vol. X.). Besides our general thanks to authors, editors, etc., whose copyrighted works are represented in the course of this series, special acknowledgment is here made to Messrs. LITTLE, BROWN & Cő., for further extracts from their edition of "Young's Chronicles."

Thanks are also due for aid derived from examination of the Collections, Memoirs, Reprints, etc., of the Mass. Hist. Society, the R. I. Hist. Society, the N. Y. Hist. Society, the Hist. Soc. of Penn., and the Va. Hist. Society; also of Force's "Historical Tracts," Shea's "Early Southern Tracts," Joseph Sabin's and W. Gowans's Reprints, Wynne's "Byrd Manuscripts," and various texts edited by S. G. Drake, J. H. Ellis, Dr. J. G. Shea, Brantz Mayer, and other scholarly antiquarians.